This volume brings together leading international scholars – from various mainstream as well as critical and interdisciplinary perspectives – to explore the historical and contemporary normative frameworks, public and private actors, and contested power relations in the ever-expanding field of transnational law. Drawing upon the groundbreaking contributions of Philip Jessup in the wake of World War II, the volume points to the innovations of current scholarship that analyse transborder legal processes as collective and discursive practice. Since many aspects of transnational law are largely unregulated by state governments, the volume rightly asks to what degree does transnational law contribute to today's crises of democratic governance. Given what is at stake, the volume is essential reading for scholars and practitioners grappling with the increasing complexities of transnational legal formations in the twenty-first century.

Eve Darian-Smith, Professor and Chair, Global and International Studies, University of California Irvine, and author of the award-winning book *Laws and Societies in Global Contexts: Contemporary Approaches* (Cambridge University Press)

From Jessup's first insights on transnational law, itself situated somewhere between the public and private international legal varieties, emerges the riddle of the 'in-between': inter-legalities, inter-normativities, intertextualities. Further questions arise: How do we understand law beyond the state, across geographical and disciplinary boundaries, if not as a motley assemblage of claims to legitimacy, soft and hard, crossing and muddling familiar boundaries, aspiring to both global and subnational validity? What exactly is being globalized as law today? What epistemologies are available in order to capture its transformations? This stimulating collection of very diverse 'multidimensional' viewpoints from around the world – by pragmatists, pluralists, feminists, postcolonialists, comparatists, historians – engages a wide selection of topics, including data flows, arbitration, sports law, environmental regulation, dispute resolution, family and others – through an equally ample range of conceptual and, indeed, emotional registers – comity, cooperation but also the drama, the unseen, the darker legacy – to enrich our legal imaginaries.

Professor Horatia Muir Watt, École de droit, Sciences Po, Paris

Jessup magisterially named a phenomenon that promises to saturate the world – the magnetic pull of law towards arrays of problems whose solution extends beyond the state. The seemingly endless proliferation of actual and aspirant legal orders in the transnational demands precisely the relentlessly creative, critical and constructive reflections in this timely volume. It is all here – transnational law as texts and institutions, form and function, drama and symbol, emotion and reason, fact and value, as it confronts food security, global sustainability, terrorism, sport and the family, and much else. No mere jurists' playground, *Many Lives* presses legal scholars into lively conversation with social scientists who also grapple with law's insatiable reach to problem-solving worldwide. *Many Lives* is a singular achievement and worthy of searching reflection by scholars and transnational lawmakers alike.

Terence C. Halliday, Research Professor, American Bar Foundation, and co-author, *Global Lawmakers: International Organizations in the Crafting of World Markets*

Transnational law is more than and different from public international law. This idea encompasses a whole world of facts, of instruments and of thoughts. Over the past sixty years, transnational law has ventured far beyond the circles of international lawyers as it continues to resonate with efforts in political science, theory and philosophy to conceptualize political order and demo-cratic legitimacy across the nation state's boundaries. The gift of writings presented here to Jessup and to the legal community at the sixtieth anniver-sary of the first publication of *Transnational Law* sketches and revisits this history and idea in a truly congenial way – dense, thoughtful and inspiring.

Professor Stefan Grundmann, European University Institute and Humboldt University, Faculty of Law, Berlin

THE MANY LIVES OF TRANSNATIONAL LAW

In 1956, International Court Justice judge Philip Jessup highlighted the gaps between private and public international law and the need to adapt the law to border-crossing problems. Today, sixty years later, we still ask what role transnational law can play in a deeply divided, postcolonial world, where multinationals hold more power and more assets than many nation states. In searching for suitable answers to pressing legal problems such as climate change law, security, poverty and inequality, questions of representation, enforcement, accountability and legitimacy become newly entangled. As public and private, domestic and international actors compete for regulatory authority, spaces for political legitimacy have become fragmented, and the state's exclusivist claim to be law's harbinger and place of origin is under attack.

Against this background, transnational law emerges as a conceptual framework and method laboratory for a critical reflection on the forms, fora and processes of lawmaking and law contestation today.

PEER ZUMBANSEN is the founding director of the Transnational Law Institute at King's College London and teaches at King's and Osgoode Hall Law School, Toronto. He is the series editor of Cambridge Studies in Transnational Law and co-editor-in-chief of *Transnational Legal Theory*.

The Many Lives of Transnational Law

CRITICAL ENGAGEMENTS WITH JESSUP'S BOLD PROPOSAL

Edited by

PEER ZUMBANSEN

King's College London
Osgoode Hall Law School

CAMBRIDGE
UNIVERSITY PRESS

CAMBRIDGE
UNIVERSITY PRESS

University Printing House, Cambridge CB2 8BS, United Kingdom

One Liberty Plaza, 20th Floor, New York, NY 10006, USA

477 Williamstown Road, Port Melbourne, VIC 3207, Australia

314–321, 3rd Floor, Plot 3, Splendor Forum, Jasola District Centre, New Delhi – 110025, India

79 Anson Road, #06–04/06, Singapore 079906

Cambridge University Press is part of the University of Cambridge.

It furthers the University's mission by disseminating knowledge in the pursuit of
education, learning, and research at the highest international levels of excellence.

www.cambridge.org
Information on this title: www.cambridge.org/9781108490269
DOI: 10.1017/9781108780582

First published 2020

Printed in the United Kingdom by TJ International Ltd. Padstow Cornwall

A catalogue record for this publication is available from the British Library.

Library of Congress Cataloging-in-Publication Data
NAMES: Zumbansen, Peer, 1966– editor.
TITLE: The many lives of transnational law : critical engagements with Jessup's bold proposal /
    [edited by] Peer Zumbansen.
DESCRIPTION: New York : Cambridge University Press, 2020. | Includes index.
IDENTIFIERS: LCCN 2019038180 (print) | LCCN 2019038181 (ebook) | ISBN 9781108490269
    (hardback) | ISBN 9781108748346 (paperback) | ISBN 9781108780582 (epub)
SUBJECTS: LCSH: International law. | Conflict of laws. | Jessup, Philip C. (Philip Caryl),
    1897-1986. | International Court of Justice.
CLASSIFICATION: LCC KZ3410 .M3625 2020 (print) | LCC KZ3410 (ebook) | DDC 341–dc23
LC record available at https://lccn.loc.gov/2019038180
LC ebook record available at https://lccn.loc.gov/2019038181

ISBN 978-1-108-49026-9 Hardback

Contents

List of Contributors   *page* xi

Preface and Acknowledgements   xvii

Introduction: Transnational Law, with and beyond Jessup   1
Peer Zumbansen

PART I   TRANSNATIONAL LAW: THE PUBLIC AND THE PRIVATE   55

1   **Jessup at the United Nations: International Legacy,**
    Transnational Possibilities   57
    Stephen Minas

2   **The Concept of a Global Legal System**   72
    Christopher A. Whytock

3   **How Comity Makes Transnationalism Work**   88
    Thomas Schultz and Niccolò Ridi

PART II   TRANSNATIONAL LAW AS REGULATORY GOVERNANCE   103

4   **Aiding and Abetting in Theorizing the Increasing**
    Softification of the International Normative Order:
    A Darker Legacy of Jessup's *Transnational Law*?   105
    Karsten Nowrot

5   **From International Law to Jessup's *Transnational Law*,**
    from Transnational Law to *Transnational Legal Orders*   126
    Gregory Shaffer and Carlos Coye

6   Transnational Law in the Pacific Century: Mapping Pesticide
      Regulation in China   153
      Francis Snyder, Hu Zhouke and Ni Lili

7   Transnational Law in Context: The Relevance of
      Jessup's Analysis for the Study of 'International' Arbitration   186
      Florian Grisel

8   Transnational Law and Adjudication: Domestic,
      International and Foreign Intersections   197
      Bryan Horrigan

9   Transnational Law and Global Dispute Resolution   224
      Shahla Ali

10   Conflicts of Law and the Challenge of Transnational
      Data Flows   240
      Paul Schiff Berman

11   What *Lex Sportiva* Tells You about Transnational Law   269
      Antoine Duval

12   Family Law: A Blind Spot   294
      Ivana Isailović

PART III TRANSNATIONAL LAW: THE FIELD'S NORMATIVE
STAKES   319

13   Locating Private Transnational Authority in the Global
      Political Economy   321
      A. Claire Cutler

14   Transnational Law as Drama   348
      Jothie Rajah

15   Transnational Law as Unseen Law   364
      Natasha Affolder

16   The *Cri de Jessup* Sixty Years Later: Transnational Law's
      Intangible Objects and Abstracted Frameworks   386
      Larry Catá Backer

17 The Private Life of Transnational Law: Reading Jessup
    from the Post-Colony   419
    Prabhakar Singh

18 After the Backlash: A New PRIDE for Transnational Law   441
    Ralf Michaels

PART IV CONCLUSION   459

**Epilogue: Difficulties for Every Solution: Defining Transnational
Law at the Edge of Transdisciplinarity**   461
Vik Kanwar

Name Index   493
Subject Index   497

Contributors

Natasha Affolder is Professor of Law at the Allard School of Law, University of British Columbia. She teaches transnational law, a mandatory part of the Allard School's first-year curriculum, as well as a range of other courses on global lawyering and professional practice, law and sustainability, and international business transactions. Her current research seeks to illuminate the rich complexity and the contradictions of transnational environmental law and practice.

Shahla Ali is Professor and Associate Dean (International) at the University of Hong Kong's Faculty of Law. Her research centres on questions of governance, development and transnational dispute resolution in East Asia. She is the author or co-editor of five books and more than forty-five articles and book chapters. She has consulted with the US Agency for International Development, the International Finance Corporation/World Bank and the United Nations on issues pertaining to access to justice, peace process negotiation training and land-use conflict resolution. She serves as a bilingual arbitrator (English/Chinese) and holds a BA from Stanford and JD/PhD from the University of California, Berkeley.

Larry Catá Backer is the W. Richard and Mary Eshelman Faculty Scholar, Professor of Law and International Affairs at Pennsylvania State University (BA, Brandeis University; MPP, Harvard University Kennedy School of Government; JD, Columbia University). He teaches and researches in the areas of globalization, corporate social responsibility (CSR), international affairs, global governance, trade and finance. He teaches courses in corporate law, CSR, multinational corporations, international institutions and transnational law, as well as on law and religion and constitutional law. He lectures globally, most recently in Panama and China. He has published extensively around a cluster of related questions central to the transnational problematique – and especially on the transnational regulation of economic activity through hard and soft law regimes, including the development of the theory and practice of CSR as philanthropy, as a human rights project and in the context of sustainability and development. He has authored or edited books on comparative corporate law, transnational law and globalization, including *Cuba's Caribbean Marxism: Essays on Ideology, Government, Society, and Economy in the Post Fidel Castro Era* (Little Sir Press, 2018); *Lawyers Making Meaning: The Semiotics of Law in Legal Education* (Springer, 2013) and *Signs in Law – a Source Book* (Springer, 2014) (both with Jan Broekman); casebooks; *Elements of Law and the U.S.: Legal System* (Carolina Academic Press, forthcoming in 2019); *Law and Religion* (West, 2015, with Frank Ravitch); *Comparative Corporate Law* (Carolina Academic Press, 2002; 2nd edn forthcoming in 2020); and an edited collection of essays, *Harmonizing Law in an Era of Globalization* (Carolina Academic Press, 2007). His work, especially on Chinese constitutional law and CSR, has been translated into Chinese, Spanish and Portuguese. Shorter essays on various aspects of globalization and governance appear on his essay site, Law at the End of the Day, at http://lcbackerblog.blogspot.com.

Paul Schiff Berman, the Walter S. Cox Professor of Law at the George Washington University Law School, is one of the world's foremost theorists on the effect of globalization on the interactions among legal systems. He is the author of over sixty scholarly works, including *Global Legal Pluralism: A Jurisprudence of Law beyond Borders*, published by Cambridge University Press in 2012. He was also among the first legal scholars to focus on legal issues regarding online activity, and he is the co-author of one of the leading casebooks in the field.

Carlos Coye is a labour attorney at the law firm Rothner, Segall & Greenstone, which specializes in representing employees and labour unions. In 2017, he graduated from the University of California, Irvine School of Law.

A. Claire Cutler is a Professor of International Law and International Relations in the Political Science Department of the University of Victoria, British Columbia. Her work is situated at the intersections of law, politics and political economy. She has published widely on private, corporate authority and international affairs, transnational law and politics, the international trade and investment regimes, and critical global political economy. A recent publication is *The Politics of Private Transnational Governance by Contract* (Routledge Series on the Politics of Transnational Law, 2017).

Antoine Duval is Senior Researcher at the Asser Institute in The Hague and obtained his doctorate at the European University Institute in Florence in 2015. His work focuses on the intersection between private actors and public interests in transnational law, using the sports sector and transnational corporations as case studies.

Florian Grisel is a Research Fellow at the French National Centre for Scientific Research (CNRS) and an Associate Professor (Reader) in Transnational Law at King's College London. He also is the Deputy-Director of the Centre de théorie et analyse du droit (Université Paris Ouest Nanterre La Défense - Ecole normale supérieure). He has published widely on the emergence of judicial governance in local and transnational settings. His latest book, *The Evolution of International Arbitration* (with Alec Stone Sweet), was published by Oxford University Press in 2018. He was the recipient of the Bronze Medal of the CNRS in 2018.

Bryan Horrigan is the Dean of the Faculty of Law at Monash University in Australia. He leads a highly world-ranked law school with hundreds of staff and approximately 4,000 students, operating from six locations on three continents. Previously a senior associate and long-standing consultant with a leading international law firm, he holds a doctorate in law from Oxford University under a Rhodes scholarship. He has both academic expertise and professional experience in various aspects of public and corporate law and governance from transnational standpoints. He has spoken and published internationally in the fields of internationalization of law, judicial decision-making, public sector governance, corporate social responsibility and good faith in commercial transactions. His work on a three-member expert panel for the Australian government resulted in changes to three major pieces of national economic regulation in which good faith issues are implicated.

Hu Zhouke was Research Assistant at the Center for Research on Transnational Law, Peking University School of Transnational Law, Shenzhen, China, where he worked with Francis Snyder on food safety in China. He received a BA from Wanjiang College, Anhui Normal University, and JM and JD degrees from the Peking University School of Transnational Law. He is particularly interested in Chinese law and politics.

Ivana Isailović is a fellow at the Max Planck Institute for Comparative and International Private Law and a visiting scholar at Northeastern Law School and the Women's, Gender and Sexuality Studies Program. Her research focuses on the interplay between globalization, family law and gender. She has taught classes on comparative family law and gender issues in Belgium,

Canada and the United States and co-organized conferences on transnational law at Sciences Po Law School (Paris) and the London School of Economics and Political Science.

Vik Kanwar currently teaches at Southwestern Law School in Los Angeles, where he serves as Associate Director of International Programs. His areas of research are social theory, law and culture, and the intellectual history of international law. He has held teaching and research posts at New York University, Harvard University, Loyola University (New Orleans) and Clemson University and was for several years at Jindal Global Law School in India, where he was Associate Professor and Founding Executive Director of the Centre on Public Law and Jurisprudence. He co-directs the Winter School on Art/Law, a transnational educational network and clearing house of legal resources for artists and other culture workers in the Global South.

Ralf Michaels is Director at the Max Planck Institute for Comparative and International Private Law in Hamburg, Professor at Hamburg University, and Professor of global law at Queen Mary University of London. Most of his research focuses on the global interaction of laws, private international law, comparative law and the theory of law and globalization.

Stephen Minas is Assistant Professor at the School of Transnational Law, Peking University, and Senior Research Fellow at the Transnational Law Institute, King's College London. He primarily publishes and works in the areas of transnational energy and climate change law, with a focus on novel forms of international organization. He holds honours degrees in law and history from the University of Melbourne, an MSc in international relations from the London School of Economics and a PhD in law from King's College London.

Ni Lily is a candidate for JD and JM degrees at the Peking University School of Transnational Law, Shenzhen, China, and Research Assistant at its Center for Research on Transnational Law. She has worked with Francis Snyder in conducting legal research and co-authoring papers related to food safety law. In addition, she also has a special interest in Chinese administrative law and international arbitration.

Karsten Nowrot is Professor of Public Law, European Law and International Economic Law; Director of the Research Institute for Economic Law and Labor Law; and the current head of the Department of Law at the School of Socio-economics of the Faculty of Business, Economics and Social Sciences at Hamburg University, Germany. He also serves as Deputy Director of the master's program European and European Legal Studies at the Institute for European Integration of the Europa-Kolleg Hamburg. His research interests include the conceptualization of transnational law, in particular in the realm of transnational economic law, on which he has published widely.

Jothie Rajah is Research Professor at the American Bar Foundation, Chicago. A law-and-language scholar, she has published widely on rule of law, with attention to transnational, global, contemporary and colonial dimensions of rule of law.

Niccolò Ridi is a lecturer in law at the University of Liverpool, a Postdoctoral Research Fellow and Visiting Lecturer at King's College London, and, when this chapter was written, a Swiss National Science Foundation Research Fellow at the Graduate Institute of International and Development Studies, Geneva. His work deals with the theory of international dispute settlement as well as with the interaction of private and public international law. He holds degrees in law and political science from the Universities of Florence (LLB/MA), Cambridge (LLM), and King's College London (PhD).

Thomas Schultz is Professor of Law at King's College London, Professor of International Arbitration at the University of Geneva, and Visiting Professor of International Law at the Graduate Institute of International and Development Studies, Geneva. Much of his work deals with the intersection of dispute settlement and transnational law. His chapter is part of a research project funded by the Swiss National Science Foundation, during which he was a research professor at the Graduate Institute of International and Development Studies.

Gregory Shaffer is Chancellor's Professor and Director of the Center on Globalization, Law and Society at the University of California, Irvine.

Prabhakar Singh is an associate professor at Jindal Global Law School, India, and writes about international law and legal theory in postcolonial ink. He holds a PhD from the National University of Singapore, an LLM from the University of Barcelona and a BA/LLB (Hons) from the National Law Institute University. He has presented papers at North American, European and Latin American universities while teaching/visiting in Thailand, Indonesia, France and Cambodia.

Francis Snyder is C. V. Starr Professor of Law, EU Jean Monnet Professor *ad personam* and Director, Center for Research on Transnational Law, Peking University School of Transnational Law. He is also Emeritus Professor, Centre of European and International Research and Studies, Aix-Marseille University, and Visiting Professor, College of Europe, Bruges. He has published widely in the areas of law and anthropology, EU law, EU–China relations, international trade and food safety. His most recent book is the award-winning *Food Safety Law in China: Making Transnational Law* (2016). In 2018 he received the national China Friendship Award and the Peking University Friendship Award.

Christopher A. Whytock is Professor of Law and Political Science at the University of California, Irvine. His research focuses on transnational litigation, conflict of laws, international law and the role of domestic law and domestic courts in global governance. He serves as Co-Director of University of California, Irvine's Center in Law, Society and Culture and Associate Reporter for the American Law Institute's (ALI's) Restatement (Third) of Conflict of Laws. He was an adviser on the ALI's Restatement (Fourth) of US Foreign Relations Law.

Peer Zumbansen is Professor of Law at Osgoode Hall Law School and served as the inaugural director of the Transnational Law Institute (TLI) at the Dickson Poon School of Law at King's College London from 2014 to 2018. Since 2018, he has been Co-director of the TLI. He has held visiting professorships at Yale Law School; Idaho College of Law; Osgoode Hall Law School; Sherbrooke University School of Law; Getúlio Vargas Foundation, São Paulo; Pontifical Xavierian University, Bogotá; the University of Paris VII, Dauphine; Lucerne Law School; the University of St Gallen; University College Dublin; Deusto Law School, Bilbao; and Melbourne Law School. He has published widely in the area of transnational corporate governance and labour law as well as transnational private regulatory governance. At King's College, he launched a new LLM pathway in transnational law, which focuses on the use of real-world examples from litigation, law reform and rights advocacy to instruct students in more than thirty areas of domestic and international law. Since 2012 he has served as the editor-in-chief of *Transnational Legal Theory* and since 2014 for the TLI Think! Papers with the Social Sciences Research Network.

Preface and Acknowledgements

The here-collected essays engage with transnational law across and beyond many of these poles. The contributors include legal scholars, anthropologists, political scientists and cultural theorists who met at King's College London for a conference to commemorate the sixtieth anniversary of Philip Jessup's landmark Storrs Lectures on transnational law at Yale Law School in 1956. In the process of writing the chapters for this book, some of the contributors found themselves taking these lectures by Jessup, who was at the time of their delivery a professor of international law and would later become appointed to the International Court of Justice, as point of origin for what has grown into much more of what might have been visible or imaginable at the time. Others understood his original text as a reference to a particular constellation of international legal theory and doctrine and policymaking, inviting both retrospective as well as future-oriented re-imagination. Altogether, the here-convened scholarship engages, challenges and refracts transnational law – with and well beyond Jessup's original and, arguably, bold proposal. As the scholars in this book show, the significance of transnational law lies foremost in its power to draw us into its immense conceptual promise as a framework through which to scrutinize the form(s) and the promise but also the limitations of law in a differentiated and deeply divided world.

The original conference was generously supported and hosted by the Dickson Poon School of Law, under the auspices of the Transnational Law Institute (TLI), and brought to life by its fearless coordinator at the time, Miss Helen Bhandari. To her and the wonderful colleagues at the school and the institute, who make such special events possible and memorable, and especially to the TLI fellows and affiliates Nik Eder, Ada Fama, Farnush Ghadery, Marius Nordby, Laura Knöpfel and Irene Valones, who helped in the organization of a wonderful conference, I am very much indebted. Further gratitude is owed to Dr Kinnari Bhatt for her editorial work in the beginning stages of this book and certainly to the contributors from near and far who accepted the invitation to reflect on Jessup and the field, the concept and methodology of transnational law sixty years after Jessup's lectures in New Haven.

Introduction

Transnational Law, with and beyond Jessup

PEER ZUMBANSEN[*]

Avant la règle, il y a le problème.[1]

He used concepts sparingly, but effectively, and he avoided windy rhetoric.[2]

A JESSUP'S LECTURES AND THE PROJECT OF 'TRANSNATIONAL LAW'

The here-presented book is an edited collection of original essays first presented at an international conference at the Transnational Law Institute, King's College London, to commemorate the sixtieth anniversary of the publication of Philip Jessup's landmark study *Transnational Law*, published by Yale University Press in 1956.[3] Philip Jessup, who was born on 5 February 1897 and died on 31 January 1986, just shy of his ninetieth birthday, was – at the time of delivering the Storrs Lectures at Yale Law School on which the book is based – the Hamilton Fish Professor of International Law and Diplomacy at Columbia Law School, while also playing a very active role in the university's Department of Public Law and Government (later renamed Department of Political Science).[4] He had previously served as assistant solicitor for the US Department of State as well as assumed different functions within and for the United Nations (UN) before being appointed, in 1960, to the International Court of Justice, where he was a judge from 1961 until 1970. In 1950, Senator Joseph McCarthy had charged Jessup with having 'an

[*] My gratitude to Priya Gupta and Vik Kanwar for comments on this chapter.
[1] CHARLES EISENMANN, LES SCIENCES SOCIALES DANS L'ENSEIGNEMENT SUPÉRIEUR, DROIT (1954), 44.
[2] Oscar Schachter, *Philip Jessup's Life and Ideas*, 80 AM. J. INT'L L. 878, 878 (1986).
[3] PHILIP C. JESSUP, TRANSNATIONAL LAW (1956).
[4] Schachter, *supra* note 2, at 881.

unusual affinity for communist causes', delaying Jessup's appointment by President Harry S. Truman as US delegate to the UN in 1951. Given the highly visible, public role Jessup was playing at the time in international diplomacy for the United States, he was one of the most prominent targets for McCarthy.[5] Eventually, Truman managed to appoint Jessup into the role of US delegate to the 1952 UN General Assembly. Jessup was eventually cleared of all charges raised by the Subcommittee on the Investigation of Loyalty of State Department Employees, commonly known as the Tydings Committee, under McCarthy.[6] In 1960, almost a decade after the McCarthy episode, Jessup was appointed to the International Court of Justice, where he assumed his role as judge in February of 1961, serving until 1970.

> Jessup was, of course, honored and pleased by the nomination and election. He must have felt, as did many of his friends, that it was a personal vindication and repudiation of the attacks on his loyalty and integrity. However, he was disappointed by the fact that the Court had few cases and appeared to be on the periphery of international affairs. He remarked in later years that he would have probably accomplished more and been happier personally if he had remained a Rockefeller Foundation associate or a Columbia professor. The relative isolation in The Hague and the personal tensions among the judges also dampened Jessup's enthusiasm. Nonetheless, Jessup remained a strong champion of the Court. It was the main subject on which he wrote and lectured during and after his term on the Court.[7]

As will become more apparent in the ensuing discussion of his 1956 lectures on transnational law, it was Jessup's commitment to facts and problems and to the identification of practical solutions that marked his approach to international law. 'However', as Oscar Schachter observed, 'his pragmatism was also imbued with a distinct teleological element. Like Elihu Root, his early mentor, Jessup saw the main trends of international society as part of an evolutionary development toward a more organized and effective legal

---

[5] *Id.* at 885: 'Writing some 20 years later in *The Birth of Nations*, Jessup commented in a footnote that "the McCarthy persecutions are now as dead and dis credited as the Spanish Inquisition." While this was probably true in 1972, the impact of the McCarthy episode on Jessup's career and, more widely, on the course of American foreign policy was surely not minor.'

[6] U.S. Dep't of State, History of the Bureau of Diplomatic Security of the United States Department of State 125 (2011), https://2009-2017.state.gov/documents/organization/176589.pdf: 'McCarthy then took aim at Ambassador-at-Large Phillip C. Jessup, and this also proved embarrassing. Jessup, a highly respected diplomat, showed up with two letters testifying to his anti-Communism and loyalty to the United States – one from former Secretary of State George C. Marshall, and one from General Dwight D. Eisenhower.'

[7] Schachter, *supra* note 2, at 889–90.

order.'[8] Jessup's 'sophisticated blend of positivism, idealism and pragmatism' has to be appreciated against the background of his belief in the significance of a notion of 'international community interest', for which he drew on Elihu Root but which he eventually understood as encompassing the protection of ocean resources and the global environment.

Schachter places *Transnational Law* in relation to Jessup's strong endorsement of 'international community', which he manifested throughout his scholarly and adjudicatory work in international law and which is based on the idea of varied degrees of 'ideas of order, responsibility and justice, while recognizing that diversity and special conditions create many different kinds of international communities with their own special interests and law'.[9] Schachter correctly credits Jessup with developing and popularizing the term 'transnational law', rather than inventing it, and underscores Jessup's intention 'to show the growing legal complexity of an interdependent world'.[10] Giving Jessup's treatment of transnational law's relative prominence amidst a concluding assessment of the scholar's, judge's and diplomat's approach to law in a global context, Schachter highlights Jessup's ability to identify areas that form part of what we today would call 'global governance'. Such areas grow out of 'new relations of interdependence'[11] and prompt the development of regulatory frameworks that do not fit into either public or private international law. While these include Jessup's references to areas such as 'European Community law, maritime law, international administrative law, war crimes, the law of economic development and the rules applicable to multinational enterprises',[12] the approach towards a fact- and problem-based understanding of law, coupled with a teleological commitment to international community's or communities' interests is justified on the basis that the law needs to be able to be effective outside of national jurisdiction.

For the conference participants and contributors to this volume, Jessup's *Transnational Law*, a slim volume of just 113 pages, served as a starting, reference and orientation point for a series of critical as well as forward-looking investigations into Jessup's elaboration and discussion of something that he defined as including 'all law which regulates actions or events that transcend national frontiers' and that included '[b]oth public and private international law [...], as are other rules which do not wholly fit into such

---

[8] *Id.* at 891; Schachter ascribes to Jessup a 'sophisticated blend of positivism, idealism and pragmatism'. *Id.*
[9] *Id.* at 893.
[10] *Id.*
[11] *Id.* at 894.
[12] *Id.*

standard categories'.[13] That said, the here-following chapters engage with
Jessup's introduction and his use of the term before an audience of internationally minded lawyers and policymakers by both contextualizing and
transcending Jessup's understanding of transnational law. Coming from different areas of law and legal theory, from comparative law, political science and
international relations, from anthropology and cultural as well as postcolonial
studies, the authors in this book provide an immensely wide spectrum of
perspectives from which they ultimately propose to engage with Jessup's bold
proposal in today's time. As should become evident from chapter to chapter as
well as from this introduction, an engagement with Jessup's *Transnational
Law* continues to occur in different layers, ranging from the textual to the
conceptual, from the historical to the critical. For some, Jessup was an
international lawyer who sought to push the frontiers of his field in order to
take a bigger-picture approach to the role that law, diplomacy and negotiation
can play,[14] while others take Jessup as someone who captures a moment in
which the demands of a fast-globalizing and decolonizing world prompt a
critical engagement with distinctions between domestic and international law
and between public and private norms. For many, the focus is less on a
continued scrutiny of Jessup himself and of his proposition but more strongly
on the field, the idea, the concept and the methodological challenge encapsulated in the term 'transnational law'. As such, and we will return to this point
again, there are today too many highly productive conceptualizations of a
transnational law to adequately trace them all back to Jessup's original contribution. We will also see that important aspects of Jessup's discussion of
transnational law – ranging from his insistence on the need to understand
law as a means to pursue policy goals and above all, as an instrument with
which to achieve practical, problem-based and problem-oriented solutions to
his acknowledgement of legal normativity outside the strict confines of domestic or international, state-based law – were not proprietary to Jessup's distinct
intellectual project but can be understood as belonging to the evolving, post–
legal realist, post–Second World War, transatlantic legal imagination at
the time.

   With that in mind, this introduction will begin by offering a brief overview
of Jessup's *Transnational Law* before picking up on some of the themes that

---

[13] JESSUP, *supra* note 3, at 2.
[14] See, for example, this observation by Schachter, *supra* note 2, at 882: 'His most influential book,
    The Modern Law of Nations, was completed in 1947. It was widely acclaimed, probably
    receiving more attention in the public media than any other book on international law ever
    had. His ideas on the international community interest, protection of individual rights and the
    regulation of force opened up vistas of a new postwar society.'

have become apparent in the discussion of transnational law in recent decades. Part literature review, part substantive argument, this part of the introduction is meant, above all, to point to the immense wealth, breadth and depth of scholarship in this area today. Finally, this introduction will conclude with a brief preview of the chapters in this book.

At the time he delivered his lectures at Yale, in 1956, Jessup offered the compelling observation that lawyers needed to find a way of expanding their legal conceptual and doctrinal repertoire in order to effectively address the growing variety of border-crossing human and institutional relations around the world. He argued that these cannot easily or can no longer adequately be grasped with the tools provided either by public international law or private international law (also known as 'conflict of laws'). Jessup was writing as both a public international lawyer and as a lawyer steeped in international economic law and diplomacy, and he was doing so at a time at which the state of the world was in disarray. The Second World War was at pains ended, and the world was rearranging itself in a mix of ideological conflict, bloc building, hegemonic aspirations and decolonization.[15] These developments reflected a variety of tensions between nineteenth-century colonizing geopolitics and the emerging development policies in the 1950s and 1960s, in which the idea and political project of the 'nation state' was pivotal.[16] Against the backdrop of European 'reconstruction', looming decolonization and the prevailing perception that the post-war creation of international law would constitute a 'clean epistemological break with the prewar international law's subservience to power and ethnocentrism',[17] who could effectively predict the way the

---

[15] Charles S. Maier, *The Two Postwar Eras and the Conditions for Stability in Twentieth-Century Western Europe*, 86 AM. HIST. REV. 327–52 (1981); Andrew Phillips, *Beyond Bandung: The 1955 Asian–African Conference and Its Legacies for International Order*, 7 AUSTRALIAN J. INT'L AFF. 329–41 (2016). *See also* Luis Eslava, Michael Fakhri & Vasuki Nesiah, *The Spirit of Bandung, in* BANDUNG, GLOBAL HISTORY AND INTERNATIONAL LAW. CRITICAL PASTS AND PENDING FUTURES (Luis Eslava, Michael Fakhri & Vasuki Nesiah eds., 2017).

[16] Martin T. Berger, *Decolonisation, Modernisation and Nation-Building: Political Development Theory and the Appeal of Communism in Southeast Asia, 1945–1975*, 34 J. SOUTHEAST ASIAN STUD. 421, 422 (2003): 'Decolonisation, the universalisation of the nation-state and the Cold War provided the crucial backdrop for the rise and elaboration of modernisation theory and closely related theories of political development and nation-building that were centred on direct or indirect US involvement in the formation and consolidation of stable anti-communist national political systems. After 1945 the nation-state became the central and unquestioned unit of study for modernisation theorists and the natural object of a burgeoning number of exercises in state-mediated national development and nation-building.'

[17] Balakrishnan Rajagopal, *International Law and the Development Encounter: Violence and Resistance at the Margins*, 93 ASIL PROCEEDINGS 16, 16 (1999).

chips would fall on the table of global geopolitics in the years and decades to come?[18]

For Philip Jessup, the diplomat and, for a long time, the US ambassador-at-large, this might have looked (and felt) like that:

> In fact, his hectic diplomatic service involved a number of developments that left their imprint on international society. The historic colonial empires were crumbling and the United Nations was faced with wars of national liberation and demands for political and economic self-determination. The ex-enemy states-Germany, Japan and Italy-were reentering the international community, each with its quota of divisive issues. Collective security, the centerpiece of the United Nations Charter, was gradually perceived as unworkable in the face of East-West hostilities; in its place, the collective defense pacts of the North Atlantic and Warsaw treaties came to dominate security relations. Jessup was close to the center of the stage as these momentous events were unfolding. It often fell to him to respond to vitriolic diatribes of the Russians and their allies. Behind the scenes, he engaged in the almost continuous negotiations that are the core of United Nations diplomacy and the mainspring of its occasional achievements.[19]

This context might explain the mixed reactions that Jessup's use of 'transnational' law provoked at the time. While some scholars endorsed his call for a distinctly 'transnational' perspective, they critiqued him for potentially underestimating the resistance on the part of nation states.[20] Others were intrigued by the consequences Jessup's lectures could have in terms of rethinking international law[21] at a time, where it was anything but certain how 'international' the still nascent field would eventually become,[22] particularly in

---

[18] For an intriguing and troubling account of political theorists' and economists' resistance against a growing human rights movement with a focus on equality and socioeconomic emancipation, see QUINN SLOBODIAN, THE GLOBALISTS 125 (2018): 'Geneva School neoliberals proposed their own version of a world of right. Against human rights, they posed the human rights of capital.'

[19] Oscar Schachter, *Philip Jessup's Life and Ideas*, 80 AM. J. INT'L L. 878, 884 (1986).

[20] See, for example, David Lehman, Book Review, 18 LA. L. REV. 219–21 (1957) (reviewing JESSUP, *supra* note 3).

[21] See, for example, C.G. Fenwick, Book Review, 51 AM. J. INT'L L. 444–45 (1957) (reviewing JESSUP, *supra* note 3), complimenting Jessup for having taken some of the mystery out of international law and for drawing a much more realistic picture of the multiplicity of global relationships than traditional international law was able to.

[22] See the hopeful reflections by MANLEY O. HUDSON, PROGRESS IN INTERNATIONAL ORGANIZATION (1932) and the supportive comments in Valentine Jobst III's review of the book, 10 IND. L.J. 106, 106 (1934): 'Covering thus hurriedly so much material, it may well be that at times Professor Hudson creates the impression of being unduly sanguine in his estimate of the results achieved or achievable under the League of Nations and the other new institutions of international government. Closer reading, however, reveals that Professor Hudson's is not the

view of the unstable global political and economic climate following the Second World War.[23] At the time, this approach received some support in that it was recognized as a timely and potentially important invitation to critically engage existing categories and frameworks.[24] Writing in 1981, Myres McDougal and Michael Reisman observed the following with regard to the making and the state of international law:

> No problem has proved more refractory to lawyers and scholars than under-standing and explaining how international law is made. Domestic analogues, whose explanatory power may be inadequate even in their own contexts, have so little relevance to the complexities of international politics that those who invoke them finish either by throwing up their hands and conceding that the model is inappropriate for the task or by painting themselves into the palpably absurd position that there is no international law. [. . .] As the world becomes pervasively more transnational and interdependent, an understanding of how international law is made and, even more to the point, how to make it, becomes a matter of greatest practical urgency.[25]

While much suggests that this debate continued with a strong emphasis on the power politics[26] that so often have called the entire project of an international

---

optimism of the impractical idealist or wishful thinker; it is, rather, the considered confidence of the man of wide actual experience in international affairs who knows that the germs of progress often lie in what for the moment looks like retrogression.' See, in our present context, the elaborate and diligent study by ANTHEA ROBERTS, HOW INTERNATIONAL IS INTERNATIONAL LAW? (2017).

[23] Thomas G. Weiss & Sam Daws, *World Politics: Continuity and Change Since 1945*, in THE OXFORD HANDBOOK ON THE UNITED NATIONS 3–34 (Thomas G. Weiss & Sam Daws eds., 2008). DANIEL YERGIN & JOSEPH STANISLAW, COMMANDING HEIGHTS: THE BATTLE FOR THE WORLD ECONOMY 75–79 (1998).

[24] See, for example, the reviews of Jessup's book by James N. Hyde (66 YALE L.J. 813–16 (1957), calling the idea 'stimulating and provocative') and by Claude L. Inis (51 AM. POL. SCI. REV. 1117–19 (1957), praising Jessup for throwing off old concepts and emancipating him from standard rigidities, whereby Jessup is able to provide a fresh stimulus to fresh thinking and to challenge in a detailed juridical analysis the validity and adequacy of old definitions and categories). But see also the review by Eric Stein (56 MICH. L. REV. 1039–43 (1958)), in which Stein recognizes Jessup's project as an 'assault on the barriers of classification and distinctions traditionally separating legal disciplines'. At the same time, Stein observes that the book contains a number of 'promising and interesting (and rather vague) suggestions' for further study and finds the book to be 'Jessup's most challenging volume'.

[25] Myres S. McDougal & W. Michael Reisman, *The Prescribing Function in the World Constitutive Process: How International Law Is Made*, in INTERNATIONAL LAW ESSAYS: A SUPPLEMENT TO INTERNATIONAL LAW IN CONTEMPORARY PERSPECTIVE 355 (Myres S. McDougal & W. Michael Reisman eds., 1981).

[26] Richard A. Falk, *The Relevance of Political Context to the Nature and Functioning of International Law: An Intermediate View*, in THE RELEVANCE OF INTERNATIONAL LAW 133, 139–40 (Karl W. Deutsch & Stanley Hoffmann eds., 1968): 'One of the inhibitions on power in

law into question,[27] 'international law' itself and in its own right resists any kind of neat, straightforward historiography. On its face more established than transnational law, international law is as kaleidoscopic, as refracted, as fragmented and as mesmerizing as its, should we say, 'younger' sibling. That is what will likely frustrate or quench any attempt to 'briefly' outline and capture the state of public international law against which Jessup sketched his idea of transnational law and which continues to provide, for many scholars in this field today, a sounding board for their engagement with the differences and the overlaps between inter- and transnational law. Similar to the manifold ways in which transnational law has been understood, right into the present time, as a framework and platform from which to place law under historical and ideological as well as interdisciplinary scrutiny, we can see such efforts carried out with regard to (public) international law with great promise.[28] The critical value of such work lies in opening up a field of legal doctrine as 'law in action',[29] as – literally – law *in context*. Rather than approaching a legal field as the collection of principles and rules, as they are elaborated, affirmed, altered and promulgated over time in a universe of legislators, governments and judges, the contextualization of a legal field and its constituent components – including its norms and processes but also its actors[30] – promises a richer and

---

world affairs is an elemental respect for some imperfect measure of symmetry – that is, the claims of right that one nation asserts must generally be available to other nations to assert. Of course, inequalities of power introduce some asymmetry as the powerful state can emphasize distinguishing features of the two contexts to establish why a claim adverse to its interests is "illegal" despite its own earlier reliance upon the legality of a similar sort of claim.'

[27] See, for example, now thirty years ago, Thomas L. Hughes, *The Twilight of Internationalism*, 61 FOREIGN AFF. 25–48 (1985), and Tom J. Farar, *International Law: The Critics Are Wrong*, 71 FOREIGN AFF. 22–45 (1988), as well as the insightful commentary by Congyan Cai, *New Great Powers and International Law in the 21st Century*, 24 EUR. J. INT'L L. 755–95 (2012), arguing that the rise of NGPs should be seen as challenge and promise to international law, specifically as it should provoke western lawyers to critically examine their 'universalist' professions with regard to the international legal order they have been promoting.

[28] See, for example, the references in note 69, below.

[29] In this regard, see, of course, the important contributions out of the University of Wisconsin School of Law, including STEWART MACAULAY, WILLIAM WHITFORD, KATHRYN HENDLEY, & JONATHAN LIPSON, CONTRACTS: LAW IN ACTION (1991); Stewart Macaulay & William C. Whitford, *The Development of Contracts: Law in Action*, 87 TEMP. L. REV. 793–806 (2015).

[30] YVES DEZALAY & BRYANT GARTH, DEALING IN VIRTUE: INTERNATIONAL COMMERCIAL ARBITRATION AND THE CONSTRUCTION OF A TRANSNATIONAL LEGAL ORDER (1996); MARY J. MOSSMAN, THE FIRST WOMEN LAWYERS: A COMPARATIVE STUDY OF GENDER, LAW AND THE LEGAL PROFESSIONS (2006); Swethaa Ballakrishnen, *Why Is Gender a Form of Diversity? Rising Advantages for Women in Indian Global Law Firms*, 20 IND. J. GLOBAL LEGAL STUD. 1261–89 (2013).

more differentiated account of the field's entanglement in varied social environments.

Contextualization leads to a legal field becoming engaged with its actual and its discursive, its empirical and its cognitive and epistemological environments. We can see this quite clearly today in international law, and this book offers compelling evidence of such advances specifically under the heading of transnational law. As for the former, it is evident how 'international law' – as field, idea and political project – has become deeply implicated in a more expanded as well as interdisciplinary engagement with law, political theory and the prospects of democratic governance in a globally interconnected world.[31] It is here where disciplinary field borders appear to have become increasingly blurry, and international lawyers – along and in engagement with their colleagues in sociology, anthropology, politics and geography, postcolonialism and philosophy – have been engaging with questions of global governance, 'world order'[32] and with the challenges of how to productively navigate – still, as lawyers – the emerging, interdisciplinary discourses.[33] These efforts manifest themselves in the conflict sites international lawyers move into to challenge and engage inherited understandings of what international law is and isn't about. Today's international lawyers illustrate, quite strikingly, their interest in law that can reach across national borders in both directions: outwards, into the fragmented spaces of 'regime' and 'coalition' building whether this concerns the 'war on terror',[34] global financial regulation[35] or climate change governance,[36] but also inwards and towards the internal, domestic political sociology of struggling democratic societies. As Philip Alston recently observed with regard to the ubiquitous rise of populism (as well as radicalized and racialized politics), 'The world as we in the human rights movement have known it in recent years is no longer. The populist agenda

---

[31] See, e.g., Emmanuelle Jouannet, *What Is the Use of International Law? International Law as a 21st Century Guardian of Welfare*, 28 MICH. J. INT'L L. 815–62 (2007), and Daniel Bodansky, *What's in a Concept? Global Public Goods, International Law, and Legitimacy*, 23 EUR. J. INT'L L. 651–68 (2012).

[32] B.S. CHIMNI, INTERNATIONAL LAW AND WORLD ORDER (2d ed. 2018).

[33] MICHEL-ROLPH TROUILLOT, GLOBAL TRANSFORMATIONS: ANTHROPOLOGY AND THE MODERN WORLD (2003); Saskia Sassen, *Spatialities and Temporalities of the Global, in* GLOBALIZATION 260–78 (Arjun Appadurai ed., 2001); William I. Robinson, *Debate on the New Global Capitalism: Transnational Capitalist Class, Transnational State Apparatuses, and Global Crisis*, 7 INT'L CRITICAL THOUGHT 171–89 (2017); RICHARD FALK, POWER SHIFT: ON THE NEW GLOBAL ORDER (2016).

[34] Ed Morgan, *Slaughterhouse Six: Updating the Law of War*, 5 GERMAN L.J. 525–44 (2004).

[35] Tony Porter, *Public and Private Authority in the Transnational Response to the 2008 Financial Crisis*, 30 POL'Y & SOC'Y 175–84 (2011).

[36] See, in this regard, Minas, in this volume.

that has made such dramatic inroads recently is often avowedly nationalistic, xenophobic, misogynistic, and explicitly antagonistic to all or much of the human rights agenda.'[37] International law, otherwise conceived as being concerned with the relations between sovereign nation states, has become deeply entangled in exercises of critical historiography, ideology critique and a self-critical evaluation of its own 'liberal' foundations and assumptions.[38]

B THE PRACTICE (NOT NECESSARILY THEORY) OF TRANSNATIONAL LAW

In order to more adequately assess the origins as well as the trajectories of today's ever more energetically unfolding engagement with transnational, it is important to first take stock of Jessup's original contribution. In this regard, it is worthwhile considering what Jessup said (and meant) and what has either been ascribed to him or presented as the result of having drawn inspiration from his ideas or having built on top of what he had lain out then, in 1956, and to recognize what he did not say and where we might identify certain limitations in his position or approach.

To begin with, it is crucial to remind ourselves that Jessup's proposal was both immensely practical as well as theoretical. On the one hand, his analysis was directed at his colleagues in public international law, international economic law and arbitration, whom he invited – in fact, encouraged – to adopt a pragmatic view of what he saw to actually be taking place all around them with regards to the nature of international and *transnational* legal problems and with view to the *actually* evolving landscape of relevant norms that are drawn upon, invoked or created in response to these problems.[39] On the other, the increasing complexity of border-crossing problems

---

[37] Philip Alston, *The Populist Challenge to Human Rights*, 9 J. Hum. Rts. Practice 1, 1–2 (2017).

[38] See the important, critical interventions by Isabel Feichtner, *Realizing Utopia Through the Practice of International Law*, 23 Eur. J. Int'l L. 1143–57 (2012), and by Christine Schwöbel-Patel, *Populism, International Law, and the End of Keep Calm and Carry on Lawyering*, Netherlands Y.B. Int'l L. (forthcoming 2019), https://ssrn.com/abstract=3300695. *See also* Vicki C. Jackson, *Paradigms of Public Law: Transnational Constitutional Values and Democratic Challenges*, 8 Int'l J. Con. L. 517–62 (2010), and, earlier, Ruth Gordon, *Critical Race Theory and International Law: Convergence and Divergence. Racing American Foreign Policy*, 94 Proc. Am. Soc'y Int'l L. 260–66 (2000).

[39] Jessup, *supra* note 3, at 30: 'To be sure, the United Nations is not a corporation and the state members are not shareholders and the analogy is very far from perfect. But the modern state, like the big corporation, has developed, for different reasons, a new sensitivity to public pressures; and the law (United Nations Charter or United States statute) has taken account of the new social consciousness.' *See also* Wolfgang Friedmann, The Changing Structure of International Law 40 (1964): 'A gradual change in the position of the individual has

arising among public, among private as well as among public and private actors provided a good enough reason for Jessup to push the envelope in testing existing legal concepts and frameworks. While his *Transnational Law* has received considerable attention in its own right, it can be seen – at least to some degree – to be standing in the context of his previous and ensuing work, which was overwhelmingly in public international law. Merely two years after his lectures at Yale, Jessup observed, in a reference to none other than himself: 'More extravagantly, the suggestion has been made that the traditional divisions between public international law and private international law and even some national law might be submerged in an ocean of "transnational law".'[40]

Challenging, thus, the two principal legal frameworks geared towards providing a regulatory architecture with which to address conflicts between either state or private parties, Jessup's proposal to think about a different approach in which one can bring ("submerge") these two together, as well as go beyond their respective restrictions, is – without a doubt – not only of practical relevance but also of immense theoretical importance. In particular, by extrapolating the already numerous examples in international and domestic legal conflict, where a resolution can be and oftentimes is found by recourse 'not by the application of law (although equally not in violation of law) but by a process of adjustment – an extralegal or metajuridical means',[41] Jessup was able to draw his listeners' attention to the coexistence and relevance of a myriad of public and private norms. Considering the challenge such a view would hold for a predominantly state-centric understanding of law, which has been an important dimension of international law's conceptual trajectory over time,[42] his invocation of a concept like 'transnational law' appears to concern a 'field' *of* law as much as a perspective *on* law per se.[43]

---

occurred, during the course of the nineteenth century, and gained far greater emphasis in the twentieth century. The individual has become a paramount object of concern, on the national as on the international level. [...] During the course of the nineteenth century, economic *laissez faire* gave way to the socially activist philosophy of the modern welfare state. This has, in our time, spread from the national to the international sphere.'

[40] PHILIP C. JESSUP, THE USE OF INTERNATIONAL LAW 63 (1959).

[41] JESSUP, *supra* note 3, at 6.

[42] Steve Charnovitz, *Two Centuries of Participation: NGOs and International Governance*, 18 MICH. J. INT'L L. 183–286 (1997), mapping the emergence of NGOs as internationally relevant actors of interest representation and mobilization along the NGOs' work on targets such as the slave trade, peace, workers' solidarity, trade, international law and NGOs themselves. *Id.* at 191–95.

[43] But note Oscar Schachter's observation regarding the late Jessup: 'He used concepts sparingly, but effectively, and he avoided windy rhetoric.' Oscar Schachter, *Philip Jessup's Life and Ideas*, 80 AM. J. INT'L L. 878, 878 (1986).

These two aspects warrant our attention as they illustrate the importance of Jessup's 'transnational' intervention in international law – and, arguably, well beyond. But while it is correct to assume that the practice-informed perspective, which Jessup emphasized in his Yale lectures as he exemplified the gaps in both public and private international law with regard to, as he called them, 'transnational problems', tended to capture the reality that lawyers working in international trade law and commercial arbitration understood to be their everyday working environment, it is fair to say that the *legal nature* – properly speaking – of 'transnational law' remained less distinctly discernible. And because this aspect of transnational law – its inherent 'legal' nature and its status *as* 'law' – remains a topic of much discussion to the present day – we need to reassess how Jessup himself engaged with this question. What we see in this regard is how Jessup kept approaching the question less as a legal philosopher or as a scholar writing in the tradition of analytical jurisprudence than as both a legal sociologist and legal cartographer and a practically minded negotiator (and diplomat) with sensibilities for the political tensions and practical impasses that characterize law's functioning in the context of great international transformation.

Well aware, at the same time, of a need to situate the idea and framework of transnational law in relation to existing doctrinal and historically evolved conceptual edifices, it appears that Jessup aimed at keeping a fine balance between relying on public and private international law as doctrinal and conceptual reference frameworks as far as they prove reliable, on the one hand, and pointing to the need for a different approach where their usefulness is cast in doubt in light of new problem developments, on the other. Early on in his exposition, he puts the complexity of the regulatory (legal?) landscape that he asks us to consider on the table:

> Some rules are made by ecclesiastical authorities as in specifying times and manners of fasting. Some are made by corporations regulating their sales agencies, as recently publicized in the hearings of the Senate Judiciary Antitrust and Monopoly Subcommittee on the practices of General Motors. Other rules are made by secret societies, by towns, cities, states. Still others are made by international organizations such as the Coal and Steel Community, the International Monetary Fund, or the OEEC. [...] Nowadays it is neither novel nor heretical to call all of these rules 'law'.[44]

'Simply', one might say, by identifying the host of competing law- and norm-making authorities as they actually operate in different sectors of

---

[44] JESSUP, *supra* note 3, at 9.

domestic and global society, Jessup is able to make transnational law more accessible, less exotic than it might otherwise seem.[45] Here, and in other places in *Transnational Law* we are directed towards a recognition of and engagement with a wider variety of relevant norms in border-crossing human and institutional interaction. At the same time, Jessup was hardly a legal pluralist in the way that other authors would take the coexistence *of* and the important tension *between* competing normative (legal and non-legal) orders not only as central to but as the decisive basis of their understanding of law as such.[46] Writing both as a public international lawyer and as an expert in transnational commercial law and arbitration, his emphasis in *Transnational Law* was on exploring the particular nature of border-crossing problems that involved confrontations and conflicts between public (state) and private (individuals, corporations) actors. A significant space in the book is occupied by the discussion of different theories of jurisdiction, through which Jessup effectively contrasts a problem-based concept of transnational law with an abstractly understood notion of state sovereignty:

> It would be the function of transnational law to reshuffle the cases and to deal out jurisdiction in the manner most conducive to the needs and convenience of all members of the international community. The fundamental approach would not start with sovereignty or power but from the premise that jurisdiction is essentially a matter of procedure which could be amicably arranged among the nations of the world. The transnational lawyer might bear in mind that even a genuine and not fictional territorial base is at times unsatisfactory, as in certain maritime situations: the problems raised by the enforcement of the United States Prohibition laws along Rum Row were not solved by a redefinition of territorial waters, but by international agreement on the procedures to be followed in apprehending smugglers on the high seas.[47]

Following this second chapter – entitled 'Power to Deal with Problems' – is an enlightening discussion in *Transnational Law*, where Jessup dives more deeply into an analysis of the *types of norms* that adjudicatory bodies find themselves confronted with in transnational law situations. Jessup's examples highlight instances where the identification of a state's uncontested jurisdictional

---

[45] This bias against transnational law as being not only not 'law' but in fact something out of the ordinary and, as such, bordering on the exotic, is still alive today.

[46] See the discussion in Peer Zumbansen, *Manifestations and Arguments: The Everyday Life of Transnational Legal Pluralism*, in THE OXFORD HANDBOOK OF GLOBAL LEGAL PLURALISM (Paul Schiff Berman ed., 2019).

[47] JESSUP, *supra* note 3, at 71.

claim on a case is absent[48] or where there is no obvious body of norms that appears to provide the legal basis of the arrangement in place. The latter can include, for example, contracts between an international organization and its employees or arbitration regimes where the parties have stipulated the application of a body of norms that can only be found to lie outside of both municipal and international law. The following observation was made by the arbitrator in an important arbitration case involving Sheikh Shakhbut of Abu Dhabi and Petroleum Development (Trucial Coast) Ltd.,[49] effectively providing 'the first controversy, public or private in nature, wherein the new legal doctrine was extensively employed'.[50] This new legal doctrine here at issue was the so-called Continental Shelf one, fundamentally concerned with 'the breadth of the territorial sea, the outer limit of the continental shelf, the extent of fishing rights, the nature of islands and archipelagos, and the kind of ocean regime required'.[51]

> What is the 'Proper Law' applicable in construing this contract? This is a contract made in Abu Dhabi and wholly to be performed in that country. If any municipal system of law were applicable, it would *prima facie* be that of Abu Dhabi. But no such law can reasonably be said to exist. The Sheikh administers a purely discretionary justice with the assistance of the Koran; and it would be fanciful to suggest that in this very primitive region there is any settled body of legal principles applicable to the construction of modern commercial instruments. Nor can I see any basis on which the municipal law of England could apply. On the contrary Clause 17 . . . repels the notion that the municipal law of any country, as such, could be appropriate. The terms of that clause invite, indeed prescribe, the application of principles rooted in the good sense and common practice of the generality of civilized nations – a sort of 'modern law of nature'.[52]

In his ensuing discussion, Jessup mentions a number of occasions where in similar situations of contracts between international organs and private parties the adjudicating bodies took recourse to '"a public law contract", whatever

---

[48] *Id.* at 76: 'Obviously, in many cases two or more states may law just claim to have such contacts with the factual situation as to justify both or all in asserting that they have jurisdiction to deal with the case.'

[49] *Matter of an Arbitration between the Petroleum Development (Trucial Coast) Limited and His Excellency Sheikh Shakhbut Bin Sultan Bin Za'id, Ruler of Abu Dhabi and Its Dependencies*, 1 Int'l & Comp. L.Q. 247 (1952).

[50] Edwin J. Cosford, Jr., *The Continental Shelf and the Abu Dhabi Award*, 1 McGill L.J. 109, 111 (1953).

[51] Harrop O. Freeman, *Law of the Continental Shelf and Ocean Resources – An Overview*, 3:2 Cornell Int'l L.J. 105, 105 (1970).

[52] Jessup, *supra* note 3, at 81.

that may imply',[53] to 'general principles'[54] as well as to 'the applicable principles of international law, justice and equity'.[55] He thus lays the groundwork for his concluding and today again relevant remarks regarding the need of a *transnational* law for transnational problems. But with a view to the language used here ('primitive'; 'generality of civilized nations') to describe a region or a legal community and their norms, we need to acknowledge and, indeed, insist on the importance of taking a radically more differentiated and sensible approach to discursively and practically engage with sociopolitical communities and their normative frameworks.[56]

As far as Jessup's repeated suggestion to adopt a *problem*-oriented attitude is concerned, it soon becomes evident how such an approach is anything but straightforward. The selection and invocation of problem-adequate and relevant norms, unavoidably, occurs from within an assembly of existing national and international, public and private legal norms that need to be identified, assessed and positioned. In the case of Jessup, reading *Transnational Law* in the context of his scholarship in international law, particularly *The Modern Law of Nations*, it is his belief in universalizable traits, shared values and generally identifiable interests relevant for the international community that ultimately shape his engagement. In it, we witness a masterful combination of legal philosophy and doctrinal–conceptual analogy between an emerging transnational law and a field, which he perceives as particularly relevant in this context – maritime law:

> But, it will be objected, one purpose of law is certainty. Individual persons, corporations, states, and international organizations must know the rules by which they should govern their conduct from day to day; such certainty cannot exist if decisions are to be rendered according to the whim of the judge who in his travels may have become fascinated by the tribal customs of Papua. The old customary law of Burma provided that if I entertain a guest at dinner who drinks well but not too wisely, and who on his way home is beaten by robbers or clawed by a tiger or bitten by a cobra, I am liable. But we do not consider it reasonable to impose such liability on the exurbanite host

---

[53] *Id.* at 91.

[54] *Id.* at 93–94: 'Here then we have judicial bodies interpreting contracts and awarding damages without being able to draw upon any specific body of law and, in general, without resorting to the rules of conflict of laws. They do draw upon general principles of law which may essentially be a good description of conflicts rules themselves.'

[55] *Id.* at 94.

[56] Boaventura de Sousa Santos, *Beyond Abyssal Thinking. From Global Lines to Ecologies of Knowledges*, Eurozine 1–41 (2007); *see also* Jonas Bens & Larissa Vetters, *Ethnographic Legal Studies: Reconnecting Anthropological and Sociological Traditions*, 50 J. Legal Pluralism & Unofficial L. 239–54 (2018).

whose housebound guest is injured through one of the hazards of the environs of New York City. Clearly the law must be specified. By whom?[57]

Jessup answers this question in the following manner:

> By the authority which has the power to control the decisions of those who will sit in judgment. Such authority may be found in the Connecticut Legislature, in the Congress of the United States, in the joint will of several states expressed through treaties or resolutions of the UN General Assembly. It may also be found in the courts themselves as when they rely on a Restatement of the American Law Institute to guide their choice of law where the controlling legislature has not prescribed the rule they must follow. The courts must have, in Judge Wyzanski's phrase, 'the robust common sense to avoid writing opinions [108] and entering decrees adapted with academic nicety to the vagaries of forty-eight States,' or, we may add here, of seventy-eight nations.[58]

We have referred to Jessup's commitment to public purpose and to community interests, and the here-cited passage points further in that direction. Throughout his book he continues to emphasize the 'procedural' and deliberative, even collaborative, dimension of transnational law creation through the interaction of members of the 'international community', and even where he directed our attention to the challenges that domestic judges face in the absence of unambiguously applicable legal norms,[59] he never seems to endorse the idea of an autonomously deciding, monadic judge. In other words, he appears not particularly interested in psychologizing or individualizing legal genius but instead insists on placing the lawyer's and judge's engagement with and, by consequence, the continuing creation of transnational law in a shared space of collective practice, discourse and contestation. Neither is nor should law for Jessup be created in what Schmitt described as the legal arcanum of power, exercised behind closed doors;[60] nor does he idealize the role of the solitary judge who finds, summons or creates the law, either by regressing into his *forum internum* or by appeal to a higher entity.[61] Jessup's judges and adjudicatory bodies are always described as

---

[57] JESSUP, *supra* note 3, at 107.

[58] *Id.* at 107–08.

[59] *Id.* at 96.

[60] CARL SCHMITT, THE CRISIS OF PARLIAMENTARY DEMOCRACY (Ellen Kennedy trans., MIT Press 1985) (1923).

[61] Nathan Isaacs, Book Review, 20 MICHIGAN LAW REVIEW 688, 688–89 (1922) (reviewing BENJAMIN CARDOZO, THE NATURE OF THE JUDICIAL PROCESS (1921)): 'In fact, many an opinion proceeds by discussing the matter "on principle" and then by "turning to the authorities," and

being part of a discursive and deliberative context, which is why it is important to acknowledge the reference to 'common sense' in his discussion of norms a judge will draw on. Because Jessup does not further elaborate on the legal theoretical or legal philosophical foundations of such common sense, we can limit ourselves at this point to a reference to the lively and ongoing discussions in legal philosophy with regard to the role of the judge in adjudication.[62]

While Jessup's reference to Lord Asquith of Bishopstone's invocation of 'common sense'[63] can be seen as indication of his acknowledgement of the psychological dimension of adjudication and, in particular, of the idea that transnational law is, in fact, being created, shaped and applied by human actors, such as judges, he does pursue neither the normative quality nor the substantive content of transnational law much further in this context or in the sense he did in his earlier, important book *The Modern Law of Nations*, in 1948. Insisting, in 1956, on the importance of 'procedure', Jessup's interest in arguing for an idea and framework of transnational law seems above all geared towards the actual *practice* of transnational law among lawyers, judges and officials as members of state governments, international organizations and private entities. This, then, is the direction the book takes in its final sections:

> Transnational law then includes both civil and criminal aspects, it includes what we know as public and private international law, and it includes national law, both public and private. There is no inherent reason why a judicial tribunal, whether national or international, should not be authorized to choose from all of these bodies of law the rule considered the most in

---

winds up by a justification on the basis of "policy." Subconscious processes must, of course, be gathered from between lines of [689] an opinion, except in the case of a very few judges who are given to the habit of dipping into autobiography in their judicial pronouncements.' But see also the intriguing discussion by Devlin, *Judges and Lawmakers*, 39 Mod. L. Rev. 1, 16 (1976): 'It is a great temptation to cast the judiciary as an elite which will bypass the traffic-laden ways of the democratic process. But it would only apparently be a bypass. In truth it would be a road that would never rejoin the highway but would lead inevitably, however long and winding the path, to the totalitarian state.'

[62] *See, e.g.*, Gregory C. Keating, *Justifying Hercules: Ronald Dworkin and the Rule of Law*, 12 Am. Bar Foundation Res. J. 525, 527 (1987): 'On the one hand, hard cases embarrass legal positivism because they show that the law is never merely a matter of social fact. What the law is, is always and everywhere partly dependent on what it ought to be. In legal decision law and morals merge. On the other hand, hard cases embarrass legal realism because they show that legal decision is not (and cannot be) merely a matter of morality. Legal decision must respect the institutional history within which it is embedded-the fabric of preexisting rights woven by prior judicial decisions and legislative choices.'

[63] Jessup, *supra* note 3, at 81.

conformity with reason and justice for the solution of any particular controversy. The choice need not be determined by territoriality, personality,
nationality, domicile, jurisdiction, sovereignty, or any other rubric save as
these labels are reasonable reflections of human [107] experience with
the absolute and relative convenience of the law and of the forum – *lex
conveniens* and *forum conveniens.*[64]

Indeed, Jessup keeps returning to 'problems' as the starting point for any
engagement with transnational law, rather than seeking to theoretically
develop a concept of transnational law as an additional, complementary *field*
besides private and public international law. In what appears to be the
pointing of a finger to the methodological nationalism that concerns him in
contemporary legal education and political science training,[65] Jessup
expresses his concern with the way in which the responsible institutions fall
short of preparing their graduates for the distinctly transnational nature of the
problems before them:

> If those who are trained, particularly in our law schools and graduate schools
> of political science, are nourished on the pap of old dogmas and fictions, it is
> not expected that they will later approach the solution of transnational
> problems with open-minded [108] intelligence instead of open-mouthed
> surprise. Within the local or national framework education has made great
> strides in seeking to convey an appreciation of the economic, social, and
> political problems which the sciences of law and government seek to adjust.
> In the international or, more broadly, the transnational area there are occa-
> sional beacons which burn brightly but there are few well-lighted avenues.[66]

Concluding his analysis and, arguably, his 'call to arms' is a short exposé of
how maritime law, in particular, can offer various insights into a transnational
regulatory regime brought about by a combination of public and private actors
in striving both for uniformity in the existing national laws and in state
governments working together towards the creation of a sensible legal framework governing the seas.[67]

[64] *Id.* at 106–07.
[65] Larry Catá Backer, *Human Rights and Legal Education in the Western Hemisphere: Legal
Parochialism and Hollow Universalism*, 21 PENN ST. INT'L L. REV. 115–55 (2002). *See also* Mary
C. Daly, *The Structure of Legal Education and the Legal Profession, Multidisciplinary Practice,
Competition, and Globalization*, 52 J. LEGAL EDUC. 480–90 (2002).
[66] JESSUP, *supra* note 3, at 108–09.
[67] *Id.* at 109–11. See also the important study by ANDREAS MAURER, LEX MARITIMA: GRUNDZÜGE
EINES TRANSNATIONALEN SEEHANDELSRECHTS (2012) and, more recently, the contributions to
STRESS TESTING THE LAW OF THE SEA: DISPUTE RESOLUTION, DISASTERS & EMERGING
CHALLENGES (Stephen Minas & Jordan Diamond eds., 2018).

Jessup's argument for transnational law should be read as a plaidoyer for international cooperation and multilateralism. This is even more significant when we consider how some of the last lines of *Transnational Law*, where Jessup voices his concern with regard to developments in US foreign policy at the time, might as well have been written in our present context:

> It may be hard to imagine that the United States would play a leading role in bringing about in broader fields agreement on rules of transnational law which would be applied in our forty-nine judicial jurisdictions. Long before Mr. Bricker* became the eponym for a new term for political and constitutional provincialism, the United States Government declined to become a party to any of the general treaties of private international law by which so many states of the world are bound.[68]

Finally, the last lines of Jessup's book merit citation, as it is here where he turns to decision makers, politicians and legislators and to scholars to effectively and productively bridge the gap between practice and theory in the area of transnational law:

> [...] if there be any virtue in developing transnational law, much more exploration and analysis would need to precede the ponderous tread of governmental action. In the words of Mr. Justice Holmes: 'The danger is that the able and practical minded should look with indifference or distrust upon ideas the connection of which with their business is remote.' So must the headlong scholar supply the proverbial characterization to himself where the foreign offices, the legislatures, and the courts still fear to tread. Seeing they themselves are wise, they may suffer the scholar gladly.[69]

C TRANSNATIONAL LAW AS PRACTICE *AND* THEORY

In what follows, we shall move away, somewhat, from Jessup and *Transnational Law* in order to take a bigger-picture look at the trajectory of ideas around something like transnational law up into our present time. As will soon

---

* The reference here is to Senator John W. Bricker, a Republican, who served in the US Senate from 1946 to 1958 after three terms as governor of Ohio. He is the originator of the 'Bricker Amendment', which would have curtailed the president's treaty-making power. While receiving support from members of both parties, the proposed bill failed in the House of Representatives.

[68] JESSUP, *supra* note 3, at 112. See, for a present-day snapshot, Michael Clarke & Anthony Ricketts, *Donald Trump and American Foreign Policy: The Return of the Jacksonian Tradition*, 36 COMP. STRATEGY 366–79 (2017).

[69] JESSUP, *supra* note 3, at 113.

become apparent, there are today numerous forms of engagements with 'transnational law', many of which manifest but the most cursory reference to the book of 1956 or, even less, to Jessup himself. Instead, what we see is to a large degree part of what Schachter observed already more than thirty years ago with regard to the growing relevance of transnational legal education in law schools.[70] Another dimension of transnational law in recent decades and today is, however, that of a continuously expanding and, in many parts, distinctly interdisciplinary, critical engagement with law, its institutions, its norms and its associated processes and procedures, in an 'age of globalization'.[71] 'Theory',[72] thus, plays a crucial role in the engagement with transnational law, especially as its status as *law* – a set of binding rules, created by a legitimate authority[73] – continues to be its Achilles' heel. With the view to a legal philosophical engagement with transnational law, Roger Cotterrell very astutely formulated this point thus:

> Since conceptual study of law has been so central to legal philosophy (insofar as it has aimed to develop philosophical theories of the nature of law), the issue is whether legal philosophy's explanations of law can cope with the new (or newly prominent) phenomena of transnational law, or whether its

[70] Schachter, *supra* note 2, at 894: 'One early consequence of the increased recognition of "transnational law" has been the growth of law school courses concerned with international transactions, human rights, international economic and social arrangements and other transnational subjects that did not fit neatly into the traditional divisions of public and private international law.' Incidentally, the Transnational Law Institute at the Dickson Poon School of Law of King's College London, which hosted the JessupTransnationalLaw@60 conference, was founded through a significant donation aimed at fostering 'transnational legal education'.

[71] *See, e.g.*, BEYOND TERRITORIALITY: TRANSNATIONAL LEGAL AUTHORITY IN AN AGE OF GLOBALIZATION (GUNTHER HANDL, JOACHIM ZEKOLL & PEER ZUMBANSEN eds., 2012).

[72] See, for example, the intriguing survey by Fleur Johns, *International Legal Theory: Snapshots from a Decade of International Legal Life*, 10 MELBOURNE J. INT'L L. 1–10 (2009), and James T. Gathii, *TWAIL: A Brief History of Its Origins, Its Decentralized Network, and a Tentative Bibliography*, 3 TRADE, L. & DEV. 26–64 (2011). See also the study by THOMAS SKOUTERIS, THE NOTION OF PROGRESS IN INTERNATIONAL LAW DISCOURSE (2009), and the contributions to the OXFORD HANDBOOK OF INTERNATIONAL LEGAL THEORY (Anne Orford & Florian Hoffmann eds., 2016).

[73] Tom Farer, *Toward an Effective International Legal Order: From Co-existence to Concert?*, 3 SUR. INT'L J. HUM. RTS. 150, 152–53 (2006): 'An authoritative legal system certainly is more than an archipelago of functional regimes. However effectively a blend of rules and principles, sometimes embedded in formal bureaucratic institutions, may as an observable matter stabilise behaviour and expectations concerning a wide array of subject areas as diverse as the uses of the seas and the protection of the chicken-breasted sloth, they will not constitute a legal order unless they are seen as instances of a general system of authority that applies reasonably effectively to all states and addresses the existential concerns of human communities which include but is not limited to the question of who may use force under what circumstances.'

ignoring of these phenomena [...] undermines the whole legal theoretical house of cards that the philosophers have built.[74]

While the globalization of human and institutional, material and immaterial affairs is widely accepted to have prompted, inter alia, significant challenges for inherited conceptual frameworks of societal ordering, the contours of what will replace them remain nebulous at best. As globalization is seen to shake the edifices – however real or 'merely' symbolic they themselves may be – of a political order based on an understanding of a relationship of interdependence between 'state' and 'society',[75] the prescriptive dimension of transnational law as a label for newly emerging regulatory formations is intimately tied to a critique of the conceptions of political, legal and economic order that had their origin in the post-revolutionary, Westphalian age of sovereignty of the eighteenth century as they unfolded through the course of the long nineteenth and the divisive twentieth centuries. Regardless of whether we draw on optimistic or critical accounts of social theory building against the backdrop of globalization,[76] we are struck by the prominence and presence of conceptual building blocks that owe their historical and symbolic capital to a long tradition of 'state theory', 'modernization' and 'development'.[77] Among those, the inherited concepts of the state and its relation to 'the market' and to 'society', or of 'the public' and 'the private',[78] constitute crucial conflict and contestation sites in the present struggle over the fate of democratic sovereignty and public regulatory competences.[79] 'The state-centrism and the nation state/inter-state framework that informs much theorization and analysis of world politics, political economy, and class structure is [172] ever more incongruent with twenty-first century world developments.'[80] Underneath this tip lies a vast iceberg of interdisciplinary work that has been unfolding over the past twenty years and that seeks to map and engage the

---

[74] Roger Cotterrell, *What Is Transnational Law?*, 37 LAW & SOC. INQUIRY 500, 504 (2012).

[75] See the first chapter in JÜRGEN HABERMAS, THE POST-NATIONAL CONSTELLATION (2001).

[76] Compare MARTIN WOLF, WHY GLOBALIZATION WORKS (2d ed. 2005), with QUINN SLOBODIAN, THE GLOBALISTS (2018).

[77] For a discussion of these dimensions, see Amanda Perry-Kessaris, *Prepare Your Indicators: Economics Imperialism at the Shores of Law and Development*, 7 INT'L J. L. CONTEXT 401–21 (2011).

[78] Friedmann, *supra* note 39, at 190: 'The neat distinction of the categories of public and private law has long ceased to be expressive of the realities of contemporary municipal, as well as international, law, even though the distinction still dominates the teaching curricula of law schools.'

[79] Walter Mattli & Ngaire Woods, *In Whose Benefit? Explaining Regulatory Change in Global Politics, in* THE POLITICS OF REGULATION 1–43 (Walter Mattli & Ngaire Woods eds., 2009).

[80] Robinson, *supra* note 33, at 171–72.

complex correlation and interdependence of global marketization and 'state transformation'.[81] This analysis *of* and critical engagement *with* the prospects and limits of transnational governance regimes, in other words, is the background and context to the research which continues to unfold in law in response to the 'globalization challenge'.[82]

The here-combined essays take their inspiration from what we understand to be at the heart of Jessup's bold proposal – namely, a distinct and decisive plug for an engagement with transnational law by seeking to identify new markers of lawmaking authorities, new authors and producers of norms and new formations of 'legal' and 'non-legal' norms. Jessup's starting point, if you will, was what he identified as a misconception with regard to what should be considered a norm that has influence over people's lives. 'As man has developed his needs and his facilities for meeting his needs, the rules become more numerous and more complicated. History, geography, preferences, convenience, and necessity have dictated dispersion of the authority to make rules men live by.'[83] In order to illustrate his point more effectively, Jessup confronted his audience with a number of scenarios in the form of small dramas, each containing two 'scenes', through which he sought to highlight the border crossing and both conceptually and doctrinally challenging materiality of contemporary legal conflicts. These illuminate the parallels between domestic and international constellations, in light of which Jessup would effectively argue for a transcending – transnational – perspective. While the first two scenes of the three dramas feature *individuals* who are caught up in disturbing, doctrinally challenging legal conflicts – variously involving

---

[81] Martin Shaw, *The State of Globalization: Towards a Theory of State Transformation*, 4 REV. INT'L POL. ECON. 497, 498 (1997): 'just as states have not always been nation-states, so their transformations in recent times have produced state forms which go far beyond the nation-state as classically understood'.

[82] *See* Harry W. Arthurs, *Law and Learning in an Era of Globalization*, 10 GERMAN L.J. 629–39 (2009) (special issue on 'Transnationalizing Legal Education'). *See also* Morag Goodwin, *Embracing the Challenge: Legal Scholarship in a Global Era*, 4 TRANSNAT'L LEGAL THEORY 686, 689 (2013): 'First, our starting point must be an acknowledgement of the magnitude of the challenge and recognition that we lack adequate responses to the need for a new, global legal perspective. We are at the beginning of our explorations and there can be no quick solutions, no simple fixes to the question of what the impact on our understanding of law is or will be, or, moreover, how we should respond as lawyers. Secondly, relatedly, we cannot therefore simply cling to the old assumptions or attempt to transpose them to the global or transnational realm. Instead, we need to recognise that the challenges to our understanding of what law is and how it functions are profound. This requires us to eschew grandiose responses or claims to have uncovered an over-arching theory of global law. Rather, an open starting position means accepting the possibility that we will fail to find shared understandings that are true in all places and at all times upon which law can rest.'

[83] JESSUP, *supra* note 3, at 8.

divorce or the exercise of membership rights in a stock corporation – the complementing second scenes invoke a very similar problem set on the *interstate* level. Set against an ensuing discussion between two art critics, Mr Orthodox and Mr Iconoclast, Jessup extrapolates the inseparability of the issues that underlie the allegedly exclusively 'domestic' versus the likewise purely 'international' constellations. The truly subversive thrust of Jessup's vision of transnational law lies in the parallels that can be drawn between supposedly local, or regional, issues in one place and those in another space, on another level. 'One's idea of what constitutes a "region" is apt to be artificial and highly subjective. The people in Boston and New York today might quite properly feel that they have a closer identity with the people of India than their grandfathers felt interest with the farmers of Iowa.'[84] With regard to stockholders, Jessup lets Mr Iconoclast point out the parallels between purportedly domestic discussions concerning 'shareholder democracy' and those involving increased demands for improved participatory rights in the United Nations and other international organizations.

Today, we are finding ourselves, on the one hand, to be heirs to Jessup's provocation in that his inherent call for a recategorization of international law is echoed throughout a lively engagement with the field's contested achievements and widely acknowledged limitations.[85] His sensitivity to the ways in which both public and private international law are called upon to respond to and to develop new ways of adequately addressing an increasingly intertwined world arena finds numerous reverberations in scholarship today.

We have already pointed to the importance of non-state norms and what Jessup calls 'extralegal or metajuridical means'.[86] As befits the lasting doubts vis-à-vis the viability of an international law in a world of violence,[87] an important manifestation of this appears to be the development of the tension-ridden relationship between international law and international

---

[84] *Id.* at 26.
[85] Martti Koskenniemi, *'The Lady Doth Protest Too Much': Kosovo and the Turn to Ethics in International Law*, 65 MOD. L. REV. 159–75 (2002); Jan Wouters, *Perspectives for International Law in the Twenty-First Century: Chaos or a World Legal Order?*, 7 ETHICAL PERSP. 17–23 (2001); Upendra Baxi, *What May the 'Third World' Expect from International Law?*, 27 THIRD WORLD Q. 713–25 (2006); Luis Eslava & Sundhya Pahuja, *Between Resistance and Reform: TWAIL and the Universality of International Law*, 3 TRADE, L. & DEV. 103–30 (2011); ARNULF BECKER LORCA, MESTIZO INTERNATIONAL LAW: AN INTELLECTUAL HISTORY 1842–1933 (2014).
[86] JESSUP, *supra* note 3, at 6.
[87] Balakrishnan Rajagopal, *International Law and the Development Encounter: Violence and Resistance at the Margins*, 93 PROC. AM. SOC'Y INT'L L 16–27 (1999). See also the new paper by Luis Eslava, *El Estado Desarrollista: Independencia, Dependencia y la Historia del Sur*, REVISTA DERECHO DEL ESTADO (forthcoming 2019), on file with author.

relations.[88] Despite an early fundamental disagreement over the focus of investigation, which distanced 'realist' international relations scholars and their interest in states' behaviour from their international law colleagues' study of the legal validity of international norms,[89] the changed geopolitical as well as ideational environment in which both groups of scholars have been operating in the breathless aftermath of 1989–90 has arguably induced a number of approximations and increased forms of interaction between the two.[90] 'International legal rules, procedures and organizations', Anne Marie Slaughter Burley wrote in 1993,

> are more visible and arguably more effective than at any time since 1945. If the United Nations cannot accomplish everything, it once again represents a significant repository of hopes for a better world. And even as its current failures are tabulated, from Yugoslavia to the early weeks and then months of the Somali famine, the almost-universal response is to find ways to strengthen it. The resurgence of rules and procedures in the service of an organized international order is the legacy of all wars, hot or cold.[91]

Another crucial battleground of Jessup's 'stress testing'[92] of public and private international law has been the today vastly proliferating activities around 'transnational human rights litigation'. Kissed back to life through a Second Circuit Appeals Court decision in 1980,[93] the until then largely forgotten procedural rule, known as the Alien Tort Statute[94] fast became the reference point for a fierce struggle over the correct jurisdictional forum for cases involving labour and human rights, having occurred predominantly in

---

[88] See the landmark contribution by INTERDISCIPLINARY PERSPECTIVES ON INTERNATIONAL LAW AND INTERNATIONAL RELATIONS. STATE OF THE ART (Jeffrey L. Dunoff & Mark A. Pollack eds., 2012).

[89] Adam Irish, Charlotte Ku & Paul F. Diehl, *Bridging the International Law–International Relations Divide: Taking Stock of Progress*, 41 GA. J. INT'L & COMP. L. 357, 362 (2013): 'Unlike their international relations colleagues, the traditional objective of international legal scholars was not to explain the behavior of states. Rather, the primary objective of most international law scholarship historically was to determine which rules or standards have acquired the status of law.'

[90] See the chapter by Claire Cutler in this volume.

[91] Anne-Marie Slaughter Burley, *International Law and International Relations Theory: A Dual Agenda*, 87 AM. J. INT'L L. 205, 205 (1993).

[92] For this term, see STRESS TESTING THE LAW OF THE SEA: DISPUTE RESOLUTION, DISASTERS & EMERGING CHALLENGES (Stephen Minas & Jordan Diamond eds., 2018).

[93] Filártiga v. Peña-Irala, 630 F.2d 876 (2d Cir. 1980).

[94] 28 U.S.C. § 1350 (1789).

Third World countries.[95] Amazingly, almost forty years on, this struggle continues, replaying the well-known and tried conflict between a formalist application of corporate law's doctrine of legal personhood and a context-based and daring assertion of corporate responsibility for rights violations in a company's sphere of influence and control.[96]

With that in mind, what appears to emerge as a series of legal doctrinal, conceptual and methodological developments since Jessup's call for a *Transnational Law* in the 1950s points to the openness and view-expanding quality of the original proposal. It takes its place among other landmark contributions in the area of international law, but it is not confined to that field. Jessup's provocative insistence on the need for a legal framework for those cases where neither public nor private international law can offer a fully satisfying answer prompts his public international law colleagues to more seriously scrutinize the existing toolkit of international law's 'subjects', 'sources' and 'actors', while pushing those working in private international law/conflict of laws to put their long-held beliefs in '*forum non conveniens*' and '*ordre public*' to a critical test. Despite the field's relative youth, such debates have already a prolonged legacy. It can be said today that his choice of 'transnational law' has had an eye-opening effect insofar that Jessup's invocation of the term over time has remained 'on the table' in our continuing efforts to conceptualize law in a global context.

True to Jessup's invocation, then, of analogies between an international organization such as the UN and a multinational stock corporation such as,

---

[95] Beth van Schaack, *The Story Behind the Case that Launched a Legal Revolution: William J. Aceves, The Anatomy of Torture: A Documentary History of Filártiga v. Peña-Irala* (2007), 30 HUM. RTS. Q. 1042, 1042–43 (2008): 'Every once in a while, a case comes along that changes everything. Filártiga v. Peña Irala was one of those cases. The Filártiga plaintiffs made an audacious assertion: that Paraguayan victims of human rights violations could bring suit in a US federal court against a Paraguayan perpetrator for acts of torture and extrajudicial killing committed in Paraguay in violation of international law. The case established many firsts: that the Alien Tort Statute (ATS) supports assertions of extraterritorial jurisdiction, that long articulated but rarely enforced human rights norms are justiciable, that the individual is front and center in international law as victim and perpetrator, and that ensuring a robust system of accountability is consistent with the interests of the United States.'

[96] Among the more recent, distressing case law examples, see Das v. George Weston Ltd., 2017 ONSC 4129 (Can. Ont. Sup. Ct. J.), in which the court was asked to assess legal claims that had been brought by survivors of the 2013 Rana Plaza collapse and where it was found that, inter alia, 'Pleadings that are irrelevant, argumentative, inflammatory, inserted only for colour, inserted only to disconcert or humiliate, or that constitute bare unfounded allegations should be struck out as scandalous' (at 18). 'Unfortunately, the Plaintiffs' Statement of Claim (and their factums) are bloated with conclusory statements that simply allege a cause of action as if it was a material fact or that provide opinions and speculations as if they were proven material facts' (at 20).

today, Google, Apple or Microsoft, we should keep an eye on the sociology of
actors and on the anthropology of agency. In that sense, the era of critically
engaging MNEs is far from over – but the vantage points from which this
engagement occurs need to be reassessed – even more so as the multinational
enterprise has become both ubiquitous and invisibilized, spatialized and part
of everyone's quotidian inventory.[97] Arguably, then, where Jessup and his
contemporaries sought to excavate the normative commitments of an international (legal) order, we have learned to shift our gaze elsewhere: 'The global
nature of transnational corporations, and the partially cosmopolitan identities
formed in response to living in a globalized world, has thinkers the world over
developing proposals for new or re-worked institutions, mechanisms, and
frameworks for engaging the new conditions brought on by this individual
and corporate trend toward a globalization of the corporation and cosmopo-
litanization of the self.'[98]

Corporations are key actors within the ever more expansive, heterogenous
landscape of 'private' regulatory governance.[99] With the proliferation of
mixed, public–private standard setting in a host of different industry sectors
operating on a global scale, there is a widely shared consensus regarding the
immense challenges this rise of 'transnational private regulatory governance'
presents for constitutional as well as administrative law frameworks developed
in the context of the nation state.[100] By consequence, there has been a lively

---

[97] Shoshana Zuboff, *Big Other: Surveillance Capitalism and the Prospects of an Information
Civilization*, 30 J. INFO. TECH. 75, 80 (2015): 'Google and the "big data" project represent a
break with this past. Its populations are no longer necessary as the source of customers or
employees. Advertisers are its customers along with other intermediaries who purchase its data
analyses. Google employs only about 48,000 people as of this writing, and is known to have
thousands of applicants for every job opening. (As contrast: at the height of its power in 1953,
General Motors was the world's largest private employer.) Google, therefore, has little interest
in its users as employees.' In her 2019 book, THE AGE OF SURVEILLANCE CAPITALISM: THE
FIGHT FOR A HUMAN FUTURE AT THE NEW FRONTIER OF POWER (2019), she observes:
'Surveillance capitalism is the puppet master that imposes its will through the medium of the
ubiquitous digital apparatus. I now name the apparatus *Big Other*: it is the sensate,
computational, connected puppet that renders, monitors, computes, and modifies human
behaviour. Big Other combines these functions of knowing and doing to achieve a pervasive
and unprecedented means of behavioural modification' (*id.* at 376).

[98] Christiana Ochoa, *Towards a Cosmopolitan Vision of International Law: Identifying and
Defining CIL Post Sosa v. Alvarez-Machain*, 74 U. CIN. L. REV. 105, 106 (2006).

[99] Gunther Teubner, *Self-Constitutionalizing TNCs? On the Linkage of 'Public' and 'Private'
Corporate Codes of Conduct*, 18 IND. J. GLOBAL LEGAL STUD. 617–38 (2011); Christian Scheper,
Labour Networks under Supply Chain Capitalism: The Politics of the Bangladesh Accord, 48
DEV. & CHANGE 106988 (2017).

[100] Peer Zumbansen, *Administrative Law's global dream: Navigating Regulatory Spaces between
'National' and 'International'*, 11 INT'L J. CONST. L. 506–22 (2013).

debate among scholars as well as practitioners in different areas of law of how to best adapt existing doctrinal tools and principles as well as conceptual frameworks to the reality of 'spatialized' legal–regulatory regimes.[101] With globalization acting as the great scene-changing event in the background, lawyers have begun, for some time now, to look to other disciplines in the search for helpful analogies, frameworks or even just categories and vocabularies to make sense of law's changing constitution in a global context. As a result, scholars presently involved in studying 'transnational law' have long been reaching out to political science and sociology in order to develop a more adequate empirical and conceptual basis for the legal de-nationalization, privatization and spatialization phenomena before them.[102] In addition, transnational legal scholars today draw on fields such as anthropology, sociology, geography and history in the attempt to widen a potentially confining, overly legalistic lens through which to study the emerging phenomena.[103] To conclude this brief aperçu, it is important to mention that a growing segment of transnational law scholarship points to the fact that the questions raised by transnational law resonate on many levels with those already raised by critical legal scholars and, in particular, legal sociologists and legal anthropologists at earlier times in the context of domestic law.[104] It turns out, then, that one of the most important promises of renewal and transformation, currently associated with 'transnational law', lies in its

[101] David Harvey, *The Sociological and Geographical Imaginations*, 18 INT'L J. POL., CULTURE & SOC'Y 211–55 (2005); Philip Liste, *Geographical Knowledge at Work: Human Rights Litigation and Transnational Territoriality*, 22 EUR. J. INT'L REL. 217–39 (2015). But see also Larry Catá Backer, in this volume, for an insightful investigation into the transnational business enterprise as the key forum of transnational law's formation.
[102] Knop, Michaels & Riles, *Foreword*, 71 LAW & CONTEMP. PROBS. 1, 10 (2008): 'The true promise of interdisciplinarity, then, is not the mere substitution of one discipline for another, but mutual enrichment. This insight becomes all the more important if we want to dramatically broaden the range of issues, questions, theoretical frameworks, methodological approaches, and historical and cultural contexts in which conflicts problems are analyzed. We believe the interdisciplinary project can be pushed further to engage a much wider range of methods and concerns, including, in particular, approaches that are noninstrumentalist in character, those that do not aim to translate immediately into technical solutions to doctrinal problems.'
[103] Laura Knöpfel, *Contesting the UN Guiding Principles on Business and Human Rights from Below* (Swisspeace, Working Paper No. 4/2017, 2017), https://www.swisspeace.ch/fileadmin/user_upload/Media/Publications/Working_Paper/SP_Working-Paper_1704-web.pdf; Matthew Canfield, *Banana Brokers: Communicative Labor, Translocal Translation, and Transnational Law*, 31 PUB. CULTURE 69–92 (2018).
[104] Sally Engle Merry, *New Legal Realism and the Ethnography of Transnational Law*, 31 LAW & SOC. INQUIRY 975–95 (2006); Peer Zumbansen, *Law after the Welfare State: Formalism, Functionalism and the Ironic Turn of Reflexive Law*, 58 AM. J. COMP. L. 769 (2008).

critical reflection impulse with regard to 'law' as such, not merely in the context of the contested relationship of 'globalization and the law':

> Over the course of the Twentieth Century, international law lost its privileged place as the primary conceptual framework for understanding the cross-border development of norms. The introduction of universal human rights standards, the recognition of interdependence among nation-states, the development of international courts and institutions, the growing diffusion of people, money, and information across territorial borders, and the increasing interest in normative development and legal consciousness outside of formal governmental spheres have collectively eroded the foundations of traditional positivist public international law, which had often been conceived only as a set of rules entered into by nation-states to govern their relationships with each other.[105]

D FROM 'GLOBALIZATION AND THE LAW' TO 'TRANSNATIONAL LAW'

The foregoing observations should have provided some background for the still evolving engagement with and debates around what is 'transnational law'. And still we seem to have skirted the expectation of offering an accessible, easy-to-use and yet all-encompassing definition of the concept. Surely, there is that by Jessup himself, as there are others.[106] It is important to draw on a number of those because even a cursory survey will further illustrate the complexity of the problem that the label 'transnational law' appears to be being attached to.

In Jessup's well-known dictum, transnational law is taken to include 'all law which regulates actions or events that transcend national frontiers. Both public and private international law are included, as are other rules which do not fit wholly into such standard categories.'[107] A crucial aspect of Jessup's definition is how he depicts the 'situation' to which a concept such as transnational law is responding:

[105] Paul Schiff Berman, *From International Law to Law and Globalization*, 43 COLUM. J. TRANSNAT'L L. 485, 555 (2005).
[106] See, for example, the definition compiled in the online Free Dictionary, according to which transnational law is '*All the law – national, international, or mixed – that applies to all persons, businesses, and governments that perform or have influence across state lines.* Transnational law regulates actions or events that transcend national frontiers. It involves individuals, corporations, states, or other groups—not just the official relations between governments of states.'
[107] JESSUP, *supra* note 3, at 2 (emphasis added).

Transnational situations, then, may involve individuals, corporations, states, organizations of states, or other groups. [...] [4] [...] One is sufficiently aware of the transnational activities of individuals, corporations, and states. When one considers that there are also in existence more than 140 intergovernmental organizations commonly described as international, one realizes the almost infinite variety of the transnational situations which may arise.[108]

What is captured by these important remarks, early on in a still continuing investigation into the nature of transnational law, is the need to place the idea and emerging field *in context*. In order to fruitfully speak of transnational law, one needs to consider the factors that drive its emergence and give it shape. As has become strikingly evident in the time since Jessup spoke to his audience in New Haven, transnational law is being engaged with across a host of scholars as well as practitioners, working in a wide range of legal subfields and different disciplines, and it is through this engagement that transnational law emerges as a combination of elements, each of which is important to the whole. As such, 'transnational law' depicts a scholarly discourse about the role, status and nature of law in a global context as well as how it is being applied to the anthropological and sociological accounts of regulatory arrangements in local settings and their interdependence with norm-setting processes that occur on and between different levels of order. While a lot of the scholarly engagement with transnational law has astutely been described as 'focusing on "subjects" (law, addressing transnational activities and situations) or on sources (law, whether international or foreign, that is imported and exported across borders)',[109] we are prompted to acknowledge this dual focus against the background of the confluence between normative and descriptive accounts of transnational law that have been produced over time. But, precisely because of the constantly recurring risk of an amalgamation of the normative and the descriptive dimensions of a 'transnational' 'law' – as for example in the already-alluded-to debates over the *lex mercatoria* – it is important to acknowledge and to accept that transnational law continues to be a contested concept that potentially stands for several different things. For some, it is simply a label for those norms that are being generated (as well as administered and adjudicated) by a host of actors not limited to state entities and that address regulatory challenges across jurisdictional borders.[110] Others accept

---

[108] *Id.* at 3–4.
[109] Gregory Shaffer, *Transnational Legal Ordering and State Change, in* TRANSNATIONAL LEGAL ORDERING AND STATE CHANGE 1, 5 (Gregory Shaffer ed., 2013).
[110] KLAUS-PETER BERGER, THE CREEPING CODIFICATION OF THE NEW LEX MERCATORIA (2d rev. ed. 2010).

the empirical accuracy of this description but challenge transnational law as not only depicting but essentially legitimizing these processes normatively.[111]

This confrontation places transnational law under bright lights and exposes its normative ambivalence. At a minimum, what this dispute highlights is that legal fields are never just a collection of value-neutral norms created through technical rule-making processes. In each newly created, amended or abdicated norm, there is a choice involved, at the heart of which lies a struggle for law.[112] And it is against this background that those engagements with transnational law carry the greatest promise and unfold in light of the concept's normative contestation and with a keen awareness of the field's deep sociological and anthropological roots.

The research done by Gregory Shaffer and Terence Halliday offers crucial insights in this regard. Their most recent conceptual work on 'transnational legal orders/ordering'[113] has to be seen against the background of an astute analysis of the norm-creating processes between different ordering levels and through the involvement of different, public and private actors. As a result, rather than positing the debate over the nature and existence of 'transnational law' somewhere in the abstract or aligning themselves with those scholars for whom the field above all represents a challenge of 'state law' against the background of competing ideas and understandings of globalization, they delve into the intricate details of how norms are actually being produced, disseminated and consolidated over time:

> The term 'global' law implies that legal norms are being created and diffused globally in different legal domains that do not necessarily involve traditional international law between nation-states. Such terminology of 'global law' is misleading because much legal ordering today is not global in its geographic reach, but it nonetheless involves variation in legal ordering beyond the nation state. Because the geographic, substantive, and organizational scope of such legal ordering varies, and because it involves both public and private actors, these processes are best captured by the concepts of *transnational legal orders* and *transnational legal ordering*.[114]

---

[111] A. Claire Cutler, Private Power and Public Authority (2010).

[112] Rudolf Ihering, Der Kampf ums Recht 34 (Felix Ermacora ed., Propyläen Verlag 1992) (1872): 'Denn das bestehende Recht, die herrschenden Rechtssätze hängen mit tausenden Wurzeln und Fäden in der Wirklichkeit, mit den Interessen zusammen, und tritt ein neuer Rechtssatz auf, dann handelt es sich nicht bloß um seine Wahrheit und Richtigkeit, sondern auch um den Gegensatz, in den er sich mit den bestehenden Interessen stellt.'

[113] Transnational Legal Orders (Terence C. Halliday & Gregory Shaffer eds. 2015).

[114] Terence C. Halliday & Gregory Shaffer, *Transnational Legal Orders, in* Transnational Legal Orders, *supra* note 113, at 3, 4.

A crucial starting point of their project is the aim at shifting 'attention from a dualist orientation toward international law and national law to a focus on how legal norms are developed, conveyed, and settled transnationally, integrating both bottom-up and top-down analyses'.[115] Applying a sociological perspective on the different human and institutional actors who are involved in mobilizing norms in an effort of creating order, Halliday and Shaffer are able, in effect, to see law as what it is, in its practical relevance and use for social processes. They break their elaboration of a transnational legal order down into three successive analyses of the elements of 'order', 'legal' and 'transnational'. Regarding the first, their take on actors' practices to identify a 'problem' for which a solution – in the form of order – must be found is particularly illuminating. Not only does it open up a vista for the infinite variety of ordering challenges that are being encountered, but, perhaps even more importantly, it highlights the role of agency, of choice and of (political) intervention that is involved in the *pairing* of 'problem' and 'order'. That is, clearly, an immensely helpful step forward from an abstract 'application' of a norm, which is otherwise so at the forefront of describing the law and the work of lawyers.

It is against this background that the elaboration of the second element of a transnational legal order – 'legal' – unfolds, not in an abstract realm but with view to the contexts in which legal actors make reference to 'law' in their struggle over a choice and creation of order. Tied, now, to the understanding that what is at the heart of the concept is its suitability to border-crossing activity in terms of norm formation, dissemination and 'settling', the first of three attributes of what constitutes a transnational *legal* order includes that 'norms are produced by, or in conjunction with, a legal organization or network that transcends or spans the nation-state'.[116] The second one requires that 'norms, directly or indirectly, formally or informally, engage legal institutions within multiple nation-states, whether in the adoption, recognition, or enforcement of the norms'.[117] Interestingly, Halliday and Shaffer here seem to feel the need to assuage eventual concerns that they associate with 'a positivist conception', that they might too readily, especially from a sociological perspective, embrace the possibility of legal norms being produced by non-legal actors. In response to such concerns, they underline with considerable emphasis that they do not contend to 'simply' bypass the nation state as 'central to lawmaking, law recognition, and law enforcement' through transnational legal ordering:

[115] *Id.* at 3.
[116] *Id.* at 12.
[117] *Id.* at 13.

The propagation of transnational legal norms can give rise to a TLO by shaping domestic statutes, regulations, and their interpretation, or through the recognition of business custom and privately made norms. TLOs are thus typically connected at some point to nation-state law and practice, including through the enforcement of private contracts and undertakings. It would be a mistake to develop a concept of transnational law that is wholly autonomous from national law and legal institutions. Private lawmaking is facilitated and structured by public lawmaking. The nation-state participates in its own transformation in transnational legal ordering. Transnational legal orders are thus not wholly autonomous of nation-state legal institutions.[118]

Together with the designation of the third criterium, which regards the idea that 'the norms are produced in recognizable legal forms',[119] the 'legal' dimension of the transnational legal order is now more clearly discernible. And so is its immense value. By carefully navigating an itself transforming state structure ('The nation-state participates in its own transformation in transnational legal ordering.') and the emergence of a multitude of new actors and norms that make up a transnationalizing regulatory landscape, Halliday's and Shaffer's insistence on keeping the nation state in play, as it were, turns out to be a crucial conceptual feat in the theory of transnational legal orders. But not only that. It appears that their attention does not rest on the state, on its legal actors and on a type of norm that is considered legal in its relation *to* and interaction *with* the state out of an appreciation of the institutional coherence of the emerging and transforming order formations but, assumingly, also for *normative* reasons.

In a refreshing departure from a legal philosophical perspective on transnational and global law formations that tends to focus on the *jurisprudential* challenges of law in a postnational context and most often renders the politics of legal ordering, the normative assertions as well as contestations that run through a legal order's veins[120], invisible, Halliday and Shaffer combine strands of sociolegal research, national and economic trade and business law, political theory and – crucially – empirical data on concrete norm creation and dissemination processes in a careful elaboration of an ambitious and yet empirically grounded conceptual framework. And in their discussion of 'legal', they compellingly invite us to refrain from the 'either-or' thinking that only too often threatens to hijack a sociological account of how norms

---

[118] *Id.*

[119] *Id.* at 15.

[120] For a compelling engagement with the normative underpinnings of the concept of the rule of law, see Jothie Rajah, *'Rule of Law' as Transnational Legal Order*, *in* TRANSNATIONAL LEGAL ORDERS, *supra* note 113, at 340–73.

work, who is involved in their creation and which processes emerge in those contexts.

In their theory of transnational legal orders, they capture the point made by Rudolf Ihering at the end of the nineteenth century, whereas each new norm is not simply 'true' or 'right' but also stands in contestation to existing interests:

> The construction of a 'problem' is closely related to the purposes or goals of salient actors in creating a TLO. If an actor's generic purposes are to produce order, the particular purposes derive from imagined alternatives to existing problems. Put another way, a struggle over definition or specification of a problem lays the foundation for a struggle over a set of prescriptions to produce a particular outcome.[121]

Theory projects such as those under the rubric of transnational law, transnational legal orders or, more widely, global governance and its different variations in social theory and political philosophy stand in the tradition of more critical and conceptual work than we will be able here to properly acknowledge. Their roots go back in history and reach deep into genealogies of practically minded critical legal, social and political thought as well as an intricate background of continuously evolving deconstruction work in terms of contesting, resisting and engaging cognitive and epistemological categories that are at play here. As such, this scholarship, however unruly and multifaceted it is and, arguably, must be, provides valuable and highly productive frameworks, platforms and laboratories for forward-going research and debate. While it is probably true that there still is a whiff of 'illegitimacy' around transnational law from a legal positivist perspective, much suggests that the debate has moved on. Centring on the manifestations of transnational legal normativity and on the arguments made in relation to the evolving actors, norms and processes associated with transnational law – writ large and broadly understood – it appears that we would be well advised to leave potentially unanswerable questions regarding the 'nature' of transnational law behind and focus instead on the 'what', the 'where' and the 'how' and – crucially – on the 'for whom'.[122] Reintroducing questions of access, inclusiveness and accountability into discussions of transnational law would also mean to engage the field with regard to its status as political theory. Here, we would be concerned with questions of agency but also with those of representation and membership. Recasting transnational law also

---

[121] Halliday & Shaffer, *supra* note 113, at 8.
[122] Peer Zumbansen, *How, Where and for Whom? Interrogating Law's Forms, Locations and Purposes*, Inaugural Lecture, King's College London, 28 Apr. 2016 (TLI *Think!* Paper No. 27, 2016).

in this way promises to connect some of the issues we identified as the field's 'life wires' with corresponding, central concerns in contemporary social and political theory. And it is there that some of the liberal, modernist assumptions that are hidden and embedded in current transnational law theorizing are bound to come under critical scrutiny. As social theory has grown wary, to say the least, of the individual, the rational actor and decision maker as reference point for an analysis of social developments, the question of agency is being asked with renewed poignancy. While the 'actually existing' world of democratically elected governments appears to be falling into ever more despair and disrepute,[123] we are hard-pressed by both social theorists and philosophers and neuro and computer scientists to turn our critical capacities to the epistemological foundations on which many of our descriptive and prescriptive interventions rest. Seeing the carpet pulled out from underneath us as theories of non-human agency, the Internet of things, of big data and algorithmic governance challenge our belief systems in their concentration on the ability of the (human) mind and the power of the human heart, we are already seeing the contours of forms of norm creation on the horizon – and in our daily midst – that prompt us to pause. As we – along with an overwhelming number of processes of political participation, market formation, production and consumption – continue to plunge into the ever-faster emerging, vastly immaterial and digital 'infrastructures' of the twenty-first century, we are hard-pressed to revisit relationships between the state and the market, between myself and others.[124]

E IN SEARCH OF A DEFINITION: TRANSNATIONAL LAW AS *QUANTITÉ IRRITANTE (ET INSPIRANTE)*

What this ongoing work on defining, conceptualizing and relating transnational law shows is that the greatest promise seems to lie in those approaches

---

[123] *See* Martin Gurri, *The Revolt of the Public and the Rise of Donald Trump*, THE FIFTH WAVE (Mar. 29 2016), https://thefifthwave.wordpress.com/2016/03/29/the-revolt-of-the-public-and-the-rise-of-donald-trump/. *See also* MARTIN GURRI, THE REVOLT OF THE PUBLIC AND THE CRISIS OF AUTHORITY IN THE NEW MILLENNIUM (2018).

[124] Philip N. Howard, Democratic Futures and the Internet of Things: how Information Infrastructure Will become a Political Constitution, in Michael X. Delli Carrpini (ed.), Digital Media and Democratic Futures 312 (2019), 316: 'This next Internet is going to make Big Data truly gargantuan, with real consequences for our political lives. . . . Public opinion polling will no longer be small survey samples with noticeable error margins and carefully worded questions, the device networks will generate many details about our lives — all the time. The end result will not be a stream of data, it will be a tsunami of information that will offer governments and politicians overwhelming evidence about our real-world behavior, not just our attitudes and aspirations.'

that attempt to grasp the *problematique* of transnational law rather than try to solve a jurisprudential riddle. In that sense, Jessup might be pleased to see how much energy continues to be invested in situating, unpacking and conceptualizing the iceberg under the 'transnational law' tip, whether that occurs against the background of public and private international law, comparative law, jurisprudence or within the fields of legal sociology, anthropology and geography. Here, scholars include but are not limited to Detlef Vagts;[125] Michael Likosky;[126] Gunther Teubner;[127] Sally Merry;[128] Richard Abel;[129] Fred Aman;[130] Francis Snyder;[131] Bryant Garth;[132] Dave Trubek, Yves Dezalay, Ruth Buchanan and John Davis;[133] Claire Cutler;[134] Gralf Calliess;[135]

---

[125] Detlev. F. Vagts, *The Multinational Enterprise: A New Challenge for Transnational Law*, 83 HARV. L. REV. 739–92 (1970); HENRY STEINER, DETLEV F. VAGTS & HAROLD HONGJU KOH, TRANSNATIONAL LEGAL PROBLEMS (1968).

[126] MICHAEL LIKOSKY, TRANSNATIONAL LEGAL PROCESSES. GLOBALISATION AND POWER DISPARITIES (2002).

[127] *See, e.g.*, Gunther Teubner, *'Global Bukowina': Legal Pluralism in the World Society, in* GLOBAL LAW WITHOUT A STATE (Gunther Teubner ed., 1997).

[128] Sally Engle Merry, *Anthropology, Law and Transnational Processes*, 21 ANN. REV. ANTHROPOLOGY 357–79 (1992); Merry, *supra* note 104.

[129] Richard L. Abel, *Transnational Law Practice*, 44 CASE W.U. L. REV. 737–870 (1994).

[130] Alfred C. Aman, *Globalization, Democracy, and the Need for a New Administrative Law*, 10 IND. J. GLOBAL LEGAL STUD. 125-155 (2003); ALFRED C. AMAN & CAROL GREENHOUSE, TRANSNATIONAL LAW: CASES AND PROBLEMS IN AN INTERCONNECTED WORLD (2017).

[131] Francis Snyder, *Governing Economic Globalisation: Global Legal Pluralism and European Law*, 5 EUR. L.J. 334–74 (1999); Francis Snyder, *Economic Globalisation and the Law, in* THE BLACKWELL COMPANION TO LAW AND SOCIETY 624–40 (Austin Sarat ed., 2004); FRANCIS SNYDER, FOOD SAFETY LAW IN CHINA: MAKING TRANSNATIONAL LAW (2016).

[132] Bryant Garth, *Transnational Legal Practice and Professional Ideology, in* 7 MICH. Y.B. INT'L LEGAL STUD. 3–21 (1986); Bryant Garth, *Introduction: Taking New Legal Realism to Transnational Issues and Institutions*, 31 LAW & SOC. INQUIRY 939–45 (2007); ; LAWYERS AND THE CONSTRUCTION OF TRANSNATIONAL JUSTICE (Yves Dezalay & Bryant Garth eds., 2012).

[133] Dave M. Trubek, Yves Dezalay, Ruth Buchanan & John R. Davis, *Global Restructuring and the Law: Studies of the Internationalization of Legal Fields and the Creation of Transnational Arenas*, 44 CASE W.U. L. REV. 407–98 (1994); *see also* YVES DEZALAY & BRYANT GARTH, DEALING IN VIRTUE: INTERNATIONAL COMMERCIAL ARBITRATION AND THE CONSTRUCTION OF A TRANSNATIONAL LEGAL ORDER (1996).

[134] A. Claire Cutler, *Legal Pluralism as the 'Common Sense' of Transnational Capitalism*, 3 OÑATI SOCIO-LEGAL SERIES 719–40 (2013); A. Claire Cutler, *The Judicialization of Private Transnational Power and Authority*, 25 IND. J. GLOBAL LEGAL STUD. 61–95 (2018); THE POLITICS OF PRIVATE TRANSNATIONAL GOVERNANCE BY CONTRACT (A. Claire Cutler & Thomas Dietz eds., 2017).

[135] Gralf-Peter Calliess, *Reflexive Transnational Law: The Privatisation of Civil Law and the Civilisation of Private Law*, 23 ZEITSCHRIFT FÜR RECHTSSOZIOLOGIE 185–216 (2002); Gralf-Peter Calliess, *Making of Transnational Contract Law*, 14 IND. J. GLOBAL LEGAL STUD. 469 (2007); Gralf-Peter Calliess, *Law, Transnational*, OSGOODE HALL L. SCH. COMP. RES. IN L. & POL. ECON. (Res. Paper Series, Paper No. 35/2010, 2010), https://papers.ssrn.com/sol3/papers

Ralf Michaels;[136] Roger Cotterrell;[137] Harold Koh;[138] Harry W. Arthurs;[139] Adelle Blackett;[140] Craig Scott;[141] Mathias Reimann;[142] William Twining;[143] Larry Catá-Backer;[144] Paul Schiff Berman;[145] Horatia Muir Watt;[146] Catherine Valcke;[147] Terence Halliday;[148] Gregory Shaffer;[149]

.cfm?abstract_id=1630348; TRANSNATIONALES RECHT. STAND UND PERSPEKTIVEN (Gralf-Peter Calliess ed., 2014).

[136] Ralf Michaels, *Law beyond the State*, in INTRODUCTION TO LAW AND SOCIAL THEORY (Reza Banakar & Max Travers eds., 2d ed. 2013).

[137] Roger Cotterrell, *Transnational Communities and the Concept of Law*, 21 RATIO JURIS 1–18 (2008); Roger Cotterrell, *Spectres of Transnationalism: Changing Terrains of Sociology of Law*, 36 J. L. & SOC'Y 481–500 (2009); Roger Cotterrell, *What Is Transnational Law?*, 37 LAW & SOC. INQUIRY 500–24 (2012).

[138] Harold Hongju Koh, *Transnational Legal Process*, 75 NEB. L. REV. 181–207 (1996); Harold Hongju Koh, *Why Transnational Law Matters*, 24 PENN ST. INT'L L. REV. 745–53 (2006).

[139] Harry W. Arthurs, *Labour Law without a State?*, 46 U. TORONTO L.J. 1–45 (1996).

[140] Adelle Blackett, *Global Governance, Legal Pluralism and the Decentered State: A Labor Critique of Codes of Corporate Conduct*, 8 IND. J. GLOBAL LEGAL STUD. 401–47 (2001); Adelle Blackett, *Transnational Labour Law*, in THE OXFORD HANDBOOK OF TRANSNATIONAL LAW (Peer Zumbansen ed., forthcoming 2019).

[141] Craig M. Scott, *A Core Curriculum for the Transnational Legal Education of JD and LLB Students: Surveying the Approach of the International, Comparative & Transnational Law Program at Osgoode Hall Law School*, 23 PENN ST. INT'L L. REV. 754–74 (2004); Craig M. Scott, *'Transnational Law' as Proto Concept: Three Concepts*, 10 GERMAN L.J. 859–76 (2009).

[142] Mathias Reimann, *From the Law of Nations to Transnational Law: Why We Need a New Basic Course for the International Curriculum*, 22 PENN ST. INT'L L. REV. 397–415 (2004); MATHIAS J. REIMANN, JAMES C. HATHAWAY, TIMOTHY L. DICKINSON & JOEL H. SAMUELS, TRANSNATIONAL LAW: CASES AND MATERIALS (2013).

[143] WILLIAM TWINING, GLOBALISATION AND LEGAL THEORY (2000); William Twinning, *Normative and Legal Pluralism: A Global Perspective*, 20 DUKE J. COMP. & INT'L L. 473–517.

[144] Larry Catá-Backer, *The Structural Characteristics of Global Law for the 21st Century: Fracture, Fluidity, Permeability, and Polycentricity*, 17 TILBURG L. REV. 177–99 (2012); Larry Catá-Backer, *Are Supply Chains Transnational Legal Orders? What We Can Learn from the Rana Plaza Factory Building Collapse*, 1 UC IRVINE J. INT'L, TRANSNAT'L & COMP. L. 11–65 (2016).

[145] Berman, *supra* note 105, and *infra* note 165.

[146] Horatia Muir Watt, *Private International Law beyond the Schism*, 2 TRANSNAT'L LEGAL THEORY 347–428 (2011).

[147] Catherine Valcke, *Global Law Teaching*, 54 J. LEGAL EDUC. 160–82 (2004); CATHERINE VALCKE, COMPARING LAW (2018).

[148] Terence C. Halliday, *Recursivity of Global Normmaking: A Sociolegal Agenda*, 5 ANN. REV. L. & SOC. SCI. 263–89 (2009); TERENCE C. HALLIDAY & BRUCE G. CARRUTHERS, BANKRUPT: GLOBAL LAWMAKING AND SYSTEMIC FINANCIAL CRISIS (2010); Gregory Shaffer & Terence Halliday, *With, Within and Beyond the State: The Promise and Limits of Transnational Legal Ordering*, in THE OXFORD HANDBOOK OF TRANSNATIONAL LAW, *supra* note 140.

[149] Gregory Shaffer, *Transnational Legal Process and State Change*, 37 LAW & SOC. INQUIRY 229–64 (2012); Gregory Shaffer, *Theorizing Transnational Legal Ordering*, 12 ANN. REV. L. & SOC. SCI. 231, 232 (2016), warning before 'a jungle without a map' with regard to existing literature that remains vague in defining what the term encompasses. *See also* TRANSNATIONAL LEGAL ORDERING AND STATE CHANGE (Gregory Shaffer ed., 2013).

Eve Darian-Smith;[150] Christopher Whytock;[151] Lars Viellechner;[152] Natasha Affolder;[153] Sujith Xavier;[154] Gavin Sullivan;[155] Gilles Lhuilier;[156] Stephen Minas;[157] Priya Gupta;[158] and Matthew Canfield.[159] They have contributed and continue to contribute crucial insights into the materiality of transnational legal formations and practices. These ongoing studies[160] offer challenging outlines of how to develop and mobilize transnational law as a combination of field, concept and critical project.

The throughout-referenced authors and their engagements with law in local and global contexts as legal scholars, political scientists, sociologists, anthropologists and geographers, all again of different backgrounds and specializations and oftentimes working in the context of unique, non-generalizable case studies, might suggest that their projects associated with transnational law are so very different that they cannot usefully be grouped

---

[150] Eve Darian-Smith, *Ethnographies of Law, in* The Blackwell Companion to Law and Society 545–68 (Austin Sarat ed., 2006). Eve Darian-Smith, Laws and Societies in Global Contexts (2013). *See also* Eve Darian-Smith & Philip McCarty, *Beyond Interdisciplinarity: Developing a Global Transdisciplinary Framework*, 7 Transcience 1–26 (2016).

[151] Christopher A. Whytock, *Conflict of Laws, Global Governance, and Transnational Legal Order*, 1 UC Irvine J. Int'l, Transnat'l & Comp. L. 117–40 (2016).

[152] Lars Viellechner, Transnationalisierung des Rechts (2013); Lars Viellechner, *Responsive Legal Pluralism: The Emergence of Transnational Conflicts Law*, 6 Transnat'l Legal Theory 312–32 (2015).

[153] Natasha Affolder, *Transnational Conservation Contracts*, 25 Leiden J. Int'l L. 443–60 (2012); Natasha Affolder, *Transnational Climate Change Law, in* The Oxford Handbook of Transnational Law, *supra* note 140.

[154] Sujith Xavier, *Learning from Below: Theorising Global Governance through Ethnographies and Critical Reflections from the South*, 33 Windsor Y.B. Access to Just. 229–55 (2016); Sujith Xavier, *Top Heavy: Beyond the Global North and the Justification for Global Administrative Law*, 57 Indian J. Int'l L. 337–56 (2017).

[155] Gavin Sullivan, *Transnational Legal Assemblages and Global Security Law: Topologies and Temporalities of the List*, 5 Transnat'l. Legal Theory 81–127 (2014); Gavin Sullivan, *'Taking on the Technicalities' of International Law – Practice, Description, Critique: A Response to Fleur Johns*, 111 AJIL Unbound 181–86 (2017).

[156] Gilles Lhuilier, Le droit transnational (2016).

[157] Stephen Minas, *Climate Change Governance, International Relations and Politics: A Transnational Law Perspective, in* The Oxford Handbook of Transnational Law, *supra* note 140.

[158] Priya S. Gupta, *Transnational Property Law, in* The Oxford Handbook of Transnational Law, *supra* note 140.

[159] Matthew Canfield, *Banana Brokers: Communicative Labor, Translocal Translation, and Transnational Law*, 31:1 Pub. Culture 69–92 (2018).

[160] The foregoing list is in no sense attempting to be comprehensive or exhaustive. At best, it should be seen as indicative in the sense of providing some evidence of the immense breadth and depth of existing work in transnational law. At a minimum, this evidence suggests that transnational law – contrary to superficial, if not persistent clichés – is by no means a pie-in-the-sky, merely theoretical undertaking.

under one unifying heading. While several among the here-cited authors offer working definitions of transnational law, their value lies more in a heuristic sense than anything else. None of the currently circulating definitions is necessarily 'better' or more 'correct' than another one, as their productive use reveals itself in the particular conceptual approach in which it is used. The reason for this, if you will, plea for relative definitional value lies in the immense and probably forever unlimited variety of approaches and circumstances that altogether constitute a scholar's engagement with transnational law over time and across changing examples and challenges. That said, while we need to recognize repeatedly voiced concerns with regard to the types of norms associated with transnational law, namely that 'nothing is law when everything is',[161] we should do so less out of belief that we could, once and for all, resolve the nature-of-law question in a way that would neither prove the analytical legal positivist or the sociolegal scholar of legal pluralism 'wrong' nor offer a solution that both would agree on. Instead, the proposal here is a different one. The relativity theory that is here defended is based on the belief that transnational law is above all a terminological stand-in for an encompassing, radical critique of law in the present context. What, in other words, would we be able to say about such a theory's, concept's or definition's coherence and about the purpose of the intended critical project if we took the qualifier 'transnational' out? What, then, if our project, and that pursued by many of the cited scholars as well as many others, concerned a critical engagement with what law *is* and *can be* in a context the physical and normative materiality of which is being described, assessed and tentatively theorized across the manifold projects in contemporary comparative law and postcolonial legal theory, in international relations, political theory, and in transnational and global legal pluralism, in cultural ethnography and literary critique? The search for a unifying theory points in the direction of a conceptual framework that combines legal, political and critical social theory while being at the same time grounded in empiricism. Scholars in transnational law, it would appear, in light of the continuing work done in its name, propose, engage and test the label across different engagements, within law and across the many interdisciplinary approaches we find today. Transnational law is mobilized as a project that combines legal and political theory, a sociology of institutions

---

[161] This is a concern expressed by many; see, for example, Ralf Michaels, *Law beyond the State, in* INTRODUCTION TO LAW AND SOCIAL THEORY (Reza Banakar & Max Travers eds., 2d ed. 2013). See also Jan Klabbers, *Reflections on Soft International Law in a Privatized World*, 16 FINNISH Y.B. INT'L L. 313–28 (2005).

and processes, an anthropology of actors and their behaviour through conceptual, philosophical and ethnographic studies.

What appears to emerge, then, is an understanding of transnational law[162] as
reference point and short formula for a critical and methodological engagement with law in a globally connected space of intersecting, overlapping and
competing processes of norm creation but also norm contestation. The drivers
of such uncounted processes are human and non-human. They include
governments and bureaucratic agencies, international organizations and
non-state actors, including expert committees, NGOs, social movements,
advocacy networks, unions, civil society groups and individuals. Non-human
drivers of transnational norm-creation/contestation processes may be situations
of violent conflict, natural and man-made disasters as well as 'problematiques'
without an easily discernible principal or agent. As we can see illustrated in
various transnational legal governance areas, from 'climate change law' to the
'war on terror', it is the recognition of a 'problem' that serves as the driver of
norm creation, policy design and political conflict.[163] This raises difficult yet
crucial questions regarding epistemology and agency, and these are at the
heart of a transnational legal critique.

The diversity of approaches to transnational law, at the same time, underscores and exposes the project's complexity and raises questions about its
limitations. What use, we might ask, can a concept have that continues to
be so unruly as far as its place in legal doctrine and legal theory is concerned?
Observations regarding the absence of a once-and-for-all-satisfying definition
are not infrequent and continue to place the project and field in an ambivalent context. On the one hand, this is both a problem of sorts and an
opportunity – a problem because doubts continue as to the *place* of transnational law in relation to many, doctrinally more or less reliably demarcated
legal 'fields', but also an opportunity for its quality as *quantité irritante* – rather
than *négligante*. In other words, transnational law's unsettling, provocative and
perhaps in fact irritating stance in the context of and in its relation to other
legal fields, theories of law and, wider even, theories of global law and order
does not lend itself to an easy solution. But, at the same time, that transnational law is, in fact, so deeply intertwined and entangled with critical

---

[162] See already Peer Zumbansen, *Transnational Law, Evolving, in* ELGAR ENCYCLOPEDIA OF
COMPARATIVE LAW 899–935 (Jan Smits ed., 2d ed., 2012).

[163] See, for example, Jacqueline Peel & Hari M. Osofsky, *A Rights Turn in Climate Change
Litigation?*, 7 TRANSNAT'L ENVTL. L. 37, 44 (2018): 'A greater focus in the international climate
regime on "adaptation" [...] and "loss and damage" [...] has inevitably directed more
attention to how individuals and communities are affected by climate change, and their
relative adaptive capacity.'

projects in legal and social theory hints at its qualities as an area of law, in which questions of doctrine, regulatory purpose and conceptual coherence are coming together – and do so against the background of a lively debate among lawyers, regardless of whether their focus is on domestic or international, on private, criminal or public law, whether or not they consider themselves legal philosophers in the analytical tradition or legal theorists with a grounding in sociology, economics or technology, about the place of 'law' in the present context.

The project of 'transnational law' emerges today at a time where a dialogue between different engagements with , both among and beyond legal scholars, is more necessary than ever – but in contrast to legal philosophy or theory, which approach law, as it were, from within and respectively focus on the foundations, principles and structures of law.

Transnational law aims at confronting the doctrinal and conceptual dimensions of law through an interdisciplinary analysis of how legal rules emerge, how they are disseminated and which actors are involved and where. It is, thus, both a theory of law in the tradition of sociolegal analysis of law's norms, actors and processes *and* a project of legal critique in the tradition of critical social theory. Combining those qualities, transnational law is at once a legal theoretical, methodological framework through which processes and actors of legal norm generation are scrutinized in local and global contexts rather than in an abstract forum of philosophical deliberation over the 'nature' of law, while it is also a critical project that seeks to understand the conditions under which invocations of 'law' are made, contested and resisted. This intersection of a *theory* of transnational norm making with a *critique* of law and rights in a global context is at the heart of transnational law and thus reveals its affinities with areas where scholars increasingly turn their attention to questions of 'sources' of law, to the actual processes of norm generation and norm contestation and to the wide variety of actors involved. Transnational law breaks the mirror of a legal conception that associated law too easily with 'the state' without scrutinizing – empirically, conceptually and epistemologically – the meaning and materiality of norm-creation processes today. It equally prompts us to follow the norm from the inchoate realities and violent struggles of its invocation into the jungle of its 'implementation', contestation or failure. Transnational law, then, emerges as a call to arms to empirically and conceptually scrutinize the actors, norms and processes as well as the pitfalls of lawmaking, on the one hand, and the conditions of accessing, challenging and using law in, through but also in contestation of the legal system, on the other.

In light of this, there might be a way to further demystify transnational law, especially as we begin to acknowledge that the concept's aspiration and promise does not lie in the design of a new and self-standing doctrinal field. It is through the invocation of something like 'transnational law' that one can point at the transformation of law's architectures through an increasing inter-penetration of local, national and international, formal and informal, state and non-state-based norm-making processes. Transnational law's doctrinal grounding follows from the functional area in which a legal conflict arises. It is in that sense that we speak of 'transnational' labour law when we refer to the border-crossing processes of hard and soft law norm production, the emergence of norm-creating and norm-resisting coalitions of workers, employ-ers, governments, unions, NGOs and activists. Similarly, we speak of trans-national climate law in order to depict the complex and constantly evolving architecture of public and private regulatory innovation that spans across forms of state regulation of tax incentives or emission standards to a wide diversity of civil society and market-based initiatives of mitigating climate change. Transnational law, in other words, offers a valuable perspective on the differentiation of lawmaking processes across a wide range of core legal–regulatory areas.

From that perspective, however, it also becomes clearer that law – seen in context – is always inherently unstable. Transnational law further emphasises the need to critically engage the idea that a particular legal field not only displays but, arguably, represents and guarantees theoretical and doctrinal coherence. Transnational law challenges the nature of such coherence by scrutinizing the dynamics that are at the heart of a legal field's achieving its regulatory purpose. The law with which we can hope to engage in this space of self-critique will never be complete. It will not ever be fully and compre-hensively visible in all its finished form. Rather, it is about the process through which we re-engage with what law is, should be, can be. The space, then, in which this self-critique and new forms of careful, open-minded and mutually respectful interaction among lawyers from different backgrounds, along with critical theorists, anthropologists, sociologists, geographers and literature the-orists,[164] can occur becomes the foundation of and the engagement with the new form and practice of law – which we here call 'transnational'.

This process occurs already, across the connection of legal subfields among themselves and with other disciplines, through the critical elaboration of problem-based and problem-driven 'new' legal areas, through legal practice

---

[164] EDWARD SAID, ORIENTALISM (1978); Amanda Ruth Waugh Lagji, *Transnational Law and Literatures: A Postcolonial Perspective*, in THE OXFORD HANDBOOK OF TRANSNATIONAL LAW, *supra* note 140.

in unchartered territories, through the fusing of different legal strategies of litigation, advocacy and reform and through a recognition of the importance of access to facts. Transnational law – as methodology of law in (global) context – then, unfolds across an ongoing engagement with manifestations of transnational regulatory normativity,[165] legal pluralism (in its domestic, transnational land global iterations),[166] non-state and "unofficial" law,[167] with intricate ethnographies of local ordering,[168] the 'spatialization' of human and institutional activities and law's varied associated adaptive processes,[169] 'recursivity' as the intricate, interloping processes of up- and downloading of norms between local, national and international regulatory levels with its challenging consequences for the shape and driving dynamics of the emerging transnational architecture of politics and the 'formal properties of global law'[170] and in the fast-evolving architectures of 'transnational legal orders'.

To some degree, then, the publication of a volume such as the here-presented one is meant to suggest that a definition of transnational law is . . . still forthcoming. More than what transnational law means, the authors here illustrate what the concept means *to them*. As such, similar to other complex conceptual frameworks – think of 'climate change law', 'cyber law' or the 'war on terror' – transnational law appears to still defy its containment in the form of its neat categorization as a field with a distinct regulatory purpose and a particular set of doctrinal rules and principles. And yet, transnational law functions as reference, as context of proliferating legal practice, advocacy

---

[165] Here, the demarcation lines between what is referred to as 'global' and 'transnational law' are oftentimes blurry. See, for a good discussion, Eric C. Ip, *Globalization and the Future of Law of the Sovereign State*, 8 INT'L J. CONST. L. 636, 643 (2010).

[166] See, for example, John Griffiths, *What Is Legal Pluralism?*, 24 J. LEGAL PLURALISM & UNOFFICIAL L. 1–55 (1986); Sally Engle Merry, *Legal Pluralism*, 22 LAW & SOC'Y REV. 869–96 (1988); Paul Schiff Berman, *Global Legal Pluralism*, 80 S. CAL. L. REV. 1155–237 (2007); Ralf Michaels, *Global Legal Pluralism*, 5 ANN. REV. LAW & SOC. SCI. 243–62 (2009); Peer Zumbansen, *Transnational Legal Pluralism* 1 TRANSNAT'L LEGAL THEORY 141–89 (2010).

[167] Boaventura de Sousa Santos, *A Map of Misreading: Toward a Postmodern Conception of Law*, 14 J. L. & SOC'Y 279–302 (1987); Ralf Michaels, *The Re-statement of Non-state Law: The State, Choice of Law, and the Challenge of Global Legal Pluralism*, 51 WAYNE ST. L. REV. 1209–59 (2005).

[168] Prabha Kotiswaran, *Sword or Shield? The Role of the Law in the Indian Sex Workers' Movement*, 15 INTERVENTIONS 530–45 (2013).

[169] PHILIP G. CERNY, THE CHANGING ARCHITECTURE OF POLITICS: STRUCTURE, AGENCY, AND THE FUTURE OF THE STATE (1990); TRANSNATIONAL LEGAL PROCESSES: GLOBALISATION AND POWER DISPARITIES (Michael Likosky ed., 2002); Saskia Sassen, *The Embeddedness of Electronic Markets: The Case of Global Capital Markets, in* THE SOCIOLOGY OF FINANCIAL MARKETS 17–37 (Karin Knorr-Cetina & Alex Preda eds., 2005).

[170] Terence C. Halliday, *Recursivity of Global Lawmaking: A Sociolegal Agenda*, 5 ANN. REV. L. & SOC. SCI. 263, 265 (2009).

and activism. As such, transnational law is here understood, above all, as a legal methodology through which we engage existing legal frameworks and principles against the background of newly emerging and evolving actors, norms and processes. Transnational law, then, should be seen as a critical methodological space and laboratory.

F TRANSNATIONAL LAW AS TRANSNATIONAL POLITICS

This leads us to the next point in this introduction to the volume. It should have become clear to which degree, and in addition to the theoretical–methodological consequences of law's engagement with globalization that are captured under the term, there is a tremendously practical dimension to the continued relevance of and interest in transnational law. As transnational law, inter alia, serves as an umbrella framework to capture the development and evolution of legal instruments applicable to border-crossing activities, the field's historical pedigree is plain to see. In considerable distance from the just-invoked varieties of theoretical sophistication, which mark (much of) the scholarly engagement with the field, legal practitioners would for a long time already have been quite comfortable seeing the label 'transnational law' applied to them or to their primary sites of operation. Crucially, however, as we have seen this seems to be the case predominantly for those lawyers working mainly in the private law arena, in areas such as commercial, corporate, contract or investment law. To give this practical reality of trans-national lawyering another twist, then, we should point out that it is precisely this rootedness of much of transnational law practice in the universe of 'private' law that continues to fuel a very frequently voiced concern that – perhaps, at the end of the day – whatever we refer to on a quotidian basis as transnational law might merely be the label for a largely self-regulatory body of norms, created, administered and controlled by those who are in the position to tailor legal instruments and norms according to their own needs.[171] The lingering concern that transnational law is just another name for the autono-mous law of a global capitalist merchant elite, as the world-renowned human rights scholar Upendra Baxi once characterized it,[172] certainly casts a dark enough shadow on the ongoing efforts to engage with the field in the sense alluded to above: namely, the way in which it would be possible to approach

[171] See, for example, the valid concerns raised by writers such as Claire Cutler, note 133, or Sol Picciotto. And see Cutler's chapter in this volume.
[172] Upendra Baxi, *Market Fundamentalisms: Business Ethics at the Altar of Human Rights*, 5 HUM, RTS. REV. (2005).

transnational law as a *laboratory*, in which – in the acknowledgement of deep-reaching societal, socio-economic, cultural and political transformation on both domestic and global levels – it should be possible (and, indeed, necessary) to place under scrutiny and to reassess the very foundational assumptions and values we associate with the 'rule of law' and with 'law', as such, as a foundation for peaceful coexistence, integration and community, for the providing of stability and certainty and for continued efforts to employ law as a force of change.

That said, the preceding observations as well as the here-following overview of the chapters in the collection should help in engaging the question of transnational law's contested politics. In contrast but also in resistance to the view that the term merely captures a neoliberal concept of law pertaining to uninhibited market exchanges, free from state 'intervention', the approach that informs this project, embodies an argument to the contrary. Well recognizing the already mentioned problem of uprooted – political, democratic – agency that haunts the emerging transnational geography of fragmented as well as privatized authority, the authors in this volume set out to provide – across an impressive range of area examples and case studies – a differentiated account of the actual formations of transnational law. As these chapters illustrate, it is really in the detail of the local context and the concrete transnational regulatory constellation that we are called upon to critically analyse the dynamics between the actors, norms, processes in play. The book should in that sense be understood also an invitation to look more closely and to dive into the multitude of emerging and evolving transnational legal problems – as Jessup called them already in 1956.

G THE STRUCTURE OF THE BOOK

This edited collection is divided into three substantive sections, preceded by this introduction and concluded by an epilogue. The first part of the book explores the public and private law dimensions that are both explicitly and implicitly making their reappearance in many of the evolving specialized fields within transnational law. Part 2, then, focuses on what has become a core field of investigation (and contention) under the larger umbrella of transnational law, namely the coexistence and co-evolution of and the relationship between what is often called 'law', on the one hand, and 'governance', on the other. By exploring different areas of 'transnational regulatory governance', this part of the collection offers a state-of-the-art assessment of current trends in transnational lawmaking. The third part of the book focuses, more particularly, on the normative implications of the field. In that regard, the chapters in this section engage with the political, democratic as well as the socio-economic 'stakes' of the field and thereby situate it centrally within the continuing debates around the erosion of state sovereignty, the crisis of democratic governance and the contested basis of legitimacy that marks global governance today.

I *Transnational Law – the Public and the Private*

At the start of this section, Stephen Minas explores the place of Jessup's project within the core field in which Jessup first introduced it, namely public international law. More specifically, Minas returns to Jessup's initial starting point to reflect on the potential of transnational law in the universe of UN-led law making on a global level today. In his 'Jessup at the United Nations: International Legacy, Transnational Possibilities', Minas examines the linkages between Jessup's legacies in diplomatic practice and legal theory in order to shed light on the degree to which 'Jessup's government service at the United Nations (UN) informed the development of his novel contributions to theory in transnational law'. In turn, the chapter considers how Jessup's concept of transnational law can inform responses to current challenges faced by the UN, as for example, in the area of implementing the Sustainable Development Goals.

Providing a mirror image to this international law(yer's) perspective, Christopher Whytock, now writing from the vantage point of a private international lawyer and interested in the forward-looking contribution that conflict of laws can make to our understanding of law in a global context, invites us to think about the nature of conceptual progression. In his contribution, entitled 'The Concept of a Global Legal System', he places Jessup's project in the very tension field that Jessup had highlighted in his lectures – namely in a space 'between' public and private international law. And it is here where he ambitiously puts forward the claim to think of transnational law as capturing a movement 'from a concept of the "international legal system" to a concept of the "global legal system"'. Whereas Jessup departed from international law because he was concerned with 'the problems of the world community' rather than with the relations between nations or states, the chapter argues for the need of a concept that reaches not only beyond international law but also beyond the international legal system. As a result, Professor Whytock points to a concept that, 'unlike transnational law, encompasses not only the law that governs cross-border problems, but also courts and other national, international and private institutions that contribute to that same function'.

Thomas Schultz's and Niccolò Ridi's 'How Comity Makes Transnationalism Work' concludes the first part in providing a powerful illustration of how a principle such as 'comity' fluctuates between public and private law connotations within transnational law. They show how the multipronged operation of comity contributes to the field's growing operational solidification. 'Comity', the authors contend, 'was developed to make sovereignty work in the face of the pragmatic transnationalism that characterizes also much of the real-world life. [...] And still today comity is used "to make things work" ... ', as it facilitates diverse adjustment processes for the law in its adaptation to transnational phenomena such as the global market, hyper-politicized situations, the proliferation of international courts and tribunals, as well as the continuing processes of legal harmonization and coordination across borders.

II *Transnational Law as Regulatory Governance*

The second, most extensive part of the book offers a series of engagements with the already-alluded-to correlation between 'law' and regulatory 'governance' in different subfields of transnational law. A core component of these hybrid legal–regulatory regimes is their high degree of functionalization, on the one hand, and their spatialization, border-crossing nature on the other. As such, much attention among scholars of transnational regulatory governance has been paid to the particular drivers and emerging constitutional features of such transboundary governance systems. As the authors of the here-included chapters effectively illustrate, our attention needs to turn to a detailed analysis of the institutional/procedural dimensions of the emerging transnational governance structures, on the one hand, while recognizing their embeddedness in ongoing debates around the legitimacy and normative orientation of the substantive lawmaking dimension of these regimes, on the other.

In that vein, Karsten Nowrot's chapter, 'Aiding and Abetting in Theorizing the Increasing Softification of the International Normative Order – a Darker Legacy of Jessup's *Transnational Law?*', is an ideal gateway into this section of the analysis. His chapter puts the finger on the terminological and conceptual trend that results and manifests itself in an increasing *softification* of the international normative order. This perspective promises crucial insights into the way in which the development of transnational regulatory regimes in both public and private law-oriented process and substance areas can be seen, since Jessup, as signs of an erosion of 'hard law'. Addressing, thus, one of the core critical contentions 'against' transnational law, namely that it might, after all, be nothing but an assemblage of privately made rules for a global marketplace, with the 'moderating' and 'enabling' state merely standing by for an occasional intervention or 'bailout', Nowrot takes the prospect of transnational law *as* soft law seriously. His analysis underscores the need for us to assess to which degree the *softification* of the international normative order actually reflects the normative realities in the present international system and whether or not, then, against this background, it should be seen as representative for the evolution of 'transboundary steering regimes'.

The second chapter in this section is co-authored by Gregory Shaffer and Carlos Coye and entitled 'From International Law to Transnational Law, from Transnational Law to Transnational Legal Orders'. The transnational legal order proposal, originally developed by Gregory Shaffer and Terence Halliday in earlier work, has been one of the most widely discussed and assessed conceptual proposals in transnational legal scholarship in recent years, and this chapter provides further and compelling support for the merits of this model. The authors of the present chapter, Shaffer and Coye, offer compelling evidence that in terms of growth drivers for transnational law, the real push has come from an expansion of *public* international law – and not from its private counterpart, *private* international law. It is here, in the proliferation of increasingly specialized bodies of public international law, that the authors identify the *locus* of the real revolution since Jessup's work. Against the background of this evidence and in drawing on the influence of international relations scholarship, Shaffer and Coye suggest that we should begin moving away from scrutinizing transnational law's ability and forms to respond to regulatory problems associated with globalization and global governance and, instead, turn our attention to the constructivist work that can and should be done under the rubric of transnational law. Concretely, their proposal is for shift of analysis away from transnational law as a body of norms addressing transnational problems and towards the investigation of emerging formations of transnational legal ordering and 'transnational legal orders'. The distinct value of their contribution can be seen in their intervention into a theoretical debate that oftentimes remains stuck in navigating competing legitimacy claims that arise from juxtaposing 'private' and 'public' ordering mechanisms. But as the authors show how the growth of specialized public international law should be understood as a core component of transnational law and transnational legal ordering, they remind us that any such conceptualization – as in the case of transnational legal orders – must remain in step with the problems of the 'real world', now understood 'as social and political constructs that, in turn, shape legal responses'.

In a perfect illustration of the merits of the approach described by Shaffer and Coye, the authors of the second chapter in this section delve into the transnational regulatory regime developments around the issue of food security. In their 'Transnational Law in the Pacific Century: Mapping Pesticide Regulation in China', Francis Snyder, Zhouke Hu and Lili Ni take the case of the regulation of risks associated with highly toxic pesticides as an example of the interactions between transnational law, global legal pluralism and other conceptualizations of global and transnational governance. Starting from an account of the recent reforms of pesticide regulation in China, which are likely to have a significant impact on food-related trade between China and the rest of the world, they advance three arguments: (1) the regulation of pesticides in China forms a transnational legal order, according to the definition offered by Halliday and Shaffer in 2015; (2) this transnational legal order is strongly and decisively conditioned by features of the Chinese political and legal system, forcing us to rethink the concept of transnational legal orders and give more importance to the national and local context; (3) pesticide regulation in China might be part of a transnational legal order, but this concept might not be sufficient to define it. Their chapter is exemplary in working out the concrete challenges in promoting conceptualizing and model-building work in the face of real-world challenges.

Florian Grisel's 'Transnational Law in Context: The Relevance of Jessup's Analysis for the Study of "International" Arbitration' follows closely on this analysis but shifts our attention to the evolving formations of the 'judiciary' in the unfolding transnational landscape. Grisel takes up the example of international arbitration to contextualize Jessup's idea of transnational law and sets out to draw a sixty-year arch from the time of Jessup's writing to the present day. Through that effort, the chapter offers invaluable insights into a core component of transnational legal ordering, namely how the branches, both domestic and transnational, private and public, in charge of conflict resolution and adjudication continued to transform and adapt amid a fast-evolving global marketplace. Pointing out that in the mid-1950s, at the time of Jessup's analysis, international arbitration was already blooming as a mechanism of dispute resolution, Grisel sheds light on the lively commercial arbitration regime that served as backdrop of Jessup's proposal. The chapter allows for a better appreciation of how, already in Jessup's elaboration and well beyond, transnational law has been serving as a laboratory for norm experimentation and institutional development.

Placing greater emphasis on the concrete interactions between domestic and transnational adjudication regimes, Bryan Horrigan, in his chapter on 'Transnational Law and Adjudication – Domestic, International and Foreign Intersections', analyses the transnationalization of law with specific regard to the implications for our understanding of the role as well as the location of the judiciary. For Professor Horrigan, then, the notion itself of 'transnational law' functions as a lens for an enquiry into debates about 'the legitimacy and the methodology of national judicial reference to international and foreign law'.

Substantively, the chapter offers an Australian perspective on judicial transnationalization of law by discussing a select series of jurisprudential, jurisdictional and topical case studies.

Shahla Ali complements and further expands the scope of analysis developed by Grisel and Horrigan as she takes up the concrete example of the application of transnational law in her chapter on 'Transnational Law and Global Dispute Resolution'. In this chapter, Ali argues that Jessup's insights, as they relate to global dispute resolution, 'can be applied to the development of cross-border arbitration as a contemporary embodiment of transnational dispute resolution'. By contending that 'as transnational awards become increasingly transparent, arbitral jurisprudence may take the role of an important contributor to the development of transnational arbitration', she opens up a powerful perspective for the system-building contribution transnational arbitration continues to make.

Shifting the perspective away from an engagement with the institutional development of transnational law, which the foregoing chapters analyse through a combination of investigating norm-creation and adjudicatory processes, the next two chapters introduce us to two evolving areas of substantive transnational law norm creation, namely 'transnational sports law' and 'transnational family law'. The immense value in these two chapters lies in their power to illuminate how transnational law continues to emerge in close proximity to well-articulated policy interests and support systems. While in the case of sports norms, we are confronted, then, with a field almost seen as an obvious, if not 'natural', contender for transnational law, the chapter on family law points to the crucial role that politics can play when interests are differently situated and represented.

In his chapter, Antoine Duval invites us to reflect on 'What *Lex Sportiva* Tells You About Transnational Law' and employs the fast-growing field of the so-called *lex sportiva* as an empirical field to study in detail how a field grows, disseminates and becomes consolidated. While the first part of the chapter focuses on how *lex sportiva* has become considered an empirical illustration of a 'pure theory of transnational law' in the meaning of representing a denationalized legal order for a truly transnational community, the second part points to the normative pitfalls in this construction. The darker side, then, of an area of transnational law with the potential of being a poster child for the field's continuing efforts of self-assertion and creation comes into view when we investigate more closely the power differentials that mark wide stretches of the *lex sportiva*'s landscapes.

A wonderful companion analysis in this regard is offered by Ivana Isailović, who investigates the competing interests in the development of effective family law rules in the transnational arena. In her chapter, 'Family Law as a Blind Spot', Isailovic argues that conversations in the field of transnational law continue to overlook family law. This omission, however, comes at a cost, as family law in substantive and policy terms continues to evolve at great speed, partly in response to law's adaption to cultural, economic and legal globalization and partly because of the field's close relations to equality rights and their ever more fervent contestation in legal cultures worldwide. The family, once again, moves into the centre of policy battles, but – as Isailovic convincingly shows – this is not yet taken up enough by transnational law scholars. In response to this finding, Isailovic forcefully argues for an approximation of critical investigations into the normative stakes of transnational law and critical family law work on the domestic level. The chapter advances that, on the one hand, studying family law through transnational law theories would help shed new light on a field, which in the case of family law is too often perceived as merely domestic, while, on the other, family law could open up new sites for a critical inquiry into the reconfiguration of law and society in the global space.

III *Transnational Law: The Field's Normative Stakes*

While the foregoing chapters give ample testimony to which degree the conceptualization of transnational law, transnational legal ordering and trans-national regulatory governance is always and inevitably entwined with a normative assessment of the existing and evolving power differentials at play, the last part of this collection sets out to make this point more explicit still. Rather than merely identifying and acknowledging 'the normative itch' in one's analysis of the evolving institutional and procedural complexities, there is a growing consensus as to the urgency to confront the field's normative stakes at face value.

By way of leading us deep into the normative contestation around trans-national law, Claire Cutler's 'Locating Private Transnational Authority in the Global Political Economy' offers a crucial and critical perspective on the operation of transnational law through an examination of what she calls 'private transnational authority'. In her chapter she takes issue with an analysis of transnational authority that fails to fully take into account the concrete operation of 'power, competition and contestation between states and a variety of private and public actors and institutions in the global political economy'. Echoing her landmark contributions to the study of private power in the transnational realm, she emphasizes how such conflicts shift the balance between and from public to private power on a global scale. Cutler's chapter is a key contribution to the ongoing analysis of law's relation to socio-economic ordering and offers crucial insights into the operation of transnational law as a battlefield of competing value systems and sociopolitical utopia.

In her remarkable chapter, 'Transnational Law as Drama', Jothie Rajah picks up on this deeper normative dimension of transnational law and transnational regulatory governance, which manifests itself, often enough, through the most persuasive forms of symbolic power. Rajah suggests a methodological rethinking of transnational law, in the spirit of 'constructively contesting (legal doctrinal) understandings of law'. For that purpose, she reaches deep into the methodological toolkits of media theory, an area that has become more and more important for a critical analysis of law. Through her close study of a photographic image that became known as the 'Situation Room photograph' (a picture showing former US president Barack Obama sitting with his national security team while receiving updates on Osama bin Laden's capture and assassination), the chapter repositions the field and project of transnational law as *drama*. Harking back to Jessup's own iteration of drama in his presentation of transnational law typical case constellations, Rajah reminds us of the importance of placing a field such as transnational law – as Jessup already illustrated – in new and different contexts.

Natasha Affolder's contribution, 'Transnational Law as "Unseen" Law', is an ideal continuation of the investigation launched in Jothie Rajah's chapter. Although Jessup's conception of transnational law promises to uncover 'unseen law' – law that is important in practice but neglected in scholarship – Professor Affolder highlights the fact that '"making visible" the actualities of law and legal practice [...] involves slippery methodological questions' that are too often sidestepped. In emphasizing that to uncover the 'unseen' aspects of transnational law leaves open the question of how to tackle the disparity between the 'known' and the 'unknowable', she directly confronts Jessup and with him the cohort of scholars, who rest content in pointing out the shortcomings of 'traditional' or 'domestic' law without, at the same time, commenting on the methodological basis on which the elaboration of a non-traditional, i.e. transnational law, might be founded. Access to sources, the chapter argues, might shape our accounts of transnational law. In a positive turn, Professor Affolder points to the valuable insights gained in that regard from engaging with the expanding scope of 'sources' that transnational law can draw upon and critically engage with.

The chapter by Larry Catá Backer focuses on Jessup's intervention with regard to our understanding of the fora in which law manifests itself and is asserted. According to Backer, Philip Jessup produced a veritable *cri de guerre* whose ramifications continue to unfold. The original *cri de Jessup* gave the transnational within law the means to distinguish itself from other legal orders. Yet even sixty years after the *cri de Jessup*, the transnational remains tied from its moorings in ancient conceptions of nation, of enterprise and of law. Backer's contribution considers the possibilities inherent in Jessup's vision liberated from its grounding in the assumption that the transnational arises only to deal with the ad hoc situation when all other efforts at resolving the issue under the law of a state, any state, fails. It first explores the contemporary approach to transnational law and its more radical possibilities, arguing that these possibilities are radical not in the sense of requiring a substantial break with the past but in the sense of suggesting the ways in which Jessup's vision ultimately requires a shifting of perspectives about the relationship of law to the state, the state to the societal sphere, and both to transnational law and the multinational enterprise. At the core of the chapter is an analysis of the parallel development of the problem of transnational law and of the transnational enterprise. To that end, it applies an actor-network (norm) process framework inward within and to the enterprise. Both transnational law and enterprise serve as a complement to domestic legal orders and its territorial boundaries. They are the embodiment for the law and space of the 'in-between' and absent the reorientation of perspective suggested in the opening section will remain at the margins of law and institutional governance.

Prabhakar Singh's chapter, 'The Private Life of Transnational Law: Reading Jessup from the Post-colony', could arguably have stood at the very beginning of this section if not of the entire volume. Written from a distinctly postcolonial perspective, Singh's chapter points to the many epistemological omissions and exclusions transnational law can rightly be accused of. As pointed out in the introduction to the volume, transnational law's colonial inheritance is only slowly being recognized more broadly, and the inclusion of a single chapter from a postcolonial scholar is by no means intended to point to 'bases covered'. Instead, Professor Singh's chapter here is as an important intervention but also a crucial reminder of the work that still must be carried out much more widely. How much there is to do becomes evident very early. Reversing, as it were, the usual perspective on transnational law as a field, which manifests itself above all in the privatization of public institutional infrastructures (and hereby raising questions of 'legitimacy' and forward-going maintenance of 'public' responsibility), Singh argues that, while seemingly progressive, the idea of challenging the role of the state as the sole maker of international law can be read to have 'sought to rob decolonized states of their new-found sovereignty acquired after decades of nationalist struggles in Africa and Asia'.

In other words, transnational law facilitated a host of institutional developments that would result in substantively weakening the newly decolonized sovereign states and contribute to a continuation of colonial control into the present day. Echoing and complementing the critical work done by colleagues such as M. S. Sornarajah in Singapore or Gus van Harten in Canada, Singh excavates the exclusionary and neocolonial effects of a transnational law that facilitates the development of the law of alien protection and the law of the economic protection of aliens.

The book's last chapter in the main section comes from Ralf Michaels, who discusses the current backlash against transnational law, as exemplified in the Brexit discussions underway in the United Kingdom. That backlash, he argues, is based on an irrational nostalgic desire for the past: there is no return to the nation state as it existed. But much contemporary transnational law suffers from a nostalgia of its own—nostalgia for the period, some sixty years ago, when transnational law was first developed. That time, the post-war area, is as irreversibly passé as is the nation state, and transnational law, Michaels suggests, can no longer rest on the ideas of its birth. Instead, he advocates for a renewal of transnational law based on a new 'PRIDE'. That PRIDE consists of a number of elements: the politicization of law, the redistribution as challenge, the inclusion of outsiders (including opponents), the democratization of lawmaking and adjudication instead of exaggerated trust in experts or seemingly natural consequences, and the energization and emotion to counter the emotionality of opponents.

H CONCLUSION

As this introduction has hopefully been able to illustrate, the study of transnational law is – if you will – only at its beginning. At the same time, we are already in its middle, navigating a project ship of doctrinal, conceptual and critical theory on high seas of changing geopolitics, a pressing crisis of local and global democratic governance and a potentially all-ending climate crisis. An academic publication can be but the smallest contribution to a conversation the importance of which the editor and authors want to contribute to and further amplify. Using a variety of approaches and taking the theory, the idea and the critical lens of transnational law to task across a range of doctrinal examples and legal fields, it is their hope to initiate further research and dialogue in this regard. Manifesting the value of creating critical analogies and comparisons between the domestic trajectories of legal theory, critical legal studies, 'law and society' and 'law in context', on the one hand,

and the emerging critical projects under the rubric of transnational law, includ-ing transnational/global legal pluralism, transnational legal anthropology, trans-national legal geography, transitional justice and – fundamentally – postcolonial and alternative epistemological studies, on the other, this book is meant as an invitation to think seriously and critically and to work empirically and conceptually in confronting the question of law's role today.

PART I

Transnational Law

The Public and the Private

1

Jessup at the United Nations
International Legacy, Transnational Possibilities

STEPHEN MINAS

A INTRODUCTION

Philip Jessup left multiple legacies, as a scholar, a diplomat and a jurist. This chapter is concerned with the interrelations of his theorizing of law and his practice of diplomacy. It is a mark of his career that the 1956 Storrs Lectures on transnational law, widely acknowledged as having launched the field of transnational legal studies, constitute but one part of Jessup's multifaceted contribution to the theory and practice of international law. This chapter will examine the linkages and feedbacks between Jessup's legacies in diplomatic practice and legal theory. In particular, it will analyse how Jessup's government service at the United Nations (UN) informed the development of his novel contributions to theory in *Transnational Law*. In addition, the chapter will consider how Jessup's scholarship can, in turn, inform responses to current challenges faced by the UN – in particular, the pan-UN-system challenge of implementing the Sustainable Development Goals (SDGs).

It will be argued that Jessup's presence at – and contributions to – the creation and operationalization of the UN left its stamp on his transnational legal scholarship, which is alive to the possibilities of novel institutional configurations, grounded in a realist appreciation of power dynamics and cognizant of both the significant roles played by non-state actors and the linkages between diplomatic and legal processes. It will be further argued that, in turn, insights from this rich store of scholarship can be productively applied to a major, current and thoroughly transnational challenge for the UN system: achieving the SDGs. If the application of lectures delivered in 1956 to goals set for 2030 may seem quixotic, it is submitted that this is less an exercise of reaching into the past than an acknowledgement of how Jessup's thinking remains relevant to current challenges in international organization.

Jessup worked at the intersection of fields of theory and practice that have
since become more specialized: public international law and transnational
law; diplomacy and judicial service. Indeed, when he delivered his Storrs
Lectures, Jessup was Hamilton Fish Professor of Law *and Diplomacy* at
Columbia University.[1] This combination of experiences yielded a familiarity
with the high stakes at play in the ongoing development of international
law, which can be bluntly evident in Jessup's writing. As Jessup warned in
A Modern Law of Nations (1948): 'Ignorance of the progress already achieved
in the development of international law over the past three centuries and
blindness to the still primitive character of the international legal system are
equally inimical to the further progress which must be made if all civilization
is not to go the way of Hiroshima and Nagasaki.'[2] It will be seen that this
preoccupation with the need for 'further progress' in the international system's
development to counter the atomic threat that hung over Jessup's time can be
extended to the broader challenges of sustainable development that have
become so much more apparent in our time.

The remainder of the chapter will be structured as follows. Section B will
examine Jessup's service at the UN. This section will recount Jessup's participation in the diplomatic activities of the newly established international
organization and how these experiences cohered with Jessup's conviction that
law and diplomacy were complementary rather than dichotomous pursuits at
the international level. Section C shifts the focus from Jessup's experiences at
the UN in the late 1940s and early 1950s to Jessup's subsequent discussion of
transnational law in his 1956 Storrs Lectures. Specifically, this section will
analyse the role that Jessup ascribes to the UN, and international organizations
generally, in his conception of transnational law. It will be seen that this strand
of Jessup's scholarship owes much to his experience of diplomatic service.
Section D applies Jessup's transnational legal scholarship to the current UN
challenge of implementing the SDGs. It will be argued that the SDGs can be
usefully conceived of as a project of transnational law in the terms given by
Jessup. Section E concludes.

B JESSUP AT THE UN

Every book is the product of its author's accumulated experiences. Early
reaction to *Transnational Law* noted its unblinkered appraisal of regulatory
practices beyond the scope of what had traditionally been considered public

---

[1]   Emphasis added.
[2]   PHILIP C. JESSUP, A MODERN LAW OF NATIONS 14 (1948).

international law. Another distinguished scholar and practitioner, Nicholas Katzenbach, wrote that Jessup had adopted a 'much more sensible' approach than traditional scholarship by unearthing 'a large and important area of rules and practices now too often arbitrarily excluded by *a priori* classification', including the decisions of international agencies.[3] C. G. Fenwick praised *Transnational Law* for taking some of the 'mystery' out of international law by drawing attention to the 'range both of jurisdiction and of law actually being made effective here and now'.[4] James Hyde identified, among *Transnational Law*'s 'thought-provoking illustrations', Jessup's comparison of 'the development and use of United Nations forums and procedures as a means for evolving a social consciousness'.[5]

The characteristics noted by Katzenbach, Fenwick and Hyde bear the mark of Jessup's service in the US government at the UN in its early years. In 1945, Jessup had been an adviser to the American delegation at the San Francisco Conference on the creation of the UN. From 1948 to 1949, he served as alternate US delegate to the UN Security Council with ambassadorial rank. From 1949 to 1953, Jessup was US ambassador-at-large and closely engaged in Cold War diplomacy as an adviser to the secretary of state. Oscar Schachter wrote that Jessup was 'severed from the mainstream of international law by diplomatic appointments'.[6] In fact, these diplomatic appointments placed Jessup in a position to assist in crafting, and then working through, the institution that would play host to more international lawmaking than any other, from his time to ours: the UN.

The optimism, ambition and novelty that attended the early years of the UN might be recalled with some bemusement after seven difficult decades for the organization. But recall we must, because it was in this atmosphere that Jessup practised diplomacy through the channels of the new international organization. In its early years, the UN was staffed and attended by officials who had been through the Second World War as politicians or civil servants or who had fought themselves. Many saw the UN as a means of preventing another such war. Indicative is the recollection of Brian Urquhart, an early staffer of the UN who went on to become undersecretary-general for political affairs:

---

[3] Nicholas Katzenbach, Book Review, 24 U. CHI. L. REV. 413, 413–14 (1956) (reviewing PHILIP C. JESSUP, TRANSNATIONAL LAW (1956)).

[4] C.G. Fenwick, Book Review, 51 AM. J. INT'L L. 444, 445 (1957) (reviewing JESSUP, *supra* note 3).

[5] James N. Hyde, Book Review, 66 YALE L.J. 813, 815 (1957) (reviewing JESSUP, *supra* note 3).

[6] Oscar Schachter, *Philip Jessup's Life and Ideas*, 80 AM. J. INT'L L. 878, 883 (1986).

The war was still vivid in everyone's mind and experience. Many of us had been in the armed forces, and others had only emerged from underground resistance movements a few months before. To work for peace was a dream fulfilled, and the fact that everything had to be organised from scratch was an additional incentive. Nothing seemed too much trouble and no hours too long. Bureaucracy, frustration, routine, empty rhetoric, political pettiness, and disillusionment were still in the future and had not yet dulled the feeling of elation and adventure.[7]

The British prime minister, Clement Attlee, went so far as to declare at the first session of the General Assembly, in 1946, that 'the United Nations Organization must become the over-riding factor in foreign policy'.[8]

There are indications that Jessup held similar views. He wrote in *A Modern Law of Nations* that the 'establishment of the United Nations presents an opportunity for innovations. The development of the organization of the international community suggests the ultimate possibility of substituting some kind of joint sovereignty, the supremacy of the common will, for the old single state sovereignty.'[9] James Hyde, who had been Jessup's assistant at the UN, recalled that

> Jessup saw international organization in general and the United Nations in particular as important elements of a modern law of nations. . . . In the early days of the United Nations, he promoted the development of 'parliamentary diplomacy,' a term for multilateral negotiation in United Nations bodies. He believed that it was a genuine type of diplomacy in which lawyers were well equipped to engage.[10]

Jessup was an energetic contributor to the early years of UN diplomacy, which dealt with the collapse of old empires, national liberation struggles, the rehabilitation of the Axis powers and, above all, the beginnings of the Cold War.[11] Dean Acheson, who as secretary of state was Jessup's superior, recalled Jessup's service as ranging from 'secret diplomatic agent' to 'editor-in-chief' of the Department of State's *China White Paper*.[12] Such was Jessup's

---

[7] BRIAN URQUHART, A LIFE IN PEACE AND WAR 92–93 (W.W. Norton & Co. 1991) (1987).

[8] *Id.* at 98.

[9] JESSUP, *supra* note 2, at 24.

[10] James N. Hyde, *Jessup: Memorials and Reminiscences*, 80 AM. J. INT'L L. 903, 903 (1986).

[11] Schachter, *supra* note 6, at 884.

[12] Dean Acheson, *Philip C. Jessup, Diplomatist, in* TRANSNATIONAL LAW IN A CHANGING SOCIETY: ESSAYS IN HONOR OF PHILIP C. JESSUP 8 (Wolfgang Friedman, Louis Henkin & Oliver Lissitzyn eds., 1972).

contribution that when a return to Columbia University was in prospect, the *New York Times* protested that 'Dr. Jessup is too valuable in action to be permitted to give all or most of his time to thinking.'[13] Jessup's role in ending the 1948–49 Soviet blockade of Berlin is a standout example of this 'action'. The United States took the matter to the UN Security Council. Jessup characterized this decision as an example of the 'emphasis placed by the United States on the use of the United Nations', in which the UK and France 'grudgingly acquiesced'.[14] In his own recollection, Jessup also emphasized the pragmatic nature of this decision: 'At the outset, recourse to the United Nations was probably endorsed by some *faute de mieux*, since we were determined not to withdraw, not to fight (although the availability of the A-bombs was not ignored) and not to negotiate under duress.'[15] Jessup emphasized the advocacy indispensable to progressing a 'case' through the UN: 'The ground was being prepared as it always must be in a case before the United Nations. Answers to possible arguments of opponents must be drafted in advance. Friends must be informed, persuaded or encouraged.'[16]

As the US deputy representative to the UN, Jessup was one of only four persons authorized by Congress to represent the United States at the Security Council, and he was given responsibility for the Berlin matter by the secretary of state.[17] Jessup played a key role in the diplomacy that resolved the crisis,[18] thus putting into practice what he had recently written in *A Modern Law of Nations*:

> There is no such dichotomy as one writer suggests between law and diplomacy. . . . To be sure, both procedures may be abused; the lawyer may become legalistic, the diplomat may become Machiavellian. But the successful practicing attorney is as much a negotiator as a citer of precedents, whether he be dealing with a corporate reorganization, a divorce suit, or the protection of national interests abroad.[19]

---

[13] Schachter, *supra* note 6, at 883.

[14] Philip C. Jessup, *The Berlin Blockade and the Use of the United Nations*, 50 FOREIGN AFF. 163, 164 (1971).

[15] *Id.* at 165.

[16] *Id.* at 170.

[17] The other authorized representatives being the president, the secretary of state and the ambassador to the UN. *Id.* at 168.

[18] The tale of Jessup's 'casual approach' to the Soviet ambassador to the UN, Yakov Malik, is recounted at DEAN ACHESON, PRESENT AT THE CREATION: MY YEARS AT THE STATE DEPARTMENT 269 (1970).

[19] Jessup, *supra* note 2, at 3–4.

C THE UN IN JESSUP'S SCHOLARSHIP

The scholarly insights of both *A Modern Law of Nations* and *Transnational Law*, which bear the stamp of Jessup's experience in participating in the UN's preparatory conference and subsequently in Security Council diplomacy, can be summarized as follows: an appreciation of the complexities of power and its interplay with law; the possibility, through the UN, to marshal a broader toolkit of modalities than was available in the context of traditional bilateral and concert diplomacy; and an openness to innovation in institutional configurations, inclusive of non-state actors. This section will highlight each of these insights.

Jessup's view of state power was essentially realist in its bottom line: 'Great powers have power because they are great and not because a skillful draftsman has invented an ingenious formula.'[20] However, the instruments of power are diverse: 'there are different kinds of power. Power, like love, is "a many splendored thing." "A nation's power can no longer be measured in terms of Francis Bacon's catalogue of 'walled towns, stored arsenals and armories, goodly race of horses, chariots of war, elephants, ordnance and artillery.'"'[21] The wielders of power are similarly diverse, with the consequence that power cannot be equated with jurisdiction. In establishing this point, Jessup gave the contrasting examples of the US Democratic Party, which acquires power through the existing organs of the US government and is therefore ignored by international law, and the Chinese Communist Party, which took power in mainland China while rejecting the legal existence of the prior organs of government of the (Nationalist-led) Republic of China, such that 'international law was ready to say here is a *de facto* government to which rules of international law apply'.[22]

---

[20] *Id.* at 30. Citing the amendment of the principle in *Animal Farm* that 'all animals are equal' to include the words 'but some animals are more equal than others', Jessup observed that the '[UN] Charter might realistically be amended in the same way'. *Id.* at n.81. Jessup's practice of diplomacy reflected these views. His account of an exchange with the Australian president of the General Assembly, H. R. 'Doc' Evatt, during the Berlin crisis is instructive: 'At the reception there came a moment when I was standing next to Evatt and no others were close at hand. He turned to me and snarled: "So you want to start another war, do you? Well, we're not going to let you do it!" I told him he was quite mistaken but I did not bother to inquire how, if we had intended to start a war, he proposed to stop us.' Jessup, *supra* note 14, at 171–72.

[21] Jessup, *supra* note 3, at 12 (quoting Sol M. Linowitz, *War for Men's Minds: The Fight We Must Not Lose*, 41 A.B.A. J. 810 (1955)).

[22] *Id.* at 12–13. Of course, international law has since gone far beyond recognition of a '*de facto* government' on mainland China, with the 1971 General Assembly resolution that recognized the People's Republic of China's representatives as 'the only lawful representatives of China to the United Nations', consequently ousting the Republic of China, which held (and holds)

Just as power defied conflation with jurisdiction, Jessup held that '[u]nlimited sovereignty' ('the quicksand upon which the foundations of traditional international law are built') was 'no longer automatically accepted as the most prized possession or even as a desirable attribute of states'.[23] Jessup illustrated this with an account of US diplomacy through the UN that laid bare the normativity of his claim. In Jessup's example, the United States advanced proposals through the UN Commission for the international control of atomic energy that were based on an 'altered attitude toward the fiction of sovereignty'. However, the US position was met with a Soviet riposte that the 'principle of sovereignty is one of the cornerstones on which the United Nations structure is built; if this were touched the whole existence and future of the United Nations would be threatened'. Jessup's conclusion: 'The path to progress may be long and thorny.'[24]

These observations concerning the complexities of power in modern state practice are arguably connected to a further insight of Jessup's scholarship: the ability, through the UN, to act through a broadened set of modalities to achieve diplomatic outcomes. Jessup makes this connection through his contention that in the absence, at the international level, of 'a governmental instrumentality whose fiat is law', there may be 'just as much power in the form of the pressures generated by Communist–non-Communist rivalries, the consciousness of need for security, and perhaps economic or humanitarian pressures'.[25] To support this contention, Jessup cited the 'successful' example of the UN technical assistance program in exercising 'sufficiently powerful leverage' to induce Soviet participation, despite the absence of legal obligation.[26] The ability to apply non-legal forms of influence through the workings of the UN is complemented, in Jessup's analysis, by a growing resort by states to international organizations when confronted by cross-border challenges: 'Governments have been accustomed to use international or transnational organizations for the solution of transnational problems. The experience is now of respectable age in dealing with postal communications, telecommunications, health, narcotics, fisheries, railways, aviation, shipping, raw materials, labor, and many others.'[27]

---

power on the island of Taiwan, from China's positions in the General Assembly and among the permanent five Security Council members. G.A. Res. 2758 (XXVI) (Oct. 25, 1971).

[23] JESSUP, *supra* note 2, at 1–2.

[24] Id. at 13.

[25] JESSUP, *supra* note 3, at 33–34.

[26] Id. at 34.

[27] Id. at 112.

This emphasis on functional cooperation, advanced through the application of real-world incentives, sidesteps the international/domestic dichotomy at the heart of the 'customary method of the study of international relations and international law', according to which '[i]f the matter does not involve the government of one state in its relations with another government or other governments, the matter is said to be "domestic"'.[28] This shift of perspective, in Jessup's telling, enables more proactive management of problems that may assume transnational dimensions.[29]

The third insight discussed here is closely related to this ability to pursue outcomes through the broadened modalities of the UN. It is the capacity for innovative institutional configurations and legal relationships to enable these modalities, including through the participation of non-state actors. This insight is consistent with *Transnational Law*'s famous assertion that 'the term "international" is misleading since it suggests that one is concerned only with the relations of one nation (or state) to other nations (or states)'.[30] Rather, observed Jessup, '[t]ransnational situations ... may involve individuals, corporations, states, organizations of states, or other groups'.[31]

According to Jessup, since transnational situations are broader than just interstate relations, transnational cooperation to address these situations can – and should – encompass coordination and agreement among other actors as well. In particular, argued Jessup in A *Modern Law of Nations*, 'collaboration between international agencies will be of great importance, and it is to be anticipated that there will be a considerable volume of agreements among them'.[32] Therefore, Jessup proposed the term 'international agreement' to 'embrace not only agreements between states but also agreements between states and individuals, between states or individuals and international organizations, and between two international organizations'.[33] Although Jessup's account of this phenomenon was broadly positive, he acknowledged the necessity of ascertaining which law governs any such particular agreement

[28] *Id.* at 11.
[29] Jessup's choice of example made clear his dissatisfaction with the logic and consequences of the traditional – and more reactive – approach: 'By and large, the orthodox approach precluded international consideration of a problem until it at least had transnational dimensions. . . . Thus a local riot not involving aliens, or agitation by citizens for the reform of their government, was not an international question. But when a dissident group inside a state was strong enough and resorted to arms, international law began to take an interest.' *Id.* at 11–12.
[30] *Id.* at 1.
[31] *Id.* at 3.
[32] JESSUP, *supra* note 2, at 130.
[33] *Id.* at 139.

in the absence of a general rule.[34] Concerning this expanded class of 'international agreements', Jessup emphasized the departure from the cumbersome processes of treaty making with an example from his own experience, concerning the UN Relief and Rehabilitation Administration (UNRRA): 'UNRRA concluded agreements with various states regarding the distribution of relief supplies. I have seen the text of one of these agreements which was to take effect on signature by a Deputy Director-General of UNRRA and by a cabinet minister of the government concerned; no ratification was required.'[35] This approach is essentially pragmatic and responsive to the urgencies and complexities of the post-war period – an attitude in keeping with the general American approach taken to the UN in its early years.[36]

D THE SDGS: APPLYING JESSUP'S TRANSNATIONAL LEGAL SCHOLARSHIP

In March 2016, Anthony Banbury, outgoing UN assistant secretary-general, slammed the UN's 'Orwellian admonitions', 'Carrollian logic', 'sclerotic personnel system' and 'minimal accountability'.[37] If the critic was unusually senior, the sentiments expressed were familiar. Lamentations about the UN's bureaucracy, opacity and meritless appointments are as old as the organization itself.[38] Such criticisms have persisted as the remit of the UN system steadily expanded from the interstate diplomacy of the Security Council and General Assembly to encompass a diverse array of subsidiary organs, specialized agencies and affiliated organizations working on peace and security, human rights and economic development. The UN's accumulation of programmatic responsibilities was already a noticeable trend by the time Jessup delivered his Storrs Lectures.[39] While the breadth and ambition of the UN's current

---

[34] *Id.* As will be seen, this is a particular challenge in contexts such as the implementation of the SDGs, which involves multiple agreements between international organizations, multistakeholder partnerships, non-state actors and states.

[35] *Id.* at 128.

[36] MARK MAZOWER, GOVERNING THE WORLD: THE HISTORY OF AN IDEA 199 (2012).

[37] Anthony Banbury, *I Love the U.N., but It Is Failing*, N.Y. TIMES, Mar. 18, 2016, https://www.nytimes.com/2016/03/20/opinion/sunday/i-love-the-un-but-it-is-failing.html?_r=0.

[38] Concerning the appointment of the first UN secretary-general, Brian Urquhart recalled: 'There was no consideration of who might be best qualified for the job.' The man who got the position, Trygve Lie, wondered in his own memoirs: 'Why had this awesome task fallen to a labor lawyer from Norway?' URQUHART, *supra* note 7, at 99, 101.

[39] Interestingly, Jessup connected this with the 'democratization of the United Nations, as the broadly based General Assembly takes on more and more authority through such measures as the Uniting for Peace Resolution and the supervision of non-self-governing territories'. JESSUP, *supra* note 3, at 27.

development agenda could not have been foreseen in Jessup's time, the insights of Jessup's transnational legal scholarship can be usefully applied to the task of implementing that agenda. This section will examine how Jessup's insights can assist the achievement of the SDGs through a UN system still wrestling with multiple shortcomings and controversies.

Jessup's conception of transnational law is particularly apt to be applied to a UN development agenda that, since the turn of the millennium, has relied on the coordination of disparate state and non-state actors to work towards broad, overarching targets. The adoption of this approach can be traced to the 2000 Millennium Summit, convened in response to member state concerns that economic development had been neglected in the UN's work.[40] The resulting Millennium Declaration identified sweeping global development goals to be met by 2015, such as halving the number of people living on less than a dollar a day and reducing maternal mortality by three-quarters.[41] The goals were itemized in the eight Millennium Development Goals (MDGs),[42] which were adopted by the General Assembly in 2002.[43] In 2012, with the 2015 deadline for meeting the MDGs approaching, the General Assembly called for the adoption of 'sustainable development goals [that] should be action-oriented, concise and easy to communicate, limited in number, aspirational, global in nature and universally applicable to all countries'.[44] In contrast to the 'top-down' creation of the MDGs, the SDGs were finalized only after a broad process of consultations involving experts and citizens from over ninety countries, enabled by digital technology.[45] The SDGs were adopted by the UN General Assembly in 2015 as the centrepiece of the 2030 Agenda for Sustainable Development.[46] They are therefore an outcome of 'parliamentary diplomacy' within the UN as championed by Jessup.[47]

---

[40] SIMON CHESTERMAN, IAN JOHNSTONE & DAVID M. MALONE, LAW AND PRACTICE OF THE UNITED NATIONS 23 (2d ed. 2016).

[41] G.A. Res. 55/2, Millennium Declaration (Sept. 8, 2000).

[42] U.N. Secretary-General, *Road Map Towards the Implementation of the United Nations Millennium Declaration*, U.N. Doc. A/56/326, annex (Sept. 6, 2001).

[43] G.A. Res. 56/95, Follow-Up to the Outcome of the Millennium Summit (Jan. 30, 2002).

[44] G.A. Res. 66/288, The Future We Want, ¶ 247 (Sept. 11, 2012).

[45] Anthony Gooch, *Digitalisation Is Not the Devil*, PROGRESSIVE POST, Feb. 5, 2019, https://progressivepost.eu/the-mag/digitalisation-is-not-the-devil.

[46] Resolution adopted by the General Assembly on 25 September 2015. G.A. Res. 70/1, Transforming Our World: The 2030 Agenda for Sustainable Development (Oct. 21, 2015).

[47] Philip C. Jessup, *Parliamentary Diplomacy*, 89 HAGUE RECUEIL DES COURS 185 (1956). In his *Transnational Law* dialogue between 'Mr Orthodox' and 'Mr Iconoclast', Jessup has Iconoclast liken 'the democratization of the United Nations, as the broadly based General Assembly takes on more and more authority', to the rise of 'corporate democracy' empowering shareholders. 'Maybe that's a general human trend', reflects Iconoclast. JESSUP, *supra* note 3, at 27.

Like their predecessors, the MDGs, the SDGs are a broad set of targets for the international community to meet over a fifteen-year period. The SDGs cannot compel states to act but can be expected to strongly influence policy and planning in many states, as well as to guide the activities of the UN development system and other organizations engaged in development work.

The SDGs have been criticized for their breadth and potential lack of focus.[48] The SDGs represent a major expansion on the subject matter treated by the MDGs, from eight to seventeen goals, from 18 to 169 targets and from 48 to 232 indicators.[49] A variety of topics that were not addressed by the MDGs, such as clean energy, sustainable use of the oceans, and peace and justice, feature prominently in the SDGs. This added complexity reflects the adoption, through the SDGs, of a 'triple-bottom-line concept' integrating economic development, social inclusion and environmental sustainability.[50] In consequence, meeting the SDGs requires coordination of a broader array of actors both within and beyond the UN system.[51]

It might be assumed that *Transnational Law* and *A Modern Law of Nations*, which are so clearly products of their time, have little to address to such an agenda. However, it is no anachronism to apply a theoretical approach developed in the 1940s and 1950s to the challenge of implementing a set of development goals adopted in 2015. For if the examples used by Jessup were necessarily from the immediate post-war period (and indeed from earlier times), the conclusions he reached emphasize the constant need for law to respond to the changing 'actualities' of international relations. Affirming the statement of Sir John Fischer Williams that it 'is obvious that international

---

[48] For example, Viñuales and colleagues charge that the 'expansive definition' of sustainable development embodied by the SDGs has 'helped to secure consensus, but more by "papering over" substantive differences, rather than truly resolving them'. J.E. Viñuales et al., *Climate Policy after the Paris 2015 Climate Conference*, 17 CLIMATE POLICY 1, 2–3 (2017). Similarly, Chesterman, Johnstone and Malone have labelled the outcome 'dismaying, ... a result of accretive drafting, seemingly more a catalogue of desiderata than architecture for a viable strategy'. CHESTERMAN, JOHNSTONE & MALONE, *supra* note 40, at 84.

[49] Global indicator framework adopted by the General Assembly (Res. 71/313) and annual refinements contained in U.N. Doc. E/CN.3/2018/2, annex II, https://unstats.un.org/sdgs/indicators/indicators-list/.

[50] J.D. Sachs, *Achieving the Sustainable Development Goals*, 8 J. INT'L BUS. ETHICS 53, 55 (2015).

[51] As captured in reports on SDG implementation: U.N., THE SUSTAINABLE DEVELOPMENT GOALS REPORT 2018, U.N. Sales No. E.18.I.6 (2018); U.N. DEP'T OF ECON, & SOC. AFFAIRS, SYNTHESIS OF VOLUNTARY NATIONAL REVIEWS 2018 (2018); and JEFFREY SACHS ET AL., SDG INDEX AND DASHBOARDS REPORT 2018 (2018).

relations are not limited to relations between states', Jessup grounded his broadening of transnational law out from interstate agreements in a pragmatic functionalism: 'The function of international law is to provide a legal basis for the orderly management of international relations. The traditional nature of that law was keyed to the actualities of past centuries in which international relations were interstate relations. The actualities have changed; the law is changing.'[52] This observation is just as relevant in 2017 as it was in 1948.

In applying Jessup's legal scholarship to the challenge of the SDGs, the key insight is that 'international agreements', expanded to include as parties non-state as well as state actors, can be used to construct novel institutional partnerships to apply resources and functional expertise to transnational challenges. As discussed in the previous section, Jessup anticipated that there would be a considerable volume of agreements among international agencies and between international agencies and states. When combined with Jessup's observation that 'individuals, corporations, states, organizations of states, or other groups' can participate in transnational situations, and with his dismissal of the international/domestic dichotomy, his insights suggest the following programmatic approach: mobilize both state and non-state actors through international agreements; use the collaboration produced by these agreements to militate against regional and functional fragmentation or duplication of effort; and employ multiple pathways for in-country implementation, including but not limited to interstate agreement.

This approach is broadly being pursued through the UN system to coordinate action on the SDGs, in particular through the modality of multi-stakeholder partnerships (MSPs). The MSP emerged as a tool of governance at the 2002 World Summit on Sustainable Development (WSSD). Defined as 'collaborations between national or sub-national governments, private sector actors and civil society actors, who form voluntary transnational agreements in order to meet specific sustainable development goals', MSPs were introduced in the WSSD to complement rather than supplant intergovernmental agreements.[53]

The Technology Facilitation Mechanism, introduced in the Addis Ababa Action Agenda of the Third International Conference on Financing for Development (which preceded and is closely related to the SDGs), is one

---

[52] JESSUP, *supra* note 2, at 16.
[53] FELIX DODDS, MULTI-STAKEHOLDER PARTNERSHIPS: MAKING THEM WORK FOR THE POST-2015 DEVELOPMENT AGENDA 6–7 (2015).

such MSP.[54] The Technology Facilitation Mechanism is composed of a UN inter-agency task team that includes thirty-two diverse agencies and pursues seven work streams;[55] an annual Multi-stakeholder Forum on Science, Technology and Innovation for the Sustainable Development Goals, which brings together governments and 'scientists, innovators, technology specialists, entrepreneurs and civil society representatives';[56] and a ten-member group to support the Technology Facilitation Mechanism, which comprises 'representatives of civil society, the private sector and the scientific community'.[57] The establishment of the Technology Facilitation Mechanism reflects the fact that technology is a means of implementation relevant to multiple SDGs. The composition of the mechanism reflects the fact that multiple international agencies and non-state actors have the ability to contribute to mobilizing technology for these purposes.

If Jessup's transnational legal insights are already well reflected in the institutional architecture of the SDGs, what purpose does it serve to illustrate that this is so? In part, applying Jessup serves as a validation that modalities that have been developed in a largely ad hoc and opportunistic manner are consistent with a valid theoretical underpinning. Bluntly, Jessup's conception of transnational law suggests that the SDG model is on the right track, insofar as the design features accommodate, rather than ignore or oppose, important realities of modern international relations and international organization. However, to the extent that Jessup is held to be a source of salient insights, his writings also serve as a reminder of the enduring centrality of states to

---

[54] The Technology Facilitation Mechanism has the broad remit of supporting the SDGs. It is 'based on a multi-stakeholder collaboration between Member States, civil society, the private sector, the scientific community, United Nations entities and other stakeholders and will be composed of a United Nations inter-agency task team on science, technology and innovation for the Sustainable Development Goals, a collaborative multi-stakeholder forum on science, technology and innovation for the Sustainable Development Goals and an online platform.' U.N. President of the G.A., Draft Resolution, Addis Ababa Action Agenda of the Third International Conference on Financing for Development, ¶ 123, U.N. Doc. A/69/L.82, annex (July 23, 2015); https://sustainabledevelopment.un.org/TFM.

[55] U.N. Division for Sustainable Dev. Goals, Terms of Reference for the UN Interagency Task Team on Science, Technology and Innovation for the Sustainable Development Goals (Oct. 22, 2015), https://sustainabledevelopment.un.org/content/documents/8569TOR%20IATT%2026%20Oct%202015rev.pdf.

[56] U.N. Econ. & Soc. Council, Multi-stakeholder Forum on Science, Technology and Innovation for the Sustainable Development Goals: Summary by the Co-chairs, U.N. Doc. E/HLPF/2016/6 (June 24, 2016).

[57] U.N. Division for Sustainable Dev. Goals, United Nations 10-Member Group to Support the Technology Facilitation Mechanism: Terms of Reference (Mar. 4, 2016), https://sustainabledevelopment.un.org/content/documents/9468TOR%2010-member%20group-final-clean.pdf.

international relations: 'The inescapable fact is that the world is today organized on the basis of the coexistence of states, and that fundamental changes will take place only through state action, whether affirmative or negative.'[58] Here, as with so much of Jessup's writing, one can hear the experienced diplomat talking.

E CONCLUSION

Transnational Law can indeed be considered a bold proposal: to move beyond the constraints on public international law that hindered its capacity to bring order to cross-border problems that had become so apparent in Jessup's time. In a different time and context, the SDGs represent an equally bold proposal: that transnational coordination of diverse stakeholders can bring measurable improvement to human and environmental conditions all across the globe. It is part of Jessup's enduring legacy that the insights he shared in the 1940s and 1950s remain relevant to meeting some of the largest contemporary challenges of international organization.

Jessup's diplomatic service informed a pragmatic scholarship of transnational law. His concern, in *Transnational Law*, to realize a 'larger storehouse of rules on which to draw'[59] reflected direct experience of the need for additional ways of managing the 'novel demands'[60] of the post-war period. Jessup identified the UN, which had shown itself to be a forum for addressing major crises and was taking on growing programmatic responsibilities, as a key body through which international cooperation could be pursued. The UN is therefore a recurring topic in Jessup's scholarship, often as an example of innovative approaches to international problems. The insights contained in that scholarship, concerning the complex interplay of power and law, the expanded toolkit of modalities for international organization and the potential contributions of both state and non-state actors, continue to be relevant to meeting the challenges of the UN and international organizations generally. As a consequence, Jessup's scholarship constitutes a rich storehouse of ideas with which to pursue improvements in the UN and a more effective implementation of its mission. The SDGs, the achievement of which depends upon the complex and sustainable collaboration of multiple actors, are an important case in point.

---

[58] JESSUP, *supra* note 2, at 17. Applied to this content, this cautionary observation serves to remind that states wield an effective veto over the implementation of SDGs in their jurisdictions.

[59] JESSUP, *supra* note 3, at 15.

[60] Acheson, *supra* note 12, at 6.

Long after his service as a diplomat there, Jessup remained clear-eyed about both the UN's value and its limitations. His observation that '[p]eople expect too much of the U.N., and that's why they're disappointed' is equally a rejoinder to the utopians and the inveterate critics.[61] But it was in a lecture given at the Hague Academy of International Law in 1970, in celebration of the twenty-fifth anniversary of the UN, that Jessup summarized best his view of the transnational possibilities of this 'supreme type of international organization':[62]

> Who can say what changes for the better this 25th year will bring about in the complex organization called the United Nations? ... The United Nations is not only a 'town meeting of the world' in which a lot of time is wasted in repetitious and bombastic orations; it is not only a rather ineffectual international policeman; it is one of the most convenient channels for serious international negotiation and 'quiet diplomacy;' it is the International Bank for Reconstruction and Development; it is the International Court of Justice; it is the World Health Organization; it is the International Labour Organization and the Universal Postal Union; it is a 'presence' in areas of tension; it is the organizational structure – efficient or inefficient – utilized for the daily operations of international life. Every improvement in the United Nations improves the quality of the life of nations.[63]

---

[61] Eric Pace, *Philip C. Jessup Dies; Helped End Berlin Blockade*, N.Y. TIMES, Feb. 1, 1986, http://www.nytimes.com/1986/02/01/obituaries/philip-c-jessup-dies-helped-end-berlin-blockade.html.

[62] Reparation for Injuries Suffered in the Service of the United Nations, Advisory Opinion, 1949, I.C.J. 174, at 179–80 (Apr. 11).

[63] Philip C. Jessup, *To Form a More Perfect United Nations*, 9 COLUM. J. TRANSNAT'L L. 177, 192–93 (1970).

2

The Concept of a Global Legal System

CHRISTOPHER A. WHYTOCK

A INTRODUCTION

The international law field of teaching and scholarship focuses – and has long focused – on the so-called "international legal system."[1] The system's parts include international law, international courts, and international organizations, and those parts are held together by foundational principles such as those governing the sources of international law and state responsibility for internationally wrongful acts.[2]

Notwithstanding its "international legal system" emphasis, international law teaching and scholarship frequently touches on national law, national courts, and nonstate actors. For example, it examines the status of international law in national courts and of nonstate actors as both potential subjects of and contributors to the development of international law.[3] But it is less common for international law teaching and scholarship to treat national law, national courts, or nonstate actors as playing independently important

---

[1] See, e.g., Mary Ellen O'Connell et al., The International Legal System: Cases and Materials (7th ed. 2015); Commitment and Compliance: The Role of Non-binding Norms in the International Legal System (Dinah Shelton ed., 2003) (2000).

[2] See James Crawford, Brownlie's Principles of Public International Law 16 (8th ed. 2012) ("International law has the characteristics of a system, not just a random collection of rules: the basic constructs of personality, sources (including treaties), interpretation, and responsibility, provide a framework within which rules may be generated, applied and, increasingly, adjudicated upon.").

[3] See, e.g., André Nollkaemper, National Courts and the International Rule of Law (2011) (discussing national courts in the international legal system); Participants in the International Legal System: Multiple Perspectives on Non-state Actors in International Law (Jean d'Aspremont ed. 2011) (discussing nonstate actors in the international legal system).

roles in global affairs, apart from any connection they may have with international law.[4]

One of the enduring and important contributions of Philip Jessup's *Transnational Law*[5] is its challenge to this concept of the international legal system. Jessup does not challenge the concept on the ground that international law is not a system, as others have.[6] Rather, he challenges it on what are essentially functionalist grounds. Rejecting the traditional doctrinal boundaries of the field of international law, his point of departure is a concern with "the problems of the world community" – not merely with "the relations of one nation (or state) to other nations (or states)" as the term "international" implies.[7] He then asks, What are the rules that regulate these problems? The answer, he argues, is not only international law but "all law which regulates actions or events that transcend national frontiers," including national law and private norms.[8] Jessup called this law "transnational law."[9]

My argument in this chapter is that a further conceptual move would be helpful, from a concept of the "international legal system" to a concept of the "global legal system." Jessup's transnational law concept is a concept of law that reaches beyond international law. But we also need a concept of legal system that reaches beyond the international legal system – one that, unlike transnational law, encompasses not only the law that governs cross-border

---

[4] *But see, e.g.,* Terence C. Halliday & Gregory Shaffer, *Transnational Legal Orders, in* TRANSNATIONAL LEGAL ORDERS (Terence C. Halliday & Gregory Shaffer eds., 2015) (developing concept of transnational legal ordering); TONYA L. PUTNAM, COURTS WITHOUT BORDERS: LAW, POLITICS, AND U.S. EXTRATERRITORIALITY (2016); Christopher A. Whytock, *Domestic Courts and Global Governance,* 84 TUL. L. REV. 67 (2009) (discussing not only relationship between national courts and international legal system but also independent role of national courts in transnational dispute resolution and global governance). In addition, several casebooks take an approach that emphasizes not only international law and international courts but also national law and national courts, as well as private norms and private forms of dispute resolution. *See, e.g.,* DONALD EARL CHILDRESS III, MICHAEL D. RAMSEY & CHRISTOPHER A. WHYTOCK, TRANSNATIONAL LAW AND PRACTICE (2015); MATHIAS W. REIMANN ET AL., TRANSNATIONAL LAW: CASES AND MATERIALS (2013); and DETLEV F. VAGTS, WILLIAM S. DODGE & HAROLD HONGJU KOH, TRANSNATIONAL BUSINESS PROBLEMS (4th ed. 2008).

[5] PHILIP C. JESSUP, TRANSNATIONAL LAW (1956).

[6] For an overview of the systemic view of international law and a discussion of critiques of that view, see Eyal Benvenisti, *The Conception of International Law as a Legal System,* 50 GERMAN Y.B. INT'L L. 393 (2008).

[7] JESSUP, *supra* note 5, at 1.

[8] *Id.* at 2.

[9] *See id.* ("I shall use instead of 'international law,' the term 'transnational law' to include all law which regulates actions or events that transcend national frontiers.").

problems, but also courts and other national, international, and private institutions that contribute to that same function.

The term "global legal system" is not new.[10] But it is usually used without definition or with only abbreviated conceptual development. Moreover, scholars sometimes use the term "global law" in a way that includes courts and other institutions beyond legal rules.[11] Indeed, the concept of a global legal system is implicit in Jessup's *Transnational Law*. It includes discussions of national courts and arbitration and of conflict-of-laws rules, which, as I will suggest below, play a central role in what I am calling the global legal system. But these discussions fit uncomfortably within Jessup's concept of transnational law, which is defined in terms of rules. A clear concept of the global legal system can accommodate and make explicit these important implications of Jessup's work.

In this chapter, I outline my concept of the global legal system and attempt to lay out a coherent and parsimonious framework for understanding and analyzing it. To preview: the global legal system consists of institutions that provide legal solutions to transnational problems. These institutions are national, international, private, and sometimes hybrid. Among the types of solutions provided by the global legal system are three generic governance functions: prescription, adjudication, and enforcement. Often more than one institution may provide solutions to a given transnational legal problem, creating a need for choice across three dimensions: national-national, national-international, and public-private. The global legal system uses three types of principles to guide these choices: principles of authority, principles of

---

[10] *See, e.g.*, Giuliana Ziccardi Capaldo, The Pillars of Global Law xvi (2008) (examining four pillars of the global legal system, including verticality and sharing of decisional processes, legality principles and common global values, integration of legal systems, and collective guarantees); Oren Perez, *Purity Lost: The Paradoxical Face of the New Transnational Legal Body*, 33 Brook. J. Int'l L. 1, 3–4 (2007); Sabino Cassese, *Global Standards for National Administrative Procedure*, 68 Law & Contemp. Probs. 109, 121 (2005); Eve Darian-Smith, *Structural Inequalities in the Global Legal System*, 34 Law & Soc'y Rev. 809 (2000); Mohamed S. Helal, *Justifying War and the Limits of Humanitarianism*, 37 Fordham Int'l L. J. 551, 555 (2014); Sung-Soo Han, *A Study on the Development of a Global Community from a Legal Perspective*, 7 BYU Int'l L. & Mgmt. Rev. 71, 72 (2010); Andreas Fischer-Lescano & Gunther Teubner, *Regime-Collisions: The Vain Search for Legal Unity in the Fragmentation of Global Law*, 25 Mich. J. Int'l L. 999, 1007 (2004); Charles H. Koch, Jr., *Envisioning a Global Legal Culture*, 25 Mich. J. Int'l L. 1, 4 (2003); Anne-Marie Slaughter, A New World Order (2004); Chris Thornhill, *The Global Legal System and the Procedural Construction of Constituent Power*, 5 Global Constitutionalism 405 (2016); Paul Schiff Berman, *From Legal Pluralism to Global Legal Pluralism, in* Law, Society and Community: Socio-legal Essays in Honour of Roger Cotterrell 255 (Richard Nobles & David Schiff eds., 2014).

[11] One of the most comprehensive accounts of "global law" to date is Ziccardi Capaldo, *supra* note 10.

allocation, and principles of party autonomy. These are among the principles that hold the global legal system together, in spite of its high degree of decentralization.

The global legal system is the system of laws, courts, and other institutions that provide legal solutions to transnational problems. This is a functional understanding of the global legal system, and it follows Jessup's functional understanding of transnational law.[12] His emphasis throughout is not on actions or events as such but on problems and the law that can be used to solve them. As he puts it on the first page of *Transnational Law*, he is interested in "analyzing the problems of the world community and the law regulating them."[13] And each of the three main parts of the book is explicitly focused on problems for which he explores legal solutions: "The Universality of the Human Problems," "The Power to Deal with the Problems," and "The Choice of Law Governing the Problems."

So to understand what transnational law is – and what the global legal system does – we need to understand what transnational problems are. Jessup defined transnational problems very broadly. Transnational problems are problems that arise out of any "actions or events that transcend national frontiers."[14] They are the problems faced by the "world community," which "begin[s] with the individual and reach[es] on up to the so-called 'family of nations' or 'society of states.'"[15] "The problems in general," he explains, "arise from conflicts of interest or desire, real or imagined."[16]

This definition of transnational problems reflects Jessup's claim that it is arbitrary to focus narrowly on international (that is, nation-to-nation) problems alone. Jessup was concerned with the problems faced by the "world community" more broadly. He argued that "the term 'international' is misleading, since it suggests that one is concerned only with the relations of one nation (or state) to other nations (or states)."[17] For Jessup, transnational problems can

---

[12] See JESSUP, *supra* note 5, at 71 (referring to "the function of transnational law"). *See also* Gralf-Peter Calliess, *Transnational Law, in* ENCYCLOPEDIA OF GLOBAL STUDIES (Helmut K. Anheier & Mark Juergensmeyer eds., 2012) ("Generally speaking, Jessup's approach to transnational law can be categorized as a functional one.").

[13] JESSUP, *supra* note 5, at 1.

[14] *Id.* at 2.

[15] *Id.* at 1.

[16] *Id.* at 11.

[17] *Id.* at 1.

involve "individuals, corporations, states, organizations of states, or other groups."[18] And he emphasized that the problems of interest to him are "after all merely human problems which might arise at any level of human society – individual, corporate, interregional, or international."[19]

Some have criticized Jessup's definition of transnational law as too broad to be useful because transnational problems are so pervasive that arguably every problem today is transnational.[20] A global legal system paradigm inspired by Jessup's notion of transnational problems might be susceptible to the same criticism. But Jessup deliberately left his definition open, suggesting that it is best to "avoid further classification of transnational problems and further definitions of transnational law."[21] This open approach is sensible. Comparative legal scholars have criticized functionalism in comparative law for its tendency to assume that all societies face similar problems that define the function of law.[22] It would also seem reasonable to resist too much generalizing about what those problems are in a functional approach to the global legal system. Moreover, human problems evolve over time. Cross-societal and intertemporal variation in human problems makes it unwise, perhaps even impossible, to specify a priori what transnational problems are.

Perhaps most important is something that Jessup did not emphasize in *Transnational Law*: the definition of transnational problems can be highly political. Different individuals and groups can disagree about what constitutes a problem and how that problem should be defined.[23] Because legal solutions almost inevitably have distributional consequences or reflect different normative values, there is contestation over whether particular phenomena count as transnational problems. The production of legal solutions depends largely on how this contestation is resolved – and how it is resolved may be strongly

---

[18] *Id.* at 3.

[19] *Id.* at 15–16. It is interesting that Jessup's insistence on a non-state-centric view came more than a decade before a similar move in US political science in the 1970s to include the study of "transnational relations" alongside international relations. *See* Joseph S. Nye, Jr. & Robert O. Keohane, *Transnational Relations and World Politics: An Introduction,* 25 INT'L ORG. 329 (1971).

[20] *See* Christian Tietje & Karsten Nowrot, *Laying Conceptual Ghosts of the Past to Rest: The Rise of Philip C. Jessup's "Transnational Law" in the Regulatory Governance of the International Economic System, in* TRANSNATIONAL LAW REVISITED: ON THE OCCASION OF THE 50TH ANNIVERSARY OF ITS PUBLICATION 17, 30 (Christian Tietje, Alan Brouder & Karsten Nowrot eds., 2006), http://www.wirtschaftsrecht.uni-halle.de/sites/default/files/altbestand/Heft50.pdf (describing, but not endorsing, this critique).

[21] JESSUP, *supra* note 5, at 7.

[22] *See* Christopher A. Whytock, *Legal Origins, Functionalism, and the Future of Comparative Law,* 2009 BYU L. REV. 1879, 1886 (2009) (discussing these criticisms).

[23] *Id.* at 1889–90.

influenced by the global distribution of power among states and between states and nonstate actors.[24]

Therefore, to define the concept of the global legal system, I suggest a broad, functionalist concept of transnational problems similar to Jessup's: transnational problems are problems that concern more than one state or persons of different nationalities. Defined this way, transnational problems include not only international problems but also problems relevant to nonstate actors. It must be a realistic functionalist concept that avoids excessive generalization and recognizes the politics of transnational problems.

C LEGAL SOLUTIONS AND GENERIC GOVERNANCE FUNCTIONS

If the first step toward defining the concept of a global legal system is to define transnational problems, the next step is to understand the nature of legal solutions to those problems. Jessup suggests that as human problems change and grow, there is growing demand for legal solutions to those problems: "As man has developed his needs and his facilities for meeting his needs, the rules become more numerous and more complicated."[25] Transnational law is the field of law that provides those solutions. Thus, as Jessup puts it, transnational law "suppl[ies] a...storehouse of rules on which to draw" to solve transnational problems.[26]

As with the definition of transnational problem, it is important not to pretend that the definition of legal solutions is apolitical. Which solutions are proposed and adopted will often be politically contested and influenced by power. It also is important not to pretend that legal solutions are necessarily effective in the sense that they actually solve the transnational problems to which they are addressed. The effect of a legal solution is an empirical question that poses difficult challenges of causal inference – and whether a particular effect makes a solution a "success" is likely to be as politically contested as the definition of the transnational problem and the selection of a solution in the first place.[27] What might be a success to one group could be viewed by another group as a failure or as making a problem worse. Even more fundamentally, law alone cannot of course solve all (or even most) transnational problems. Therefore, it is best not to think of legal solutions as

---

[24] This contestation may occur national and transnationally. *See generally* Halliday & Shaffer, *supra* note 4.

[25] JESSUP, *supra* note 5, at 8.

[26] *Id.* at 15.

[27] *See generally* Whytock, *supra* note 22, at 1879.

necessarily effective but rather to think of them as potential solutions to be assessed based on evidence.

Jessup made no effort to catalog transnational problems in detail, and he made no effort to list the solutions offered by transnational law either. Yet it is helpful to think about solutions to transnational problems at a very general level, with a focus on a trio of generic governance functions: prescription (the making of rules), adjudication (the authoritative resolution of disputes), and enforcement (namely, the enforcement of rules and the outcomes of adjudication).[28] These generic functions may help address many different transnational problems, ranging from transnational crime to cross-border environmental harm and from human rights abuses to international child custody disputes. They are not the only functions, but they are a good point of departure for thinking about the functions of the global legal system.[29]

D SUPPLIERS OF LEGAL SOLUTIONS: THE INSTITUTIONS OF THE GLOBAL LEGAL SYSTEM

The next step in honing the concept of a global legal system is to ask, Who supplies legal solutions? Jessup emphasized that the suppliers of transnational law include not only states but also international organizations and private actors. He includes in his concept of transnational law rules made by "ecclesiastical authorities," corporations, "secret societies," towns, cities, states, and international organizations.[30]

Likewise, the suppliers of legal solutions in the global legal system include not only states but also other institutions. These institutions can be differentiated functionally (Table 2.1) and organizationally (Table 2.2). Functionally, there are institutions that correspond to each of the generic functions of the

---

[28] *See* Anne Mette Kjaer, Governance (2004) (defining governance as "the setting of rules, the application of rules, and the enforcement of rules"). These functions roughly correspond to the three types of authority addressed by the customary international law of jurisdiction. *See* Sean D. Murphy, Principles of International Law 313–44 (2d. ed. 2012) (discussing jurisdiction to prescribe, jurisdiction to adjudicate, and jurisdiction to enforce).

[29] *See, e.g.,* Lung-chu Chen, An Introduction to Contemporary International Law: A Policy-Oriented Perspective (2015) (identifying seven functions of the international legal system: the intelligence (information) function, the promoting function, the prescribing (lawmaking) function, the invoking function, the applying function, the terminating function, and the appraising function).

[30] Jessup, *supra* note 5, at 8–9. In this way, Jessup's concept of transnational law can be considered a precursor to the concept of global legal pluralism. *See generally* Ralf Michaels, *Global Legal Pluralism*, 5 Ann. Rev. L. & Soc. Sci. 1–35 (2009); Paul Schiff Berman, *Global Legal Pluralism*, 80 S. Cal. L. Rev. 1155 (2007).

TABLE 2.1 *Institutions of the global legal system differentiated by generic governance function*

Prescription
Adjudication
Enforcement
Hybrid

TABLE 2.2 *Institutions of the global legal system differentiated by organizational level*

National
International
Private
Hybrid

global legal system: institutions that prescribe rules (e.g., legislatures and sometimes courts), institutions that adjudicate (e.g., courts and private dispute-resolution bodies, such as arbitral tribunals), and institutions that enforce (e.g., groups of nations or private groups taking law into their own hands).

Organizationally, the institutions of the global legal system include national institutions (e.g., national legislatures and national courts), international institutions (e.g., the United Nations), and private institutions (e.g., private rule-making bodies and private dispute resolution bodies, such as arbitral institutions). Often, institutions are hybrid, with a combination of prescriptive, adjudicative, and enforcement functions, or a combination of national, international, and private elements.

There are also subsystems of the global legal system. Subsystems vary by participants and the types of problems they address. National legal systems are subsystems in which participation is limited to a given state. International legal subsystems often have a limited number of participating states, with those limits often defined regionally (e.g., the African Court on Human and Peoples' Rights), and many are focused on particular types of problems (e.g., the World Trade Organization and the International Criminal Court).

The global legal system is highly decentralized – so decentralized that some might hesitate to call it a "system" at all.[31] Needless to say, there is no global

---

[31] The status of international law as a system has been widely discussed, along with the implications of fragmentation for that status. *See, e.g.,* JAN KLABBERS, ANNE PETERS & GEIR

court or global legislature. However, centralization is not necessary for a system to exist.[32] Rather, centralization is a variable, such that a system can be more or less centralized (or more or less fragmented). In any event, some subsystems of the global legal system are quite centralized (e.g., most national legal systems and, one might add, the European Union). Most fundamentally, there are legal rules that are part of the global legal system that contribute to the coordination of its different parts, including national (and, increasingly, international) conflict-of-laws rules; public international law's principles of jurisdiction to prescribe, adjudicate, and enforce; the national and international law of arbitration; and the host of principles that govern the relationships between different rules of international law (such as the maxims of *lex specialis derogat legi generali* and *lex posterior derogat legi priori* and the concept of jus cogens norms).[33]

E LEGAL RULES: BEYOND TRADITIONAL DOCTRINAL DISTINCTIONS

One type of legal solution provided by the institutions of the global legal system is the production of legal rules – that is, prescription, which is one of the generic functions of the global legal system. Nations create national law. Acting together, nations create international law, including customary international law and treaty law. And private actors also create rules. All three types of rules are part of transnational law, according to Jessup.

This conception of transnational law was – and to a significant degree still is – innovative in several ways.[34] First, it challenges the distinction between national law and international law. As Jessup argued, "the line between the international and the national should be questioned as a basis for legal

ULFSTEIN, THE CONSTITUTIONALIZATION OF INTERNATIONAL LAW (2009); Int'l Law Comm'n, FRAGMENTATION OF INTERNATIONAL LAW: DIFFICULTIES ARISING FROM THE DIVERSIFICATION AND EXPANSION OF INTERNATIONAL LAW, U.N. Doc. A/CN.4/L.682/Corr.1 (Aug. 11, 2006) (finalized by Martti Koskenniemi).

[32] *Cf.* Giuliana Ziccardi Capaldo, *Managing Complexity within the Unit of the Circular Web of the Global Law System: Representing a "Communal Spider Web,"* 1 GLOBAL COMMUN. Y.B. INT'L L. & JUR. xxi (2011) (affirming that "[t]he global law system is highly fragmented" but nevertheless treating it as a system).

[33] *Cf.* Int'l Law Comm'n, *supra* note 31, at 7 (noting that notwithstanding fragmentation, international law is a system due largely to these and other principles of international law).

[34] For an overview of the concept, its evolution, and its adoption by different theoretical schools of international law, see HAROLD HONGJU KOH, TRANSNATIONAL LITIGATION IN UNITED STATES COURTS ch. 1 (2008).

classification ... ."[35] The distinction may in many situations be doctrinally relevant, but from Jessup's functional perspective, the essential commonality is that both national law and international law can provide potential solutions to transnational problems. Second, Jessup challenged the distinction between public international law and private international law. According to Jessup, "[b]oth public and private international law are included" in the concept of transnational law.[36] Third, Jessup didn't hesitate to include private rules in his definition of transnational law.[37]

It is not obvious whether to include concepts like "soft law" and "nonstate law" in the concept of a global legal system. On the one hand, there are good reasons to reserve the term "law" for rules that are produced by a recognized lawmaking process – such as those defined in a national constitution or international law's doctrine of sources – and intended to be legally binding in the sense that a court would consider them to be binding rules of decision in adjudication. Legal scholars and social scientists have long sought to understand what is distinctive about law. Normatively, is there a difference between legal obligations and other types of obligations? Behaviorally, do legal rules affect behavior in ways that are systematically different from other types of rules? And how do legal rules affect, and how are they affected by, nonlegal rules?[38] But if one conflates legal and nonlegal rules into a single concept of law, this type of analysis is not possible.

On the other hand, so-called soft law and nonstate law play a crucial role in solving transnational problems, as Jessup emphasized.[39] They are also so closely linked to legally binding rules as to make it difficult to consider the role of one without the other.[40] For example, non–legally binding and private rules may influence the development of law, and private rules that take the form of, or are incorporated into, contracts may be legally enforceable as a

---

[35] JESSUP, *supra* note 5, at 70.

[36] *Id.* at 2.

[37] He downplayed this move, saying that "[n]owadays it is neither novel nor heretical to call all of these rules 'law.'" *Id.* at 9. But actually, this may have been one of the more novel aspects of Jessup's concept at the time.

[38] *See* Martha Finnemore, *Are Legal Norms Distinctive?*, 32 N.Y.U. J. INT'L L. & POL. 699, 701 (2000) (arguing that one of the most important questions for political scientists and policy makers is whether "legal norms, as a type, operate differently from any other kinds of norms in world politics").

[39] *See, e.g.,* COMMITMENT AND COMPLIANCE, *supra* note 1 (on nonbinding rules) and TIM BÜTHE & WALTER MATTLI, THE NEW GLOBAL RULERS: THE PRIVATIZATION OF REGULATION IN THE WORLD ECONOMY (2011) (on private forms of governance).

[40] *See* Christopher A. Whytock, *Private-Public Interaction in Global Governance: The Case of Transnational Commercial Arbitration*, 12:3 BUS. & POL. (2010).

matter of contract law. And from Jessup's functional perspective, the differences between legally binding rules, non–legally binding rules, and private rules are not as fundamental as what they all have in common: they are all potential solutions to transnational problems. I therefore include non–legally binding rules and private rules as among the rules of the global legal system; but in an effort to avoid the analytical problems posed by conflating them with law, I do not use the terms *soft law* or *nonstate law* to describe them.

F DIMENSIONS OF CHOICE

An important implication of a global legal system concept based on Jessup's functionalist concept of transnational law is that a wide variety of legal solutions may be available for a given transnational problem. As Jessup explains:

> There are rules, or there is law, bearing upon [transnational problems]. There may be a number of applicable legal rules and they may conflict with each other. When this is the case, still other rules may determine which law prevails. In certain types of situations we may say this is a question of "choice of law" which is to be determined by the rules of "Conflict of Laws" or "Private International Law." The choice usually referred to here is between rules of different national laws; and the choice, we assume, is to be made by a national court. In other types of situations the choice may be between a rule of national law and a rule of "Public International Law," and the choice may be made by a national tribunal or by some nonjudicial decision maker.[41]

In other words, since nations, international institutions, and private actors can all provide legal solutions to transnational problems, there are multiple dimensions to choosing a legal solution (see Figure 2.1). First, will a national or international solution be used? Second, will a national or private solution be used? Third, will an international or private solution be used?[42] And beyond these three basic dimensions, there are others: among multiple national solutions, international solutions, or private solutions, which will be used?

These dimensions intersect with the three generic functions of prescription, adjudication, and enforcement (Table 2.3).[43] Which rules should be applied?

---

[41] JESSUP, *supra* note 5, at 4–5.

[42] *See* Whytock, *Domestic Courts and Global Governance, supra* note 4.

[43] *See* id. As noted above, there are of course other functions of the global legal system. For example, both the Human Rights Council's universal periodic review process (at the international level) and nongovernmental human rights organizations (at the private level) perform what Chen calls an "intelligence" function, a function that does not fit neatly into the category of prescription, adjudication, or enforcement. *Cf.* CHEN, *supra* note 29 (listing the UN Human Rights Council's reporting system as an example of the "intelligence" function).

TABLE 2.3 *Institutions of the global legal system: functions and organization (with examples)*

		Organizational level		
		National	*International*	*Private*
	Prescription	National legislatures	Treaty-making, regulations of regional (e.g., EU) or specialized (e.g., ILO) organizations	Private rulemaking bodies (e.g., ISO)
Governance Function	Adjudication	National courts	International courts (e.g., ICJ)	Transnational arbitral institutions (e.g. ICC)
	Enforcement	Police, national executive agencies	UN Security Council, economic sanctions	Reputational monitoring and reciprocity

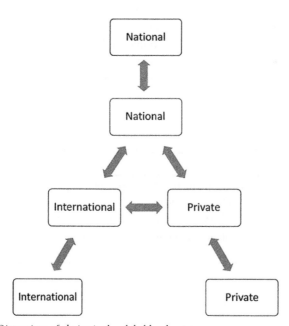

FIGURE 2.1 Dimensions of choice in the global legal system

Which court or other body should adjudicate? Who should enforce? And for each of these generic governance functions, the questions are as follows: Which nation? National or international? Private or public? To understand the global legal system, it is essential to understand these dimensions of choice.

G METHODS OF CHOICE

But how are these choices made? Whether through national law, public international law, or private international law, argued Jessup, one "function of transnational law [is] to reshuffle the cases and to deal out jurisdiction in the manner most conducive to the needs and convenience of all members of the international community."[44] The global legal system uses three basic methods to guide choices across these dimensions: authority, allocation, and party autonomy (Table 2.4). First, a choice may be included or excluded from consideration based on whether the supplier has the authority to apply a particular solution. This method is most familiar in public international law, a branch of which provides principles limiting the jurisdiction of states to prescribe, adjudicate, and enforce. A given nation either has or lacks authority to prescribe, adjudicate, or enforce.

Second, a choice may be made based on rules of allocation. The question is not whether a given supplier has authority but rather which solution among several will be applied to a transnational problem. Ordinarily, this method assumes – implicitly or explicitly – that the suppliers of the solutions under consideration have the requisite authority, and in that way authority and allocation are related.[45] Perhaps the most familiar example of allocation as a

TABLE 2.4 *Methods of choice in the global legal system (with examples)*

Method	Examples
Authority	Customary international law principles of jurisdiction to prescribe, adjudicate, and enforce
Allocation	Choice-of-law branch of conflict of laws (private international law)
Party autonomy	Choice-of-law and forum-selection clauses

---

[44] Jessup, *supra* note 5, at 71.
[45] *See* Christopher A. Whytock, *Toward a New Dialogue between Conflict of Laws and International Law*, 110 Am. J. Int'l L. Unbound 150 (2016).

method of choice is the choice-of-law branch of conflict of laws (or "private international law"), which attempts to guide judges and lawyers in figuring out which state's law to apply.[46]

Third, a choice may be made not based on rules of authority or allocation but instead based on party autonomy.[47] The most common examples are choice-of-law clauses in contracts, whereby parties choose a particular nation's law (or even rules other than national law, such as the UNIDROIT Principles of International Commercial Contracts), or dispute resolution clauses, whereby parties choose a particular nation's courts or a private dispute-resolution method such as arbitration. There can also be some degree of party autonomy regarding enforcement, such as through private escrow arrangements.

The branch of law that most explicitly deals with choice – conflict of laws – deals primarily with the international dimension (and, to a lesser extent, with the private-public dimension).[48] For example, choice of law deals with which nation's law to apply, not whether to apply national law or international law. But each nation has domestic rules that help determine when one of its courts will apply international law rather than national law, which is an example of the national-international dimension; and most nations have rules that help determine when one of its courts will enforce a choice-of-law or forum-selection clause, which is an example of the private-public dimension.

These methods of choice are important in legal practice, yet they are contested and vary significantly across legal systems. The future development of the global legal system will thus depend largely on the further development of rules of authority, allocation, and party autonomy. But the choices themselves are not merely legal but also political: they distribute governance power among states, between national and international institutions, and between private and public actors. For this reason, these choices – like the definition of problems and the evaluation of solutions – inevitably have a political aspect.

---

[46] *See* Alex Mills, The Confluence of Public and Private International Law: Justice, Pluralism and Subsidiarity in the International Constitutional Ordering of Private Law (2009) and Whytock, *Domestic Courts and Global Governance, supra* note 4 (discussing allocation of governance authority by conflict of laws).

[47] *See* Alex Mills, Party Autonomy in Private International Law (2018). Of course, rules governing party autonomy also can be understood as involving allocation – namely, allocation between state and private authority.

[48] Conflict of laws can also deal with choice among the governmental subunits of federal systems (e.g., among US states in the US federal system).

H FROM INTERNATIONAL LAW AND INTERNATIONAL RELATIONS
TO LAW AND WORLD POLITICS

The global legal system concept can benefit teaching, legal practice, and scholarship by providing a coherent way of thinking about the multiple transnational problem-solving functions of a legal system (including prescription, adjudication, and enforcement) and the multiple levels at which those functions are performed (including national, international, and private). For teaching, the global legal system concept can help train students to identify legal solutions without limiting themselves to national (or international) law. For lawyers, it can offer a coherent way to make sense of the complex legal environment in which they try to help clients solve their transnational problems.

For scholars, it puts in focus a wide range of questions about coordination among the different institutions of the global legal system and about the appropriate roles of authority, allocation, and party autonomy in the choice of legal solutions to transnational problems. And it helps to highlight weaknesses – such as the relative underdevelopment of principles for allocating between national and international solutions, among different international solutions, and between national and private solutions. The global legal system concept also brings into focus questions about contestation over the definition of transnational problems, the design of legal solutions, the measurement of outcomes, and the assessment of solutions, o and that there is an additional (but separate) set of questions about the legal and political determinants of decisions regarding the allocation of governance authority.

More broadly, the global legal system concept implies a move away from the current international law and international relations (IL/IR) paradigm in interdisciplinary international law scholarship.[49] As its label suggests, IL/IR research tends to be state-centric and focuses primarily on international law and international courts. It therefore tends to neglect the two other principal dimensions of the global legal system: the national and the private.

But interdisciplinary scholarship is increasingly taking what I call a "law and world politics" (L/WP) approach.[50] Moving beyond the somewhat narrow focus on international law and international courts indicated by the "IL" in

---

[49] *See* INTERDISCIPLINARY PERSPECTIVES ON INTERNATIONAL LAW AND INTERNATIONAL RELATIONS: THE STATE OF THE ART (Jeffrey L. Dunoff & Mark A. Pollack eds., 2012).

[50] *See* Christopher A. Whytock, *From International Law and International Relations to Law and World Politics, in* OXFORD RESEARCH ENCYCLOPEDIA OF POLITICS (William R. Thompson ed., 2018).

IL/IR scholarship, L/WP scholars are bringing national law and national courts into the analysis, shedding light not only on how they support (and sometimes undermine) international law and international courts but also on their direct role in core areas of international relations, such as international conflict and foreign policy. Moving beyond the state-centric tendencies reflected by the "IR" in IL/IR scholarship, scholars are bringing research on law up to speed with the broader world politics trend in political science by studying aspects of law – including extraterritoriality, conflict of laws, private international law, and the law of transnational commercial arbitration – that govern the transnational activity of private actors and that support (and sometimes undermine) private governance. And moving beyond the domestic-international divide, political scientists are increasingly rejecting the traditional distinction between "hierarchical" domestic law and "anarchical" international law and beginning to take advantage of theoretical convergence across the domestic, comparative, and international politics subfields to develop a better general understanding of law and politics that does not rely on the traditional hierarchy/anarchy distinction.[51]

This L/WP trend in interdisciplinary scholarship is consistent with (and might even seem necessary) from the perspective of Jessup's functionalist concept of transnational law. It promises to provide a richer understanding of the global legal system than a largely state-centric approach that revolves primarily around international law and international courts.

---

[51] *See* Christopher A. Whytock, *Thinking beyond the Domestic-International Divide: Toward a Unified Concept of Public Law*, 36 GEO. J. INT'L L. 155 (2004) and Wayne Sandholtz & Christopher A. Whytock, *The Politics of International Law*, *in* RESEARCH HANDBOOK ON THE POLITICS OF INTERNATIONAL LAW 1, 14–17 (Wayne Sandholtz & Christopher A. Whytock eds., 2017). *See also* Daryl J. Levinson & Jack L. Goldsmith, *Law for States: International Law, Constitutional Law, Public Law*, 122 HARV. L. REV. 1791–868 (2009); Shalev Roisman, *Constraining States: Constitutional Lessons for International Courts*, 55:3 VA. J. INT'L L. 729–82 (2015); and Jeffrey K. Staton & Will H. Moore, *Judicial Power in Domestic and International Politics*, 65 INT'L ORG. 553–87 (2011).

3

How Comity Makes Transnationalism Work

THOMAS SCHULTZ AND NICCOLÒ RIDI

Once upon a time, Real-World Pragmatism was a happy but wild and destructive fellow. After a particularly ferocious rampage, powerful forces decided it should get married. Sovereignty, they thought, would make a perfect spouse, bringing it order and control and peace. So the wedding was celebrated, with great fanfare – the fairy tale says it was in 1648, but fairy tales, as we know, are not to be trusted. What was bound to happen happened: very quickly the relationship descended into constant tension and bickering. The couple turned to a rabbi for counselling. The rabbi listened intently to Sovereignty and its complaints about territory and borders, about respect, about the importance of orderliness and maintaining appearances. And the rabbi said, 'Yes, you're right.' He then turned to Real-World Pragmatism and listened, just as intently, to grievances about the need for flexibility and spontaneity, about human relations that cannot systematically be boxed in and made to fit some theory, hard feelings about freedom. And again the rabbi said, 'Yes, you're right.' At that stage the rabbi's wife, who was listening in on the conversation from an adjacent room, stepped in and admonished her husband: 'You can't say that! You can't say they are both right!' The rabbi smiled benignly and answered, 'Yes, you, my dear, you are right too.' Slightly perplexed but essentially content with the recognition they received, all parties left the rabbi with earnest thanks. A friend then came in. 'I've bumped into Sovereignty and Real-World Pragmatism on my way over', he said. 'They both seemed reassured and pacified. How did you pull that off?' The rabbi chuckled and responded, 'I've used comity.' 'Huh?' came the response. 'Ah, comity – so you don't know what it is. That's good. Most people don't. That's part of why it works.'

A INTRODUCTION

Lawyers, normally, like law.

Lawyers, normally, understand law to be rules or at least principles, things that tell them what the (legal) solution is in a given situation, commands that say what should now happen, as precisely as possible, in a concrete case or in a set of possible cases.

Lawyers, normally, like to articulate these rules and principles around categories (public law and private law, national law and international law, and a great many more), even if these categories have limited analytical purchase, even if they are somewhat artificial and dogmatic. Ordering the world may here not come second to understanding it. 'Doctrine' is not a dirty word for lawyers.

Jessup was not normal. That is a good thing. It means not being within the norm. An exceptional lawyer by definition is. And so Jessup thought about the 'universality of the human problems', precisely with the purpose of knocking down categories he perceived as artificial and dogmatic, or at least reconsidering them in light of the fact that the same problems arise across orders, across borders, across categories.[1]

And from problems Jessup went on to think about rules, and wrote this:

> To envisage the applicability of transnational law it is necessary to avoid thinking solely in terms of any particular forum, since it is quite possible, as we shall see, to have a tribunal which does not have as its own law either a body of national law or the corpus of international law. A *problem may also be resolved* not by the application of law (although equally not in violation of law) but *by a process of adjustment* – an extralegal or metajuridical means.[2]

A process of adjustment by which a problem is resolved; that is precisely what comity is. And that is precisely why comity is often (that is, normally) said to be 'grating to the ear when it proceeds from a court of justice'.[3] That these are the words of an eighteenth-century attorney from the US South is not out of line.

And this is the irony of comity. It is notable for its perceived obscurity and vagueness and for its unusually bad press. It is, as Lord Collins puts it, 'a discredited concept in the eyes of the text-writers'. Yet, as Lord Collins also points out, comity 'thrives in the judicial decisions'.[4] Indeed, as our own research confirms, literally thousands upon thousands of judicial decisions

---

[1] PHILIP C. JESSUP, TRANSNATIONAL LAW 8 (1956).
[2] *Id.* at 6.
[3] SAMUEL LIVERMORE, DISSERTATIONS ON THE QUESTIONS WHICH ARISE FROM THE CONTRARIETY OF THE POSITIVE LAWS OF DIFFERENT STATES AND NATIONS 26 (1828).
[4] Laurence Collins, *Comity in Modern Private International Law, in* REFORM AND DEVELOPMENT OF PRIVATE INTERNATIONAL LAW: ESSAYS IN HONOUR OF SIR PETER NORTH 95 (James Fawcett ed., 2002).

refer to the notion, and many if not most of them turn on the notion.[5] Now if it is obscure and vague and incurs widespread odium, then why does it still sit so comfortably in the toolbox of (some of) those who have to make things legal work, namely courts? One reason may precisely be this: it just makes things work.

As in the story of our rabbi, comity might not contribute much to the construction of a neat theoretical edifice, one that agrees with (predominantly Western) binary, Cartesian, logical thinking. It might even undermine such a construction. But it helps to just make things work. This indeed is why comity was developed in the first place – that is, to make sovereignty work in the face of the pragmatic transnationalism that characterizes so much of real-world life. And this is one of the purposes comity is used for today – that is, to make things work, as an adjustment process for mostly transnational things, things such as the global market, hyper-politicized situations, the proliferation of inter-national courts and tribunals, and legal harmonization and coordination across borders.

This article is an experimentation of this idea. It starts with sovereignty – a nice idea in theory that required comity to work well in practice – and then proceeds with a discussion of how comity helps the operations of the trans-national things we just mentioned.

B SOVEREIGNTY

Comity was to a large extent fathered by Dutch scholars in the seventeenth century, in the wake of – and as a reaction to – the development of the Westphalian paradigm. That story is simple: territorial sovereignty and free-dom from interference were consecrated as fundamental pillars of the new 'Westphalian' system, in which the rule of personal statuses became largely trumped by the force of the territorial law of the state. Good fences make good neighbours; that was in essence the idea. But good fences (good in the sense of clear, strict, binary) proved to be at odds with the transnational relations of seventeenth-century European society and commerce.[6]

---

[5] Thomas Schultz & Jason Mitchenson, *Navigating Sovereignty and Transnational Commercial Law: The Use of Comity by Australian Courts*, 12 J. PRIV. INT. LAW (2016); Thomas Schultz & Niccolò Ridi, *Comity and International Courts and Tribunals*, 50 Cornell International Law Journal 577–610 (2017).

[6] KURT LIPSTEIN, PRINCIPLES OF THE CONFLICT OF LAWS: NATIONAL AND INTERNATIONAL 8 (1981); Thomas Schultz & David Holloway, *Retour sur la comity (Première partie)*, J. DROIT INT. 863–66 (2011); Thomas Schultz & David Holloway, *Retour sur la comity, deuxième partie: La comity dans l'histoire du droit international privé*, J. DROIT INT. 571, 571, 574 (2012);

The comity doctrine was then conceived as an instrument capable of mitigating these contrasts. In its most influential statement, contained in a treatise penned by Ulrik Huber, comity was presented as an exception to the territoriality rule: sovereigns were expected to 'so act by way of comity that rights acquired within the limits of a government retain their force everywhere so far as they do not cause prejudice to the power or rights of such governments or of its subjects'.[7]

The idea, then, was that sovereigns graciously concede that their territorial law should be set aside, thus reconciling their sovereignty with mutual convenience. Yet a domestic public policy element remained at the heart of it, in the sense that deference would be granted only to the extent it was tolerable.

From there on, the doctrine influenced the development of the common law in the United Kingdom and, to a greater extent, in the United States, where it has been hailed as the foundation of American private international law.[8] It was also there that the currently most influential statement of the doctrine sprang from Justice Gray's majority opinion in *Hilton v. Guyot*, the 'lodestar for all transnational enforcement doctrines in the US'.[9] Here's the influential statement: Comity

> in the legal sense, is neither a matter of absolute obligation, on the one hand, nor of mere courtesy and goodwill, upon the other. But it is the recognition which one nation allows within its territory to the legislative, executive, or judicial acts of another nation, having due regard both to international duty and convenience and to the rights of its own citizens or of other persons was are under the protection of its laws.[10]

Hilton framed the problem of comity and private international law in general firmly within the realm of international law.[11] In that regard, these were different, less dogmatic times: Joseph Story, whose work was so influential in the adoption of the doctrine in the United States, did not believe in a

---

RODOLFO DE NOVA, HISTORICAL AND COMPARATIVE INTRODUCTION TO CONFLICT OF LAWS 441 (1966); Schultz & Ridi, *supra* note 5.

[7] This translation can be found in Ernest G. Lorenzen, *Story's Commentaries on the Conflict of Laws: One Hundred Years After*, HARV. LAW REV. 15–38, 403 (1934).

[8] Joel R. Paul, *Comity in International Law*, 32 HARV. INT'L L.J. 1, 78 (1991); Joel R. Paul, *The Transformation of International Comity*, LAW & CONTEMP. PROBL. 19, 19 (2008) [hereinafter Paul, *The Transformation of International Comity*].

[9] HAROLD HONGJU KOH, TRANSNATIONAL LITIGATION IN UNITED STATES COURTS 206 (2008).

[10] Hilton v. Guyot, 159 U.S. 113, 163–64 (1895).

[11] *Id.*

sharp division between public and private international law and cited Vattel alongside the Dutch scholar.[12] The latter too was very much a Grotian thinker and described the operation of his comity doctrine very much in terms of an international usage, if not as a custom, an operation not so far away from what the Permanent Court of International Justice's held in *Serbian and Brazilian Loans*.[13] *Hilton* too proceeded along these lines. Comity could thus remain a sound basis for private international law, which it did, until the rise of 'positivism' (to level the charge broadly) reduced it to a vestige of historical interest only – or so it claimed.[14]

For, indeed, today comity is still employed quite often to address situations in which transnationalism bumps into sovereignty and is thereby centrally instrumental to the development of what Harold Koh calls the 'transnationalist jurisprudence' of certain countries.[15] For example, comity has been invoked as an upper limit to restrain the reach of domestic law, in cases concerning issues as diverse as competition and human rights; it has been considered a relevant factor in the granting of recognition to foreign and international judicial decisions and interpreted as counselling restraint in passing judgment on the sovereign acts of other states; and it has also been considered a compelling reason to refrain from adjudicating in cases of international litispendence (actual or simply foreseen) and a significant parameter for the granting of anti-suit injunctions. In yet other cases, it has been considered the foundation of sovereign immunity and the privilege of bringing suit.

Such is the conventional nature of comity, or comity in its sovereignty-related dimension: a doctrine (or a principle) in the name of which states – mostly through their courts – often fine-tune the reach of their national substantive law and jurisdictional rules, refrain from questioning the lawfulness of another sovereign state's acts and restrict themselves from issuing such judgments and orders when to do so would amount to an unjustifiable interference.[16] All of this comity has been enabled by paying homage to sovereignty.

---

[12] JOSEPH STORY, COMMENTARIES ON THE CONFLICT OF LAWS, FOREIGN AND DOMESTIC: IN REGARD TO CONTRACTS, RIGHTS, AND REMEDIES, AND ESPECIALLY IN REGARD TO MARRIAGES, DIVORCES, WILLS, SUCCESSIONS, AND JUDGMENTS § 11 (1834).

[13] Hessel E. Yntema, *The Comity Doctrine*, MICH. LAW REV. 9, 30 (1966). Serbian and Brazilian Loans (Fr. v. Yugoslavia, Fr. v. Braz.), 1929, P.C.I.J. (ser. A) Nos. 20–21).

[14] ALBERT VENN DICEY, A DIGEST OF THE LAW OF ENGLAND WITH REFERENCE TO THE CONFLICT OF LAWS 10 (1896).

[15] Harold Hongju Koh, *International Law as Part of Our Law*, 98 AM. J. INT. LAW 43, 52–53 (2004).

[16] Adrian Briggs, *The Principle of Comity in Private International Law*, 354 RECUEIL DES COURS DE L'ACADÉMIE DE DROIT INT'L 65, 85–86; Schultz & Ridi, *supra* note 5.

Then again, perhaps comity has enabled this by paying lip service, rather than homage, to sovereignty.

Let us consider, for example, those cases in which the pendency of foreign proceedings concerning the same dispute prompts local courts to discontinue local ones – or decline to exercise their jurisdiction altogether. Comity is often invoked as a justification for doing so, counselling restraint when the local proceedings would amount to an undue interference with the activity of the foreign court, an affront to sovereignty by reason of the sovereign nature of the act of adjudication. But looking closely at the modern life of the concept, is this really the best explanation? Does comity only have a sovereignty-related dimension?

Quite possibly not.

Comity has quite possibly gone beyond being a simple remedy to the inflexibility of sovereignty. To a significant extent, it has become unstuck from the latter notion, of which it was once a corollary. As the following sections will endeavour to highlight, the way comity has been used casts real doubts upon the idea of sovereignty as the only – or even the main – protected good.

C THE GLOBAL MARKET

Comity, we observed, entered the picture as a way to pay homage to sovereignty. But is that it? One way to tackle the problem is to follow Jessup in considering the topic of his second essay in *Transnational Law*, titled 'The Power to Deal with the Problems'.[17] The piece, it will be recalled, meant 'to examine which authorities deal effectively with which transnational situations. In familiar language this question may be approached as a matter of jurisdiction'. The term was here adopted in its public international law sense, that is as 'an aspect of sovereignty: it refers to a state's competence under international law to regulate the conduct of natural and juridical persons. The notion of regulation includes the activity of all branches of government: legislative, executive, and judicial.'[18]

In Jessup's days, the traditional view of jurisdiction in international law was still founded on the PCIJ decision in *Lotus*, notable for being 'based on a highly contentious metaphysical proposition of the extreme positivist school that the law emanates from the free will of sovereign independent States'.[19]

---

[17] JESSUP, *supra* note 1, at 35.

[18] JAMES CRAWFORD, BROWNLIE'S PRINCIPLES OF PUBLIC INTERNATIONAL LAW 456 (8th ed. 2012).

[19] James L. Brierly, *The Lotus Case*, 44 L.Q. REV. 154–56, 155 (1928).

Lacking an international law prohibition, the dictum may be paraphrased as 'states can do whatever pleases them' – no longer quite true, if it ever was, one might point out.[20] Jessup, in any event, went beyond that, skipping the otiose question of whether *Lotus* was correct and rather tested its helpfulness in understanding the allocation of authority in cross-border issues.[21]

Now how does comity enter the picture? In very general terms, the doctrine of comity has provided the basis for rules of private international law and rules of jurisdiction, the former being a species of the latter.[22] Further, comity has frequently been invoked as a canon of statutory construction to determine the reach of the domestic law of a state. While it might be argued that such construction canons are qualitatively distinct from questions of jurisdictional power properly-so-called, the distinction is quite immaterial for a transnational outlook on the point: either way, comity has been a key concept in the treatment by domestic courts of their jurisdictional limits.

In *Transnational Law*, Jessup cited Justice Holmes's decision in *American Banana* – an opinion notable for the bewilderment of his drafter at the plaintiff's 'several rather startling propositions' suggesting that a matter occurring in Costa Rica should be subject by United States antitrust law.[23] But it was precisely down this road that the United States became the 'world's antitrust policeman'.[24]

Indeed, come the early 1990s, comity had lost much weight in competition matters on both sides of the Atlantic. *Deference*, deference to sovereign authorities as expressed by comity, had lost much of its weight in competition matters on both sides of the Atlantic, with one shore calling comity irrelevant, the other appearing unsure of what it was to begin with.[25] In the American

[20] *See generally* Alex Mills, *Rethinking Jurisdiction in International Law*, 84 Brit. Y.B. Int'l. L. 187–239 (2014).

[21] Jessup, *supra* note 1, at 36.

[22] Alex Mills, The Confluence of Public and Private International Law: Justice, Pluralism and Subsidiarity in the International Constitutional Ordering of Private Law 303 (2009).

[23] Am. Banana Co. v. United Fruit Co. 213 U.S. 347, 355 (1909).

[24] Spencer Weber Waller, *The Twilight of Comity*, 38 Col. J. Transnat'l L. 563, 566 (1999).

[25] *See* Case C-89/85, Ahlström v. Comm'n (Woodpulp II), 1993 E.C.R. 1307 ('As regards the argument relating to disregard of international comity, it suffices to observe that it amounts to calling in question the Community's jurisdiction to apply its competition rules to conduct such as that found to exist in this case and that, as such, that argument has already been rejected'); Hartford Fire Ins. Co. v. Cal. 509 U.S. 764, 798 (1993) (we need not decide that question here, however, for even assuming that in a proper case a court may decline to exercise Sherman Act jurisdiction over foreign conduct (or, as Justice Scalia would put it, may conclude by the employment of comity analysis in the first instance that there is no jurisdiction), international comity would not counsel against exercising jurisdiction in the circumstances

context, Koh saw this approach as a product of what he called 'nationalist jurisprudence', one that 'refuses to look beyond US national interests when assessing the legality of extraterritorial action'.[26]

Yet, in the following decade, a few shouts of 'full reverse astern' were given to steer this jurisdictional approach towards a more cooperative model, transcending – to some extent – parochial and domestic interests and rather invoking comity to consider the 'mutual interests of all nations in a smoothly functioning international legal regime' and must 'consider if there is a course that furthers, rather than impedes, the development of an ordered international system'.[27] More recent cases have confirmed as much.[28] And if the application of comity has progressively become less overt, one may argue that this is only because 'its advocates won'.[29]

Now could we possibly think that this result has been achieved in pursuit of 'a harmony particularly needed in today's highly interdependent *commercial* world'?[30] Could we possibly consider that 'the market' is a new 'sovereignty' that comity is designed to pay homage to?[31]

The idea seems credible in the operation of comity as a principle of recognition. As we observed, comity has also provided a basis for courts to give effect to choice-of-law provisions, but concerns of domestic public policy had traditionally constituted the upper limit of any such accommodation, for indeed foreign sovereignty was to be respected but not at the cost of giving up one's own. And yet, some cases clearly seem to fail to be explained by this paradigm. Let us consider, for example, the 1985 landmark case *Mitsubishi Motors Corp.* v. *Soler Chrysler-Plymouth*. In its decision, the US Supreme Court chose to give effect to an arbitration clause that covered antitrust matters, traditionally considered non-arbitrable. To justify its holding, the court argued that

> [c]oncerns of international comity, respect for the capacities of foreign and transnational tribunals, and sensitivity to the *need of the international commercial system* for predictability in the resolution of disputes, all require

alleged here – the only substantial question in this litigation is whether 'there is in fact, a true conflict between domestic and foreign law').
[26] Koh, *supra* note 15, at 53.
[27] Harold Hongju Koh, *Why Transnational Law Matters*, 24 PENN ST. INT'L L. REV. 745, 749 (2005).
[28] F. Hoffman-LaRoche, Ltd. v. Empagran S.A., 542 U.S. 155 (2004).
[29] Waller, *supra* note 24, at 566.
[30] *Empagran*, 542 U.S. at 166 (emphasis added).
[31] Paul, *The Transformation of International Comity*, *supra* note 8, at 36.

enforcement of the arbitration clause in question, even assuming that a contrary result would be forthcoming in a domestic context.[32]

So: cases such as this show the limits of a theory of comity strictly focused on the concept of sovereignty.

D HYPER-POLITICIZED SITUATIONS

Part of the very nature of comity is that it offers a pot of flexibility that can be dipped into when needed. Accordingly, comity may help mitigate the ill effects of adjudication in hyper-politicized situations. Let us consider, for example, the string of cases in the Third Reich industry litigation. Recall: a 'foundation' was created in Germany in the year 2000 to hear the claims and provide compensation of the victims of Nazi forced labour programs, 'the product of intense diplomatic negotiation in which officials of the United States as well as representatives of German industry and government played the most important roles'.[33] When claims were also filed in the United States, American courts by and large declined to hear them: the purpose was to channel litigation into the foundation. As Scott and Wai argue, this was textbook transnational legal process, in both the creation of the mechanism and the effort of feeding cases into it.[34] Comity, in this regard, was the perfect tool.

This was expressly confirmed in one of the more recent decisions in the same string of cases, where the traditional reliance on the political question doctrine left its place to a more elaborate and transnationally oriented conception of 'prospective' comity, based on 'the interests of our government, the foreign government and the international community in resolving the dispute in a foreign forum'.[35]

Now does, or should, the same approach apply to transnational human rights litigation? The conclusion and aftermath of the *Kiobel* case seem to serve as a cautionary tale on this very problem. Let us consider the facts of the

[32] Mitsubishi Motors Corp. v. Soler Chrysler-Plymouth, Inc., 473 U.S. 614, 615 (1985) (emphasis added).
[33] Libby Adler & Peer Zumbansen, *The Forgetfulness of Noblesse: A Critique of the German Foundation Law Compensating Slave and Forced Laborers of the Third Reich*, 39 HARV. J. ON LEGIS. 1, 2 (2002).
[34] Craig Scott & Robert Wai, *Transnational Governance of Corporate Conduct through the Migration of Human Rights Norms: The Potential Contribution of Transnational 'Private' Litigation*, in TRANSNATIONAL GOVERNANCE AND CONSTITUTIONALISM 309 (Christian Joerges, Inger-Johanne Sand & Gunther Teubner eds., 2004).
[35] Ungaro-Benages v. Dresdner Bank AG, 379 F.3d 1227 (11th Cir. 2004).

case to be known. What matters in this context is that there was no question of the substantive law that should have applied to the case (the 'law of nations'): the killer blow to the Alien Tort Statute was struck by a decision not to extend its application extraterritorially. Indeed, Horatia Muir-Watt described this resurfacing of territoriality as 'a spectacular backlash against the open-ended or functional approaches which these intrinsically deterritorialised jurisdictional conflicts seemed to call for'.[36] Once again, comity contributed a good deal to achieving this result.

In a sense, comity made things work in these cases too. But making things work comes at a price. For is it appropriate for the same jurisdictional approaches that guide 'antitrust imperialism' to also inform judicial protection of human rights? In one case a remedy was granted; in the other no solution was given to the dispute. A reminder, to be sure, that the substantive law of the case must matter and that the regulation of jurisdictional competence is not value agnostic.

E PROLIFERATION OF INTERNATIONAL COURTS AND TRIBUNALS

There is one more situation where it is not helpful to reduce the notion of comity to a mere corollary of sovereignty: its use within international dispute settlement.

For a long time, the idea of competition among international jurisdiction was not perceived to be a problem of any real significance. And yet, had Jessup discussed the topic in the early 2000s, international dispute settlement might have proved a rather good setting for a scene in one of his 'little dramas'.

Its heading might have read as follows: 'Exterior, the International System – soon after the publication of the International Law Commission's report on the "fragmentation" of international law.'[37] The plot would have revolved around the phenomenon of the proliferation of international courts and tribunals: in the days of old, international jurisdictions were not numerous, and it was difficult enough to bring a state to accept the competence of one. But in recent years, states have been more willing to submit to international

---

[36] Horatia Muir Watt, *A Private (International) Law Perspective: Comment on 'A New Jurisprudential Framework for Jurisdiction'* 109 AM. J. INT'L L. UNBOUND 75, 77–78 (2015).

[37] Int'l Law Comm'n, *Fragmentation of International Law: Difficulties Arising from the Diversification and Expansion of International Law*, U.N. Doc. A/CN.4/L.682 (Apr. 13, 2006) (finalized by Martti Koskenniemi).

dispute-settlement mechanisms, bringing about a plurality of international jurisdictions to better cope with the growing quantity and complexity of the rules of international law.[38] This disposition has further brought about a shift from a consensual to a compulsory paradigm in international adjudication, which has made international jurisdictions more extensive and difficult to elude.[39] And to add to the mix, these jurisdictional rules of international courts and tribunals are usually characterized by some rigidity so that jurisdictional conflict is a definite possibility.[40] In other words, what could once qualify as an embarrassment of riches is now a full-fledged issue with significant consequences. Does comity help make things work?

Lacking clear jurisdiction-regulating rules, there is no reason why, as a matter of principle, an international judicial body should not be able to use comity as a *technique*. Indeed, international courts and tribunals normally do have the power *not* to exercise 'a jurisdiction they have'.[41] And if securing a theoretical underpinning matters, the argument is easily made that while traditional comity reasoning, based on respect for sovereignty and non-interference, is incompatible with the context of international adjudication, the true basis of comity is in fact the horizontal arrangement of jurisdictions – which is, respectively, a consequence of the Westphalian paradigm of sovereign equality in the interstate system, of the lack of hierarchical principles in the international one.[42]

International judicial bodies have occasionally employed comity in this sense, discussing, for example, 'considerations of mutual respect and comity which should prevail between judicial institutions' to justify a stay of proceedings in the face of a virtually certain involvement of another international

---

[38] CHESTER BROWN, A COMMON LAW OF INTERNATIONAL ADJUDICATION 22 (2007); YUVAL SHANY, THE COMPETING JURISDICTIONS OF INTERNATIONAL COURTS AND TRIBUNALS 10 (2003); Cesare P.R. Romano, *The Proliferation of International Judicial Bodies: The Piece of the Puzzle*, 31 N.Y.U. J. INT'L L. & POL. 709 (1999); Ibrahim F.I. Shihata, *Towards a Greater Depoliticization of Investment Disputes: The Roles of ICSID and MIGA*, 1 ICSID REV. 1–25 (1986); Geir Ulfstein, *International Courts and Judges: Independence, Interaction, and Legitimacy*, N.Y.U. J. INT'L L. & POL. 858–59 (2014).

[39] Cesare P.R. Romano, *The Shift from the Consensual to the Compulsory Paradigm in International Adjudication: Elements for a Theory of Consent*, 39 N.Y.U. J. INT'L L. & POL. 791, 795 (2006).

[40] JAMES CRAWFORD, CHANCE, ORDER, CHANGE: THE COURSE OF INTERNATIONAL LAW, GENERAL COURSE ON PUBLIC INTERNATIONAL LAW 211 (2014).

[41] Legality of the Use of Force (Serb. & Montenegro v. Belg.), Judgment on Preliminary Objections, 2004 I.C.J. Rep. 1307, 1361, para. 10 (Dec. 15) (separate opinion of Judge Higgins).

[42] CRAWFORD, *supra* note 18, at 445; CAMPBELL McLACHLAN, LIS PENDENS IN INTERNATIONAL LITIGATION 229–30 (2009).

forum.[43] Conversely, resorting to considerations of comity might also contribute to mitigating the ill effects of certain strong assertions of exclusive jurisdictions, which seem to be at odds with the principle of *Kompetenz-Kompetenz* in international adjudication, and help neutralize attempts to conduct abusive litigation and forum shopping.[44] Interestingly, references to comity have not been less common when the relation between jurisdictions was less obviously horizontal. For example, arbitration tribunals dealing with investor-state disputes have sometimes discussed comity to justify a stay – or decision not to stay – of their proceedings on comity grounds when the matter was pending before a domestic court.[45]

Generally, there are indications that international tribunals have been welcoming of uses of comity that benefit the propagation of a transnational system but less so of comity as a matter of homage and respect for sovereign authority, mitigating to a great extent the traditional 'stress on the state or nation factor' in international dispute settlement.[46]

F HARMONIZATION

When the rules of the game are not satisfactory, changing them usually seems the best solution. It is certainly not by chance that Jessup devoted the third essay in his landmark book to issues of choice of law or, rather, of applicable law.[47] The surfacing of transnational legal orders may be qualified as one such operation: it occurs slowly, if unavoidably, all the players trying to make the most of their position in the field while the rule book is amended. Much has been written on these topics, and we will restrict ourselves to a couple of remarks, advancing one specific – at this point unsurprising – proposition: in this context too, comity makes things work.

Indeed, broadly speaking, comity constitutes an important principle for the alignment of different legal orders and, on a different plane, the making of transnational ones. So what is the nature of comity's contribution?

---

[43] MOX Plant (Ir. v. U.K.), Suspension of Proceedings on Jurisdiction and Merits, and Request for Further Provisional Measures, 42 I.L.M. 1187 (Perm. Ct. Arb. 2003).

[44] *See generally* Schultz & Ridi, *supra* note 5; Joost Pauwelyn & Luiz Eduardo Salles, *Forum Shopping before International Tribunals: (Real) Concerns, (Im)Possible Solutions*, 42 CORNELL INT'L L.J. (2009); McLachlan, *supra* note 42, at 455.

[45] S. Pac. Properties (Middle East) Ltd. v. Arab Republic of Egypt, ICSID Case No. ARB/84/3, Decision on Jurisdiction (Nov. 27, 1985).

[46] JESSUP, *supra* note 1, at 11.

[47] *Id.* at 72.

As a first example, courts have in some cases referred to comity to adopt transnationally consistent interpretations of international instruments, not only public[48] but private too, so long as they have transnational application.[49] In so doing, courts have appeared mindful of this necessity to the extent that they have felt obliged to follow foreign precedents.[50]

Secondly, and perhaps most importantly, comity constitutes a key concept for the understanding of judicial networks. Anne-Marie Slaughter's work has convincingly relied on the notion to explain certain dynamics.[51] To Slaughter, comity constitutes one of the building blocks of judicial dialogue occurring in the 'global community' of national and international courts. Indeed, according to her model, courts would respect foreign courts 'qua courts, rather than simply as the face of a foreign government', recognizing them as co-equals in the global task of judging', though with a distinctive emphasis on individual rights and the judicial role in protecting them.[52] To be sure, Slaughter's theory is not without its critics, and it has been suggested that it is, to a large extent, quite starry-eyed.[53] It bears noting that this author first addressed the topic discussing the implications of the *Breard* case[54] and – specifically – the fact that, regardless of the nature (binding or not) of the provisional measures granted by the International Court of Justice, domestic courts should have accorded (and did not accord) them 'full faith and credit'.[55]

Irrespective of the above, there are strong indications that comity is becoming an important item in the toolboxes of international courts. This, it must be observed, goes beyond both simple institutional dialogue[56] and a qualification

---

[48] Morris v. KLM Dutch Airlines [2002] 2 AC 628 [81] (Lord Hope) (UK).

[49] Leonie's Travel Pty Ltd v Qantas Airways Ltd [2010] FCAFC 37 (Austl.).

[50] *See generally* Schultz & Mitchenson, *supra* note 5.

[51] Anne-Marie Slaughter, *Judicial Globalization*, 40 VA. J. INT'L L. 1103 (1999) [hereinafter Slaughter, *Judicial Globalization*]; Anne-Marie Slaughter, *A Global Community of Courts*, 44 HARV. INT'L L.J. 191 (2003) [hereinafter Slaughter, *Global Community of Courts*]; ANNE-MARIE SLAUGHTER, A NEW WORLD ORDER (2004).

[52] SLAUGHTER, *supra* note 51, at 87; many of these aspects had been dealt with in Slaughter, *Judicial Globalization*, *supra* note 51, and Slaughter, *Global Community of Courts*, *supra* note 51.

[53] *See* Alex Mills & Tim Stephens, *Challenging the Role of Judges in Slaughter's Liberal Theory of International Law*, 18 LEIDEN J. INT'L L. 1–30 (2005).

[54] Breard v. Greene, 523 U.S. 371 (1998).

[55] Anne-Marie Slaughter, *Court to Court*, 92 AM. J. INT'L L. 708 (1998).

[56] *See, e.g.,* Rosalyn Higgins, *A Babel of Judicial Voices? Ruminations from the Bench*, 55 INT'L & COMP. L.Q. 791–804 (2006); Cesare P.R. Romano, *Deciphering the Grammar of the International Jurisprudential Dialogue*, 41 N.Y.U. J. INT'L L. & POL. 755 (2008); and, relying almost exclusively on the concept of comity, Elisa D'Alterio, *From Judicial Comity to Legal Comity: A Judicial Solution to Global Disorder?*, 9 INT'L J. CONST. L., 394–424 (2011).

as 'an emerging general principle of international procedural law'.[57] More significantly, it is not confined to a role of a flexible jurisdictional-regulating rule we have discussed above, showing the potential to counteract the ill effects of fragmentation, thus going – as Elisa d'Alterio puts it, from *judicial* comity to *legal* comity.[58] Granting certain decisions the force of res judicata does, of course, go a long way; but there have been examples of tribunals referring to the concept to justify the need to rely on external precedent – and, specifically, precedent set by the judicial institution perceived as central in the international legal system.[59]

G CONCLUSION

Despite what some private international lawyers may choose to believe, comity's demise does not seem to be approaching. The doctrine is very much alive and constitutes an important tool in the management of cross-border and cross-regime situations. To be sure, it has evolved; inescapably, its contours have become blurred and fused with those of other principles. Yet, it remains part of the judicial and legal discourse of national and international courts dealing with transnational issues and regime interaction.

Lawyers are not normally thrilled by a game ending in a draw. And yet, never ceasing to pay homage to the very essence of positivism, in the sense of 'an adherence to what is, rather than to what a priori principle says should be'[60], we have attempted to highlight how comity makes this result easier to attain. The current study tends to suggest that comity does so by greasing cogs and gears that are prone to friction and preventing the resulting heat. This does not mean that there was something wrong with the two models in whose quarrel we stumbled at the outset. Rather, it means that sometimes some indeterminacy can be of assistance in the quest for compromise, to make things work, between two opponents. Especially when they are both right.

---

[57] Bruno Simma, *Universality of International Law from the Perspective of a Practitioner*, 20 EUR. J. INT'L. L., 265, 287 (2009).

[58] D'Alterio, *supra* note 56.

[59] Tulip Real Estate Inv. & Dev. Neth. BV v. Turk., ICSID Case No. ARB/11/28, Decision on Bifurcated Jurisdictional Issue, ¶ 45 (Mar. 10, 2014).

[60] Roger O'Keefe, *Curriculum Vitae: A Prequel (Part I)*, EJIL: TALK! (Jan. 4, 2016), http://www .ejiltalk.org/curriculum-vitae-a-prequel-part-i/.

Transnational Law as Regulatory Governance

PART II

Transnational Law as Regulatory Governance

4

Aiding and Abetting in Theorizing the Increasing Softification of the International Normative Order: A Darker Legacy of Jessup's *Transnational Law*?

KARSTEN NOWROT

A SOFT BECOMES BEAUTIFUL: ON THE CHANGING STRUCTURE OF THE INTERNATIONAL NORMATIVE ORDER

'The only thing that is constant is change.' And indeed, the truth of this ancient saying frequently attributed to Heraclitus of Ephesus is also confirmed by the evolution of the international normative order being currently – once again – in a phase of undergoing quite substantial changes. This time, however, these developments do not seem to support a kind of linear narrative of progress,[1] at least when viewed and assessed from the perspective of traditional public international law. Unlike in some previous periods, the respective processes of reformation do not find their manifestation in an ever-expanding legal regime extending its mandatory scope of application to areas that were formerly thought to be in the exclusive competence of individual states.[2] Almost to the contrary, international law in the narrow sense of the meaning is by now frequently considered as having more recently, in particular since the beginning of the twenty-first century, entered a phase first and foremost characterized by stagnation.[3] Not only has, for example,

---

[1] Generally, on progress narratives in international law, see, e.g., Matthew Windsor, *Narrative Kill or Capture: Unreliable Narration in International Law*, 2 LEIDEN J. INT'L L. 743, 748 *et seq.* (2015), with further references.

[2] On this previous perception, see, e.g., Jost Delbrück, *A More Effective International Law or a New 'World Law'? – Some Aspects of the Development of International Law in a Changing International System*, 68 IND. L.J. 705, 706 *et seq.* (1993); Christian Tomuschat, *International Law: Ensuring the Survival of Mankind on the Eve of a New Century*, 281 RECUEIL DES COURS 9, 63 *et seq.* (1999); KARSTEN NOWROT, GLOBAL GOVERNANCE AND INTERNATIONAL LAW 15 (2004).

[3] *See, e.g.*, Joost Pauwelyn, Ramses A. Wessel & Jan Wouters, *When Structures Become Shackles: Stagnation and Dynamics in International Lawmaking*, 25 EUR. J. INT'L L. 733, 734 (2014) ('Formal international law is stagnating in terms of both quantity and quality.'); Timothy

with regard to the institutional dimension of the international normative order, the creation of new international organizations considerably slowed down in recent years.[4] The same applies, from a substantive perspective, to the processes of formal lawmaking that are at present in the international system frequently replaced or at least supplemented by the adoption of steering instruments that are not directly legally binding but nevertheless often quite rigorously adhered to by the respective actors and thus most certainly not entirely devoid of normative value and effectiveness.[5]

As a consequence of this current rise of informal rule-making in the international system, the normative expectations of how actors ought to behave on the global plane are presently in many areas of international social life – more than ever[6] – based on and determined by what might appropriately be described as a mixture or network of various different types of legally binding as well as non-binding steering mechanisms resulting from cooperative efforts of governmental, supra-governmental, intermediate and non-governmental entities.[7] These developments have already for a number of years given rise to the perception that the distinction between so-called hard law and non-binding regulatory instruments is now more and more blurred.[8]

Meyer, *Shifting Sands: Power, Uncertainty and the Form of International Legal Cooperation*, 27 Eur. J. Int'l L. 161–85 (2016).

[4] Kenneth W. Abbott, Jessica F. Green & Robert O. Keohane, *Organizational Ecology and Institutional Change in Global Governance* 3 (2015), http://papers.ssrn.com/sol3/papers.cfm?abstract_id=2293678; Pauwelyn, Wessel & Wouters, *supra* note 3, at 736.

[5] *See, e.g.*, Meyer, *supra* note 3, at 161; Pauwelyn, Wessel & Wouters, *supra* note 3, at 734 *et seq.*; Dinah Shelton, *Normative Hierarchy in International Law*, 100 Am. J. Int'l L. 291, 319 *et seq.* (2006); Arnold N. Pronto, *Understanding the Hard/Soft Distinction in International Law*, 48 Vand. J. Transnat'l L. 941, 945 (2015). *See also* Gralf-Peter Calliess & Peer Zumbansen, Rough Consensus and Running Code 271 (2010) ('deeper trend towards a *deformalisation* of international law') (emphasis in the original).

[6] It seems appropriate to recall at this point that the normatively relevant steering processes in the international system have in principle always also comprised governance mechanisms of a non-legal character. On this perception, see, e.g., Jost Delbrück, *Die Entwicklung außerrechtlicher internationaler Verhaltensnormen unter den Bedingungen nuklearer Abschreckung, in* Nukleare Abschreckung – Politische und ethische Interpretationen einer neuen Realität 353, 358 *et seq.* (Uwe Nerlich & Trutz Rendtorff eds., 1989); Christian Tietje, *Recht ohne Rechtsquellen? Entstehung und Wandel von Völkerrechtsnormen im Interesse des Schutzes globaler Rechtsgüter im Spannungsverhältnis von Rechtssicherheit und Rechtsdynamik*, 24 Zeitschrift für Rechtssoziologie 27, 31 *et seq.* (2003).

[7] From the truly numerous contributions on this issue, see, e.g., Paul S. Berman, *From International Law to Law and Globalization*, 43 Colum. J. Transnat'l L. 43, 485, 492 *et seq.* (2005); Nowrot, *supra* note 2, at 5 *et seq.*, each with further references.

[8] On this perception, see, e.g., Francisco Orrego-Vicuña, *Law Making in a Global Society: Does Consent Still Matter?, in* Internationale Gemeinschaft und Menschenrechte – Festschrift für Georg Ress zum 70. Geburtstag 191, 200 (Jürgen Bröhmer et al. eds.,

In addition, and taken together, they have also – from the viewpoint of traditional public international law – resulted in an overall increasing and probably unprecedented softification of the international normative order as a whole.[9]

In the ongoing discourses on how to understand and systemize the implications of what is not infrequently perceived as paradigmatic changes in the international system,[10] its ever more diverse actors and its legal structure, a growing number of scholars have advanced the view that the respective conceptualizations cannot take recourse to classical state-centred models developed in the context of domestic law or traditional public international law. Rather – precisely in order to overcome the 'perseverance of the "touch of stateness"'[11] – this task necessitates employing new terms and the development of equally unprecedented analytical concepts.[12] In a sense, their argumentation thereby finds itself in line with an advice given by Philip C. Jessup in the 1960s, namely that adequately describing and conceptualizing the evolving normative structures beyond the state 'require that old concepts be constantly re-examined with a mind unfettered by blind acceptance of traditional classifications and labels'.[13] However, this is most certainly not the only connection to be drawn between the rise of informal rule-making, on the one hand, and the question as to the current importance of 'Jessup's bold proposal' on the

2005) ('The classical distinction between lex lata and lex ferenda thus also becomes increasingly blurred.'); Dinah Shelton, *Law, Non-law and the Problem of 'Soft Law'*, in Commitment and Compliance – The Role of Non-Binding Norms in the International Legal System 1, 10 (Dinah Shelton ed., 2000) ('The line between law and not-law may appear blurred.'); Harold Hongju Koh, *Why Do Nations Obey International Law?*, 106 Yale L.J. 2599, 2630 *et seq.* (1997) ('International law now comprises of a complex blend of customary, positive, declarative, and "soft" law, which seeks not simply to ratify existing practice, but to elevate it.').

[9] On this view, see also, e.g., Meyer, *supra* note 3), at 162 ('In short, we are living in an age in which soft law – non-binding rules that have legal consequences – is assuming an increasingly important place in international governance.').

[10] Eckart Klein, *Globalisation and International Law*, in Polis und Kosmopolis – Festschrift für Daniel Thürer 409, 419 (Giovanni Biaggini, Oliver Diggelmann & Christine Kaufmann eds., 2015) ('International law making has entered a new phase.').

[11] Jo Shaw & Antje Wiener, *The Paradox of the 'European Polity'*, in 5 The State of the European Union 64, 65 *et seq.* (Maria G. Cowles & Michael Smith eds., 2000).

[12] On this 'sui generis approach', see, e.g., Karsten Nowrot, *Towards 'Open' Transnational Administrative Networks: Emerging Structural Features*, in Transnational Administrative Rule-Making: Performance, Legal Effects, and Legitimacy 255, 258 *et seq.* (Olaf Dilling, Martin Herberg & Gerd Winter eds., 2011).

[13] Philip C. Jessup, *The Concept of Transnational Law: An Introduction*, 3 Colum. J. Transnat'l L. 1 (1964).

occasion of the sixtieth anniversary of his work *Transnational Law*, on the other hand. Rather, an even more notable feature linking these two subjects is indicated by the observation that prominently among the terms and concepts suggested in the literature to describe the phenomenon of what is referred to here as an increasing softification of the international normative order stands the idea and approach of an emerging transnational law, either applied to the normative structures of transboundary relations as a whole or, in particular, to an ever-growing number of their legal sub-systems.[14]

Against this background, the present contribution intends to assess, and to present some thoughts on, this terminological and conceptual trend, thereby also attempting to make a small contribution to a more nuanced understanding of transnational law and the appropriateness of this ordering idea in the ongoing debates on an adequate characterization of the international system and its changing legal structure. For the present purposes, I intend to approach this research topic in three main steps. The first part presents and describes the more recent emergence of different areas of 'transnational (...) law' as an important strand in the scholarly discussions on the concept of transnational law (section B). Based on the findings made in this section, the subsequent second part will be devoted to the question of whether this trend and its underlying conceptual approach can rightly be regarded as a notable legacy of Jessup's work (section C). Finally, the third and main section of this contribution will be devoted to an assessment of whether this terminological and conceptual trend to theorize the softification of the international normative order on the basis of emerging areas of 'transnational (...) law' – first and foremost perceived to be characterized by an increasing blurring of the boundaries between hard law and non-binding steering instruments – can legitimately be regarded as, first, an approach adequately reflecting the normative realities in the present international system and, second, as a desirable guiding idea for the future evolution of transboundary steering regimes (section D).

---

[14] *See also, e.g.*, Roger Cotterrell, *What Is Transnational Law?*, 37 LAW & SOC. INQUIRY 500 *et seq.* (2012) ('For many scholars, a new term has seemed necessary to indicate new legal relations, influences, controls, regimes, doctrines, and systems that are not those of nation-state (municipal) law but, equally, are not fully grasped by extended definitions of the scope of international law. The new term is "transnational law", widely invoked but rarely defined with much precision.'); Carrie Menkel-Meadow, *Why and How to Study 'Transnational' Law*, 1 UC IRVINE L. REV. 97, 117 (2011) ('The recent turn to the term "transnational", rather than international, law connotes a conceptual change in how we look at what we are studying in law ....').

B CONCEPTUALIZING THE BEAUTY OF SOFTNESS: FROM THE
SCIENTIFIC DISCOVERY OF INFORMAL STEERING INSTRUMENTS TO
THE RISE OF 'TRANSNATIONAL (...) LAW'

Commenting on the so-called republican revival among scholars in the late
1970s, the American historian Joyce Appleby remarked in 1985: 'The recent
discovery of republicanism as the reigning social theory of eighteenth-century
America has produced a reaction among historians akin of the response of
chemists to a new element. Once having been identified, it can be found
everywhere.'[15] To a certain extent, the same could be said of the more recent
'transnational law revival'. Admittedly, this claim also warrants some qualification. First, recourse to this term and concept in the literature as well as an
explicit reference to Jessup in this connection is not entirely new and can be
occasionally found, for example, in scholarly works published in the 1960s.[16]

Second, surely not all – past and contemporary – uses of the phrase
'transnational law' are directly related to the present context of describing an
emerging mixture of legally binding and non-binding steering mechanisms. In
addition to characterizing, for example, the direct effect of legal acts adopted
by the European Union and the internal lawmaking competences of organs of
international organizations[17] or the 'union of rules taken from many legal
systems',[18] it is well known that this term is frequently applied by legal scholars
as a synonym for the autonomous body of trade law, which is commonly
known as the *lex mercatoria*,[19] thereby excluding in particular traditional

---

[15] Joyce Appleby, *Republicanism and Ideology*, 37 AM. Q. 461 (1985).
[16] *See, e.g.*, Georg Erler, *Das Grundgesetz und die öffentliche Gewalt internationaler Staatengemeinschaften*, 18 VERÖFFENTLICHUNGEN DER VEREINIGUNG DER DEUTSCHEN STAATSRECHTSLEHRER 7, 22 *et seq.* (1960); Berthold Goldman, *Frontières du droit et 'lex mercatoria'*, ARCHIVES DE PHILOSOPHIE DU DROIT 177–92 (1964).
[17] Erler, *supra* note 16, at 22 *et seq.*
[18] Sandeep Gopalan, *Transnational Commercial Law: The Way Forward*, 18 AM. U. INT'L L. REV. 803, 809 (2003). For a rather distinctive understand of transnational law, see also, e.g., Lawrence M. Friedman, *Borders: On the Emerging Sociology of Transnational Law*, 32 STAN. J. INT'L L. 65, 66 (1996) ('I will describe a regime as "transnational" only if it has the force of law, or the force of force, behind it.').
[19] *See, e.g.*, Klaus Peter Berger, *The New Law Merchant and the Global Marketplace – A 21st Century View of Transnational Commercial Law*, in THE PRACTICE OF TRANSNATIONAL LAW 1–22 (Klaus Peter Berger ed., 2001); Clive M. Schmitthoff, *Nature and Evolution of the Transnational Law of Commercial Transactions*, in THE TRANSNATIONAL LAW OF INTERNATIONAL COMMERCIAL TRANSACTIONS 19, 20 *et seq.* (Norbert Horn & Clive M. Schmitthoff eds., 1982); see thereto also, e.g., Christian Tietje & Karsten Nowrot, *Laying Conceptual Ghosts of the Past to Rest: The Rise of Philip C. Jessup's 'Transnational Law' in the Regulatory Governance of the International Economic System*, in PHILIP C. JESSUP'S TRANSNATIONAL LAW REVISITED – ON THE OCCASION OF THE 50TH ANNIVERSARY OF ITS

public international law from its scope of application.[20] Furthermore, the notions of transnational public law litigation in general as well as of transnational human rights law in particular (or the combined concept of transnational human rights litigation)[21] are referred to by Harold Hongju Koh and other scholars to describe, among others, the relations between domestic and international human rights regimes, the processes of applying international human rights law within state boundaries, the 'consolidated corpus of international and domestic human rights'[22] and thus only the interactions between the respective transboundary and national 'hard law' instruments.[23] Moreover, the concept of transnational legal orders as recently advanced by Terence C. Halliday and Gregory Shaffer also involves normative processes initiated by private actors and, more generally, takes into account hard law as well as soft law instruments. Nevertheless, these categories of steering mechanisms are not considered as 'equals' since informal norm-generation processes are only regarded as relevant under this (consequently more narrow) approach in so far as the respective actors 'aim to catalyze through these instruments the adoption, recognition, and enforcement of binding authoritative legal norms in nation-states'.[24]

That said, for a considerable and currently ever-increasing number of legal scholars invoking the idea of an emerging transnational law 'is to suggest that

PUBLICATION 17, 30 (Christian Tietje, Alan Brouder & Karsten Nowrot eds., 2006), with further references.

[20] *See also, e.g.,* Gralf-Peter Calliess, *Law, Transnational, in* 3 ENCYCLOPEDIA OF GLOBAL STUDIES 1035, 1036 (Helmut K. Anheier & Mark Juergensmeyer eds., 2012) ('This, however, implies a definition of transnational law that is much narrower and much more specific than the one Jessup suggested. The transnational law of cross-border commerce is thus conceptualized as a third category of law besides national law and international law.'). To the contrary, the term is also occasionally – and narrowly – taken recourse to as a synonym for public international law itself; *see, e.g.,* Sally Engle Merry, *New Legal Realism and the Ethnography of Transnational Law,* 31 LAW & SOC. INQUIRY 975–95 (2006).

[21] See thereto, e.g., SARAH JOSEPH, CORPORATIONS AND TRANSNATIONAL HUMAN RIGHTS LITIGATION (2004).

[22] Samantha Besson, *Human Rights and Constitutional Law – Patterns of Mutual Validation and Legitimacy, in* PHILOSOPHICAL FOUNDATIONS OF HUMAN RIGHTS 279, 297 (Rowan Cruft, S. Matthew Liao & Massimo Renzo eds., 2015).

[23] *See, e.g.,* Kristen Hessler, *Resolving Interpretive Conflicts in International Human Rights Law,* 13 J. POL. PHIL. 29, 37 (2005) ('I will use the phrase "transnational human rights law" to refer to international human rights law as it applies within state boundaries.'), as well as more generally Harold Hongju Koh, *Transnational Public Law Litigation,* 100 YALE L.J. 2347–402 (1991); Harold Hongju Koh, *Why Transnational Law Matters,* 24 PENN ST. INT'L L. REV. 745–53 (2006).

[24] Terence C. Halliday & Gregory Shaffer, *Transnational Legal Orders, in* TRANSNATIONAL LEGAL ORDERS 3, 11 *et seq.* (Terence C. Halliday & Gregory Shaffer eds., 2015).

law has new sources, locations, and bases of authority'[25] with one of the typical elements of these new normative frameworks and their assessment being the above mentioned 'relativization of the law versus non-law distinction'.[26] Although occasionally also applied in a manner transcending specific legal areas of the international system such as the ordering idea of a transnational community of responsibility,[27] the perception that steering regimes beyond the state are increasingly characterized by a linkage of hard and soft law seems to be particularly prominent in more recent conceptual analyses on an ever-growing number of individual legal sub-systems of the international normative order. This has given rise to what might be labelled as the emergence of various different areas of 'transnational (. . .) law'. A vivid example is the notion of an emerging transnational economic law adhered to by Christian Tietje and a number of other scholars whose structural features include not only, for example, an increasing number of different categories of governmental, supra-state, intermediate and non-state actors actively involved in the lawmaking and law-realization processes but, albeit closely related to this characteristic, first and foremost also a 'more and more vanishing distinction between traditional legally binding norms on the one hand and rules that are in a strict sense

---

[25] Cotterrell, *supra* note 14, at 502; *see also, e.g.*, Craig Scott, *'Transnational Law' as a Proto-Concept: Three Conceptions*, 10 GERMAN L.J. 859, 873 *et seq.* (2009).

[26] Peer Zumbansen, *Defining the Space of Transnational Law: Legal Theory, Global Governance, and Legal Pluralism*, 21 TRANSNAT'L L. & CONTEMP. PROBS. 305, 309 (2012); *see also, e.g.*, Gralf-Peter Calliess & Andreas Maurer, *Transnationales Recht – eine Einleitung, in* TRANSNATIONALES RECHT 1, 24 (Gralf-Peter Calliess ed., 2014); Menkel-Meadow, *supra* note 14, at 113 ('a hybrid of hard and soft law'); JAN KLABBERS, INTERNATIONAL LAW 351 (2d ed. 2017) ('the norms of an emerging "transnational law"; rules and standards, whether hard or soft, public or private'); Peer Zumbansen, *Transnational Private Regulatory Governance: Ambiguities of Public Authority and Private Power*, 76 LAW & CONTEMP. PROBS. 117, 132 (2013); CALLIESS & ZUMBANSEN, *supra* note 5, at 20 *et seq.*, 274 *et seq.* and *passim*; Calliess, *supra* note 20, at 1035 ('Transnational law . . . is structured as a plurality of functionally specialized transnational law regimes, which in a pragmatic approach combine different governance mechanisms of private (norms, alternative dispute resolution, social sanctions) and public (laws, courts, enforcement) origin').

[27] See thereto KARSTEN NOWROT & YVONNE WARDIN, LIBERALISIERUNG DER WASSERVERSORGUNG IN DER WTO-RECHTSORDNUNG – DIE VERWIRKLICHUNG DES MENSCHENRECHTS AUF WASSER ALS AUFGABE EINER TRANSNATIONALEN VERANTWORTUNGSGEMEINSCHAFT 48 *et seq.* (2003); Karsten Nowrot, *Die Transnationale Verantwortungsgemeinschaft im Internationalen Wirtschaftsrecht, in* VERFASSUNGSRECHTLICHE DIMENSIONEN DES INTERNATIONALEN WIRTSCHAFTSRECHTS 57, 97 *et seq.* (Christian Tietje & Karsten Nowrot eds., 2007) as well as, *e.g.*, JAN KLABBERS, ANNE PETERS & GEIR ULFSTEIN, THE CONSTITUTIONALIZATION OF INTERNATIONAL LAW 261 (2009); KATJA FREY, GLOBALE VERSORGUNGSSICHERHEIT 26 *et seq.*, 171 *et seq.* (2013); Christian Tietje, *Begriff, Geschichte und Grundlagen des Internationalen Wirtschaftssystems und Wirtschaftsrechts, in* INTERNATIONALES WIRTSCHAFTSRECHT 1, 65 *et seq.* (Christian Tietje ed., 2d ed. 2015).

non-legally binding on the other' with the normative framework in the transnational economic system thus 'characterized by a mixed composition of "hard", "semi-hard" and "soft" regulations'.[28] A related perception can also be found specifically with regard to a transnational company law comprising, according to Peer Zumbansen, 'the law governing the global business corporation through a multilevel and multipolar legal regime of hard and soft law, statutes and recommendations, command-and-control structures of mandatory rules as opposed to an ever expanding body of self-regulatory rules'.[29] The same applies to the concept of a transnational labour law, understood, for example, by Ulrich Mückenberger as a global hybrid labour law in the sense of a new transnational type of law whose hybrid character finds its manifestation in linkages between hard and soft labour law.[30]

However, these conceptual approaches are not only confined to the realm of economic and business law as well as the normative framework on industrial and employment relations. Radu Mares, for example, has more recently advanced the idea of a transnational human rights law in the present sense of the meaning by highlighting the 'emergence of a transnational regulatory regime that, by mobilizing new sources of public and private authority, creates a new regulatory dynamic that augments the traditional state-centered and territory-based protection of human rights'.[31] At its core lies the realization that '[c]onceptual treatments of human rights in a less state-centered global order do not seek mistakenly to reinforce distinctions such as those between hard and soft law, between legal and nonlegal, private and public, territorial and extraterritorial, but to transcend such distinctions with a decisive focus on root

---

[28] Tietje & Nowrot, *supra* note 19, at 28 *et seq.*; *see also, e.g.*, Christian Tietje, *Transnationales Wirtschaftsrecht aus öffentlich-rechtlicher Perspektive*, 101 ZEITSCHRIFT FÜR VERGLEICHENDE RECHTSWISSENSCHAFT 404, 417 (2002); Christian Tietje, *Transnationalisierung des Wirtschaftsrechts*, in TRANSNATIONALES RECHT 239, 253 *et seq.* (Gralf-Peter Calliess ed., 2014); Christian Tietje & Karsten Nowrot, *Forming the Centre of a Transnational Economic Legal Order? Thoughts on the Current and Future Position of Non-state Actors in WTO Law*, 5 EUR. BUS. ORG. L. REV. 321, 341 *et seq.* (2004); KARSTEN NOWROT, NORMATIVE ORDNUNGSSTRUKTUR UND PRIVATE WIRKUNGSMACHT 650 *et seq.* (2006); BIRGIT ROST, DIE HERAUSBILDUNG TRANSNATIONALEN WIRTSCHAFTSRECHTS AUF DEM GEBIET DER INTERNATIONALEN FINANZ- UND KAPITALMÄRKTE 68 *et seq.* (2007).

[29] Peer Zumbansen, *Transnational Law, Evolving*, in ELGAR ENCYCLOPEDIA OF COMPARATIVE LAW 898, 906 (Jan M. Smits ed., 2d ed. 2012).

[30] Ulrich Mückenberger, *Ein globales Hybridarbeitsrecht*, in TRANSNATIONALES RECHT 457–77 (Gralf-Peter Calliess ed. 2014).

[31] Radu Mares, *Decentering Human Rights from the International Order of States: The Alignment and Interaction of Transnational Policy Channels*, 23 IND. J. GLOBAL LEGAL STUD. 171, 174 (2016).

causes and a search for new regulatory arrangements to tackle them'.[32] Equally of more recent origin is the notion of an emerging transnational environmental law, a regime that is, according to Olaf Dilling and Till Markus, characterized, among others, by the fact that no clear boundaries exist between legally binding and non-binding steering instruments.[33] Finally, another notable example is the transnational legal approach towards international humanitarian law as advocated by Math Noortmann and Ioannis Chapsos in particular, with a view to incorporate private military and security companies into this area of the international normative order. Arguing that the 'development of bottom-up transnational social responsibilities within the business sector'[34] on the basis of non-binding steering instruments like the International Code of Conduct for Security Service Providers of 9 November 2010[35] or the Sarajevo Code of Conduct for Private Security Companies of September 2006[36] 'constitutes a robust and workable alternative to the concept of legal accountability',[37] the authors ultimately envision and support the rise of a kind of transnational humanitarian law characterized by a normative framework that increasingly blurs the distinction between traditional hard law and more informal regulatory mechanisms.

C DID JESSUP ALREADY CONSIDER SOFT AS BEAUTIFUL? ON ATTRIBUTION

These more or less randomly chosen examples serve as an illustration that the understanding of transnational law as an approach to theorize the increasing levelling of binding and non-binding steering instruments and thus the evolving softification of the international normative order has undoubtedly more recently become an important, albeit not necessarily dominant,[38] strand in the

---

[32] Mares, *supra* note 31, at 195.

[33] Olaf Dilling & Till Markus, *Transnationalisierung des Umweltrechts*, 27 ZEITSCHRIFT FÜR UMWELTRECHT 3–16 (2016).

[34] Math Noortmann & Ioannis Chapsos, *Private Military and Security Companies: A Transnational Legal Approach, in* 100 YEARS OF PEACE THROUGH LAW: PAST AND FUTURE 257, 259 (Andreas von Arnauld, Nele Matz-Lück & Kerstin Odendahl eds., 2015).

[35] The code is available under http://www.icoca.ch/en/the_icoc (last visited Apr. 15, 2017).

[36] Available under http://www.seesac.org/res/files/publication/544.pdf (last visited Apr. 15, 2017).

[37] Noortmann & Chapsos, *supra* note 34, at 259; see also in this regard, for example, Evgeni Moyakine, *From National and International Frustrations to Transnational Triumph? Hybrid Transnational Private Regulatory Regimes in the Industry of Private Military and Security Companies and Their Effectiveness in Ensuring Compliance with Human Rights*, 28 PAC. MCGEORGE GLOBAL BUS. & DEV. L.J. 209–25 (2015).

[38] On the widely and rightly held perception that there is currently neither consensus on, nor at least a dominant approach to, the concept of transnational law in the scholarly literature, see,

more general debate on the concept of transnational law. In light of the fact that most of the above-mentioned authors explicitly take recourse to Jessup's Storrs Lectures on Jurisprudence of 1956, the question arises whether this understanding is indeed attributable to Jessup in the sense that it could be legitimately argued that his work *Transnational Law* has objectively aided and abetted the above-mentioned attempts aimed at theorizing the increasing softification of the international normative order. In other words, can this conceptual approach rightly be regarded as a notable legacy of Jessup sixty years after the publication of his ideas?

It is by now comparatively well known and recognized that although Jessup, as he recognized,[39] did not invent the term 'transnational law', he was responsible for introducing the term to a larger scholarly public within his 'delightful little volume'[40] bearing the same title.[41] In his search for the 'law applicable to the complex interrelated world community', he highlighted that 'there is really much more to international legal relations than merely public international law'[42] and, as a consequence, rejected the name 'international law' as being 'misleading since it suggests that one is concerned only with the relations of one nation (or state) to other nations (or states)'.[43] This 'world community' is, according to Jessup, increasingly shaped by the emergence of 'transnational situations' that involve a considerable diversity of actors, such as 'individuals, corporations, states, organizations of states, or other groups'.[44] Given this necessarily broader and more inclusive approach to transboundary interactions, he famously describes the term 'transnational law' – being the normative framework governing these situations – 'to include all law which

e.g., CALLIESS & ZUMBANSEN, *supra* note 5, at 79; ANDREAS MAURER, LEX MARITIMA 13 *et seq.* (2012). See in this connection also the observation by Gregory Shaffer, *Transnational Legal Process and State Change*, 37 LAW & SOC. INQUIRY 229, 233 (2012) ('Although the term transnational law is increasingly used, authors are not always careful in specifying what they mean by it.').

[39] See in retrospective Philip C. Jessup, *The Present State of Transnational Law*, *in* THE PRESENT STATE OF INTERNATIONAL LAW AND OTHER ESSAYS 339 (Maarten Bos ed., 1973) ('the term was not new – it was not an original creation of the author's').

[40] C.G. Fenwick, Book Review, 51 AM. J. INT'L L. 444 (1957) (reviewing PHILIP C. JESSUP, TRANSNATIONAL LAW (1956)).

[41] On this perception, see, e.g., Harold Hongju Koh, *Transnational Legal Process*, 75 NEB. L. REV. 181, 186 (1996); Zumbansen, *supra* note 29, at 898 ('locus classicus'); Dennis Patternson, *Transnational Governance Regimes*, *in* INTERNATIONAL LEGAL POSITIVISM IN A POST-MODERN WORLD 401, 414 (Jörg Kammerhofer & Jean D'Aspremont eds., 2014).

[42] See the respective characterization in the book review by H.B. Jacobini, Book Review, 19 J. POLITICS 681 (1957) (reviewing JESSUP, *supra* note 40).

[43] PHILIP C. JESSUP, TRANSNATIONAL LAW 1 (1956). For an assessment of this perception, see, e.g., Tietje & Nowrot, *supra* note 19, at 27, with additional references.

[44] JESSUP, *supra* note 43, at 3.

regulates actions or events that transcend national frontiers. Both public and private international law are included, as are other rules which do not wholly fit into such standard categories.'[45]

Nevertheless, what is today equally well known and acknowledged among legal scholars is the absence of a more in-depth systematic conceptualization and theorization of transnational law in Jessup's work that – at least 'for the time being; – explicitly 'avoid[s] further classification of transnational problems and further definition of transnational law'.[46] This finding first and foremost also holds true with regard to his understanding of the character of 'other rules which do not wholly fit into such standard categories' and thus the type of transnational norms that are not only, but most certainly also, of particular relevance in the present context.[47] To find a substantiated answer to the question of whether the residual class of 'other rules' also encompasses non-binding steering instruments and thus whether the conceptual approach to 'transnational (…) law' as discussed here can indeed be attributed to Jessup's Storrs Lectures, it seems useful to follow Peer Zumbansen's advice 'to re-read the slim but nevertheless immensely rich volume'[48] as a whole. And indeed, despite the fact that Jessup has not explicitly elaborated on the scope of what he labelled 'other rules', an assessment of his writings reveals some notable indications as to his understanding of 'rules' or 'law' for the purposes of *Transnational Law*. Although some of his statements may also legitimately be interpreted as expressing a more narrow understanding of transnational law in the sense of only comprising domestic and international hard law,[49] it is submitted that there are in particular two paragraphs in the first section of his work in which he makes sufficiently – and almost beyond reasonable doubt – clear that his treatment of transnational law is in fact based on a more encompassing idea of 'rules' and 'law' very much in line with the approaches to what is referred to here as 'transnational (…) law' introduced above.

---

[45] Id. at 2.

[46] *Id.* at 7. *See* thereto also already Math Noortmann, *Transnational Law: Philip Jessup's Legacy and Beyond, in* NON-STATE ACTORS IN INTERNATIONAL LAW 57–74 (Math Noortmann, August Reinisch & Cedric Ryngaert eds., 2015); Scott, *supra* note 25, at 859 *et seq.*

[47] See generally also Noortmann, *supra* note 46, at 59 ('The ultimate question is not, whether transnational legal scholars can overcome the traditional split of the international legal realm into a public and private one, but whether they can envisage, identify and formulate "other rules which do not wholly fit into such standard categories".'); Scott, *supra* note 25, at 873; LARS VIELLECHNER, TRANSNATIONALISIERUNG DES RECHTS 168 (2013).

[48] Zumbansen, *supra* note 29, at 900.

[49] *See, e.g.*, JESSUP, *supra* note 43, at 106 ('Transnational law then includes both civil and criminal aspects, it includes what we know as public and private international law, and it includes national law, both public and private.').

Jessup highlights that '[a]s man has developed his needs and his facilities for
meeting his needs, the rules become more numerous and more complicated.
History, geography, preferences, convenience, and necessity have dictated
dispersion of the authority to make the rules men live by. Some rules are
made by the head of the family, whether it be father or mother, such as "Wash
your hands before supper". Some rules are made by ecclesiastical authorities
as in specific times and manners of fasting. Some are made by corporations
regulating their sales agencies . . . . Other rules are made by secret societies, by
towns, cities, states. Still others are made by international organizations such
as the Coal and Steel Community, the International Monetary Fund, or the
OEEC.'[50] Against the background of this exemplary list of binding as well as
non-binding, societal steering instruments, he continues by recalling that
'[n]owadays it is neither novel nor heretical to call all of these rules "law"'
and, moreover, declares that he also – in the exercise of 'scholarly freedom' –
'rest[s] for the time being on this broad description of the sense in which
I speak of law in general and of transnational law in particular'.[51] It can validly
be inferred from this proposition that Jessup's understanding of 'all law which
regulates actions or events that transcend national frontiers' encompasses
binding legal rules as well as other steering mechanisms[52] and is thus rightly
referred to by modern authors in approaches aimed at conceptualizing the
increasing softification of the international normative order.

D IS SOFT REALLY BEAUTIFUL? IT (AGAIN) SEEMS TO DEPEND ...

In light of these findings, the third and final step of my analysis will address
whether this terminological and conceptual trend in theorizing the softification of the international normative order on the basis of emerging areas of
'transnational (...) law' – perceived to be characterized by an increasing
blurring of the boundaries between hard law and non-binding steering instruments – can legitimately be regarded as, first, an approach appropriately
reflecting the normative realities in the present international system, and,
second, a desirable guiding idea for the future evolution of transboundary
steering regimes.

---

[50] *Id.* at 8 *et seq.*
[51] *Id.* at 9.
[52] Generally on this perception, *see also, e.g.*, Zumbansen, *supra* note 29, at 900 *et seq.*; Peer
      Zumbansen, *Transnational Law and Societal Memory, in* LAW AND POLITICS OF
      RECONCILIATION 129, 132 *et seq.* (Scott Veitch ed., 2007); MAURER, *supra* note 38, at 16.

Before doing so, however, some brief remarks on two preliminary and underlying issues seem to be in order. First, although being mindful of the well-known difficulties we still face when trying to identify and agree upon a precise understanding of what exactly law is,[53] the present analysis is based on the assumption that it is nevertheless in principle possible – and already, in order to maintain law's autonomy vis-à-vis the realms of politics and morality,[54] also conceptually important – to clearly distinguish between legally binding stipulations, on the one hand, and non-law, on the other hand,[55] without denying the possibility, and indeed actuality, of attributing legally relevant effects also to this later class of non-binding rules of behaviour. Second, despite adhering to this binary distinction between law and other steering instruments as being in principle separable and not always equal, I do not intend to bother the reader with some kind of broad positivistic critique of non-binding norms in general and soft law in particular because, first, much

[53] The famous finding by Immanuel Kant in his 'Critique of Pure Reason' that jurists are still searching for a definition of their concept of law thus still appears to be valid; *see* IMMANUEL KANT, CRITIQUE OF PURE REASON 639 (Paul Guyer & Allen W. Wood eds. & trans., Cambridge Univ. Press 1998) (1787). *See also*, for example, more recently, HERBERT L.A. HART, THE CONCEPT OF LAW 1 (2d ed. 1997) ('Few questions concerning human society have been asked with such persistence and answered by serious thinkers in so many diverse, strange, and even paradoxical ways as the question "What is law?".').

[54] On the autonomy of law in this regard, see already, e.g., Ulrich Fastenrath, *A Political Theory of Law: Escaping the Aporia of the Debate on the Validity of Legal Argument in Public International Law*, *in* FROM BILATERALISM TO COMMUNITY INTEREST – ESSAYS IN HONOUR OF JUDGE BRUNO SIMMA 58, 61 *et seq.* (Ulrich Fastenrath et al. eds., 2011); Joost Pauwelyn, *Is It International Law or Not, and Does It Even Matter?*, *in* INFORMAL INTERNATIONAL LAWMAKING 125, 130 (Joost Pauwelyn, Ramses A. Wessel & Jan Wouters eds., 2012); Prosper Weil, *Towards Relative Normativity in International Law?*, 77 AM. J. INT'L L. 413, 417 (1983) ('the specific nature of the legal phenomenon'), as well as from the realm of international judicial practice, for example South West Africa Cases (Eth. v. S. Afr.; Liber. v. S. Afr.), Second Phase, 1966 I.C.J. Rep. 6, 34 (July 18) ('The Court must now turn to certain questions of a wider character. Throughout this case it has been suggested, directly or indirectly, that humanitarian considerations are sufficient in themselves to generate legal rights and obligations, and that the Court can and should proceed accordingly. The Court does not think so. It is a court of law, and can take account of moral principles only in so far as these are given a sufficient expression in legal form. Law exists, it is said, to serve a social need; but precisely for that reason it can do so only through and within the limits of its own discipline. Otherwise, it is not a legal service that would be rendered.').

[55] See thereto, also from the perspective of state practice, Dinah Shelton, *International Law and 'Relative Normativity'*, *in* INTERNATIONAL LAW 137, 161 (Malcolm D. Evans ed., 4th ed. 2014); Weil, *supra* note 54, at 415 *et seq.*; Pauwelyn, *supra* note 54, at 127 *et seq.*; Jan Klabbers, *The Redundancy of Soft Law*, 65 NORDIC J. INT'L L. 167–82 (1996); for a quite different perception, *see* the already famous Richard R. Baxter, *International Law in 'Her Infinite Variety'*, 29 INT'L & COMP. L.Q. 549, 564 (1980) ('I hope, [I] have persuaded the reader that it is excessively simplistic to divide the written norms into those that are binding and those that are not.').

ink has been spilled on this topic in particular since the beginning of the 1980s,[56] and, second, I do not share this criticism in its entirety. In particular, in so far as it results in qualifications of soft law as, for example, a thoroughly undesirable phenomenon as far as international law as a whole is concerned.[57]

Rather, I would like to give a typical lawyer's answer to the questions raised above concerning the appropriateness and desirability of theorizing the soft-ification of the international normative order on the basis of emerging areas of 'transnational (...) law': it depends. This might sound to many readers like a cliché, but one has to bear in mind that not all clichés are always false and that this particular cliché answer seems rather fitting in the present context, since it implies the need for a differentiated assessment. It is submitted that the recently advanced 'transnational (...) law' approaches are not equally suitable for all branches of the international normative order.

To illustrate this proposition, I would like to start by drawing attention to two areas of public international law that have proven themselves to be quite immune to tendencies of softification and thus to processes of transnationali-zation in the present sense of the meaning. The first one concerns the field of international criminal law, understood as the branch of the global normative order that deals with the direct criminal responsibility of individuals.[58] The label 'transnational criminal law' or variations thereof are not without prece-dent in the respective legal discourses.[59] However, I'm not aware of anybody

[56] From the almost countless contributions on this topic, see, in addition to the publications already cited in the footnotes above, also, for example, Christine M. Chinkin, *The Challenge of Soft Law: Development and Change in International Law*, 38 INT'L & COMP. L.Q. 850–66 (1989); Gregory C. Shaffer & Mark A. Pollack, *Hard vs. Soft Law: Alternatives, Complements, and Antagonists in International Governance*, 94 MINN. L. REV. 706–99 (2010); Hartmut Hillgenberg, *A Fresh Look at Soft Law*, 10 EUR. J. INT'L L. 499–515 (1999), each with further references.

[57] See, in particular, Jan Klabbers, *The Undesirability of Soft Law*, 67 NORDIC J. INT'L L. 381–91 (1998); see in this connection also, e.g., Weil, *supra* note 54, at 415 *et seq.*; László Blutman, *In the Trap of a Legal Metaphor: International Soft Law*, 59 INT'L & COMP. L.Q. 605, 623 *et seq.* (2010).

[58] On this definition of international criminal law, as well as alternative or more encompassing understandings of this branch of public international law, see, e.g., Robert Cryer, *International Criminal Law*, in INTERNATIONAL LAW 752 (Malcolm D. Evans ed., 4th ed. 2014); MALCOLM N. SHAW, INTERNATIONAL LAW 288 *et seq.* (8th ed. 2017).

[59] See thereto, e.g., Neil Boister, *'Transnational Criminal Law'?*, 14 EUR. J. INT'L L. 953, 955 (2003), who suggests the (restrictive) use of this term in order to describe 'the indirect suppression by international law through domestic penal law of criminal activities that have actual or potential trans-boundary effects'. For additional meanings and references, see also Florian Jeßberger, *Transnationales Strafrecht, Internationales Strafrecht, Transnationale Strafrechtsgeltung – eine Orientierung*, in TRANSNATIONALES RECHT 527, 528 (Gralf-Peter Calliess ed., 2014).

using this term in the sense of indicating a relativization of the law versus non-law distinction. And this situation is not the result of a kind of deplorable wilful neglect of an important conceptual issue. Rather, it merely reflects the regulatory reality that individual criminal responsibility is simply not determined on the basis of a melange of hard law and softer steering mechanisms[60] – and rightly so in light of our cherished rule of law and the principle of legality, since nobody wants and expects to be criminally indicted for, inter alia, not complying with the rules of behaviour laid down in a code of conduct.

The second example of an area of the international normative order that has not been affected by processes of transnationalization is the jus ad bellum, the transboundary regime governing recourse to force. In this regard, already from the perspective of terminology, the present author is not aware of any voices in the literature advocating for a 'transnational law on the use of force' or related terms and concepts. This finding does not imply that this field of law comprises clear and unambiguous rules whose interpretation is based on a broad global consensus and where soft steering mechanisms are virtually non-existent. On the contrary, it hardly needs to be recalled that the precise scope of international hard law stipulations on the use of force are frequently highly contested[61] and that soft law instruments do at times exercise quite notable legal effects in the processes of creating and concretizing these provisions.[62] In addition, it has been emphasized – and rightly criticized – that the application of the jus ad bellum is, more recently, suffering from the problematic challenge of a visible rise of what might be referred to as 'twilight zone' arguments. This argument submits that certain uses of force may for example be 'illegal but justifiable',[63] thereby ultimately attempting to overcome the distinction

---

[60] On the inappropriateness to speak of a 'transnational criminal law' in the present sense of the meaning, see also already, for example, Calliess & Maurer, *supra* note 26, at 27; Ingeborg Zerbes, *Transnationales Korruptionsstrafrecht, in* TRANSNATIONALES RECHT 539 (Gralf-Peter Calliess ed., 2014).

[61] On this perception, see also, e.g., Christian J. Tams & Antonios Tzanakopoulos, *Use of Force, in* INTERNATIONAL LEGAL POSITIVISM IN A POST-MODERN WORLD 498 (Jörg Kammerhofer & Jean D'Aspremont eds., 2014); Jörg Kammerhofer, *Introduction: The Future of Restrictivist Scholarship on the Use of Force*, 29 LEIDEN J. INT'L L. 13 (2016); Oliver Dörr, *Use of Force, Prohibition Of*, para. 2, MAX PLANCK ENCYCLOPEDIA OF PUBLIC INTERNATIONAL LAW (Rüdiger Wolfrum ed., Sept. 2015), www.mpepil.com/ ('repeatedly the subject of controversy').

[62] This is evident, for example, in a number of judgments of the International Court of Justice where the court referred to UN General Assembly resolutions as evidence of state practice for the formation of customary international law. *See, e.g.,* Military and Paramilitary Activities in and Against Nicaragua (Nicar. v. U.S.), Merits, 1986 I.C.J. Rep. 14, 99 *et seq.*; Armed Activities on the Territory of the Congo (Congo v. Uganda), 2005 I.C.J. Rep., 168, 226 *et seq.*

[63] THOMAS M. FRANCK, RECOURSE TO FORCE 174 *et seq.* (2002).

between legality and illegality.[64] Nevertheless, and although these and other current challenges have the potential to result in an increased legal uncertainty in the regime governing recourse to force, the incontrovertible fact remains that the question of whether the use of force presents itself as lawful in individual cases has always been answered in light of the applicable hard law and most certainly not with regard to 'relevant' soft law instruments alone.

When trying to generalize these findings with the aim of applying them to other areas of international law, it appears potentially quite promising to enquire why the distinction between hard law and non-binding steering instruments is not blurred but in fact still very much present and alive in some branches of the international normative order. Among these underlying reasons, one can initially identify certain individual, sector-specific aspects that appear – at least at first sight – not transferable to other fields of international law. In the realm of international criminal law, for example, the principle of legality, given that the human rights of suspects are at issue, excludes recourse to any other source of punishment than hard law in force at the time when the crime was committed (*nullum crimen sine lege*) and, inter alia, sufficiently precise as well as accessible to the alleged perpetrator.[65] However, viewed from an overarching structural perspective and thus transcending these more sector-related aspects, it is submitted that the above-mentioned examples also serve as indications for the potential suitability of a novel binary distinction to be applied to the international normative order as a whole, between what might be labelled as *consequential and formalistic* areas of international law, on the one hand, and more *flexible and encompassing* fields of international law, on the other hand.

The characterization as consequential for those branches of the international normative order like international criminal law and the legal regime

[64] For a critical account of these approaches, see Tams & Tzanakopoulos, *supra* note 61, at 516 *et seq.*

[65] Thereto as well as generally on the central role played by the principle of legality in the normative design of international criminal law, see Dov Jacobs, *International Criminal Law, in* INTERNATIONAL LEGAL POSITIVISM IN A POST-MODERN WORLD 451–74 (Jörg Kammerhofer & Jean D'Aspremont eds. 2014); ANTONIO CASSESE ET AL., CASSESE'S INTERNATIONAL CRIMINAL LAW 22 *et seq.* (3d ed. 2013), each with further references. On the special position enjoyed by this area of law in realm of transboundary rules, see also, e.g., Anne Peters, *Transnational Law Comprises Constitutional, Administrative, Criminal and Quasi-private Law, in* MAKING TRANSNATIONAL LAW WORK IN THE GLOBAL ECONOMY – ESSAYS IN HONOUR OF DETLEV VAGTS 154, 166 (Pieter H.F. Bekker, Rudolf Dolzer & Michael Waibel eds., 2010) ('interstate law needs quite a lot of flexibility, whereas criminal law, quite to the contrary, requires very detailed, clear and unambiguous rules, given that the fundamental rights of suspects are at stake').

on the use of force, which have proven themselves to be quite immune to tendencies of softification and transnationalization, seems appropriate because it rightly draws attention to the fact that it is in particular the frequently rather severe consequences that these steering regimes and especially their violations have for individuals (with regard to international criminal law and the regime governing recourse to force), as well as for political communities as a whole (like in the case of the use of force) and ultimately also for the violator and its population themselves (being, for example, subject to measures taken in exercise of the right of self-defence), that can be regarded as a primary reason why these legal regimes do not comprise of a melange of hard law and softer steering instruments being on an equal normative footing. The emphasis on the consequences for individuals either considered for themselves or as members of a political community seems warranted based on the increased recognition of natural persons as legally relevant actors in the international system and its normative order – a development that has already given rise to the perception of public international law being in process of continued 'individualization'.[66] The additional qualification of the respective fields of the global normative order as formalistic is thereby intended to convey the message that their design and progressive development is strongly guided by an insistence on certain formalities and their observance such as the capacity, authority and intent of the involved international actors to create binding international normative rules.

Against this background, the question obviously arises whether there are also other branches of the international normative order, aside from the already mentioned fields of international criminal law and the legal regime governing the use of force, that deserve to be characterized as consequential and formalistic areas of public international law. In this regard, an argument could validly be made that, for example – and contrary to more recently advanced views by a number of international legal scholars as outlined above[67] – the normative realms of international human rights law as well as international humanitarian law are too consequential to the lives of individuals to legitimately consider their design and normative ordering structures as being shaped by a melange of hard law and softer steering instruments on an equal normative level. And indeed, to confine myself to but one example, the distinction between law and non-binding rules of behaviour seems to be quite influential and even appears to lie at the heart of the highly polarized debate

---

[66] For a general and comprehensive discussion, see ANNE PETERS, BEYOND HUMAN RIGHTS – THE STATUS OF THE INDIVIDUAL IN INTERNATIONAL LAW (2016).

[67] See section B.

on the extent to which transnational or multinational corporations should also
contribute to the promotion of global community interests like the protection
of human rights and, in particular, whether the fulfilment of such expectations should be secured also on the basis of respective legal obligations. In
discourse of this issue, all of the various relevant state, supra-state and non-state
actors clearly differentiate – explicitly or at least implicitly – between hard law
obligations on the one hand and more or less voluntary commitments on the
other hand.[68] This is, for example, evidenced as early as in the middle of the
1970s by the controversial debates prior to the adoption of the voluntary
OECD Guidelines for Multinational Enterprises that were originally envi-
sioned by some OECD countries, among them Canada, the Netherlands and
Scandinavian states, to become a legally binding steering instrument.[69] More
recently, the same applies to the polarized discussions in connection with the
activities of the Open-Ended Intergovernmental Working Group on Transnational Corporations and Other Business Enterprises with Respect to Human
Rights, established in June 2014 by the UN Human Rights Council and
entrusted with the mandate 'to elaborate an international legally binding
instrument to regulate, in international human rights law, the activities of
transnational corporations and other business enterprises'.[70]

Although consequential and formalistic branches of the international normative order also seem to be beneficial, in addition to a number of advantages
already referred to above, by allowing a precise identification of existing legal
gaps and thereby enabling a more focused discussion of whether and how to
fill them,[71] it is by now increasingly recognized – and indeed beyond reasonable doubt – that the normatively relevant steering practice in current international relations also rightly and legitimately provides room for the existence
of more *flexible and encompassing* fields of international law. The labelling as

---

[68] On this observation, see also, e.g., KARSTEN NOWROT, THE RELATIONSHIP BETWEEN NATIONAL
LEGAL REGULATIONS AND CSR INSTRUMENTS: COMPLEMENTARY OR EXCLUSIONARY
APPROACHES TO GOOD CORPORATE CITIZENSHIP? 10 *et seq.* (2007), with further references.

[69] See thereto, for example, PETER MUCHLINSKI, MULTINATIONAL ENTERPRISES AND THE LAW
659 (2d ed. 2007); BEATRIZ HUARTE MELGAR, KARSTEN NOWROT & YUAN WANG, THE
2011 UPDATE OF THE OECD GUIDELINES FOR MULTINATIONAL ENTERPRISES: BALANCED
OUTCOME OR AN OPPORTUNITY MISSED? 9 *et seq.* (2011).

[70] Human Rights Council Res. 26/9, U.N. Doc. A/HRC/RES/26/9, at para. 1 (July 14, 2014). On
the activities of this working group, see also, e.g., more recently, Human Rights Council,
Report on the Second Session, U.N. Doc. A/HRC/34/47 (Jan. 4, 2017).

[71] On this perception, see also, already, Michael Bothe, *Legal and Non-legal Norms –
A Meaningful Distinction in International Relations?*, 11 NETH. Y.B. INT'L L. 65, 94 (1980)
('Their danger [of non-legal norms] lies in the fact that they enable the salutary difficulties
involved in the *law*-making process to be circumvented, and that law is thereby not created
where it could and should be.') (emphasis in the original).

flexible thereby indicates a reduced emphasis on the observance of otherwise indispensable formalities in the processes of creating international steering instruments, thus also including, for example, normative rules of behaviour developed by non-state actors lacking the authority to adopt public international hard law. Closely related by being a more or less direct result of this first aspect, the term 'encompassing' captures the more inclusive character of these areas of international law that are with regard to their normative structures and the implementation in practice characterized by notable relativization of the law versus non-law distinction and due to this strong linkages of hard and soft law thus rightly considered as emerging branches of 'transnational (. . .) law'. Compared to the consequential and formalistic fields of public international law, these flexible and encompassing sub-systems are overall not less important for the international system and its normative order as a whole. However, for example, due to their often quite technical character as well as the generally less direct, less fundamental and less elementary effects of these steering regimes – as well as of respective violations of the rules of behaviour stipulated by them – for natural persons, they can be considered as ultimately less consequential for individuals and political communities. Arguably, this description applies, inter alia, to the normative regime governing transboundary economic relations and a number of its sub-systems, like the legal framework dealing with global business corporations that are thus rightly and legitimately captured by the notions of an emerging transnational economic law or an evolving transnational company law respectively.[72]

In sum, it is submitted that the differentiated approach towards the identification of emerging areas of 'transnational (. . .) law' suggested here is, compared to wider generalizing claims recently advanced in the legal literature, not only more accurately reflecting the normative realities in the international system but in particular also a considerably more appropriate guiding vision for the future development of transboundary steering regimes rightly regarded as being first and foremost also instrumental in realizing a continued individualization of public international law as a whole to the benefit of humankind.

E CONCLUDING OBSERVATIONS

In the hope that the findings made in this contribution have the potential to appear to some readers as not entirely unconvincing, I finally intend, in

---

[72] On these perceptions, see section B.

evaluating some facets of the current importance of 'Jessup's bold proposal' on the occasion of the sixtieth anniversary of his work *Transnational Law*, to briefly turn to the question of whether this eminent legal scholar is quasi to 'blame' for the currently often comparatively undifferentiated recourse to a purportedly widespread rise of 'transnational (...) law'. Could this trend somehow be considered as a kind of 'darker legacy' of his 'delightful little volume'[73]? Has he – figuratively speaking – aided and abetted in opening the 'floodgates' for the respective approaches aimed at theorizing the increasing softification of the international normative order? I would like to conclude with providing my answer to these issues by addressing three sub-questions.

First, is this tendency in parts of the legal literature attributable to Jessup's understanding of transnational law? The answer is yes, because – as already indicated above[74] – it can be directly traced back to his broad and intentionally undertheorized[75] description and application of this term and concept in *Transnational Law*. Second, could he have known or at least anticipated that a more differentiated and thus less encompassing understanding of transnational law might have more appropriately reflected the current state and desirable future evolution of the international normative order? The answer is again yes, since although the process of 'individualization' of public international law was still in its infancy in the first half of the 1950s, in particular the proclamation of the Universal Declaration of Human Rights by the UN General Assembly on 10 December 1948 as well as, inter alia, the adoption of the Convention for the Protection of Human Rights and Fundamental Freedoms by the members of the Council of Europe in November 1950 and the signing of the four Geneva Conventions in August 1949 codifying and progressively developing international humanitarian law already served as clear indications for an emerging trend in this direction. In addition, the development of international criminal law, further evidencing an increased individual orientation of the transboundary legal order and being one of the natural reference fields for consequential and formalistic branches of public international law, had clearly made a 'great leap forward' at the time of writing *Transnational Law* as a result of the creation of the international war crimes tribunals of Nuremberg and Tokyo in the second half of the 1940s. It hardly needs to be recalled that the same applies to the international legal regime on

[73] Fenwick, *supra* note 40, at 444.
[74] See section C.
[75] On this view, see also, already, e.g., Noortmann, *supra* note 46, at 57 *et seq.*; Scott, *supra* note 25, at 859 *et seq.*

the use of force based on the respective stipulations enshrined in the Charter of the United Nations, signed on 26 June 1945 in San Francisco.

Finally, and more generally, should Jessup, being a lawyer, have known that aiming at a nuanced understanding of transnational law would have been at least a suitable path worth exploring on the way to an adequate development of this concept? Once more, the answer is yes, because it is still common knowledge among lawyers that 'it depends', indicating the appropriateness of a differentiated approach, has always been the best answer to most legal questions, most certainly including questions relating to the proper perception, role and functions of transnational law in the global normative order.

5

From International Law to Jessup's *Transnational Law*, from Transnational Law to *Transnational Legal Orders*

GREGORY SHAFFER AND CARLOS COYE

A INTRODUCTION

In his path-breaking 1956 Storrs Lectures, Judge Philip Jessup shifted attention from international law, as governing relations between states, to transnational law, as governing transnational activities. He famously defined *transnational law* as "all law which regulates actions or events that transcend national frontiers," which includes public international law, private international law, and "other rules which do not wholly fit into such standard categories."[1] Much recent scholarship on transnational law has focused on that residual category of "other rules" and their "private" character.[2] There has, however, been a parallel revolution in public international law since Jessup's lectures, which needs to be theorized in transnational terms. It is best done through shifting attention from the concept of *transnational law* to the concepts of *transnational legal ordering* and *transnational legal orders*.

Jessup wrote of the concept of transnational law as problem-solving during the Cold War, when hope in public international law and public international institutions had withered. Jessup had served on the US delegation to both the 1943 Bretton Woods conference that led to the creation of the International Monetary Fund and World Bank and the 1945 San Francisco charter conference that created the United Nations (UN). By 1956, however, the prospect of international institutions and international law as problem solvers had collapsed. Jessup himself had been investigated and attacked as a Communist sympathizer by US Senator Joseph McCarthy, undermining Jessup's reputation and explaining the Senate's refusal to approve him as the US

---

[1] PHILIP C. JESSUP, TRANSNATIONAL LAW (1956).

[2] Gregory Shaffer, *Theorizing Transnational Legal Ordering*, 12 ANN. REV. L. & SOC. SC. 231 (2016).

representative to the UN.[3] Jessup turned to analyze other means of fostering international problem-solving through the concept of transnational law that incorporated, but went beyond, public international law. Jessup's lectures focused primarily on private international law. As reflected in his three lectures' titles ("The Universality of Human Problems," "The Power to Deal with the Problems," and "The Choice of Law Governing the Problems"), Jessup was drawn to private international law's functional ability to resolve individual transnational "problems" (lecture 1) through its decentralized system of allocating jurisdictional "power" among national courts (lecture 2), which, in turn, use "choice of law" techniques to decide on the applicable law (lecture 3).

This article has two main targets for its audience: first, it responds to theorists who conceive of transnational law either exclusively or predominately as a private lawmaking phenomenon, and second, it addresses the relation of public international law to the concepts of transnational legal ordering and transnational legal orders. The article's thesis is twofold. First, the scope of public international law has exploded since Jessup's time, arguably more than the other two prongs of his conceptualization.[4] Second, we should shift our conceptual analysis from *transnational law* as a body of law addressing transnational problems to transnational legal ordering and transnational legal orders, so as to capture these processes' deeper political, social, and legal implications. The term *transnational legal ordering* refers to the transnational construction, flow, settlement, and unsettlement of legal norms in particular domains.[5] By *transnational legal orders*, we mean "a collection of formalized legal norms and associated organizations and actors that authoritatively order the understanding and practice of law across national jurisdictions" in these domains.[6] These developments in public international law and their implications have catalyzed a populist backlash, which could, at least in the near term, lead to a renewed turn toward the other two prongs of Jessup's concept, private international law and private rulemaking (part E).

---

[3]   Oscar Schachter, *Philip Jessup's Life and Ideas*, 80 AM. J. INT'L L. 879, 885–89 (1986).
[4]   To recall, the three prongs are public international law, private international law, and other rules.
[5]   Gregory Shaffer, *Transnational Legal Ordering and State Change, in* TRANSNATIONAL LEGAL ORDERING AND STATE CHANGE (Gregory Shaffer ed., 2013), 1, 5–9.
[6]   Terence C. Halliday & Gregory Shaffer, *Transnational Legal Orders, in* TRANSNATIONAL LEGAL ORDERS (Terence C. Halliday & Gregory Shaffer eds., 2015), 3, 5 (elaborating the concept); Terence C. Halliday & Gregory Shaffer, *Researching Transnational Legal Orders, in* TRANSNATIONAL LEGAL ORDERS, *supra*, at 475.

This article shows how public international law has become a much more central component of transnational law and transnational legal ordering since Jessup wrote and now increasingly permeates state boundaries. Formally, international law does so when it has direct effect in national legal systems, when it is enacted by state legislatures in statutes or adopted by state regulators as administrative regulations, and when it shapes national courts' interpretation of national law.[7] Informally, public international law also has significant effects through iterative processes engaging international organizations, soft law norms, indicators, information sharing, expert consultation, peer review, and other technologies of governance that facilitate social interaction and produce and diffuse knowledge, norms, and practices that transnationally shape law and legal ordering. Private actors are central in driving the development and application of international law, as when they participate in norm making that is eventually incorporated into international law, when they bring claims before national courts derived from international law, and through their practices that apply and interpret these norms.

The result is much deeper implications of international law than ad hoc problem-solving applied to transnational situations, as theorized by Jessup. International law deeply implicates what the state does (in relation to the market and social ordering), states' institutional architecture (by affecting the allocation of authority among executives, legislatures, courts, administrative bodies, and central and federal institutions), the role of professions and private parties in governance (creating new professional stakes), mechanisms of accountability (including to international bodies and transnational networks of public officials and private stakeholders), and social identities.[8]

This article follows Jessup in asserting that real-world problems should be the starting point for analysis. However, it problematizes the conceptualization of problems as involving human agency, so that the problems themselves should be viewed as social and political constructs that, in turn, shape legal

---

7   Pierre-Hugues Verdier & Mila Versteeg, *International Law in National Legal Systems: An Empirical Investigation*, 109 AM. J. INT'L L. 514 (2015); Pierre-Hugues Verdier & Mila Versteeg, *Modes of Domestic Incorporation of International Law*, in RESEARCH HANDBOOK ON THE POLITICS OF INTERNATIONAL LAW 149 (Wayne Sandholtz & Christopher A. Whytock eds., 2017) (comparing national judicial systems regarding "how treaties and custom are received and interpreted, and their status vis-à-vis other sources of domestic law"). For highly cited cases regarding the doctrine of avoiding non-compliance with international law through statutory construction, see Murray v. Schooner Charming Betsy, 6 U.S. 64, 118 (1804) (in the US legal system); Case C-61/94 Comm'n v. Germany 1996 E.C.R. I-3989, ¶ 52 (in the EU legal system).

8   TRANSNATIONAL LEGAL ORDERING AND STATE CHANGE, *supra* note 6; Gregory Shaffer, *How the World Trade Organization Shapes Regulatory Governance*, 9 REG. & GOVERNANCE 1 (2015); Harold Hongju Koh, *Transnational Legal Process*, 75 NEB. L. REV. 181 (1996).

responses. With Jessup, we also contend that public international law is a part of the study of transnational law. Yet we build from his analysis by focusing on international law's permeation of national legal systems and local practices so that international law is not viewed on a separate plain, as conventionally viewed in the international relations / international law scholarship, but rather as part of a recursive transnational legal process.[9] While a major prong of transnational legal theorizing rightly focuses on private law and private law-making (which are important and critical areas of study), public law components of transnational law also remain central and critically important.[10]

B THE CONCEPTUAL TURN FROM TRANSNATIONAL LAW TO TRANSNATIONAL LEGAL ORDERS: TWO EXAMPLES

Once we turn from assessing transnational law as law applied to transnational problems to assessing processes of transnational legal ordering and the development of transnational legal orders, we cannot start with a stipulated problem but must ask how that problem was framed. Problems are not natural since issues can exist for long periods before they are conceptualized as problems, much less as "transnational problems." That conceptualization reflects shifting ideologies and interests over time.[11] Law responds to such conceptualizations, and thus the very definition of a problem shapes the ensuing legal response to it. This section illustrates our thesis with two examples, one involving powerful actors and the other marginalized groups, and both engaging a combination of bottom-up, top-down, and recursive processes. The first involves intellectual property law norms advanced by powerful countries and private actors. The second involves indigenous rights norms advanced by marginalized groups, including against powerful states and commercial interests.

I *Intellectual Property as a Transnational Legal Order*

Take first the example of intellectual property, which for a long time was a relatively sleepy, self-contained regime, including at the time Jessup wrote.

---

[9] TRANSNATIONAL LEGAL ORDERS, *supra* note 7, at 5, 18–21, 37–42; Koh, *supra* note 9, at 183–86.

[10] Shaffer, *supra* note 3, at 231 (providing a critical literature review of different modes of theorizing the transnational).

[11] TRANSNATIONAL LEGAL ORDERS, *supra* note 7, at 7–11. For an example, see Gregory Shaffer, Nathaniel H. Nesbitt & Spencer W. Waller, *Criminalizing Cartels: A Global Trend?, in* COMPARATIVE COMPETITION LAW 301–44 (John Duns, Arlen Duke & Brendan Sweeney eds., 2015) (noting the shift in the conceptualization of cartels as evil).

Under the 1889 Paris Convention for the Protection of Industrial Property, countries were given great discretion regarding the content of patent law as long as they applied it on a nondiscriminatory basis.[12] In the 1980s, however, a group of private entrepreneurs in the United States formed a national association and then a transnational network of private stakeholders to enroll the United States to press other countries to link intellectual property law to trade agreements.[13] The movement successfully prompted the US government to amend its national trade regulation (section 301 of the 1974 Trade Act) to authorize US unilateral sanctions against countries that did not protect US intellectual property rights. The United States then used this leverage to press countries to agree to common public international trade law rules to protect intellectual property, such as patents, in return for the United States not acting unilaterally as prosecutor, judge, and executioner of trade law. The movement successfully gave rise to the Agreement on Trade-Related Aspects of Intellectual Property Rights (TRIPS Agreement) of the World Trade Organization (WTO) in 1995. Encountering resistance at the level of implementation in many countries, the United States continues to press for new requirements and review mechanisms through bilateral and plurilateral agreements and mechanisms.

The TRIPS Agreement is transnational law, in Jessup's definition, in that it resolves a transnational problem – that of a conflict between US industrial and commercial interests and developing countries regarding the recognition of intellectual property and the payment of royalties. Yet the TRIPS Agreement is also transnational in a deeper sense as reflected in the socio-legal concepts of "transnational legal ordering" and "transnational legal orders." These concepts help unpack how the problem was framed (as a private property right implicating trade), by whom (by US and European private parties and their governments), and where the legal response derived (from norms developed in US and European law). And it shows the immense transnational implications of the change in international law – including the creation of new institutions to monitor enforcement at the multilateral level, giving rise to new transnational accountability mechanisms under a particular normative frame; the creation of new institutions within states to ensure compliance with TRIPS obligations (such as patent-examining agencies and administrative bodies and

---

[12] Laurence Helfer, *Pharmaceutical Patents and the Human Right to Health: The Contested Evolution of the Transnational Legal Order on Access to Medicines, in* TRANSNATIONAL LEGAL ORDERS, *supra* note 7, at 311; Gregory Shaffer & Susan K. Sell, *Transnational Legal Ordering and Access to Medicines, in* PATENT LAW IN GLOBAL PERSPECTIVE (Ruth L. Okediji & Margo A. Bagley eds., 2014), 97–126.
[13] JOHN BRAITHWAITE & PETER DRAHOS, GLOBAL BUSINESS REGULATION (2000), 203–04.

courts to hear and enforce patent claims); and the rise and empowerment of new professions of patent examiners and intellectual property lawyers who have a professional stake in the application of these legal norms. These developments, moreover, are dynamic, involving interactions with domestic institutions, professions, commercial interests, and social movements over time.

To give one example of domestic transformations, China did not recognize the concept of intellectual property until recent decades, yet today it has created and expanded intellectual property institutions and trained judges and administrators in these issues, and intellectual property is now an important part of curricula in its law schools. Between 1997 and 2011, patent filings in China increased 3,245 percent. China increased the number of patent examiners in its State Intellectual Property Office, from 2,700 patent examiners in 2007 to 6,000 in 2011.[14] By 2016, the numbers increased to over 9,000 patent inspectors in China,[15] who received 6,058,575 applications for recognition of Chinese patents (based on inventions), and who granted 1,464,115 patents.[16] China is now the largest issuer of patents in the world, surpassing the United States.[17] In 2017, it ranked second in terms of international patent applications and third in terms of international trademark registrations.[18]

At the judicial level, China created specialized intellectual property divisions within courts and, in 2014, specialist intellectual property courts in Beijing, Shanghai, and Guangzhou.[19] These courts have directly applied the TRIPS Agreement in dozens of private disputes.[20] In 2015 alone, these

---

[14] Shaffer, *supra* note 9, at 1. Regarding similar processes in India, *see* Gregory Shaffer, James Nedumpara & Aseema Sinha, *State Transformation and the Role of Lawyers: The WTO, India, and Transnational Legal Ordering*, 49 L. & Soc'y Rev. 595 (2015).

[15] St. Intell. Prop. Off. of the P.R.C. (中华人民共和国国家知识产权局), 2016 Annual Report (年度报告) 43 (2016), http://www.sipo.gov.cn/gk/ndbg/2016/201705/P020170505541250020396.pdf.

[16] *Distribution of Inventions Received from Home and Abroad*, St. Intell. Prop. Off. of the P.R.C. (2016), http://english.sipo.gov.cn/statistics/2016/12/201704/t20170407_1309327.html; *Distribution of Grants for Inventions Received from Home and Abroad*, St. Intell. Prop. Off. of the P.R.C. (2016), http://english.sipo.gov.cn/statistics/2016/12/201704/t20170407_1309323.html.

[17] WIPO, *Who Filed the Most PCT Patent Applications in 2017?* (2018), https://www.wipo.int/export/sites/www/ipstats/en/docs/infographic_pct_2017.pdf.

[18] WIPO, *Who Filed the Most Madrid Trademark Applications in 2017?* (2018), http://www.wipo.int/export/sites/www/ipstats/en/docs/infographic_madrid_2017.pdf; WIPO, *supra* note 18.

[19] Kristie Thomas, Assessing Intellectual Property Compliance in Contemporary China (2017), 143 (on specialized courts).

[20] Congyan Cai, *International Law in Chinese Courts During the Rise of China*, 110 Am. J. Int'l L. 269, 286–87 (2016).

specialist courts concluded 9,872 cases.[21] In 2018, China decided to establish a specialized intellectual property court of appeal at the national level in order to foster uniform jurisprudence in intellectual property law.[22] Housed in the Supreme People's Court and headed by its vice president, the new court will hear all appeals against patent-related decisions from lower courts from January 1, 2019.[23] In three years, it is expected that appeals on other intellectual property cases, such as copyright and trade secrets, also will be made to the new court.[24] Paradoxically, China "has emerged as the world's most litigious country in the intellectual property area," with 16,010 new patent cases, 37,946 new trademark cases, and 137,267 new copyright cases reportedly filed in 2017.[25] These developments are remarkable and involve much more than "transnational problem-solving."

These developments in China are not simply foreign "transplants." From a top-down vantage, the government created its own domestic "indigenous innovation" policies, to the consternation of the United States and Europe.[26] From a bottom-up perspective, Chinese individuals invested in new professional careers focused on intellectual property, and Chinese companies hired and worked with them. In parallel, domestic constituencies that embraced intellectual property protection and became rights holders engaged in information campaigns and enforcement actions.[27] They worked to shape public awareness and attitudes toward intellectual property, including among new generations of Chinese. In addition, as the Chinese became wealthier, consumers became more interested in consumer protection, such as against trademark fraud.

---

[21] Thomas, *supra* note 20, at 144.
[22] *The Supreme People's Court Issued the 'Regulations on Certain Issues of the Intellectual Property Tribunal*, Sup. People's Ct., Dec. 28, 2018, http://www.court.gov.cn/zixun-xiangqing-137461.html.
[23] *The Supreme Law Intellectual Property Court Unveiled the Relevant Cases in Accordance with the Law*, Tencent, Jan. 1, 2019, https://new.qq.com/omn/20190101/20190101A0FHFB.html.
[24] Guo Liqin, *SPC Establishes IP Court, Paving the Road for a Uniform National Appeal Court*, Yicai, Oct. 23, 2018, https://www.yicai.com/news/100045081.html.
[25] Supreme People's Court of the People's Republic of China, *The Status of Judicial Protection of Intellectual Property Rights in Chinese Courts* 2 (2017–2018), https://chinaipr2.files.wordpress.com/2018/06/2017e799bde79aaee4b9a6–2018041.docx; Peter Yu, *Building Intellectual Property Infrastructure Along China's Belt and Road*, 14 U. Pa. Asian L. Rev. 8 (forthcoming 2019).
[26] Office of the U.S. Trade Rep., Findings of the Investigation into China's Acts, Policies, and Practices Related to Technology Transfer, Intellectual Property, and Innovation Under Section 301 of the Trade Act of 1974, at 16 (Mar. 22, 2018), https://ustr.gov/sites/default/files/Section%20301%20FINAL.PDF.
[27] Thomas, *supra* note 20, at 139.

In other words, new public international law supported the dynamic development of a *transnational legal order* for the governance of intellectual property that shaped state institutions and professions, which, in turn, interacted with new constituent demands.[28] Once one turns from the concept of transnational law (and the more formalist connotation that concept conveys) to those of transnational legal ordering and transnational legal order, one shifts one's focus to the deeper processes through which legal norms are constructed, framed, propagated, resisted, adapted, settled, and unsettled.

II *Indigenous Rights as an Emerging Transnational Legal Order*

The indigenous rights movement provides an example of how traditionally marginalized groups within states also have been able to harness public international law to develop and transform legal norms and accountability mechanisms within states. We illustrate these processes in a small developing country in Central America (Belize) and a highly industrialized country in East Asia (Japan). In these cases, indigenous groups (the Maya and Ainu respectively) have been able to use evolving public international law to advance their aims through transnational processes.

1 The Maya in Belize

In 2007, the UN General Assembly adopted the UN Declaration on the Rights of Indigenous People (UNDRIP).[29] UNDRIP, in combination with regional instruments and regional and international organizations, played a major role in catalyzing the Belizean state's recognition of the communal property rights of the Maya of Southern Belize. The Maya of Southern Belize, namely the Ke'kchi and Mopan Maya, have been practicing traditional land use and occupation since precolonial times, giving rise to claims of customary land rights. The Belizean government, however, refused to recognize these claims and began granting logging concessions and oil-exploration licenses in the mid-1990s.[30]

---

[28] Helfer, *supra* note 13, at 322–24; Shaffer & Sell, *supra* note 13, at 103–15.
[29] G.A. Res. 61/295, U.N. Doc. A/RES/61/295, Declaration on the Rights of Indigenous Peoples (Sept. 13, 2007), 46 I.L.M. 1013 (2007).
[30] Aurelio Cal et al. v. Att'y Gen. of Belize, Supreme Court of Belize (Claims Nos. 171 & 172) (Oct. 18, 2007), ¶ 18, http://www.belizejudiciary.org/web/supreme_court/judgements/2007/Claims%20Nos.%20171%20and%20172%20of%202007%20%28Consolidated%29%20re%20Maya%20land%20rights.pdf.

In the 2000s, the Maya found allies for the recognition of their land rights in regional institutions and Belizean courts by making claims under international law. Because of the initial judicial inertia in Belize, and with the hope that an international body's finding in their favor would jump-start domestic courts handling their claims, leaders of the Maya rights movement petitioned the Inter-American Commission on Human Rights of the Organization of American States (OAS) in August 1998.[31] They requested that the commission find that Belize was violating the human rights of the Maya under the 1948 American Declaration of the Rights and Duties of Man and make recommendations to resolve and prevent any future violations.[32] The Inter-American Commission investigated and issued a merits report, delivered in October 2004, finding that the government of Belize had violated the Maya's communal property rights under article XXIII of the American Declaration. It maintained that "the right of property has an autonomous meaning in international human rights law," which include "indigenous communal property ... grounded in indigenous custom and tradition."[33] It also found that the Mopan and Ke'kechi Maya people had demonstrated communal property rights to the lands they inhabit in the Toledo district and Belize's government had violated these rights by failing to demarcate the Maya's lands and by granting, without first consulting the Maya, logging and oil concessions that could lie within these lands.[34] The report cited case law of the Inter-American Court of Human Rights, opinions of the UN Human Rights Committee, the UN Committee on the Elimination of Racial Discrimination, and the Inter-American Commission and provisions of international human rights law.

Unsatisfied with the government's response, the Maya continued litigation before the Belize Supreme Court. In 2007, Chief Justice Conteh of the Supreme Court recognized that the commission report was not binding but

[31] Christina Coc, Director & Co-founder, Julian Cho Society, Address at Native American Law Students Association at University of California, Irvine School of Law Symposium: Blood Quantum, Sovereignty, and Identity: Contemporary Legal Battles in Indigenous Communities (Mar. 24, 2017).
[32] Maya Indigenous Communities & Their Members v. Belize, Case 12.053, Admissibility Rep. No. 78/100, ¶ 6 (2000), http://cidh.org/annualrep/2000eng/ChapterIII/Admissible/Belize12.053.htm.
[33] Maya Indigenous Communities & Their Members v. Belize, Case 12.053, Merits Rep. No. 40/04, ¶ 117 (2004), http://cidh.org/annualrep/2004eng/Belize.12053eng.htm.
[34] Id. at ¶¶ 127, 153. The commission also found violations of article 2 of the American Declaration regarding equal protection of the law and article 28 regarding failure to provide judicial protection on account of undue delay. Id. at ¶¶ 171, 186, 192–96.

found it "persuasive" for his determinations[35] and "fortified" his conclusions.[36] In his decision, the chief justice dedicated an entire section to the Belizean government's obligations under international law, which the government had violated. He observed that Belize is a party to, and bound by, a series of international treaties that require the recognition and respect for indigenous peoples' property rights, including the International Covenant on Civil and Political Rights (ICCPR), the Convention on the Elimination of All Forms of Racial Discrimination (CERD), and the Charter of the OAS.[37] He cited determinations of UN human rights bodies on these issues, including the UN Committee on the Elimination of All Forms of Racial Discrimination, which found that nonrecognition of indigenous people's rights violates CERD's prohibition against discrimination.[38] He noted "that both customary international law and general principles of international law would require that Belize respect the rights of its indigenous people to their lands and resources," including as reflected in the 2007 UN General Assembly Declaration 61/295 on the Rights of Indigenous Peoples (UNDRIP).[39] He recognized that UNDRIP, as a General Assembly resolution, was nonbinding but concluded that, as it is contained general international law principles and had been adopted by over 143 states at the time, including Belize, it had special "resonance and relevance in the context of [the] case,"[40] and the Government of Belize could not disregard it.[41]

The Maya continued to press their legal claims before the Belize courts and the Caribbean Court of Justice (CCJ),[42] the final court of appeal in

---

[35] Aurelio Cal et al. v. Att'y Gen. of Belize, *supra* note 31, at ¶ 22.

[36] Id. at ¶ 100.

[37] *Id.* at ¶¶ 118–34. He wrote: "I conclude therefore, that the defendants are bound, in both domestic law in virtue of the Constitutional provisions that have been canvassed in this case, and international law, arising from Belize's obligation thereunder, to respect the rights to and interests of the claimants as members of the indigenous Maya community, to their lands and resources which are the subject of this case." *Id.* at ¶ 134.

[38] *Id.* at ¶ 123 (referencing General Recommendation XXIII: Rights of Indigenous Peoples, ¶ 5, U.N. Doc. A/52/18, annex V (Aug. 18, 1997); *id.* at ¶ 126 ("These considerations, engaging as they do Belize's international obligation towards indigenous peoples, therefore weighed heavily with me in this case in interpreting the fundamental human rights provisions of the Constitution agitated by the cluster of issues raised, particularly, the rights to property, life, security of the person, the protection of the law and the right not to be discriminated against.").

[39] *Id.* at ¶ 127.

[40] *Id.* at ¶ 131.

[41] *Id.* at ¶ 132 (where the CJ references article 26 of UNDRIP; according to article 26, "States shall give legal recognition and protection to these lands, territories and resources. Such recognition shall be conducted with due respect to the customs, traditions and land tenure systems of the indigenous peoples concerned").

[42] The CCJ is Belize's final court of appeal since 2010, when Belize amended its constitution to abolish appeals to the Judicial Committee of the Privy Council in London.

Belize, referencing international law. In 2014, in a claim challenging the Belize government's granting of a permit for road construction and oil drilling in a national park, the Belize Supreme Court enjoined the government from proceeding until it consulted and obtained the prior consent of the Maya in relation to their property claims. It held that "it is incumbent on the Government of Belize to put in place the legal mechanisms necessary to recognize and to give effect to those rights belonging to the Maya which have already been recognized by ... the International Commission of Human Rights" under the American Declaration.[43] It further held that "Belize, as a member state of the United Nations which voted in favor of the [UNDRIP] is clearly bound to uphold the general principles of international law contained therein" regarding consultation and prior informed consent.[44]

In 2015, just before the CCJ began hearing the final appeal, the Belize government entered a settlement in which it committed "to create an effective mechanism to identify and protect the property and other rights arising from Maya customary land tenure, in accordance with Maya customary laws and land tenure practices."[45] As a representative of the Maya people told us, it was the condemnation before international bodies and domestic courts that created the pressure on the government to settle before the CCJ decided. In her words:

> While the government looks down on us domestically, when we are in the international front, it is hard for them to ignore us. And so we have used the international mechanisms strategically .... We are using a tool that does not belong to us to prove to the rest of the world that we exist and deserve full protection of the laws for our lands.[46]

Because of the settlement agreement, the CCJ only decided whether the government violated the Maya's rights under the Belize Constitution and owed damages. In interpreting the Belize Constitution, the CCJ stressed that it was

---

[43] Sarstoon Temash Institute for Indigenous Management et al. v. Att'y Gen. of Belize, Supreme Court of Belize (Claim No. 394) (Apr. 3, 2013), ¶ 13, http://www.belizejudiciary.org/web/wp-content/uploads/2014/01/Supreme-Court-Claim-No-394-of-2013-Sarstoon-Temash-Institute-for-Indigenous-Management-et-al-v-The-Attorney-General-of-Belize-et-al-.pdf.

[44] *Id.*

[45] Maya Leaders Alliance et al. v. Att'y Gen. of Belize, Caribbean Court of Justice (Appeal No. BZCV2014/002) (Oct. 30, 2015), ¶¶ 9–10, http://www.caribbeancourtofjustice.org/wp-content/uploads/2015/10/2015-CCJ-15AJ.pdf.

[46] Coc, *supra* note 32.

aware of and accord[ed] great significance to relevant international law jurisprudence, particularly the 2004 Report of Inter-American Commission on Human Rights (the IACHR) which made findings on the application of Articles II and XXIII of the American Declaration on the Rights and Duties of Man (the American Declaration) to the claim by the Maya people to protection of their customary land rights (the *Maya Communities case*).[47]

It referenced rulings of the Inter-American Court of Human Rights, together with the Universal Declaration of Human Rights and the 2007 UNDRIP.[48] In the end, it found that the Belize Government had violated the Maya's constitutional rights and ordered the government "to establish a fund of BZ$300,000.00 as a first step toward compliance with its undertaking" in its 2015 settlement with the Maya.[49] International law, in other words, provided tools that helped shift the balance of power between the Belizean state and indigenous groups through its penetration into the Belizean legal system, backed by oversight by regional and international institutions to which Belize is accountable.

Implementation was contested. After the CCJ's decision, the Belizean government delayed, for several years, taking meaningful steps to pass legislation to effectuate the terms of the parties' consent decree.[50] The Belizean government continued to issue logging and oil-exploration permits without first consulting with or receiving consent from the Maya. As a result, the Maya returned to the CCJ for further help in compelling the Belizean government to implement the consent decree and a dispute resolution framework.[51] Because of the Belizean government's foot-dragging in developing the legislative and administrative structure to demarcate, recognize, and protect Maya land rights, the Maya continue to utilize procedures before international bodies to pressure the Belizean government to adhere to its domestic,

---

[47] Maya Leaders Alliance et al. v. Att'y Gen. of Belize, *supra* note 46, at ¶ 8.
[48] *Id.* at ¶¶ 54, 59.
[49] *Id.* at ¶ 79.
[50] *Belize: Hearing at International Courts Demonstrates Belize's Noncompliance in Landmark Maya Land Rights Case*, CULTURAL SURVIVAL (Oct. 26, 2017), https://www.culturalsurvival.org/news/belize-hearing-international-courts-demonstrates-belizes-noncompliance-landmark-maya-land.
[51] Glenn Tillett, *Caribbean Court Justice "Exasperated" with GOB's Delay in Implementing Maya Court Order*, AMANDALA (Feb. 24, 2018), http://amandala.com.bz/news/caribbean-court-justice-exasperated-gobs-delay-implementing-maya-court-order/; Micah Goodin, *CCJ Orders Barrow Administration to Get Serious About Respecting Maya Rights*; AMANDALA (Nov. 1, 2017), http://amandala.com.bz/news/ccj-orders-barrow-administration-respecting-maya-rights/.

regional, and international legal obligations.[52] In light of the Maya's persistence before the CCJ and international bodies, the parties are making progress in realizing the terms of the consent decree and the CCJ's decisions.[53]

2 The Ainu in Japan

Indigenous communities have mobilized throughout the world, including in countries that were not subject to colonial occupation and thus did not view themselves as constrained by indigenous rights law. For example, the Japanese government long viewed itself as a homogenous society and refused to recognize the existence of the Ainu, an indigenous group on the island of Hokkaido, as a minority group, much less as one protected by indigenous rights. Indeed, so powerful were the government's assimilationist policies that the Ainu dropped the word *Ainu* from their association's name in 1961 because of the word's derogatory implications at the time.[54]

In 1979, the Japanese government ratified both the ICCPR and the International Covenant on Economic, Social, and Cultural Rights (ICESCR), which required the Japanese government to report to these treaties' respective monitoring bodies.[55] The government also served on UN human rights committees, which placed it under more scrutiny from international human rights groups and bodies.[56] In 1980, when the government was required to submit its first mandatory report to the Human Rights Committee regarding minority rights protected under ICCPR article 27, it brazenly claimed that "minorities of the kind mentioned in the Covenant do not exist in Japan."[57] In the meantime, the Ainu had visited and formed linkages with indigenous groups in North America and Scandinavia. These encounters helped catalyze and invigorate a greater sense of pride in their indigenous identity.[58] Japan's

---

[52] *Maya Leaders Alliance Advocates at United Nations Urging Respect for Rule of Law Belize*, CULTURAL SURVIVAL (May 8, 2018), https://www.culturalsurvival.org/news/maya-leaders-alliance-advocates-united-nations-urging-respect-rule-law-belize.

[53] *Progress in Maya Land Tenure Policy*, CHANNEL 5 (Mar. 15, 2019), http://edition.channel5belize.com/archives/182042.

[54] Kiyoteru Tsutsui, *Human Rights and Minority Activism in Japan: Transformation of Movement Actorhood and Local-Global Feedback Loop*, 122 AM. J. SOCIOLOGY 1050 (2017); KIYOTERU TSUTSUI, RIGHTS MAKE MIGHT: GLOBAL HUMAN RIGHTS AND MINORITY SOCIAL MOVEMENTS IN JAPAN (2018).

[55] TSUTSUI, *supra* note 55, at 1059.

[56] Id. at 1063.

[57] *Id.* at 1066.

[58] In his detailed empirical study, Kiyoteru Tsutsui concludes, "[i]f not for Ainu's encounter with international indigenous rights activities, it is highly unlikely that *movement initiation* would have happened for Ainu, especially as an indigenous rights movement." *Id.* at 1070.

claim prompted the Ainu to organize a response. In 1986, with the assistance of an international nongovernmental organization, the Ainu initiated a procedure before the new UN Human Rights Committee to report Japan's violations of the group's rights.[59]

International human rights law helped transform the Ainu movement's sense of "actor-hood" and empowered and opened new opportunities for it.[60] In 1987, the Japanese government first acknowledged the Ainu as a distinct group.[61] In 1992, it acknowledged that Ainu "may be called minorities under (Article 27)" of the ICCPR in its third report to the Human Rights Committee. In 1997, Japan enacted an Ainu Cultural Promotion Law.[62] By 2008, the year after UNDRIP's adoption, fearful of embarrassment at Japan's universal periodic review before the UN Human Rights Council and from potential protests at the Hokkaido G-8 summit, the Japanese Diet passed a unanimous resolution that acknowledged the Ainu as an indigenous group.[63] A year later, the Hokkaido Utari Association changed its named back to the Hokkaido Ainu Association out of a sense of pride and strengthened identity.[64] The Ainu's engagement, in turn, reciprocally helped consolidate indigenous rights norms and diffuse them for use by other indigenous groups in Asia.[65]

Human rights activists and attorneys often use international institutions such as the Inter-American Commission on Human Rights, the UN Human Rights Council, and the UN Human Rights Committee as leverage to bring countries to the table, including when they formally lose their human rights law claims in domestic courts. These bodies can be fruitful in effecting change and in obtaining favorable settlements for their clients.[66] As these case

---

[59] *Id.* at 1066–67.

[60] *Id.* at 1066–69.

[61] *Id.* at 1067.

[62] *Id.* at 1068.

[63] *Id.*

[64] *Id.* at 1069.

[65] *Id.* at 1083.

[66] James L. Cavallaro, *Toward Fair Play: A Decade of Transformation and Resistance in International Human Rights Advocacy in Brazil*, 3 CHINA J. INT'L L. 481, 486–87 (2002) ("After eight years of litigation in which the Brazilian state consistently and repeatedly missed deadlines and failed to engage the system seriously, the Commission prepared a final report condemning the state of Brazil for violations of the American Declaration and the American Convention on Human Rights. Shortly before that report was in its final phase of consideration for publication, the Brazilian government expressed its interest in reaching a friendly solution."); James L. Cavallaro & Stephanie Erin Brewer, *Reevaluating Regional Human Rights Litigation in the Twenty-First Century: The Case of the Inter-American Court*, 102 AM. J. INT'L L. 768, 787–88, 793 (2008); James L. Cavallaro & Emily J. Schaffer, *Less as More: Rethinking Supranational Litigation of Economic and Social Rights in the Americas*, 56 HASTINGS L.J. 217, 238–39 (2004)("In varying degrees, states in the Americas (and in the rest of

studies illustrate, by turning our conceptual focus to that of transnational legal
ordering and transnational legal orders, we see how norms penetrate and
shape law, legal practice, and social identity within states. International law,
in sum, is not simply a technology that exists to solve discrete transnational
problems; it shapes state law, institutions, professions, and social identity. It
does so dynamically and recursively, often in response to considerable
resistance.[67]

C PUBLIC INTERNATIONAL LAW'S BROADER SCOPE AND DEEPER IMPACT COMPARED TO JESSUP'S TIME

We started with concrete examples in two discrete subject areas of the broader
and deeper implications of public international law today for law, institutions,
professions, social identity, and accountability within states. Quantitative data
illustrate the broader implications of public international law across most areas
of social life since Jessup's time. International law has expanded far beyond
interstate relations as then understood.[68] It is now a key component in
transnational legal ordering and the creation of transnational legal orders.

In recent years, with the relative decline of US and European economic
power, the rise of emerging economies, and the turn to security concerns
since the destruction of the World Trade Center in New York on September
11, 2001, some have posited a stagnation and decline of traditional modes of
public international law. For example, in a 2014 article, Pauwelyn, Wessel,
and Wouters argue that "formal international law is stagnating in terms both of
quantity and quality."[69] They point to the decline in the number of new

the world) legitimate themselves through their insertion in international organizations,
structures and discourse. This internal legitimization process can empower actors – whether
social movements, NGOs, or lawyers – to the extent they are able to tap into the strength of
international networks and intergovernmental oversight bodies. ... [T]he force of oversight
bodies goes far beyond their legal powers, which are rarely, if ever, what matters most within
the country whose abuses are subject to adjudication. It is the fact of international rebuke or
condemnation that is of greatest import to those seeking to challenge state abuses within a
given country.").

[67] Gregory Shaffer, *Transnational Recursivity Theory: A Review Essay of Halliday & Carruthers'
Bankrupt*, 9 Socioeconomic Rev. 371 (2011); Halliday & Shaffer, *Researching Transnational
Legal Orders*, *supra* note 7, 500–03, 513–16. *See infra* part E.
[68] Jessup, *supra* note 1, at 1 (preferring the term transnational law because "the term
'international' is misleading since it suggests that one is concerned only with the relations of
one nation (or state) to other nations (or states)").
[69] Joost Pauwelyn, Ramses A. Wessel & Jan Wouters, *When Structures Become Shackles:
Stagnation and Dynamics in International Lawmaking*, 25 Eur. J. Int'l L. 733, 733–34 (2014).
In 2014, *AJIL Unbound* likewise organized a special agora on "The End of Treaties?"

multilateral treaties deposited with the UN secretary-general from an average of thirty-five treaties per decade between 1950 and 2000 to twenty from 2000 to 2010.[70] They cite parallel decreases in bilateral treaties, which dropped from 12,566 in the 1990s to 9,484 in the 2000s, treaties transmitted to the US Senate, and international agreements reported to the US Congress.[71] Overall, they highlight a turn toward informal lawmaking through nonbinding soft law.

These numbers, however, reflect neither a decline of public international law nor in the ongoing role of treaties and (more broadly) other forms of international agreements. First, the number of new treaties is still significant. Second, the aggregate number of treaties continues to grow. The comparison with the number of treaties in Jessup's time is striking. In 1959, there were 7,779 treaties on deposit with the UN secretary-general, with 105 of them being multilateral treaties.[72] As of 2014, around 56,500 treaties were on deposit with the UN secretary-general,[73] with over 560 being multilateral treaties.[74] Third, Pauwelyn et al. did not include amendments, protocols, and annexes to treaties in their calculations.[75]

Decline in the annual growth rate of new treaties also does not capture trends in state ratification of treaties across issue areas. In trade law, the original membership of General Agreement on Tariffs and Trade (GATT) was 23 countries when it was created in 1948; by the end of 2018, the WTO had 164 members.[76] In parallel, plurilateral and bilateral trade agreements proliferated. In 1956, there were only two preferential trade agreements notified to the GATT,[77] but by 2016, 419 were in force, and 625 had been notified.[78]

Humberto Cantú-Rivera, *The Expansion of International Law beyond Treaties*, AM. J. INT'L L. UNBOUND (May 9, 2014), https://www.asil.org/blogs/expansion-international-law-beyond-treaties-agora-end-treaties.

[70] Pauwelyn, Wessel & Wouters, *supra* note 70, at 734.
[71] *Id.* at 735.
[72] Adolf Sprudzs, *Status of Multilateral Treaties – Researcher's Mystery, Mess or Muddle?*, 66 AM. J. INT'L L. 365, 365 (1962) (noting that these are just treaties on deposit at the UN).
[73] Christian J. Tams, Antonios Tzanakopoulos & Andreas Zimmermann, *Introduction* to RESEARCH HANDBOOK ON THE LAW OF TREATIES x (Christian J. Tams, Antonios Tzanakopoulos & Andreas Zimmerman with Athene E. Richford eds., 2014).
[74] *Overview*, UNITED NATIONS TREATY COLLECTION, https://treaties.un.org/Pages/Overview.aspx?path=overview/overview/page1_en.xml (last visited Apr. 2, 2019).
[75] Pauwelyn, Wessel & Wouters, *supra* note 70, at 734.
[76] *Understanding the WTO: The Organization*, WORLD TRADE ORGANIZATION, https://www.wto.org/english/thewto_e/whatis_e/tif_e/org6_e.htm (last visited Apr. 2, 2019).
[77] WTO, WTO ANALYTICAL INDEX 88 (2012).
[78] *Regional Trade Agreements*, WORLD TRADE ORGANIZATION, https://www.wto.org/english/tratop_e/region_e/region_e.htm (last visited Apr. 2, 2019).

For commercial arbitration, the UN Convention on the Recognition and Enforcement of Foreign Arbitral Awards had only 25 parties on December 31, 1958, the year it went into effect, but 153 countries are parties today.[79] Ratification of the six core human rights treaties likewise increased significantly, rising by over 50 percent, from 927 ratifications in 2000 to 1,586 ratifications by 2012. That number increases by about another 50 percent, to approximately 2,000 ratifications if one includes the treaties' optional protocols.[80]

Likewise, there were no bilateral investment treaties (BITs) signed at the time of Jessup's lecture in 1956, as the first was signed between the Federal Republic of Germany and Pakistan in 1959.[81] Since then, the number soared to almost 2,500 by the end of 2005[82] and then rose more slowly (as the number of remaining pairings decreased) to 2,860 BITs by mid-2013.[83] Overall, the international investment regime consists of more than 3,300 agreements, which includes over 2,900 BITs and over 350 other treaties with such investment provisions. Litigation has soared under them: in 1987, there was no recorded litigation under bilateral investment treaties, but by 2018 the number had climbed to over 900, rising rapidly.[84]

Ratifications of these treaties are not about ad hoc problem-solving; rather, the aim is to reach deep within state law, institutions, and practices. Take human rights treaties, which are the subject of considerable empirical research. Elkins, Ginsburg, and Simmons show their impact on national

---

[79] Paolo Contini, *International Commercial Arbitration: The United Nations Convention on the Recognition and Enforcement of Foreign Arbitral Awards*, 8 Am. J. Comp. L. 283, 291 (1959); *Status of Treaties: Chapter XXII: Commercial Arbitration*, United Nations Treaty Collection, https://treaties.un.org/pages/ViewDetails.aspx?src=TREATY&mtdsg_no=XXII-1&chapter=22&lang=en (last visited Apr. 2, 2019).

[80] Navnethem Pillay, Strengthening the United Nations Human Rights Treaty Body System 17 (2012), http://www2.ohchr.org/english/bodies/HRTD/docs/HCReportTBStrengthening.pdf.

[81] U.N. Conference on Trade and Development, *Bilateral Investment Treaties 1995–2006: Trends in Investment Rulemaking* 1 (2007), http://unctad.org/en/docs/iteiia20065_en.pdf. During this time, there were some commercial treaties, such as the US signature of treaties of friendship, navigation, and commerce, but they were not of the same nature in terms of the depth and breadth of commitments and in terms of giving rights to private investors to directly bring claims against host states.

[82] Id.

[83] U.N. Conference on Trade and Development, *International Investment Policymaking in Transition: Challenges and Opportunities of Treaty Renewal* (Jan. 15, 2010), http://unctad.org/en/PublicationsLibrary/webdiaepcb2013d9_en.pdf.

[84] Since many cases are kept confidential, the number is higher in reality. For statistics, see the UNCTAD Investment Policy Hub at https://investmentpolicyhub.unctad.org/ISDS?status=1000.

constitutions. After the passage of the Universal Declaration of Human Rights (UDHR) and the ICCPR, the number of rights found in national constitutions almost doubled.[85] The inclusion of a right in the UDHR correlates with its inclusion in a national constitution by as much as 50 percent.[86] After a country ratified the ICCPR, the similarity of the rights included in the constitution to those in the ICCPR increased by almost ten points, controlling for other factors.[87] In terms of state practice, Simmons shows that for states in a period of democratic transition, human rights treaties have significant effects by shaping executive agendas, supporting activist groups litigating before domestic courts, and mobilizing domestic support.[88] As regards the European Convention of Human Rights, Madsen shows its significant impacts within Europe.[89] Litigation before the European Court of Human Rights, for example, transformed the unwritten constitution of the United Kingdom (UK).[90] The UK "domesticated" treaty responsibility by shifting authority for it from the Foreign Office to the Home Office. The treaty also catalyzed the development of a new profession in the UK, that of "specialized human rights lawyers," which has since spread to other European states.[91]

Environmental law shows similar trends. The modern period of major international environmental agreements began in 1972 with the Stockholm

---

[85] Zachery Elkins, Tom Ginsburg & Beth Simmons, *Getting to Rights: Treaty Ratification, Constitutional Convergence, and Human Rights Practice*, 54 HARV. INT'L L.J. 63, 76–80 (2013) (while "nine constitutions written in 1947 contain an average of 17.6 rights, . . . the six written in 1949 contain an average of 31 rights").

[86] *Id.* at 80.

[87] *Id.* at 87–88 (such as "controlling for the era and a country's prior constitutional tradition vis-à-vis the ICCPR").

[88] BETH A. SIMMONS, MOBILIZING FOR HUMAN RIGHTS: INTERNATIONAL LAW IN DOMESTIC POLITICS 112–55 (2009); Gregory Shaffer & Tom Ginsburg, *The Empirical Turn in International Legal Scholarship*, 106 AM. J. INT'L L. 1, 22–25 (2012).

[89] Mikael Madsen, *The Challenging Authority of the European Court of Human Rights: From Cold War Legal Diplomacy to the Brighton Declaration and Backlash*, 79 LAW & CONTEMP. PROBS. 141, 166–67 (2016) ("Institutionally, the ECtHR became a de facto constitutional court for most member states because the Convention – although in most dualist countries only having the status of statutory law – effectively governed human rights at a transnational constitutional level.").

[90] Alec Stone Sweet, *A Cosmopolitan Legal Order: Constitutional Pluralism and Rights Adjudication in Europe*, 1 GLOBAL CONSTITUTIONALISM 53, 71–72 (2012) ("Under the UK Human Rights Act (2000), individuals may challenge all acts, including Parliamentary legislation; if a Parliamentary statute is found to be incompatible with the ECHR, the high courts are obligated to issue a ruling of incompatibility – but they may not set aside the offending legislative provisions. Declarations of incompatibility are addressed to the Parliament, which must indicate what remedial legislation, if any, will be proposed.").

[91] Madsen, *supra* note 90, at 157.

Conference on the Human Environment.[92] Since then, the growth of international environmental law instruments increased steadily, with the
number of multilateral environmental agreements more than doubling over
the twenty years leading up to the 1992 UN Conference on Environment
and Development in Rio de Janeiro.[93] As of July 2013, the International
Environmental Agreements Database Project reports over 1,190 multilateral
environmental agreements, 1,550 bilateral environmental agreements, and
250 other environmental agreements on deposit at the UN,[94] including nine
new multilateral environmental agreements since 2012.[95] In contrast, no
multilateral environmental agreements were in force at the time of Jessup's
lectures.[96]

In addition, a decrease in the rate of new treaties does not indicate a decline
in treaties' role. The number of new amendments to the US Constitution is
nonexistent, yet no one would suggest the end of US constitutional law.
Analogously, international courts and analogous bodies have proliferated,
and they interpret and apply treaties to new contexts. According to Alter, if
we exclude the GATT's noncompulsory dispute system, only two operative
permanent international courts existed in 1956 – the International Court of
Justice (ICJ) and the European Court of Justice (ECJ).[97] By 1956, these two
courts together had issued only twenty-two binding judgments.[98] In 1989, at
the tail end of the Cold War, the number of permanent international courts
had increased to six.[99] Alter reports that by 2013 there were at least twenty-four
permanent international courts that had collectively issued 37,000 binding

[92] Daniel Bodansky, Jutta Brunnée & Ellen Hey, *International Environmental Law: Mapping the Field*, in The Oxford Handbook of International Environmental Law (Daniel Bodansky, Jutta Brunnée & Ellen Hey eds., 2007), 1, 3.
[93] Peter H. Sand, *Evolution of International Environmental Law*, in The Oxford Handbook of International Environmental Law, *supra* note 93, at 29, 35.
[94] *Data from Ronald B. Mitchell.* 2002–2016, International Environmental Agreements (IEA) Database Projects, http://iea.uoregon.edu/page.php?file=home.htm&query=static (last visited Apr. 2, 2019) (note that they started recording MEAs from 1950).
[95] *Id.*
[96] *Relationship Between WTO and MEA Rules*, World Trade Organization, https://www.wto.org/english/tratop_e/envir_e/envir_neg_mea_e.htm (last visited Apr. 2, 2019).
[97] Karen J. Alter, *The Evolving International Judiciary*, 7 Ann. Rev. L. & Soc. Sci. 387, 388 (2011); E-mail from Karen J. Alter, Professor, Department of Policy Science, Northwestern University, to Gregory Shaffer, Chancellor's Professor of Law, UC Irvine School of Law (Aug. 18, 2016) (on file with author).
[98] *Id.* The ICJ issued ten, and the ECJ issued twelve. Even if we include the GATT's sixteen decisions by 1956, these three adjudicatory bodies collectively only issued thirty-eight binding judgments by the time of Jessup's lectures.
[99] Alter, *supra* note 98, at 388.

legal judgments.[100] And over 100 other international bodies interpret international rules, complementing these courts.[101] In sum, amendments, protocols, and annexes, coupled with treaty interpretation and application, show that international treaties continue to be used to respond to an expanding scope of contexts.

The work of Pauwelyn and others, moreover, posits not a move away from international public lawmaking but rather a move to soft law and informal means of advancing transnational legal ordering. The institutional architecture for international lawmaking has broadened and deepened, giving rise to secondary lawmaking and in particular involving soft law and informal modes of reporting and peer review to oversee implementation of these norms.[102] These developments have enhanced the scope and depth of international law across almost all areas of social life. In 1956, the year of Jessup's lectures, the Union of International Associations' *Yearbook of International Organizations* reported there were 132 intergovernmental organizations (IGOs) and 985 international nongovernmental organizations (INGOs).[103] By 2018, the numbers had skyrocketed to at least 7,726 IGOs and 62,621 INGOs.[104] Even more importantly, early IGOs were much more constrained in their power and area of coverage.[105] IGOs now play a much more significant role in establishing norms, procedures, peer review mechanisms, dispute settlement, and other forms of intergovernmental interaction, coordinating resources and expertise.[106]

---

[100] Karen J. Alter, The New Terrain of International Law: Courts, Politics, Rights 4 (2014).

[101] Alter, *supra* note 98, at 388.

[102] Gregory Shaffer & Mark Pollack, *Hard and Soft Law: What Have We Learned?*, in International Law and International Relations: Insights from Interdisciplinary Scholarship (Jeffrey L. Dunoff & Mark A. Pollack eds., 2012).

[103] UIA Yearbook of International Organizations 2015–2016, Union of International Associations, http://www.uia.org/allpubs?combine=&field_pub_year_value=&items_per_page=20&page=8&order=field_uia_publication_nr_&sort=asc (last visited Apr. 2, 2019).

[104] UIA Yearbook of International Organizations 2018–2019, Union of International Associations, https://uia.org/sites/uia.org/files/misc_pdfs/pubs/yb_2018_vol2_lookinside.pdf (last visited Apr. 2, 2019) (reports data collected in 2017). The Union of International Associations' Yearbook defines an intergovernmental organization as one "composed primarily of sovereign states, or of other intergovernmental organizations." The yearbook counts self-identified IGOs as IGOs. *Id.* at § 1.3.

[105] Esref Ertürk, *Intergovernmental Organizations (IGOs) and Their Roles and Activities in Security, Economy, Health, and Environment*, 8 J. Int'l Soc. Research 333, 334 (2015) (as an example of an early IGO, the Central Commission for the Navigation of the Rhine was established in 1815).

[106] Jose E. Alvarez, International Organizations as Law-Makers (2005), 589–619.

The development of international institutions has empowered INGOs, who are their frequent interlocutors and partners. IGOs grant INGOs "observer or consultative status, access to documents, and even on occasion, other forms of institutional voice such as the power to distribute compromise legal texts during a treaty negotiation or to file amicus briefs in institutionalized dispute settlement forums."[107] INGOs, in turn, reciprocally help intergovernmental organizations by diffusing international hard and soft law norms through INGO networks within states, helping bring the norms home. They serve as intermediary norm conveyors.

These international organizations have been active in creating soft law, which aims to shape national law and practice. Such soft law affects governance of areas traditionally seen as strictly domestic, such as "financial regulation, consumer protection, and law enforcement."[108] Accurately measuring the amount of soft law is impossible, but there is general consensus that it has been on the rise for some time, with some arguing that it has become more important than hard law.[109] The proliferation of transnational legal orders comes not just from formal public international (hard) law but arguably even more from the explosion of soft law and the increased scope that soft law instruments and mechanisms provide for creating, expanding, and deepening transnational legal orders.

To view how a soft law process works, take the example of bankruptcy law. The UN Commission on International Trade Law (UNCITRAL) has created principles and model codes for bankruptcy law for all UN members. Those who participate most actively in the UNCITRAL process are only a handful of members, such as the US and European Union (EU), complemented by professional associations, such as INSOL International (a global federation of national associations of insolvency accountants and lawyers) and specialized sections of the International Bar Association and the American Bar Association.[110] These actors help define the problems that need to be addressed and set the legal norms to resolve them. Some of the problems are of a

---

[107] Jose E. Alvarez, *Governing the World: International Organizations as Lawmakers*, 31 SUFFOLK TRANSNAT'L L. REV. 591, 597 (2008).

[108] Jean Galbraith & David T. Zaring, *Soft Law as Foreign Relations Law*, 99 CORNELL L. REV. 735, 747 (2014).

[109] Pauwelyn, Wessel & Wouters, *supra* note 70, at 738–44; Timothy Meyer, *Collective Decision-Making in International Governance*, AM. J. INT'L L. UNBOUND (Apr. 28, 2014), https://www.asil.org/blogs/collective-decision-making-international-governance-agora-end-treaties.

[110] Terence C. Halliday & Bruce G. Carruthers, *The Recursivity of Law: Global Norm-Making and National Law-Making in the Globalization of Corporate Insolvency Regimes*, 112 AM. J. SOCIOLOGY 1135 (2007).

"transnational nature," as contemplated by Jessup, in that some bankruptcies are multijurisdictional. Some of the impetus is also "transnational" because of broader concerns regarding economic spillovers if financial crises are not contained through improved national bankruptcy law. In all cases, however, the intended impact is much deeper than resolving discrete transnational problems, as with private law. Rather, the impact is to reach deep within the institutional architecture of the state, affecting the power of different state institutions, including executives, legislatures, courts, independent agencies, and professions regarding corporate bankruptcy law.[111]

D THE INTERACTION OF PUBLIC INTERNATIONAL LAW WITH PRIVATE INTERNATIONAL LAW AND OTHER RULES IN TRANSNATIONAL LEGAL ORDERING

The concepts of transnational legal ordering and transnational legal orders do not examine public international law in isolation from Jessup's other two components of transnational law: private international law and "other rules." Public international law interacts with them as part of broader processes of transnational legal ordering, giving rise to the settlement and unsettlement of legal norms in transnational legal orders defined by functional as opposed to territorial logics.[112] These transnational legal orders may be constituted by a mix of public international law, private international law, and private ordering. Some transnational legal orders rest on configurations that rely more on public international law and others less so. Empirical research is needed to assess variations and their relative importance for the institutionalization of legal norms in response to different types of social problems.

At times, public international law and institutions operate as orchestrators by delegating authority to and monitoring private legal ordering initiatives. Abbott, Snidal, and their collaborators trace such orchestration processes in the fields of international health, environmental, finance, telecommunications, and labor law.[113] Reciprocally, private actors orchestrate public international law and institutions, as exemplified by the role of private actors behind the adoption of the TRIPS Agreement,[114] in drafting legal texts such

---

[111] Terence C. Halliday, *Architects of the State: International Organizations and the Reconstruction of States in East Asia, in* Transnational Legal Ordering and State Change, *supra* note 6, at 89, 89–120.

[112] Poul Kjaer, Constitutionalism in the Global Realm: A Sociological Approach (2014).

[113] Kenneth W. Abbott, Philipp Genschel, Duncan Snidal & Bernhard Zangl, International Organizations as Orchestrators (2015).

[114] Braithwaite & Drahos, *supra* note 14, at 87.

as for bankruptcy law,[115] and in driving interpretation through directly bringing claims, such as under indigenous rights law and investment-state dispute settlement or doing the legal work for states to bring claims such as in trade law.[116] Public and private actors endorse and borrow from one another's texts to advance their goals. The WTO Agreement on Technical Barriers to Trade, for example, incorporates the standards of the International Organization for Standardization; international investment tribunals reference the International Bar Association's guidelines for conflicts of interest and rules for taking evidence;[117] and the International Tropical Timber Organization has endorsed the Forest Stewardship Council's standards.[118] Reciprocally, GLOBALG.A.P., a private organization that certifies agricultural products, incorporates the Hazard Analysis and Critical Control Points guidelines published by the UN Food and Agricultural Organization.[119]

Public international law also interacts with private international law. It authorizes the privatization of dispute settlement through arbitration that displaces national courts. The 1958 Convention on the Recognition and Enforcement of Arbitral Awards recognizes, facilitates, and legitimizes these privatized processes.[120] International treaties also govern some choice of law norms, whether regionally (in Europe and to a lesser extent Latin America) or functionally (in family law, with some developments in commercial law).[121] Public international law, private international law, and private legal ordering are not simply alternative forms of transnational legal ordering. They shape, complement, and support each other.

---

[115] Halliday & Carruthers, *supra* note 111, 1148–55.
[116] GREGORY SHAFFER, DEFENDING INTERESTS: PUBLIC-PRIVATE PARTNERSHIPS IN WTO LITIGATION (2003) (on the private interests behind WTO claims); Sergio Puig, *Tobacco Litigation in International Courts*, 57 HARV. INT'L L.J. 383 (2016); Gregory Shaffer, *How Business Shapes Law: A Socio-legal Framework*, 42 CONN. L. REV. 149 (2009).
[117] *See* Pauwelyn, Wessel & Wouters, *supra* note 70, at 761.
[118] Tim Bartley, *Institutional Emergence in an Era of Globalization: The Rise of Transnational Private Regulation of Labor and Environmental Conditions*, 113 AM. J. SOCIOLOGY 297 (2007).
[119] Errol Meidinger, *Private Import Safety Regulation and Transnational New Governance, in* IMPORT SAFETY: REGULATORY GOVERNANCE IN THE GLOBAL ECONOMY (Cary Coglianese, Adam M. Finkel & David Zaring eds., 2009), 233.
[120] Christopher A. Whytock, *Private-Public Interaction in Global Governance: The Case of Transnational Commercial Arbitration*, 12 BUS. & POL. 1 (2010); Gregory Shaffer & Terence Halliday, *with, within and beyond the State: The Promise and Limits of Transnational Legal Ordering, in* OXFORD HANDBOOK OF TRANSNATIONAL LAW (Peer Zumbansen ed., forthcoming 2019).
[121] Christopher A. Whytock, *Conflict of Laws, Global Governance, and Transnational Legal Order*, UCI J. INT'L, TRANSNAT'L & COMP. L. (forthcoming).

E RESISTANCE: THE RISE AND FALL OF TRANSNATIONAL
LEGAL ORDERING

Transnational legal orders are not inexorable. They settle and unsettle; they rise and fall. They often, if not typically, encounter strong resistance.[122] Such resistance arises because of transnational legal ordering's deep implications within states, especially when involving public law. Those marginalized from centers of power resist, as do powerful countries when they feel constrained. Resistance can come from any direction, locally, nationally, and transnationally, including through the engagement of other international organizations. Local actors may develop legal doctrines or extralegal strategies to foil transnational powers.[123] Nongovernmental groups may work to develop counternorms at the international level, as done in the struggle to ensure access to medicines to thwart internationally required patent protection through pressing for responses from the World Health Organization and UN human rights committees.[124]

Contests arise because of a transnational legal order's successes. Its institutionalization raises awareness that the stakes are high. The increased scope of public international law and its penetration into domestic legal systems can catalyze populist, nationalist responses, as illustrated in the United States and Europe, punctuated by the election of President Donald Trump in the United States, the vote in the UK to leave the EU, and the rise of nationalist/populist parties and leaders in a number of EU countries, such as Hungary and Poland.[125] Ironically, the United States and Europe were the architects of much of the transnational legal ordering that has catalyzed such popular resistance.

Within national legal systems, legislatures and courts have raised screens to the legal effects of public international law. Verdier and Versteeg code domestic legal system's reception of international law, and find "that while

---

[122] Halliday & Shaffer, *Researching Transnational Legal Orders, supra* note 7, 500–03.
[123] *Id.*
[124] Helfer, *Pharmaceutical Patents and the Human Right to Health*, 325–34; Shaffer & Sell, *supra* note 13, at 116–26.
[125] Gregor Aisch, Adam Pearce, & Bryant Rosseau, *How Far Is Europe Swinging to the Right?*, N.Y. TIMES (Mar. 20, 2017), https://www.nytimes.com/interactive/2016/05/22/world/europe/europe-right-wing-austria-hungary.html; JAMES KIRCHICK, THE END OF EUROPE: DICTATORS, DEMAGOGUES, AND THE COMING DARK AGE 5 (2017) ("authoritarian populist parties (of both the left and right) hold almost 20 percent of the seats in European national parliaments, nearly twice as many as they did thirty years ago, and they sit in a third of Europe's governments") (citing Andreas Johansson Heinö, *Timbro Authoritarian Populism Index 2016*, TIMBRO, June 29, 2016, https://timbro.se/allmant/timbro-authoritarian-populism-index-2016/).

domestic rules generally give the national executive the leading role in
negotiating and concluding treaties, this power is increasingly constrained
by legislative approval requirements, constitutional review of treaties, and
other procedures that allocate authority – and sometimes veto power – to
legislatures, courts and other domestic actors."[126] In the United States, the
Supreme Court has created a presumption that international treaties do not
create rights of action before domestic courts and tightened doctrine regarding
the direct effect of treaties in US law without congressional implementation.[127] The Court has signaled that constitutional allocations of power to
subfederal states could also limit US domestic application of treaties,[128] and
appellate court judges have signaled a narrowing of existing doctrine that takes
account of treaties in interpreting domestic statutes.[129] Within Europe,
national supreme courts have become more resistant to accepting judgments
of the ECJ and the European Court of Human Rights.[130] In December 2016,

[126] Verdier & Versteeg *Modes of Domestic Incorporation of International Law, supra* note 8, at 150
(coding the systems of one hundred one national judicial systems regarding "how treaties and
custom are received and interpreted, and their status vis-à-vis other sources of domestic law");
Pierre-Hugues Verdier & Mila Versteeg, *International Law in National Legal Systems: An
Empirical Investigation*, 109 Am. Jo. Int'l L. 514, 522 (2015) (pointing out that "the nascent
trend towards cumulating ex ante and ex post legislative intervention may be seen as a
corrective to the insufficient coverage of ex post implementation alone").

[127] Medellín v. Texas, 552 U.S. 491, 506–20 (2008); Curtis A. Bradley, *Intent, Presumptions, and
Non-self-executing Treaties*, 102 Am. J. Int'l L. 540, 540 (2008).

[128] Bond v. United States, 134 S. Ct. 2077, 2102 (2014) (Scalia, J., concurring in judgment) ("All this
to leave in place an ill-considered *ipse dixit* that enables the fundamental constitutional
principle of limited federal powers to be set aside by the President and Senate's exercise of the
treaty power. We should not have shirked our duty and distorted the law to preserve that
assertion; we should have welcomed and eagerly grasped the opportunity – nay, the
obligation – to consider and repudiate it.")

[129] Fund for Animals, Inc. v. Kempthorne, 472 F.3d 872, 880 (D.C. Cir. 2006) (Kavanaugh, J.,
concurring) ("In other words, because non-self-executing treaties have no legal status in
American courts, there seems to be little justification for a court to put a thumb on the scale in
favor of a non-self-executing treaty when interpreting a statute."). In 2018, Judge Kavanaugh
was appointed to the US Supreme Court.

[130] R. Daniel Kelemen, *The Court of the European Union in the Twenty-First Century*, 79 Law &
Contemp. Probs. 117, 133–37 (2016); Nico Krisch, *The Backlash Against International Courts*,
Verfassungsblog: On Matters Constitutional (Dec. 16, 2014), http://verfassungsblog.de/
backlash-international-courts-2/; Madsen, *supra* note 90, at 144 ("With the Court increasingly
overburdened and backlogged – yet still progressively expanding the scope of the Convention –
a number of member states launched, for the first time since the Court's creation in 1959, a
systematic critique of both the Court's power over national law and politics and the quality of
the Court's judges and their judgments. This discontent climaxed with the 2012 Brighton
Declaration, adopted by all forty-seven member states, which began an institutionalized
process that aimed to limit the ECtHR's power."). *Id.* at 174 ("In the legal field, highly critical
voices speak out in every single European state. Even presidents of national supreme courts are
openly voicing their opposition to the ECtHR – most recently, the Supreme Court Presidents

for example, the Danish Supreme Court frontally defied the ECJ by refusing to apply the ECJ's judgment in the AJOS case (concerning the application of an EU directive on age discrimination) in light of existing Danish law.[131]

Nonetheless, where policy makers and stakeholders continue to view problems in transnational terms, they often turn to law to address them. Given public international law's deep implications within states, there may be a turn to less formal, stealthier means of transnational legal ordering, including greater relative use of soft law, private international law, and private legal ordering to address transnational problems. The secular trend, we contend, will involve more than ad hoc problem-solving and will continue to entail deeper processes of legal ordering that transcend national borders to permeate legal practice within states.

F CONCLUSION

Public international law remains central to the concept of transnational law, both empirically and normatively. It is even more central than when Jessup wrote his seminal lectures and included public international law within his broader concept. Public international law is a critical part of the concept today because of its deep implications for transnational legal ordering and the creation of transnational legal orders. Empirically, international law has critical implications for the role of markets (and thus what the state does), the allocation of power among state institutions, the creation and role of professions, and the development of transnational accountability mechanisms operating under particular normative frameworks.

This chapter stresses the bottom-up, top-down, and recursive nature of transnational legal processes that give rise to transnational legal orders. It shows how the development of public international law is a place where domestic problems and domestic struggles – whether over human rights, commercial law, or regulatory reform – get played out in international arenas

from the United Kingdom, Belgium, and Finland. Although bashing the ECtHR is not new, the generalization of the discourse across Europe and its application to very different human rights situations is quite novel.").

[131] Hójesteret [Supreme Court] Case No. 15/2014, Dansk Industri (DI) Acting for Ajos A/S v. The Estate Left by A (2016) (Den.), http://www.supremecourt.dk/supremecourt/nyheder/ pressemeddelelser/Documents/Judgment%2015-2014.pdf. For discussion, *see* Mikael Rask Madsen, Henrik Palmer Olsen & Urska Sadl, *Legal Disintegration? The Ruling of the Danish Supreme Court in Ajos*, VERFASSUNGSBLOG: ON MATTERS CONSTITUTIONAL, Jan. 30, 2017, http://verfassungsblog.de/legal-disintegration-the-ruling-of-the-danish-supreme-court-in-ajos/ (highlighting that "*Ajos* is illustrative of a turn towards a greater national patrolling of the limited mandate given to the EU, including its judicial organ").

alongside domestic ones. States and private actors seek to "upload" domestic legal norms to advance policies as well as to "download" and institutionalize them within and across domestic jurisdictions. These processes are dynamic and recursive.

Public international law should not be viewed in isolation of private international law, national law, and private legal ordering. Rather, much of public international law consists of the uploading and export of national and privately developed legal norms, whether from powerful states, professions, or other private actors. The resulting public international law norms interact with private legal ordering and private international law, from arbitration to private standard setting, from trade to human rights. Together, they give rise to transnational legal orders governing different legal domains.

Normatively, the problems (and thus the issues at stake) are socially and politically constructed, involving contests among actors. Public international law, as law more generally, tends to have a slant in favor of the privileged. It accordingly must be subject to empirically grounded, normative critique. At the same time, law is needed for ordering and the institutional alternatives for ordering involve trade-offs. Law constrains power as well as reflects power, and power is needed to accomplish social ends. It is important to retain a public law element to transnational legal ordering because otherwise the concept of transnational law, as conceived by Jessup, risks becoming disconnected from the public sphere. Public international law and institutions are needed to address transnational problems, in complement with private international law and private norm making. A critical role for transnational scholars is both to reveal the place and roles of international law and institutions while critiquing their processes. An essential way of proceeding is to evaluate transnational legal ordering through which legal norms are constructed, conveyed, resisted, implemented, and have effects. Only then might we participate effectively in improving the way things are.

6

Transnational Law in the Pacific Century

Mapping Pesticide Regulation in China

FRANCIS SNYDER, HU ZHOUKE AND NI LILI

A INTRODUCTION

The regulation of risks associated with highly toxic pesticides in the world today is a good example of how transnational law, global legal pluralism and relations between numerous sites of governance interact with one another.[1] In this chapter we discuss the regulation of pesticides in China. China is the leading producer, user and exporter of pesticides in the world. Currently the system for regulating pesticides in China, including laws and institutions, is subject to major reforms. During the coming years, these reforms are likely to reshape this area of risk regulation in China and to have a significant impact on trade in food between China and the rest of the world.

Our objective is to map China's regulatory regime for pesticides, focusing mainly on public rather than private standards. We use the term 'regime' here in a loose sense, rather than in a state-centric sense drawn from the realist political science literature; the Chinese regulatory system exemplifies transnational law in that international and transnational measures now are interlocked with the national legal system rather than simply regulating relations among nation states. We identify the multiple institutional and normative

[1] A draft of this chapter was presented on 10 May 2017 at the Faculty Scholarship Workshop, Peking University School of Transnational Law, Peking University Shenzhen Graduate School. We are grateful for many helpful comments on that occasion. We also wish to thank Cao Fei, Susan Finder, Wei Gong, Norman Ho, K. S. Leung, Imelda Maher, Thomas Yunlong Man, Qianlan Wu and Ting Xu for detailed comments. We are grateful to Du Qifang, He Jian, Yi Seul Kim, Anne-Lise Strahtmann and Tian He for their contributions to the chapter. We thank Peking University School of Transnational Law and Peking University Shenzhen Graduate School for financial support. We remain solely responsible for the contents. The chapter does not take account of recent administrative reforms except to note that the former Ministry of Agriculture (MoA) is now part of the Ministry of Agriculture and Rural Affairs (MARA).

sources for the regulation of pesticides in China. We introduce the veritable
labyrinth of relevant rules, ranging from public international agreements to
national law to notices adopted by Chinese cities. The subject is vast, and our
discussion is necessarily selective. We aim not only to illustrate some of the
distinctive features of the Chinese regulatory system but also to contribute to
the development of theories of transnational law and global legal pluralism.

We make three main arguments. First, the regulation of pesticides in China
forms part of a transnational legal order (TLO), in the sense of 'a collection of
formalized legal norms and associated organizations and actors that authoritatively order the understanding and practice of law across national
jurisdictions'.[2] Second, the TLO for pesticide regulation is conditioned
strongly and in some respects shaped decisively by specific features of the
Chinese political and legal system, thus urging us to reframe the concept of
TLO so as to give more emphasis to national and local contexts. Third, and
consequently, the regulation of pesticides in China can be conceived of as
part of a TLO, but this concept by itself may not be a very good fit. To give
more force to the conjunction of our three arguments, we sketch in conclusion the evolution of the normative shape of the pesticide TLO, from the
development of sites of governance to global legal pluralism to international
normative repertoires to transnational law, emphasizing in particular the
specific features of China and perhaps other Asia-Pacific countries.

The chapter is divided into three main parts, each corresponding to a semi-
autonomous legal field.[3] The first part discusses international and regional
measures on the regulation of pesticides. The second part considers Chinese
national measures. The third part introduces selected provincial and municipal regulatory measures in China. A conclusion summarizes the discussion.

B INTERNATIONAL AND REGIONAL AGREEMENTS AND STANDARDS

The regulation of pesticides is the subject of numerous international measures. We mention these first because this may be more convenient for most
legal readers, who may begin instinctively from the premise that international
measures predominate in the hierarchy of norms. Here, however, this order is

---

[2]   Terence C. Halliday & Gregory Shaffer, *Transnational Legal Orders, in* Transnational
      Legal Orders 3 (Terence C. Halliday & Gregory Shaffer eds., 2015).
[3]   On semi-autonomous social fields, see Sally Falk Moore, *Law and Social Change: The Semi-
      autonomous Social Field as an Appropriate Subject of Study*, 7:4 Law & Soc'y Rev., 719–45
      (1973), *reprinted in* Sally Falk Moore, Law as Process: An Anthropological Approach,
      (1978); and Francis Snyder, Food Safety Law in China: Making Transnational Law
      15–107 (2016).

not intended to recognize any priority or hegemonic status of international measures, either in law or in practice; this is an empirical question. We can distinguish legally binding measures from those that are not legally binding. Here we consider only those measures that directly concern China. The measures in each category are considered in chronological order according to date of adoption.

I *Legally Binding International Agreements*

The first major international measure is the Basel Convention on the Control of Transboundary Movements of Hazardous Wastes and Their Disposal, adopted on 22 March 1989 and entered into force on 5 May 1992.[4] It seeks to reduce the generation of hazardous waste and to promote environmentally sound management of such wastes, to restrict their transboundary movements except in accordance with principles of environmentally sound waste management and to establish a system for regulating permissible movements of hazardous wastes.[5] It covers '[w]astes from the production, formulation and use of biocides and phytopharmaceuticals, including waste pesticides and herbicides which are off-specification, outdated, or unfit for their originally intended use'.[6] China signed the convention on 22 March 1990 and ratified it on 17 December 1991, with the convention coming into force on 5 May 1992.[7] Dealing primarily with trade, the Basel Convention is very significant for the Chinese government and Chinese pesticide exporters.[8] In 2016 China exported about USD 5.6 billion worth of pesticides, of which almost half

---

[4] Basel Convention on the Control of Transboundary Movements of Hazardous Wastes and Their Disposal, http://www.basel.int/Portals/4/Basel%20Convention/docs/text/ BaselConventionText-e.pdf (last visited Apr. 5, 2017). On additional annexes, see http://www .basel.int/TheConvention/Overview/TextoftheConvention/tabid/1275/Default.aspx (last visited Apr. 5, 2017).

[5] *Overview*, BASEL CONVENTION, http://www.basel.int/TheConvention/Overview/tabid/1271/ Default.aspx (last visited Apr. 5, 2017).

[6] Basel Convention on the Control of Transboundary Movements of Hazardous Wastes and Their Disposal, *supra* note 4, at annex VIII, list A, 4030.

[7] *Parties to the Basel Convention on the Control of Transboundary Movements of Hazardous Wastes and Their Disposal*, BASEL CONVENTION, http://www.basel.int/Countries/ StatusofRatifications/PartiesSignatories/tabid/4499/Default.aspx (last visited Apr. 5, 2017).

[8] See Mark Bradford, *The United States, China, & the Basel Convention on the Transboundary Movements of Hazardous Wastes and Their Disposal*, 8 FORDHAM ENVTL. L. REV. 304, 349 (2011), http://ir.lawnet.fordham.edu/cgi/viewcontent.cgi?article=1445&context=elr. On implementation for exports and imports, see Ministry of Envtl. Prot. of P.R. China, *Implementation of Basel Convention in China*, file:///C:/Users/admin/Downloads/UNEP-FAO-IMPL.4-CP05.En.pdf (last visited May 14, 2017). We do not deal with imports of toxic waste into China.

went to Asia and Latin America.[9] In order to implement the Basel Convention with regard to its exports, China enacted in 2008 the Administrative Measures for Examination and Approval of the Export of Hazardous Waste.[10]

Second, the Convention Concerning Safety in the Use of Chemicals at Work (Chemicals Convention) was adopted by the International Labour Organization (ILO) on 25 June 1990 and entered into force on 4 November 1993.[11] It establishes a classification system for hazardous chemicals, required appropriate labelling, marking and chemical data sheets to be given by suppliers to employers and sets out responsibilities of suppliers, employers and exporting states and duties of employees. China ratified this convention on 11 January 1995, and the convention is in force.[12] China was a founding member of the ILO in 1919, withdrew from active participation between 1949 and 1981 and returned to active participation in 1983, with involvement in technical 'non-core' labour standards like the Chemicals Convention. Such standards have had very important effects on domestic Chinese law.[13] The 1996–7 report of the ILO director-general noted that China was seeking to implement the convention fully in domestic law, for example by developing a classification and labelling system for chemicals,[14] which is now incorporated in China's Catalogue of Hazardous Chemicals.[15]

Third, the Rotterdam Convention on the Prior Informed Consent Procedure for Certain Hazardous Chemicals and Pesticides in International Trade

---

[9] *Overview of Chinese Pesticide Exportation in 2016*, CHEMLINKED, https://agrochemical .chemlinked.com/news/news/overview-chinese-pesticide-exportation-2016 (last visited Apr. 10, 2017).

[10] Weixian Feiwu Chukou Hezhun Guanli Banfa (危险废物出口核准管理办法) [Administrative Measures for Examination and Approval of the Export of Hazardous Wastes] (promulgated by the State Envtl. Prot. Admin., Jan. 25, 2008, effective Mar. 1, 2008), http://en .pkulaw.cn/display.aspx?cgid=102001&lib=law.

[11] Int'l Labour Org., Chemicals Convention, Convention No. 170 (1990), http://www.ilo.org/dyn/ normlex/en/f?p=NORMLEXPUB:12100:0::NO::P12100_ILO_CODE:C170.

[12] *Ratifications for China*, INT'L LABOUR ORG., http://www.ilo.org/dyn/normlex/en/f?p= 1000:11200:0::NO:11200:P11200_COUNTRY_ID:103404 (last visited May 13, 2017).

[13] See A.C. Neal, *Implementing ILO Fundamental Labour Rights in China : A Sensitive Meeting of Form and Substance in* FUNDAMENTAL LABOUR RIGHTS IN CHINA: LEGAL IMPLEMENTATION AND CULTURAL LOGIC 19, 38–52 (Ulla Liukkunen & Yifeng Chen eds., 2016); *China and the ILO: Formalistic Cooperation Masks Rejection of Key Labour Rights*, HUMAN RIGHTS IN CHINA (Jan. 20, 2001), http://www.hrichina.org/en/content/4804.

[14] Int'l Labour Org., Activities of the ILO 1996–97: Report of the Director-General, ILO, International Labour Conference, 86th Session, at 99 (1998).

[15] English Edition of the Catalogue of Hazardous Chemicals (2002), CHEM. INSPECTION & REGULATION SERV. (2011), http://www.cirs-reach.com/China_Chemical_Regulation/Catalog_ of_Hazardous_Chemicals_China_2002_English.xlsx.

was adopted on 10 September 1998.[16] It applies to banned or severely restricted chemicals and severely hazardous pesticide formulations. It provides for the establishment of a list of such chemicals and for agreement by each party on prior informed consent procedures for import and export. It covers potentially hazardous chemicals so far as they form part of international trade. China signed the Rotterdam Convention on 24 August 1999 and ratified it on 22 March 2005, and with regard to China, the convention entered into force 20 June 2005.[17] The Rotterdam Convention deals mainly with trade.

Fourth, the Stockholm Convention on Persistent Organic Pollutants (POPs) was adopted on 22 May 2001 and entered into force on 17 May 2004.[18] It aims to reduce, eliminate and prevent health and environmental effects of pesticides that resist degradation, accumulate in soil or water, and may be transported or released far from their place of origin. It deals with production, trade, marketing, agricultural use and management of stockpiles of POPs. China signed and ratified the convention on 23 May 2001 and 13 August 2004, respectively, and the convention entered into force for China on 11 November 2004.[19] China adopted a national implementation plan (NIP) in April 2007.[20] The NIP evaluated the status of POPs in China as of 2004 and set forth objectives, a strategy and a detailed action plan for achieving different objectives by 2010 and 2015. The Regional Centre for the Asia Pacific Region is located at Tsinghua University, Beijing.[21]

A fifth measure is the ILO Convention on Safety and Health in Agriculture, which was adopted by the ILO on 21 June 2001 and, for signatories having ratified the convention, entered into force on 20 September 2003.[22] It lays

---

[16] *Text of the Convention*, ROTTERDAM CONVENTION, http://www.pic.int/TheConvention/ Overview/TextoftheConvention/tabid/1048/language/en-US/Default.aspx (last visited Apr. 4, 2017).

[17] *Status of Ratifications*, ROTTERDAM CONVENTION, http://www.pic.int/Countries/ Statusofratifications/tabid/1072/language/en-US/Default.aspx (last visited Apr. 4, 2017).

[18] *History of the Negotiations of the Stockholm Convention*, STOCKHOLM CONVENTION, http:// chm.pops.int/TheConvention/Overview/History/Overview/tabid/3549/Default.aspx (last visited Apr. 5, 2017).

[19] *Status of Ratifications*, STOCKHOLM CONVENTION, http://chm.pops.int/Countries/ StatusofRatifications/PartiesandSignatoires/tabid/4500/Default.aspx (last visited Apr. 4, 2017).

[20] State Envtl. Prot. Admin., National Implementation Plan for the Stockholm Convention on Persistent Organic Pollutants (China), http://www.pops.int/documents/implementation/nips/ submissions/china_nip_en.pdf (last visited Apr. 4, 2017).

[21] *Basel and Stockholm Convention Regional Centre for the Asia and Pacific Region in China (BCRC-SCRC China)*, STOCKHOLM CONVENTION, http://chm.pops.int/?tabid=648 (last visited Apr. 4, 2017).

[22] Int'l Labour Org., Safety and Health in Agriculture Convention, Convention No. 184 (2001), http://www.ilo.org/dyn/normlex/en/f?p=NORMLEXPUB:12100:0::NO::P12100_ILO_CODE: C184.

down detailed obligations concerning the sound management of chemicals used in agriculture and of chemical waste. China has not ratified this convention.[23] The Chinese government considered that the convention's objective of guaranteeing an equal level of health protection to urban and rural workers 'cannot be achieved in China because of its present level of productivity' and in light of China's dual rural and urban economic structure that produces a large economic gap between urban and rural areas. However, given that one objective of the government is to ensure that rural and urban employees enjoy equal rights, entry into the convention has since been 'a matter for a Recommendation'.[24] The All-China Federation of Trade Unions, a party-state organization, agreed that '[i]nternational instruments will contribute to promoting' the Chinese government efforts to achieve its objective.[25] More recently, the Chinese government has given its backing to the proposal in favour of an ILO recommendation[26] and in favour of a preamble referring to the Tripartite Declaration of Principles Concerning Multinational Enterprises and Social Policy, adopted by the ILO Governing Body.[27]

II *Non–Legally Binding International Agreements*

Subsequently, in October 2010 an ILO international group of experts adopted a non–legally binding Code of Practice on Safety and Health in Agriculture, which was endorsed and approved for publication in March 2011 by the ILO Governing Body.[28] The code complements the convention and its supplementing Recommendation No. 192.[29] On 1 May 2013, the code was published

---

[23] *Ratifications for China, supra* note 12.

[24] Int'l Labour Org., Safety and Health in Agriculture, International Labour Conference, 88th Session, 2000, Report VI(2), Sixth Item on the Agenda, at 10 (2000), http://www.ilo.org/public/english/standards/relm/ilc/ilc88/pdf/rep-vi-2.pdf.

[25] *Id.* On China's relationship with the ILO and China's negotiating position at the time, *see* ANN KENT, CHINA, THE UNITED NATIONS, AND HUMAN RIGHTS: THE LIMITS OF COMPLIANCE 117–45 (1999).

[26] Int'l Labour Org., *supra* note 24, at 13.

[27] *Id.* at 15–16.

[28] Int'l Labour Org., Code of Practice on Safety and Health in Agriculture, Meeting of Experts to Adopt a Code of Practice on Safety and Health in Agriculture, Geneva, Oct. 25–29, 2010, http://www.ilo.org/wcmsp5/groups/public/—dgreports/—dcomm/—publ/documents/publication/wcms_159457.pdf.

[29] Int'l Labour Org., Safety and Health in Agriculture Recommendation, Convention No. 192, (2001), http://www.ilo.org/dyn/normlex/en/f?p=NORMLEXPUB:12100:0::NO::P12100_ILO_CODE:R192.

in Chinese by the Chinese Labour and Social Security Publishing House.[30] It contains provisions on strategies to control chemical risks; the transport, storage and disposal of pesticides; exposure to pesticides; medical and health surveillance of workers; and atmospheric and environmental controls.[31] The soft law character of the ILO measures made possible their translation into soft national measures. From the standpoint of both the ILO and the Chinese government, the use of soft law permitted the government to maintain control of transnational law and rendered it less rigid and more easily adaptable to Chinese conditions and thus more likely to endure.

As the debate about ILO measures suggested, it often is easier, for domestic political and economic reasons, for governments to accept non–legally binding measures instead of legally binding ones.[32] It is not surprising, therefore, that pesticides are the subject of numerous non–legally binding measures, led by the United Nations (UN). With the ILO Convention, the Chinese government did not accept the legally binding instrument and proposed instead to accept an accompanying non–legally binding code of practice. Similarly, there is the example of GLOBALG.A.P.[33] This is a set of international voluntary guidelines, established in 1997 by UK and continental European supermarkets in the Euro-Retailer Produce Working Group to develop a certification system for good agricultural practices and food quality, including pesticide use, which is now used worldwide.[34] As adopted in China, ChinaGAP consists of voluntary standards that are benchmarked to GLOBALG.A.P. However, the ChinaGAP standards are public standards, and certification is governed and supervised by the national Certification and Accreditation Administration,[35] under the authority of the State Council.[36] From a purely legal perspective, the normative processes in the

---

[30] *Code of Practice on Safety and Health in Agriculture Available in Chinese*, Int'l Labour Org., July 12, 2013, http://www.ilo.org/safework/cis/WCMS_217636/lang–en/index.htm (Chinese version: http://www.ilo.org/safework/info/standards-and-instruments/codes/WCMS_217558/lang–en/index.htm).

[31] Int'l Labour Org., *supra* note 28, at 66–92.

[32] On international soft law, see Kenneth W. Abbott & Duncan Snidal, *Hard and Soft Law in International Governance*, 54 Int'l Org., 421–56 (2000).

[33] On GLOBALG.A.P. and other international private standards covering pesticides, see Nicolien van der Grijp, Regulating Pesticide Risk Reduction: The Practice and Dynamics of Legal Pluralism 101–35, 247 (2008).

[34] *GLOBALG.A.P. History*, GLOBALG.A.P., http://www.globalgap.org/uk_en/who-we-are/about-us/history/ (last visited Apr. 11, 2017).

[35] Int'l Trade Centre, *China – GAP*, http://www.agromedquality.eu/public/img_upload/file/ChinaGAP.pdf (last visited Apr. 11, 2017).

[36] See the website of the Certification and Accreditation Administration of the People's Republic of China, http://english.cnca.gov.cn/ (last visited 11 Apr. 11, 2017).

transformation of the private (soft) GLOBALG.A.P. into the public (soft) ChinaGAP differ from those involved in the transformation of the hard ILO Convention into a soft code of practice subsequently published in Chinese as soft law. However, both sets of processes were ways of reframing international measures as national measures. Moreover, in both the private-to-public translation and the hard-to-soft translation of international measures into domestic measures, the Chinese government was able to maintain control and shape the measures to suit the local context.

In 1992 the UN Conference on Environment and Development (UNCED) adopted a mandate that spurred work to develop the Globally Harmonized System of Classification and Labelling of Chemicals (GHS). It culminated in the publication of a first edition of GHS in 2003, as amended in 2004 and 2006.[37] The GHS provided for a classification of hazardous chemicals and the communication of hazards by labelling and safety data sheets. It also identified environmental hazards and specific health hazards, such as acute toxicity, germ cell mutagenicity, carcinogenicity and reproductive toxicity. China has followed the GHS, most recently by publishing the Catalogue of Hazardous Chemicals (2015), Regulations on the Safe Management of Hazardous Chemicals in China (Decree No. 591), the State Administration of Work Safety (SAWS) Measures for the Administration of Physical Hazard Identification and Classification of Chemicals, and the SAWS 2015 trial version of the Guidance for the Implementation of the Catalogue of Hazardous Chemicals.[38] The national strategy is led by the Ministry of Industry and Information Technology (MIIT), with the participation of many other ministries and governmental organizations, including SAWS. The Ministry of Agriculture is the lead organization in '[d]eveloping the legislation and enforcement of GHS for pesticides'.[39]

The Food and Agriculture Organization (FAO) International Code of Conduct on the Distribution and Use of Pesticides was adopted on

---

[37] UNITED NATIONS, GLOBALLY HARMONIZED SYSTEM OF CLASSIFICATION AND LABELLING OF CHEMICALS (GHS) (2d rev. ed. 2007), http://www.unece.org/fileadmin/DAM/trans/danger/publi/ghs/ghs_rev02/English/00e_intro.pdf.

[38] Lily Hou, *China Publishes GHS Catalogue for the Classification for the Catalogued Hazardous Chemicals*, CHEMADVISOR, https://www.chemadvisor.com/china-publishes-ghs-classifications-for-the-catalogued-hazardous-chemicals-2015/ (last visited May 14, 2017).

[39] Luo Qiming, *GHS in China*, PowerPoint prepared for the GHS Review Conference for Southeast Asia, Kuala Lumpur, 21–23 May 2013, MINISTRY OF INDUS. & INFO. TECH. OF P.R. CHINA, http://www.miit.gov.cn/n973401/n974339/n974347/n974349/c3786019/part/3786022.pdf (last visited May 14, 2017).

28 November 1985 and updated in 2002.[40] It was addressed to 'international organizations, governments of exporting and importing countries, pesticide industry, application equipment industry, traders, food industry, users, and public-sector organizations such as environmental groups, consumer groups and trade unions'.[41] The code was intended to be especially useful for countries that then had no regulatory regime for pesticides and also to provide a basis for national legislation.[42] It laid down voluntary standards for distribution and use of pesticides. These standards included Good Agricultural Practice (GAP) and Integrated Pesticide Management (IPM).[43] The code exhorted governments to enact and enforce legislation for the regulation of pesticides and provided detailed regulatory and technical requirements.[44] In June 2013 the FAO approved the International Code of Conduct on Pesticide Management[45] and related guidelines.[46] It replaced and updated the earlier code and added specific provisions on public health pesticides, highly hazardous pesticides, integrated vector management of diseases and maximum pesticide residue limits (MRLs). The code of conduct provides that the '[prohibition of the importation, distribution, sale and purchase of highly hazardous pesticides may be considered if, based on risk assessment, risk mitigation measures or good marketing practices insufficient to ensure that

---

[40] FOOD AND AGRICULTURE ORGANIZATION [FAO], CODE OF CONDUCT ON THE DISTRIBUTION AND USE OF PESTICIDES (rev. version 2002), http://www.fao.org/docrep/005/y4544e/y4544e00 .htm [hereinafter FAO, CODE OF CONDUCT ON THE DISTRIBUTION AND USE OF PESTICIDE]. *See also* FAO, PREVENTION AND DISPOSAL OF OBSOLETE PESTICIDES: CODES AND CONVENTIONS, http://ww.fao.org/agriculture/crops/obsolete-pesticides/how-deal/codes-and-conventions/en/ (last visited May 15, 2017).

[41] FAO, CODE OF CONDUCT ON THE DISTRIBUTION AND USE OF PESTICIDE, Article 1.5.

[42] *Id.*

[43] Defined in *id.* Article 2. GAP was not included in the original code; *see* FAO, CORPORATE DOCUMENT DEPOSITORY, E. INTERNATIONAL CODE OF CONDUCT ON THE DISTRIBUTION AND USE OF PESTICIDES, http://www.fao.org/docrep/x5562E/X5562e0a.htm.

[44] FAO, CODE OF CONDUCT ON THE DISTRIBUTION AND USE OF PESTICIDES, Article 6. *See also* JESSICA VAPNEK, ISABELLA PAGOTTO & MARGARET KWOKA, DESIGNING NATIONAL PESTICIDE LEGISLATION, FAO Legislative Study 97 (2007), http://www.fao.org/3/a-a1467e.pdf. For a list of other relevant documents, see Intergovernmental Forum on Chemical Safety (IFCS) VI, *The Central Role of the International Code of Conduct on the Distribution and Use of Pesticides in Achieving Sustainable Chemicals Management*, Panel, Wednesday, 17 September 2008, Dakar, Senegal, WHO, www.who.int/entity/ifcs/documents/forums/. . ./code_flyer.doc?ua.

[45] FAO & WORLD HEALTH ORGANIZATION [WHO], AGP – INTERNATIONAL CODE OF CONDUCT ON PESTICIDE MANAGEMENT (2014), http://www.fao.org/agriculture/crops/thematic-sitemap/ theme/pests/code/en/.

[46] FAO & WHO, INTERNATIONAL CODE OF CONDUCT ON PESTICIDE MANAGEMENT: ANNOTATED LIST OF GUIDELINES FOR THE IMPLEMENTATION OF THE INTERNATIONAL CODE OF CONDUCT ON PESTICIDE MANAGEMENT (2014), http://www.fao.org/fileadmin/templates/ agphome/documents/Pests_Pesticides/Code/Annotated_Guidelines2014.pdf.

the product can be handled without unacceptable risk to humans and the environment'.[47] As discussed later, China's Regulations on Pesticide Administration, promulgated in 1997, amended in 2001 and revised substantially in 2015, follow essentially the same trajectory.

The Rio Declaration on Environment and Development was proclaimed by the UN Conference on Environment and Development in 1992.[48] Consistent with the aim of sustainable development, its basic principles stated that governments should enact effective environmental legislation, 'develop national law regarding liability and compensation for the victims of pollution and other environmental damage' (principle 13) and apply the precautionary principle according to their capacities. China's recently adopted Environmental Protection Law does not incorporate the precautionary principle.[49]

Together with the Rio Declaration, Agenda 21 – the Global Programme of Action on Sustainable Development – was also adopted at the UNCED conference in Rio from 3–14 June 1992. Chapter 14 concerned the promotion of sustainable agriculture and rural development. Chapter 19 dealt specifically with environmentally sound management of toxic chemicals, including prevention of illegal international traffic in toxic and dangerous products. It proposed the following programme areas:

a.   Expanding and accelerating international assessment of chemical risks;
b.   Harmonization of classification and labelling of chemicals;
c.   Information exchange on toxic chemicals and chemical risks;
d.   Establishment of risk reduction programmes;
e.   Strengthening of national capabilities and capacities for management of chemicals
f.   Prevention of illegal international traffic in toxic and dangerous products.[50]

It proposed strengthening international risk assessment, capacity building, exchange of information on toxic chemicals and the establishment of

[47]   FAO & WHO, The International Code of Conduct on Pesticide Management, Article 7.5 (2014), http://www.fao.org/fileadmin/templates/agphome/documents/Pests_Pesticides/Code/CODE_2014Sep_ENG.pdf.
[48]   *Report of the United Nations Conference on Environment and Development, Rio de Janeiro, 3–14 June 1992*, U.N. Doc. A/CONF.151/26 (Vol. I) (Aug. 12, 1992), http://www.un.org/documents/ga/conf151/aconf15126-1annex1.htm.
[49]   Lei Zhang, Guizhen Je & Arthur P.J. Mol, *China's New Environmental Protection Law: A Game Changer?* 13 Envtl. Dev. 1, 2 (2015).
[50]   *Report of the United Nations Conference on Environment and Development, Rio de Janeiro, 3–14 June 1992, supra* note 48, at para. 19.4.

risk-reduction programmes, including 'integrated pest management, includ-ing the use of biological control agents, as alternatives to toxic pesticides'.[51] Chinese pesticide regulation has aimed to follow this pattern; for example, under the most recent reforms, so-called natural-enemy pesticides are exempt from registration and marketing license requirements.[52]

In considering the TLO concerning pesticides, it is essential to include the international non-governmental organization PAN (Pesticides Action Network) International, the most important lobbying group in the field. Founded in 1982, PAN 'now links over 600 groups, institutions and individuals in more than 90 countries ... [and] work[s] through five independent, collaborating regional centers'.[53] It has 103 partner organizations in the Asia-Pacific region;[54] the Pesticide Eco-Alternatives Centre (PEAC) in China's Yunnan Province is on the PAN Asia Pacific Governing Body.[55] The PAN database, which has exhaustive information on toxicity and pesticide regula-tion,[56] and the PAN International List of Highly Hazardous Pesticides,[57] are essential tools for any serious law and policy initiatives on pesticides. PAN has played a significant role in the development of the pesticides TLO. For example, lobbying by PEAC contributed to the decision by the Fourth Meeting of the Twelfth National People's Congress to ratify an amendment

---

[51] *Id.*
[52] Lin Fan, *Summary on the 5 Draft Supporting Rules for Chinese New Pesticide Registratio*, CHEMLINKED (Apr. 20, 2017), https://agrochemical.chemlinked.com/node/3007 (last visited Apr. 22, 2017).
[53] PAN (Pesticide International Network), at http://www.panna.org/pan-international (last visited May 17, 2017).
[54] PAN ASIA PACIFIC, http://panap.net/ (last visited May 17, 2017).
[55] *See PAN Asia Pacific Steering Council*, PAN ASIA PACIFIC, http://panap.net/steering-council/ (last visited May 17, 2017). On the work of PEAC, see http://panchina.org/en_index.aspx (last visited May 17, 2017); GOKUNMING, http://www.gokunming.com/en/listings/item/31614/ pesticide_eco_alternative_center_peac (last visited May 17, 2017); Yang Yang, *A China Environmental Health Factsheet: Pesticides and Environmental Health Trends in China*, WILSON CENTER, https://www.wilsoncenter.org/sites/default/files/pesticides_feb28.pdf (last visited May 17, 2017) ('produced as part of the China Environment Forum's partnership with Western Kentucky University on the USAID-supported China Environmental Health Project'); Jakob A. KLEIN, *Eating Green: Ecological Food Consumption in Urban China, in* RE-ORIENTING CUISINE: EAST ASIAN FOODWAYS IN THE TWENTY-FIRST CENTURY 238, 243–44 (Kwang-Ok Kim ed., 2015); Katherine Morton, *Transnational Advocacy at the Grassroots: Benefits and Risks of International Cooperation, in* CHINA'S EMBEDDED ACTIVISM: OPPORTUNITIES AND CONSTRAINTS OF A SOCIAL MOVEMENT 195, 206–09 (Peter Ho & Richard Edmonds eds., reprinted 2012).
[56] PAN PESTICIDE DATABASE, http://www.pesticideinfo.org/ (last visited May 17, 2017).
[57] *PAN International List of Highly Hazardous Pesticides (PAN List of HHPs)*, PAN GERMANY (June 2015), http://www.pan-germany.org/download/PAN_HHP_List_150602_F.pdf.

to add endosulfan to the list of POPs in the Stockholm Convention.[58] Endosulfan is a highly toxic pesticide that was frequently used in the production of tea for domestic consumption and export[59] and, though banned today for agricultural use, is still used in cotton and tobacco production.[60] PEAC (PAN China) has also contributed to the decision of the Chinese government to ban the highly hazardous chemical paraquat.[61]

III *International Standards*

These international measures provide a general policy context for pesticide management, indicate directly operational actions for pesticide management and often supply a template for or correspond to Chinese law. A first step in the adoption of precise norms was taken by the Codex Alimentarius Commission (CAC or Codex), which was established in 1963 by the FAO and the World Health Organization (WHO).[62] Codex works through a combination of commodity-specific (vertical) committees and cross-cutting (horizontal) committees.[63] The most important committee concerning pesticides is the Codex Committee on Pesticide Residues (CCPR).[64] A horizontal committee, the CCPR is composed of 40–60 national delegations, FAO and WHO and other governmental and non-governmental organizations,

---

[58] *See* Xinhua News Agency, http://roll.sohu.com/20130830/n385489891.shtml (in Chinese; English translation at http://www.panna.org/sites/default/files/ 3ChinaApprovesEndosulfanAmendmentStockholm.pdf) (last visited May 17, 2017).

[59] *See Victory in China!*, PAN (PESTICIDE ACTION NETWORK NORTH AMERICA) (Sept. 17, 2013), http://www.panna.org/blog/victory-china.

[60] *Endosulfan Phasing-Out in China*, UNDP IN CHINA, http://www.cn.undp.org/content/china/ en/home/library/environment_energy/issue-brief–endosulfan-phasing-out-in-china.html (last visited Feb. 21, 2017). The trade website Made-in-China.com currently lists thirteen endosulfan manufacturers and suppliers, with thirty-nine products in China. *Supplier Discovery*, MADE-IN-CHINA.COM, http://www.made-in-china.com/manufacturers/endosulfan.html (last visited Feb. 21, 2017). This information is taken from Francis Snyder & Ni Lili, *A Tale of Eight Pesticides : Risk Regulation and Public Health in China*, 8 EUR. J. RISK REG. 469–505 (2017).

[61] *See PAN China Takes Down Paraquat*, PAN (PESTICIDE ACTION NETWORK NORTH AMERICA), http://www.panna.org/blog/pan-china-takes-down-paraquat (last visited May 17, 2017).

[62] Codex Alimentarius, *International Food Standards*, FAO, http://www.fao.org/fao-who-codexalimentarius/codex-home/en/ (last visited Apr. 6, 2017).

[63] See MARIELLE D. MASSON-MATHEE, THE CODEX ALIMENTARIUS COMMISSION AND ITS STANDARDS (2007); Tim Büthe, Institutionalization and Its Consequences: The TLO(s) for Food Safety, *in* TRANSNATIONAL LEGAL ORDERS, *supra* note 2, at 258–86.

[64] On CCPR procedures, see http://www.codexalimentarius.org/procedures-strategies/procedural-manual/en/ (last visited Apr. 10, 2017).

including industry associations, such as CropLife International.[65] In 2006, five years after joining the World Trade Organization (WTO), China chaired the CCPR, a position it still holds. China experts have worked actively to develop Codex MRLs, to elaborate corresponding Chinese MRLs and most recently to provide scientific data based on Chinese risk assessments as the basis for international standards.

CCPR works in close cooperation with the FAO-WHO Joint Meeting on Pesticide Residues (JMPR).[66] An international scientific expert committee, the JMPR provides scientific risk assessments that eventually form the basis for international and international food safety standards, including those regarding MRLs and those to estimate acceptable daily intakes (ADI) for pesticide residues in food.[67] On the basis of CCPR proposals based on JMPR assessments, the Codex elaborates standards in the form of MRLs for pesticide residues in food. So far, the Codex has adopted approximately 4844 MRLs for pesticide residues in numerous food commodities.[68] In December 2016 China updated its national standard for pesticide residues and now has a total of 4160 MRs for 433 active ingredients in thirteen categories of food.[69]

In principle Codex standards are not legally binding, but in practice they exercise great influence on national standards-making, for at least three reasons. First, as a result of the WTO Appellate Body report in the *EC – Hormones* case,[70] they are the principal source of international food safety standards. Second, de facto they provide guidelines for national food safety standards, which put pressure on countries involved in international food trade and which often exercise a virtually magnetic attraction, especially for countries that lack resources to generate their own standards. Third, international trade, global food networks and WTO monitoring create pressure and

---

[65] CropLife International represents the major agro-chemical companies and related regional organisations: *see* its website, https://croplife.org/about/ (last visited Apr. 10, 2017).

[66] WHO, Food Safety, Joint FAO/WHO Meeting on Pesticide Residues (JMPR), at http://www.who.int/foodsafety/areas_work/chemical-risks/jmpr/en/ (last visited Apr. 6, 2017).

[67] For an inventory of JMPR evaluations, *see Inventory of Evaluations performed by the Joint Meeting of Pesticide Residues (JMPR)*, WHO, http://apps.who.int/pesticide-residues-jmpr-database/Home/Range/All (last visited Apr. 6, 2017).

[68] See Codex Alimentarius, *International Food Standards, Pesticide Residues in Food and Feed*, Codex Pesticides Residues in Food Online Database, FAO, http://www.fao.org/fao-who-codexalimentarius/standards/pesticide-mrls/en/ (last visited Apr. 6, 2017).

[69] GB2763-2016 Standard of Maximum Residue Limits for Pesticide in Food: see https://food.chemlinked.com/news/food-news/china-releases-107-national-food-safety-standards-related-pesticide-mrls-and-determination-methods (last visited Apr. 10, 2017).

[70] Appellate Body Report, *EC – Measures Concerning Meat and Meat Products (Hormones)*, WTO Doc. WT/DS23/AB/R (adopted Feb. 13, 1998).

momentum for alignment and implementation of Codex standards.[71] Consequently, they have direct operational implications for pesticide management
in China, for example for POPs.[72] In practice, the Chinese National Health
and Family Planning Commission, which proposes food safety standards,
takes Codex standards as persuasive unless suggested to be inappropriate by
local dietary habits.

IV *Regional Measures*

Regional measures are a subset of international measures, in this case limited
to the Asia-Pacific region, either legally binding or more commonly soft law.
The main actor is the Asia-Pacific Economic Cooperation (APEC)
Secretariat. While recognizing the great diversity within the Asia-Pacific
region, APEC has elaborated guidelines for the voluntary alignment or harmonization of MRL standards on imported products. The guidelines are
designed to encourage regulatory convergence, in particular focusing on
Codex standards.[73] China is a member of APEC. In addition, the Association
of South East Asian Nations (ASEAN) has prepared voluntary guidelines for
the preparation, use and trade of pesticides and other biological control agents
(BCAs).[74] China is not a member of ASEAN but signed a Framework
Agreement on Comprehensive Economic Partnership with ASEAN on
5 November 2002; the agreement entered into force on 1 July 2003.[75] China's
large population, enormous market, economic strength, political power, position as chair of the Codex CCPR and general preference for soft international
measures give it a unique position in the development of regional guidelines
on pesticides.

[71] On WTO monitoring, see Francis Snyder, *No Country Is an Island: How the WTO Monitors Chinese Food Safety Law Through the Trade Policy Review Mechanism (TPRM)*, 14 J. INTEGRATIVE AGRI. 2142–56 (2015).
[72] On the interaction of international and domestic measures, see Melody Hoi Yin Lau et al., *Environmental Policy, Legislation and Management of Persistent Organic Pollutants (POPs) in China*, 165 ENVTL. POLLUTION 182, 185–88 (2012).
[73] ASIA-PACIFIC ECONOMIC COOPERATION, IMPORT MRL GUIDELINES FOR PESTICIDES: A GUIDELINE ON POSSIBLE APPROACHES TO ACHIEVE ALIGNMENT OF INTERNATIONAL MRLS (2016), http://publications.apec.org/publication-detail.php?pub_id=1750.
[74] ROY BATEMAN, SULAIMAN GINTING, JAN MOLTMANN & THOMAS JÄKEL, ASEAN GUIDELINES ON THE REGULATION, USE AND TRADE OF BIOLOGICAL CONTROL AGENTS (BCAs) (2014), http://www.asean.org/storage/images/Community/AEC/AMAF/OtherDocuments/ASEAN%20Guidelines%20on%20Biological%20Control%20Agents.pdf.
[75] *See* FRANCIS SNYDER, THE EU, THE WTO AND CHINA: LEGAL PLURALISM AND INTERNATIONAL TRADE REGULATION 340–45 (2010).

C NATIONAL MEASURES

I *Relation to International Law*

China is a dualist country with regard to international law, meaning that international law is not self-executing or directly applicable in China. National measures are required to bring a duly signed and ratified international treaty into force under Chinese law. The Chinese point of doctrinal reference for litigants thus is mainly national law. An example is WTO law,[76] which after conclusion and ratification of the WTO agreements was been brought into Chinese law by much legislation and by the Supreme People's Court Provisions on Several Issues Concerning the Adjudication of Administrative Cases Relating to International Trade.[77] With regard to pesticides, this national sovereignty orientation applies not only to legally binding measures but also to non–legally binding international measures. The latter may be imported into the Chinese regulatory regime for pesticides by soft law, as in the case of the ILO Code of Practice on Health and Safety in Agriculture, or by nationally legally binding standards, as in the case of MRLs derived from Codex standards.

II *Rule-Making*

The Chinese system of making legislation and other norms is extremely complex. Its legal basis is the Legislation Law (2015 Amendment),[78] supplemented by the Regulations on Procedures for the Formulation of Rules.[79] The Legislation Law provides:

> Article 7 The National People's Congress and its Standing Committee shall exercise the legislative power of the State.
> [...]

---

[76] *See, e.g.,* ZHANG XIN, IMPLEMENTATION OF THE WTO AGREEMENTS IN CHINA (2005); Donald C. Clarke, *China's Legal System and the Prospects for WTO Compliance*, 2 WASH. U. GLOBAL STUD. L. REV. 97, 99–104 (2003).

[77] Issued 27 August 2002, effective 1 October 2002.

[78] Lifa Fa (立法法) [Law on Legislation] (promulgated by the Standing Comm. Nat'l People's Cong., Mar. 15, 2000, effective July 1, 2000) (China) *translated in* China Law Translate, http://www.chinalawtranslate.com/2015lawlaw/?lang=en.

[79] Guizhang Zhiding Chengxu Tiaoli (规章制定程序条例) [Ordinance Concerning the Procedures for the Formulation of Administrative Rules] (promulgated by the St. Council, Nov. 16, 2001, effective Jan. 1, 2002) (China).

Article 9 Where laws have not been developed on any matters specified in Article 8 of this Law, the National People's Congress or its Standing Committee may make a decision to empower the State Council to first develop administrative regulations as actually needed on certain matters, except for matters involving criminal offense and penalties, compulsory measures and penalties involving deprivation of a citizen's political rights or restriction of personal freedom, and the justice system.

[...]

Article 72 The people's congress and its standing committee of a province, autonomous region, or municipality directly under the Central Government may, according to the specific circumstances and actual needs of the administrative region, develop local regulations, provided that such regulations do not contravene the Constitution, laws, and administrative regulations.'

Article 9 thus provides for the *delegation* of norm-making power from the national legislative authority to the national administrative authority, including the State Council itself and its departments (ministries). Article 72 provides for the *specification* of norms by subordinate governmental units to adapt national norms to local conditions or adopt new norms appropriate for local conditions, provided that such norms are not contrary to the Chinese constitution, national laws or national administrative regulations. It goes without saying that national, delegated or specifying norms must be compatible with the Constitution of the Communist Party of China (CPC)[80] and CPC policy.

Numerous authorities, in addition to the CPC, may adopt norms. The institutions and the types of norms that they may adopt include NPC legislation (*jiben falu*) and State Council regulations (*xingzheng fagui/guizhang*), decisions (*jueding*) and orders (*mingling*), which may be either definitive or provisional (*zanxing*).[81] State Council departments (ministries) and commissions may issue regulations (*guizhang*), directives (*zhishi*), orders (*mingling*), provisions (*guiding*), rules (*shishi xize*), circulars (*tongzhi*) and other normative documents, which may be known as orders (*mingling*), decrees (*ling*), directives (*zhiling*), resolutions (*jueyi*), decisions (*jueding*), instructions (*zhishi*) or announcements (*gong gao*). Provincial and lower levels of government may issue local regulations (*difangxing fagui*), resolutions (*jueyi*), decisions (*jueding*), local administrative rules (*difangxing xingzheng guizhang*) or

---

[80] XIANFA [Constitution] (China), *translated in* CONSTITUTION OF THE COMMUNIST PARTY OF CHINA (CHINESE–ENGLISH) (Foreign Languages Press, 2001).

[81] On flexibility, adaptation to local conditions and trial legislation in Chinese governance, see MAO'S INVISIBLE HAND: THE POLITICAL FOUNDATIONS OF ADAPTIVE GOVERNANCE IN CHINA (Sebastian Heilman, Elizabeth J. Perry & Patricia M. Thornton eds., 2011).

other normative documents (*guifanxing wenjian*).[82] In addition to the numerous norm-making authorities and types of acts, the lines of lawmaking authority and the normative status of particular acts are not always clear.[83]

In addition to legislative and administrative authorities,[84] the Supreme
People's Court (SPC) and the Supreme People's Procuratorate (SPP) are
entitled to issue interpretations, which unlike regular court judgments have
independent normative force.[85] In 2013 the SPC and the SPP issued interpretations on several issues concerning the Application of Law in the Handling of
Food-Related Criminal Cases.[86] They stated that food containing pesticide
residues that exceeded the standard limits was 'enough to cause serious food
poisoning or other food-borne diseases' within the meaning of Article 143 of
the Chinese Criminal Code. They also interpreted Article 144 of the Criminal
Code to include 'using forbidden pesticides in planting, cultivation, selling,
transportation or storage of edible agricultural products'.

III Hard Law and Soft Law

According to our calculations, there are more than 135 different acts currently
in force in the Chinese legal system about pesticides; this does not include
either international or regional measures or general policy documents, which
in China often are recognized to have legal force.[87] This number itself is a
severe underestimate because our research includes acts of only two provinces
and one municipality. We can summarize this normative complex as being
composed of the following types and numbers of acts: *ji ben fa lu* (laws), three;

---

[82] List reconstructed from PETER HOWARD CORNE, FOREIGN INVESTMENT IN CHINA: THE
ADMINISTRATIVE LEGAL SYSTEM (1997).

[83] *See, e.g.*, Randall Peerenboom, *Globalization, Path Dependency and the Limits of Law:
Administrative Law Reform and Rule of Law in the People's Republic of China*, 19 BERKELEY
J. INT'L. L. 161–264 (2001). On types of administrative rules in the Chinese legal system, *see*
PETER HOWARD CORNE, FOREIGN INVESTMENT IN CHINA: THE ADMINISTRATIVE LEGAL
SYSTEM (1997); WEI LUO, CHINESE LAW AND LEGAL RESEARCH 109–17 (2005); JIANFU CHEN,
CHINESE LAW: CONTEXT AND TRANSFORMATION 191, 252–54 (2008); Chaoyang Jiang,
Departmental Rule-Making in the People's Republic of China, in LAW-MAKING IN THE
PEOPLE'S REPUBLIC OF CHINA 105–16 (Jan Michiel Otto, Maurice V. Polak, Jianfu Chen &
Yuwen Li eds., 2000).

[84] In China, '[t]he power to interpret rules belongs to the formulating organs of rules': Guizhang
Zhiding Chengxu Tiaoli, *supra* note 79.

[85] *See* JIANFU CHEN, CHINESE LAW: CONTEXT AND TRANSFORMATION 200–02 (2008).

[86] *China Releases Punishment Standards for Food-Related Crimes*, CHINA BRIEFING (May 28,
2013), http://www.china-briefing.com/news/2013/05/28/china-releases-punishment-standard-for-
food-related-crimes.html.

[87] The principal domestic measures on pesticides are outlined in Snyder & Ni, *supra* note 60.

guo ji tiao ye (international treaties), two; *xing zheng fa gui* (administrative regulations), five; *tong zhi* (circulars), forty-one; *fa gui jie shi* (interpretations), two; *jue ding* (decisions), one; *zhi dao yi jian* (guidance opinions), three; *mingling* (orders), eleven; *xing zheng gui zhang* (provisions), seven; *gong gao* (announcements), thirty-two; *shi shi xi ze* (rules), two; *gui hua* (proposals), one; *zheng ce jie xian* (department regulatory documents), one; *gui ding* (provisions), five; *di fang xing fa gui* (local regulations), one; *gui fan xing wen jian* (normative documents), five; and *di fang xing xing zheng gui* (local administrative rules), twelve. The term for the act does not always indicate the norm-making authority; sometimes the same term may be used for norms made by different authorities. Clearly, however, the extremely complex system for regulating pesticides is a prime example of a 'hybrid state hard and soft law structure'.[88] More than one-third of all the norms identified above (47 out of 135) are soft law.[89]

China's national measures concerning pesticides include two legislative measures and one administrative measure: the 2006 Law on the Quality and Safety of Agricultural Products (Law on Agricultural Product Quality Safety),[90] the 2015 Food Safety Law (FSL 2015)[91] and Chinese State Council Regulations on Pesticide Administration.[92] The Pesticides Regulation

---

[88] According to the terminology of Luo Haocai & Song Gongde, Soft Law Governance: Towards an Integrated Approach 321–432 (Ben Armour & Tong Hailong trans., 2013). Under the heading 'Regulations on the Control of Agricultural Chemicals', the authors (at p. 412) counted ten soft law measures out of a total of forty-nine provisions as of November 2001.

[89] We classify the following as soft law: many *tong zhi* (circulars), *zhi dao yi jian* (guidance opinions), many *gong gao* (announcements), *gui hua* (proposals) and *gui fan xing wen jian* (normative documents). There is no universally agreed definition of soft law. In addition, the Chinese legal system includes many more types of norms, of varying normative status, than do Western legal systems. Institutional origin and nomenclature of the act do not always indicate hard or soft law status. The normative status of act may also depend on which unit within an institution issues the act. Here we draw mainly on the definition of soft law as 'rules of conduct which, in principle, have no legally binding force but which, nevertheless, may have practical [and even] legal effects': Francis Snyder, *The Effectiveness of European Community Law* 56 Modern L. Rev. 19, 32 (1993), further developed in Francis Snyder, *Soft Law and Institutional Practice in the European Community*, in The Construction of Europe : Essays in Honour of Emile Noël 197–225 (Stephen D. Martin ed., 1994). Particularly useful for classification was Luo Haocai & Song Gongde, Soft Law Governance : Towards an Integrated Approach (Ben Armour & Tang Hailong trans., 2013), especially pp. 365–423.

[90] Nongchanpin Zhi Liang Anquan Fa (农产品质量安全法,) [Agricultural Product Quality Safety Law] (promulgated by the Standing Comm. Nat'l People's Cong., Apr. 29, 2006, effective Nov. 1, 2006), CLI.1.76285(EN) (Lawinfochina).

[91] Shipin Anquan Fa (食品安全法) [Food Safety Law] (promulgated by the Standing Comm. Nat'l People's Cong., Apr. 24, 2015, effective Oct. 1, 2015), CLI.1.247403(EN) (PKUlaw).

[92] Nongyao Guanli Tiaoli (农药管理条例) [Regulations on Pesticide Administration], (promulgated by the St. Council, May 8 May, 1997, effective Nov. 29, 2001 CLI.2.38098(EN)

expressly refers to international law, stating that '[w]here an international treaty related to pesticide that the People's Republic of China has conclude [d] or acceded to contains . . . provisions different from those of these Regulations, the provisions of the international treaty shall apply, unless the provisions are those on which the People's Republic of China has declared reservations'.[93] It embraces legally binding measures but not soft law, though the Chinese government appears to have taken both types of international measures seriously. A new Regulation on Pesticide Administration, now known as the Regulation on Control of Agrochemicals (State Council Decree 677), was released on 1 April 2017.[94] It consolidates the central role of the Ministry of Agriculture in pesticide regulation and abolishes temporary registration of pesticides. Taken together, these measures aim to severely limit the use of highly toxic pesticides in agricultural production and hence as residues in food.

In addition to this basic framework, China has specific domestic legislation on chemicals.[95] The Measures on Environmental Administration of New Chemical Substances (MEANCS) were originally issued in 2003 and were revised by Order No. 7 (the 'New MEANCS') by the Ministry of Environmental Protection (MEP) 19 January 2010).[96] They are known as 'China REACH', because they are modelled on the EU's Regulation on Registration,

(PKUlaw); *see Pesticides and Biocides Compliance*, CHEM. INSPECTION & REG. SERV., http://www.cirs-reach.com/China_Chemical_Regulation/China_Pesticides_Herbicides_Registration.html (last visited Mar. 31, 2017).

[93] Nongyao Guanli Tiaoli, *supra* note 92, art. 48.

[94] Lin Fang, *China Promulgates New Pesticide Regulation*, (Apr. 5, 2017), https://agrochemical .chemlinked.com/news/news/china-promulgates-new-pesticide-regulation. Mi Gao, *A Comparative Analysis of China's New and Old Pesticide Regulation*, CHEMLINKED (Mar. 6, 2017), https://agrochemical.chemlinked.com/agro-analysisexpert-article/comparative-analysis-chinas-new-and-and-old-pesticide-regulation. *Inter-ministerial Consultations on Implementing Rules Are in Progress*, Webinar, CHEMLINKED (Apr. 25, 2017; notice received by email (on file with the authors). *See also* Lin Fang, *Summary of the 5 Draft Supporting Rules for Chinese Pesticide Regulation*, CHEMLINKED (Apr. 20, 2017), https://agrochemical.chemlinked.com/node.

[95] Measures on chemicals are listed and described at https://agrochemical.chemlinked.com/chempedia/chinese-pesticide-legislation-overview#Expert (last visited Oct. 18, 2016). *See also New Chemical Substance Notification in China – China REACH*, CHEM. INSPECTION & REG. SERV. (2016), http://www.cirs-reach.com/China_Chemical_Regulation/IECSC_China_REACH_China_New_Chemical_Registration.html; and ICAMA, CHINA PESTICIDE INFORMATION NETWORK, http://www.chinapesticide.gov.cn/ywb/index.jhtml (last visited Oct. 18, 2016).

[96] *New Chemical Substance Notification in China – China REACH*, *supra* note 95.

Evaluation, Authorisation and Restriction of Chemicals ('the REACH Regulation').[97] Companies are required to notify the MEP Chemical Registration Centre (CRC) of the production or import of new chemical substances to be used as ingredients or intermediaries for pesticides and other chemicals. Supporting documents for the New MEANCs were issued in September 2010.[98] In 2016, China notified the WTO of a proposed revision of China REACH by a non–legally binding guidance document[99] stating that except for the production and importation of new chemical substances,[100] China REACH will not apply to pesticides.[101] Instead, supplementing the basic legislative framework, a host of other laws and regulations shall govern the management and use of pesticides in domestic agriculture.

IV *Standards and Alignment*

National food safety standards in China are legally binding, so the adoption of national Chinese standards about pesticide residues transforms non–legally binding Codex standards into legally binding norms. Due partly to a lack of resources, the alignment of domestic standards with international standards has been a difficult challenge for the Chinese government but one that it is gradually meeting, while still leaving room for differing national standards where necessary. MRLs in China are set by the National Health and Family Planning Commission (NHFPC) of the Ministry of Agriculture (MOA) and announced jointly by the NHFPC and the MOA. The basic Chinese national food safety standard on pesticide residues is currently GB 2763-2016 National Food Safety Standard – Maximum Residue Limits for Pesticides in Food.[102]

[97] Commission Regulation 1907/2006 of Dec. 18 2006, Registration, Evaluation, Authorisation and Restriction of Chemicals, 2006 O.J. (L 396) 1, http://eur-lex.europa.eu/legal-content/EN/TXT/?uri=CELEX:32006R1907.

[98] These documents as of 2012 are listed in Hoi et al., *supra* note 72, at 188, Table 5.

[99] *China Looks Set to Finalize Technical Document on New Chemical Substance Declaration and Registration*, CʜᴇᴍADVISOR (2016), https://www.chemadvisor.com/news/604-china-looks-set-to-finalize-technical-document-on-new-chemical-substance-declaration-and-registration.

[100] On importation and exportation of pesticides, *see* Ema Huang, *Chinese Pesticide Import/Export Management*, CʜᴇᴍLɪɴᴋᴇᴅ (June 25, 2014), https://agrochemical.chemlinked.com/agro-analysisexpert-article/china-pesticide-importexport-management.

[101] *New Chemical Substance Notification in China – China REACH, supra* note 95.

[102] *See* Summer Jiang, *China Releases 107 National Food safety Standards Related to Pesticide MRLs and Determination Methods*, CʜᴇᴍLɪɴᴋᴇᴅ (Jan. 4, 2017), https://food.chemlinked.com/news/food-news/china-releases-107-national-food-safety-standards-related-pesticide-mrls-and-determination-methods.

The code 'GB' indicates that the standard is a national, legally binding standard.

The pace of alignment of national MRLs with international standards was slow in the early years after Chinese accession to the WTO. By 2005 China had established only 478 MRLs for 136 pesticides used in more than thirty agricultural products.[103] By 2007, the number had increased slightly to 484 standards – very few compared to the United States (more than 8600), the EU (more than 22 000) or Japan (more than 9000). At the time, fewer than 20 per cent of Chinese pesticide residue standards conformed to international standards; Codex had already adopted more than 2500 MRLs.[104]

Since China began to chair the CCPR in 2006, however, the pace of alignment has quickened dramatically.[105] GB 2763-2014 was announced by the National Health and Family Planning Commission and the MOA on 28 March 2014 and entered into force on 1 August 2014. It set 3650 MRLs for 387 pesticides, including 473 new MRLs for fruit and now covering 'almost all food categories and all pesticides used in China'.[106] It was updated on 18 December 2016 by the current GB 2763-2016.[107] The new standard specified 4160 MRLs in thirteen food categories;[108] this included 184 MRLs for twenty-

---

[103] Yibing He, *Pesticide Residue Evaluation in China*, PowerPoint Presentation, http://www.gmu .org/presentation pdf/day2HE.pdf (last visited Mar. 15, 2017).

[104] Fengxia Dong & Helen H. Jensen, *Challenges for China's Agricultural Exports: Compliance with Sanitary and Phytosanitary Measures*, 22 CHOICES 19, 20 (2007).

[105] For a thorough review, see FOOD SAFETY IN CHINA: SCIENCE, TECHNOLOGY, MANAGEMENT AND REGULATION, (Joseph J. Jen & Chen Junshi eds., 2017).

[106] *China GB 2763-2014 Maximum Residue Limits for Pesticide in Food Published*, CHEM. INSPECTION & REG. SERV. (May 29, 2014), http://www.circs-group.com/food/news/GB_2763- 2014_maximum_residue-pesticide.html. For GB 2763-2014, an unofficial English translation may be found in M. MEADOR & MA JIE, U.S. DEP'T OF AGRIC., FOREIGN AGRIC. SERV., CHINA – PEOPLE'S REPUBLIC OF: MAXIMUM RESIDUE LIMITS FOR PESTICIDE IN FOOD (2014), http://gain.fas.usda.gov/Recent%20GAIN%20Publications/Maximum%20Residue%20Limits% 20for%20Pesticides%20in%20Food_Beijing_China%20-%20Peoples%20Republic%20of_4-30- 2014.pdf. It replaced GB 2763-2012 and was implemented as of 1 August 2014.

[107] See also Ministry of Agriculture Press Office, National Food Safety Standards for Pesticide Residues in Food, 2016 Version of the Release of Pesticide Residues in China to 4140 Standard Limit, Jan. 13, 2017; Lin Fang, *490 Pesticide MRLs Newly Added into China's National Food Safety Standard*, CHEMLINKED AGROCHEMICAL REGULATORY NEWS & DATABASE (Jan. 6, 2017), https://agrochemical.chemlinked.com/node/2963.

[108] According to USDA statistics, GB 2763-2016 set 4140 standards for 433 pesticides for ten product categories: JENNIFER CLEVER & MA JIE, U.S. DEP'T OF AGRIC., FOREIGN AGRIC. SERV., CHINA, PEOPLES REPUBLIC OF, FOOD AND AGRICULTURAL IMPORT REGULATIONS AND STANDARDS – NARRATIVE FAIRS COUNTRY REPORT 14 (2015), https://gain.fas.usda.gov/Recent %20GAIN%20Publications/Food%20and%20Agricultural%20Import%20Regulations%20and% 20Standards%20-%20Narrative_Beijing_China%20-%20Peoples%20Republic%20of_12-30-2015 .pdf.

four prohibited and restricted pesticides designed to control illegal pesticide use. Following international practice, it also exempted thirty-three risk-free pesticides from MRLs. The NHFPC and the MOA also jointly issued a new standard under the GB 23200-2016 series of standards on 106 mandatory test methods of detecting pesticide residues. China's thirteenth Five-Year Plan foresees the establishment of 6000 new MRLs and pesticide-residue-testing standards, with additional MRLs for imported foods and a goal of 20 000 MRLs by 2020.[109] China is now among the leaders in setting international standards for pesticide residues, and Chinese risk assessments are used as a basis of Codex standards.

D PROVINCIAL AND MUNICIPAL MEASURES

I *Subnational Rule-Making*

China has twenty-three provinces, four municipalities linked directly to central government, five autonomous regions and two special administrative regions. In total, at least thirty-four subnational units have the power to adopt legislative and administrative acts, not counting other cities that have local legislation and administrative powers. The Legislation Law (Article 72) provides for specification or adaptation of national measures by provincial and municipal legislatures according to local conditions. Moreover, Article 82 of the same law provides for analogous powers by provincial or other local administrative authorities. It states that '[t]he people's government of a province, an autonomous region, a municipality directly under the Central Government, a districted city, or an autonomous prefecture may develop rules in accordance with laws, administrative regulations, and the local regulations of the province, autonomous region, or municipality'. As with ministerial acts, the acts of these units are designed to specify general national rules to take account of the size and diversity of different parts of China.[110] The potential for tension and conflict is inherent in both central–local relations and in the Chinese administrative system, often characterized as 'fragmented authoritarianism', and by the distinction between vertical *(tiao)* and horizontal *(kuai)* relations, which is the basic structuring principle of Chinese bureaucracy but differs fundamentally from Western, Weberian conceptions.[111]

---

[109] Jiang, *supra* note 102.
[110] On specification by local government and local functional departments, see PETER HOWARD CORNE, FOREIGN INVESTMENT IN CHINA: THE ADMINISTRATIVE LEGAL SYSTEM 124–35 (1997).
[111] See SNYDER, *supra* note 3, at 65–78.

II A *Tale of Two Provinces*

We give examples of measures from two of the most important agricultural provinces, Shandong and Shaanxi, and from the city of Xi'an, which is located in Shaanxi Province and is universally known as the home of the famous terracotta warriors. We selected these provinces (and one city) for two reasons. First, both Shandong and Shaanxi are major producers of apples, the agricultural product that we initially chose to study, because of its importance for public health and food safety. Second, the two provinces differ substantially in basic economic and demographic characteristics, thus permitting a comparison of different approaches to pesticide regulation. It is not surprising that the two provinces differ in the extent to which they adopt local measures, with the number of local measures being correlated roughly with population density, wealth and complexity of agricultural economy.

1 Shandong Province

Shandong is the third wealthiest province in China. It has a population of 97 333 900 people (2014 census) for an area of 157 100 km^2, or a population density of 620/km^2, fifth in the country. In 2016 its GDP was CNY 6.7 trillion (USD 1.0 trillion), and the per capita GDP was CNY 67.364 or USD 10 144, ninth in the country.[112] In contrast, Shaanxi Province has a population of 37 327 378 (2010 census) for an area of 205 800 km^2, or a population density of 180/km^2, less than a third of that of Shandong Province and twenty-first in the country. In 2016 its GDP was CNY 1.92 trillion (USD 289 billion), or USD 7.609, fifteenth in the country.[113]

Shandong Province promulgates many more local regulations to respond to and to specify administrative rules from the central government. In response to the Regulations on Pesticide Administration promulgated by the State Council, Shandong prescribed the Shandong Regulations on Pesticide Administration to localize the upper-level law. They confirm the governing departments, especially concerning supervision, and require them to check the pesticide market and punish illegal production, sale and use. They also

---

[112] This information is taken directly from Wikipedia: *Shandong*, WIKIPEDIA, https://en.wikipedia .org/wiki/Shandong (last visited May 15, 2017).
[113] This information is taken directly from Wikipedia: *Shaanxi*, WIKIPEDIA, https://en.wikipedia .org/wiki/Shaanxi (last visited May 15, 2017).

require specified contents on pesticide labels and prohibit use of banned or illegal pesticides.[114]

The Shandong Agricultural Product Quality Regulation (Provincial Order No. 277) aims to improve the quality of agricultural products by improved coordination among and increased supervision by government departments. The order refers to the agricultural department, forest department, environmental department, industry and commerce department, quality and tech-supervising department, food- and drug-monitoring department and others.[115] Lack of coordination among local government departments has been a continuing problem in the implementation of law in China. The order also prohibits the use of highly toxic pesticides in natural reserve areas, agricultural product protection areas and water source areas. After public consultation, county and municipal governments may prohibit the production and sale of highly toxic pesticides in their districts.

As a coastal province, Shandong has also promulgated the Shandong Import Agricultural Product Administration Order (Provincial Order No. 189). It mainly requires farmers to use the standard of import countries as the criteria for selecting and using pesticides, thus reflecting the 2015 Food Safety Law (Article 99). Government departments are urged to cooperate in supervision, service and guidance in order to establish leading commercial brands and high-quality agricultural products.[116] It also emphasizes the importance of environmental protection.

Based on the international Globally Harmonized System of Classification and Labelling of Chemicals and the national catalogue of hazardous chemicals, Shandong also has promulgated a Directory of High-Risk Pesticides and related management methods, including more stringent requirements for governmental supervision and reporting.[117] The directory includes

---

[114] Shandong Nongyao Guanli Banfa (山东农药管理办法) [Shandong Province Regulations on Pesticide Administration/Management] (Provincial Order No. 121), http://www.shandong.gov .cn/art/2006/1/8/art_284_180.html (last visited Dec. 13, 2016).

[115] Shandong Sheng Nongchanpin Zhi Liang Anquan Jiandu Guanli Guiding (山东省农产品质量安全监督管理规定)[Shandong Province Agricultural Product Quality and Safety Supervision and Management Regulations], http://www.shandong.gov.cn/art/2014/4/15/art_ 285_5755.html (last visited Dec. 13, 2016).

[116] Shandong Chukou Nongchanpin Zhi Liang Anquan Jiandu Guanli Guiding (山东出口农产品质量安全监督管理规定) [Shandong Province Import Agricultural Product Administrative Order] (Order No. 189), http://www.shandong.gov.cn/art/2006/10/23/art_285_6104.html (last visited Dec. 13, 2016).

[117] Shandong Sheng Gao Fengxian Nongyao Mulu (山东省高风险农药目录) [Shandong Province High-Risk Pesticide Directory], http://www.moa.gov.cn/zwllm/zcfg/dffg/201411/ t20141119_4213537.htm (last visited Dec. 13, 2016).

dimethoate, methidathion and omethoate.[118] Shandong has specified detailed sanctions for misuse of pesticides according to which the monetary sanction is correlated to the value of the pesticide. Promulgated by the Shandong Agricultural Department, it sets standards for administrative punishments by specifying rules in relevant articles of the national Regulations on Pesticide Administration, the national rules on the Implementing of the Regulations on Pesticide Administration and the Shandong Agricultural Product Quality Regulation. It defines five levels of illegality: slight, general, serious, above serious and extremely serious.[119]

Shandong Province has adopted a notice procedure to enable improvement of ploughed land by, for example, dramatically lowering the use of toxic pesticides.[120] It sets forth four principles: overall planning with step-by-step implementation, adjustment of measures to local conditions, priority to prevention and combining prevention and treatment, and governmental guidance with popular participation. It also identifies specific districts for special treatment regarding pesticide residues. Shandong has also promulgated specific rules governing supervision and spot checking of pesticide use[121] and detailed rules to regulate registration of pesticide sales. Both are designed to prevent sales of counterfeit pesticides.[122]

2 Shaanxi Province

In contrast to Shandong, Shaanxi Province relies mainly on national measures, such as the MOA Implementation Measures for the State Council Regulations on Pesticide Administration, for which it has adopted local

---

[118] These are three of the eight highly toxic pesticides studied in Snyder & Ni, *supra* note 60.

[119] Shandong Sheng Nongye Ting Xingzheng Chufa Cailiang Jizhun (山东省农业厅行政处罚裁量基准) [Shandong Provincial Department of Agriculture Discretionary Administrative Penalties], http://www.sdny.gov.cn/zwgk/tfwj/fgc/201602/t20160229_376062.html (last visited Dec. 13, 2017).

[120] Shandong Xing Renmin Zhengfu Bangong Ting Guanyu Yinfa Shandong Sheng Gengdi Zhiliang Tisheng Guihua De Tongzhi (2014–2020) (山东省人民政府办公厅关于印发山东省耕地质量提升规划的通知 (2014–2020)) [Notice of the General Office of the People's Government of Shandong Province on Printing and Distributing the Planning of Cultivated Land Quality in 2014–2020], http://www.shandong.gov.cn/art/2014/12/23/art_285_6753.html (last visited Dec. 13, 2016).

[121] Shandong Sheng Nongyao Jiandu Choucha Guanli Banfa (山东省农药监督抽查管理办法) [Shandong Province Pesticide Supervision and Inspection Management Measures], http://www.moa.gov.cn/zwllm/zcfg/dffg/201411/t20141119_4213600.htm (last visited Dec. 13, 2016).

[122] Shandong Sheng Nongyao Jingying Gaozhi Guanli Banfa (山东省农药经营告知管理办法) [Shandong Province Measures to Regulate Pesticide Sales], http://www.moa.gov.cn/zwllm/zcfg/dffg/201411/t20141119_4213598.htm (last visited Dec. 13, 2016).

implementation measures.[123] However, it has adopted Regulations on Pesticide Administration and Measures for the Implementation of Pesticide Management Regulation, a provincial measure that specifies the national Pesticide Management Regulation. This measure sets financial penalties for selling pesticides without registration or production license, pesticides whose registration or license is outdated or has been cancelled, unlabelled or mislabelled pesticides, and counterfeit pesticide or unsafe use of pesticides. As with the analogous Shandong Province measure, penalties vary according to the value of the pesticide.[124] Shaanxi Province has also adopted a trial governmental policy document, not binding for citizens but binding on the government, to guide governmental action and encourage structural adjustment through differentiated pesticide registration policy. It is intended to facilitate registration by high-tech pesticide companies and to eliminate the use of highly toxic pesticides.[125]

III *Xi'an City*

The city of Xi'an in Shaanxi Province has adopted further specification measures. A first measure sets registration fees for foreign companies at the same level as for domestic companies, removing the previous advantage for foreign companies.[126] A second measure is a municipal notification[127] that aims to reduce the use of highly toxic pesticides by setting detailed standards

[123] Shaanxi Province, Nongyao Guanli Tiaoli Shishi Banfa (农药管理条例实施办法) [Pesticide Management Regulations Implementation Measures], http://fgk.chinalaw.gov.cn/article/bmgz/200712/20071200270072.shtml (last visited Dec. 13, 2016).

[124] Shaanxi Province, Xingzheng Chufa Cailiang Jizhun (行政处罚裁量基准) [Administrative Penalty Discretion Benchmark], http://www.xaagri.gov.cn/xxgk/bmwj/flfg/32515.htm & http://www.xaagri.gov.cn/xxgk/bmwj/flfg/32507.htm (last visited Dec. 13, 2016).

[125] Shanxi Xing Renmin Zhengfu Bangong Ting Guanyu Tuijin Gengdi Lunzuo Xiugeng Shixing Huafei Nongyao Shiyong Jian Liang Hua Yijian (陕西省人民政府办公厅关于推进耕地轮作休耕实行化肥农药使用减量化的意见) [Opinions of the General Office of the People's Government of Shaanxi Province on Promoting the Reduction of Use of Chemical Fertilizers and Pesticides], http://knews.shaanxi.gov.cn/o/sxzb/8963.htm (last visited Dec. 13, 2016).

[126] Xi'an Mun. People's Gov't, Nongyao Dengji Fei (农药登记费) [Pesticide Registration Fee], http://www.xa.gov.cn/ptl/def/def/index_1121_6774_ci_trid_1250608.html (last visited Dec. 13, 2016).

[127] Xi'an Mun. People's Gov't, Xi'an Shi Renmin Zhengfu Bangong Ting Guanyu Tiaozheng Youhua Zhongzhi Jiegou Shixing Huafei Nongyao Shiyong Jian Liang Hua De Yijian (西安市人民政府办公厅关于调整优化种植结构实行化肥农药使用减量化的意见) [Notification [Executive Order] on the Adjustment and Optimization of Planting Structure and Reduction of the Use of Chemical Fertilizers and Pesticides], http://www.xa.gov.cn/ptl/def/def/index_1121_6774_ci_trid_2118743.html (last visited Dec. 13, 2016).

for the use of agricultural land, encouraging high-tech companies to develop less toxic pesticides and improving supervision and monitoring of pesticide marketing and use. Both measures apply only to the jurisdiction of the municipal government.

E CONCLUSION

The regulation of pesticides in China is a prime example of transnational law in light of the definition given by Philip Jessup in his 1956 Storrs Lectures as 'all law which regulates actions or events that transcend national frontiers'.[128] In effect this covers most if not all PRC measures because almost every measure has at least an indirect effect on trade. However, the world has changed profoundly in the past sixty years, and the label 'transnational law' by itself no longer suffices alone to dissect modern regulatory law concerning pesticides in China or elsewhere.

In this chapter we used Halliday and Shaffer's concept of TLO to map the labyrinth of rules that constitute pesticide regulation in China. From this perspective, three features are striking in the Chinese example. First, the normative complex includes both legally binding norms and a great variety of soft law norms. Second, legally binding norms and soft law norms are to a great extent 'settled' or institutionalized at the transnational, national and local levels. Third, the institutionalized norms at the three levels of rule-making are highly concordant, so the textual meaning of measures at the three levels virtually identical.[129] This is due partly to the highly technical nature of the subject. In addition, the Chinese government has aimed to demonstrate that it is a good player on the international stage as well as in the domestic regulatory arena and is committed to economic and legal globalization. Given limited resources, such a strategy is sound because often it is easier and less expensive to translate international measures than to invest in independent national measures. Being situated within a TLO may therefore be good policy for less wealthy countries, though much better for 'rule makers' than for 'rule-takers'. It is important to bear in mind that today China is among the leaders in the elaboration of international standards for pesticide regulation. While concluding provisionally that the concept of TLO is a sufficient fit in this context, we consider that it needs to be supplemented by more attention both to global legal pluralism and to local contexts. For this reason, we find it useful to sketch our view of the evolution of its normative shape in the context of

---

[128] Philip C. Jessup, Transnational Law 2 (1956).
[129] On settling and concordance, see Halliday & Shaffer, *supra* note 2, at 43–46.

increasing globalization. Such a sketch will help to trace the logic by which we reach our conclusion. It may also shed light on potential reformulation of the concept of TLO and its place in the study of transnational law.

Recapping previous arguments made by one of the present authors,[130] a first step is to recognize that economic globalization is governed not simply by nation states but rather by sites of governance. This represents a decisive break with a state-centred view of law and also with a previously exclusive focus on private law in governing globalization. A site of governance is 'a locus of decision-making with the authority to settle disputes'. According to this broad definition, a site may include but is not limited to nation states. Its normative production may be legally binding, soft law or a combination of the two. Sites are not necessarily linked with territory; they may be public, or private or hybrid, and they are not necessarily hierarchically ordered in relation to one another. Moreover, each site has two dimensions, a structural dimension and a relational dimension. Here we have been concerned with both but especially with the relational dimension. The latter too often has been considered only by scholars wedded to state-centred public international law or working in private international law (conflict of laws); both groups consequently neglect transnational law.

The second step is to conceive of relations between sites in terms of global legal pluralism: 'the totality of strategically determined, situationally specific and often episodic conjunctions of a multiplicity of sites throughout the world'.[131] This view aggregates the multiplicity of sites, but in contrast to the concept of TLO, it emphasizes the potentiality of putting existing but inert institutions, norms and dispute-handling processes into play (*potentiel de réalisation*); regulatory competition as well as settledness and concordance; the often conflicting legal strategies of many actors; and the relative fluidity and unpredictability of social life rather than assumed order and stability. The main foundations of global legal pluralism are globalization, international competition and legal strategies and their unintended consequences; they are interrelated in that 'there is a correlation between international economic integration and trade, the disintegration and fragmentation of production, and

---

[130] Starting in 1999, with Francis Snyder, *Governing Economic Globalisation: Global Legal Pluralism and European Law* 5:4 EUR. L.J. 334–74 (1999) [hereinafter Snyder, *Governing Economic Globalisation*]. For further elaboration, *see* SNYDER, *supra* note 75. The following quotations are from this book at pp. 49, 42, 89 and 260, respectively.

[131] Snyder, *Governing Economic Globalisation*, *supra* note 130, at 334, 371.

the use of global legal pluralism'.[132] For example, the growth of today's transnational agrochemical industry has been accompanied by the rapid development of legal pluralism in the regulation of pesticides.

The third step is to admit the importance in lawmaking and regulatory policy of what has been called an 'international normative repertoire'. This refers to 'the constitution of a conceptual and normative repertoire, drawing on national legislation, multilateral negotiations and administrative decisions in several jurisdictions within a particular historical context'.[133]. International organizations, national governments and lower-level governments and other actors all may draw from this international normative repertoire in developing political and legal strategies, policymaking, legal argument, negotiations and rule-making. Such a repertoire need not be particularly coherent or systematic. This view pays more attention to the 'bits and pieces' of available concepts and norms – or 'assemblages'[134] – than to any ascribed systematic character. The creation of such a repertoire, as for international regimes, may be 'an evolutionary form of development, punctuated and crystallised by periodic "contractarian moments"'.[135] This seems to have been the case for pesticides.

The fourth step is to recognize the potential existence of a TLO – 'a collection of formalized legal norms and associated organizations and actors that authoritatively order the understanding and practice of law across national jurisdictions'[136] – and then to go beyond it. China's system of pesticide regulation may be envisaged as an increasing coalescence, coordination and coherence of norms deriving from a variety of sites of governance. The most recent manifestations of these processes are institutionalization, settling and concordance. The conception of these developments as a TLO, however, gives too much emphasis to formal legal norms and authoritative ordering. Implicitly or explicitly, it conceives of transnational law as analogous to a national legal system, emphasizing the state as the main source of legitimation and the important role of national jurisdictional boundaries. It gives too little

---

[132] This view is consistent with the concept of transnational legal pluralism advanced by Peer Zumbansen, *Transnational Legal Pluralism*, 10 Transnat'l Legal Theory 141–89 (2010), CLPE Research Paper No. 01/2010, https://ssrn.com/abstract=1542907.

[133] Francis Snyder, *The Origins of the 'Nonmarket Economy': Ideas, Pluralism and Power in EC Ant-Dumping Law About China*, 7 Eur. L.J. 369, 420 (2001).

[134] See Saskia Sassen, Territority, Authority, Rights: From Medieval to Global Assemblages (2008).

[135] Oran R. Young, *International Regimes: Problems of Concept Formation*, 32 World Pol. 331–56 (1980).

[136] Halliday & Shaffer, *supra* note 2, at 3.

emphasis to private regulation, which for reasons of space could not be studied here. Nor does it consider the ways in which internal structures of sites of governance influence the relations of a site with other sites. At international, regional, national, provincial and municipal levels of governance, the normative complex of pesticide regulation includes a great variety of hard law and soft law. To understand the working interconnections between these different types of rules, we need further research not only on international, national and local relations or local, national and international relations but also on so-called horizontal relations between different international, regional or national organizations,[137] for example between China and other Asia-Pacific countries. A basic hypothesis can be represented as follows: structures condition, shape or determine relations, and vice versa [structures ← → relations].[138] This applies in both 'vertical' and 'horizontal' relations; indeed, this terminology is not very useful in the context of legal pluralism. In other words, the concept of TLO conceives of transnational law as a type of legal system or a field of law, instead of using transnational law more fruitfully as a method or perspective.[139]

Concerning pesticide regulation, the next step is to conduct further empirical research on relations between sites of governance and on implementation of and compliance with national and local law. These processes concern both hard law and soft law and include both rule-making and dispute settlement. Empirical research on these topics is urgently required, particularly in the Chinese context.[140] Only then can we assess the empirical validity of the concept of TLO. This will help us to advance in our thinking about transnational law as a method or perspective.

In empirical as well as theoretical research, it is fundamentally important to move away from assumptions based on Western legal systems and to understand the specific features of Asia-Pacific countries, as well as the features which they share with other countries. For example, in China the relationship between state and society is fundamentally different from that in Western

---

[137] An example is the study of relations between the WTO and many other sites of governance: SNYDER, *supra* note 75, at 381–423.

[138] *See* SNYDER, *supra* note 3, at 485–86.

[139] For similar reflections, *see* PEER ZUMBANSEN, *Transnational Law, Evolving, in* ENCYCLOPEDIA OF COMPARATIVE LAW (Jan Smits ed., 2d ed. 2012), 899–925; also available as King's College London Dickson Poon School of Law, Legal Studies Research Paper Series, Paper No. 2014-29, https://papers.ssrn.com/sol3/Papers.cfm?abstract_id=1975403.

[140] *See* Francis Snyder, Hu Zhouke, Wang Jiayi & Zhu Dianmeng, *The Judicial Struggle Against Fake Pesticides in China: A Geography of Law and Public Health, 1997–2017* (forthcoming). On compliance, *see* HUIQI YAN, PESTICIDE LAW AND COMPLIANCE DECISION MAKING: A CASE STUDY OF CHINESE FARMERS (2017).

countries. Predominant on the normative stage are the political line, norms and policies of the CPC. According to a leading Chinese scholar, 'there is no such thing as government policy independent from the CCP'.[141] In Asia-Pacific countries, our research needs to take full account of the features of societies, polities and legal systems that often differ profoundly from our idealized versions of Western countries.

How can we explain the development in China of such energetic participation in pesticide regulation? A fundamental marker is the beginning of reform and opening under Deng Xiaoping as paramount leader starting in December 1978. This signalled the beginning of China's legal reforms and the development of new normative frameworks for technical standards.[142] More recently, in addition to general environmental and public health concerns, there seem to have been four precipitating events. First, China joined the WTO in 2001, becoming part of the international community concerned with regulating international trade. Second, the 2002–3 SARS crisis revealed serious gaps in the legal framework for dealing with health emergencies.[143] Third, China assumed the chair of the CCPR in 2006, learning about international standards on pesticides and then contributing to their development. Finally, the 2008 melamine food safety scandal demonstrated the shortcomings of administrative fragmentation, corruption and lack of regulation, and it stimulated the Chinese government to adopt China's first Food Safety Law.[144] Chinese government policies then evolved to incorporate, reflect and affect internationally agreed norms and to integrate transnational law successfully into the domestic legal system, at least on the books.

It is tempting to conceive of pesticide regulation and food safety regulation as two interconnected but distinct TLOs or regimes. Pesticide regulation and food safety regulation in China overlap. Normatively, the

---

[141] Zhu Suli, *Political Parties in China's Judiciary*, Fifth Annual Herbert Bernstein Memorial Lecture in International and Comparative Law, 2 November 2006, published as 1 DUKE L. CENTER FOR INT'L & COMP. L. OCCASIONAL PAPERS (CiCLOPS) 85–110 (2009), http://www.law.duke.edu/cicl/ciclops. *See also* Harro von Senger, *Ideology and Law-Making, in* LAW-MAKING IN THE PEOPLE'S REPUBLIC OF CHINA 41–54 (Jan Michiel Otto, Maurice V. Polak, Jianfu Chen & Yuwen Li eds., 2000).

[142] On the development of Chinese measures on standards, *see* SNYDER, *supra* note 3, at 186–202.

[143] *See* YANZHONG HUANG, *The SARS Epidemic and Its Aftermath in China : A Political Perspective, in* LEARNING FROM SARS: PREPARING FOR THE NEXT DISEASE OUTBREAK (Stacey Knobler et al. eds., 2004), https://www.ncbi.nlm.nih.gov/books/NBK92462/, and YANZHONG HUANG, GOVERNING HEALTH IN CONTEMPORARY CHINA 89–95 (2013).

[144] *See* SNYDER, *supra* note 3.

2006 Law on Agricultural Product Quality Safety regulated the use of pesticides in agricultural production until the 2015 Food Safety Law carved out significant exceptions.[145] In terms of regulation, the regulation of agricultural use of pesticides has a direct impact on pesticide residues in edible agricultural products. In terms of bureaucratic jurisdiction, the MOA is responsible for supervision of the Agricultural Product Safety Law, while formerly the Ministry of Health was and now the National Health and Family Planning Commission (NHFPC) is responsible for administration of the Food Safety Law; they serve different constituencies and frequently compete in policymaking processes. In both fields, international, national and local norms are settled and largely concordant, though more so with regard to pesticides than with regard to food safety. Private measures remain to be investigated.

Strong domestic political leadership has been crucial in mediating and maintaining these boundaries. Xi Jinping's unrivalled position (since 2012) as general secretary of CPC, chairman of the CPC Central Military Committee and head of the Standing Committee of the Politburo of the Eighteenth CPC Central Committee, and (since 2013) as president of the People's Republic of China has facilitated significant governmental and legal reforms. Li Bin assumed the new position of minister of the NHFPC, which was established in 2013 when the former Ministry of Health was dissolved; the previous minister of health was the distinguished Dr Chen Zhu, then the only minister in the State Council who was not a member of the CPC. Han Changfu has been minister of agriculture since 2009; he is also a leading expert on agriculture and migrant workers.[146] Both are of the same generation, born in 1954, and both previously had been provincial governors, Li Bin of Anhui Province and Han Changfu of Jilin Province. They also previously worked together in Jilin Province, where Han Changfu served as deputy provincial party secretary (2006–9), acting governor (2006–7) and governor (2007–9) and Li Bin served as vice governor from 2001 to 2007, member of the Provincial Government (2001–7) and member of the Provincial CPC Standing Committee (2007). Both are members of the Eighteenth CPC Central Committee.[147] Their appointments were consistent with the current Chinese pattern of choosing national leaders from among governors

[145] *See* Snyder & Ni, *supra* note 60.
[146] *See* HAN CHANGFU, MIGRANT WORKERS IN CHINA (2011), based on the early Chinese version GAI GE YU NONG CUN GONG QING TUAN GONG ZUO (1990).
[147] On Li Bin, see *Biography of Li Bin*, CHINA VITAE, http://www.chinavitae.com/biography/Li_Bin/full (last visited May 16, 2017). On Han Changfu, see *Biography of Han Changfu*, CHINA VITAE, http://www.chinavitae.com/biography/Han_Changfu/full (last visited May 16, 2017).

of provinces.[148] They piloted significant legal reforms in the form of the 2015 Food Safety Law and the current continuing reforms of pesticide regulation, which have given the MOA sole responsibility for the regulation of pesticides. So far at least, these reforms have managed to focus on converging policy objectives and to avoid major public conflicts. In China, bureaucratic politics in the form of inter-ministerial competition, which is supervised and coordinated by central government and complemented if possible by good personal relations, is an important means by which the legal and social meanings of norms are contested and evolve.

Pesticide regulation in China hence represents only a part of a more complex map of interlocking regulatory regimes and normative processes, which call upon a wide variety of sites of governance. In China today, the node that links the pieces of the map together is Chinese central government, comprised of the dual rule of the CCP and the Chinese government. In the case of China's pesticide regulatory regime, the role of Chinese central government, relations between central and local government and the multi-plicity and the diversity of norms are crucially important for understanding the law on the books and the law in practice. It is too early to ascertain the impact of very recent Chinese reforms, but it is likely that these reforms will reinforce the transnational aspects of Chinese regulation of pesticides while not entirely eradicating many of the current system's basic features, which are deeply embedded in Chinese society.

---

[148] *See* Cheng Li, *Xi Jinping's Inner Circle (Part 3: Political Protegés from the Provinces)*, BROOKINGS, https://www.brookings.edu/wp-content/uploads/2016/06/Xi-Jinpings-Inner-Circle-Political-Proteges-from-the-Provinces.pdf (last visited May 16, 2017).

7

Transnational Law in Context

The Relevance of Jessup's Analysis for the Study of 'International' Arbitration

FLORIAN GRISEL[1]

A INTRODUCTION

When Philip Jessup's Storrs Lectures were published in 1956 under the title *Transnational Law*, Cecil Olmstead, who was teaching international law at New York University at the time, wrote the following review of the book:

> The urgent necessity is for a recognition and understanding by international and national decision-makers of the kind of comprehensive analysis of world community interrelations and interactions described by Professor Jessup in chapter one. [...] Although recognized by Professor Jessup, the principal objection to the choice of law method he suggests is, nevertheless, injury to the concept of precedent and predictability in decision-making. The advocate who must prepare a case for argument and decision pursuant to transnational law must indeed be no less than a modern Blackstone.[2]

Olmstead emphasized the relevance of Jessup's comprehensive analysis of transnational law for the understanding of global relations and the challenges it raised for its practitioners. Olmstead particularly considered that the new contracting practices with regard to choice of law would require no less than a modern Blackstone in order to be workable once a dispute has arisen. As will be seen further below, the paths of Jessup and Olmstead would cross again decades later in ways that would involve Jessup's rare set of skills as a practitioner and thinker of transnational law.

This chapter aims at highlighting the relevance of Jessup's analysis based on the example of international arbitration. At the time Jessup wrote his Storrs Lectures, international arbitration was already blooming as a mechanism of

---

[1] The author warmly thanks Eloise Glucksmann for her invaluable research at the Library of Congress. He also thanks Dr Hans Blix for sharing his personal insights on Philip Jessup.
[2] Cecil J. Olmstead, *Jessup: Transnational Law*, 32 N.Y.U. L. REV. 1024, 1026–27 (1957).

dispute resolution involving businesses and states. Private and public institutions actively collaborated to support international arbitration involving
various states and corporations. For instance, the International Chamber of
Commerce (ICC) actively supported (and influenced) the treaty negotiations
that led to the New York Convention on the Recognition and Enforcement of
Foreign Arbitral Awards (1958).[3] During the same time period, the World
Bank intervened as a third party to solve prominent disputes involving investors and states, thus anticipating the creation of the International Centre for the
Settlement of Investment Disputes (ICSID) in 1965.[4] In this chapter, I will use
the example of international arbitration to contextualize the notion of transnational law and its potential relevance as an analytical tool. I will do so by
intertwining two analyses. I will consider, on the one hand, the ways in which
international arbitration was a source of inspiration for Jessup when elaborating
the notion of transnational law. On the other hand, I will consider how the
notion of transnational law constitutes a relevant tool for the analysis of international arbitration and its subsequent developments. Jessup, who was not only
an academic but also, first and foremost, a practitioner of international relations,
demonstrated the necessity of establishing such a dialogue between theory and
practice. To carry out the first analysis, I will rely in particular on the documents
gathered in the Philip C. Jessup Collection at the Library of Congress. These
documents include early drafts and preparatory works for the Storrs Lectures at
Yale University. My analysis will rely on three discrete stories that will each
illustrate one salient aspect of the notion of transnational law.[5]

The first aspect of the analysis concerns rules. According to Jessup, the
notion of transnational law comprises a variety of rules, whether private,
public, domestic or international, which have traditionally been defined in
isolation from (and often as counterpoints to) one another. This process of
seclusion, which resulted from ingrained traditions that have progressively
been built into the legal unconscious,[6] prevented lawyers from fully capturing

---

[3] See Florian Grisel, *Treaty-Making between Public Authority and Private Interests: The Genealogy of the Convention on the Recognition and Enforcement of Foreign Arbitral Awards*, 28 Eur. J. Int'l L. 73–87 (2017).

[4] See Florian Grisel, *Arbitration as a Dispute Resolution Process: Historical Developments, in* Cambridge Compendium of International Commercial and Investment Arbitration (Andrea Björklund, Franco Ferrari & Stefan Kröll eds., forthcoming).

[5] These stories cast light on the norms, actors and processes of transnational law. *See* Peer Zumbansen, *Where the Wild Things Are: Journeys to Transnational Legal Orders, and Back*, 1 UC Irvine J. Int'l, Transnat'l & Comp. L. 161–94.

[6] See, for instance, on the notion of 'legal order' and its prominence in the civil law world, Florian Grisel, L'arbitrage international ou le droit contre l'ordre juridique (2011).

the reality of the legal globalization that unfolded after the Second World War. Jessup emphasized how the term 'transnational' law comprises 'all law which regulates actions or events than transcend national frontiers', including 'both public and private international law' as well as 'other rules which do not wholly fit into such standard categories'.[7]

The second aspect concerns actors. Transnational law does not solely regulate the interactions between private actors or public actors but extends to various categories of legal persons, whether they are individuals, corporations, non-governmental organizations, governmental organizations or states. Jessup clarified that transnational law did not merely involve a single type of actor but could involve 'individuals, corporations, states, organizations of states, or other groups'.[8]

Finally, the third aspect of the analysis concerns processes. Transnational law not only focuses on rules and actors but also on the processes through which various actors generate these rules at the intersection of distinct legal networks and systems. Jessup mentioned various examples of these processes: an American oil company does business in Venezuela; the United Nations (UN) ships milk for UNICEF or sends a mediator to Palestine.[9] Building on Jessup's analysis, Harold Koh defined transnational legal processes as the 'theory and practice of how public and private actors – nation-states, international organizations, multinational enterprises, non-governmental organizations, and private individuals – interact in a variety of public and private, domestic and international fora to make, interpret, enforce, and ultimately internalize rules of transnational law'.[10]

The following stories will illustrate these distinct aspects and show how international arbitration has informed Jessup's notion of transnational law, which in turn lays a proper theoretical foundation for the analysis of international arbitration.

B TRANSNATIONAL RULES IN INTERNATIONAL ARBITRATION

The first story concerns the rules that apply to the merits of disputes arising between investors and states. These disputes were infrequently brought before arbitral tribunals at the time when Philip Jessup wrote *Transnational Law*. ICSID had not yet been created, and most investor-state disputes were

---

[7]   PHILIP C. JESSUP, TRANSNATIONAL LAW 2 (1956).
[8]   *Id.* at 3.
[9]   *Id.* at 3–4.
[10] Harold Hongju Koh, *Transnational Legal Process*, 75 NEB. L. REV. 181, 183–84 (1996).

resolved (or typically left unresolved) through diplomatic means, military intervention or by proceedings before national and international tribunals. However, investors and states began incorporating arbitration clauses and choice-of-law clauses in their concession agreements, thus inaugurating a contracting practice that further developed in the subsequent decades. This contracting practice was noted by Jessup when preparing his Storrs Lectures. For instance, Jessup reviewed the (in)famous settlement agreement that was concluded between a conglomerate of Western investors and the government of Iran in 1954.[11] This contractual agreement included a choice-of-law clause that compiled different sources of applicable law:

> In view of the diverse nationalities of the parties to this Agreement, it shall be governed by and interpreted and applied in accordance with principles of law common to Iran and the several nations in which the other parties to this Agreement are incorporated, and in the absence of such common principles, then by and in accordance with principles of law recognized by civilized nations in general, including such of those principles as may have been applied by international tribunals.[12]

Jessup relied on this extract in *Transnational Law* to illustrate the variety of rules that may apply in the transnational space.[13] Jessup's insights anticipated how arbitral tribunals would later construe the rules applicable to investor-state disputes. The difficulty in reconciling the needs of foreign investors (who insisted on the applicability of international law) and those of host states (who deemed their own law to be applicable) led to a mix of applicable rules. Many subsequent tribunals would decide disputes by applying similar choice-of-law clauses and by abstaining from creating hierarchies among the rules referred to in these clauses. For instance, the arbitral tribunal in the *Kuwait v. Aminoil* case determined, on the basis of a similar clause, that it would apply both Kuwaiti law and public international law.[14] More importantly, a similar approach was adopted by the drafters of the ICSID Convention, as reflected in its Art. 42(1):

> The Tribunal shall decide a dispute in accordance with such rules of law as may be agreed by the parties. In the absence of such agreement, the Tribunal

[11] This settlement agreement put an end to the major political crisis that followed the expropriation of the Anglo-Iranian Oil Company in Iran.

[12] Philip C. Jessup Collection, Library of Congress, Box I-220, p. 105.

[13] JESSUP, *supra* note 7, at 14–15.

[14] *Award in the Matter of an Arbitration between Kuwait and the American Independent Oil Company*, 21 INT'L LEGAL MATERIALS 976, 999–1001 (1982) (the arbitrators emphasized the 'international, or rather transnational character; of the case).

shall apply the law of the Contracting State party to the dispute (including its rules on the conflict of laws) and such rules of international law as may be applicable.[15]

This remarkably broad choice-of-law provision illustrates the relevance of transnational law for the analysis of contemporary arbitration. Art. 42(1) of the ICSID Convention refers to state law and international law *without* creating a hierarchy between these rules.[16] This 'cumulative' treatment of the rules applicable to the merits of investor–state disputes offers a stark contrast with the 'hierarchical' ways in which international tribunals have treated situations involving both domestic law and international law (typically resulting in the prevalence of international law over domestic law).[17] The 'cumulative' approach also reveals the detachment of arbitral tribunals from the legal system of their forum, contrary to international or national tribunals (which deem themselves bound to apply – in priority – the law of their forum). This detachment results from the impossibility of resolving the question of knowing which legal system – national or international – prevails over the other when the disputes involve actors who are traditionally deemed to be subject to different legal systems.

C TRANSNATIONAL ACTORS IN INTERNATIONAL ARBITRATION

The second story concerns actors of international arbitration. Investment arbitration is again a prime example of the relevance of transnational law as an analytical framework. For the contemporary observer, the possibility for foreign investors – whether individuals or multinational corporations – to sue states is quite normal: hundreds of investment arbitrations have been initiated against states in the last decades.[18] However, this possibility was quite unusual when Jessup delivered his Storrs Lectures in 1956. At that time, foreign investors were often deemed to lack the legal standing to sue states in the international arena, which was the exclusive turf of governmental actors. As emphasized by Jessup, in this view, 'the individual is not a subject but an

---

[15] Convention on the Settlement of Investment Disputes between States and Nationals of Other States art. 42(1), Mar. 18, 1965, 575 U.N.T.S. 159.

[16] *See* Emmanuel Gaillard & Yas Banifatemi, *The Meaning of 'And' in Article 42(1), Second Sentence, of the Washington Convention: The Role of International Law in the ICSID Choice of Law Process*, 18 ICSID Rev. – Foreign Investment L.J. 375–411 (2003).

[17] *See* Grisel, *supra* note 6.

[18] Seven hundred seventeen arbitration cases have been filed before ICSID since 1972 (*see* https://icsid.worldbank.org/en/Pages/cases/AdvancedSearch.aspx, last visited Feb. 22, 2019).

object of international law'.[19] Consequently, states brought disputes on behalf of their investors through the use of diplomatic protection. For instance, in the *Barcelona Traction* case, which was initiated in 1950 before the International Court of Justice (ICJ), Belgium brought claims against Spain on behalf of the Belgian shareholders of the Barcelona Traction Co. The case raised the question of knowing whether Belgium could exercise diplomatic protection on behalf of the shareholders of a company incorporated in another country (Canada). The ICJ gave a negative answer to this question in 1970, dismissing the case for lack of jurisdiction.[20] Interestingly, Jessup was, at the time, a judge at the ICJ, and he wrote a separate opinion in this case. In this opinion, Jessup emphasized that the decision of the court in *Barcelona Traction* was susceptible to limited jurisprudential effect, as it ignored the reality of modern business practices:

> [. . .] joint business ventures, State guarantees of foreign investment, the use of international organizations such as the IBRD and UNDP, may in the course of time relegate the case of Barcelona Traction to the status now occupied by *Delagoa Bay* – a precedent to be cited by advocates if helpful to the pleading of a cause, but not a guiding element in the life of the international business community.[21]

Jessup's prediction that *Barcelona Traction* would not become 'a guiding element in the life of the international business community' turned out to be accurate: states now rarely, if ever, exercise diplomatic protection in favour of investors against foreign states. These investors, as transnational actors, now benefit from the right to directly sue these states before arbitral tribunals. The ICJ subsequently recognized the importance of transnational arbitration in one of those (rare) cases of diplomatic protection:

> This Court is bound to note that, in contemporary international law, the protection of the rights of companies and the rights of their shareholders, and the settlement of the associated disputes, are essentially governed by bilateral or multilateral agreements for the protection of foreign investments, such as the treaties for the promotion and protection of foreign investments, and the Washington Convention of 18 March 1965, which created an International Centre for Settlement of Investment Disputes (ICSID), and also by contracts between States and foreign investors. In that context, the role of diplomatic

---

[19] JESSUP, *supra* note 7, at 7.
[20] *See* Barcelona Traction, Light & Power Co., Ltd. (Belg. v. Spain), Judgment, 1970 I.C.J. Rep. 3, 3–53 (Feb. 5).
[21] Belg. v. Spain, 1970 I.C.J. at 166, ¶ 12 (separate opinion by Jessup, J.).

protection somewhat faded, as in practice recourse is only made to it in rare cases where treaty regimes do not exist or have proved inoperative.[22]

In addition, the principle recognized in *Barcelona Traction* that corporations have the nationality of the state in which they are incorporated (Canada in the *Barcelona Traction* case) was softened to account for the complex shareholding situations (involving investors of various nationalities) that commonly arise in global business affairs. For instance, the parties may determine the nationality of an investor by agreement under Art. 25 of the ICSID Convention (when shareholders of country X exercise 'foreign control' over the investor of country Y).[23]

Jessup anticipated the changes brought by globalized markets where investors acquire an equal standing with states when making foreign investments and where their complex shareholding structures (in the case of investing corporations) make issues of nationality more challenging for global adjudicators. This was illustrated by the *Barcelona Traction* case, where the traditional approach under public international law (determining the nationality of a corporation in the sole light of its place of incorporation) overlooked the reality of the underlying business relation (with the involvement of shareholders of different nationalities and a principal place of business located in yet another country). In other words, Jessup's approach took account of the complex business reality that emerged after the Second World War by recognizing the legal authority of individual corporations and the necessity to elevate them to the same level as traditional actors in public international law. For instance, in the arbitration system put in place within the Union of International Transport by Rail, Jessup reported that 'no distinction is made between the governmental and nongovernmental administrations, both of which are members'.[24] Jessup probably did not anticipate how business actors would feel empowered to the point of excess, as in when they tweak their shareholding structure for the sole purpose of benefiting from the arbitration provisions of a favourable investment treaty.[25]

---

[22] Ahmadou Sadio Diallo (Guinea v. Dem. Rep. Congo), Preliminary Objections, Judgment, 2007 I.C.J. Rep. 582, 614, ¶ 88 (May 24).

[23] Convention on the Settlement of Investment Disputes between States and Nationals of Other States, *supra* note 15, art. 25(2)(b). On this provision, see Christoph H. Schreuer, Loretta Malintoppi, August Reinisch & Anthony Sinclair, The ICSID Convention – A Commentary 422–23 (2d ed. 2009).

[24] Jessup, *supra* note 7, at 15.

[25] *See, e.g.*, Phoenix Action, Ltd. v. Czech Republic, ICSID Case No. ARB/06/5, Award (Apr. 15, 2009).

D TRANSNATIONAL PROCESSES IN INTERNATIONAL ARBITRATION

The third story concerns transnational legal processes. Jessup anticipated the ways in which transnational private actors could influence normative processes that are traditionally deemed insulated from private authority. In *Transnational Law*, Jessup referred to several examples of transnational legal processes, for instance, when major oil companies negotiate concession agreements head-to-head with countries.[26] Another example given by Jessup, which has remained unexplored until recently,[27] is the 'International Chamber of Commerce exercising its privilege of taking part in a conference called by the Economic and Social Council of the United Nations'.[28] The ICC is a private organization headquartered in Paris with 91 national committees[29] and 12 000 affiliated business chambers around the world.[30] As part of its mission to promote cooperation among businesses,[31] the ICC created a Court of Arbitration in 1923, which has since become the most prominent (and global) arbitral institution in the world.[32] The ICC is also the first business organization to have obtained consultative status at the Economic and Social Council (ECOSOC) of the UN in 1946[33] and is the only business organization to have obtained observer status at the General Assembly of the UN.[34] The unique position of the ICC at the public–private, international–domestic junctures makes it a prime example of a transnational institution as defined by Jessup. The anecdote told by Jessup concerning the intervention of the ICC at the ECOSOC in the mid-1950s is one of the most powerful, yet unknown, examples of transnational legal process that one can find. This process led to

[26] JESSUP, *supra* note 7, at 13–14.
[27] See Florian Grisel, *Treaty-Making between Public Authority and Private Interests: The Genealogy of the Convention on the Recognition and Enforcement of Foreign Arbitral Awards*, 28:1 EUR. J. INT'L L. 73–87 (2017).
[28] JESSUP, *supra* note 7, at 4.
[29] See http://www.iccwbo.org/worldwide-membership/national-committees/ (last visited Feb. 22, 2017).
[30] See http://www.iccwbo.org/about-icc/organization/world-chambers-federation/ (last visited Feb. 22, 2017).
[31] See International Chamber of Commerce [ICC] Constitution art. 1(2), http://www.iccwbo.org/constitution/#Article%201 (last visited Feb. 22, 2017).
[32] See ALEC STONE SWEET & FLORIAN GRISEL, THE EVOLUTION OF INTERNATIONAL ARBITRATION – JUDICIALIZATION, GOVERNANCE, LEGITIMACY 45–46 (2017).
[33] See http://www.iccwbo.org/global-influence/international-organizations/working-with-the-un/ (last visited Feb. 22, 2017).
[34] See https://icc-ccs.org/news/1216-un-general-assembly-grants-observer-status-to-international-chamber-of-commerce-in-historic-decision (last visited Feb. 22, 2017).

the adoption in 1958 of the Convention on the Recognition and Enforcement of Foreign Arbitral Awards (also known as the New York Convention), which has been described as the 'cornerstone of current international commercial arbitration'.[35] The New York Convention indeed provides an international framework for securing the enforcement of arbitration agreements and awards in the territories of its 156 member states. Arbitration experts often assume that states wilfully chose to restrict the grounds upon which their courts can resist the enforcement of arbitral awards (thus promoting the effectiveness of international arbitration). However, this story disregards the strong reluctance of at least some states to move in that direction as well as the active efforts of the ICC to promote a text that strongly supports the autonomy of international arbitration.[36] In fact, the ICC elaborated the first draft of the New York Convention and sent it to the UN in 1953. A committee of states gathered within the ECOSOC unanimously rejected this draft in 1955, deeming it too close to the interests of arbitration and contrary to their own interests. Despite the strong opposition from these states, the treaty that was eventually adopted in New York in June 1958 was very close in substance to the original draft prepared by the ICC. The ICC indeed lobbied state representatives in skilful ways, even having two of its active members, Pieter Sanders and René Arnaud, represent the Netherlands and France, respectively, during the negotiations of the treaty. [37] As a result of this discreet lobbying, the ICC successfully matched public authority and private interests in a transnational legal process where states no longer held a monopoly. [38] A narrow view of this process, focusing on the states' formal consent to the New York Convention, would miss the complex interaction of various policy makers in the elaboration of a treaty that supported the development of transnational law (through the consolidation of commercial arbitration).

E CONCLUSION

In conclusion, Jessup not only found a source of great inspiration in international arbitration when drafting *Transnational Law*; in many respects, his analysis also anticipated the ways in which international arbitration would

---

[35] ALBERT JAN VAN DEN BERG, THE NEW YORK ARBITRATION CONVENTION OF 1958 1 (1981).
[36] Grisel, *supra* note 3.
[37] *Id.*
[38] *Id.*

unfold to become the main method for the settlement of international business disputes in subsequent decades.[39] Jessup even took an indirect part in this development. One must keep in mind the 'very broad attitude'[40] that Jessup nurtured towards the law as an individual who occupied high-level positions in international diplomacy (as an ambassador-at-large), law practice (as a judge at the ICJ) and academia (as a professor at Columbia University). In a fascinating turn of events, Jessup was contacted many years after writing *Transnational Law* by Cecil Olmstead, the former New York University professor who had moved on to become in-house counsel and vice president of Texaco, one of the largest oil companies in the world at the time. Olmstead approached Jessup in order to have him write a legal opinion on behalf of Texaco in a landmark arbitration case against Libya.[41] The case arose out of the nationalization of oil concessions by the government of Muammar Gaddafi in the early 1970s, resulting in the expropriation of Texaco and Calasiatic's assets in Libya. This was a typical transnational case involving public and private matters, two multinational companies, a state, and complex regulatory issues. When gathering Texaco's legal team, Olmstead turned towards Jessup as a modern Blackstone who would defend 'the applicability of international law to the type of agreement, investment and transactions [Texaco] had with Libya, i.e., in the language of the concession deed principles of law common to Libyan law and to international law'.[42] Jessup's legal opinion has never been published but is available at the Library of Congress in Washington, DC. This legal opinion illustrates how important – and indeed premonitory – Jessup's analysis of transnational law was for the future developments of international arbitration. The rise of private entities as actors of public international law and the growing importance of private rules in the settlement of arbitral disputes, which led to the evolution of international arbitration towards a full-fledged system of global governance, could not have been properly theorized and

---

[39] See also, on Jessup's legacy, Peer Zumbansen, *Transnational Law, in* ENCYCLOPEDIA OF COMPARATIVE LAW 738–54 (Jan Smits ed., 2006).

[40] Phone interview of the author with Hans Blix (9 June 2016). One of Jessup's research assistants was Hans Blix, a future director general of the IAEA and foreign minister of Sweden (who gained international fame when leading the UN Monitoring, Verification and Inspection Commission in 2002–3). Blix insisted on the very broad vision that Jessup entertained towards the law.

[41] *See* Julien Cantegreil, *The Audacity of the Texaco/Calasiatic Award: René-Jean Dupuy and the Internationalization of Foreign Investment Law*, 22 EUR. J. INT'L L. 441–58 (2011).

[42] Letter from Cecil J. Olmstead to Philip C. Jessup dated 1 April 1975, in Philip C. Jessup Collection (Library of Congress), Box II-65.

understood without the analytical tools introduced by Jessup.[43] His words in
Texaco Calasiatic v. *Libya* confirm his view that the notion of transnational
law was necessary to capture the complex situations arising from international
business disputes but also that it was contested and perhaps even too far ahead
of his time:

> The international juridical position of the corporation has developed *pari
> passu* with that of the individual and of the international organization.
> Because much of international law now deals with the rights of corporations
> and because there are semantic difficulties in applying the term 'inter-
> national' to relations between states and individuals or corporations,
> I suggested in 1956 the term 'transnational law' but that term is not meant
> to deny the applicability of international law to the interrelationships in
> question.[44]

---

[43] STONE SWEET & GRISEL, *supra* note 32.
[44] Opinion on Certain Issues in Topco-Calasiatic/Libya Arbitral Tribunal by Professor Philip
C. Jessup, dated 1 June 1975, p. 4, in Philip C. Jessup Collection, Library of Congress,
Box II-68.

8

Transnational Law and Adjudication: Domestic, International and Foreign Intersections

BRYAN HORRIGAN

A INTRODUCTION: THE JESSUP TRADITION AND TRANSNATIONAL ADJUDICATION

Approaching the field and continuing discussion around 'transnational law' through an engagement with Jessup's work in the 1950s, and the scholarship that has drawn on Jessup, promises fresh insights into the prospects of law on a global scale.[1] Jessup laid the ground for an approach to law that moves beyond conventional categorization of different legal systems and orders, departments of law, and kinds of legal entities while inviting us to look more closely at how all of those different legal subjects and objects interact. Viewed from that perspective, transnational law acknowledges but also transcends conventional legal demarcation of boundaries between state and non-state entities, 'international law' and 'national law', 'foreign law' and 'national law', 'public international law' and 'private international law', 'monist' and 'dualist' theories of international law, and 'incorporation' and 'transformation' accounts of the international–domestic law nexus.

This chapter uses transnational law in the Jessup tradition as a lens for engaging with debates about the legitimacy and methodology of national judicial reference to international and foreign law.[2] It does so, in particular, through a discussion of a select series of jurisprudential, jurisdictional and topical viewpoints. In a collection that is itself transnational in character, it offers an additional Australian perspective on judicial transnationalization of

[1] The author gratefully acknowledges the research and editing assistance of his research assistants, Nicholas Young, Zoe Tripovich, Jarryd Shaw and Michael Adams. This chapter contains the preliminary results of research on transnational judicial decision-making from an Australian perspective, funded by the Australian Research Council (ARC).
[2] Hereinafter described mainly as 'judicial transnationalization of law' and 'transnational adjudication'.

law, as an additional contribution in its own right and for positioning within the preponderance of academic scholarship and judicial decisions from other countries on the topic.

Transnational law both subsumes and challenges conventional accounts of the interaction between different legal orders, norms and actors. It is a multidimensional concept and evades complete capture by any single concept, definition or explanation. Accordingly, it can be viewed on various planes of analysis and from a multitude of angles. No one knew these fundamentals about transnational law better than Professor Philip Jessup. Like a favourite book or religious text, his famous 1956 Storrs Lectures at Yale Law School, recorded in *Transnational Law*, reveal new nuances, fresh insights and different interpretative possibilities on every reading.

Sixty years on, few (if any) have matched the elegance, simplicity and profundity of his understanding of transnational law as 'all law which regulates actions or events that transcend national frontiers', including but not limited to 'public and private international law [and] other rules which do not wholly fit into such standard categories', as a notion of law for 'the complex interrelated world community' encompassing everyone from individual legal persons to entire nation states.[3] Such a simultaneously overarching, innovative and radical understanding repays careful study in illuminating present and future directions for the study and practice of transnational law.

In his 1956 Storrs Lectures, Jessup uses a hypothetical 'Mr Orthodox' and 'Mr Iconoclast' to personalize the discussion of three postulated dramas with related scenes, as a means of testing the limits of trying to separate domestic and international levels of concern. So there should be no surprise in seeing his notion of transnational law as a fundamental disruption of conventional mapping of international, comparative and national law. In a nutshell, Jessup rejects a rigid pigeonholing approach to legal systems and departments of law. Instead, he offers a vision of law whose point is grounded in the common problems of humanity and a holistic account of legal orders, norms and entities.

Referring to the limits of conventional views of national legal systems in addressing regulation of an increasingly global economy, Jessup outlines the kernel of his world-view as follows:[4]

---

[3] PHILIP C. JESSUP, TRANSNATIONAL LAW 1–2 (1956).
[4] *Id.* at 15–16; for an example of extrajudicial consideration of Jessup's work in this context, see Anthony Mason, *The Influence of International and Transnational Law on Australian Municipal Law, in* THE MASON PAPERS 256, 266 (Geoffrey Lindell ed., 2007).

The use of transnational law would supply a larger storehouse of rules on which to draw, and it would be unnecessary to worry whether public or private law applies in certain cases. We may find that some of the problems we have considered essentially international, inevitably productive of stress and conflict between governments and peoples of two different countries, are after all merely human problems which might arise at any level of human society – individual, corporate, interregional, or international. In spite of the vast organisational and procedural differences between the national and the international stage, if we find there are common elements in the domestic and the international dramas, may not the greater experience with the solution of the former aid in the solution of the latter?

In their specific context, those comments and their accompanying dramas and scenes are directed at illuminating what greater collective experience in domestic contexts of nation states might contribute at a sufficient level of comparability towards lesser collective experience in international matters between nation states.

Accordingly, as Peer Zumbansen has argued, 'transnational law presents a radical challenge to all theorizing about law as it reminds us of the very fragility and unattainedness of law' in transitioning from a postcolonial to a twenty-first century account of law globally, because it 'breaks with the separation of domestic and international legal (economic, social, cultural, political) problems and, instead, seeks to assess the inner connections and resemblances in their alleged differences [under] a more radical legal theory conceptualisation of denationalised human and institutional interaction'.[5] On his view, Jessup is taken to conceive that 'transnational law should encompass and simultaneously challenge public and private international law', thereby 'shaping and informing a much wider field of work on legal concepts ... for illuminating the overwhelming complexity of decentred and highly frag-mented socio-legal and political discourse around transnational activity'.[6]

In other words, a theory of transnational law challenges multiple orthodox-ies and blunt dichotomies simultaneously, all of which are nested and working within (democratic) government's formal architecture and substantive oper-ation – yet another orthodox dichotomy.[7] Conceived in that way, the idea of transnational law therefore challenges conventional notions of law as emanat-ing only from designated sovereign authorities, involving the exercise of

---

[5] Peer Zumbansen, *Transnational Law, in* ENCYCLOPEDIA OF COMPARATIVE LAW 738, 739, 741, 743 (J. Smits ed., 2006).

[6] *Id.* at 740, 743–44.

[7] *Id.* at 738.

official power, within delineated jurisdictional and territorial boundaries, based upon enforceable legal norms and backed by one nation state or others in the international legal community. Courts must be positioned (and repositioned) in that landscape too.

Transnational law therefore straddles boundaries between nation states and other legal entities, categories of applicable norms, modes of relevant reasoning and decision-making, varieties of legal and regulatory actors, departments of law, and forms of regulation and enforcement, as a matter of categorization. Indeed, from the standpoint of courts working at the interface between the law of their own country and other legal systems and bodies of law that are potentially applicable for domestic purposes, transnational law both reflects and mediates interactions with other legal orders – in other words, between international law conceived as 'the law of (and between) nations', foreign law conceived as 'the *laws* of (other) nations', and domestic law conceived as 'the laws of *a* nation'.[8] Beyond matters of categorization, the lens of transnational law also provides a basis for rethinking the exclusivity of the nation state in defining and deciding the authority, content and limits of the rule of law and its antecedents (e.g. territorial and jurisdictional sovereignty, as conventionally conceived).[9]

The point of the preceding discussion is that analysis in the Jessup tradition increasingly exposes the limits of traditional taxonomies and demarcations concerning international, foreign and domestic law. Recasting and even replacing such taxonomies and demarcations remains a global work in progress. Much of the work that has been done on this front owes a significant debt to Jessup and the impetus in this direction created by his Storrs Lectures. National courts do not operate in a vacuum, free from such influences, and their frames of reference for adjudication and its place in interconnected global systems of governance, regulation and responsibility must adapt accordingly.

B THE RELATIONSHIP BETWEEN INTERNATIONAL, FOREIGN AND NATIONAL LAW IN ADJUDICATION

As a starting point, the terms on which international and foreign law relate to the domestic law of a nation state in adjudication by its courts are set by every

---

[8] On the nuances and limits of related definitions, see JEREMY WALDRON, PARTLY LAWS COMMON TO ALL MANKIND: FOREIGN LAW IN AMERICAN COURTS 28–30 (2012).

[9] On this point in the context of sovereignty, see RICHARD JOYCE, COMPETING SOVEREIGNTIES 2 (2013).

sovereign nation under its own constitutional arrangements.[10] In other words, domestic law determines whether and how its jurisdiction reflects and uses international and foreign law, including the conditions under which something that is external to the domestic legal order can have a meaningful influence, although rarely (if ever) a determinative one on its own.

Unless a country's constitutional arrangements specifically mandate or permit reference to foreign and international law, judicial transnationalization of law characteristically occurs where non-domestic citation offers an insight or contrast for an interpretative option that is inherently possible under domestic law and as one link in a chain of reasons supporting an outcome.[11] In his 2009 Hamlyn Lectures, for example, Lord Bingham nominates 'two situations in which foreign authority may exert a significant if not decisive influence'.[12] The first situation is 'where domestic authority points towards an answer that seems inappropriate or unjust'.[13] The second situation is 'where domestic authority appears to yield no clear answer'.[14] Each of these situations remains anchored in a primary focus upon national law and interpretations to which that law is legitimately open.

Similarly, Professor John Bell argues that most national judicial references to foreign law simply offer 'a perspective on arguments already available within domestic law', given 'the divergent ways in which the rules can be legitimately formulated and interpreted'.[15] In this way, foreign judicial decisions meet certain preconditions for their domestic use – they can assist in framing potential problems and solutions, they form part of many strands of reasoning and rarely function as a persuasive reason on their own, and they reflect legal possibilities that are immanent in domestic law in the first place.[16]

---

[10] GILLIAN TRIGGS, INTERNATIONAL LAW: CONTEMPORARY PRINCIPLES AND PRACTICES 155 (2d ed. 2011); Phillip Sales & Joanne Clement, *International Law in Domestic Courts: The Developing Framework*, 124 L.Q. REV. 388, 389 (2008); HILARY CHARLESWORTH ET AL., NO COUNTRY IS AN ISLAND: AUSTRALIA AND INTERNATIONAL LAW 49 (2006). The author is also grateful for insights on this point in discussion with Professor Gillian Triggs at the 2010 workshop for the author's research project on judicial transnationalization of law, funded by the ARC.

[11] John Bell, *The Argumentative Status of Foreign Legal Arguments*, 8 UTRECHT L. REV. 8–19 (2012).

[12] TOM BINGHAM, WIDENING HORIZONS: THE INFLUENCE OF COMPARATIVE LAW AND INTERNATIONAL LAW ON DOMESTIC LAW 8 (2010).

[13] *Id.*

[14] *Id.*

[15] John Bell, *The Relevance of Foreign Examples to Legal Development*, 21 DUKE J. COMP. & INT'L L. 431, 459 (2011).

[16] Bell, *supra* note 11.

Views such as those posited by Lord Bingham and Professor Bell from a UK perspective resonate with the reaction by a former chief justice of Australia, Robert French, that 'the interpretation of domestic laws of one country by reference to judicial decisions and legal scholarship of the laws of another' is a practice that is unlikely to raise 'any real issue of principle', although it generates a need for 'care and discrimination' in its use.[17] Describing the use of comparative material as 'a non-issue in Australia', for reasons including its non-extensiveness, the absence of a constitutional bill of rights and the risks attached to judicial invocation of community values, Chief Justice French contemplates greater use of comparative material where a national constitution or statute is based upon one elsewhere, with particular reference to the influence of US and UK constitutional arrangements in designing the Australian Constitution.[18]

Nevertheless, speaking generally but with a clear view to courts in countries with a common legal tradition, Chief Justice French systematizes the potential use of transnational decisions and scholarship by a national court, as follows:[19]

> There are a number of circumstances in which decisions of the courts or the writing of jurists in other countries may arguably play a legitimate part in decision making by a domestic court:
>
> 1. When the decision of the foreign court or foreign legal scholarship has played a part in the developmental history of the domestic law, be it constitutional or statutory or common law.
> 2. When the decision of the foreign court or foreign legal scholarship has been concerned with the same legal question as that before the domestic court.
> 3. When the decision of the foreign court or legal scholarship involves the construction and explanation of a treaty or a statute made under a treaty to which the domestic jurisdiction is a party.
> 4. When the content of a foreign law is an issue to be determined by the domestic court.

These four contexts for transnational resort and citation might be conveniently categorized respectively in terms of genealogy, commonality, comity and

---

[17] Robert French, *Home Grown Laws in a Global Neighbourhood: Australia, the United States and the Rest*, 85 AUSTL. L.J. 147, 157 (2011).

[18] *Id.* at 157–58.

[19] *Id.* at 157. His successor as chief justice of Australia has also added to scholarship on this topic, with comparable views; *see* Susan Kiefel, *Comparative Analysis in Judicial Decision-Making: The Australian Experience*, 75 RABEL J. COMP. & INT'L PRIVATE L. 354, 366 (2011).

elementality. By comparison, Waldron's theory[20] raises the prospect of at least another (or related) category for recognition – harmonization – based on a relevant cross-jurisdictional community of peoples with a legitimate expectation that the courts in that community will strive for harmonization of their approaches on matters as universal as fundamental human rights.

So it is important to keep everything in proportion when debating or using the citation of foreign and international law, notwithstanding fears in some quarters that judicial transnationalization improperly distorts the 'true' meaning and scope of domestic law. Here, as elsewhere in legal interpretation and argument, establishing the 'truth' or correctness of a position under the law is hardly ever self-evident and usually contestable. In the end, 'infusion' or 'infection' of domestic law by non-domestic law is ultimately a matter of characterization *and* in the eye of the beholder.

At the broadest conceptual level, different parts and sources of transnational law have a potential interface with different parts and sources of national legal interpretation, mediated through different modes of usage.[21] For example, the ratification of international conventions and their enactment in national legislation, to be interpreted and applied in adjudication, offers a different point of global–national interface from that provided by what national courts might learn from one another's approach to universal human problems or common constitutional features.

Similarly, in common law countries, rules of constitutional, statutory and common law interpretation might require or permit judicial reference to relevant international and foreign laws and precedents for domestic adjudicative purposes. For example, many national (and, in Australia's case, subnational) charters or bills of rights provide for legislation to be construed in rights-sensitive ways,[22] with recourse to relevant human rights jurisprudence beyond the immediate jurisdiction.[23]

Anglo-Commonwealth common law contains protection to varying degrees of at least some fundamental human rights recognized under international law, especially through norms of interpretation that are encapsulated in what

---

[20] WALDRON, *supra* note 8.

[21] Decisions of national courts can be *sources* of international law too, under Art. 38 of the Statute of the International Court of Justice, for example; *see* ROSALYN HIGGINS, PROBLEMS AND PROCESS: INTERNATIONAL LAW AND HOW WE USE IT 208 (1994).

[22] *E.g.*, Human Rights Act 1998, c. 42, § 3 (Eng.) [hereinafter Human Rights Act]; *Charter of Human Rights and Responsibilities Act* 2006 (Vic), s 32(1) (Austl.) [hereinafter *Charter of Human Rights and Responsibilities Act*].

[23] *E.g.*, Human Rights Act, § 2; *Charter of Human Rights and Responsibilities Act*, s 32(2).

has been termed a 'common law bill of rights'.[24] In other words, national judges face choices at multiple levels about whether and how to engage with international and foreign law. The considerations in making those choices are multidimensional and context dependent, as are the points of interface between the different legal orders.

Until recently, the prevailing view of international law in much national adjudication in the common law world has reflected judicial mindsets framed mainly around the monism–dualism debate, state-centricity and authority-based legal regulation.[25] However, this traditional frame of reference is under increasing pressure on multiple fronts.[26] The focus of international law is also shifting.

Individuals and other non-state actors (e.g. business enterprises) have assumed greater significance in international law than ever before in history. Stimuli for that development include the universalization of human rights, the reorientation of some doctrines of international law beyond a purely state-centric focus, the emergence of areas covered by international law that increasingly have corporations in their sights (e.g. intellectual property, investment, arbitration and climate change) and other transnational standard setting focused upon multinational business activity (e.g. *OECD Guidelines for Multinational Enterprises*). In addition, international law is increasingly infused with a variety of regulatory forms and actors, such as standard-setting initiatives involving coalitions of nation states, non-governmental organizations and others (e.g. *UN Guiding Principles on Business and Human Rights*).

C THE LANDSCAPE OF THE JUDICIAL TRANSNATIONALIZATION OF LAW

The last two decades of the twentieth century and the first two decades of the twenty-first century have witnessed an avalanche of global scholarship and adjudication on the general topic of national judicial engagement with

[24] James Spiegelman, Statutory Interpretation and Human Rights 4 (2008).
[25] E.g., Michael Kirby, *The Growing Rapprochement between International Law and National Law*, in Legal Visions of the 21st Century: Essays In Honour of Judge Christopher Weeramantry 333, 333–34 (Antony Anghie & Garry Sturgess eds., 1998), citing Higgins, *supra* note 21, at 205–07; Charlesworth et al., *supra* note 10, at 50.
[26] E.g., Triggs, *supra* note 10, at 152–56; Annemarie Devereux & Sara McCosker, *International Law and Australian Law*, in 23–26 International Law in Australia (Donald Rothwell & Emily Crawford eds., 3d ed. 2017); Robert McCorquodale, *International Community and State Sovereignty: An Uneasy Symbiotic Relationship*, in Towards an International Legal Community: The Sovereignty of States and the Sovereignty of International Law 241–65 (Colin Warbrick & Stephen Tierney eds., 2006).

international and foreign law.[27] Nevertheless, the collective judicial and academic work on this topic reveals a number of fundamental imbalances. Comparative judicial reference to decisions of other national courts does not treat all countries and courts equally in practice, for reasons that await further revelation and justification.[28] The ideal of a truly transnational institutional dialogue between the courts of different countries through citation and use of one another's decisions is compromised by the reality of the historical, cultural and other adjudicative biases that affect the choices of foreign countries and courts that find favour with domestic courts from one country to another.[29]

At the same time, the global scholarship is overwhelmingly concerned with conceptual questions of 'why' (i.e. rationales) and 'where' (i.e. which jurisdictions), with far less attention given to operational concerns of 'when' (i.e. under what conditions) and 'how' (i.e. uses in practice).[30] In Ganesh Sitaraman's pithy summary, '(t)he use of foreign law . . . has had many critics and defenders, but the debate over foreign law could be furthered if scholars

---

[27] For example, major texts include RICHARD POSNER, HOW JUDGES THINK ch. 12 (2008); BASIL MARKESINIS & JÖRG FEDTKE, ENGAGING WITH FOREIGN LAW (2009); CASS SUNSTEIN, A CONSTITUTION OF MANY MINDS: WHY THE FOUNDING DOCUMENT DOESN'T MEAN WHAT IT MEANT BEFORE (2009); ERIC POSNER, THE PERILS OF GLOBAL LEGALISM (2009); VICKI JACKSON, CONSTITUTIONAL ENGAGEMENT IN A TRANSNATIONAL ERA (2010); BINGHAM, *supra* note 12; HIGHEST COURTS AND GLOBALISATION (Sam Muller & Sidney Richards eds., 2010); DAVID SLOSS, MICHAEL RAMSEY & WILLIAM DODGE, INTERNATIONAL LAW IN THE U.S. SUPREME COURT: CONTINUITY AND CHANGE (2011); WALDRON, *supra* note 8; THE USE OF FOREIGN PRECEDENTS BY CONSTITUTIONAL JUDGES (Tania Groppi & Marie-Claire Ponthoreau eds., 2013); MICHAL BOBEK, COMPARATIVE REASONING IN EUROPEAN SUPREME COURTS (2013); THE CONTRIBUTION OF INTERNATIONAL AND SUPRANATIONAL COURTS TO THE RULE OF LAW (Geert De Baere & Jan Wouters (eds.), 2015); and STEPHEN BREYER, THE COURT AND THE WORLD: AMERICAN LAW AND THE NEW GLOBAL REALITIES (2015).

[28] Se-Shauna Wheatle, *Comparative Law and the 'Ius Gentium'*, 3 CAMBRIDGE J. INT'L & COMP. L. 1060–83 (2015).

[29] *Id.* at 1075.

[30] This typology builds upon the basic contrast in the literature's focus upon 'the *why* of foreign law' at the expense of 'the *how* of foreign law', as identified in Ganesh Sitaraman, *The Use and Abuse of Foreign Law in Constitutional Interpretation*, 32 HARV. J. L. & PUB. POL'Y 653, 654, 656 (2009). In Sitaraman's typology, 'why' questions go to the *legitimacy* of judges using foreign law and 'how' questions go to their *methodology* in doing so. However, methodology itself operates on a number of levels beyond basic 'varieties of foreign law usage' (i.e. the core of Sitaraman's 'how' questions), including operative questions about the choice of appropriate jurisdictions and areas of law for judicial transnational of law (i.e. 'where' questions), the preconditions for courts to engage in judicial transnationalization of law (i.e. 'when' questions) and the characterization of the different approaches over time of different national courts and their members in their use or non-use of foreign law at different periods (i.e. 'what' questions).

focused more narrowly on particular ways in which foreign law is used'.[31]
However, suitable frameworks and tools for this enterprise remain elusive.

Much of the academic and judicial theorizing about transnational
adjudication has a strong European, UK and North American focus, as well
as a bias towards particular areas of law (public law generally and constitutional law in particular) and associated topics (mainly the connection
between the state and human rights). In particular, the transnational controversy over international and foreign law's influence upon constitutionally
protected human rights exerts a strong gravitational pull upon the focus of
debate and the volume of material written about it, especially through
American eyes.

Both the US Supreme Court itself and informed commentary about its
constitutional jurisprudence have moved beyond the initial rush of reactions
earlier this century to the court's controversial reference to international and
foreign law as a factor influencing decisions about constitutional rights. The
furore inside and outside the US Supreme Court on this issue has abated
progressively, after initial reactions to a group of decisions surrounding capital
punishment for intellectually disabled offenders in 2002 (*Atkins* v. *Virginia*[32]),
the criminality of homosexual sexual conduct in private in 2003 (*Lawrence*
v. *Texas*[33]) and capital punishment for juvenile offenders in 2005 (*Roper*
v. *Simmons*[34]).

The controversy has taken some new turns and the opposing judicial
positions have crystallized in two subsequent decisions in 2008 (*District of
Columbia* v. *Heller*[35]) and 2010 (*McDonald* v. *Chicago*[36]), on the constitutional right to keep and bear arms, and a 2010 decision on the constitutionality
of imprisonment without parole for juvenile offenders (*Graham* v. *Florida*[37]).

The controversy over transnational legal material in death penalty
jurisprudence concerned the use of that material in confirming or alternatively distorting judicial assessments of a national legal consensus about capital

---

[31] *Id.* at 692–93. Sitaraman identifies ten uses, grouped in sets with different degrees of
controversy: 'Quoting Language', 'Illustrating Contrasts', 'Logical Reinforcement' and 'Factual
Propositions' (all of which are not controversial); 'Empirical Consequences', 'Direct
Application' and 'Persuasive Reasoning' (all of which are potentially controversial); and
'Authoritative Borrowing', 'Aggregation' and 'No Usage' (all of which are definitely
controversial). *See id.* at 5–16.
[32] Atkins v. Virginia, 536 U.S. 304 (2002).
[33] Lawrence v. Texas, 539 U.S. 558 (2003).
[34] Roper v. Simmons, 543 U.S. 551 (2005).
[35] District of Columbia v. Heller, 554 U.S. 570 (2008).
[36] McDonald v. Chicago, 561 U.S. 742 (2010).
[37] Graham v. Florida, 560 U.S. 48 (2010).

punishment as constitutionally prohibited 'cruel and unusual punishment' in particular contexts, under the test of 'evolving standards of decency in a civilised society'.[38] By the time that same-sex marriage's constitutionality was settled in *United States* v. *Windsor*[39] and *Obergefell* v. *Hodges*,[40] much of the heat had gone out of the US Supreme Court's internal debate about judicial reference to transnational law, with the opposing positions well defined and debate refocusing upon constitutional provisions in their own context, notwithstanding earlier judicial references to transnational law and material on sexual orientation and conduct.[41]

As a result of the American-centric concentration of cases and scholarship on this topic, there has been a less extensive discussion of the full range of potential interactions between international, foreign and national law within a coherent framework for exercising the necessary judicial choices that arise across public and private law, as well as constitutional, legislative and other sources of law (e.g. judge-made law in common law jurisdictions). Yet, the theory-building work of two of the foremost modern scholars in transnational law and adjudication – Sir Basil Markesinis[42] and Professor Jeremy Waldron[43] – respectively covers both American and European law as well as public and private law. This fact alone suggests the need and possibility of a theoretical framework and correlative tools of analysis that transcend particular jurisdictions and areas of law.[44]

There are considerable jurisdictional, jurisprudential and doctrinal challenges in developing a framework for transnational adjudication, given that nobody is an expert in every area of theory, doctrine and practice in every area of law in every jurisdiction. However, the magnitude of these challenges results in some parts of the conceptual and operational landscape of transnational adjudication being more cultivated and illuminated than others.

---

[38] Quoting Justice Stevens in *In re* Stanford, 537 U.S. 968, 971 (2002). For an analysis of US Supreme Court jurisprudence on 'evolving standards of decency', see Matthew Matusiak et al., *The Progression of 'Evolving Standards of Decency' in U.S. Supreme Court Decisions*, 39 Crim. Just. Rev. 253–71 (2014).

[39] United States v. Windsor, 570 U.S. ___ (2013).

[40] Obergefell v. Hodges, 576 U.S. ___ (2015).

[41] This section amplifies and updates material covered in Bryan Horrigan, *Global and Jurisprudential Dimension of Natural Law, Human Rights, and the Common Good, in* Jurisprudence as Practical Reason (2013).

[42] Basil Markesinis, Foreign Law and Comparative Methodology: A Subject and a Thesis (1997); Markesinis & Fedtke, *supra* note 27.

[43] Waldron, *supra* note 8.

[44] The broad fields of commercial and business law are therefore important in testing the application and reach of any theory of transnational adjudication, as significant parts of private law with considerable transnational economic significance.

While there are obviously key differences between international law and foreign law that affect their respective use in different areas of domestic adjudication,[45] judges often refer to both bodies of law meaningfully in particular cases, and both need positioning within an overall framework for the interaction between domestic and non-domestic law.[46]

The kind of theory building that is necessary here must reach beyond standard doctrinal and even jurisprudential analysis, in search of a more holistic approach across jurisdictions, whole systems and even disciplines. Such an enterprise can usefully start with the courts of the common law world as a successful modern example of an interconnected transnational judicial network. As a system of law with its own distinctive features, it offers a model for the characteristics of a reliable system of transnational adjudication. First, the member countries share *'a common legal heritage'*[47] through their historical or ongoing links with the British legal system. Secondly, as part of the broader Commonwealth, they have relationships of sufficient 'thickness' to provide a coherent basis for *commonality in their group identity* that can be justified from a range of political, legal and moral standpoints.

Thirdly, with the common law being a source of law in its own right in such countries, along with constitutional and statutory law, the common law as developed within and between them constitutes *a distinct body of law* too, even allowing for diversity of approach in its exposition and application across jurisdictions. Fourthly, the courts in common law countries are both contributors and beneficiaries of *a common judicial methodology* based upon the common law tradition and its modes of reasoning. Finally, it has *a system of precedent* and accompanying judicial hierarchies that govern adjudication within each member country and from a systemic standpoint as well, as in the Privy Council's status as a historical or ongoing ultimate appeal court for some Commonwealth countries. It is a live jurisprudential question whether or not other kinds of communities make sense (and if so, under what conditions) in the judicial transnationalization of law.[48]

---

[45] Cheryl Saunders, *The Use and Misuse of Comparative Constitutional Law*, 13 IND. J. GLOBAL LEGAL STUD. 37–76 (2006); Cheryl Saunders, Judicial Engagement in the High Court of Australia, High Court of Australia Public Lecture Series (2012); Robert Reed, *Foreign Precedents and Judicial Reasoning: The American Debate and British Practice*, 124 L.Q. REV. 253–73 (2008); Sitaraman, *supra* note 30.

[46] WALDRON, *supra* note 8, at 8, 32–33.

[47] *Id.* at 20; emphasis added.

[48] For related discussion of the features of a transnational system of adjudication, the Commonwealth model, and other global communities of sufficient cohesion, see id. at 17–20, 210–14.

As the then chief justice of Australia, Chief Justice Murray Gleeson, reminded an Australian Bar Association conference at the turn of this century, both evangelists and sceptics of legal globalization's impact upon the judiciary need to accommodate the reality that the reception of English common law throughout the common law world meant that 'our legal system developed as part of a great international network', embracing the UK, United States, Canada, India, Ireland, New Zealand and others.[49] Judges from those countries are now participants in a worldwide phenomenon of 'judicial internationalization' of law, which has multiple prongs beyond the relations between courts throughout the common law world.[50]

Other prongs include, most significantly, (a) national use and citation of foreign judicial decisions across civilian and common law jurisdictions; (b) transnational harmonization of laws across jurisdictions by national legislatures and courts (especially in economically significant areas for transnational business); (c) formal and informal transnational 'networks' for shared dialogue and standard setting between judges from different countries; (d) increasing national judicial attention to legal review of governmental actions in matters that also affect diplomacy and foreign affairs (such as counterterrorism); (e) cross-jurisdictional judicial cooperation and coordination in harmonizing the conduct of litigation; and (f) transnational enculturation of a judicial outlook of openness to shared judicial learning and harmonization in adjudication.[51] Considered from the standpoint of inter-systemic governance and regulation, all of these prongs inform theories and frameworks for why and how judges interact with legal orders beyond their own.

For example, focusing upon transnational law and adjudication invites consideration of courts in terms of interconnected systems and networks of norm development, beyond but also consistent with their location and operation within judicial and precedential hierarchies in national political systems and under country-specific constitutional arrangements. Professor Anne-Marie Slaughter presents a challenging alternative to the conventional view of the place of national courts in the international legal order. Looking at them through a broader governance and regulatory lens, she points to 'a system composed of both horizontal and vertical networks of national and

---

[49] Murray Gleeson, *Global Influences on the Australian Judiciary*, 22 Australian B. Rev. 184, 184 (2002).
[50] Sam Muller & Sidney Richards, *Introduction: Globalisation and Highest Courts, in* Highest Courts and Globalisation, *supra* note 27, at 1, 3–4.
[51] *Id.*

international judges', who all share 'the recognition of one another as participants in a common judicial enterprise'.[52]

Those judicial networks are of various kinds, including 'information networks', 'enforcement networks' and – interestingly, in the light of more recent theory building on transnational adjudication[53] – 'nascent harmonisation networks'.[54] She identifies five categories of judicial interactivity through such networks, comprising 'constitutional cross-fertilisation', a global human-rights-protection community, relations between courts regionally in the European Union, judicial roles in 'private transnational litigation' and personal judicial meetings and contacts worldwide.[55]

In the transnational commercial arena, a series of developments related to adjudication also straddle national political and legal borders. Those developments include (a) the rise of international commercial courts;[56] (b) the constituent components of international commercial law and regulation (including the *lex mercatoria*); (c) shifting competitive dynamics between courts and others forms of transnational business dispute resolution (e.g. arbitration and mediation);[57] (d) the nature of multinational corporations as borderless enterprises;[58] (e) multiple transnational forms of regulation for corporate social responsibility;[59] and (f) the maturing contribution of

---

[52] ANNE-MARIE SLAUGHTER, A NEW WORLD ORDER 67–68 (2004).

[53] WALDRON, *supra* note 8.

[54] SLAUGHTER, *supra* note 51, at 69. For a judicial view of transnational judicial networks and dialogue from an Australian perspective, see, e.g., Michael Kirby, *Transnational Judicial Dialogue, Internationalisation of Law, and Australian Judges*, 9:1 MELBOURNE J. INT'L L. 171–89 (2008).

[55] SLAUGHTER, *supra* note 51, at 69.

[56] E.g., Marilyn Warren & Clyde Croft, An International Commercial Court for Australia: Looking Beyond the New York Convention, Paper for the Commercial Court CPD Seminar Series, Monash University Law Chambers (Apr. 13, 2016).

[57] E.g., Sundaresh Menon, Judicial Attitudes Towards Arbitration and Mediation in Singapore, Speech for the ASEAN Law Association Malaysia (ALA) and Kuala Lumpur Regional Centre for Arbitration (KLRCA) (2013); James Allsop, International Commercial Arbitration – the Courts and the Rule of Law in the Asia Pacific Region, Paper for the Second Annual Global Arbitration Review, Sydney (Nov. 11, 2014).

[58] E.g., Larry Cata Backer, *Multinational Corporations as Objects and Sources of Transnational Regulation*, 14 ILSA J. INT'L & COMP. L. 499–523 (2008).

[59] E.g., BRYAN HORRIGAN, CORPORATE SOCIAL RESPONSIBILITY IN THE 21ST CENTURY: DEBATES, MODEL, AND PRACTICES ACROSS GOVERNMENT, LAW, AND BUSINESS (2010); Larry Cata Backer, *Multinational Corporations, Transnational Law: The United Nation's Norms on the Responsibilities of Transnational Corporations as Harbinger of Corporate Responsibility in International Law*, 37 COLUM. HUM. RTS. L. REV. 287–379 (2006).

international and national law to a distinct body of transnational economic regulation.[60] They all contribute to the impetus for a transnational view of national courts.

D NATIONAL COURTS AND MULTI-MODAL GOVERNANCE, REGULATION AND DEMOCRACY

The key obstacle to political and public acceptance of judges being allowed to adjudicate in ways that are informed by global law is the fundamental objection that national judges have no business looking beyond their own country and its prevailing laws, unless authorized to do so by the prevailing constitutional arrangements for their country's governance. Objections of that kind are grounded commonly in notions of territorial sovereignty, democratic legitimacy, jurisdictional relevance, constitutional validity, comparative reliability and judicial capability.

Such objections can cut both ways. For example, arguments about democracy can be framed from different angles – the undesirability of unelected judges supplanting elected legislatures by infusing national law with norms from other jurisdictions versus the desirability of judges holding the executive and legislative branches of government to account under judicial review for meeting basic democratic preconditions (including respect for universal human rights) on behalf of a sovereign people under a country's constitution.[61] Grouping the basic arguments for and against national judicial transnationalization of law under the two categories of 'arguments about liberal democratic values and arguments about accuracy', for example, one

---

[60] *E.g.*, GOOD FAITH AND INTERNATIONAL ECONOMIC LAW (Andrew Mitchell et al. eds., 2015).

[61] In an American context, Professor Ronald Dworkin famously rejected majoritarian democracy as the only or best account of democracy, in favour of a 'moral reading' of the American Constitution and its enshrined Bill of Rights. He argued for a notion of democracy that encompassed the role of courts in assessing governmental laws and actions against the benchmark of such democratic preconditions, as enshrined in national constitutional arrangements; *see* RONALD DWORKIN, FREEDOM'S LAW: THE MORAL READING OF THE AMERICAN CONSTITUTION 7–12, 15–18, 20–24 (1996). In an Australian context, former chief justice of Australia Sir Anthony Mason has been a strong public advocate of the idea that democracy has evolved in Australia and elsewhere to encompass both a formal and a substantive concern for protection of an individual's fundamental rights and liberties from misuse of official power by the nation state; *see* MASON, *supra* note 4. So every objection, response, and counter-response in this field of debate must be unpacked at a deeper level of analysis by reference to the particular conception of democracy upon which it depends; *see also* Sitaraman, *supra* note 30.

US academic commentator proceeds to turn opposing arguments on their head under each category as follows:[62]

> The first category encompasses both the argument that liberal democracy is undermined when judges rely upon the decisions of foreign courts or statements of international bodies, and the corresponding counterargument that the existence of a democratic society depends on preconstitutional values in the form of basic human rights or conditions for democratic participation. The second category includes both the argument that considering foreign materials has innumerable methodological problems such as selective or shallow use of sources, and the corresponding counterargument that considering foreign law provides more information and thus better judicial decision making.

As foreign and international law and decisions sit outside the domestic legal and judicial system, the interface between different legal systems raises the challenging prospect of different bases for legal authoritativeness, with the legal world beyond national borders lacking a readily identifiable sovereign authority, single legal system and jurisdiction, and coherent set of governing legal norms for adjudication.[63] At the same time, features such as the lack of a centralized lawmaking and enforcement authority are also said to be indicative of the supposed divide between international and domestic law being replaced by a divide between 'public law regimes' (including both international law *and* constitutional law) that regulate nations and governments, on one hand, and 'ordinary domestic law' regimes that are administered by state organs of government, on the other.[64]

How might an account of transnational law in the Jessup tradition challenge the conventional frame of reference for much political and legal discussion of national judicial recourse to international and foreign law? The conventional frame of reference for such discussions posits a self-contained system of positive law, in which the judiciary as a branch of government exercises a particular form of jurisdiction, which is conferred by that system's constitutional arrangements, to adjudicate matters according to the law applicable to that jurisdiction. In other words, it is a jurisdiction-

[62] Sitaraman, *supra* note 30, at 657.
[63] Bosko Tripkovic, *Judicial Comparativism and Legal Positivism*, 5 TRANSNAT'L LEGAL THEORY 285–313 (2014).
[64] Jack Goldsmith & Daryl Levinson, *Law for States: International Law, Constitutional Law, Public Law*, 122 HARV. L. REV. 1792, at 1792 (2009). For extrajudicial criticism of this view in an Australian context, see Robert French, *Oil and Water? International Law and Domestic Law in Australia*, in THE INTERNATIONALISATION OF LAW: LEGISLATING, DECISION-MAKING, PRACTICE, AND EDUCATION 211, 215 (Mary Hiscock & William Van Caenegem eds., 2010).

bound, state-based, law-exclusive and authority-focused frame of reference for judicial responsibility and accountability.

Under this frame of reference, there is a complete correlation between each of *sovereignty* and national territorial jurisdiction, *democracy* and its formal institutional architecture, *governance* and organs of (democratic) government, *regulation* and the law, and *responsibility* and enforceable legal compliance. On this view, international law and foreign law both lie outside this frame of reference for national courts, except to the extent that something within that frame of reference makes those different legal orders relevant for national adjudicative purposes.

National courts can be repositioned within a twenty-first-century inter-systemic view of governance, regulation and democracy under a view of transnational law. Five propositions provide a baseline for the kind of inter-systemic view that transnational law fosters. First, governance of any nation and the world at large now involves more than just government (i.e. an account of governance that both includes and transcends formal organs of government). Secondly, regulation now involves a variety of means and norms for influencing human behaviour that are not limited to what is done by legislatures and courts through and with posited law (i.e. an account of regulation that both includes and transcends formal (or 'hard') law).

Thirdly, and most importantly, the practice of democracy is adapting itself in multiple ways to those paradigm shifts in the understanding and practice of governance and regulation, along with other drivers of its evolution (i.e. an account of democracy that works with and also transcends its formal architecture). Contemporary democracy is defined historically and constitutionally – but not necessarily exhausted in its operation – by reference to concepts such as the sovereignty of the people, the separation of powers between different arms of government, representation of the people by elected representatives, lawmaking by majority vote, free popular elections and the rule of law.

Arguably, democratic governance now extends further, to embrace the related aspects of institutional respect for the preconditions of democracy and substantive values of the rule of law, accountability holding across arms of government and to the people in accordance with those values, systemic protection of fundamental human rights and freedoms, and publicly available and reasoned justification of encroachment upon basic democratic features.[65] On this view, the evolution of democracy transcends legislative majoritarian-ism to embrace the role of government as a guardian of universal human

---

[65] See generally the discussion and sources of different notions of democracy below. *See also* Bryan Horrigan, *The Social Responsibility of Everyone*, 37 Monash U. L. Rev. 155–75 (2011).

rights as well.[66] A question then arises about the conditions within *and* across jurisdictions for securing the universal human rights of people – the sovereign people in mono-national terms or sovereign *peoples* in transnational terms.[67]

In this way, the formal machinery of constitutional government in a democracy is increasingly understood to allow for substantive interactions involving a wide range of institutional and societal actors that give effect to other interests associated with the multidimensional notion of democracy too. For example, the legitimacy of power to affect others rests upon those people who are affected by exercises of power and suffer its consequences having proper avenues of consideration, influence and accountability for their legitimate interests. In short, the conditions for the legitimacy of institutional forms of power wielding are a product of the relation of those who wield power and those who are affected by power. This complex relation does not treat the people simply as the passive objects of governmental or corporate power as forms of institutional power wielding. Rather, the people in a variety of individual and collective forms are active subjects in the conferral, conditioning and proper use of power.[68]

Various emanations of 'the people' within and beyond a governing jurisdiction interact with one another, working also through and with the official arms of government. A pointer to further theory building, institutional architecture setting and community measures (at least from an Australian standpoint) is foreshadowed in the statement by former chief justice of Australia Sir Anthony Mason that '[j]ust as we have recognised that sovereignty resides in or derives from the people and that the representatives of the people exercise their powers for and on behalf of the people, so we must recognise that the courts are institutions which belong to the people and that the judges exercise their powers for the people'.[69] Extrapolating the sovereignty of one nation's people to the sovereignty of peoples in free and democratic societies generally, their commitment to 'freedom and democracy as such' arguably forms the basis for the kind of collective community and its commitments to justice upon which a theory of judicial transnationalization of law can be seen to depend.[70]

[66] See ANTHONY MASON, *Future Directions in Australian Law*, in THE MASON PAPERS, *supra* note 4, at 11, 26.
[67] For a recent example of theory building for transnational adjudication that addresses such questions of commonality and universality in the context of transnational protection of human rights, *see* WALDRON, *supra* note 8.
[68] E.g., Paul Finn, *Public Trusts, Public Fiduciaries*, 38:3 FED. L. REV. 335–51 (2010).
[69] ANTHONY MASON, *The Role of the Judge at the Turn of the Century*, in THE MASON PAPERS, *supra* note 4, at 46, 58.
[70] WALDRON, *supra* note 8, at 198.

In short, under an evolving understanding of democracy in current practice, there is an emerging emphasis upon how the formal machinery of democracy interacts with systems of governance, regulation and responsibility that not only embrace a wider range of participants but also broaden democracy's interaction with various networks of rights protection, power sharing, standard setting and behaviour influencing. In other words, there is a heightened focus upon multi-order and multi-constituency accountability of all arms of government for all exercises of public power over others under twenty-first-century conditions of what is variously called 'participatory', 'deliberative' and 'monitory' democracy.[71] The organs and actors of government (including courts and judges) are thereby exposed to enhanced standards of public contestability, deliberation and justification in their official decisions and reasons for action.[72]

At the same time, single nation states suffer from an incapacity to regulate everything arising from the globalization of law, resulting in a 'democratic deficit' on two fronts for 'international decision-making infrastructure', to the extent that the latter remains 'government-based, not popularly based, and the democratic governance of the nation state does not carry through to the international infrastructure'.[73] So any viable account of transnational law for the twenty-first century must not only grapple with the evolution of the concept and manifestations of democracy in general but also address the implications of legal globalization for regulation across democratic systems.

Doing so creates an additional and important connection that must be made in theory building between transnational law, inter-systemic democratic governance and transnational adjudication. Accordingly, transnational law must accommodate a fourth proposition of inter-systemic governance, regulation and democracy. In terms of institutional and societal responsibilities flowing from intertwined strands of governmental, cross-governmental and non-governmental architecture for democratic governance and regulation, transnational law brings a different and broader lens to notions of judicial responsibility and accountability. On this view, judges play roles, generate outputs and make public contributions that are (or could be) themselves the subject or object of a variety of norm-shaping and accountability mechanisms

---

[71] JOHN KEANE, THE LIFE AND DEATH OF DEMOCRACY (2009); AMY GUTMANN & DENNIS THOMPSON, WHY DELIBERATIVE DEMOCRACY? (2004).

[72] GUTMANN & THOMPSON, *supra* note 70.

[73] ANTHONY MASON, *Decline of Sovereignty: Problems for Democratic Government, in* THE MASON PAPERS, *supra* note 4, at 276, 293–94.

within various co-extensive systems (i.e. an account of judges as both legal norm shapers and other kinds of socio-ethical and politico-legal actors).

Finally, the contemporary conditions of governance, regulation and democracy that bear upon the judiciary, and the interplay between these four essential components, have both 'thick' and 'thin' dimensions. An understanding of these dimensions also assists in unpacking some of the issues surrounding judicial transnationalization. Viewed another way, one of the key issues in theorizing about transnational law is the reconceptualization of sovereignty, democracy, governance, regulation and responsibility under the rule of law so that both 'thick' (i.e. 'substantive' or 'maximalist') and 'thin' (i.e. 'formal' or 'minimalist') notions of those concepts operate together, rather than at odds with each another.[74]

The key question for courts engaged in judicial transnationalization of law then becomes one of simultaneously navigating these 'thick' and 'thin' notions without denying, diluting or compromising any of them. If a law or other purported legally relevant norm that is being urged upon a national court lies outside its constituent systems of law and precedent, for example, the fact that it is not part of the law of that country (as a matter of *description*) does not alone settle the question of the relevance and use of that law or norm in national adjudication (as a matter of *normativity*).[75]

Is a universal theory of judicial transnationalization of law even possible? Chief Justice French argues that, at least for his country, 'the engagement of international law and domestic law [is] multi-faceted, complex, and difficult to encompass within any all-embracing theory'.[76] In his landmark 2012 book on this topic, *'Partly Laws Common to All Mankind': Foreign Law in American Courts*,[77] Professor Jeremy Waldron sets the preconditions that a credible theory of judicial transnationalization of law must meet, including (a) the basis of non-domestic law's adjudicative authority and relevance in national

---

[74] For recent definition and discussion of 'thick'/'substantive'/'maximalist' and 'thin'/'formal'/ 'minimalist' notions of the rule of law, see, e.g., Simon Chesterman, *Lies, Damned Lies, and the International Rule of Law*, OPINIO JURIS (May 17, 2016), commenting on Robert McCorquodale, *Defining the International Rule of Law: Defying Gravity?*, 65 INT'L & COMPAR. L.Q. 277–304 (2016).

[75] This point draws upon the classic distinction between law's 'double life' (i.e. its descriptive and normative guises) in 4 JOHN FINNIS, *Adjudication and Legal Change, in* COLLECTED ESSAYS 397–403 (2011); *cf.* the discussion of Waldron's positive and critical modes of the jus gentium in Steven Calabresi & Bradley Silverman, *Hayek and the Citation of Foreign Law: A Response to Professor Jeremy Waldron*, 1 MICH. ST. L. REV. 1, 15–16 (2015).

[76] French, *supra* note 63, at 212, 229, citing the author and the contributions of MARKESINIS & FEDTKE, *supra* note 27; POSNER, *supra* note 27; and SUNSTEIN, *supra* note 27.

[77] WALDRON, *supra* note 8.

adjudication; (b) the range of areas of law that are appropriate for transnational adjudication; (c) the kinds of jurisdictions and constitutional systems that are amenable to transnational judicial recourse; and (d) the justification of transnational adjudication in terms of the nature and institutions of law.[78]

In developing a working approach to judicial responsibility and accountability from an inter-systemic perspective, transnational law is sensitive to courts as one among many players and law as one among many forms of politico-regulatory influences, as reflections of societal ordering that both inform and shape one another. The institutional and explanatory accountability of national judges to the people of their nation for the choices that those judges make in using or declining to use international and foreign law in national adjudication, for example, has features and requirements that must operate under national constitutional arrangements (and prevailing legal and judicial cultures) but are rarely outlined explicitly in them.

In the end, for national courts faced with a choice of whether or not to engage with international and foreign law, what looks on the surface to be a dispute about the existence of a unified global legal order (as in the 'monist' view of law) or multiple distinct checkpoints between international and domestic legal orders (as in the 'dualist' view of law) is really a debate at another level about democratic lawmaking roles and boundaries that are implicated in any influence of international and foreign law upon domestic law.[79] Accordingly, there is all the more reason under each of a 'culture of justification' (as itself 'a particular conception of democratic legal culture'[80]) and accounts of 'deliberative', 'participatory' and 'monitory' democracy[81] to take judicial exposition of arguments for and against transnationalization of law to another level of explanatory accountability.

In short, the lens offered by an account of transnational law in the Jessup tradition presents a frame of reference for challenging many of the underlying premises and arguments that inform much conventional debate about judicial transnationalization of law. The mediation between national law and each of international and foreign law through the judicial branch of democratic government therefore transcends single legal orders and borders and engages broader considerations of sovereignty, constitutionality, institutionality and

---

[78] *Id.* at 22; original emphasis.

[79] David Dyzenhaus, Murray Hunt & Michael Taggart, *The Principle of Legality in Administrative Law: Internationalisation as Constitutionalisation*, 1 OXFORD U. COMMONWEALTH L.J. 5–34 (2001).

[80] *Id.* at 6.

[81] See generally the discussion and sources on 'participatory', 'deliberative' and 'monitory' democracy in Horrigan, *supra* note 64.

society within contemporary notions of inter-systemic governance, regulation and democracy.

E JURISDICTIONAL CASE STUDY – AUSTRALIA

Australia serves as a useful jurisdictional case study for judicial transnationalization of law, for various reasons. Being a leading common law jurisdiction, it offers a point of contrast with the predominate judicial and academic focus upon the US legal system, EU law, and pre-Brexit and post-Brexit approaches to non-UK law in UK courts. As a major democratic country without a constitutional or legislative bill of rights at the national level, and hence without the major legal architecture under which the courts of other countries engage with universal human rights, Australia's jurisprudence throws into sharp relief a range of other ways in which national courts employ international and foreign law in adjudication.

At the same time, Australia's constitutional system draws upon some British and American constitutional features, and some Australian laws are based to some extent upon laws in other legal systems, especially the UK.[82] As a member of a significant transnational judicial network comprising the courts of common law countries, Australia provides an example of how rules of precedent operate in a system of adjudication operating both within and across jurisdictions. Australia features prominently as a jurisdiction in the scholarship of transnational adjudication.[83] Finally, in terms of theory building for judicial transnationalization of law, it offers an example of a legal and judicial culture that is still struggling with the intersections between the jurisprudence of legal formalism, the influence of legal positivism and the international–domestic legal dichotomy.[84]

In many countries, judicial eras are often characterized and evaluated in terms of successive chief justices and the benches they lead, and Australia is no exception. For example, the last quarter of the twentieth century and the first quarter of the twenty-first century so far collectively spans the Mason Court (1987–95), the Brennan Court (1995–8), the Gleeson Court

---

[82] John Basten, International Influences on Domestic Law: Neither Jingoistic Exceptionalism nor Blind Servility, The Community of Law: Law's Dependence on Social Values Lecture Series, New South Wales Bar Association (2010).

[83] E.g., AHARON BARAK, THE JUDGE IN A DEMOCRACY 197 (2006); SUNSTEIN, *supra* note 27, at 207; JACKSON, *supra* note 27, at 17; and WALDRON, *supra* note 27, at 18–19.

[84] E.g., see Justice John Perry's extrajudicial reflections to this effect in John Perry, Courts Versus the People: Have the Judges Gone Too Far?, Paper for the Judicial Conference of Australia Colloquium, Launceston (2002).

(1998–2008), the French Court (2008–17) and the Kiefel Court (from 2017 onwards).[85] The spirit of the Jessup tradition and transnational law's rethinking of conventional legal demarcations and dichotomies lives on in Australian recognition that 'the interface between domestic and international law cannot be easily described according to the familiar, orderly typologies favoured by international and domestic lawyers, such as transformation/incorporation or monism/dualism'.[86]

An earlier Australian study this century noted 'a level of anxiety on the part of [Australian] judges about the potential effect of international norms on the domestic legal system'.[87] A more recent longitudinal study suggests that, while the High Court of Australia has entered a downturn period in explicit reliance on international and foreign law, conversely, select courts on the world's stage are engaging more rather than less with Australian adjudication.[88] Here, inbound and outbound uses of material from particular legal jurisdictions are equally important areas of study.

For much of its first century in existence, almost all of the High Court of Australia's judges who have considered non-Australian law in their reasons for judgment have either used and cited international and foreign law without controversy or justification of the practice or else denounced the practice outright and again without much exposition of the normative justification of their stance, beyond simply repeating the basic dualist view of the separation between national and international law. Yet, the Australian High Court's overwhelming rhetorical refusal to countenance judicial globalization of municipal constitutional law through an infusion of international human rights jurisprudence stands in stark contrast to the numerous occasions when its judges have made reference to global law for reasons other than to reject its interpretative relevance.[89]

---

[85] See the diagram appearing later in this chapter.

[86] Hilary Charlesworth et al., *International Law and National Law: Fluid States, in* THE FLUID STATE: INTERNATIONAL LAW AND NATIONAL LEGAL SYSTEMS 1, 16 (Hilary Charlesworth et al. eds., 2005).

[87] CHARLESWORTH ET AL., *supra* note 10, at 50.

[88] These are preliminary results from the ARC-funded study by the author of the two-way interaction between decisions of the High Court of Australia and decisions of a select range of non-Australian courts over a twenty-five-year period (1990–2014).

[89] For example, the High Court of Australia has referenced global law when incorporating foreign legal principles. *See Amalgamated Society of Engineers v Adelaide Steamship Co Ltd* (1920) 28 CLR 129, 145–146; [1920] HCA 54 per Isaacs, Rich and Starke JJ, drawing upon decisions from the US Supreme Court to demonstrate the primacy of federal power. To inform the interpretation of domestic law, for example, see *Australian Capital Television Pty Ltd v Commonwealth* (1992) 177 CLR 106; [1992] HCA 45, 41–42 per Mason CJ, looking to foreign jurisdictions to prove the essentiality of freedom of communication coexisting with a

Nevertheless, the High Court of Australia has been an active institutional participant in the last twenty-five years in a pervasive worldwide practice of national courts making reference to international and foreign law in their judgments about numerous areas of public and private law. In turn, judicial decisions and arguments from the High Court of Australia have featured to varying degrees, in the jurisprudence of other ultimate national courts and international institutions. Increasingly, evidence-based analysis is emerging of high-level Australian judicial engagement with international and foreign law in periods straddling the end of the twentieth century and the beginning of the twenty-first century that tests what, until now, have been anecdotal impressions and arguments.[90]

Two of these recent studies focus upon foreign citations in constitutional decisions of the High Court of Australia over different periods of time.[91] Even with different methodologies and timescales, the result in each case is that the High Court of Australia cites foreign law from the UK, United States, Canada and New Zealand, in that descending order of frequency. Preliminary analysis from the author's own study affirms this pattern over a twenty-five-year period, (1990–2014), across both public and private law.

At the very least, the prevalence of those four jurisdictions in Australian judicial citations might be partly a product of the area of law concerned (i.e. constitutional law) and partly a product of their status in the community of common law countries. While these results are unsurprising, given the status of all five as major common law countries and the combined influence of UK and US influences in Australia's own constitutional development, there is value in converting anecdotal impressions into data-based reality,[92] with

---

democratic constitution. To ensure congruence with international legal standards, for example, see *Polyukhovich v Commonwealth* (1991) 172 CLR 501; [1991] HCA 32, 105 per Toohey J, referring to international human rights agreements to evaluate the international position on retrospectively operating criminal legislation.

[90] See Paul von Nessen, *Is There Anything to Fear in Transnationalist Development of Law? The Australian Experience*, 33 PEPP. L. REV. 883–924 (2006); Brian Opeskin, *Australian Constitutional Law in a Global Era*, in REFLECTIONS ON THE AUSTRALIAN CONSTITUTION 171–91 (Robert French, Geoffrey Lindell & Cheryl Saunders eds., 2003); Wayne Sandholtz, *How Domestic Courts Use International Law*, 38 FORDHAM INT'L L.J. 595–637 (2015); Cheryl Saunders & Adrienne Stone, *Reference to Foreign Precedents by the Australian High Court: A Matter of Method*, in THE USE OF FOREIGN PRECEDENTS BY CONSTITUTIONAL JUDGES, *supra* note 27, at 13–38; and the author's own study of how the High Court of Australia engages with foreign and international law and also how decisions of the High Court of Australia are received in other jurisdictions over a twenty-five-year period (1990–2014).

[91] Opeskin, *supra* note 89; Saunders & Stone, *supra* note 89.

[92] See, e.g., Justice Paul Finn's comparative assessment of the High Court of Australia's reference to foreign contract law in different eras ('while the level of regard given to the decisions and

flow-on implications for refining judicial methodology in the selection and use of relevant foreign material in national adjudication.

One of these studies also records a decreasing trend in foreign citations and an increasing trend in Australian citations in a select range of constitutional decisions of the High Court of Australia over the course of its first century, but with a noticeable increase again in foreign citations in the last two decades of the twentieth century.[93] The other study focuses upon foreign citations in Australian constitutional cases in the 2000–8 period and records a downwards trend in foreign citations, except for an upwards 'spike' in 2004.[94] A third study records the high correlation between an overall increase in the citation of international law during Justice Michael Kirby's tenure on the High Court of Australia (1996–2009) and his own record in being both the leading judicial citer of international law on that court by a long margin, as well as the outlier among his judicial colleagues in accepting the role of international law in constitutional law involving human rights questions.[95]

Many factors are in play to produce such results, with courts having little control over when cases might arise that raise the question of reference to foreign and international law. Nevertheless, all of this data suggests that eligible factors for consideration as significant influences upon these results include changes in the modes of reasoning from one judicial period to another that affect judicial amenability to citing international and foreign law,[96] the abnormal influence of individual judges (such as Justice Kirby and former chief justice of Australia Sir Anthony Mason) in raising the profile of foreign and international law in Australian adjudication, and the

---

literature of foreign jurisdictions [in the Gleeson era] remains relatively similar to that of the Mason era, it too is markedly doctrinal in character'). Paul Finn, *Internationalisation or Isolation: The Australian Cul de Sac? The Case of Contract, in* THE INTERNATIONALISATION OF LAW: LEGISLATING, DECISION-MAKING, PRACTICE, AND EDUCATION, *supra* note 63, at 145, 149.

[93] Opeskin, *supra* note 89.

[94] Saunders & Stone, *supra* note 89, at 32.

[95] Sandholtz, *supra* note 89, at 618, 621.

[96] For example, one much-quoted study of successive benches of the High Court of Australia from the time of Chief Justice Dixon to the time of Chief Justice French concludes that '[t]he Gleeson Court offered a largely untheorised form of legalism that embraced neither the theoretical assumptions of Dixonian legalism nor the realist based jurisprudence of the Mason era', or, in other words, that '[t]he Gleeson Court's reliance upon legalism has, at times, been seen as a reaction to the activism of the Mason era and a return to a more confined approach that is associated with Sir Owen Dixon's legalism'. *See* RACHAEL GRAY, THE CONSTITUTIONAL JURISPRUDENCE AND JUDICIAL METHOD OF THE HIGH COURT OF AUSTRALIA: THE DIXON, MASON AND GLEESON ERAS 78, 260 (2008). This conclusion cannot sensibly be unpacked without also addressing differences during each of these judicial eras in the citation and treatment of foreign and international law.

correlation between US and Australian outbreaks of controversy at the highest judicial levels in the first decade of the twenty-first century over the relevance of universal human rights jurisprudence in adjudicating constitutional rights.[97]

Preliminary analysis of trends over a twenty-five-year period tends to support the broad thematic thrust of the earlier evidence-based studies, even allowing for differences in timescales, departments of law, research methodology and areas of focus.[98] The following diagram juxtaposes the tenure of individual judges of the High Court of Australia with both the relevant judicial era(s) to which their tenure belongs and trends in the citation of international and foreign law by the High Court of Australia during their tenure. In broad terms, the patterns of judicial referencing of foreign and international adjudication occurring during and in the immediate aftermath of the Mason and Brennan eras, co-extensively with the tenure of Chief Justice Mason and Justice Kirby as public advocates of greater legal globalization, as well as public critics of the kind of textual and legalistic analysis associated with the methodology of strict legalism, stand in marked contrast to the pattern in subsequent judicial eras.

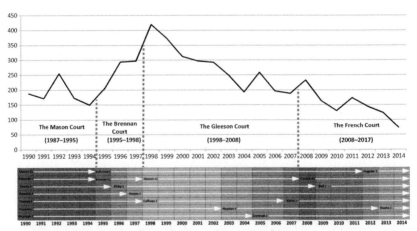

FIGURE 8.1 High Court references to foreign and international courts

97 For further discussion and comparative analysis on this point, see, e.g., Saunders & Stone, *supra* note 89; Mark Rahdert, *Exceptionalism Unbound: Appraising American Resistance to Foreign Law*, 65 CATH. U. L. REV. 537–603 (2016).
98 These are preliminary results, based upon the author's ARC-funded research project on judicial transnationalization of law involving the High Court of Australia.

F FUTURE DIRECTIONS

The judicial transnationalization of law provides fertile ground yet to be explored, beyond the well-tilled domains of universal human rights and comparative constitutional law. Even in those domains, the development of 'a more sophisticated comparative method' might now be warranted,[99] in the wake of the new level that both theory building and evidence-based jurisdictional case studies have reached on judicial transnationalization of law. The connections between international economic law[100] and domestic corporate, business and commercial law seem ripe areas for similar case studies and ongoing framework building and theory testing, as are the decisions of courts beyond those in Europe and the United States. In doing so, the community of judges, lawyers and others who study transnational adjudication pays homage to the Jessup tradition.

---

[99] Saunders & Stone, *supra* note 89, at 35.

[100] *E.g.*, FRANK GARCIA, GLOBAL JUSTICE AND INTERNATIONAL ECONOMIC LAW (2013).

9

Transnational Law and Global Dispute Resolution

SHAHLA ALI*

A INTRODUCTION

In February 1956, the Hamilton Fish Professor of International Law and Diplomacy of Columbia University, Professor Philip C. Jessup, delivered the Storrs Lectures on Jurisprudence at Yale Law School. The three lectures he had delivered were reduced into the volume *Transnational Law*, published by Yale University Press.[1] In this volume, Jessup examines the universality of the human problem and explores the idea that the relationships between states could be analogical to the relationships between individuals. He examines the source and exercise of legal power to deal with transnational problems, theories of jurisdiction (both civil and criminal) and how to approach the choice of law.

Philip Jessup's groundbreaking work *Transnational Law* (1956) identifies the evolution of law as emerging from a concern with regulation of events confined within national boundaries to events 'transcend[ing] national frontiers'.[2] His identification of this new realm of interaction, absent the corresponding existence of a world state, has led to a useful analytic framework for a number of important issues extending Cardozo's observation that 'we must enlarge [law] until it is broad enough to answer to realities'.[3] This framing has important implications for the study of developments in transnational dispute resolution and corresponding questions of adaptation, harmonization and diversity in global practice.

* The author thanks the Government of Hong Kong's University Grants Committee for its kind support through its GRF Grant (HKU 17604318).
[1] PHILIP C. JESSUP, TRANSNATIONAL LAW (1956).
[2] *Id.*
[3] *Id.*

Jessup's insights can be applied to the development of cross-border arbitration as a contemporary embodiment of transnational dispute resolution.

B JESSUP'S INSIGHTS AS THEY RELATE TO GLOBAL DISPUTE RESOLUTION

The idea of 'transnational law' as put forward by Jessup was considered to be broader and more accurate than the concept of 'international law'. He argued that the term 'international' was only concerned with the relations of one nation or state to other nations or states.[4] This concept therefore was inadequate in describing most problems and disputes involving more than one nation. He observed that such disputes 'may involve corporations, states, organizations of states or other groups'.[5] Moreover, disputes between a national and an individual from another nation, or between an international organization and a corporate body, may arise, as we see commonly today. Hence, he suggests that the term 'transnational law', inclusive of 'both public and private international law' and 'other rules which do not wholly fit into such standard categories', is a more accurate term for such situations.[6]

In considering the 'choice of law' question, Jessup puts forward the possibility that a solution might be reached by extralegal means, such as via commercial arbitration noting we should 'avoid further classification of transnational problems and further definitions of transnational law'.[7] By analysing how some international conflicts are merely human problems recognizable in the interactions between two individuals, Jessup suggests that certain approaches to resolution might be universally applicable at the transnational, domestic and personal levels.[8]

In examining theories of jurisdiction, Jessup suggests that jurisdiction is essentially a matter of procedure and not subject to exclusive and absolute analysis.[9] He considers five criteria that might give rise to the exercise of jurisdiction, namely the individual's physical presence within the state, domicile, nationality, consent and whether he 'has by acts done by him within the state subjected himself to its jurisdiction'.[10] The distinction between international and national, as well as the distinction between criminal and civil,

---

[4]　*See id.* at 1.
[5]　*See id.* at 3.
[6]　*See id.* at 2.
[7]　*See id.* at 7.
[8]　*See id.* at 15–16.
[9]　*See id.* at 42.
[10]　*See id.* at 65–68.

are, according to Jessup, merely legal fictions.[11] Transnational law should be responsible for shaping cases into procedural matters and coming to international agreement on procedure, such that the exercise of authority of a state in handling transnational cases is recognized and given effect by other states.[12] Applying this to transnational arbitration, today we see that jurisdiction is often arrived at by mutual agreement of parties.

With respect to choice of law, Jessup proposes that if there is no indication as to what law should apply in the constituent instrument, general principles of law and equity might apply.[13] He also suggests that 'principles rooted in the good sense and common practice of the generality of civilized nations' is indeed the 'modern law of nature'.[14] In practice, mixed arbitral tribunals established under peace treaties often resort to such general principles of law and equity where international law is inapplicable.[15] Similarly, arbitration clauses shift the burden of examining choice of law questions to the arbitration tribunal.[16] Therefore, according to Jessup, transnational law can be regarded as including civil and criminal, national and international, public and private law.[17] A judicial tribunal should therefore be authorized to choose from all of these bodies of law, considering which one is most in conformity with reason and justice in that particular dispute, with the aim being 'the search for a just decision'.[18]

Applying this to transnational arbitration, arbitrators should seek a solution that is just and reasonable and resort to general principles of law and equity where appropriate. Yet, more importantly, as a general practice, arbitration agreements must clearly state the choice of jurisdiction and law in order to ensure legal certainty.

C TRANSNATIONALIZATION OF INTERNATIONAL DISPUTE RESOLUTION

'Transnational commercial law [...] has become a reality, in legal theory as well as in commercial practice.'[19] Such transnational transactions call for

---

[11] *See id.* at 70.
[12] *See id.* at 70–71.
[13] *See id.* at 78–80.
[14] *See id.* at 81.
[15] *See id.* at 95–96.
[16] *See id.* at 100 n.1.
[17] *See id.* at 106.
[18] *Id.*
[19] Klaus Peter Berger, The Creeping Codification of the Lex Mercatoria 234 (1999).

'flexible legal instruments'.[20] Parties conclude arbitration agreements to privatize their dispute resolution while the laws governing arbitration often are developed by national legislators,[21] at times based on global models. However, because international commercial arbitration may be characterized as a lever that recomposes justice within the commercial field,[22] there is a need for arbitral practice, its laws and instruments to increasingly adapt to transnational tendencies. Because the notion of transnational arbitration is 'more than an academic quibble'[23] and has various practical implications, it remains a controversially debated topic. The following sections will examine some of the transnational dynamics in legal practice as they relate to the development of transnational arbitration. Key forces influencing the design of transnational arbitration, including the UNCITRAL Model Law, will be examined.

D HISTORIC DEVELOPMENTS OF TRANSNATIONAL LAW IN THE GLOBAL COMMERCIAL DISPUTE RESOLUTION FIELD

Jessup's insights regarding the continuing development of transnational law are particularly significant when viewed in light of historic developments in the field of transnational dispute resolution. While some authors believe that the question of the applicable body of law in international commerce has been the subject of debate for more than 600 years,[24] others consider that significant transnational dynamics in legal practice were only traceable to the seventeenth century.[25] On the European continent, a specialized autonomous law for merchants, which was subsequently accepted as customary law, developed in the eleventh century.[26] In northern Europe, the so-called Law of the Hanse, a medieval trade association immune from local authorities' jurisdiction, was developed around the same time period.[27] As early as 1300,

---

[20] Peer Zumbansen, *Piercing the Legal Veil: Commercial Arbitration and Transnational Law*, 8 Eur. L.J. 401 (2002).

[21] *See id.* at 402.

[22] Yves Dezalay & Bryant G. Garth, Dealing in Virtue: International Commercial Arbitration and the Construction of a Transnational Legal Order 126 (1996).

[23] William W. Park, *The Lex Loci Arbitri and International Commercial Arbitration*, 32 Int'l & Comp. L.Q. 21, 28 (1983).

[24] Uwe Blaurock, *The Law of Transnational Commerce, in* The Unification of International Commercial Law 9 (Franco Ferrari ed., 1998).

[25] Klaus Peter Berger, *The New Law Merchant and the Global Market Place: A 21st Century View of Transnational Commercial Law, in* The Practice of Transnational Law 3–4 (Klaus Peter Berger ed., 2001).

[26] *See* Blaurock, *supra* note 24, at 10–11.

[27] *See id.* at 11.

the term *lex mercatoria* appeared for the first time in English law, namely in
the 'Fleta', which comprised commercial customs.[28] Subsequent to the enactment of the Carta Mercatoria in 1301, the law merchant was integrated into
the common law by the leading case of *Pillans v. van Mierop* in 1765.[29] Berger
notes several 'milestones' contributing to an evolving theory of transnational
law.[30] In 1622, Malynes defined the *lex mercatoria* in a treatise called *Con-
suetudo Vel Lex Mercatoria, or the Ancient Law-Merchant*.[31] While this
treatise dealt with customary law,[32] Blackstone wrote in its commentary on
the laws of England in the eighteenth century that municipal laws were
insufficient to regulate commercial affairs due to their complexity and exten-
siveness. Rather, such affairs should be determined by the *lex mercatoria*,
which was a separate law.[33]

In the nineteenth century, the content of the *lex mercatoria* was captured by
a wave of codifications.[34] In the late nineteenth and early twentieth centuries,
Zitelmann sketched out the idea of a 'world private law'.[35] Because this body
of law was thought to encompass all areas of private law, it was suggested that
at its inception, it was insufficiently detailed to survive.[36] In the late 1950s and
1960s, the *lex mercatoria* underwent a revival with the so-called French School
founded by Goldman, Fouchard and Kahn.[37] Clive Schmitthoff contributed
heavily to the revival of the *lex mercatoria*.[38] Subsequently, the UNCITRAL
Working Group took up its mandate in 1971, seeking to satisfy the 'need for a
real *ius commune mercatorum*'.[39] In addition to UNCITRAL's endeavours,
Teubner, Dezalay and Garth and Zumbansen adopted and developed a
sociolegal approach to transnational law. Teubner sought to explain the *lex
mercatoria* as a product of rule-making happening 'at the periphery of the legal
process'.[40] He noticed that international arbitral tribunals are the important
external instances that control and thereby validate the principles of the

---

[28] *See id.* at 13.
[29] *Id.*
[30] *See* Berger, *supra* note 25, at 3.
[31] *See id.* at 4.
[32] *Id.*
[33] *Id.*
[34] *See id.* at 5.
[35] *Id.*
[36] *Id.*
[37] *See id.* at 6.
[38] *See id.* at 7.
[39] *See id.* at 8.
[40] *See id.* at 11.

autonomous legal system *lex mercatoria*.[41] Teubner did not agree with the common criticism of the *lex mercatoria* doctrine, namely that it lacked precision and suffered from ambiguity.[42] In his view, the doctrine of transnational law depends on whether the law community accepts the latter as a 'self-organized process of the creation of law', as opposed to imposing on transnational law a requirement that it consist of legal rules and principles that ought to be 'well-structured and detailed'.[43] Dezalay and Garth offer a multi-faceted approach to the development of a transnational legal order. In their view, the *lex mercatoria* must be examined as an autonomous and universal 'international legal field' subordinated 'to economic and political power'.[44] Since 1994, Berger detected a phenomenon that he described as 'informal creeping codification of transnational commercial law'.[45] In 1994 the UNIDROIT Principles were published.[46] One year later, the Commission on European Contract Law published part 1 of the Principles of European Contract Law.[47] In 1996, the Center for Transnational Law (CENTRAL), which claims to be 'devoted to the research, teaching and study of transnational commercial law, the "new lex mercatoria"',[48] founded trans-lex.org, a platform containing purported principles and standards of the *lex mercatoria*.[49] These three references suggest that transnational commercial law has increasingly been developed by private parties.[50] As Zumbansen observes, it is actors in international commercial transactions and arbitral tribunals who codify the law by reproducing it through arbitral decisions.[51]

In summarizing the historic developments of transnational law, it is important to note that predecessors of modern international commercial law were somewhat geographically and regionally contained.[52] While modern theories stress self-regulation and a movement towards legal unification, the theories of

---

[41] *See id.* at 11–12.
[42] *See id.* at 12.
[43] *Id.*
[44] *See* DEZALAY & GARTH, *supra* note 22, at 65.
[45] *See* Berger, *supra* note 25, at 12–14.
[46] INTERNATIONAL INSTITUTE FOR THE UNIFICATION OF PRIVATE LAW, PRINCIPLES OF INTERNATIONAL COMMERCIAL CONTRACTS (1994).
[47] *See* Berger, *supra* note 25, at 12–13.
[48] Available at http://www.central.uni-koeln.de/en_ID122 (last visited Dec. 25, 2015).
[49] *See* Berger, *supra* note 25, at 13.
[50] *See* Blaurock, *supra* note 24, at 15.
[51] *See* Zumbansen, *supra* note 20, at 417; Blaurock, *supra* note 24, at 22.
[52] FILIP DE LY, INTERNATIONAL BUSINESS LAW AND LEX MERCATORIA 317 (1992).

ancient law merchants were commonly used within one specific legal system and were thus not autonomous in today's terms.[53]

E CURRENT DISCUSSION AND ISSUES IN TRANSNATIONAL LAW

Legal processes in international commercial law in the twenty-first century have increasingly become de-nationalized such that state sovereignty loses paramount significance in the 'traditional theory of legal source'.[54] Lawmaking is no longer a centralized process, and international commercial contracts in the modern age are genuine sources of law.[55] While we witness a developing global civil society, Berger observes that the doctrinal discussion no longer revolves around questions of justifying *lex mercatoria* but around questions of how it may be properly codified and whether distinct transnational business and trade areas possess different commercial laws.[56] Similarly, Gaillard argues that it is no longer a question of whether *lex mercatoria* exists.[57] Other authors affirm this by stating that the law arising out of the practice of international trade can be described as transnational law or independent global commercial law, a 'new lex mercatoria'.[58] The latter has further been described as constituting an 'international legal field', which is both autonomous and universal.[59] While some have noted that rather than a 'new law' being born, a proceduralized law has emerged, capable of meeting the demands of autonomy, through 'manifestations of transnational actors and their regulations'.[60] Nevertheless, the international trade practice in the form of standard contracts based on party autonomy contributes to a 'de facto harmonization' of the *lex mercatoria*.[61] Several authors are of the opinion that the *lex mercatoria* is an

---

[53] *Id.*
[54] *See* Berger, *supra* note 25, at 17; *see also* Roy Goode, *Is the Lex Mercatoria Autonomous?*, *in* COMMERCIAL LAW CHALLENGES IN THE 21ST CENTURY: JAN HELLNER IN MEMORIAM 75 (Ross Cranston, Jan Ramberg & Jacob Ziegel eds., 2007).
[55] *See* Berger, *supra* note 25, at 19.
[56] *Id.* at 21.
[57] Emmanuel Gaillard, *Transnational Law: A Legal System or a Method of Decision-Making*, *in* THE PRACTICE OF TRANSNATIONAL LAW 53–54 (Klaus Peter Berger ed., 2001); *see also* BERGER, *supra* note 19, at 230.
[58] *See* Blaurock, *supra* note 24, at 21.
[59] *See* DEZALAY & GARTH, *supra* note 22, at 65.
[60] *See* Zumbansen, *supra* note 20, at 417.
[61] Filip De Ly, *De Facto Harmonization by Means of Party Autonomy and Model Contract Clauses (Lex Mercatoria)*, *in* UNIFICATION AND HARMONIZATION OF INTERNATIONAL COMMERCIAL LAW: INTERACTION OR DEHARMONIZATION? 160 (Morten M. Fogt ed., 2012).

autonomous legal system,[62] while others see the autonomy of the lex mercatoria in the parties' freedom to choose said law, rather than 'in the alleged free-
floating of legal rules and principles'.[63] While a few authors have queried the
extent to which the *lex mercatoria* is 'a legal system of its own',[64] others have
noted that 'lex mercatoria is a source of law made up of custom, practice,
convention, precedent, and many national laws ... an alternative to a conflict
of laws search which is often artificial and inconclusive'.[65]

The 'renewed debate on the lex mercatoria' focuses on two questions. First,
whether the *lex mercatoria* is defined by its content or its sources,[66] and
second, whether the *lex mercatoria* may be characterized as a list or a method.
According to Gaillard, the specificity of the rules of the *lex mercatoria* stems
from the sources of the *lex mercatoria*, being various legal systems, implying
that the *lex mercatoria* is more accurately defined by its sources rather than its
content.[67] With regards to the second question, Gaillard sees the *lex mercatoria* as a 'method of decision-making' rather than a 'list of creeping codification', which can either be static or open-ended.[68] In Gaillard's view, the
content of transnational law is derived from 'a comparative law analysis',
leading the arbitrator to the rules which are 'most widely accepted'.[69] Ultimately, Gaillard concludes that the transnational rules distilled through this
method 'perform a function strikingly similar to that of a genuine legal
system',[70] which consists of the four characteristics of completeness, structured
character, ability to evolve and predictability.[71] This is in contrast to the view
put forward by Berger of a 'creeping codification of the lex mercatoria'
through an ever-evolving list of principles.[72] The list approach bears the
advantage of a dynamic development of transnational law as opposed to

---

[62] *See* Goode, *supra* note 54, at 83, advocating for a de facto autonomy of the *lex mercatoria*;
Gaillard, *supra* note 57, at 65; Berger, *supra* note 25, at 19; Berthold Goldman, *Nouvelles
réflexions sur la Lex Mercatoria, in* Études de Droit International en l'Honneur de
Pierre Lalive 247–48 (Christian Dominicé, Robert Patry & Claude Reymond eds., 1993).

[63] *See* Zumbansen, *supra* note 20, at 406.

[64] Thomas Schultz, *Some Critical Comments on the Juridicity of Lex Mercatoria*, 10 Y.B. Private
Int'l L. 709 (2008).

[65] Andreas F. Lowenfeld, *Lex Mercatoria: An Arbitrator's View, in* Lex Mercatoria and
Arbitration 82 (Thomas E. Carbonneau ed., 1998).

[66] On this question, see Goode, *supra* note 54, at 75, who states that there is no consensus among
scholars with regards to the *lex mercatoria*'s nature and sources.

[67] *See* Gaillard, *supra* note 57, at 55.

[68] *Id.* at 57.

[69] *Id.*

[70] *Id.* at 65.

[71] *Id.* at 59 *et seq.*

[72] *See* Berger, *supra* note 19, at 233.

codifications that comprise a 'static element'.[73] According to Berger, all actors in international trade form part of the community in finding said law.[74] The list approach has been critiqued based on the view that such a codification remains incomplete as it neglects developments in the legal world outside of the list.[75] The method approach of Gaillard has been similarly criticized. Although such an approach bears more flexibility than any codification, it places significant power in the hands of arbitrators whose decisions are rarely subject to review.[76]

The question of whether more formal codification of *lex mercatoria* is required continues to be actively examined. Zumbansen observes that given its special nature, a complete codification of said rules may not even be the primary goal,[77] while some see that the United Nations Convention on Contracts for the International Sale of Goods,[78] the International Chamber of Commerce (ICC) Incoterms, the UNIDROIT Principles[79] and the ICC Uniform Customs for Documentary Credits as representing a 'ready sourc[e] of the lex mercatoria'.[80] In view of recent developments in the field of transnational arbitration, some have observed a process of formalization of the *lex mercatoria* in the decline of arbitral awards applying the 'force majeure' doctrine to resolve contractual disputes.[81]

In recent years, the *lex mercatoria* of the twenty-first century has been described as transnational and comprising elements both of 'national and non-national law'.[82] While the 'reality of lex mercatoria' is still disputed, the theories about it have developed a certain degree of sophistication.[83] What has been described as the 'new lex mercatoria', namely codifications such as the

---

[73] *Id.*

[74] *Id.*

[75] *See* Zumbansen, *supra* note 20, at 407.

[76] *Id.*

[77] *See* Zumbansen, *supra* note 20, at 427.

[78] Joseph Lookofsky & Ketilbjørn Hertz, 3 Transnational Litigation and Commercial Arbitration. An Analysis of American, European, and International Law 841 (2011).

[79] Michael Joachim Bonell, *The UNIDROIT Principles and Transnational Law, in* Klaus Peter Berger ed., The Practice of Transnational Law 33 (2001) lists ICC Cases No. 8873, No. 9029 and No. 9419 as examples where the tribunal denied to follow the view that the UNIDROIT Principles stand for the *lex mercatoria*.

[80] Richard Garnett, *International Arbitration Law: Progress Towards Harmonisation*, 3 Melbourne J. Int'l L. 412 (2002).

[81] Luke R. Nottage, *The Vicissitudes of Transnational Commercial Arbitration and the Lex Mercatoria: A View from the Periphery*, 16:1 Arb. Int'l 60 (2000).

[82] Ralf Michaels, *The True Lex Mercatoria: Law beyond the State*, 14:2 Ind. J. Global Legal Stud. 447 (2007).

[83] *See id.* at 449.

UNIDROIT Principles, can be characterized as a form 'global law without a state'.[84] While such a system is not fully independent from national law, there is no doubt that the arbitral system has become more and more autonomous over time.[85]

The question of whether the *lex mercatoria*'s internal structure 'reflects that of the political [...] or the economic system'[86] has implications for the relationships between political systems consisting of states within a transnational economic system.[87] Although we witness the beginning of an adaptation of the law to the economic system, some argue that a transnational legal system will never be truly independent of states.[88] The terminology of 'law beyond the state', rather than 'law without a state', captures the ongoing tensions within this transition.[89]

Critiques have been raised suggesting that the rules of the transnational *lex mercatoria* system are too general, giving arbitrators too broad a discretion in deciding disputes in a 'laissez-faire' manner.[90] While it has been put forward that the concept of 'general' as used in 'general principles of law' points towards the level of acceptance of these rules rather than towards their specificity,[91] nevertheless it has been suggested that the *lex mercatoria* concept is too vague and incomplete;[92] accordingly, it can therefore not form 'an objective legal system'[93] but rather can be described as 'a myriad mixture of legal sources than as a clearly constructed legal pyramid'.[94]

The increasing popularization of *lex mercatoria* has been viewed in reaction to the initial constraints national laws imposed on arbitration.[95] Because national laws and conflict-of-law rules restrictively prescribed that any dispute

---

[84] *See id.* at 457.
[85] *Id.*
[86] *See id.* at 464.
[87] *See id.* at 465.
[88] *Id.*
[89] *See id.* at 468.
[90] Michael Mustill, *The New Lex Mercatoria: The First Twenty-Five Years*, 4 ARB. INT'L 117 (1988), http://www.trans-lex.org/126900#head_7; for a comment on Mustill's position in connection with the English view on *lex mercatoria*, see Lowenfeld, *supra* note 65, at 73–74; in this sense, see PIERRE MAYER, L'ARBITRE ET LA LOI, ETUDES OFFERTES À PIERRE CATALA. LE DROIT PRIVÉ FRANÇAIS À LA FIN DU XXe SIÈCLE 236 (2001).
[91] EMMANUEL GAILLARD, LEGAL THEORY OF INTERNATIONAL ARBITRATION 55 (2010).
[92] *See* Zumbansen, *supra* note 20, at 405.
[93] Harold J. Berman & Felix J. Dasser, *The 'New' Law Merchant and the 'Old': Sources, Content, and Legitimacy*, in LEX MERCATORIA AND ARBITRATION 54 (Thomas E. Carbonneau ed., 1998).
[94] *See* Zumbansen, *supra* note 20, at 406.
[95] Roy Goode, *The Role of the Lex Loci Arbitri in Commercial Arbitration*, 17:1 ARB. INT'L 21 (2001).

before a tribunal must be decided according to a specific national law, there was a 'drive for freedom [...] towards resurrection [...] of the medieval *lex mercatoria* as a supposedly free-floating, autonomous body of law which was neutral in character ... obviat[ing] the need to resort to national legal systems, and, in consequence, rules of private international law'.[96] This striving for independence within applicable substantive law has been viewed as emerging alongside the concept of delocalized arbitration or the notion that the arbitral procedure itself has no connection to specific national law.[97]

F DEVELOPMENT OF TRANSNATIONAL COMMERCIAL ARBITRATION

While Jessup made several specific references to arbitration in his early work, the idea of transnational arbitration has always proved to be controversial.[98] Dezalay and Garth locate the starting point of transnational arbitration as being around 1970, when special historical circumstances called for a legal system independent from involved states.[99] Commercial arbitration has been regarded as the 'institutional crystallization of transnational economic law'.[100]

Measuring the effects of the *lex mercatoria* on transnational arbitral practice poses difficulties because documentary evidence of such practice is at most fragmentary.[101] Such documents include arbitration rules or transnational contracts that refer to international trade usages and thus to the *lex mercatoria*.[102] Inversely, arbitration awards, it has been suggested, stimulate the creation of transborder commercial law.[103] *Lex mercatoria* has been criticized in the arbitration context on an ideological, theoretical and practical basis.[104]

Because the application of transnational law in international arbitration is today a matter of fact, its theoretical legal foundations and merits have become the subject of empirical studies. CENTRAL has conducted the 'CENTRAL enquiry' on the use of transnational law in international arbitration. The enquiry presented two hypotheses. First, whether or not the 'repeated use of certain contract clauses in international commerce and [the] reliance [. . .]

---

[96] *Id.* at 21–22.
[97] *Id.* at 21.
[98] *See* Zumbansen, *supra* note 20, at 403.
[99] *See* GAILLARD, *supra* note 91, at 59.
[100] *See* Zumbansen, *supra* note 20, at 429.
[101] *See* DE LY, *supra* note 52, at 267.
[102] *Id.*
[103] Thomas E. Carbonneau, *The Ballad of Transborder Arbitration*, 56 U. MIAMI L. REV. 777, 807 (2002).
[104] Emmanuel Gaillard, *Thirty Years of Lex Mercatoria: Towards the Selective Application of Transnational Rules*, 10 ICSID REV. – FOREIGN INV. L.J. 209 (1995).

[on] such clauses has led to the formation of a transnational legal system, i.e. a new lex mercatoria', and second, whether or not 'the specificity of this third legal system satisfies all elements of the classic theory of the sources of law'.[105] Although the enquiry claims not to be representative,[106] the survey shows that practitioners are aware of the use of transnational law in legal practice[107] and that the respondents in the category of arbitration quite consistently refer to general principles of law, *lex mercatoria* and/or the UNIDROIT Principles when asked about the subject matters of transnational law.[108]

Fundamental to a tribunal's willingness to apply transnational law as substantive law in arbitration in the absence of an express choice of law by the parties represents a slight but essential change in institutional and ad hoc arbitration rules. While such rules previously allowed tribunals to determine applicable 'law', now provisions addressing applicable substantive law allow tribunals to determine the applicable 'rules of law'.[109] Bearing in mind continuing calls for a justiciability analysis of *lex mercatoria* in fulfilling the notions of an autonomous legal system,[110] *lex mercatoria* now falls within the term of 'rules of law'[111] and is thus a viable substantive law applicable to a dispute.[112]

What might explain the growing reference by arbitral tribunals to transnational law and commercial custom in place of national law? It has been suggested that arbitrators are 'particularly apt to apply commercial custom' because not only are they often experts in the respective trade and thus familiar with its usages but also because the majority of arbitration laws and rules refer to trade usages when defining which laws arbitrators shall take into account.[113] With respect to transnational law, according to Goode, tribunals aim to demonstrate neutrality through abstaining from preference for a

---

[105] Klaus Peter Berger, Holger Dubberstein, Sascha Lehmann & Viktoria Petzold, *The Central Enquiry on the Use of Transnational Law in International Contract Law and Arbitration, in* The Practice of Transnational Law 95 (Klaus Peter Berger ed., 2001).

[106] *Id.* at 96.

[107] *Id.* at 103.

[108] *Id.* at 105.

[109] *See* Gaillard, *supra* note 91, at 38; Klaus Peter Berger & Catherine Kessedjian, The New German Arbitration Law in International Perspective 13 (2000), discussing Article 28 of the UNCITRAL Model Law; Yves Derains, *Transnational Law in ICC Arbitration, in* The Practice of Transnational Law 43 (Klaus Peter Berger ed., 2001); Schultz, *supra* note 64, at 669.

[110] *See* I.2. above; Mayer, *supra* note 90, at 88.

[111] However, see Schultz, *supra* note 64, at 671, 679–84, which concludes that the concept of the *lex mercatoria* being 'rules of law' is flawed.

[112] *See* Berman & Dasser, *supra* note 93, at 66.

[113] *Id.* at 65.

national law of either of the parties.[114] It has similarly been suggested that tribunals believe that their arguments carry a higher degree of persuasiveness if they are not based on domestic law but rather on a 'non-domestic standard[s] of adjudication'.[115] Others take a more general approach holding that *lex mercatoria* became increasingly prominent because national laws were no longer suitable to decide international disputes referred to arbitration.[116] Applying transnational law has been regarded as permissible if it reflected the parties' agreement, if there was no agreement with regards to the applicable law or when the tribunal found that applying transnational law was appropriate.[117] The tribunal in the *Dow Chemical* award summarized the latter approach in the following words[118]: 'The decisions [rendered by arbitrators] gradually make up a body of case law which must be taken into account, as it reflects the consequences of economic reality and complies with the needs of international trade, which call for specific rules, also developed gradually, of international arbitration.'

It is undisputed that a tribunal may apply the *lex mercatoria* as substantive law where parties have made an explicit choice of that law.[119] However, even in the absence of such choice of law, arbitrators have increasingly been inclined to apply *lex mercatoria* to render awards[120] through a systematic method of analysis.[121] Arbitrators apply transnational law rules either to fill gaps within the chosen national law or to supplement the latter or because international public policy calls for the non-application of the chosen law and substitution by transnational rules.[122]

Several prominent arbitral awards applying *lex mercatoria* have been upheld against subsequent court challenges. In the case of *Fougerolle*, the Appellate Court of Paris confirmed an arbitral award that made reference to 'general principles generally applicable in international trade'.[123] Similarly, the arbitral

[114] See Goode, *supra* note 54, at 78.
[115] Filip De Ly, *Uniform Commercial Law and International Self-Regulation*, in The Unification of International Commercial Law 60 (Franco Ferrari ed., 1998).
[116] See Gaillard, *supra* note 91, at 46.
[117] Id.
[118] See Gaillard, *supra* note 91, at 47.
[119] See Mayer, *supra* note 90, at 410.
[120] Matthew T. Davidson, The Lex Mercatoria in Transnational Arbitration – An Analytical Survey of the 2001 Kluwer International Arbitration Database (2002), http://www.cisg.law.pace.edu/cisg/biblio/davidson.html, referring to ICC Case No. 3540.
[121] See Berger & Kessedjian, *supra* note 109, at 45–48.
[122] See Gaillard, *supra* note 91, at 48–51 with a detailed analysis.
[123] See Goldman, *supra* note 62, at 244–45 (author's translation).

award in the case of *Pabalk Ticaret Ltd.* v. *Norsolor S.A.*, which was based on *lex mercatoria*, was ultimately enforced[124] following annulment proceedings in Austria. The Oberster Gerichtshof of Austria enforced the award, reversing the previous partial annulment by an Austrian court, which had held that the *lex mercatoria* was 'a world law of uncertain validity'.[125] The Oberster Gerichtshof held that a decision based on the *lex mercatoria* was a decision in law rather than in equity.[126] Proceedings to set aside the same award in France were suspended by the French Cour de Cassation while awaiting the Austrian courts' findings.[127] Ultimately, the French courts enforced the award and thus gave effect to an award based on transnational law.[128] In the similar case of *Deutsche Schachtbau und Tiefbohrgesellschaft G.m.b.H.* v. *Rakoil*, the English Court of Appeal affirmed the enforceability of an award that was decided based on *lex mercatoria* reasoning that such a decision was not merely based on equity.[129] Similarly, the Appellate Court of Paris held that the sole arbitrator in the *Valenciana* case, who decided a dispute on the basis of *lex mercatoria* in the absence of any choice of national law selection by the parties, had decided the case 'within its mission'.[130] In the case *Fratelli Damiano* v. *August Töpfer & Co.*, the arbitral tribunal had rendered an unreasoned award in accordance with English customs despite the fact that the Italian party had requested such reasoning. The Corte di Cassazione held that although the disputing parties had not agreed to apply the Geneva Convention of 1961, according to which providing reasons in an award is mandatory, because said convention was generally accepted 'by the international community of merchants', it was nevertheless applicable as *lex mercatoria*.[131] A growing body of arbitral awards have similarly been upheld in cases where tribunals have applied transnational law.[132]

---

[124] *See* LOOKOFSKY & HERTZ, *supra* note 78, at 843 n.138.
[125] *Id.*; *see also* BERGER, *supra* note 19, at 56.
[126] *See* Blaurock, *supra* note 24, at 23.
[127] *See* LOOKOFSKY & HERTZ, *supra* note 78, at 843 n.138.
[128] *Id.*
[129] *See* Blaurock, *supra* note 24, at 24.
[130] *See* Goldman, *supra* note 62, at 245–46 (author's translation).
[131] *See* Blaurock, *supra* note 24, at 24.
[132] A selection of such ICC awards (ICC Cases No. 7110, No. 7365, No. 7375, No. 8261 and No. 8502) where the transnational law was connected to UNIDROIT Principles is discussed by Michael Joachim Bonell, *The UNIDROIT Principles and Transnational Law, in* THE PRACTICE OF TRANSNATIONAL LAW 30–32 (Klaus Peter Berger ed., 2001).

G THE UNCITRAL MODEL LAW AS FORCE CONTRIBUTING TO
TRANSNATIONAL INTERNATIONAL ARBITRATION

Regulating, as Jessup describes, transactions 'transcend[ing] national frontiers' the UNCITRAL Model Law provides a framework for adaptation and modernization of arbitration legislation across diverse jurisdictions.[133] It codifies worldwide practices governing arbitration and thus embodies a consensus 'on the essential principles of arbitration law and of the rules pertaining to the arbitral trial'.[134] The UNCITRAL Model Law, including Art. 2A, contributes to the development of a transnational arbitral practice by acknowledging its international origin and 'the need to promote uniformity in its application'.[135] The fact that the Model Law provides for minimal court intervention[136] while enhancing the scope of action on the part of the arbitral tribunal[137] thus reduces the influence of national variation and contributes to the development of transnational practice.[138] Inspired by the UNCITRAL Arbitration rules, the Model Law puts great weight on party autonomy,[139] which is among the major drivers of transnational development.[140]

Although nation states are not obliged to adopt the provisions of the Model Law, to advance the achievement of harmonization, contribute to a stable trading environment[141] and accommodate the 'needs of international commercial arbitration practice',[142] such adoption has been widely encouraged. Since its inception, the Model Law had a significant impact in the arbitration world.[143] UNCITRAL currently lists over seventy jurisdictions that have either adopted the Model Law or based legislation on it.[144] Some have suggested that this wide-scale adoption reflects the emergence of a transnational law,[145] while

[133] See BERGER & KESSEDJIAN, *supra* note 109, at 3.
[134] See Carbonneau, *supra* note 103, at 807.
[135] Art. 2A of the UNCITRAL Model Law 2006.
[136] See BERGER & KESSEDJIAN, *supra* note 109, at 4.
[137] See Nottage, *supra* note 81, at 54.
[138] See SHAHLA F. ALI, RESOLVING DISPUTES IN THE ASIA PACIFIC REGION: INTERNATIONAL ARBITRATION AND MEDIATION IN EAST ASIA AND THE WEST (2011).
[139] See MAYER, *supra* note 90, at 407; *see, e.g.*, Article 19 of the UNCITRAL Model Law.
[140] Id.
[141] See MAYER, *supra* note 90, at 400–01.
[142] Recommendation in G.A. Res. 40/72 (Dec. 11, 1985).
[143] Vratislav Pechota, *The Future of the Law Governing the International Arbitral Process, in* LEX MERCATORIA AND ARBITRATION 260 (Thomas E. Carbonneau ed., 1998).
[144] Available at http://www.uncitral.org/uncitral/en/uncitral_texts/arbitration/1985Model_arbitration_status.html (last visited Jan. 16, 2016).
[145] See Pechota, *supra* note 143.

others have suggested that the Model Law may eventually develop into 'customary rules of universal application' due to its broad acceptance.[146]

UNCITRAL recommends that nations make as few amendments to the Model Law as possible in order to 'increase the visibility of harmonization, thus enhancing the confidence of foreign parties as the primary users of international arbitration'.[147] Nevertheless, countries are free to amend the Model Law when incorporating its provisions into its national legislation.[148] This can be explained by the concept of informed divergence, giving effect to a national legal systems' particularities. Advantages can be found in regional as well as national differences between institutions and market regulations.[149]

H CONCLUSION

'Corporations have neither bodies to be punished, nor souls to be condemned. They therefore do as they like'. [150] Philip Jessup's groundbreaking work *Transnational Law* (1956) identifies the evolution of law as emerging from a concern with regulation of events confined within national boundaries to events 'transcend[ing] national frontiers'. His identification of this new realm of interaction, absent the corresponding existence of a world state, has led to a useful analytic framework for a number of important issues, extending Cardozo's observation that 'we must enlarge [law] until it is broad enough to answer to realities'. This framing has important implications for developments in transnational dispute resolution and corresponding questions of adaptation, harmonization and diversity in global practice.

In particular, as transnational awards become increasingly transparent, arbitral jurisprudence may take the role of an important contributor to the development of transnational arbitration.[151]

---

[146] *Id.*

[147] Explanatory note by the UNCITRAL secretariat on the 1985 Model Law on International Commercial Arbitration as amended in 2006, at 24.

[148] *See* ALI, *supra* note 138.

[149] *See* Zumbansen, *supra* note 20, at 411, with further references.

[150] Baron Thurlow, *quoted in* William Dalrymple, *The Original Evil Corporation*, N.Y. Times (Sept. 4, 2019), https://www.nytimes.com/2019/09/04/opinion/east-india-company.html.

[151] *See* Zumbansen, *supra* note 20, at 411, with further references.

10

Conflicts of Law and the Challenge of Transnational Data Flows*

PAUL SCHIFF BERMAN

A INTRODUCTION

Phillip Jessup's *Transnational Law*,[1] though generally phrased in the reassuring tones of a treatise, presented a bold vision for law in the twentieth century and beyond. In his very first paragraph, Jessup asserted the existence of a "complex interrelated world community" and a set of legal problems that involve more than just state-to-state relations.[2] Thus, his vision was both cosmopolitan and pluralist from the get-go, recognizing that human community affiliations cut across traditional territorial lines and that states are not the only relevant actors on the world stage of law. Jessup then spent the remainder of the book identifying both conflict-of-law principles and possible alternative legal and political forums where what he called transnational law was being made.

In this chapter, I wish to update Jessup's vision for the twenty-first century. Jessup correctly observed sixty years ago that multinational corporate activity created new challenges for nation states and their territorially based rules for jurisdiction, choice of law, and recognition of judgments. Those challenges are exponentially more difficult in the twenty-first century because electronic data – everything from emails and text messages to Facebook and Instagram posts to Twitter pronouncements to drone warfare data to search algorithms to financial transactions to cloud data storage – travels around the globe with

---

* Special thanks to Samuel Wenzel for helpful research assistance in the preparation of this chapter. Some material in this chapter is derived from PAUL SCHIFF BERMAN, GLOBAL LEGAL PLURALISM: A JURISPRUDENCE OF LAW BEYOND BORDERS (2012) and Paul Schiff Berman, *Legal Jurisdiction and the Deterritorialization of Social Life, in* RESEARCH HANDBOOK ON THE LAW OF VIRTUAL AND AUGMENTED REALITY (Woodrow Barfield et al. eds., 2019).
[1] PHILLIP JESSUP, TRANSNATIONAL LAW (1956).
[2] *Id.* at 1.

little relationship to physical territory. In addition, this data is often in the custody and control of data intermediaries such as Google, Facebook, Twitter, Apple, Microsoft, Amazon, private military contractors, and so on.

Three important consequences flow from this ubiquitous technology-enabled, data-driven global societal activity. First, the territorial location of data becomes increasingly arbitrary and substantively unimportant. If I, as a US citizen based in Maryland, have a Gmail account and Google, a US corporation, decides to store my archived emails in Ireland or France or Indonesia (or indeed to split up the data fragments that make up each email message among data warehouses in all three countries), that decision seems irrelevant to any question of whether I have somehow affiliated myself with any of those communities or governments for purposes of jurisdictional or choice-of-law analysis. Second, because of this deterritorialization of data, it will often be the case that territorially based courts (or law enforcement authorities generally) are unable to easily enforce their decisions because those decisions require cooperation from relevant actors in far-flung communities. Third, as a direct result of the first two problems, governmental and judicial authorities are increasingly turning to multinational corporate data intermediaries to carry out and enforce their orders because only those companies have sufficient global reach to make legal rulings effective. But deputizing these intermediaries to become enforcement agents, while logical and possibly effective, raises new problems regarding the scope of governmental authority and the distortions involved in privatizing law enforcement.

These are the sorts of concerns that surely would have occupied Phillip Jessup were he still alive today. Interestingly, even though scholars first began raising these issues at the dawn of the commercial internet era as far back as 1995, the jurisprudential solutions we see so far are still largely unsatisfying, both conceptually and practically. Indeed, as with many conflicts-of-law problems that have bedeviled courts and commentators for hundreds of years, there *may not be* a fully satisfactory solution. Moreover, even if there were a single unifying theory for conflicts of law in the information age, it's not at all clear that everyone would agree on what that theory should be. Thus, as legal pluralist scholars have long realized, there is never a stable "solution" to the reality of legal pluralism. Instead, legal pluralism is an inevitable (and perhaps not even an undesirable) result of a world with multiple communities and multiple legal and quasi-legal systems.

Yet, even if there is no single unifying theory that could put an end to legal conflicts, we can still survey the types of cases that are arising and analyze the efforts of courts and others to navigate the problems that arise from the deterritorialization of information. This chapter aims to do that, providing a series of real-life case studies that any consideration of twenty-first-century conflicts of law (and transnational law) must face.

What is perhaps most striking about all of these cases, taken together, is that we see in the legal decisions very little serious engagement with the doctrines, principles, values, and policies that historically underlie the conflicts-of-law doctrines of jurisdiction, choice of law, or recognition of judgments. Instead, courts simply tend to assume that because something is arguably located within a territorial boundary, that is enough to assert jurisdiction or apply local law. Or they assume that because local application of a legal regime is appropriate, worldwide application of that same regime is also appropriate. Or they assume that in recognizing a foreign judgment, local public policies automatically apply and trump any other concerns. And even in the rare case of a court refraining from applying its local law, such a decision not to apply norms extraterritorially may still be based on an arbitrary territorial localization, not on a sustained grappling with the core values underlying conflicts-of-law doctrines.

But conflicts-of-law doctrines are not just mechanical rules based on territorial location or raw power. They implicate fundamental questions about community affiliation, membership, and effects, as well as governmental sovereignty, relative authority, and cosmopolitan cooperation. The conundrums raised by the deterritorialization of data and the rise of data intermediaries afford a useful opportunity to ask these fundamental questions and begin to forge new conceptions of conflicts of law for the new information age that is already transforming our world.

B INTERNET CONFLICTS-OF-LAW CASES: 2000–03

1 *LICRA v. Yahoo!*

It is perhaps fitting that the most famous legal dispute of the early internet era implicated all three conflicts doctrines: jurisdiction, choice of law, and judgment recognition. On May 22, 2000, the Tribunal de Grande Instance de Paris issued a preliminary injunction against Yahoo.com, ordering the site to take all possible measures to dissuade and prevent access in France to Yahoo! auction sites that sell Nazi memorabilia or other items that are sympathetic to Nazism or constitute Holocaust denial.[3] Undisputedly, selling such

---

[3] UEJF & LICRA v. Yahoo!, Inc. & Yahoo France, Tribunal de grande instance [TGI] [ordinary court of original jurisdiction] Paris, May 22, 2000, 00/05308, https://perma.cc/738B-V9BM.

merchandise in France would violate French law,[4] and there would be no jurisdictional dispute had the French authorities limited their prosecution to the French end users who were downloading the illegal materials from Yahoo!'s auction sites. But even in this early internet era, legal authorities were already realizing that it is often far more effective to proceed against an intermediary such as Yahoo!, both because the intermediary is usually a larger corporate actor and therefore easier to find and because one legal action can address a broader problem rather than requiring separate enforcement actions against each end user. In effect, the intermediary becomes the enforcement agent of whatever legal authority issues the order.

In this case, the intermediary question had two parts, however. Certainly the French court had undisputed jurisdictional authority over Yahoo.fr, Yahoo!'s French subsidiary, and Yahoo.fr complied with requests that access to such sites be blocked.[5] What made this action noteworthy was that the suit was brought not only against Yahoo.fr but against Yahoo.com, an American corporation, and the court sought to enjoin access to non-French websites stored on Yahoo.com's non-French servers.

Of course, one can easily see why the court and the complainants in this action would have taken this additional step. Shutting down access to web pages on Yahoo.fr does no good at all if French citizens can, by entering a slightly different URL in their search box, simply go to Yahoo.com and access those same pages. On the other hand, Yahoo! argued that the French assertion of jurisdiction was impermissibly extraterritorial in scope.[6] According to Yahoo!, in order to comply with the injunction, it would need to remove the pages from its servers altogether (not just for the French audience), thereby denying such material to non-French citizens, many of whom have the right to access the materials under the laws of their countries.[7] Most importantly, Yahoo! argued that such extraterritorial censoring of American web content would run afoul of the First Amendment of the US

---

[4]   *See* Code Pénal [C. Pén] [Penal Code] art. R.645-1 (Fr.) (prohibiting the public display of Nazi memorabilia except for the purposes of a historical film, show, or exhibit), https://perma .cc/BL8T-4J3A.

[5]   *See* LICRA & UEJF v. Yahoo!, Inc. & Yahoo France, TGI Paris, Nov. 20, 2000, 00/05308 (noting that Yahoo! France had posted warnings on its site that the user could access revisionist sites through Yahoo! U.S. and that the visiting of such sites is prohibited and punishable by French law), https://perma.cc/ALK9-XM6A.

[6]   *Id.*

[7]   *Id.*

Constitution.[8] Thus, Yahoo! and others[9] contended that the French assertion
of jurisdiction was an impermissible attempt by France to impose global rules
for internet expression. As Greg Wrenn, associate general counsel for Yahoo!'s
international division, put it at the time, "We are not going to acquiesce in the
notion that foreign countries have unlimited jurisdiction to regulate the
content of U.S.-based sites."[10]

Yet, it is easy to see that the extraterritoriality charge runs in both directions.
If France is *not* able to block the access of French citizens to proscribed
material, then the United States will effectively be imposing First Amendment
norms on the entire world. And though geographical tracking software might
seem to solve the problem by allowing websites to offer different content to
different users, such a solution would still require the sites to analyze the laws
of all jurisdictions to determine what material to filter for which users.

The arguments in the *Yahoo!* case therefore establish the basic dichotomy
that we then see repeated in case after case subsequently. On the one hand,
legal authorities wish to assert jurisdiction anywhere a community is affected
by web-based content. This tends to push in the direction of universal
jurisdiction because content uploaded anywhere in the world can potentially
cause harmful effects anywhere else in the world. In response, defendants
argue for jurisdiction only where content is uploaded or only where their
servers are located or only in their home jurisdiction. This theory of jurisdiction tends to result either in arbitrary or easily manipulable jurisdictional
principles (such as where a server is located) or a system where actors
impacting communities across the globe can only be sued or regulated in
their home jurisdiction. Both of these solutions seem unsatisfying. And finding some other non-web-based territorial nexus to bolster an assertion of
jurisdiction can also be problematic. For example, regardless of how one
resolves the jurisdictional question in the Yahoo! case, it seems clear that
where in the world the actual paper share certificate by which Yahoo! owned
Yahoo.fr seems irrelevant to the underlying jurisdictional issues at stake.

In the end, rather than filter out French users, Yahoo! chose a two-pronged
strategy. First, it decided to remove the auction sites from its servers altogether,

---

[8]   *Id.*
[9]   *See, e.g.,* Carl S. Kaplan, *Experts See Online Speech Case as Bellwether,* N.Y. TIMES (Jan. 5,
      2001), http://www.nytimes.com/2001/01/05/technology/05CYBERLAW.html (quoting the
      warning of Barry Steinhardt, associate director of the American Civil Liberties Union, that if
      "litigants and governments in other countries ... go after American service providers ... we
      could easily wind up with a lowest common denominator standard for protected speech on the
      Net").
[10] *Id.*

but it claimed that such a decision was "voluntary" and unrelated to the French court ruling.[11] Second, it filed suit in US District Court in the Northern District of California, seeking a declaratory judgment that the French court's orders were not enforceable in the United States pursuant to the First Amendment.[12] Accordingly, what had started as a jurisdictional dispute was transformed into its flip side: a question of recognition of judgments.

Faced with the question of whether or not to enforce the French court's order, the district court started from the assumption that US law (and US constitutional norms) must apply. Thus, the court framed the issue for decision solely in US constitutional terms: "What is at issue here is whether it is consistent with the Constitution and laws of the United States for another nation to regulate speech by a United States resident within the United States on the basis that such speech can be accessed by Internet users in that nation."[13]

Conceptualized in this way, the district court had little difficulty determining that enforcement of the French court order would violate the First Amendment, concluding both that the French judgment constituted impermissible viewpoint discrimination and that it was unconstitutionally vague. The court therefore concluded that a US court could not have issued such an order in the first instance without violating constitutional free speech norms.[14] But of course, in a judgment recognition case, that is not the appropriate inquiry. Indeed, in the domestic context, the Full Faith and Credit Clause *requires* recognition of judgments that might be completely unavailable or even potentially illegal in the state where recognition is sought.[15] Thus, the

---

[11] *See* Press Release, Yahoo!, Yahoo! Enhances Commerce Sites for Higher Quality Online Experience (Jan. 2, 2001), https://perma.cc/H9RS-QGTN (announcing new product guidelines for its auction sites that prohibit "items that are associated with groups which promote or glorify hatred and violence"). *But cf.* Troy Wolverton & Jeff Pelline, *Yahoo to Charge Auction Fees, Ban Hate Materials*, CNET (Jan. 2, 2001), https://perma.cc/LGE4-RDMX (noting that Yahoo!'s new policy regarding hate-related materials followed action by the French court).

[12] Yahoo!, Inc. v. La Ligue Contre le Racisme et l'Antisémitisme, 169 F. Supp. 2d 1181, 1186 (N.D. Cal. 2001), *rev'd on other grounds*, 433 F.3d 1199 (9th Cir. 2006) (en banc).

[13] *Id.* at 1186 (emphasis omitted).

[14] *Id.* at 1189–90, 1192–93.

[15] *See, e.g.*, Estin v. Estin, 334 U.S. 541, 546 (1948) (finding that the Full Faith and Credit Clause "ordered submission ... even to hostile policies reflected in the judgment of another State, because the practical operation of the federal system, which the Constitution designed, demanded it"); Milwaukee County v. M.E. White Co., 296 U.S. 268, 277 (1935) ("In numerous cases this Court has held that credit must be given to the judgment of another state, although the forum would not be required to entertain the suit on which the judgment was founded . . . ."); Fauntleroy v. Lum, 210 U.S. 230, 237 (1908) (holding that the judgment of a

real question is whether this is the type of judgment that should be *recognized*, not whether the court could have issued the ruling *as an original matter.*

To its credit, the district court did include a brief discussion of the judgment recognition issue in a section titled "Comity."[16] And the court acknowledged that "United States courts generally recognize foreign judgments and decrees unless enforcement would be prejudicial or contrary to the country's interests."[17] Yet, after reiterating that the French judgment "clearly would be inconsistent with the First Amendment if mandated by a court in the United States,"[18] the district court judge concluded that because the foreign order would unconstitutionally chill speech occurring within US borders, "the principle of comity is outweighed by the Court's obligation to uphold the First Amendment."[19]

Thus, while ostensibly addressing principles of judgment recognition, the court ultimately returned to the idea that if a judgment would be unconstitutional if issued in the United States, enforcing that judgment also would be unconstitutional, or at least sufficiently contrary to state interests as to overwhelm any principles of comity. By eliding the difference between *issuing* a judgment and *enforcing* a judgment, however, the court neglected to apply in more detail the various principles of judgment recognition or to consider more carefully those circumstances in which US interests might *not* truly be threatened by the application of a foreign norm.

An en banc panel of the Ninth Circuit ultimately reversed, on other grounds, by a six-to-five vote.[20] Three judges in the majority determined that the District Court did not have personal jurisdiction over the French defendants until those defendants actually came to the United States seeking to enforce the French judgment. The other three judges making up the majority also dismissed, but they did so on ripeness grounds, similarly concluding that the enforcement issue should not be decided until the French defendants actually sought enforcement. Thus, the Court of Appeals majority never addressed the judgment recognition issues upon which the district court had relied.

Missouri court was entitled to full faith and credit in Mississippi even if the Missouri judgment rested on a misapprehension of Mississippi law).
[16] *Yahoo!*, 169 F. Supp. 2d at 1192–93.
[17] *Id.* at 1192.
[18] *Id.*
[19] *Id.* at 1193.
[20] *Yahoo!*, 433 F.3d 1199 (9th Cir. 2006) (en banc).

II *GlobalSantaFe Corp.* v. *Globalsantafe.com*

Transnational data flows also impact choice of law. For example, historically, the boundaries of trademark law have been delineated in part by reference to physical geography.[21] Thus, if I own a store in New York City called Berman's, I will not, as a general matter, be able to prevent a person in Australia from opening a store that is also called Berman's, even if I have previously established a trademark in my name. The idea is that customers would be unlikely to confuse the two stores because they are in markets that are spatially distinct.[22] In the online world, such clear spatial boundaries are collapsed because, as the domain name system is currently organized, there can be only one bermans.com domain name, and it can only point to one "location."[23]

In the early to mid-1990s, as corporations and entrepreneurs began to understand the potential value of a recognizable domain name, pressure increased to create trademark rights in such names. In response, Congress first passed the Federal Trademark Dilution Act[24] and then the Anticybersquatting Consumer Protection Act (ACPA), which provides an explicit federal remedy to combat so-called cybersquatting.[25] According to the congressional reports, the ACPA is meant to address cases where non–trademark holders

---

[21] *See* Graeme B. Dinwoodie, *Trademarks and Territory: Detaching Trademark Law from the Nation-State*, 41 HOUS. L. REV. 885, 887 (2004) ("[I]t is an axiomatic principle of domestic and international trademark law that trademarks and trademark law are territorial.").

[22] *See* Stone Creek, Inc. v. Omnia Italian Design, Inc., 875 F.3d 426, 438 (9th Cir. 2017), *petition for cert. filed* ("[W]here two parties independently are employing the same mark upon goods of the same class, but in separate markets wholly remote the one from the other, the question of prior appropriation is legally insignificant . . . [except in cases of bad faith].") (quoting Hanover Milling Co. v. Metcalf, 240 U.S. 403, 415 (1916)). This is not an absolute rule, of course, because "famous or well-known marks may well leap oceans and rivers, cross national borders, and span language barriers to achieve international recognition." Dan L. Burk, *Trademark Doctrines for Global Electronic Commerce*, 49 S. C. L. REV. 695, 720 (1998). *See also* Vaudable v. Montmartre, Inc., 193 N.Y.S.2d 332, 332 (N.Y. Sup. Ct. 1959) (enjoining the use by a restaurant in New York of the name and decor of Maxim's Restaurant in Paris). Nevertheless, the likelihood-of-confusion standard historically has tended to imbed a geographical limitation.

[23] Of course, users going to www.bermans.com could be shown an introductory screen that provides a choice of which Berman's site they wish to access.

[24] Federal Trademark Dilution Act of 1995, Pub. L. No. 104-98, 109 Stat. 985 (codified at 15 U.S.C. §§ 1125, 1127 (Supp. 1996)).

[25] Anticybersquatting Consumer Protection Act, Pub. L. No. 106-113, § 3002, 113 Stat. 1501A-545 (1999) (codified at 15 U.S.C. § 1125(d) (2000)); *see* H.R. REP. NO. 106-412 (1999) (detailing the act).

register well-known trademarks as domain names and then try to "ransom" the names back to the trademark owners.[26]

This application of trademark law to domain names means that trademark law has become unmoored from physical geography and is now more likely to operate extraterritorially. Potentially, even those who are legitimately using a website that happens to bear the name of a famous mark held by an entity across the globe could be forced to relinquish the name. In addition, this unmooring of trademarks from territory creates the possibility that individual countries will interpret their trademark laws expansively, thereby reducing trademark rights "to their most destructive form": the mutual ability to block (or at least interfere with) the online use of marks recognized in other countries. Moreover, each of the parties claiming ownership in a trademark could sue in a different country, and because of differences in substantive law, each party could win.[27]

This is the backdrop for *GlobalSantaFe Corp. v. Globalsantafe.com.*[28] On September 3, 2001, Global Marine Inc. and Santa Fe International Corp. announced their agreement to merge into an entity to be known as Global-SantaFe Corp. Less than a day later, Jongsun Park, a citizen of South Korea, registered the domain name globalsantafe.com with the Korean domain name registrar Hangang. In response, Global Marine and Santa Fe filed an in rem action in the Eastern District of Virginia under the ACPA. The ACPA provides in rem jurisdiction over a domain name wherever that name is registered.[29] Thus, for example, if people register domain names online via a website owned by Network Solutions, a domain name registrar[30] corporation located in Virginia, they potentially can be forced, under the ACPA, to defend a trademark action in Virginia whether or not they have ever set foot in Virginia or knew Network Solutions was a Virginia corporation.

---

[26] *See* H.R. Rep. No. 106-412, at 5–7 (1999) (noting that "[s]ometimes these pirates put pornographic materials on theses sights [*sic*] in an effort to increase the likelihood of collecting ransom by damaging the integrity of a [trade]mark"); S. Rep. No. 106-140, at 4–7 (1999) (highlighting testimony regarding attempts to ransom domain names to the highest bidder).

[27] *See, e.g.*, Mecklermedia Corp. v. D.C. Cong. GmbH, 1998 Ch. 40, 53 (Eng.) (noting that the cause of action for using trademarked language is different in Germany and England and, thus, simultaneous proceedings could continue).

[28] GlobalSantaFe Corp. v. Globalsantafe.com, 250 F. Supp. 2d 610 (E.D. Va. 2003).

[29] 15 U.S.C. § 1125(d)(2)(C) (2000) ("In an *in rem* action ... a domain name shall be deemed to have its situs in the judicial district in which ... the domain name registrar, registry, or other domain name authority that registered or assigned the domain name is located ...").

[30] A registrar is one of several entities for a given top-level domain (such as .com, .edu, .gov, .uk, etc.) that is authorized by the Internet Corporation for Assigned Names and Numbers to grant registration of domain names. David Bender, Computer Law § 3D.05[3], at 3D-104 (2002).

In this case, however, jurisdiction was further complicated by the fact that Park had not even registered the domain name with a US registrar but with a South Korean one. Nevertheless, the ACPA also authorizes in rem jurisdiction in the judicial district where the overall domain name *registry* is located.[31] Based on this provision, the district court determined that it could exercise jurisdiction because VeriSign, which administers the entire ".com" registry, is located in Virginia.[32] And having determined that the substantive provisions of the ACPA had been met, the court therefore ordered both Hangang and VeriSign to "take all appropriate steps to transfer the domain name" to GlobalSantaFe.[33]

Approximately a week later, Park filed an application for an injunction in the District Court of Seoul, South Korea, seeking an order preventing Hangang from transferring the domain name.[34] Ruling that the Virginia court did not have proper jurisdiction, the Korean court provisionally granted the injunction, and Hangang, presumably responding to the Korean court's injunction, subsequently refused to transfer the domain name.[35] In an effort to resolve this transnational stalemate, GlobalSantaFe returned to the court in Virginia seeking an additional order directing VeriSign to cancel the infringing domain name from the ".com" registry.[36]

The district court reaffirmed that it had proper in rem jurisdiction over the case pursuant to the ACPA because VeriSign is located in Virginia.[37] The court also reiterated that Park had violated the substantive provisions of the ACPA.[38] And after a lengthy discussion of the mechanics concerning how a registry company would effectively cancel or transfer a domain name,[39] the court concluded that such a remedy was both available under the ACPA and appropriate given the unwillingness of Hangang to act in violation of the Korean court's order.[40]

---

[31] For each top-level domain (such as ".com," ".gov," ".edu," ".uk," etc.), a single registry company is responsible for keeping the records and a directory of all the domain names within that domain. When an individual or corporation company wants the rights to a new domain name, it contacts a registrar. The registrar submits the domain name to the registry, which enters the assigned domain name into a database. At the time, VeriSign Global Registry Services was the sole registry for ".com" domain names.

[32] *GlobalSantaFe*, 250 F. Supp. 2d at 614–15.

[33] *Id.* at 614.

[34] *Id.*

[35] *Id.*

[36] *Id.*

[37] *Id.* at 614–15.

[38] *Id.* at 615–16.

[39] *Id.* at 617–24.

[40] *Id.* at 623.

From a conflicts perspective, what is most striking about the decision is that the court focuses almost exclusively on its jurisdiction to hear the case but never questions that the ACPA is the only possibly relevant legal regime. Indeed, the court seems to assume that the ACPA's legal reach is limited solely by the scope of the court's jurisdiction, not by any choice-of-law considerations. Thus, in the court's view, the only significant gap in the ACPA's trademark enforcement regime is for domain names registered under top-level domains whose registry is located outside the United States. Never does it seem to occur to the court that even if it had jurisdiction over the action, it might nevertheless choose South Korean (or some other) law as providing the operative legal norms for resolving the dispute.

This single-minded focus on jurisdiction (and therefore the physical location of registry companies) poses potential problems for ACPA enforcement in the future. As the court recognizes, if jurisdiction is all, then the ACPA can only provide a broad-based remedy in domain name trademark cases so long as the registries of the most popular top-level domains remain in the United States.[41] Thus, if the registries for generic domains such as ".com" and ".net" were relocated outside the physical territory of the United States, then US trademark rights in domain names would face serious enforcement challenges.

Such difficulties are a natural consequence of laws that are deemed to apply to the full extent of their territorially based jurisdictional reach. But, of course, as choice-of-law scholars have long recognized, laws need *not* be applied to the full extent of their jurisdictional reach, and concerns about the establishment of competing or conflicting trademark systems on the internet are precisely the sorts of concerns that might animate a more restrained application of forum law.

In any event, having concluded that the case was within its jurisdiction and that, therefore, US law necessarily applied, the court only at the very end of its opinion asked whether "concerns of international comity" might dictate deference to the injunction issued by the Korean court.[42] Even here, however, the court did not ask about the *content* of South Korean trademark law; it only asked whether deference was owed to the court decision granting the actual injunction.[43] Having framed the issue in this way, the court resolved it by reference to a principle that in rem cases should generally be decided by the

---

[41] *Id.*
[42] *Id.* at 624.
[43] *Id.*

first court to exercise jurisdiction over the property in question.[44] And since the original Virginia court order preceded the Korean court injunction, the Virginia court found deference inappropriate.[45]

The vision of choice of law that emerges from the decision, therefore, is founded solely on jurisdictional power and a race to the courthouse. A state can enact legal norms with extremely broad extraterritorial reach, and courts within that state are bound to apply those norms to a multinational dispute so long as the case was commenced there first. Needless to say, this is not a particularly thoughtful or nuanced choice-of-law regime,[46] nor does it take into account the possible long-term benefits that might accrue from adopting a more restrained application of forum law or from considering the forum's own interest in harmonious international adjudicatory processes.

III *Barcelona.com, Inc.* v. *Excelentisimo Ayuntamiento de Barcelona*

Whereas the choice-of-law issues in *GlobalSantaFe* were made more complicated by the fact that the parties were from different countries, in *Barcelona. com*, all of the principal actors in the dispute were from Spain.[47] Yet even here the Fourth Circuit, reversing a contrary ruling of the district court,[48] eschewed Spanish law and insisted on applying the ACPA.[49] Moreover, this decision was again reached without significant consideration of choice-of-law issues.

The case involved the right to the domain name barcelona.com. In 1996, Mr. Joan Nogueras Cobo ("Nogueras"), a Spanish citizen, registered barcelona.com with the Virginia-based domain name registrar Network Solutions.[50]

---

[44] *See id.* at 624–26 (referring to the first-in-time rule known as the *Princess Lida* doctrine.)

[45] *Id.* at 625.

[46] It should be noted that this first-in-time principal, also known as *lis pendens*, is used in many civil law jurisdictions around the world.

[47] Barcelona.com, Inc. v. Excelentisimo Ayuntamiento de Barcelona, 330 F.3d 617 (4th Cir. 2003).

[48] Barcelona.com, Inc. v. Excelentisimo Ayuntamiento de Barcelona, 189 F. Supp. 2d 367 (E.D. Va. 2002), *rev'd* 330 F.3d 617 (4th Cir. 2003).

[49] *Barcelona.com*, 330 F.3d at 630. To be sure, because the claim at issue sought only a declaratory judgment as to the plaintiff's rights under the Lanham Act, it is possible to construe the Fourth Circuit decision as merely clarifying US law without requiring that this law be the ultimate rule of decision in the case. However, nowhere does the court state that it is rendering such a limited ruling and instead explicitly reverses the district court's application of Spanish law and remands so that the district court can "grant the appropriate relief under [the Lanham Act]." *Id.* at 630. In addition, the appellate opinion states that the ACPA can be used specifically to reverse arbitration decisions "grounded on principles foreign or hostile to American law." *Id.* at 626. Both of these statements strongly imply that the Fourth Circuit considered its application of US law to be dispositive.

[50] *Id.* at 620.

Subsequently, Nogueras formed a corporation under US law, called Bcom, Inc.[51] Despite the US incorporation, however, the company had no offices, employees, or even a telephone listing in the United States.[52] Nogueras (and the Bcom servers) remained in Spain.[53]

The Barcelona City Council asserted that Nogueras had no right to use barcelona.com under Spanish trademark law and demanded that he transfer the domain name registration to the city council.[54] When Nogueras refused, the city council filed a complaint with the World Intellectual Property Organization (WIPO).[55] Several months later, the WIPO panelist ruled in favor of the city council.[56] Instead of transferring the domain name, however, Bcom filed suit in federal court, again in Virginia, seeking a declaratory judgment that the registration of barcelona.com was not unlawful.[57]

Having decided that the WIPO administrative proceedings would be given "no weight,"[58] the district court then turned to the elements of the ACPA, first considering whether either party possessed a valid trademark for the name *Barcelona*. Significantly, the district court sought to answer this question by reference to *both* US and Spanish law.[59] And although the court concluded that neither party possessed a US trademark in the name *Barcelona*, it did find that the city council possessed multiple Spanish trademarks containing the term *Barcelona*, such as *Barcelona Teatre*, *Barcelona Canal*, and *Barcelona Television*.[60] The court also noted that under Spanish law, if a trademark consists of two or more words, the operative issue is which word creates the dominant impression in the mind of the consumer. Here, that word obviously would be *Barcelona*.[61] Finally, the court determined that under Spanish law, the names of communities, municipalities, and provinces cannot be registered as trademarks without authorization by municipal officials, and neither

---

[51] *Id.*

[52] *Id.*

[53] *Id.*

[54] *Id.*

[55] *Id.* at 621. Every domain name issued by Network Solutions is issued under a contract, the terms of which include a provision requiring resolution of disputes through the Uniform Domain Name Dispute Resolution Policy (UDRP) promulgated by the Internet Corporation for Assigned Names and Numbers. *Id.* The WIPO complaint was filed in accordance with the terms of the UDRP. *Id.*

[56] *Id.*

[57] *See id.*

[58] *See Barcelona.com*, 189 F. Supp. 2d at 371.

[59] *See id.* at 371–72.

[60] *See id.* at 371–72 & n.3.

[61] *See id.* at 372.

Nogueras and Bcom had received such authorization.[62] Thus, the court ruled that the city council possessed a "legally valid Spanish trademark" for the word *Barcelona*.[63] The district court then turned to the other elements of the ACPA, finding both likelihood of consumer confusion and the requisite bad-faith intent to profit from the domain name registration.[64] Accordingly, the district court ruled in favor of the city council and refused to issue the declaratory judgment Bcom had sought.[65]

The Fourth Circuit reversed.[66] Significantly, the major issue on which the appellate court disagreed with the trial court was the use of Spanish law to determine whether the city council had a valid trademark. Citing section 1114 (2)(D)(v) of the ACPA, the Fourth Circuit emphasized that the principal issue to be decided is whether "plaintiff's registration or use of the domain name is not unlawful *under the Lanham Act*."[67] According to the appellate panel, this language makes clear that only US law may be used to determine the existence of a valid trademark or its possible infringement.[68] Having decided to apply US trademark law, the court then concluded that *Barcelona* is "a purely descriptive geographical term entitled to no trademark protection" under the ACPA.[69] Accordingly, the court found nothing unlawful in Nogueras's registration of barcelona.com and therefore reversed the district court's ruling.[70]

Thus, the Fourth Circuit, like the court in *GlobalSantaFe Corp.*, applied US law to an international trademark dispute, invoking principles of territoriality. Indeed, despite the fact that the principal actors in the dispute were all in Spain, the appellate court opined that the ACPA, "by requiring application of United States trademark law to this action brought in a United States court by a United States corporation involving a domain name

---

[62] *See id.*
[63] *See id.*
[64] *See id.* at 372–73.
[65] *See id.* at 373. The court also ruled in favor of the city council on an ACPA counterclaim against Nogueras, finding that Nogueras had engaged in bad-faith intent to profit from the city council's valid trademark. *See id.* at 373–77.
[66] *Barcelona.com*, 330 F.3d 617 at 619–20.
[67] *Id.* at 626 (emphasis added).
[68] *See id.* at 627–28.
[69] *Id.* at 629.
[70] *Id.* The Fourth Circuit also vacated the district court's decision concerning the city council's counterclaim (without reaching the merits) because the appellate panel concluded that no counterclaim had actually been filed. *See id.*

administered by a United States registrar" was consistent with "the fundamental doctrine of territoriality upon which our trademark law is presently based."[71]

This doctrine of territoriality likely derives from the 1883 Paris Convention for the Protection of Industrial Property[72] (upon which the Fourth Circuit relied[73]). Indeed, the concern animating the convention was that absent a doctrine of territoriality, a country could create a "world mark" simply by granting a trademark under its local law and thereby prevent anyone anywhere in the world from using that name.[74] Such an extraterritorial encroachment was unacceptable in an era when it was presumed that trademarks could easily operate locally because the use of a trade name in one country would have no significant impact on the use of the same name by a different entity in another country.

When considering trademarks in domain names, however, a single-minded emphasis on territoriality may itself create law with substantial *extra*territorial effects. For example, by applying the ACPA in *GlobalSantaFe*, the US District Court necessarily imposed US trademark law on a South Korean domain name registrant and a South Korean domain name registrar, even though neither had any significant contact with the United States. Likewise, in *Barcelona.com*, the Fourth Circuit applied US trademark law to a dispute where all the principal actors were Spanish and where the issue concerned a domain name associated with the name of a major city in Spain. Both of these cases demonstrate that, by applying a rigid conception of territoriality to international trademark disputes (at least in the context of domain names), courts run the risk of imposing US law extraterritorially and creating precisely the sort of world mark that the principle of territoriality was originally designed to avoid.

Accordingly, we need to reconsider the traditional assumption that trademark disputes must always be resolved by applying the law of the forum country. Instead, cases involving international actors require courts to use choice-of-law principles in order to determine the appropriate legal norms. Moreover, such cases may help suggest choice-of-law frameworks that take

[71] *Id.* at 628.
[72] *See* Convention Revising the Paris Convention of March 20, 1883, as Revised, for the Protection of Industrial Property, July 14, 1967, art. 10bis, 21 U.S.T. 1583, 828 U.N.T.S. 305.
[73] *See Barcelona.com*, 330 F.3d at 628.
[74] *See, e.g.*, Tortsten Bettinger & Dorothee Thum, *Territorial Trademark Rights in the Global Village – International Jurisdiction, Choice of Law and Substantive Law for Trademark Disputes on the Internet (Part Two)*, 31 INT'L REV. INTELL. PROP. & COMPETITION L. 285, 286 (2000) (explaining the basis of the doctrine of territoriality with regard to trademarks).

proper account of the actual community affiliations of the parties, as well as the interests nation states have in being a functioning part of an interlocking international network of domestic trademark regimes.

C INTERNET CONFLICTS-OF-LAW CASES: 2013–17

Lest we think that these three cases from the early years of the twenty-first century represent simply the growing pains associated with applying law to a new technology, it is worth considering the following group of cases. Although they each arose a decade or more later, the issues they raise will immediately be familiar based on the paradigm cases discussed so far.

Indeed, more and more of our social identity is now stored remotely by third parties, far from our physical location. Whether it be our emails, our social media posts, our musical preferences, our virtual world activities, our online search histories, or our banking and health data, very little of our data identity actually remains tied to our person anymore. This increasing deterritorialization of data and identity is resurfacing many of the same conundrums for jurisdiction, choice of law, and judgment recognition that were identified in the early days of the commercial internet.

I *United States* v. *Microsoft*

In 2013 US officers conducting a criminal drug investigation sought a search warrant under federal law to seize the emails of a Microsoft customer. This is usually a relatively routine process, and as long as the search warrant is valid, then data storage companies such as Microsoft generally comply. And in fact Microsoft did turn over all account information it had that was being stored in the United States. However, in this case the actual emails and their contents were stored overseas in Dublin, Ireland. Microsoft refused to turn over this content, arguing that the federal law pursuant to which the search warrant was issued, the Stored Communications Act, could not be applied extraterritorially.

The US Court of Appeals for the Second Circuit agreed, albeit reluctantly.[75] Applying the presumption against extraterritoriality, the court determined that because Congress had not, in the Stored Communications Act,[76] contemplated cloud-based data storage, it had made no provision for warrants to apply beyond US borders. Significantly, the physical location or the

---

[75] Microsoft v. United States, 829 F.3d 197 (2d Cir. 2016).
[76] 18 U.S.C. §§ 2701–12 (2012).

nationality of the underlying *person* who was the subject of the investigation was irrelevant. Thus, as interpreted by the Second Circuit, the Stored Communications Act might not permit authorities to obtain a search warrant and seize email records of a US citizen located in the United States who sent emails to other US citizens from a computer located in the United States. The only relevant territorial nexus is where the email data happens to be stored. And significantly, this storage decision is entirely within the control of the storage provider, leaving open the possibility of manipulation in order to avoid the law of a particular sovereign.

In contrast, a district court in Pennsylvania subsequently ruled the opposite way on a similar warrant involving Google.[77] Here, the data question was in some ways even more difficult because Google does not store customers' data in one location, such as Ireland. Instead, Google uses an algorithm that divides an individual's user data across data centers and even splinters the data such that an email is not stored as a "cohesive digital file" but in "multiple data 'shards,'" each in a separate location around the world. Accordingly, even if US law enforcement sought the data through a government-to-government treaty, there would be no one government to whom to address the request.

Unlike the Second Circuit, the court in the *Google* case reasoned that if the Stored Communications Act is meant to protect Fourth Amendment privacy interests, then the relevant question is where the potential invasion of privacy takes place, not where the data is located. And given that Google can move customers' data at will around the globe, the court reasoned that forcing Google to reterritorialize the data in the United States does not violate any privacy interest. Then, once the data is repatriated, the warrant can issue just as it would in any other domestic situation.

In order to resolve this ambiguity, the US Congress in 2018 enacted the CLOUD Act.[78] Under this statute US data and communication companies must provide stored data for US citizens on any server they own and operate when requested by warrant, regardless of where in the world that data happens to be stored. Thus, the statute sensibly looks at the underlying community affiliation of the *user* rather than the arbitrary territorial location of the *data*. On the other hand, the act does provide mechanisms for the communications companies or the courts to challenge or reject warrants if they believe the request violates the privacy rights of the foreign country where the data is stored. This caveat still seems to unduly reify the physical location of data even

---

[77] *In re* Search Warrant No. 16-960-M-01 to Google, *In re* Search Warrant No. 16-1061-M to Google, 232 F. Supp. 3d 708 (E.D. Pa. 2017).
[78] CLOUD Act, H.R. 4943, 115th Cong. (2018).

though that physical location may be arbitrary and completely unrelated to the social reality of the person whose data is at issue.

II *Google Spain SL* v. *Agencia Española de Protección de Datos*

As with data, online searches are part of our social identity. And, as with data, searches are fundamentally deterritorialized, linking searchers anywhere in the world with websites located anywhere in the world. But what if a territorially based sovereign wants to block certain search results because the sovereign objects in some way to the underlying website that would otherwise be retrieved in the search? In such circumstances, as in the *Yahoo!* case, regulators may focus on the intermediary – here the search company – rather than the offending website because it is far easier to find the search company and deputize it to leverage the regulation.

In 2014 the European Court of Justice (ECJ) took this approach in a case involving Google.[79] A 1995 European Council data privacy directive[80] had recognized that individuals possess privacy rights in data. As interpreted by the ECJ, such a right allows individuals to object to old reputation-damaging online information about them that is no longer relevant and not of sufficient public concern to continue to be searchable.

Significantly, rather than apply the directive against the website operator, the court ruled that it was Google, as the search operator, who bore responsibility for ensuring that websites containing this sort of obsolete private information be blocked from search results. Moreover, again as with the *Yahoo!* case, the court deemed it insufficient only to apply its ruling to google.es, the Spanish subsidiary, instead ruling that google.com must also block offending websites from its search results.

By making Google responsible for enforcing this right to be forgotten, the ECJ effectively deputized Google as a sort of administrative agency. Henceforth, any individual seeking to have a website blocked from Google search must first file a notice with Google. Then, it will be Google's legal team that will apply the ECJ's balancing test to see if the elements of the right to be forgotten are satisfied and there is insufficient countervailing public interest in the information remaining accessible. If the individual disagrees with Google's decision, then that decision can be challenged in court. Given that Google is constantly altering its search algorithms anyway, one can understand

---

[79] Case C-131/12, Google Spain SL v. Agencia Española de Protección de Datos (AEPD) and Mario Costeja González, 2014 E.C.R. 317 (May 13, 2014), https://perma.cc/2367-44E8.

[80] Council Directive 95/46, 1995 O.J. (L 281) 31 (EC).

why the court would view this as an effective division of labor. Moreover, Google is not jurisdictionally constrained regarding the websites it blocks from its search algorithms, as a government regulator would be if it sought to have a website taken down. Nevertheless, the fact is that a European court has required Google, a US corporation, to perform a quasi-governmental adjudicatory function on a worldwide basis (albeit only at the request of EU citizens).

This case, therefore, not only illustrates issues of jurisdiction but also the increased importance of intermediaries such as virtual world operators, online service providers, social media companies, and search engines. Given that our social lives are conducted through or stored with such intermediary companies, it is increasingly clear that those companies are likely to become the brokers that territorially based governments use to pursue regulation. And, of course, as the ubiquitous power of those companies over data grows, we can expect that they will often be the target of complaints by individuals and governments.

III *Procureur-General* v. *Yahoo! Inc.; Procureur-General* v. *Skype*

Meanwhile, Belgian authorities in 2009 reprised the French efforts against Yahoo! from 2000, requiring Yahoo! to disclose subscriber information about Yahoo! users as part of a fraud investigation. Yahoo! once again argued that the application of the Belgium statute to a company without a physical presence in Belgium was impermissibly extraterritorial.[81] And Yahoo!'s argument was perhaps even more compelling than in the French case because, although there was a country-specific yahoo.be website, unlike in the French case, it does not appear that Yahoo! even had a Belgium subsidiary operating locally.

Nevertheless, the Supreme Court of Belgium rejected Yahoo!'s argument.[82] Significantly, the court took an extremely broad view both regarding the scope of the statute and Belgian law enforcement authority more generally. First, according to the court, the Belgian law at issue covered "any operator or provider that actively aims its economic activities on [Belgium] consumers," regardless of whether or not the operator or provider has a physical presence in Belgium.[83] And the court reasoned that enforcing the law would not require

---

[81] Procureur-Général v. Yahoo! Inc., Hof van Cassatie [Cass.] [Court of Cassation], Dec. 1, 2015, No. P.13.2082.N (Belg.), *translated in* 13 DIGITAL EVIDENCE & ELECTRONIC SIGNATURE L. REV. 156 (2016).

[82] *Id.* at 157.

[83] *Id.*

Belgian authorities to act extraterritorially because the statute at issue did not "require the performance of any physical act abroad." From this perspective, the authorities were simply staying in Belgium asking for data to be provided by Yahoo![84] Interestingly, whereas the Second Circuit had ruled that US law enforcement authorities could not collect information held abroad because it was akin to traveling beyond their territorial boundaries, the Belgian court emphasized that the Belgian authorities were simply remaining in the jurisdiction receiving data from elsewhere.

Subsequently, a lower court in Belgium has applied the logic of the *Yahoo!* case to assert jurisdiction over Skype in a case where Belgian authorities sought not only subscriber information but the content of communications as well.[85] Skype complied with regard to registration information, but argued that because Skype is a Luxembourg company, there was no jurisdiction in Belgium. Instead, according to Skype, any request for communications content must proceed via a mutual legal assistance request of the Luxembourg government.

The Belgian court rejected this argument. The court ruled that even though Skype was based in Luxembourg, it was "actively participating in the economic life in Belgium" by offering services there and was therefore subject to Belgian jurisdiction.[86] Echoing the Belgian Supreme Court's decision in *Yahoo!*, the court characterized the enforcement action as occurring within Belgium because presumably the requested data would be handed over there, regardless of where that data might have been collected or stored and regardless of whether or not the underlying target of the investigation was a Belgian citizen.

Thus, the two Belgian cases go far beyond what even the US government argued in the *Microsoft* case, because at least with Microsoft, the government clearly had jurisdiction over the intermediary, which was indisputably based in Washington state. In contrast, neither Yahoo! nor Skype had either a physical presence in Belgium or even a subsidiary there. And if the test is merely whether a company "participates in the economic life of Belgium" by offering services to Belgian customers, then jurisdiction may potentially extend to any web page viewed in Belgium regardless of where the content originated. Such a position mirrors early internet jurisdiction cases in the United States that

---

[84] *Id.*

[85] Procureur Général v. Skype, Tribunal de Première Instance [Civ.] [Tribunal of First Instance], Mechelen, Oct. 27, 2016, No. ME 20.4.1 105151-12, ¶¶ 1.2–1.5 (Belg.), https://perma.cc/C5Z7-EZ9Y.

[86] *Id.*

asserted jurisdiction over websites wherever they were viewed or viewable, conceptualizing a website as a twenty-four-hour-a-day advertisement "entering" every jurisdiction where the website was accessible.[87]

IV *Google* v. *Equustek*

Finally, we turn to a 2017 Canadian Supreme Court decision that in many respects reprises elements of both the *Google Spain* case and the original *Yahoo! France* case with which we began.

In this case, Equustek, a small Canadian technology company, brought a trademark suit in Canada against another company, Datalink, which had been distributing its products. Equustek claimed that Datalink had begun to relabel one of Equustek's products in order to sell the product as its own. Ultimately, Datalink left Canada, and although Equustek was able to secure Canadian court orders enjoining Datalink from continuing to sell Equustek's products on its websites, those orders were ineffectual because Datalink no longer had any presence or assets in Canada and simply ignored the orders.

Thus, we see an inherent difficulty a territorially based sovereign has in enforcing its judgment. If the relevant party has insufficient presence in the jurisdiction, there will be limited means of enforcing any order. In such a circumstance, as we have seen already, a global data intermediary becomes a useful way to leverage power. Accordingly, it is not surprising that the Canadian courts would turn to Google, just as the ECJ did in the "right to be forgotten" context. As in that case, the courts recognized that if a website exists but can't be found in a Google search, the utility of that website will be reduced to almost zero. Thus, following the court order against Datalink and a request from Equustek, Google agreed to deindex some but not all of Datalink's web pages so that they would not be found if they were being searched for on Google's Canadian site, google.ca. However, those same pages could still be found by searching on google.com or other countries' Google search sites. Thus, as with blocking Nazi memorabilia on yahoo.fr, the Canada-specific remedy was insufficient.

Accordingly, Equustek sought a preliminary injunction against Google requiring the company to deindex Datalink's websites through any of its search portals worldwide. Google argued in response that such an injunction

---

[87] Bochan v. La Fontaine, 68 F. Supp. 2d 692, 701 (E.D. Va. 1999) ("Federal courts in Virginia in particular have generally found that Internet advertising accessible to Virginia residents 24 hours a day constitutes solicitation of business in Virginia sufficient to satisfy the requirements of § 8.01–328.1(A)(4)" (personal jurisdiction)).

would be improperly extraterritorial as it would mean that Canada's judgment would dictate search results around the world.

The Canadian Supreme Court rejected Google's argument. According to the court,

> [w]here it is necessary to ensure the injunction's effectiveness, a court can grant an injunction enjoining conduct anywhere in the world. The problem in this case is occurring online and globally. The Internet has no borders – its natural habitat is global. The only way to ensure that the interlocutory injunction attained its objective was to have it apply where Google operates – globally.

Accordingly, the court took a purely functionalist approach. Because there was no other way to make its injunction against Datalink effective, it must require Google, a nonparty to the suit, to act as its global enforcement mechanism, just as the European court had in the *Google Spain* case.

Significantly, unlike the *Yahoo! France* case, the concerns about chilling free speech in this case were far less strong because the websites in question were sales sites, and though commercial speech receives First Amendment protection under US Constitutional law, that protection is arguably less stringent.[88] Moreover, if the websites to be deindexed were in fact infringing trademark, deindexing them would be unlikely to be the basis for a successful First Amendment claim. And, of course, since Datalink is not a US corporation, it is not clear it would have valid First Amendment rights to assert in any event. As to Google, it is an open question whether search results count as speech for First Amendment purposes.

Nevertheless, despite the lessened First Amendment concerns at stake, Google took the same path that Yahoo! had sixteen years earlier, filing for a declaratory judgment in a US court that would declare the Canadian judgment unenforceable under US law. This time, however, the law in question was section 230 of the Communications Decency Act, which generally immunizes internet service providers against liability arising from content created by third parties.[89] And as in the *Yahoo!* case, the district court granted the declaratory judgment.[90]

---

[88] *See* Central Hudson Gas & Elec. Corp. v. Public Svc. Comm'n of New York, 447 U.S. 557 (1980) ("Because 'commercial speech' is afforded less constitutional protection than other forms of speech, it is important that the commercial speech concept not be defined too broadly lest speech deserving of greater constitutional protection be inadvertently suppressed.").

[89] 47 U.S.C. § 230 (2012).

[90] Google v. Equustek Solutions, No. 5:17-cv-04207, 2017 WL 5000834 (N.D. Cal. Nov. 2, 2017).

The US District Court's declaratory judgment decision is questionable on a number of grounds. First, because no real liability was being imposed on Google, it is possible section 230 would not apply. Moreover, no party was yet seeking to enforce the Canadian court judgment in the United States, arguably rendering Google's suit unripe or requiring dismissal for lack of personal jurisdiction over the defendant, Equustek. It was on those grounds, after all, that the Ninth Circuit had ultimately overruled the district court order in the *Yahoo!* case.[91] Finally, as noted previously, even if the Canadian Supreme Court order would violate US federal law if the order had been issued by a US court, that does not answer the question of whether it would likewise violate federal law to enforce another court's judgment to the same effect. After all, the judgment recognition decision is based on different considerations from those that are involved in issuing an order in the first instance.

In the end, although the district court's declaratory judgment order seems to create a jurisdictional stalemate, the reality is that Equustek need not ever seek enforcement of the Canadian Supreme Court judgment in the United States anyway because Google presumably wants to continue to do business in Canada as an ongoing commercial enterprise there, and so it is highly likely that Google will comply with the order just as Yahoo! did in France. Thus, the declaratory judgment action may be more a public relations ploy than a serious effort to thwart extraterritorial enforcement.

V *Global Electronic Currencies and Transactions*

Search engines are, of course, not the only piece of deterritorialized infrastructure that operates in online interaction. Consider the general ledger technology known as blockchain. Although the global alternative currency Bitcoin has generated the most attention, it is only one instantiation of this technology. Blockchains store data in distributed computers and chain them together to form an unbroken record of that information.[92] The information stored could be currency transactions, but it could also be any automated executable set of instructions, such as an insurance contract that pays out automatically if a given event occurs. Two features make blockchain technology valuable. First, identical copies of the particular blockchain (or ledger) are stored on and accessed from potentially thousands of computers around the

---

[91] *Yahoo!*, 433 F.3d at 1253.
[92] CLYDE & CO., BLOCKCHAIN AND THE LAW: AN UNCHARTED LANDSCAPE 1 (2016), https://perma.cc/7D7A-DHV4.

world. Any changes to information on one is immediately and automatically authenticated by the others, and any authenticated change immediately updates on all computers in the chain. Second, the information is encrypted so that, in combination with its decentralization, it is difficult to hack.

On the other hand, those same features make blockchains potentially difficult to regulate. Not only do blockchain transactions cross borders, but it will often to be difficult to identify a particular computer or entity that is responsible if there is a dispute or problem. As one commenter has described it, "the infrastructure does not fall under any traditional jurisdiction, but the users of the infrastructure also naturally evade any sense of traditional jurisdiction. All parties may transact entirely anonymously on a public blockchain."[93]

So far, blockchain technology has not been deployed sufficiently for us to know precisely how legal challenges are likely to be resolved. And the assumption that blockchain transactions completely lack connection to a territorially based entity may be overstated. That is because the parties to a blockchain transaction are still physically located somewhere on Earth. And to the extent that money changes hands, that money is in some form sent from one physical place to another, creating a territorial nexus.

For example, in *Greene v. Mizuho Bank, Ltd.*,[94] the plaintiff wired money from a Wells Fargo branch account in California to a bank in Japan, which then held the funds in an account used by a Bitcoin exchange. So although the Bitcoin transactions themselves might not have a location, the exchange interacted with a bank chartered in Japan, and that bank in turn interacted with a bank in California, making all of the defendants potentially subject to jurisdiction in California.

Of course, when we say that money was "sent from California to Japan," we are really talking about metaphysical electronic signals crossing borders, and so we are in a sense using what is already a fictional connection to the physical world to territorially ground a Bitcoin transaction, which is an even more fictional connection to the physical world. It remains to be seen at what point all that is solid will melt into air and legal jurisdiction based on territory will cease to be meaningful as a way to describe and regulate electronic transactions at all.

---

[93] Wulf A. Kaal & Craig Calcaterra, *Blockchain Technology's Distributed Jurisdiction*, MEDIUM, June 20, 2017, https://perma.cc/3PMT-T98E.
[94] Green v. Mizuho Bank, Ltd., 169 F. Supp. 3d 855 (N.D. Ill. 2016).

D THE NEED FOR A COSMOPOLITAN PLURALIST APPROACH TO
CONFLICT OF LAWS

As difficult as the cases discussed above may be to resolve, if anything, the future holds issues that may be tougher still. Similar questions can, and almost certainly will, be raised by automation in vehicles and by machine-learning-based robotics and drones for commercial, consumer, and military use. These new deployments will likely reshape legal rules regarding product liability, insurance, contract, jurisdiction, criminal law, and other areas. Indeed, the movement of our social activity into various forms of the virtual is a major trend that is not likely to reverse, and it is a trend that is bound to unsettle previously settled legal principles. Yet, a time of flux is also a time of opportunity. As judges, legislators, and scholars struggle to apply old legal principles to new contexts, they are – in a far more self-conscious way than usual – questioning whether those old legal principles really work in the brave new world they are encountering. Such a time of self-conscious inquiry opens the conceptual space to allow one to go back to first principles and ask important jurisprudential and sociologically charged questions that run throughout all of law.

With regard to conflicts of law, rather than simply adapt existing jurisdictional models to the new social context in order to "solve" tensions in particular situations, we need to reflect on the conflicts principles we are seeking to adapt. By doing so, we can perhaps lay the groundwork for a theoretical model that will allow us better to understand and evaluate the increasing transnationalization of data flows.

To construct such a model, we first need to remind ourselves that conceptions of legal jurisdiction (by which I mean to include both the jurisdiction to decide a dispute and the determination that a jurisdiction's law will apply) are more than simply ideas about the appropriate boundaries for state regulation or the efficient allocation of governing authority. Jurisdiction is also the locus for debates about community definition, sovereignty, and legitimacy. Moreover, the idea of legal jurisdiction both reflects and reinforces social conceptions of space, distance, and identity. Too often, however, contemporary frameworks for thinking about jurisdictional authority unreflectively accept the assumption that nation states defined by fixed territorial borders are the only relevant jurisdictional entities, without examining how people actually experience allegiance to community or understand their relationship to geographical distance and territorial borders. Moreover, by sidestepping these questions of community definition, borders, and the experience of place, legal thinkers are ignoring a voluminous literature in anthropology, cultural studies, and the social sciences concerning such issues.[95]

Indeed, even a cursory examination reveals that our current territorially based rules for jurisdiction (and conflicts of law) were developed in an era when physical geography was more meaningful than it is today and during a brief historical moment when the ideas of nation and state were being joined by a hyphen to create a historically contingent Westphalian order. Yet if the ideas of geographical territory and the nation state are no longer treated as givens for defining community,[96] an entirely new set of questions can be asked. How are communities appropriately defined in today's world? In what ways might we say that the nation state is an *imagined* community,[97] and what other imaginings are possible? How do people actually experience the idea of membership in multiple overlapping communities? Should citizenship be theorized as one of the many subject positions occupied by people as members of diverse, sometimes nonterritorial, collectivities? In what ways are our sense of place and community membership constructed through social forces? And if ideas such as "place," "community," "member," "nation," "citizen," "boundary," and "stranger"[98] are not natural and inevitable but are instead constructed, imagined, and (sometimes) imposed, what does that say about the presumed "naturalness" of our geographically based jurisdiction and choice-of-law rules?

We need to ask these questions, drawing on humanities and social science literature that complicates many of the premises most lawmakers and legal scholars take for granted concerning jurisdiction. This literature insists that we recognize the constructed nature of our ideas about boundaries and

---

[95] For a more detailed discussion of this literature as applied to issues of legal jurisdiction, see generally Paul Schiff Berman, *The Globalization of Jurisdiction*, 151 U. PA. L. REV. 311 (2002).

[96] *See* Akhil Gupta, *The Song of the Nonaligned World: Transnational Identities and the Reinscription of Space in Late Capitalism, in* CULTURE POWER PLACE: EXPLORATIONS IN CRITICAL ANTHROPOLOGY 179 (Akhil Gupta & James Ferguson eds., 1997) ("The nation is so deeply implicated in the texture of everyday life and so thoroughly presupposed in academic discourses on 'culture' and 'society' [and jurisdiction] that it becomes difficult to remember that it is only one, relatively recent, historically contingent form of organizing space in the world.").

[97] *See generally* BENEDICT ANDERSON, IMAGINED COMMUNITIES (Rev. ed. 2006) (analyzing the nation state as an imagined community).

[98] *See, e.g.*, Georg Simmel, *The Stranger, in* THE SOCIOLOGY OF GEORG SIMMEL 402, 402 (Kurt H. Wolff ed., 1964) (arguing that the stranger "is fixed within a particular spatial group, or within a group whose boundaries are similar to spatial boundaries," but that "his position in this group is determined, essentially, by the fact that he has not belonged to it from the beginning, that he imports qualities into it, which do not and cannot stem from the group itself").

community definition and that we acknowledge the historical contingency of the nation state. Moreover, by analyzing the social meaning of our affiliations across space, we can think about alternative conceptions of community that are subnational, transnational, supranational, or cosmopolitan. Such an analysis provides a better understanding of the world of experience on which the legal world is mapped and is therefore essential in order to develop a richer descriptive account of what it means for a juridical body to assert jurisdiction over a controversy.

In addition, moving from the descriptive to the normative, can we conceptualize the idea of jurisdiction in a way that might take into consideration the contested and constantly shifting process by which people imagine communities and their membership in them? Just as Phillip Jessup noted many of the ways a rigidly territorial conception of jurisdiction eventually gave way in the first part of the twentieth century to the idea of jurisdiction based on contacts with a sovereign entity, so too a contacts-based approach must now yield to a conception of jurisdiction based on community affiliation. In the past, I have offered one such conception, which I have termed a cosmopolitan pluralist conception of jurisdiction.[99]

A *cosmopolitan*[100] approach allows us to think of community not as a geographically determined territory circumscribed by fixed boundaries, but as "articulated moments in networks of social relations and understandings."[101] This dynamic understanding of the relationship between the "local" community and other forms of community affiliation (regional, national, transnational, international, cosmopolitan) permits us to conceptualize legal jurisdiction in terms of social interactions that are fluid processes, not motionless demarcations frozen in time and space.

In addition, if nation states are imagined, historically contingent communities defined by admittedly arbitrary geographical boundaries, and if those

---

[99] *See* PAUL SCHIFF BERMAN, GLOBAL LEGAL PLURALISM: A JURISPRUDENCE OF LAW BEYOND BORDERS (2012).

[100] By "cosmopolitan," I refer to a multivalent perspective that recognizes the wide variety of affiliations people feel toward a range of communities, from the most local to the most global. I therefore distinguish cosmopolitanism from a universalist vision (often associated with cosmopolitanism), which sees people solely, or primarily, as members of one world community. Cosmopolitanism, as I use the term, involves an ideal of multiple attachments; it does not necessarily entail the erasure of nonglobal community affiliations. *See, e.g.,* Bruce Robbins, *Introduction Part I: Actually Existing Cosmopolitanism, in* COSMOPOLITICS: THINKING AND FEELING BEYOND THE NATION 1, 3 (Pheng Cheah & Bruce Robbins eds., 1998) ("[I]nstead of an ideal of detachment, actually existing cosmopolitanism is a reality of (re) attachment, multiple attachment, or attachment at a distance.").

[101] DOREEN MASSEY, SPACE, PLACE, AND GENDER 154 (1994).

nation states – because of transnational flows of information, capital, and people – no longer define unified communities (if they ever did), then there is no conceptual justification for conceiving of nation states as possessing a monopoly on the assertion of jurisdiction. Instead, any comprehensive theory of conflicts of law must acknowledge that *nonstate* communities also assert various claims to jurisdictional authority and articulate alternative norms that are often incorporated into more "official" legal regimes. This *pluralist*[102] understanding of jurisdiction helps us to see that law is not merely the coercive command of a sovereign power but a language for imagining alternative future worlds. Moreover, various norm-generating communities (not just the sovereign) are always contesting the shape of such worlds.

Finally, as this survey of cases makes clear, in a world of deterritorialized data, the role of intermediaries as lawmakers and law enforcers has radically increased. When Facebook enforces terms of service, or Twitter is asked (or required) to police hate speech, or Google implements an ECJ ruling, we can call these acts of intermediaries law or not, but a pluralist would argue that it doesn't matter how you define it; the fact is that it affects the behavior of real people in the real world. Indeed, the actions of intermediaries can have more impact than the sometimes empty commands of a sovereign. A pluralist perspective has the advantage of not getting caught up in definitions of law but instead recognizing that the quasi-law created, imposed, and/or applied by nongovernmental entities should always remain within our legal analytical purview.

E CONCLUSION

No fixed conflicts-of-law principles will ever completely solve the conflicts problems raised by increasing transnational data flows. Indeed, there are no perfect solutions, and the factual settings whereby these sorts of problems may arise are so multifaceted and unpredictable that trying to develop a comprehensive set of rules to govern all eventualities strikes me as a fool's errand. Moreover, even if we could discover a grand scheme for handling these questions, it is unlikely that all communities in the world (or their judicial bodies) would agree. Therefore, no amount of analysis will ever wipe out the reality of legal pluralism and its attendant uncertainties.

Nevertheless, just as Phillip Jessup did sixty years ago when he sketched out a set of conflicts-of-law problems under the rubric he called transnational law,

---

[102] *See* Paul Schiff Berman, *The New Legal Pluralism*, 2009 ANN. REV. L. & SOC. SCIENCES 225 (providing an overview of the trajectory of legal pluralism scholarship).

so too it is incumbent on legal scholars today to recognize the new challenges arising in this increasingly data-driven world and to build new cosmopolitan pluralist legal models that may, over time, become simply the way we conceptualize law in the twenty-first century. After all, law and society are forever like a Mobius strip, each turning into the other, and what seems unsettled and new to us now may become the commonplace assumptions of future generations. In that regard, Jessup's bold proposal of sixty years ago seems largely uncontroversial and even obvious to most scholars today; that is the force of Jessup's ideas. But neither law nor society ever stop moving, and to do justice to Jessup's vision, we must push forward to develop new models to respond to new practices in new contexts.

11

What *Lex Sportiva* Tells You about Transnational Law

ANTOINE DUVAL

A INTRODUCTION

When Philip C. Jessup died in 1986, the *New York Times'* obituary coined him an 'authority in International Law'.[1] It is an ironical, though enlightening, portrayal for a man who believed that to tackle the problems of our times 'the term "international" is misleading since it suggests that one is concerned only with the relations of one nation (or state) to other nation (or states)'.[2] His famous 1956 Storrs Lectures on transnational law were a quest to find the 'appropriate word or term' to qualify the law applicable to these pressing problems, and in which he famously stated that he 'shall use, instead of "international law," the term "transnational law" to include all law which regulates actions or events that transcend national frontiers'.[3] As the *Times'* obituary illustrates, his proposal remained *lettre morte* outside of a select group of scholars.[4] Surely, transnational law found its way in the name of some American law journals[5] and a few titles of books,[6] but it remained an

---

[1] Eric Pace, *Philip C. Jessup Dies; Helped end Berlin Blockade*, N.Y. TIMES (Feb. 1, 1986), https://www.nytimes.com/1986/02/01/obituaries/philip-c-jessup-dies-helped-end-berlin-blockade.html.

[2] PHILIP C. JESSUP, TRANSNATIONAL LAW 1 (1956).

[3] *Id.* at 2.

[4] In fact, if one does a quick comparative exercise of the *New York Times'* use of the concept of international law versus transnational law, the results are striking. Since 1851, international law features in 27 253 articles, while transnational law was used in only 49 pieces.

[5] Notably, the *Columbia Journal of Transnational Law*, established in 1961; the *Vanderbilt Journal of Transnational Law*, established in 1967; the *Suffolk Transnational Law Review*, established in 1976, *Transnational Law & Contemporary Problems*, established in 1989; and the *Journal of Transnational Law & Policy*, established in 1991.

[6] For a while, only TRANSNATIONAL LAW IN A CHANGING SOCIETY: ESSAYS IN HONOR OF PHILIP C. JESSUP (Wolfgang Friedmann et al. eds., 1972) and EUGEN LANGEN, TRANSNATIONAL COMMERCIAL LAW (1973). *See also* EUGEN LANGEN, TRANSNATIONALES RECHT (1981) and THE

extremely marginal concept in both the academic and public discourse. At the time of his death, Jessup's lectures were an almost forgotten footnote in the history of international law that in any case deserved only a short mention in the great man's obituary. In recent years, however, the idea of transnational law has been revived by a strong scholarly movement dealing with the legal transformations triggered by globalizing societies.[7] The references to transnational law have become more frequent, and Jessup's forward-looking conceptual intuition seems almost vindicated at last.

What is meant when the notion of transnational law is used remains deeply unsettled.[8] In this chapter, I would like to reflect on the diversity of usages of the idea of transnational law in legal scholarship. To do so, I will focus on the *lex sportiva* as a fruitful empirical field to study *in concreto* the use of the concept. Indeed, the regulation of international (often based on competitions between teams of different nations, but not exclusively) sports is nowadays

---

TRANSNATIONAL LAW OF INTERNATIONAL COMMERCIAL TRANSACTIONS (Norbert Horn & Clive M. Schmitthoff eds., 1982).

[7] This scholarly dynamic was crowned by the launch of the *Transnational Legal Theory* journal in 2010. It is also reflected in the publication of numerous books referring to transnational law in their titles over the last ten years; *see, e.g.,* among a burgeoning literature, DAVID SZABLOWSKI, TRANSNATIONAL LAW AND LOCAL STRUGGLES: MINING, COMMUNITIES AND THE WORLD BANK (2007); FRANCK LATTY, LA LEX SPORTIVA: RECHERCHE SUR LE DROIT RANSNATIONAL (2007); NILS C. IPSEN, PRIVATE NORMENORDNUNGEN ALS TRANSNATIONALES RECHT? (2009); MORITZ RENNER, ZWINGENDES TRANSNATIONALES RECHT: ZUR STRUKTUR DER WIRTSCHAFTSVERFASSUNG JENSEITS DES STAATES (2010); THE LIMITS OF TRANSNATIONAL LAW: REFUGEE LAW, POLICY HARMONIZATION AND JUDICIAL DIALOGUE IN THE EUROPEAN UNION (Guy Goodwin-Gill & Hélène Lambert eds., 2010); FROM TRANSNATIONAL RELATIONS TO TRANSNATIONAL LAWS: NORTHERN EUROPEAN LAWS AT THE CROSSROADS (Anne Hellum, Shaheen Sardar Ali & Anne Griffiths eds., 2010); MAKING TRANSNATIONAL LAW WORK IN THE GLOBAL ECONOMY: ESSAYS IN HONOUR OF DETLEV VAGTS (Pieter H. F. Bekker, Rudolf Dolzer & Michael Waibel eds., 2010); DETLEF VON DANIELS, THE CONCEPT OF LAW FROM A TRANSNATIONAL PERSPECTIVE (2010); COMPARATIVE LAW AS TRANSNATIONAL LAW: A DECADE OF THE GERMAN LAW JOURNAL (Russel A. Miller & Peer C. Zumbansen eds., 2011); CLIMATE CHANGE LIABILITY : TRANSNATIONAL LAW AND PRACTICE (Richard Lord et al. eds., 2012); TRANSNATIONAL LAW OF SPORTS (James A.R. Nafziger & Thomas B. Stoel eds., 2013); MATHIAS REIMANN, JAMES HATHAWAY & TIMOTHY L. DICKINSON, TRANSNATIONAL LAW, CASES AND MATERIALS (2013); TRANSNATIONALES RECHT: STAND UND PERSPEKTIVEN (Gralf-Peter Calliess ed., 2014); TRANSNATIONAL LAW: RETHINKING EUROPEAN LAW AND LEGAL THINKING (Miguel Maduro, Karlo Tuori & Suvi Sankari eds., 2014); THE FUTURE OF TRANSNATIONAL LAW: EU, USA, CHINA AND THE BRICS (Francis Snyder & Lu Yi eds., 2015); DONALD EARL CHILDRESS III, MICHAEL D. RAMSAY & CHRISTOPHER A. WHYTOCK, TRANSNATIONAL LAW AND PRACTICE (2015); GILLES LHUILLIER, LE DROIT TRANSNATIONAL (2016); TRANSNATIONAL LAW OF PUBLIC CONTRACTS (Mathias Audit & Stephan W. Schill eds., 2016).

[8] For a first attempt at mapping its meanings, see Craig Scott, '*Transnational Law*' as Proto-concept: Three Conceptions, 10 GERMAN L.J. 859–76 (2009).

often referred to as *lex sportiva* and deemed an example of transnational law.[9] The first part of this chapter will focus on exhibiting how *lex sportiva* has been used as an empirical support for what I call the 'pure' theory of transnational law[10], a conception of transnational law as denationalized legal order of a transnational community. The second part will aim to show how *lex sportiva* can also be used to support an 'impure' theory of transnational law. This refers to the idea that the concept of transnational law primarily captures the messy process of transnational interactions between multiple actors, norms and institutions that characterizes much of contemporary legal practice.

B *LEX SPORTIVA* AND THE PURE THEORY OF TRANSNATIONAL LAW

Jessup's concept of transnational law was quickly picked up and, as I aim to show in the first section, inspired a pure theory of transnational law relying heavily on the concept of transnational legal order (in particular in the context of the rediscovery of the *lex mercatoria*). Previously, before Jessup's lectures and starting with the work of Santi Romano in the early twentieth century, the private regulations of sports had been identified as a legal order in its own right. Thus, it seems quite natural that these two positions were more recently united to ascertain the transnational legal order(s) of sports, called *lex sportiva* in reference to *lex mercatoria*.

I *The Emergence of a 'Pure' Theory of Transnational Law*

The notion of transnational law quickly becomes from the 1960s onwards embroiled in a controversial doctrinal dispute over the existence of a *lex mercatoria* of the transnational community of merchants. This discussion started with the work of a French scholar, Berthold Goldman, and his famous article of 1964, 'Frontières du droit et "lex mercatoria"'.[11] In this piece he claims that international arbitrators are seeking to apply 'transnational law', which he perceives as a 'receptacle' for the principles shared among national laws and a 'melting pot' of the specific rules called for by international trade,

---

[9] See LATTY, *supra* note 7.

[10] In reference to Hans Kelsen's 'pure' theory of law. Indeed, the pure theory of transnational law is influenced by the Kelsenian vision of a hierarchical, unified and coercive legal order.

[11] Berthold Goldman, *Frontières du droit et 'lex mercatoria'*, 9 ARCHIVES DE PHILOSOPHIE DU DROIT 177–92 (1964).

to international commercial disputes.[12] This article was the result of a research programme initiated in the late 1950s at the Université de Dijon in France that led to the revival of the then almost forgotten *lex mercatoria*.[13] It gave way to a never-ending debate among specialists on the existence of the *lex mercatoria*.[14]

Yet, it is François Rigaux, a Belgium scholar of both public and private international law, who first theorized the change in the usage of Jessup's concept. In his book *Droit public et droit privé dans les relations internationales*,[15] published in 1977, Rigaux dedicates a full chapter to discussing the 'transnational space' and in particular the added value of the concept of transnational compared to international and multinational.[16] In this chapter, Rigaux devotes some of his reflections to the notion of transnational law. He evokes the possibility of 'the constitution of a new type of law specifically tailored to the needs of "transnational" relations, a law stemming from the specific community of international business and on which multinational enterprises exercise a decisive influence'.[17] In the concluding remarks of the same chapter, Rigaux comes back to the notion of transnational law; he strongly criticizes its legitimacy but at the same time he recognizes that '[a]s long as economic agents exercise a form of power and organize their inter-actions, they constitute a society [or community] abiding by certain rules'.[18] Thus, for him, the 'notion itself of "transnational law" designates a non-territorial order, of which the agents of an economic power diffused across the globe are the subjects'.[19] He considers that these economic agents have succeed in creating a 'domaine reservé'[20] analogous to the state's own domain,

[12] In Goldman, *supra* note 11, at 189 n.5, Goldman refers directly to Jessup's book as the inspiration for his use of the concept.

[13] See, reminiscing on the project, Philippe Kahn, *Toward the Quest for the Lex Mercatoria: The Contribution of the Dijon School, 1957–1964*, in THE CREEPING CODIFICATION OF THE NEW LEX MERCATORIA 363–67 (Klaus Peter Berger ed., 2010). On the 'Dijon school', see also Thomas Schultz, *The Concept of Law in Transnational Arbitral Legal Orders and Some of Its Consequences*, 2 J. INT'L DISP. SETTLEMENT 59–85 (2011).

[14] For a good historical genealogy of this debate, see Nikitas E. Hatzimihail, *The Many Lives – and Faces – of Lex Mercatoria: History as Genealogy in International Business Law*, 71 LAW & CONTEMP. PROBS. 169 (2008).

[15] FRANÇOIS RIGAUX, DROIT PUBLIC ET DROIT PRIVÉ DANS LES RELATIONS INTERNATIONALES (1977).

[16] *Id.* at 366–402.

[17] *Id.* at 371 (the author's translation). In the footnote supporting this statement, he refers primarily to authors working on the *lex mercatoria*. See *id.* at 371–72 nn.10 & 13.

[18] *Id.* at 400 (the author's translation).

[19] *Id.* (the author's translation).

[20] *Id.*

inside which they obey exclusively to their self-made rules. In his ensuing chapter on legal pluralism, Rigaux aims to demonstrate that this form of transnational law can be considered law. He believes it 'inexcusable' to negate the legal quality of this emerging transnational law and adds that '[o]nly a narrow legalistic conception of law and a theory identifying law with the state lead to the negation of the autonomy and spontaneity of the legislative and enforcement processes of a positive law which is indebted only to the states for their abstention and for the freedom to act they have left to private economic agents'.[21] In sum, Rigaux, relying empirically on the burgeoning literature on the revival of the *lex mercatoria*, was the first to theorize transnational law as law without the state. An interpretation, as we will see in greater length below, that was foreign to Jessup's own understanding of transnational law. Rigaux in his later work, especially in his Hague Academy lecture entitled *Les situations juridiques individuelles dans un système de relativité générale*,[22] elaborated on his understanding of transnational law. Instead of transnational law, he developed the concept of transnational legal order derived from Santi Romano's institutional theory of the legal order.[23] Rigaux's aim was to highlight the plurality of legal orders applying to transnational situations and to emphasize the 'general relativity' in private international law.[24] He regrets deeply that a 'purely statist vision of this discipline [the legal discipline]' leads to the neglect of numerous 'non-state "galaxies"'.[25] In this regards, the lecture relies on the concept of 'transnational legal orders'[26]. He identifies transnational legal orders in three fields in particular – sporting legal orders, canonical law and the international economic space. Rigaux's view is not one of a single transnational legal order active in each field; rather, he discerns a multiplicity of orders. These transnational legal orders

---

[21] *Id.* at 413.

[22] FRANÇOIS RIGAUX, LES SITUATIONS JURIDIQUES INDIVIDUELLES DANS UN SYSTÈME DE RELATIVITÉ GÉNÉRALE (1989).

[23] Santi Romano is a key inspirer, in particular in France, for scholars actively engaging in the theorization of transnational law as transnational legal order. The translation of his book *L'ordinamento giuridico* into French in 1975, by Lucien François and Pierre Gothot, was a source of inspiration for many French-speaking authors interested in the emergence of private legal orders.

[24] In other words: 'Emprunté aux sciences de la nature, le principe de relativité générale a paru seul apte à énoncer la condition actuelle du droit international privé: divers systèmes institutionnels appréhendent les situations juridiques transfrontières.' RIGAUX, *supra* note 22, at 20.

[25] *Id.* at 26.

[26] *Id.* at 61–69.

have a life of their own and do not require the recognition of the state to be deemed law.

This emergence of transnational legal orders alongside the national and international legal order had a certain success in continental legal scholarship. The idea of a 'tiers droit' was endorsed by influential contributors to the doctrinal debates surrounding the *lex mercatoria*.[27] Indeed, much of these debates revolved around the question of whether the *lex mercatoria* constitutes a proper transnational legal order or not.[28] In this process of doctrinal repackaging, the transnational law referred to by Jessup lost much of its original meaning to become synonymous with transnational legal orders without the state.[29] This view is still widespread nowadays.[30] For example, Gralf-Peter Calliess defines transnational law as 'a third-level autonomous legal system beyond municipal and public international law created and developed by the law-making forces of an emerging global civil society, founded on general principles of law as well as societal usages administered by private dispute resolution service providers, and codified (if at all) by private norm formulating agencies'.[31] The purity of this approach lies in its interpretation of transnational law as embodying an autonomous legal order or system of a specific 'transnational community'.[32] The emphasis is put on coherence, closure and exclusivity of transnational law and on its societal, bottom-up origins. In a nutshell, the empirical claim is that transnational communities are relying on

[27] Michel Virally, for example, refers both to transnational law and transnational legal order to qualify the *lex mercatoria* in Michel Virally, *Un tiers droit? Réflexions théoriques*, in LE DROIT DES RELATIONS ÉCONOMIQUES INTERNATIONALES. ETUDES OFFERTES À BERTHOLD GOLDMAN 373–85 (1982). *See also* Alain Pellet, *La Lex Mercatoria, 'Tiers ordre juridique'? Remarques ingénues d'un internationaliste de droit public*, in SOUVERAINETÉ ETATIQUE ET MARCHÉS INTERNATIONAUX À LA FIN DU 20ÈME SIÈCLE, ÉLANGES EN L'HONNEUR DE PHILIPPE KAHN 53–74 (2000).
[28] Debating this question at the turn of the last century, see FILIP DE LY, INTERNATIONAL BUSINESS LAW AND LEX MERCATORIA (1992); URSULA STEIN, LEX MERCATORIA: REALITÄT UND THEORIE (1995); KLAUS-PETER BERGER, THE CREEPING CODIFICATION OF THE NEW LEX MERCATORIA (1999).
[29] Or 'global law without the state' for Gunther Teubner; *see* GLOBAL LAW WITHOUT THE STATE (Gunther Teubner ed., 1997).
[30] *See*, more generally, MATH NOORTMANN, *Transnational Law: Philip Jessup's Legacy and Beyond*, in NON-STATE ACTORS IN INTERNATIONAL LAW 57–74 (Math Noortmann, August Reinisch & Cedric Ryngaert eds., 2015).
[31] Gralf-Peter Calliess, *Reflexive Transnational Law – the Privatisation of Civil Law and the Civilisation of Private Law*, 23 ZEITSCHRIFT FÜR RECHTSSOZIOLOGIE 185, 188 (2002).
[32] For a sociolegal elaboration on the connection of the concept of law with transnational communities, see Roger Cotterrell, *Transnational Communities and the Concept of Law*, 21 RATIO JURIS 1, 12–13 (2008).

transnational legal orders to regulate their activities and resolve their disputes outside of the purview of the state.

II *The* Lex Sportiva: *The Transnational Legal Order(s) of Sport*

As discussed in the previous section, the pure theory of transnational law is primarily a product of the debate on the *lex mercatoria*. Yet, long before, scholars were already discussing the prevalence of non-state legal orders in national and international sports (as well as in religious communities). The Italian doctrine,[33] building on Santi Romano's work on the 'ordinamento giuridico',[34] was the first to theorize and analyse the rise of a separate legal order in the sporting context. This idea irrigates until today the way sports regulation is conceived in Italy.[35]

This Italian scholarship slowly made its way outside of the peninsula, especially after Santi Romano's book was translated into French in 1975,[36] and emulated across Europe. Firstly in Belgium, where Luc Silance, a theoretically minded jurist, disciple of the 'Ecole de Bruxelles' under the leadership of the legal logician Chaïm Perelman and also legal counsel at the International Olympic Committee, had argued since the early 1970s in favour of the existence and legitimacy of an autonomous sporting legal order.[37] As we have seen above, Rigaux, influenced by Silance, used sports

---

[33] See in particular Cesarini Sforza, *La teoria degli ordinamenti giuridici e il diritto sportivo*, FORO ITALIANO (1933) and Massimo Giannini, *Prime osservazioni sugli ordinamenti giuridici sportivi*, 1 RIVISTA DI DIRITTO SPORTIVO 10 (1949).

[34] *See* SANTI ROMANO, L'ORDINAMENTO GIURIDICO: STUDI SUL CONCETTO, LE FONTI E I CARATTERI DEL DIRITTO (1918).

[35] For an enlightening introduction to the Italian doctrine, see LORENZO CASINI, DIRITTO GLOBALE DELLO SPORT 18–25 (2010).

[36] *See* S. ROMANO, L'ORDRE JURIDIQUE (1975). Romano's influence on transnational legal thinking perseveres until today in French scholarship and is not as forgotten as some may think; see Filippo Fontanelli, *Santi Romano and 'L'ordinamento giuridico': The Relevance of a Forgotten Masterpiece for Contemporary International, Transnational and Global Legal Relations*, 2 TRANSNAT'L LEGAL THEORY 67–117 (2011).

[37] For a first hint in that direction before being acquainted with the work of Santi Romano, see Luc Silance, *The Rules of the International Olympic Committee and Law*, OLYMPIC REVIEW 50–51 (1971). Thereafter, he embraced the sporting legal order view in numerous publications, citing Santi Romano as a reference; Luc Silance, *La logique, le sport, et les ordres juridiques, in* JUSTICE ET ARGUMENTATION. ESSAIS À LA MÉMOIRE DE CHAÏM PERELMAN 29–46 (Guy Haarscher & Léon Ingber eds., 1986), with a reference to Romano at pp. 43–44; LUC SILANCE, *Les ordres juridiques dans le sport, in* SPORT ET DROIT 107–19 (Eric Bournazel ed., 2002). See also, in general, the section on legal orders in LUC SILANCE, LES SPORTS ET LE DROIT 79–135 (1998).

as a key example for the existence of transnational legal orders.[38] Rigaux was not familiar with the concept of *lex sportiva*, but he is definitely one of the forefathers to the proposition that sports regulations could constitute transnational legal orders or transnational law. This discussion spread thereon to French academia, where Gérald Simon popularized the idea of a sporting legal order during the 1990s.[39]

However, it is only in 1990 with the book of a German scholar, Thomas Summerer, that the concept of *lex sportiva* was crafted.[40] In his PhD thesis, Summerer introduced a section on the '*Lex Sportiva Internationalis Sui Generis*' and coined the term.[41] From thereon, authors started to pick up the concept,[42] which was also quickly introduced by the Court of Arbitration for Sport (CAS) in its awards and publications.[43] Nowadays, the reference to *lex sportiva* is almost ubiquitous in the literature.[44] In its minimalist dimension, it is used to qualify the jurisprudence of the CAS on general principles of law.[45] In its maximalist understanding, it is synonymous of a transnational legal order

---

[38] In his Hague lecture, he refers directly to Luc Silance's work. *See, e.g.*, RIGAUX, *supra* note 22, at 290.

[39] *See* GÉRALD SIMON, PUISSANCE SPORTIVE ET ORDRE JURIDIQUE ÉTATIQUE: CONTRIBUTION À L'ÉTUDE DES RELATIONS ENTRE LA PUISSANCE PUBLIQUE ET LES INSTITUTIONS PRIVÉES 5–6 (1990) and Gérald Simon, *Existe-t-il un ordre juridique du sport?*, 33 DROITS 97–106 (2001). *See also* more recently Mathieu Maisonneuve, *Les ordres juridiques sportifs transnationaux*, 3 REVUE DE LA RECHERCHE JURIDIQUE – DROIT PROSPECTIF 1564–96 (2005).

[40] THOMAS SUMMERER, INTERNATIONALES SPORTRECHT VOR DEM STAATLICHEN RICHTER (1990).

[41] *Id.* at 95.

[42] Gérald Simon used the concept of *lex sportiva* to qualify the emergence of a jurisprudence of the CAS in Gérald Simon, *L'arbitrage des conflits sportifs*, 2 REVUE DE L'ARBITRAGE 185, 210–18 (1995). While Gunther Teubner popularized the concept beyond the narrow field of sports lawyers in Gunther Teubner, '*Global Bukowina*': *Legal Pluralism in the World Society*, in GLOBAL LAW WITHOUT THE STATE 4 (Gunther Teubner ed., 1996).

[43] The first mention of *lex sportiva* in a published CAS award was in CAS 2002/O/373 Canadian Olympic Committee & Beckie Scott v. International Olympic Committee, Award of 18 December 2003. However, a *Digest of CAS Awards*, published in 2002 by the CAS secretary general Matthieu Reeb, referred to CAS jurisprudence as 'a real *lex sportiva* in development' on its back cover; *see* DIGEST OF CAS AWARDS II 1998–2000 (Matthieu Reeb ed., 2002).

[44] See, in the latest years, among a fast-growing literature, LEX SPORTIVA: WHAT IS SPORTS LAW? (Robert C.R. Siekmann & Janwillem Soek eds., 2012); Antoine Duval, *Lex Sportiva: A Playground for Transnational Law*, 19 EUR. L.J. 822–42 (2013); Klaus Dieter Wolf, *The Non-existence of Private Self-Regulation in the Transnational Sphere and Its Implications for the Responsibility to Procure Legitimacy: The Case of the Lex Sportiva*, 3 GLOBAL CONSTITUTIONALISM 275–309 (2014); Alfonso Valero, *In Search of a Working Notion of Lex Sportiva*, 14 INT'L SPORTS L.J. 3–11 (2014); LEX SPORTIVA (Klaus Vieweg ed., 2015).

[45] For a typical example of this view, see Matthew J. Mitten, *The Court of Arbitration for Sport and Its Global Jurisprudence: International Legal Pluralism in a World without National Boundaries*, 30 OHIO ST. J. ON DISP. RESOL. 1–44 (2014–15) and Richard W. Pound, *Sports Arbitration: How It Works and Why It Works*, 1 McGILL J. OF DISP. RES. 82 (2015).

of sport, or transnational law.[46] In fact, it was only with the publication of Franck Latty's PhD thesis in 2007 that *lex sportiva* and transnational law became intimately entwined in many authors' minds.[47]

Furthermore, with the rise of the CAS as a central dispute resolution body in international sports, numerous authors familiar with the discourse on the *lex mercatoria* were prompt to compare it with an emerging *lex sportiva*.[48] The paradox being that from a strictly Hartian perspective on the concept of law, the *lex sportiva* seems more likely to fit a denationalized concept of law than its older sibling.[49] Despite the widespread view that the *lex sportiva* is just a less 'well-established'[50] *lex mercatoria*, it can be argued that in practice it relies on a more centralized and hierarchic network of rules and institutions than the rather chaotic field of international arbitration.[51] The Sports Governing Bodies (SGBs) play a fundamental role as legislative and executive powers in the day-to-day operations of sporting regulations, while the judicial power is mainly in the hands of the internal dispute resolution mechanisms of the SGBs and the CAS. The force of the SGBs depends on their monopolistic position and their capacity to exclude a person, a team, a country from sporting competitions worldwide.[52] The tangled hierarchy of power is never clearer as when a Swiss association (formally no different than a local chess club) is able to force a national government into passing certain laws or abstaining from certain regulations.[53]

---

[46] This is the thesis advanced in LATTY, *supra* note 7.

[47] *Id.* I have aimed to highlight how *lex sportiva* could become a fruitful playground for transnational lawyers in Duval, *supra* note 44.

[48] Explicitly drawing the analogy, see, e.g., ANTONIO RIGOZZI, L'ARBITRAGE INTERNATIONAL EN MATIÈRE DE SPORT 633 (2005) or JAMES A.R. NAFZIGER, *Defining the Scope and Structure of International Sports Law: Four Conceptual Issues, in* LEX SPORTIVA 178 (Klaus Vieweg ed., 2015).

[49] *See* Duval, *supra* note 44, at 828–30.

[50] Matthew J Mitten & Hayden Opie, *'Sports Law': Implications for the Development of International, Comparative, and National Law and Global Dispute Resolution*, 85 TUL. L. REV. 269, 289 (2010).

[51] Noting this specific quality of international sports organisations, see, e.g., Michael R. Will, *Les structures du sport international, in* CHAPITRES CHOISIS DU DROIT DU SPORT 21–32 (Louis Dallevès & Margareta Baddeley eds., 1993). *See also* LATTY, *supra* note 7.

[52] See, e.g., on the power of FIFA, Henk Erik Meier & Borja Garcia, *Protecting Private Transnational Authority against Public Intervention: FIFA's Power over National Governments*, 93 PUB. ADMIN. 890–906 (2015).

[53] See, in the context of the Olympics, Thomas Schultz, *La lex sportiva se manifeste aux jeux olympiques de Turin: Suprématie du droit non étatique et boucles étranges*, JUSLETTER (2006), and Mark James & Guy Osborn, *London 2012 and the Impact of the UK's Olympic and Paralympic Legislation: Protecting Commerce or Preserving Culture?*, 74 MOD. L. REV. 410–29 (2011).

Thus, at first glance, *lex sportiva* might fit better the theoretical premises underlying the idea of an autonomous transnational legal order.[54] In fact, some authors rejecting on empirical grounds the existence of a *lex mercatoria*, such as Pierre Mayer, are more open to the existence of a *lex sportiva*.[55] Where *lex mercatoria* lacks a coherent and stable body of rules, the sporting world relies on stable and identifiable authoritative texts, such as the Olympic Charter or the FIFA Statutes. Where its users create the *lex mercatoria* contract after contract, the *lex sportiva* relies on stable procedures of lawmaking not unlike those used in national parliaments. Where a multitude of commercial arbitral tribunals are empowered to secretly apply the *lex mercatoria* in practice, the CAS is a monopolist seated at the apex of the *lex sportiva*'s judicial pyramid and relies on a relatively stable and accessible jurisprudence.[56] Where commercial awards have often to be recognized and enforced by national courts, the SGBs can implement themselves the sanctions adopted and impose compliance with CAS awards. All those practical differences illustrate why the *lex sportiva* offers an ideal (probably better than the *lex mercatoria*) example for scholars in search of empirical support for the pure theory of transnational law.

This approach to the *lex sportiva*, and transnational law in general, leads to endless debates on its autonomy (or not) and to heated black-or-white arguments regarding its (in)existence.[57] Thinking in terms of pure theory of transnational law encourages Manichean assessments unlikely to do justice to the many nuances and shades of law in the transnational age. Instead, it might hide many of the legal transformations and challenges that Jessup aimed to highlight when he decided to have recourse to the notion of transnational law in the first place. In particular, as I aim to show in the next

---

[54] Antoine Duval, *The Olympic Charter: A Transnational Constitution without a State?*, 45 J.L & Soc'y 245–69 (2018).

[55] *See* PIERRE MAYER, LE PHÉNOMÈNE DE LA COORDINATION DES ORDRES JURIDIQUES, (2007). He is critical on the existence of a *lex mercatoria* at pp. 64–71 and more favourable to the *lex sportiva* at pp. 72–3.

[56] On the emergence of a jurisprudence at the CAS, see Gabrielle Kaufmann-Kohler, *Arbitral Precedent: Dream, Necessity or Excuse?*, 23 ARB. INT'L 357, 365–66 (2007).

[57] The famous words of the Frankfurt court comes to mind: "eine von jedem staatlichen Recht unabhängige lex sportiva gibt es nicht' [there is no lex sportiva entirely independent from state law], in Oberlandesgericht [OLG] [Higher Regional Court] Frankfurt, Decision from Apr. 18, 2001, Az. 13 U 66/01 (Ger.). This view resonates among many (in particular German) authors denying forcefully the existence of autonomous sporting legal orders. *See, e.g.,* Thomas Summerer, *Internationales Sportrecht – eine dritte Rechtsordnung?*, *in* FESTSCHRIFT FÜR HANS HANISCH 267–79 (Eltje Aderhold et al. eds., 1994); PETER SCHLEITER, GLOBALISIERUNG IM SPORT (2009); and IPSEN, *supra* note 7.

section, it can obfuscate the complexity, relativity and fluidity of the *lex sportiva* and downplay its blended origins and institutions.

C *LEX SPORTIVA* AND THE IMPURE THEORY OF TRANSNATIONAL LAW

Jessup's theory of transnational law was recently criticized as 'confusing'[58] and as having failed 'to constitute an inter-subjective understanding of transnational law as a separate legal category.'[59] Yet, one could also acknowledge his vague and all-encompassing understanding of transnational law as a prescient recognition of the fluid, pluralistic and, to some extent, chaotic legal universe that we are (sixty years later) currently facing. Jessup's transnational law was impure and unsettled, but, as we will see, so is the *lex sportiva*.

I *The Impure Theory of Transnational Law: From Jessup to Zumbansen*

1 Jessup's Transnational Law

Jessup's account of transnational law was consciously blurry and almost all-inclusive. In his own words: 'I shall use, instead of "international law," the term "transnational law" to include all law which regulates actions or events that transcend national frontiers.'[60] His transnational law covers public and private, international and national law. The core objective of the lectures was to break old dogmatic frames in order to deal with new transnational problems. As '[t]he more wedded we become to a particular classification or definition, the more our thinking tends to become frozen and thus to have a rigidity which hampers progress towards the ever needed new solutions of problems whether old or new'.[61] Instead of replacing the old frames with new ones, Jessup decided to 'avoid further classification of transnational problems and further definitions of transnational law'.[62] There is something inherently pragmatic in his approach, departing from the messy reality to elaborate concepts, instead of trying to force the reality into preconceived conceptual boxes. His turn to transnational law is premised on the empirical intuition that the transnationalization of life and law had, already in 1956, rendered the

---

[58] Noortmann, *supra* note 30, at 61.
[59] *Id.* at 57.
[60] JESSUP, *supra* note 2, at 2.
[61] *Id.* at 7.
[62] *Id.*

concept of international law (and the public–private distinction) inadequate to usefully capture the complexity of legal interactions in a transnational context.

Moreover, his account was given from the point of view of a problem-solver, having mainly the position of the judge in mind. Thus, he dedicated the second part of his book to the question of jurisdiction – which institution has the power to deal with a specific dispute. His main take is that strict principles of territoriality and sovereignty are obsolete in practice. Instead, '[t]he fundamental question is to determine which national authorities may deal effectively with which transnational situations – effectively in the sense that authorities of other states will recognize that the exercise of authority is reasonable and will therefore give effect to judgments rendered or refrain from protests through the diplomatic channel'.[63] In fact, '[i]t would be the function of transnational law to reshuffle the cases and to deal out jurisdiction in the manner most conducive to the needs and convenience of all members of the international community'.[64]

The third and final part of the book discusses the question of the judge's choice of law to deal with transnational problems. Here again, Jessup endorses a broad legal ecumenism and affirms that there is 'no inherent reason why a judicial tribunal, whether national or international, should not be authorized to choose from all of these bodies of law the rule considered to be most in conformity with reason and justice for the solution of any particular controversy'.[65] This 'choice need not be determined by territoriality, personality, nationality, domicile, jurisdiction, sovereignty, or any other rubric save as these labels are reasonable reflections of human experience with the absolute and relative convenience of the law and of the forum – *lex conveniens* and *forum conveniens*'.[66] Thus, it seems Jessup was advocating for pragmatism in a transnational legal context rather than for a separate transnational legal order that would provide separate judicial institutions and applicable law.

Twenty years later, when reminiscing on the Storrs Lectures, Jessup indicated that 'the basic thesis of a plea for the evolution of a transnational law is the desirability of eliminating distinctions between different branches of law which have been compartmentalized in judicial practice',[67] adding that 'as one so frequently reads the word "transnational" in writings on what we used

---

[63] *Id.* at 70.
[64] *Id.* at 71.
[65] *Id.* at 106.
[66] *Id.*
[67] Philip C. Jessup, *The Present State of Transnational Law, in* The Present State of International Law 342 (Maarten Bos ed., 1973).

to call simply "international law", one realizes that our international legal realm no longer concentrates on relationships between states themselves'.[68] Jessup's concept of transnational law did not aim at arguing for the existence of denationalized transnational legal orders; rather, his modest ambition was to help lawyers think about the transformations of law in a transnationalizing context. In his own words, '[i]t is to ease the transmission of thought in its approach to legal problems which transcend national frontiers that the term "transnational" has recently come to be used more and more widely'.[69] Jessup would probably have been comfortable with Scott's first two conceptions of transnational law as proto-concept: 'Transnationalized Legal Traditionalism' and 'Transnationalized Legal Decisionism'. The former holds that 'it is "law" as we know it that must deal with various phenomena consisting of "actions or events that transcend national frontiers"'.[70] In the latter instance, 'transnational law is understood as the resulting (institutionally generated) interpretation or applications of domestic and international law to transnational situations'.[71] Jessup's eclectic approach to transnational law went almost lost, if not for the scholarship of Detlev Vagts in the United States[72] and, to a more distant extent, Eugen Langen's work in Germany.[73]

2   Transnational Legal Pluralism: Reconciling Jessup with Transnational Law

As we have seen in the first part of this chapter, the most popular use of transnational law quickly diverged from the original meaning ascribed to it by Jessup. It became, at least in continental Europe, very much synonymous with autonomous transnational legal orders. Yet, in a profoundly renewed fashion, Peer Zumbansen recently revived Jessup's heuristic ambition for transnational law. Inspired by Jessup's essay, but going beyond it by adopting a resolutely interdisciplinary outlook, Zumbansen argued for a new pluralist and methodological turn in transnational legal studies. This he referred to as

---

[68]   *Id.* at 344.

[69]   Philip C. Jessup, *The Concept of Transnational Law: An Introduction*, 3 COLUM. J. TRANSNAT'L L. 1 (1963–1964).

[70]   Craig Scott, 'Transnational Law' as Proto-concept: Three Conceptions, 10 GERMAN L.J. 868 (2009).

[71]   *Id.* at 871.

[72]   *See* HENRY J. STEINER & DETLEV F. VAGTS, TRANSNATIONAL LEGAL PROBLEMS (1976).

[73]   Whom Jessup helped publish his main monograph on transnational law, as recalled in LANGEN, *supra* note 6, at XI.

'transnational legal pluralism'.[74] For Zumbansen, transnational law 'must be seen in the context of a vibrant interdisciplinary discourse about the status and role of law in an increasingly inchoate, globe-spanning web of regulatory regimes, actors, norms and processes'.[75] His theory excludes the reduction of transnational law to a separate transnational legal order of a functional community. Indeed, '[a]pproaching transnational law from a methodological perspective should help us in refraining from too quickly depicting the "transnational" as a distinct regulatory space, which would differ from the national and the international due to its de-territorial scope and its hybrid, public–private constitution'.[76] Instead, 'transnational law emerges as a particular *perspective on law* as part of a society that itself cannot sufficiently be captured by reference to national or de-nationalized boundaries'.[77] In other words, 'transnational law can be conceived of as a way of questioning and reconstructing the project of law between places and spaces, precisely because it helps to relativize law's association with particular institutional frameworks'.[78] In doing so, Zumbansen embraces Jessup's willingness to 'unpack the intricate combination of state/non-state and public/private dimensions inherent to the emerging transnational regulatory landscape'.[79] In a nutshell, transnational 'depicts the space in which the legal pluralist analysis of legal and non-legal regulation occurs'.[80] It is 'the space that is left empty between conceptualisations of a legal order from either a "national" or "international" perspective'.[81]

This interdisciplinary, openly ironic and relativistic perspective on transnational law stands in contraposition to the ideals of coherence, hierarchy and autonomy advanced by the purists. It does not consider transnational law as a denationalized legal order floating above national law and beside international law but as a complex regime emerging out of and reaching through

---

[74] Peer Zumbansen, *Transnational Legal Pluralism*, 1 TRANSNAT'L LEGAL THEORY 141–89 (2010). *See also* Peer Zumbansen, *Defining the Space of Transnational Law: Legal Theory, Global Governance & Legal Pluralism*, *in* BEYOND TERRITORIALITY: TRANSNATIONAL LEGAL AUTHORITY IN AN AGE OF GLOBALIZATION 53–86 (Günther Handl, Joachim Zekoll & Peer Zumbansen eds., 2012).

[75] Peer Zumbansen, *Transnational Law, Evolving*, *in* ELGAR ENCYCLOPEDIA OF COMPARATIVE LAW 898 (Jan Smits ed., 2012).

[76] Zumbansen, *supra* note 75, at 74.

[77] *Id.*

[78] *Id.*

[79] *Id.* at 84.

[80] *Id.* at 150.

[81] *Id.*

national legal and political orders. It is reminiscent of Sassen's 'global assemblages'[82], which 'integrate territorial and de-territorial, vertical and horizontal ordering patterns to produce a structured regime of societal activities'.[83] This view is also closely related to the recent sociolegal work on transnational legal orders done by Terence Halliday and Gregory Shaffer.[84] Transnational legal orders in their mind have to be sharply distinguished from the concept used in the first part of this chapter. They mean 'a collection of formalized legal norms and associated organizations and actors that authoritatively order the understanding and practice of law across national jurisdictions'[85] and focus their scholarly attention on what they refer to as the process of transnational legal ordering. In their view, the state still plays a central role inside transnational legal processes. As put by Shaffer, '[w]hat we are witnessing [...] is variable pressures and convergences that give rise to transnational legal ordering, with considerable variation within national contexts in light of different institutional and socio-cultural legacies and configurations of power'[86]. In fact, '[i]t is this varying, pluralist interaction of different national, international, and transnational legal orders, of different geographic and substantive scope, which is of growing importance for the empirical study of how law operates today'.[87] In other words, '[t]he legal ordering that we see is transnational because it implicates multiple states and constituencies within them, but it is not post-national in that states remain central to the creation, implementation, and contestation of transnational legal ordering'.[88]

Jessup's original refusal to pin down transnational law to a precise field, order or system of law is paradoxically an analytical strength. Indeed, the lacking analytical trenchant of his concept enables it to better capture the complexity, relativity and fluidity of the current transnational legal landscape.

---

[82] *See* Saskia Sassen, Territory, Authority, Rights: From Medieval to Global Assemblages (2008). And for a shorter elaboration of her theory, Saskia Sassen, *Neither Global nor National: Novel Assemblages of Territory, Authority and Rights*, 1 Ethics & Global Pol. 61–79 (2008).

[83] Zumbansen, *supra* note 75, at 181.

[84] *See* Transnational Legal Orders (Terence C. Halliday & Gregory Shaffer eds., 2014) and Transnational Legal Ordering and State Change (Gregory Shaffer ed., 2012). *See also* Shaffer's chapter in this book.

[85] Transnational Legal Orders, *supra* note 84, at 5.

[86] Gregory Shaffer, A *Transnational Take on Krisch's Pluralist Postnational Law*, 23 Eur. J. Int'l L. 565, 579 (2012).

[87] *Id.*

[88] *Id.*

II *The* Lex Sportiva: *A Playground for the Impure Theory of Transnational Law*

Is there a 'third legal realm beyond the nation state',[89] as Math Noortmann claims? Or a 'tiers droit', as Virally argued earlier? *Lex sportiva* (like the *lex mercatoria*) is often perceived as entirely autonomous from, and floating above (or beside), (inter)national law.[90] Instead, I will aim to show that *lex sportiva* and its operation can be used to support empirically an impure theory of transnational law. To do so, I will briefly highlight the complexity and overlapping nature of the transnational legal regime(s) of international sports in three key domains: the fight against doping, the transfers of football players and the resolution of sporting disputes at the CAS.

1 The World Anti-doping System: 'Glocal' Law in Action

The world anti-doping system is a suitable place to start this concise inquiry into the empirics of *lex sportiva*. It is well known for its complex, public–private and network-like structure and, therefore, has been used by global administrative law scholars as a case study to empirically ground some of their theories.[91] Furthermore, Latty argued that it is a crucial addition to support and reinforce an autonomous *lex sportiva*.[92]

In practice, the World Anti-doping Code,[93] which is the single global text supposed to rule anti-doping worldwide, is adopted by the World Anti-doping Agency (WADA) – a Swiss foundation with a mixed governing structure

---

[89] Noortmann, *supra* note 30, at 57.
[90] Already in 1996, Gunther Teubner invoked the existence of an autonomous *lex sportiva internationalis* in Teubner, *supra* note 42, at 4. See also the reference of Lars Viellechner to *lex sportiva* to challenge Shaffer's approach to transnational law in his review published in 26 EUR. J. INT'L LAW 767, 772 (2015).
[91] *See* Lorenzo Casini, *Global Hybrid Public–Private Bodies: The WADA*, 6 INT'L ORG. L. REV. 421–46 (2009). The World Anti-doping Agency (WADA) is also referred to multiples times in Benedict Kingsbury, Nico Krisch & Richard Stewart, *The Emergence of Global Administrative Law*, LAW & CONTEMP PROBS. 15–62 (2005).
[92] In other words: 'L'Agence mondiale antidopage apporte une contribution de première importance à la *lex sportiva*, dans la mesure où le droit antidopage de la quasi-totalité des organisations sportives transnationales est imité ou inspiré des normes qu'elle sécrète.' LATTY, *supra* note 7, at 411.
[93] The latest 2015 edition of the World Anti-doping Code is available at https://www.wada-ama.org/sites/default/files/resources/files/wada-2015-world-anti-doping-code.pdf (last visited May 10, 2017).

involving state representatives and SGBs.[94] In traditional formalistic legal terms, this code is just a piece of paper with no binding value upon states or individuals. It does not amount to international law or national law. In fact, its binding force is mainly imposed through networks of private contracts. The SGBs are compelling their members (and their members' members) to comply with the code through their private rules.[95] Accordingly, the members of the SGBs are required to abide with the code to be admitted to international competitions. Thus, in theory at least, by controlling access, SGBs impose norm observance. Yet, the actual enforcement of the code relies on a complex enmeshment of implementing regulations and institutions at local, national and transnational level.[96] Similarly, the issuance of sanctions is highly decentralized (on a geographical and sport-by-sport bases), even though WADA disposes of the right (but not the material ability) to appeal any local anti-doping decision involving an international athlete to the CAS.[97]

In principle, at least, all international athletes around the world are subjected to the same obligations and fall under a common world anti-doping system de-fragmenting the fight against doping.[98] Yet, this is not the whole story, as the recent Russian doping scandal has shown.[99] The pluralism of the living transnational law prevails as the bite of these uniform anti-doping rules is geographically variable and highly dependent on each regulatory level's enforcement capabilities and willingness to implement the code.[100] National

[94] The statutes of WADA are available at https://www.wada-ama.org/sites/default/files/resources/files/new_statutes_-11_april_2016.pdf (last visited May 10, 2017).

[95] For a concrete example of how these contractual networks is holding in practice, see CAS 2007/A/1370 & 1376, WADA & FIFA v. STJD & Superior Tribunal de Justiça Desportiva do Futebol (STJD) & Confederação Brasileira de Futebol (CBF) & Mr Ricardo Lucas Dodô, 11 September 2008.

[96] This diversity of enforcers is very well reflected in WADA's 2015 *Anti-doping Rule Violations (ADRVs) Report* and especially in the figures related to the testing authorities responsible for the adverse analytical aindings (AAF) at pp. 17–24. The full report is available at https://www.wada-ama.org/sites/default/files/resources/files/2015_adrvs_report_web_release_0.pdf (last visited May 10, 2017).

[97] See Art. 13, WADC.

[98] On this 'defragmentation', see Franck Latty, *Les Règles applicables aux relations sportives transnationales. Le regard de l'internationaliste publiciste, in* LA FRAGMENTATION DU DROIT APPLICABLE AUX RELATIONS INTERNATIONALES. REGARDS CROISÉS D'INTERNATIONALISTES PRIVATISTES ET PUBLICISTES 83–94 (Jean-Sylvestre Bergé et al. eds., 2011).

[99] On the doping scandal and its consequences, see Antoine Duval, *Tackling Doping Seriously – Reforming the World Anti-doping System After the Russian Scandal*, ASSER POLICY BRIEF No. 2016-02, https://papers.ssrn.com/sol3/Papers.cfm?abstract_id=2836388 (last visited May 10, 2017).

[100] A variability already highlighted by Dag Vidar Hanstad, Eivind A. Skille & Sigmund Loland, *Harmonization of Anti-doping Work: Myth or Reality?*, 13 SPORT IN SOC.: CULTURES, COM.,

anti-doping agencies and anti-doping laboratories, which conduct the brunt of the testing, are often controlled by states.[101] Even if they do not willingly aim at favouring their national champions, states are not born equal, and neither are their anti-doping operations. The world anti-doping fight is, thus, in practice still differentiated on national fault lines and hostage to an inescapable transnational legal pluralism. This illustrates how scratching under the polish of seemingly global rules, one can observe the complex, heterarchical and pluralist nature of the *lex sportiva* in action. The world anti-doping system is public–private in essence but also rather 'glocal' than global in practice, insofar as the global text is reappropriated and reinterpreted at many local levels by various actors and institutions. Does this mean that the states are sovereign and master of their anti-doping policy? No. The Russian doping scandal has shown that the feedback loop can work both ways.[102] Local institutions can shape the practical meaning of the code, but global institutions can also fight back what they believe are pathologic implementations of the code. The unsettled and uncertain 'jeu'[103] of transnational law is played in this space of tension between global and local.

2 The FIFA Regulations on the Status and Transfer of Players: Transnational Lawmaking in the Shadow of EU Law

My second example concerns the transfer system introduced by the Fédération Internationale de Football Association (FIFA). As any football fan knows, a global transfer market for the services of football players is taking place every summer and winter (mainly in Europe, where the football/soccer money still lies).[104] Interestingly, the operation of this market is not solely regulated by national labour law or private international law but also through a

---

MEDIA, POL. 418–30 (2010) and Bastien Soule & Ludovic Lestrelin, *The Puerto Affair: Revealing the Difficulties of the Fight against Doping*, 35 J. SPORT & SOC. ISSUES 186–208 (2011).

[101] On the Russian laboratory's close contacts with the Russian government, read the detailed confession of the former head of the laboratory to the *New York Times* in Rebecca Ruiz & Michael Schwirtz, *Russian Insider Says State-Run Doping Fueled Olympic Gold* (N.Y. TIMES), May 12, 2016, https://www.nytimes.com/2016/05/13/sports/russia-doping-sochi-olympics-2014.html?_r=0.

[102] On the CAS's strong reaction to the scandal, see Antoine Duval, *The Russian Doping Scandal at the Court of Arbitration for Sport: Lessons for the World Anti-doping System*, 16 INT'L SPORTS L.J. 177–97 (2017).

[103] On the 'jeu' as a fruitful legal paradigm, see François Ost & Michel van de Kerchove, *Le jeu: un paradigme fécond pour la théorie du droit?*, 17–18 DROIT ET SOCIÉTÉ 173–205 (1991).

[104] In fact, we are talking about 14 591 transfers for $4.79 billion declared to the FIFA TMS in 2016. *See* Press Release, FIFA, FIFA TMS Global Transfer Market 2017: Record International

set of private regulations issued by FIFA: the Regulations on the Status and Transfer of Players (RSTP).[105] Players and clubs are forced to abide by those rules due to the existence of an International Transfer Certificate (ITC) issued by national federations. As a matter of FIFA's rules, players must obtain an ITC to be allowed to move from a club in one national federation to a club in another.[106] In other words, FIFA introduced an additional requirement to state migration laws for professional football players to move transnationally for work-related reasons. Hence, in order to obtain this ITC, players and clubs have to respect specific conditions enshrined in the RSTP to terminate labour contracts and are restricted in the way they can structure their contractual arrangements.[107] For example, FIFA recently banned a particular contractual practice referred to as third-party ownership, thus outlawing its use on the football transfer market as clubs are being threatened with substantial fines and sporting (thus economic) sanctions, even if this investment practice might be considered legal under national laws.[108] On a daily basis, the transfer market is monitored by a FIFA subsidiary – the FIFA TMS Gmbh – systematically gathering the contractual documents linked to the transfers.[109] This could, at first sight, appear to constitute a perfect example of an autonomous transnational legal order regulating economic exchanges in a particular sector or field.[110]

Transfers in 2016, http://www.fifa.com/governance/news/y=2017/m=1/news=fifa-tms-global-transfer-market-2017-record-international-transfers-in-2865353.html (last visited May 10, 2017).

[105] The latest 2016 version of the FIFA Regulations on the Status and Transfer of Players is available at https://resources.fifa.com/mm/document/affederation/administration/02/70/95/52/regulationsonthestatusandtransferofplayersnov2016weben_neutral.pdf (last visited May 10, 2017).

[106] See Art. 9, RSTP. See Annexe 3, RSTP, for the details regarding the procedure of obtention of such an ITC.

[107] On the implementation of the RSTP's specific labour rules, see Jan Kleiner, Der Spielervertrag im Berufsfussball (2013); Markus Zimmerman, Vertragsstabilität im internationalen Fussball (2015); and Frans De Weger, The Jurisprudence of the FIFA Dispute Resolution Chamber (2016).

[108] See Press Release, Several Clubs Sanctioned for Breach of Third-Party Influence, Third-Party Ownership Rules, FIFA, Mar. 29, 2016, http://www.fifa.com/governance/news/y=2016/m=3/news=several-clubs-sanctioned-for-breach-of-third-party-influence-third-par-2772984.html.

[109] For more information, see the website of the FIFA TMS Gmbh at https://www.fifatms.com/ (last visited May 10, 2017).

[110] Not unlike the insulated world of the Diamond industry chronicled by Lisa Bernstein more than twenty years ago. See Lisa Bernstein, *Opting Out of the Legal System: Extralegal Contractual Relations in the Diamond Industry*, 21 J. Legal Stud. 115–57 (1992). Transposing this idea to FIFA, see Suren Gomtsian et al., *Between the Green Pitch and the Red Tape: The Private Legal Order of FIFA*, 43 Yale J. Int'l L. (2018).

Nonetheless, the reality is slightly more complex. In 1995, the *Bosman*[111] ruling of the then European Court of Justice not only recognized the right of EU players not to be discriminated against in European football, but it also challenged the then applicable transfer regulations imposed by UEFA and FIFA. Indeed, the court found

> that Article 48 of the Treaty [now Article 45 TFEU] precludes the application of rules laid down by sporting associations, under which a professional footballer who is a national of one Member State may not, on the expiry of his contract with a club, be employed by a club of another Member State unless the latter club has paid to the former club a transfer, training or development fee.[112]

The ruling was followed quickly thereafter by the opening by the European Commission of an investigation under EU competition law against the 1997 FIFA RSTP.[113] In 2000 and 2001, political negotiations took place in the shadow of the complaint between the EU Commission, FIFA, UEFA and FIFPro, the football players' union.[114] The basic principles that underlie the operation of the current version of the RSTP were agreed in March 2001 under considerable political pressure and public controversy.[115] Thus, despite the fact that the FIFA transfer system seems to run smoothly outside of any state control, it is in its present form mainly the result of the legal intervention of the EU institutions. Interestingly, the CAS, which is solely competent to deal on appeal with disputes involving the application by FIFA's judicial bodies of the RSTP, refers to this EU legislative history to interpret the RSTP.[116] Furthermore, a recent case in front of German courts, the *SV Wilhelmshaven* case, has shown that EU law remains a potent legal weapon to check the

---

[111] Case C-415/93, Union Royale Belge des Sociétés de Football Ass'n v. Bosman, ECLI:EU: C:1995:463 (Dec. 15, 1995).

[112] *Id.* at para. 114.

[113] On the detailed trajectory of the complaint, see Antoine Duval, *The FIFA Regulations on the Status and Transfer of Players: Transnational Law-Making in the Shadow of Bosman*, in THE LEGACY OF BOSMAN 81–116 (Antoine Duval & Ben Van Rompuy eds., 2016).

[114] *Id.*

[115] The main principles of the agreement are enshrined in the EU Commission's press release announcing the closing of the investigation. *See* Press Release, European Commission, Commission Closes Investigations into FIFA Regulations on International Football Transfers (June 5, 2002), http://europa.eu/rapid/press-release_IP-02-824_en.htm.

[116] See most prominently in CAS 2013/A/3365 Juventus FC v. Chelsea FC and CAS 2013/A/3366 A.S. Livorno Calcio S.p.A. v. Chelsea FC, Award of 21 January 2015. *See also* my commentary of the case in Y.B. INT'L SPORTS ARB. 2015 155–68 (Antoine Duval & Antoinio Rigozzi eds., 2016).

private enforcement of the FIFA transfer system.[117] The German club, which was sanctioned by the FIFA Dispute Resolution Chamber and the CAS to pay compensation to two Argentinean clubs, successfully challenged the CAS award in front of the German Bundesgerichtshof.[118]

It is easy to mistake the operation of the FIFA transfer system for a purely autonomous, denationalized system of economic regulation specific to football and its transnational activity. Yet, in practice its legislative history, crucial to its current interpretation by the CAS, is intertwined with EU law. Hence, it is impossible to dissociate the current operation of the system from the *Bosman* ruling and the ensuing negotiations under the umbrella of the European Commission. The FIFA transfer system is undoubtedly more centralized and privatized than the world anti-doping system. In fact, its implementation is almost exclusively in the hands of FIFA bodies – the FIFA TMS for the monitoring and the FIFA Players' Status Committee and Dispute Resolution Chamber in case of a dispute. Nevertheless, in practice it is embedded in national and European law. The FIFA transfer system is premised on an unlikely normative assemblage weaving together EU law, Swiss law (and sometimes other national labour laws) and private regulations. While FIFA plays a central role in its operation, the EU institutions as well as national courts have also their say in it. In this context, complexity, hybridity and relativity better embody the empirical reality of the operation of the FIFA transfer system than the idea of an autonomous transnational legal order.

3 The Court of Arbitration for Sport and the Importance of Swiss Law

The operation of the CAS will provide my final example to illustrate the 'impurity' of the *lex sportiva*. The CAS is a recent institutional actor in the sporting world. It started operating in 1984 under the patronage of the International Olympic Committee and rendered its first award in 1987.[119] After the *Bosman* ruling, it rapidly became a popular venue to circumvent the jurisdiction of national courts, and nowadays, almost all international sporting

---

[117] In general, on the importance of EU law to control the CAS, see Antoine Duval, *The Court of Arbitration for Sport and EU Law. Chronicle of an Encounter*, 22 MAASTRICHT J. EUR. AND COMP. L. 224–55 (2015).

[118] *See* OLG Bremen, 2 U 67/14, SV Wilhelmshaven v. Norddeutscher Fußball-Verband e.V, 30 December 2014 and BGH, II ZR 25/15, 20 September 2016.

[119] For a short official history of the CAS, see http://www.tas-cas.org/en/general-information/history-of-the-cas.html (last visited May 10, 2017).

disputes fall under its competence.[120] Its appeal procedure enables SGBs to pick the CAS as the sole competent body where their internal decisions can be challenged.[121] The CAS is formally a private arbitral tribunal seated in Lausanne and subjected to the Swiss Private International Law Act (PILA). Under Art. 187 of PILA, an arbitral tribunal 'shall decide the dispute according to the rules of law chosen by the parties'. This provision is interpreted as allowing the parties to select non-state rules as applicable law.[122]

Thus, Art. 58 of the CAS Code of Sports-Related Arbitration, defining the applicable law in appeal proceedings, provides that a CAS panel

> shall decide the dispute according to the applicable regulations and, subsidiarily, to the rules of law chosen by the parties or, in the absence of such a choice, according to the law of the country in which the federation, association or sports-related body which has issued the challenged decision is domiciled or according to the rules of law the Panel deems appropriate.

Based on this provision, so a purist's argument could go, CAS panels can enforce the self-made rules of the *lex sportiva* and close the autopoietic transnational legal system or order on itself. Unsurprisingly, the CAS is also often hailed as the maker or fabricator of a *lex sportiva*.[123] Moreover, the fact that it is formally an arbitral tribunal has (quite naturally) encouraged many to assume that the *lex sportiva* is, like the *lex mercatoria*, a product of arbitral jurisprudence.[124] The latter view is certainly empirically misleading, as it would disregard the peculiar set-up of the CAS appeal procedure and the crucial role played by the rules and the political influence of the SGBs in CAS

[120] As Jack Anderson argued in 2000, it was very successful in taking sports out of the courts, see Jack Anderson, 'Taking Sports Out of the Courts': Alternative Dispute Resolution and the *International Court of Arbitration for Sport*, 10 J. LEGAL ASPECTS SPORT 123–28 (2000). In 2016, the CAS handled 599 cases, while in 1995, the year of the *Bosman* ruling, only thirteen cases were submitted. The official CAS statistics are available at http://www.tas-cas.org/fileadmin/user_upload/CAS_statistics_2016_.pdf (last visited May 10, 2017).

[121] On the appeal procedure, *see* Antonio Rigozzi & Erika Hasler, *Special Provisions Applicable to the Appeal Arbitration Procedure (Arts. R47–R59), in* ARBITRATION IN SWITZERLAND 982–1060 (Manuel Arroyo ed., 2013).

[122] *Id.* at 1048.

[123] Arguing in this direction, see Maisonneuve, *supra* note 59, at 1596; LATTY, *supra* note 7, at 260–359; Lorenzo Casini, *The Making of a Lex Sportiva by the Court of Arbitration for Sport*, 12 GERMAN L.J. 1317–40 (2011).

[124] See, e.g., among numerous authors, Louise Reilly, *Introduction to the Court of Arbitration for Sport (CAS) & the Role of National Courts in International Sports Disputes*, 2012 J. DISPUTE RESOLUTION 63–81 (2012); Rowan Platt, *The Appeal of Appeal Mechanisms in International Arbitration: Fairness over Finality?*, 30 J. INT'L ARB. 531, 556 (2013). Pound, *supra* note 45; Mitten & Opie, *supra* note 50, at 287–89; Nafziger, *supra* note 48.

awards. However, portraying the CAS as a simple 'bouche' of a *lex sportiva* stemming exclusively from the rules of the SGBs would also be unsatisfactory.

In practice, the CAS can be best described as a legal alchemist. In its awards it fuses the rules of the SGBs with considerations of Swiss law (and more rarely other national laws or EU law). Swiss law plays a central role due to the fact that SGBs are often based in Switzerland and CAS awards are exclusively appealable, on extremely narrow grounds, at the Swiss Federal Tribunal (SFT).[125] The fact that CAS awards rarely require recognition by national courts to be enforced, as SGBs can easily implement them through their private monopoly on sporting competitions, places an important responsibility on the shoulders of the SFT. When integrating elements of national (Swiss or otherwise) law to the private norms of the *lex sportiva*, the CAS relativizes the private nature of the *lex sportiva* and renders it more palatable to other legal contexts. This does not entail that the CAS and the *lex sportiva* are entirely subservient to Swiss law (and lawyers); the SFT's control remains extremely marginal and the CAS panels know it. Moreover, Switzerland has proclaimed its ambition to support its 'Silicon Valley of Sports'.[126] Hence, the CAS operates neither in a radically denationalized environment nor under the absolute control of Swiss law and institutions. Instead, the CAS works as a peculiar transnational legal fabric weaving together different, sometimes contradictory, legal texts, logics and objectives. This alchemist function of the CAS is crucial to turn the *lex sportiva* into legitimate law.

In fine, the pluralist perspective on transnational law is helpful to capture the intricacy of the *lex sportiva*, whereas a purist lens would hide (or at least understate) its embeddedness in an ensemble of public rules and institutions at the national, European and international level. Yet, this should not lead to denying the prominence of private actors and their rules; rather it highlights their transnational integration and collaboration with national and European laws and institutions.

---

[125] On the centrality of Swiss law in CAS arbitration, see Antonio Rigozzi, *L'importance du droit suisse de l'arbitrage dans la résolution des litiges sportifs internationaux*, 132 REVUE DE DROIT SUISSE 301–25 (2013). *See also* Despina Mavromati, *Applicability of Swiss Law in Doping Cases Before the CAS and the Swiss Federal Tribunal*, *in* Y.B. INT'L SPORTS ARB. 2015 155–68 (Antoine Duval & Antonio Rigozzi eds., 2016). On the procedure to challenge CAS awards, see Antonio Rigozzi, *Challenging Awards of the Court of Arbitration for Sport*, 1 J. INT'L DISP. SETTLEMENT 217–65 (2010).

[126] *See* Rebecca Ruiz, *Swiss City Is 'the Silicon Valley of Sports'*, N.Y. TIMES (Apr. 22, 2016), https://www.nytimes.com/2016/04/23/sports/olympics/switzerland-global-sports-capital-seeks-new-recruits.html.

D CONCLUSION

More than sixty years ago, Philip Jessup put the spotlight on a new idea, the concept of transnational law. My intention was to show that his lectures were only the beginning of an ongoing conceptual journey to define the scope and implications of transnational law. Hence, this chapter was meant as a concise travel guide for the world of transnational legal scholarship. Highlighting, through a study of its use in the context of the *lex sportiva*, two different, and to some extent opposite, ways in which legal scholars received and operational-ized the concept of transnational law.

First, almost immediately after Jessup's book was published, the notion was mobilized by a powerful scholarly movement engaged in reviving the spectre of the medieval law merchant in the guise of the new *lex mercatoria*. In this context, it became a synonym for a denationalized transnational legal order of the merchant community. It is this approach that was then transposed to the sporting community. In fact, the *lex sportiva* might better fit the model of a transnational legal order of a transnational community, as in the context of international sports identifying a stable set of secondary rules, and a commu-nity of officials monopolizing their interpretation and implementation is empirically more credible than in the anarchic commercial world. Trans-national law is thus conceived as mirroring the attributes of the law in national states, only sovereignty moved from a territorial basis to a functional one. The pluralism often invoked in this context is one of a multitude of transnational functional communities producing their own legal systems. Ironically, it resonates with the pluralism enshrined in the traditional state-based under-standing of the international order, the states being simply replaced by func-tional communities and their legal systems in an updated billiard ball model.

The second approach, which I believe is more in line with what Jessup had in mind in his lectures, has rejuvenated the idea of transnational law as a methodological, pluralist and process-oriented perspective. Transnational law, in this regard, is not a specific, clearly delineable legal system but a complex, network-like transnational construct reflecting the current practice of law. The emphasis is on the plurality and relativity of transnational authorities, norms and processes that collaborate to make law. Thus, transnational law does not constitute a separate legal order above and beyond national law but rather embodies the mindset necessary to see and grasp the complexity of law's transnational practice in a globalizing world. While *lex sportiva* was mainly mobilized to support the pure theory of transnational law, it was seldom invoked to illustrate the impure perspective. This is a want I strived to remedy in the second part of this chapter.

Which vision of transnational law is more adequate to navigate the law of the twenty-first century will be decided by experience. For my part, I believe the emergence of the concept, in both its pure and impure fashion, was crucial to break the frames of (almost) exclusively state-centric legal studies. Yet, it is easy to fall prey to the opposite framing, one that dogmatically sidelines the state as being already passé. Instead, transnational lawyers should aim to better apprehend the complexity and enmeshment of legal practice in a multiplicity of social contexts – at local, national, regional and global levels. To do so, they must gear up methodologically (and linguistically) to navigate a challenging variety of legal phenomena, discourses and institutions.

12

Family Law

A *Blind Spot*

IVANA ISAILOVIĆ*

A INTRODUCTION

Scholarly conversations about transnational law, or law and globalization often ignore family law.[1] While a majority of early transnational law scholars focused mostly on regulatory issues predominantly concerning economic matters, family law questions have only more recently become the object of interdisciplinary and transnational analysis.[2]

Why do scholars of transnational law overlook family law? The reasons are varied and may be related to one's understanding of family law or of the scope of 'transnational law' itself. A first reason is that family law is still predominantly perceived as a domestic field of inquiry, embedded within local religious or cultural values; a transnational analysis of the field may therefore seem unappealing.[3] A second reason may be that family law is often understood to

---

* I am very grateful to Peer Zumbansen for extremely helpful comments on this chapter and his support. This is part of a broader project on globalization and family law, which was presented at the Emile Noël fellows' forum at Jean Monnet Center at NYU Law in the fall 2016. I thank the participants for their feedback, and Gráinne de Búrca and Joseph Weiler for their continuing support. Many of these ideas were developed while I was teaching the comparative family law seminar at Northeastern Law School in spring 2018 and the seminar on transnational activism, gender and social justice at Northeastern University in fall 2018, and I thank my students for helping me sharpen my arguments.

[1] This chapter does not discuss in depth the substantive differences that exist between various theoretical approaches to transnational law that are coloured by the doctrinal and disciplinary backgrounds of those who participate in the discussion. For a discussion about these different approaches, *see* Peer Zumbansen's introduction to this volume.

[2] Daphna Hacker, Legalized Families in the Era of Bordered Globalization (2016). *See also* Sally Engle Merry, Human Rights and Gender Violence: Translating International Law into Local Justice (2006).

[3] *See, e.g.,* David Bradley, *A Family Law for Europe? Sovereignty, Political Theory and Legitimation* in Perspectives for the Unification and Harmonisation of Family Law in Europe 573 (Katharina Boele-Woelki ed., 2003) (noting that family law is 'commonly

be distinct from market regulation,[4] while transnational law is often characterized as predominantly interested in legal norms and actors related to market governance.[5]

Over the past few years, however, family law scholars have started examining families' everyday lives and family law in relation to globalization dynamics by looking at how domestic family law rules get influenced by human rights regimes, how different states and non-state jurisdictions regulate families and the plurality of values these different orders represent, and how transnational families whose lives span across jurisdictions interact with global legal pluralism.[6] This scholarship weaves together comparative, private, public and international and domestic law and strives to evaluate family laws in their social contexts.

All of the above strongly suggest that family law should be seen as an excellent example of a legal field deeply shaped by and implicated in the regulatory transformation processes that a new generation of transnational law scholarship has become more interested in. Different transnational law approaches discussed in this book – from Jessup's landmark analysis[7] to more recent methodological projects critically analysing the myriad of actors, norms and processes that intervene within the conflictual and plural transnational

---

presented as reflecting deeply embedded differences between states themselves' and arguing that this is so because family law is a 'component of political economy' insofar as it reinforces 'a particular system of social organisation'.).

[4]   Janet Halley & Kerry Rittich, *Critical Directions in Comparative Family Law: Genealogies and Contemporary Studies of Family Law Exceptionalism*, 58 Am. J. Comp. L. 753 (2010).

[5]   This is not to say that economic relations are the only focus of the transnational law field. Scholars have also analysed very a diverse range of topics going from human rights, environmental law regulation or global counterterrorism measures. *See, e.g.*, Veerle Heyvaert & Thijs Etty, *Introducing Transnational Environmental Law*, 1 Transnat'l Envtl L. 1 (2012); *Transnational Criminal Law*, 6 Transnat'l Legal Theory (Special Issue) (2015).

[6]   *See, e.g.*, Hacker, *supra* note 2; Routledge Handbook of International Family Law (Barbara Stark & Jacqueline Heaton eds., 2018) D. Marianne Blair, Merle H. Weiner, Barbara Stark, Solangel Maldonado, Family Law in the World Community, Cases, Materials and Problems in Comparative and International Family Law (2015); Routledge Handbook of Family Law and Policy (John Eekelaar & Rob George eds., 2014). *See also* the European family law harmonization project in the context of European integration, Common Core and Better Law in European Family Law (Katharina Boele-Woelki ed., 2005); Perspectives for the Unification and Harmonisation of Family Law in Europe (Katharina Boele-Woelki ed., 2003). In the European private international law context, see Horatia Muir Watt, *Les modèles familial face à la mondialisation (aspects de droit international privé)*, 45 Arch. phil. droit (2001).

[7]   Philip C. Jessup, Transnational Law (1956).

regulatory space in relation to specialized areas of social activity – all point out to important opportunities to study family law in the global context.[8]

The translation law perspective brings to the fore the production of family norms beyond, below and across legal jurisdictional boundaries, by supra-national courts, human rights bodies, international organizations and trans-national networks of human rights activists and other – for instance religious – communities, while also allowing us to trace the migration of family norms across different jurisdictions and to account for the formation of new regula-tory assemblages around family issues. To take two examples discussed below, we can only fully understand the relationship between religious and secular family norms or the adoption of same-sex marriage reforms if such a trans-national legal plural approach is taken as a starting point of our legal inquiry.

But the study of family law using transnational law methodologies also urges us to examine family law in light of the question of legitimacy.[9] Transnational law, as understood here, is a critical project, building on and connecting domestic critical approaches with a variety of projects bringing together different yet connected disciplines – such as history, colonial and postcolonial studies, sociology or political economy – to examine the asymmetries consti-tutive of global governance dynamics.[10] Transnational law therefore invites us to contextually analyse norms, legal actors and process in light of social and legal conflicts around the meaning of law, rights and justice.[11]

Thus, transnational law helps us improve our understanding of the role family law plays in this new continuously evolving transnational legal context. It invites us, for instance, to deploy the emerging field of transnational feminisms straddling feminist theories, postcolonial studies and political econ-omy to evaluate how family law creates, reproduces and legitimizes gender

---

[8]   *See* Peer Zumbansen, *Introduction* to this book [hereinafter Zumbansen, *Introduction*]; Peer Zumbansen, *Transnational Law as Socio-legal Theory: The Challenges for 'Law and Society' in a Divided World*, 67 BUFF. L. REV. (forthcoming 2019) [hereinafter Zumbansen, *Transnational Law as Socio-legal Theory*]; Peer Zumbansen, *Where the Wild Things Are: Journey of Transnational Legal Orders, and Back*, 1 U.C. IRVINE J. INT'L TRANSNAT'L & COMP. L. 161 (2016) [hereinafter Zumbansen, *Where the Wild Things Are*]; Peer Zumbansen, *Defining the Space of Transnational Law: Legal Theory, Global Governance and Global Pluralism*, 21 TRANSNAT'L. L. & CONTEMP. PROBS. 305, 323 (2012) [hereinafter Zumbansen, *Defining the Space of Transnational Law*] (describing transnational law as a conceptual laboratory); Gregory Shaffer, *Transnational Legal Ordering and State Change*, in TRANSNATIONAL LEGAL ORDERING AND STATE CHANGE 5 (Gregory C. Shaffer ed., 2012).

[9]   Zumbansen, *Where the Wild Things Are*, *supra* note 8.

[10] Zumbansen, *Transnational Law as Socio-legal Theory*, *supra* note 8 (describing the critical dimension of transnational law in light of postcolonial studies).

[11] *See* Zumbansen, *Introduction*, *supra* note 8; Zumbansen, *Defining the Space of Transnational Law*, *supra* note 8.

inequalities in the transnational context. It prompts us to mobilize colonial and postcolonial studies to assess family law's role in maintaining empires and continuing colonial legal imposition or to inquire into how the global expansion of neo-liberal transformations[12] shape family regulations. In short, the transnational law framework accentuates how the field of family law is part of broader global regulatory transformative processes and how it is deeply enmeshed with the global distribution of power, privilege and wealth.

But family law is not unilaterally benefiting from transnational law. Studying the transformations of family law in the transnational context enriches our understanding of how law interacts with society in the new regulatory environment. It reveals new regulatory assemblages situated at the intersection of global and local spaces, showing, from an under-explored vantage point, how transnational processes, norms and actors affect the most intimate aspects of human existence.[13] Similarly, as I will discuss in this chapter, by connecting transnational law themes to family law evolving regulation, we can appreciate the 'local' embeddedness of legal transformations that are often associated with globalization, namely law's embrace of global neo-liberal economic model and rationality,[14] the ongoing changes affecting the production of state law and the proliferation of human rights regimes.

In order to substantiate these different claims, in this chapter, I study three prominent critical themes in transnational law scholarship: legal pluralism, the politics of the private–public distinction and the continuing transformation of welfare states. In each instance, I intend to show the parallels – and, indeed, the correlations – between critical approaches common to both family and transnational law[15] but also the mutual learning opportunities that are often under-explored by scholars on both sides of the disciplinary divide. In order to make these different arguments more concrete, in each part I discuss different contemporary family law case studies, including the legal recognition of Muslim family law in multicultural and postcolonial societies, the regulation of transnational surrogacy agreements and the proliferation of same-sex

---

[12] WENDY BROWN, UNDOING THE DEMOS: NEOLIBERALISM'S STEALTH REVOLUTION (2015). DAVID HARVEY, A BRIEF HISTORY OF NEOLIBERALISM (2005). On the birth of neo-liberalism, see QUINN SLOBODIAN, THE GLOBALISTS: THE END OF EMPIRE AND THE BIRTH OF NEOLIBERALISM (2018).

[13] *See, e.g.*, THE GLOBAL AND THE INTIMATE: FEMINISM IN OUR TIME (Geraldine Pratt & Victoria Rosner eds., 2012).

[14] *See infra* D.II.

[15] For the argument to short-circuit domestic and transnational critical legal theory, see Peer Zumbansen, *Law after the Welfare State: Formalization, Functionalism and the Ironic Turn of Reflexive Law*, 56 AM. J. COMP. L. 769 (2008) [hereinafter Zumbansen, *Law after the Welfare State*].

marriage reforms across jurisdictions. My goal is not to provide definitive arguments and methodologies or to offer a complete picture of family law's evolutions in the global context. Rather, this chapter should be read as tentatively providing one of the many building blocks of the emerging trans-national interdisciplinary conversation that sketches out some of the overlaps between family and transnational law, hints at questions that necessitate further legal research and points to the many ways in which the insights from one field can enrich our understanding of the other.

B TRANSNATIONAL LEGAL PLURALISM

I Legal Pluralism and Transnational Law

In his landmark 1956 lectures, Philip Jessup used the family to illustrate the many limits of the narrow approach to international law adopted at the time by fellow scholars.[16] According to Jessup, the family is one of the many sites of norm production, along with corporations, ecclesiastical authorities and secret societies.[17] By making this claim, Jessup challenges the prevalence of state law within the legal imaginary. To do so, he adopts a more sociolegal lens to the study of law as it is applied to disputes with a transnational dimension by incorporating in its legal analysis questions regarding how law gets produced and by whom,[18] echoing claims made by anthropologists and sociologists focusing on legal pluralism in domestic contexts.[19]

Legal pluralism remains a central trope in transnational law scholarship[20] and within the broader legal globalization literature, which still grapples with questions of legal fragmentation and legitimacy of newly formed legal struc-tures, operating beyond and across state's boundaries.[21] An important theme in legal pluralism, which returns in transnational law, has been the analysis of the interrelationships between non-hierarchical plural 'traditional'/'state' and

---

[16] Jessup, *supra* note 7.

[17] *Id.*

[18] *Id.*

[19] Sally Engle Merry, *Legal Pluralism* 22 L. & Soc'y Rev. 869 (1988); John Griffiths, *What Is Legal Pluralism?* 18 J. Legal Pluralism & Unofficial L. 1 (1986).

[20] *See, e.g.,* Eve Darian-Smith, Law and Societies in Global Contexts (2015); Peer Zumbansen, *Transnational Legal Pluralism,* 1 Transnat'l Legal Theory 141 (2010).

[21] This literature is extensive; *see, e.g.,* Andreas Fischer-Lescano & Gunther Teubner, *Regime Collisions: The Vain Search for Legal Unity in the Fragmentation of Global Law,* 25 Michigan J. Int'l L. 999 (2004); Paul Schiff Berman, *Global Legal Pluralism,* 80 S. Cal. L. Rev. 1155 (2007); Gunther Teubner, *Global Bukowina: Legal Pluralism in the World Society, in* Global Law without the State 3 (G. Teubner ed., 1996).

'informal'/'customary' legal orders.[22] This has been an important theme for legal pluralist scholars, who reject the idea of a bright line between 'official' state law and 'unofficial' law, and it has been important in the context of postcolonial legal theory, where this critique has been extended to historical trajectories of colonial imposition as it manifests itself today. Today, transnational law scholars are engaged with these insights, analysing the encounters and the interrelationships between 'official' and 'non-official' in relation to a myriad of social and legal orderings beyond, below and across states.[23]

Transnational law then proposes a lens for the study of multiple overlapping lawmaking processes. This mapping includes the identification of the various communities that are competing for a space in which to shape the regulatory environment. Such spaces are seen to move in and out and across jurisdictional divides, constituting, thus, new normative spaces between what is traditionally understood as the 'domestic' and the 'international' field[24] and connecting the global with the local.[25] The end point of the legal analysis is not to insist on a categorical answer to the endless jurisprudential question regarding law's *nature and form*. Instead, the here-endorsed approach to transnational law urges us to question the role of the state as the main legal actor, by reading *all* legal relations against the background of broader globalizing forces of cultural, political and economic interactions[26] in order to grasp the complexity of norm making in the global context. As I argue below, transnational law can function as a powerful lens through which these new normative spaces related to family regulation can be made visible and comprehensible.

II *Transnational Legal Pluralism in Family Law*

Rather than being only a domestic discipline, family regulation is actually shaped by a plurality of overlapping and competing legal orders, which applying a transnational law lens allows us to account for. This lens heightens

---

[22] Merry, *supra* note 19 (distinguishing between 'classic legal pluralism' and 'new legal pluralism'). *See also* Boaventura de Sousa Santos, *A Map of Misreading: Toward a Postmodern Conception of Law*, 14 J. L. & SOC'Y 279 (1987).

[23] For different approaches in that regard, see Ralf Michaels, *Global Legal Pluralism*, 5 ANNUAL REV. L. & SOC. SCIENCE 243 (2009), and Peer Zumbansen, *Transnational Legal Pluralism*, *supra* note 20.

[24] Zumbansen, *Introduction*, *supra* note 8.

[25] DARIAN-SMITH, *supra* note 20; Zumbansen, *Transnational Law as Socio-legal Theory*, *supra* note 8.

[26] DARIAN-SMITH, *supra* note 20, at 5; Zumbansen, *Defining the Space of Transnational Law*, *supra* note 8.

our awareness to the multiplicity of norm-generating authorities by prompting us to apply a multifaceted approach to what at first sight appear to be merely singular domestic or isolated international cases.[27] It invites us to map, in a much more detailed fashion, the various state and non-state actors that intervene in norm-generating processes that take place inside and outside of official state lawmaking institutions. Meanwhile, it is through this more detailed scrutiny of the sites and processes of norm production that we are able to appreciate the different actors' interactions with one another and identify the different dynamics of norm migration in this context. Instead of scrutinizing a norm-production process within 'official' state-based institution, we focus on transnational legal processes, which appear as frameworks making visible struggles among different groups for political recognition, spaces for multi-sited norm contestation, fora for the formulation of new claims and creations of new interpretations of 'rights'.

Transnational legal pluralism aptly describes how family is regulated. At the 'domestic' level, legal pluralism is unquestionably a contemporary reality and manifests itself in relation to religious or ethnic orders in states that accommodate different groups by allowing the application of non-state family norms when these groups are involved in family law disputes.[28] In other countries, legal pluralism is a consequence of settler colonialism, as indigenous legal orderings exist side by side with the settler's law.[29] Pluralism is also a reality in most contemporary family laws to the extent that states allow, and sometimes encourage, individuals to *contract out* from state norms and to define their family relationships through private ordering.[30] Finally, private international

---

[27] DARIAN-SMITH, *supra* note 20.

[28] This is for instance the case in India or Israel, where each religious community is regulated by its particular family rules. See, for an overview of different examples, Hadas Tagari, *Personal Family Law Systems — A Comparative and Human Rights Analysis*, 8 INT'L J. L. CONTEXT 231 (2012). A different example is South Africa, where state law accommodates, to a certain extent, customary family law. *See, e.g.,* DAVID L. CHAMBERS, *Civilizing the Natives: Customary Marriage in Post-apartheid South Africa,* in ENGAGING CULTURAL DIFFERENCES: THE MULTICULTURAL CHALLENGE IN LIBERAL DEMOCRACIES 81 (Richard Shweder, Martha Minow & Hazel Rose Markus eds., 2002).

[29] *See, e.g.,* Annelise Riles, *Cultural Conflicts,* 71 LAW & CONTEMP. PROBS. 273 (2008) (analysing conflicts between Native American Navajo marriage rules and US criminal law).

[30] CONTRACTUALISATION OF FAMILY LAW: GLOBAL PERSPECTIVES (Frederik Swennen ed., 2015) (examining private ordering across several jurisdictions). On how some states encourage private ordering, see, e.g., Katharina Boele-Wolkie & Merel Jonker, *Family Law Contractualisation in the Netherlands-Changes and Trends,* in CONTRACTUALISATION OF FAMILY LAW: GLOBAL PERSPECTIVES 311 (Frederic Swennen ed., 2015).

law has been dealing for a long time with legal pluralism as regards the recognition of foreign marriages, divorces, parental or property rights.[31]

Besides these examples, transnational legal regimes, which operate beyond and across states, also influence domestic family laws and practices. One prominent example is human rights law. As will be discussed below, equality and non-discrimination human rights norms have played a crucial role in transnational legal advocacy and in prompting states to adopt reforms legalizing same-sex marriage.[32] Similarly, human rights courts – such as the European Court of Human Rights (ECTHR) – have influenced family law regulations. One example are 'domestic' rules pertaining to the filiation of children born out of transnational surrogacy agreements.[33] In the midst of an ongoing explosive debate about transnational surrogacy in France,[34] the ECTHR has condemned France for refusing to recognize the foreign birth certificate and the filiation between the biological father and children born out of surrogacy agreements, arguing that this amounted to a violation of children's right to private and family life.[35] Accordingly, in order to satisfy its human rights obligations, in subsequent cases, the French Cour de cassation – the supreme court in criminal and civil matters – has adopted this legal interpretation.[36] Recently, the court also asked the ECTHR for an advisory opinion regarding the legal status of intended mother under French law. The Cour de cassation has typically refused to register the intended mother as the 'legal mother' while opening for her the possibility to adopt the child. The Cour de cassation asked therefore whether this legal solution was contrary to the right to children's private and family life, to which the answer was no.[37] Thus the short description of the case already illustrates some of the

---

[31] *See, e.g.,* R. LEA BRILMAYER, JACK L. GOLDSMITH, ERIN O'HARA O'CONNOR, CONFLICT OF LAWS: CASES AND MATERIALS (7th ed. 2015); LES GRANDS ARRÊTS DE LA JURISPRUDENCE FRANÇAISE DE DROIT INTERNATIONAL PRIVÉ (Bertrand Ancelle & Yves Lequette eds., 5th ed. 2006).

[32] *See infra* D.I.

[33] *See infra* C.III.

[34] *Protests in Paris for and against Surrogacy and Medically Assisted Reproduction*, EURONEWS, May 10, 2014, https://www.euronews.com/2014/10/05/protests-in-paris-for-and-against-surrogacy-and-medically-assisted-reproduction.

[35] Mennesson v. France, App. No. 65192/11, Eur. Ct. H.R. (2014); Labassee v. France, App. No. 65941/11, Eur. Ct. H.R. (2014).

[36] Ass. plén., July 3, 2015, https://www.courdecassation.fr/jurisprudence_2/assemblee_pleniere_22/619_3_32230.html.

[37] Recognition in Domestic Law of Parent-Child Relationship between a Child Born through a Gestational Surrogacy Arrangement Abroad and the Intended Mother, Advisory Opinion, Eur. Ct. H.R. (Apr. 10, 2019), https://hudoc.echr.coe.int/eng#{%22itemid%22:[%22003-6380464-8364383%22]} .

transnational processes through which norms migrate between domestic and international jurisdictions through multiple forms of influence that different authorities exert on each other.

Within the global context, a particularly controversial and heated debate, driven by 'the politics of recognition'[38], concerns the application or recognition of Sharia in family law cases.[39] As Ayelet Shachar argued, these are 'privatized diversity' claims according to which respect for cultural and religious identities requires the (secular) state to adopt a non-interventionist attitude towards family law questions, which should be left outside the public sphere.[40] These demands have triggered much controversy – in particular, those concerning the establishment or the legal recognition of faith based religious arbitration.[41] Seen as potentially in tension with the respect for gender equality,[42] these arbitrations were banned by the Canadian provinces of Quebec and Ontario.[43] In other states, like the UK, the controversial Sharia councils, which apply religious laws to family disputes, seem to exist today outside the official legal system. The law does not prohibit these alternative

---

[38] CHARLES TAYLOR, MULTICULTURALISM: EXAMINING THE 'POLITICS OF RECOGNITION' (1992); NANCY FRASER & AXEL HONNETH, REDISTRIBUTION OF RECOGNITION? A POLITICAL PHILOSOPHICAL-EXCHANGE (2003).

[39] HACKER, *supra* note 2, at 80–101; PASCALE FOURNIER, MUSLIM MARRIAGE IN WESTERN COURTS: LOST IN TRANSPLANTATION (2010) (showing how Western courts use different frameworks – legal pluralism, legal equality and substantive equality – to deal with the reception of *mahr* – formally a gift that the bride receives from the bridegroom in consideration of marriage and that becomes the property of the wife.); AYELET SHACHAR, MULTICULTURAL JURISDICTIONS: CULTURAL DIFFERENCES AND WOMEN'S RIGHTS (2001); Ivana Isailović, *Political Recognition and Transnational Law: Gender Equality and Cultural Diversification in French Courts, in* PRIVATE INTERNATIONAL LAW AND GLOBAL GOVERNANCE (D. Arroya & H. Muir Watt eds., 2014) (examining the reception of talaq in French courts in light of gender equality claims); Ayelet Shachar, *Privatizing Diversity: A Cautionary Tale from Religious Arbitration in Family Law* 9 THEORETICAL INQ. L. 573 (2008) (providing a conceptual framework for understanding and addressing religious arbitration, drawing on Canadian legal debates).

[40] Shachar, *supra* note 39, at 577.

[41] See on debates concerning religious tribunals: Machteld Zee, *Five Options for the Relationship Between the State and Sharia Councils: Untangling the Debate on Sharia Councils and Women's Rights in the United Kingdom,* 16 J. RELIG. & SOC'Y 1 (2014); Caryn Lyte Wolff, *Faith-Based Arbitrations: Friend or Foe? An Evaluation of Religious Arbitration Systems and Their Interaction with Secular Courts,* 75 FORDHAM L. REV. 427 (2006).

[42] HACKER, *supra* note 2 at 96-97. Shachar, *supra* note 39.

[43] The Family Law Amendment Act, 2006, S.O. 1991, ch. 1, para. 2.1; Civil Code of Quebec, S.Q. 1991, art. 2639. For debates concerning religious arbitration in Canada, *see* Shachar, *supra* note 37.

modes of dispute settlement but neither explicitly legally recognizes their jurisdiction.[44]

Another similarly controversial – although less high profile – case is the legal recognition by domestic courts of foreign family law norms that are influenced by Sharia.[45] A particularly interesting case study is provided by the transnational recognition of talaq divorces, according to which the husband has a unilateral right to end the marital union without the necessary interventions of courts.[46] In these cases, spouses are typically foreign or dual nationals domiciled in the state that is asked to recognize the foreign talaq. To take the example of France, in a series of cases decided in 2004 that settle the question of talaq recognition, the French Cour de cassation has refused to recognize foreign talaq divorces, arguing that they were contrary to the French public order to the extent that they were in conflict with the gender equality principle protected by the European Convention on Human Rights, which is applicable in France. Unlike in its previous decisions,[47] the court adopted a formal understanding of gender equality violation, no matter the context surrounding the application of foreign law. In line with the arguments of some feminist scholars reflecting on the tension between gender equality and multiculturalism,[48] gender equality was here understood as *formal equality of rights*, which necessarily trumps the respect for cultural or religious identity.[49]

This understanding of talaq as a violation of gender equality seems to gain traction transnationally. In a recent preliminary reference case before the Court of Justice of the European Union,[50] involving the recognition of talaq pronounced before religious authorities in Syria, the advocate general

---

[44] On legal debates surrounding the regulation of sharia councils, see Zee, *supra* note 41. A recent report recommended that sharia councils should not be prohibited, but that different pieces of legislation should be changed in order to decrease the recourse to these councils, see *The Independent Review into the Application of Sharia Law in England and Wales*, Feb. 2018, https://assets.publishing.service.gov.uk/government/uploads/system/uploads/attachment_data/file/678478/6.4152_HO_CPFG_Report_into_Sharia_Law_in_the_UK_WEB.pdf.

[45] For a comparative approach to the reception of *mahr*, see Fournier, *supra* note 39. For a comparative approach that analyses different state family laws based on sharia and the reception of talaq by different courts in Western Europe, see Pauline Kruiniger, Islamic Divorces in Europe: Bridging the Gap between European and Islamic Legal Orders (2015).

[46] For differences between national laws influenced by sharia, see Kruiniger, *supra* note 45.

[47] For a historical account of the recognition of talaq in France, see Roula El Husseini Begdache, Le droit international privé français et la répudiation islamique (2002).

[48] Susan Moller Okin, Is Multiculturalism Bad for Women? (1999).

[49] One of the proponent of this solution is Léna Gannagé, for whom talaq violates a fundamental right, Cass. 1e civ, July 12, 2001 (2001) Revue Critique de Droit International Privé 704, note L. Gannagé. See, for a critical appraisal of this position, Isailovic, *supra* note 39.

[50] Case C-372/16 Soha Sahyouni v. Raja Mamisch (Dec. 20, 2017).

Saugmandsgaard Øe, along with the EU Commission and several state governments, was of the opinion that a foreign law that does not grant the same procedural and substantive divorce rules to spouses should not be recognized by EU courts.[51] At this stage, however, more empirical legal research is needed to gain a comprehensive view of the conflicts, if adopted in the future, this solution could create between EU legal regime, states that adopt a more contextual approach to the issue of foreign talaq recognition[52] and different international, transnational advocacy actors[53] but also community-level actors involved in shaping transnational norms related to talaq.

As all of these examples show us, only a focus on multilayered interactions between domestic, international and transnational legal orders, related to different religious and epistemic communities, allows us to truly appreciate how family regulation and underlying values evolve and how norms and discourses migrate across jurisdictions. Transnational law also prompts us to reflect critically on the conflictual nature of different actors' legal demands analysing how they relate to the question of right allocation, subordination and power distribution. This is visible in the example of talaq, where different actors compete within different processes for defining what constitute law (can religious law be law on par with secular state law?), rights (does gender equality only entails a formal understanding of equality?) and identity (what is the scope of recognition in law of culturally hybrid identities?).

C THE GLOBAL POLITICS OF THE PUBLIC–PRIVATE DISTINCTION

I *The Public–Private Distinction in Transnational Law*

Related to the distinction in legal pluralism in transnational law scholarship between state and non-state norms is the debate surrounding the analytic and normative purchase of the private–public distinction.[54] Public law is closely associated with public interests, state power and unequal relations. By

---

[51] Case C-372/16 Soha Sahyouni v. Raja Mamisch, Opinion of Advocate General Saugmandsgaard Øe (Sept. 14, 2017).

[52] KRUINIGER, *supra* note 46.

[53] For instance, the transnational NGO Equality Now, which uses a combination of transnational legal advocacy and community mobilization to force governments to adopt laws that protect the rights of women and girls, has recently singled out *talaq* as being one of the main violations of gender equality in family law relations. Council on Foreign Relations, Women and the Law: Levelling the Economic Playing Field, New York, Dec. 12, 2018.

[54] Peer Zumbansen, *Transnational Law, in* ENCYCLOPEDIA OF COMPARATIVE LAW 738, 740–42 (Jan Smits ed., 2006).

contrast, private law is identified as regulating relations between private parties and as protecting 'private rights'. Unlike public legal relations, private legal relations are seen as autonomous from the state and are characterized by horizontality.[55]

Building on the extensive critical legal literature,[56] which exposed the illusory nature of this divide by showing that private law actually involves public interests and has distributional consequences that structure and perpetuate power relations,[57] some transnational law scholars argue that this classification performs a problematic, de-politizing function in the global regulatory space.[58] This distinction ends up promoting and legitimizing the legal unaccountability of private economic actors, who are 'isolated' from public law interventions and invested with major regulatory powers without bearing states' obligations, such as respect for human rights or labour law.[59] Thus, the distinction directly contributes to the persistence of an unequal distribution of power at the global level in favour of transnational private actors. Besides obfuscating true power differentials, transnational scholars argued that the private–public distinction is also descriptively flawed. It fails

---

[55] Ralf Michaels & Nils Jansen, *Law beyond the State? Europeanization, Globalization, Privatization*, 54 AM. J. COMP. LAW 843, 847–53 (2006) (noting that this classification may be far more prevalent in the European legal context than it is elsewhere and listing different concepts which define private law's specific rationality).

[56] Zumbansen, *Transnational Law as Socio-legal Theory, supra* note 8.

[57] *See* Robert Hale, *The Coercion and Distribution in a Supposedly Non Coercive State*, 38 POL. SCI. Q. 470 (1923). For critical legal scholars' interventions, see MORTON J. HORWITZ, THE TRANSFORMATION OF AMERICAN LAW 1870–1960: THE CRISIS OF LEGAL ORTHODOXY (1977); Duncan Kennedy, *The Stages of Decline of the Public/Private Distinction*, 130 U. PA. L. REV. 1349 (1982).

[58] A. CLAIRE CUTLER, PRIVATE POWER AND GLOBAL AUTHORITY (2003); A. Claire Cutler, *The Judicialization of Private Transnational Power and Authority*, 25 IND. J. GLOBAL LEGAL STUD. 61 (2018); Zumbansen, *Where the Wild Things Are, supra* note 8. For a critique of the public/private distinction in the context of private international law, Horatia Muir Watt, *Private International Law's Shadow Contribution to the Question of Informal Transnational Authority*, 25 IND. J. GLOBAL LEGAL STUD. 37 (2018); Horatia Muir Watt, *Private International Law beyond the Schism*, 2 TRANSNAT'L LEGAL THEORY 347 (2011); Robert Wai, *Transnational Liftoff and Juridical Touchdown*, 40 COLUM. J. TRANSNAT'L L. 29 (2002). See similar critiques on the international 'public' side of the disciplinary divide: JOHN LINARELLI, MARGOT E. SALOMON & M. SORNARAJAH, THE MISERY OF INTERNATIONAL LAW, CONFRONTATIONS WITH INJUSTICE IN THE GLOBAL ECONOMY (2018) (analysing how international trade law, international investment law, the regulation of global finance and human rights law perpetuate neo-liberalism and entrench social inequalities); Martti Koskenniemi, *Empire and the International: The Real Spanish Contribution*, 61 U. TORONTO L.J. 1 (2011) (showing how the universalization of private law concepts of property and contract were critical in the making of 'informal empire').

[59] *See* Backer, in this volume.

to account for recent legal evolutions, namely new types of actors and norms that cannot be mapped along the public–private categories. Some of these evolutions include the expansion of private actors' norm making, the growth of hybrid regulatory transnational regimes[60] and the proliferation of transnational private governance through contracts.[61]

II *The Private–Public Distinction in Family Law*

Family law scholars and legal feminists have pointed out similar descriptive and conceptual flaws of the private–public distinction. Although the field still tends to be described as 'private', this description has always been contested. For instance, historians have shown how family law is deeply involved in nation state building projects, making family law norms highly public matters, rather than private, individualized issues.[62] Similarly, recent comparative family law scholarship has focused on 'constitutionalization' processes examining how family laws are being profoundly shaped by constitutional notions of individual rights and equality.[63] Parallel evolutions are also at play in the international context. For instance, under the pressure of equality and non-discrimination human rights norms, domestic family laws across jurisdictions have evolved beyond heterosexual family law models.[64]

---

[60] *See, e.g.,* Fabrizzio Caffagio, *New Foundations of Transnational Private Regulation*, 38 J. L. & Soc'y 20 (2011).

[61] *See, e.g.,* THE POLITICS OF PRIVATE TRANSNATIONAL GOVERNANCE BY CONTRACT (A. Claire Cutler & Thomas Dietz eds., 2017); Jody Freeman, *The Contracting State*, 28 FLA. ST. U. L. REV. 155 (2000–2001).

[62] NANCY COTT, PUBLIC VOWS: A HISTORY OF MARRIAGE AND THE NATION (2000); Philomila Tsoukala, *Marrying Family Law to the Nation*, 58 AM. J. COMP. L. 873 (2010).

[63] MARY ANN GLENDON, THE TRANSFORMATION OF FAMILY LAW: STATE, LAW AND FAMILY IN THE UNITED STATES AND WESTERN EUROPE 88–89 (1989). For an analysis of U.S. law, *see* David D. Meyer, *The Constitutionalization of Family Law*, 42 FAM. L.Q. 529 (2008).

[64] In the European regional context: Orlandi & Others v. Italy, App Nos. 26431/12, 26742/12, 44057212, 60088/12, Eur. Ct. H.R. (Dec. 14, 2017); Oliari & Others v. Italy, App. Nos. 18766/11, 36030/11, Eur. Ct. H.R. (July 21, 2015) (finding that Italy has breached article 8 protecting the right to private and family life). *See also* Vallianatos & Others v. Greece, App. Nos. 29381/09, 32684/09, Eur. Ct. H.R. (Nov. 7, 2013) (concluding that the law that recognizes different sex unmarried couples is discriminatory on the basis of sexual orientation); Case C-267/06, Tadao Maruko v. Versorgungsanstalt der deutschen Bühnen (Apr. 1, 2008) (holding that same-sex partners should be treated like spouses with regard to survivor's pension scheme); C-147/08, Romer (May 10, 2011) (finding that there is discrimination on the ground of sexual orientation if a pensioner who has entered into a registered life partnership with a person of their own gender receives a supplementary retirement pension lower than that granted to a married, not permanently separated, pensioner, in cases in which registered partner is comparable to marriage). In the inter-American system of human rights, Atala Riffo & Daughters v. Chile, Inter-Am. Ct. H.R. (Feb. 24, 2012) (finding that the state violates its human rights obligations by

Feminist legal scholars have repeatedly argued that the public–private distinction creates, obscures and legitimizes women's subordination across different sectors.[65] By relegating family matters to the 'private' sphere of the home, seen as reserved for women, and by classifying family relations as 'private' matters, the law disadvantages women and perpetuates women's unequal position in society.[66] The entire legal structure, they argue – from contract, tort, to criminal, family and tax law – is geared towards legitimizing the ideology of male domination, leading the state to condone violence against women and depriving women of dignity, autonomy and equal citizenship.[67] These critiques have been relatively successful, inspiring a range of domestic and transnational policies concerning domestic violence.[68]

---

denying custody to a parent because of his or her sexual orientation); Advisory Opinion OC-24/17, Inter-Am. Ct. H.R. (ser. A) No. 24 (Nov. 24, 2017) (finding that states should legalize same-sex marriage in application of the right to equality).

[65] Frances Olsen, *Constitutional Law: The Feminist Critiques of Public/Private Distinction*, 10 CONST. COMMENT. 319 (1993) [hereinafter Olsen, *Constitutional Law: The Feminist Critiques of Public/Private Distinction*]; Frances E. Olsen, *The Family and the Market: A Study of the Ideology and Legal Reform*, 96 HARV. L. REV. 1497 (1983) [hereinafter Olsen, *The Family and the Market*].

[66] Olsen, *Constitutional Law: The Feminist Critiques of Public/Private Distinction, supra* note 65; NADINE TAUB & ELIZABETH M. SCHNEIDER, *Perspectives on Women's Subordination and the Role of Law, in* THE POLITICS OF LAW: A PROGRESSIVE CRITIQUE 151 (David Kairys ed., 2d ed. 1990).

[67] CATHARINE A. MACKINNON, TOWARD A FEMINIST THEORY OF THE STATE 193 (1989) ('[T]he legal concept of privacy can and has shielded the place of battery, marital rape, and women's exploited domestic labor. It has preserved the central institutions whereby women are deprived of identity, autonomy, control, and self-definition. It has protected a primary activity through which male supremacy is expressed and enforced.'); Sylvia A. Law, *Rethinking Sex and the Constitution*, 132 U. PA. L. REV. 955, 1020 (1984) ('The rhetoric of privacy . . . reinforces a public/private dicotomy [sic] that is at the heart of the structures that perpetuate the powerlessness of women.'). *See also* Suzanne A. Kim, *Reconstructing Family Privacy*, 57 HASTINGS L.J. 557 (2006) (examining the conflict between radical feminists that challenge privacy as a basis for asserting rights and liberal feminists' defence of privacy, and proposing how privacy could be reconstructed independently from its gendered origins). Reva B. Siegel, *'The Rule of Love': Wife Beating as Prerogative and Privacy*, 105 YALE. L.J. 2117 (1996).

[68] Melissa Murray, *Strange Bedfellows: Criminal Law, Family Law and the Construction of Intimate Life*, 94 IOWA L. REV. 1253, 1263 (2009) (noting that 'the reform project was remarkably successful' insofar that domestic violence is a crime throughout the United States, some states have adopted mandatory arrest policies that require police to arrest upon probable cause, and 'no-drop policies' according to which prosecution of domestic violence is required even if the victim does not cooperate). For the critiques of feminists' turn to the criminalization of the domestic sphere, see Aya Gruber, *The Feminist War on Crime*, 92 IOWA L. REV. 741 (2007). For transnational legal changes, *see* MERRY, *supra* note 2; Sally Engle Merry, *Constructing a Global Law – Violence against Women and the Human Rights System*, 28 LAW & SOC. INQUIRY 941 (2003).

Moreover, by treating the home as 'private' and different from the market, which is coded as 'public', the distinction has also occluded how domestic work, such as caregiving activities, usually performed by women, is treated as acts of 'love', and ends up being legally and economically unrecognized,[69] despite the obvious benefit to the state[70] and its being a condition for capitalism to thrive.[71] Feminist counterproposals have ranged from demanding wages for housework[72] to alimony reforms and to policies that would change the distribution of labour between partners at home.[73]

From the perspective of transnational law, as understood here, these critiques invite us to (re)consider the role that family law plays in the broader global social context and to assess the global politics of private family law.

III *The Global Politics of 'Private' Family Law*

Transnational law scholarship's invitation to bridge domestic and transnational legal debates, by connecting 'private' law (i.e. family law) questions with issues of legitimacy, alerts us to the global distributive effects of family law, legal discourses and practices surrounding family law. The critical approach requires a close examination of how transnational actors, institutions and processes are involved in the design and struggle over family law norms

---

[69] Olsen, *The Family and the Market, supra* note 65. In the global context, *see* Catherine Hoskyns & Shirin M. Rai, *Recasting the Global Political Economy: Counting Women's Unpaid Work*, 12 New Polit. Econ. 297 (2007).

[70] Martha A. Fineman, The Autonomy Myth: A Theory of Dependency (2004); Martha Fineman, *Cracking the Foundational Myths, Independence, Autonomy and Self-Sufficiency, in* Feminism Confronts Homo Economicus 180 (M. Fineman & T. Dougherty eds., 1991) ('Not only is the family perceived as occupying the private sphere. It is conceptualized as embodying values and norms very different from the institutions occupying the public sphere, particularly those of the market. Family relationships are cast as different in functioning and form than relationship existing in the public world. Families are altruistic institutions held together by affectional bonds. Of course, any serious consideration of the family reveals that it is a very public institution, assigned an essential public role within society.'). *See also* Katharine Silbaugh, *Turning Labour into Love: Housework and the Law*, 91 Nw. U. L. Rev. 1 (1996); Olsen, *The Family and the Market, supra* note 89.

[71] See the contributions of materialist feminism on how social reproduction is complementary to and necessary for capitalism to operate; *see, e.g.*, Materialist Feminism: Reader in Class, Difference and Women's Lives (Rosemary Hennessy & Chris Ingraham eds., Routledge 1997).

[72] Sylvia Federici, Revolution at Point Zero: Housework, Reproduction and Feminist Struggles (2012).

[73] *See Symposium on the Structure of Care*, 76 Chi.-Kent L. Rev., 1389 (2001).

and values and how these processes legitimize or challenge prevailing dynamics of inequality and domination.

From the emerging field of transnational feminist perspective, which bridges and integrates feminist theory, colonial and postcolonial studies and political economy,[74] it becomes possible to bring to the fore the interactions between gender, race and sexuality in the analysis of global contemporary family law evolutions. This interdisciplinary framework can help us revisit the contemporary heated legal and political debates surrounding key family law regulatory areas such as the regulation of transnational surrogacy, which, from a domestic phenomenon,[75] has become a truly global concern.[76]

---

[74] *See, e.g.*, Chandra Talpade Mohanty, Feminism without Borders: Decolonizing Theory, Practicing Solidarity (2003); Women's Activism and Globalization: Linking Local Struggles and Global Politics (Nancy A. Naples & Manisha Desai eds., 2002); Feminist Genealogies, Colonial Legacies, Democratic Futures (M. Jaqui Alexander & Chandra Talpade Mohanty eds., 1997), Maylei Blackwell, *Geographies of Difference: Transborder Organizing and Indigenous Women's Activism*, 42 Soc. Just. 137 (2016); Maylei Blackwell, Laura Briggs & Mignonette Chiu, *Transnational Feminisms Roundtable*, 36 Frontiers 1 (2015); *Gender, Justice and Neoliberal Transformations*, S&F Online (2013), http://sfonline.barnard.edu/gender-justice-and-neoliberal-transformations/ *Gender, Globalization and Social Change in the 21st Century*, 18 Int'l Soc. (Special Issue) (2003); *Globalization and Gender*, 26 Signs (Special Issue) (2001).

[75] See, for instance, in the US context, Darren Rosenblum et al., *Pregnant Men? A Conversation*, 22 Yale J. L. & Feminism 207 (2010); Elizabeth S. Scott, *Surrogacy and the Politics of Commodification*, 72 Law & Contemp. Probs. 109 (2009) (describing how in the US legal actors and feminist movements framed surrogacy over time and showing how feminists gradually lost interest in the issue of surrogacy, accepting a more pragmatic approach to its regulation).

[76] On the rise of transnational surrogacy agreements, *see* Hague Conference on Private International Law, A Study of Legal Parentage and the Issues Arising from International Surrogacy Arrangements (Mar. 2014), https://assets.hcch.net/docs/bb90cfd2-a66a-4fe4-a05b-55f33b009cfc.pdf. There is an extensive literature on the legal regulation of transnational surrogacy: International Surrogacy Arrangements: Legal Regulation at the International Level (Katarina Trimmings & Paul Beaumont eds., 2012); Sital Kalantry, *Regulating Markets for Gestational Care: Comparative Perspectives on Surrogacy in the United States and India*, 27 Cornell J. L. & Pub. Pol'y 685 (2018); Cyra Akila Choudhury, *The Political Economy and Legal Regulation of Transnational Commercial Surrogate Labor*, 48 Vand. J. Transnat'l L. 1 (2015); Yasmine Ergas, *Babies without Borders: Human Rights, Human Dignity and the Regulation of International Commercial Surrogacy*, 27 Emory Int'l L. Rev 117 (2013); Katarina Trimmings & Paul Beaumont, *International Surrogacy Arrangements: An Urgent Need for Legal Regulation at the International Level*, 7 J. Private Int'l L. 627 (2011); Barbara Stark, *Transnational Surrogacy and International Human Rights Law*, 18 ILSA J. Int'l & Comp. L. 369 (2012); Daniel Gruenbaum, *Foreign Surrogate Motherhood: Mater Semper Certa Erat*, 60 Am. J. Comp. L. 475 (2012); Ruby L. Lee, *New Trends in Global Outsourcing of Commercial Surrogacy: A Call for Regulation*, 20 Hastings Women's L.J. 275 (2009).

The transnational law perspective, as understood here, urges us to identify different norm-generating actors involved in the regulation of transnational surrogacy – from states and state courts to international organizations such as the Hague Conference on Private International Law and human rights courts,[77] to the plethora of industry actors as well as transnational human rights activists groups[78] – and assess how the multiplicity of conflicting norms-regulating surrogacy agreements play out in this multilayered context.[79] More importantly, the transnational critical perspective leads us to engage and revisit the 'scandal'[80] that over the recent years became associated with transnational surrogacy.

For many feminists and legal scholars, surrogacy is contrary to gender equality because it leads to the commodification of surrogate mothers and deprives them of their autonomy and harms their dignity.[81] This normative analysis is reflected in Daphna Hacker's recent critique of surrogacy in the context of Israeli parents' experiences that had recourse to Indian surrogates. According to Hacker, the contractual practices leave the surrogate mothers without bargaining power and amount to 'extreme legal objectification' in which surrogates are perceived as *outside the law* as humans and only *inside the law* as for-rent baby ovens'.[82] Another critique voiced by feminists is that

---

[77] Mennesson v. France, App. No. 65192/11, Eur. Ct. H.R. (June 26, 2014); Labassee v. France, App. No. 65941/11, Eur. Ct. H.R. (June 26, 2014); Paradiso & Campanelli v. Italy, App. No. 25358/12, Eur. Ct. H.R. (Jan. 27, 2017) (finding that Italian authorities' removal of the child born out of surrogacy did not violate intended parents' private and family life).

[78] *See, e.g.*, Cornell Int'l Human Rights: Policy, Advocacy Clinic, Nat'l Law Univ.-Delhi, Should Compensated Surrogacy Be Permitted or Prohibited? (2017), https://scholarship.law.cornell.edu/cgi/viewcontent.cgi?referer=&httpsredir=1&article=2685&context=facpub; Aparna Chandra, Mrinal Satish & Sital Kalantry, Memorandum on the Surrogacy (Regulation) Bill, 2016 (Apr. 13, 2017), https://cpb-us-e1.wpmucdn.com/blogs.cornell.edu/dist/2/7529/files/2017/08/CLPG-NLU-Delhi-Cornell-Memorandum-on-Surrogacy-Bill-2016-1s985d1.pdf.

[79] On the interplay between 'domestic' 'private' international family law and human rights law, see, e.g., Ivana Isailović, *The ECtHR and the Regulation of Transnational Surrogacy Agreements*, EIJL Talk! (July 25, 2014), https://www.ejiltalk.org/author/iisailovic/.

[80] Prabha Kotiswaran, *Do Feminists Need an Economic Sociology of Law?* 40 J. L. & Soc'y 115, 133 (2013).

[81] Hacker, *supra* note 2, at 138 (listing problematic contractual practices in India before the country closed itself to international surrogacy); Muriel Fabre Magnan, La gestation pour autrui: Fictions et réalité (2013); Susan Markens, Surrogate Motherhood and the Politics of Reproduction (2007); Margaret Jane Radin, Contested Commodities: The Trouble with Trade in Sex, Children, Body Parts, and Other Things (1996). This is also the position of some European states, like France, Germany and Switzerland; see Ergas, *supra* note 76, at 155–56.

[82] Hacker, *supra* note 2, at 138.

transnational surrogacy fuels a global market for cheap labour[83] and that it constitutes neocolonial forms of oppression of women of colour.[84]

But other feminist scholars have complicated this dominant subordination/objectification narrative. Prabha Kotiswaran, for instance, used her ethnographic work in India to point to the structural similarities between sex work, bar dancing and surrogacy and the ways in which women experience this kind of labour. She argues that the current feminist category of 'reproductive labour' is too narrow and should be extended to include these different forms of work performed outside traditional affective relational networks.[85] Similarly, Cyra Choudhury has analysed different domestic legal regimes and discourses influencing the regulation of transnational surrogacy and concludes that none of the traditional feminist normative framings (i.e. subordination/objectification) provides a compelling description of surrogates' everyday lives. Minimizing neither the problem of exploitation associated with surrogacy nor the stigma that surrogates bear, she convincingly argues that surrogate mothers are not women without agency and that surrogacy could be a rational and preferable economic choice in some contexts.[86] Instead of objectification/exploitation frame, she argues, the surrogate should be perceived as a *worker* performing hazardous work that should be regulated through more protective labour and contract law provisions.[87]

D TRANSFORMATIONS OF THE WELFARE STATE

Within this legally fragmented and plural context, transnational scholars have demonstrated the continuous transformations of states and their law.[88] The final part of this chapter looks at two conceptualizations of state change that are of interest here and how they can explain ongoing family law evolutions: the first one is the notion of 'transnational legal ordering', developed by Gregory Shaffer and Terence Halliday. The second one is the erosion of the welfare state in the context of pervasive neo-liberalism, characterized by privatization, fiscal austerity and the cultural triumph of economic rationality

---

[83] *See* Choudhury, *supra* note 76, at 22–24.

[84] *Id.* at 24–26 (describing different arguments according to which surrogacy constitutes the oppression of women of colour).

[85] Prabha Kotiswaran, *The Laws of Social Reproduction: A Lesson in Appropriation.* 64 N. IR. LEGAL Q. 317 (2013).

[86] *Id.* at 30.

[87] *Id.* at 58–60.

[88] *See, e.g.*, SASKIA SASSEN, LOSING CONTROL? SOVEREIGNTY IN AN AGE OF GLOBALIZATION (1996).

across different sectors of the society.[89] Here, my primary aim is to show how
transnational law scholars' critical findings can help us theorize some of the
contemporary evolutions in family law. I argue that the recent proliferation of
same-sex marriage across different jurisdictions is an excellent example of
'transnational legal ordering'. Similarly, by identifying how domestic legal
evolutions enable the expansion of neo-liberal policies and rationality,[90] the
transnational perspective invites us to better understand how domestic family
law has made possible neo-liberal transformations and, vice versa, how transnational neo-liberal policies have influenced family regulations.

I *Same-Sex Marriage Reforms as Transnational Legal Ordering*

Transnational legal ordering refers to the process of production, flow and
consolidation of transnational norms – namely, norms that originate in
treaties, private codes of conduct or standards – in a particular field through
the action of multiple actors, including governmental officials, business officials but also civil rights activists. This transnational constellation in turn
generates transnational legal orders, which can be more or less salient or
fragmented, depending on whether norms are clear and coherent and
whether or not they are supported by transnational practice. How does domestic change happen within the process of transnational legal ordering? For
Shaffer and Halliday, the answer can be found in the process of 'recursivity',
denoting 'a multidirectional, diachronic process of legal change'[91], where 'the
transnational and local are held in tension, the actors engaged in transnational
legal processes seek to influence local lawmaking and practice, and the
national legal norms, adaptations, and resistances provide models for and feed
back into transnational lawmaking'.[92]

How does this model allow us to evaluate changes in family law? A good
example of transnational ordering is the adoption of same-sex marriage
reforms across various jurisdictions. Domestic, comparative and human rights
legal scholars often adopt the convergionist narrative to account for this legal

---

[89] BROWN, *supra* note 12; HARVEY, *supra* note 12.
[90] Peer Zumbansen, *Law after the Welfare State, supra* note 15, at 768 ('The challenges of
      globalization to domestic state-originating welfare programs ... had a very domestic face ....
      Globalization ... further accentuated and fuelled a transformation of public governance that
      was already beginning to unfold from within the cores of western welfare states.')
[91] Gregory C. Shaffer, *Transnational Legal Process and State Change,* 37 LAW & SOC. INQUIRY
      229, 238 (2012).
[92] *Id.*

transformation,[93] emphasizing the 'incremental path' followed by different jurisdictions, the influence of human rights, and the role that cross-fertilization between domestic and international courts played in the process. In this narrative, same-sex marriage follows the decriminalization of homosexuality and the adoption of anti-discrimination laws and does so in a context in which different courts and legislators observe each other and then mobilize similar legal arguments. Among those is the promotion of equality and the prohibition of discrimination.[94] The work of David Paternotte on same-sex marriage reforms, which bears important similarities with Halliday's and Shaffer's transnational legal order model, however, complicates this narrative by providing a more granular description of transnational processes, institutions and actors who are involved in the construction of same-sex marriage as a transnational equality law norm.[95]

Paternotte describes the role of transnational advocacy networks in the adoption of same-sex marriage in very different jurisdictions and how these networks interact with states and international institutions.[96] Without minimizing the importance of legal and political processes on the domestic level, Paternotte argues that the usual domestic justifications – such as secularization, a relative decrease in homophobia or the influence of international norms on domestic law – cannot fully account for the recent rapid diffusion of same-sex marriage reforms. Instead, he argues, legal changes should be understood in light of what he calls 'global politics of same-sex marriage'.[97] This denotes the decisive role that transnational formal and informal networks of advocates and (mainly European) legal experts have played in forging the success of same-sex marriage claims in a growing number of jurisdictions around the world.

In this transnational context, legal experts played a crucial role by acting as legal advisers for various countries and by using their contacts with NGOs to frame same-sex marriage as a human rights issue, namely as a question of legal

---

[93] Ivana Isailović, *Same Sex but Not the Same: Same-Sex Marriage in the U.S. and France and the Universalist Narrative*, 66 AM. J. COMP. L. 267 (2018) (describing the convergionist legal narrative, and providing its conceptual and descriptive critique).

[94] For a recent example of this argument, see ANGIOLETTA SPERTI, CONSTITUTIONAL COURTS, GAY RIGHTS AND SEXUAL ORIENTATION EQUALITY (2017).

[95] DAVID PATERNOTTE, REVENDIQUER LE 'MARIAGE GAY': BELGIQUE, FRANCE, ESPAGNE (2011). David Paternotte, *Global Times, Global Debates? Same-Sex Marriage Worldwide*, 22 SOC. POL.: INT'L STUD. GENDER, ST. & SOC'Y 653 (2015) [hereinafter Paternotte, *Global Times, Global Debates?*].

[96] Paternotte, *Global Times, Global Debates?*, *supra* note 95.

[97] *Id.*

discrimination on the basis of sexual orientation.[98] According to Paternotte, it was the translation of claims supporting same-sex marriage into the legal language of equality and discrimination that explains the transnational proliferation of same-sex marriage reforms. Moreover, human rights claims connected same-sex marriage to democratic principles, making same-sex marriage the yardstick against which the modernity of a state is evaluated, which in turn put a normative (and economic) pressure on states.[99] Same-sex marriage is thus an example of 'transnational legal ordering', to the extent that its adoption at the domestic level is a consequence of a combination of transnational and local legal and political processes, involving the deployment of international, European and domestic legal norms challenging domestic practices and definitions of gender and sexuality.

II Neo-liberalism and Family Law

Another focus of transnational law scholarship is the relationship between the *welfare state* and *law*, or the relationship between law and political economy. Since the 1980s, neo-liberal precepts have become the unquestioned 'background ideas' that guide political action and provide frames through which people see or make sense of their social environment.[100] Peer Zumbansen provides one illustration of how transnational law engages with the law's role in the continuous transformations of welfare states. He argues that the triumph of economic rationality has been considerably driven by legal changes inside welfare states.[101] Tracing the evolutions of different legal theories from the nineteenth century onwards, Zumbansen shows how formalism and functionalism, which were initially in tension, ended up justifying the turn from public to private regulation, limiting state interventions and legitimizing the depoliticization of law, which came to be perceived as a neutral tool in the hands of experts.[102] Thus, he argues, today's revival of legal formalism limits law's intervention in order to allow for social self-governance, while

---

[98] *Id.* at 659 (noting that 'historically European, this network is increasingly active at the global level'). For a critique of law's emancipatory role in the global context, see, e.g., Ivana Isailović, *Beyond Marriage, in* OXFORD RESEARCH ENCYCLOPEDIA, LGBT POLITICS AND POLICY (forthcoming 2019).

[99] Paternotte, *Global Times, Global Debates?, supra* note 95, at 667–68.

[100] Vivien A Schmidt, *The Roots of Neo-liberal Resilience: Explaining Continuity and Change in Background Ideas in Europe's Political Economy,* 18 BRIT. J. POL. & INT'L REL. 318, 320 (2016).

[101] Peer Zumbansen, *Law after the Welfare State, supra* note 15.

[102] *Id.* at 796.

legal neo-functionalism is associated with market needs, detached from polit-ical conflicts that used to define law's goal.[103]

Family laws and policies seem to be an excellent vantage point from which to observe the global legal transformations and erosion of welfare states, given that – as political economists and historians have demonstrated – family laws and norms are central to the functioning of welfare states.[104] For political economists, understanding the provision of welfare necessitates studying sim-ultaneously the role family, the labour market and the welfare state play in the distribution of resources.[105] The analysis of the 'family wage', at the heart of the industrial era welfare states, according to which economic resources – welfare and wage – are allocated primarily to male-headed, nuclear, hetero-sexual families, in which the husband is the main breadwinner while women's domestic work remains unpaid, helps understand the interplay between family law, gender, race and political economy. The demise of welfare states also implies an economic and gendered model for the family. In her fascinating study of the economic and family values changes in the United States, political scientist Melinda Cooper recently showed how the neo-liberal assault on the welfare state is closely associated with the promotion of conservative family values in law and the notion that family – the nuclear married family – should be economically self-sufficient.[106] Similarly, examining how the global economy operates requires understanding the role of households in subsidiz-ing capital accumulation through unpaid work.[107]

For the most part, however, family law scholars still typically understand family law as being distinct from 'the market'.[108] This complicates the critical study of how neo-liberalism, as an economic theory and cultural worldview, interacts with family law doctrines, rules and practices. In contrast, recent interventions in family law[109] and transnational feminist

---

[103] *Id.*

[104] Susan Pedersen, Family, Dependence, and the Origins of the Welfare State in the UK and France 1914–1945 (1993); Gøsta Esping-Andersen, The Three Worlds of Welfare Capitalism (1990); Immanuel Wallerstein & Joan Smith, *Households as an Institution of the World-Economy, in* Creating and Transforming Households: The Constraints of the World Economy 3 (Immanuel Wallerstein & Joan Smith eds., 1992).

[105] Esping-Andersen, *supra* note 104.

[106] Melinda Cooper, Family Values: Between Neoliberalism and New Social Conservatism (2017).

[107] Wallerstein & Smith, *supra* note 104.

[108] Halley & Rittich, *supra* note 4.

[109] *See, e.g.,* June Carbone & Naomi R. Cahn, Marriage Markets: How Inequality Is Remaking the American Family (2014); Philomila Tsoukala, *Household Regulation and European Integration: The Family Portrait of a Crisis,* 63 Am. J. Comp. L. 747, 754, (2015); Anne L. Alstott, *Neoliberalism in U.S. Family Law: Negative Liberty and Laissez Faire Markets*

scholarship[110] indicate ways in which to start drawing connections between
family law, transnational advocacy and processes of norm creation, migration
and implementation, suggesting a more comprehensive agenda of resistance
against neo-liberal policies. For instance, the above-mentioned discussions
about the transnational regulation of surrogacy needs to be considered in light
of a broader analysis of how law structures the global market for reproductive
services and how law can address inequalities that inhere in the global
surrogacy market.[111]

Other examples illustrate how domestic family law evolutions enable global
neo-liberal reforms and are subordinated to neo-liberal tenets. For Alison
Alstott, neo-liberalism in the United States permeates family law by focusing
on negative liberties rather than on positive rights.[112] To illustrate her claim,
she contrasts major constitutional law cases in family law that protect individual rights from state intrusion, on the one hand, and courts' rejection of
positive rights that would allow individuals to obtain resources needed to
conduct family life, on the other.

Another way of critically assessing the role of family law in enabling a neo-
liberal agenda is to analyse the way in which transnational economic organizations influence family regulation.[113] One such example is Philomila
Tsoukala's work on Greek households regulation in the context of the Greek
sovereign debt crisis in 2008–9.[114] One of Tsoukala's main arguments of
interest here is that EU austerity measures – namely, the conditions attached
to the loans received by Greece – affected the regulation of the family by

---

in the Minimal State, 77 Law & Contemp. Probs. 25 (2014); Kerry Rittich, *Black Sites:
Locating the Family and Family Law in Development*, 58 Am. J. Comp. L. 1023 (2010); Chantal
Thomas, *Migrant Domestic Workers in Egypt: A Case Study of the Economic Family in Global
Context*, 58 Am. J. Comp. L. 987 (2010); Hila Shamir, *The State of Care: Rethinking the
Distributive Effects of Familial Care Policies in Liberal Welfare States*, 58 Am. J. Comp. L. 953
(2010).

[110] *Gender, Justice and Neoliberal Transformations, supra* note 74; Manisha Desai, *Transnational
Solidarity, Women's Agency, Structural Adjustments and Globalization, in* Women's Activism
and Globalization: Linking Local Struggles and Global Politics (Nancy A. Naples &
Manisha Desai eds., 2004) (examining the gendered effects of structural adjustment programs
and transnational mobilization challenging neo-liberal policies).

[111] *See supra* C.II.

[112] Alstott, *supra* note 109.

[113] *See, e.g.*, Rittich, *supra* note 109, at 1026 (arguing that 'the family itself is increasingly an object
of direct policy intervention and legal reform'). See also, for an example of how the European
Union work-life balance measures promote and legitimize the neo-liberal turn underway in the
EU, Ivana Isailović, *Neoliberalism, the EU and the Question of 'Work-Life Balance'*, Legal
Form (Nov. 4, 2018), https://legalform.blog/2018/11/04/neoliberalism-the-european-union-and-
the-question-of-work-life-balance/

[114] Tsoukala, *supra* note 109.

dramatically weakening the role of families as precarious safety nets within Greek society, without replacing previous safety measures with alternative welfare mechanisms.

One such measure imposed by the EU concerns annual property taxes, aimed at increasing labour mobility. As Tsoukala argues, given the high rate of home ownership in Greece, this measure, paired with a new policy adopted by the Greek government facilitating expropriations, had the effect of notably decreasing the household's capacity of accommodating its members' needs. In a context in which austerity measures have become central to EU economic governance and are imposed through the economic policies coordination mechanism throughout the eurozone,[115] similar measures concerning housing policies migrate across EU member states. Their aim is to increase the labour mobility and incentivize individuals to move around in order to take up jobs. But as Tsoukala shows, the same economic policies risk having different effects in light of the various role families play in the organization of the welfare. They risk crippling households' ability to provide basic welfare in states in which the provision of welfare relies essentially on the household, like in Greece. In other cases, these measures target the provision of welfare by the state and can have the effect of putting pressure on low-to-middle-income households that cannot rely on the provision of welfare by the state, as was the case, for instance, in the Netherlands.[116]

The transnational perspective, as understood here, directly builds on this kind of interdisciplinary scholarship. It does so in two ways: on the one hand, we are invited to analyse the multiplicity of local, national, regional and transnational actors, norms and processes that are involved in the evolutions of family law norms towards a neo-liberal model, and identify the plurality of modes of resistance and struggles surrounding neo-liberal family law, on the other.

E CONCLUSION

In this chapter, I have argued that although conversations about transnational law have for a long time omitted questions concerning family law, there seems to be a reciprocal learning opportunity where the two fields meet. The here-offered examples provide compelling evidence for the argument that family law could and, indeed, should inform transnational legal theory, and vice

---

[115] Philomial Tsoukala, *Eurozone Crisis Management and the New Social Europe*, 20 COLUM. J. EUR. L. 31 (2013).
[116] Tsoukala, *supra* note 109 at 792–93.

versa. The variations of transnational law, with a focus on new but also 'old'
actors, norms and processes of transnational legal ordering with an interest in
the continued role of the state in the production, the dissemination and the
'settling' of transnational legal normativity, along with the continuously
expanding body of scholarship in critical theory, could prove instrumental
in the study of family law against the backdrop of border-crossing policies and
emerging regulatory assemblages. Given the importance of the family in most
individuals' lives and the intricate connections between family law and
broader economic, cultural and political transformations, a thus-conceived
transnational family law might offer crucial insights into the future study of
law and society in a global, plural and increasingly unequal world.

PART III

Transnational Law

The Field's Normative Stakes

13

Locating Private Transnational Authority in the Global Political Economy

A. CLAIRE CUTLER

A INTRODUCTION

The growing literature on transnational law and politics takes as a reference point the emergence and deepening of a transnational authoritative politico-juridical space. This space is represented variously by liberal-inspired analyses of a 'transnational public arena',[1] 'transnational policy regimes',[2] 'transnational policy space'[3] and the 'global public'.[4] For some, increasing legal pluralism and the transnationalization of law are welcome by-products of the functional differentiation of the global political economy[5] and reflect the progressive emergence of a global rule of law.[6] At issue is an 'inquiry into the conditions of global or transnational governance'[7] and a scrutiny of the differentiated orders that constitute transnational legal ordering.[8] The emergence of transnational actors in the regulation of trade, investment, finance, food and agriculture, the

---

[1] John Ruggie, *Reconstituting the Global Public Domain: Issues, Actors and Practices*, 10 EUR. J. INT'L REL. 499–531 (2004) [hereinafter Ruggie, *Reconstitutiong the Global Public Domain*].

[2] Edgar Grande, *Cosmopolitan Political Science*, 57 BRIT. J. SOC'Y 87, 89 (2006).

[3] William Coleman, *Globality and Transnational Policy-Making in Agriculture: Complexity, Contradiction, and Conflict, in* COMPLEX SOVEREIGNTY: RECONSTITUTING POLITICAL AUTHORITY IN THE TWENTY-FIRST CENTURY (Edgar Grande & Louis Pauly eds., 2005), 93–119.

[4] Gerard Delanty, *The Cosmopolitan Imagination: Critical Cosmopolitanism and Social Theory*, 57 BRIT. J. SOC'Y 25–47 (2006).

[5] *See* Peer Zumbansen, *Transnational Legal Pluralism*, 1 TRANSNAT'L LEGAL THEORY 141–89 (2010); and Johsua Karton, *Contractual Governance and Sectoral Fragmentation of Transnational Contract Law, in* THE POLITICS OF PRIVATE TRANSNATIONAL GOVERNANCE BY CONTRACT (A. Claire Cutler & Thomas Dietz eds., 2017).

[6] Paul Schiff Berman, *Global Legal Pluralism*, 80 S. CAL. L. REV. 1155–237 (2007).

[7] GRALF-PETER CALLIESS & PEER ZUMBANSEN, ROUGH CONSENSUS AND RUNNING CODE 5 (2010).

[8] TRANSNATIONAL LEGAL ORDERS (Terrence Halliday & Gregory Shaffer eds., 2015).

environment, human rights and international security are regarded as ushering in a new era of global governance.[9]

Embedded in each referent is the belief that we are in the midst of transformations associated with globalization and resulting in changes in political authority. The effects include altering relations between public and private actors, domestic and international politics, as well as national and transnational political economies, societies and legal systems. For some, these transformations mark the dawning of exciting opportunities for human emancipation[10] and even for the 're-invention of political science'.[11] However, others are more sceptical, identifying a related and disturbing increase in the power and authority of private actors, institutions and laws that strengthen corporate power, governmentality and the hegemony of global capitalism.[12] They question the existence of a 'transnational public space', suggesting that the ontology of 'the transnational' is heavily contested. This inquiry seeks to problematize the notions of transnational political authority by treating it as a hypothetical construct that requires analytical, theoretical and normative interrogation. Following the insight of the Italian political thinker Antonio Gramsci[13], history is regarded as a social process of 'becoming which ... does not start from unity, but contains in itself the reason for a possible unity'. Central to understanding this potential unity or solidarity, its history is conceived of as the philosophy of praxis.[14] The philosophy of praxis, also known as

---

[9]   See THE POLITICS OF PRIVATE TRANSNATIONAL GOVERNANCE BY CONTRACT (A. Claire Cutler & Thomas Dietz eds., 2017); and TRANSNATIONAL ACTORS IN GLOBAL GOVERNANCE: PATTERNS, EXPLANATIONS AND IMPLICATIONS (Christer Jönsson & Jonas Tallberg eds., 2010).

[10] See DAVID HELD, DEMOCRACY AND THE GLOBAL ORDER: FROM THE MODERN STATE TO COSMOPOLITAN GOVERNANCE (1995); and DAVID HELD, GLOBAL COVENANT: THE SOCIAL DEMOCRATIC ALTERNATIVE TO THE WASHINGTON CONSENSUS (2004).

[11] Grande, supra note 2, at 88.

[12] See SUSAN STRANGE, THE RETREAT OF THE STATE: THE DIFFUSION OF POWER IN THE WORLD ECONOMY (1996); Roland Robertson, Open Societies, Closed Minds? Exploring the Ubiquity of Suspicion and Voyeurism, 4 GLOBALIZATIONS 399–416 (2007); Hans-Martin Jaeger, 'Global Governance' and the Depoliticization of Global Governance, 1 INT'L POL. SOC. 257–77 (2007); Ulrich Brand, Order and Regulation: Global Governance as a Hegemonic Discourse of International Politics?, 12 REV. INT'L POL. ECON. 155–76 (2005); and William Robinson, Gramsci and Globalization: From Nation-State to Transnational Hegemony, 8 CRITICAL REV. INT'L SOC. & POL. PHIL. 559–74 (2005).

[13] ANTONIO GRAMSCI, SELECTIONS FROM THE PRISON NOTEBOOKS OF ANTONIO GRAMSCI 356 (Quintin Hoare & Geoffrey Nowell Smith eds. & trans., 1971).

[14] The philosophy of praxis, as formulated by Gramsci, 'expresses' his 'epistemology' and 'represents Gramsci's most original and lasting contribution to Marxists theoretical self-understanding'. (See Wolfgang Fritz Haug, Rethinking Gramsci's Philosophy of Praxis from One Century to the Next, 26 BOUNDARY 101, 115 (1999)). Haug notes that 'Immanentism', as in a philosophy of immanent critique, posits a potentially active, or immanent historical role for

historical materialism, contemplates the world historically and dialectically, as comprised by multiple contradictory social forces.[15]

The idea here is that transnational governance might best be approached as incipient or immanent in contemporary political economy and society while recognizing that there is no teleological certainty of its maturation into a unified transnational state and civil society. Nor would such a state necessarily be desirable from a normative perspective. This is particularly pertinent in light of what is generally regarded to be an expansion and deepening of

---

philosophy. (*See id.* at 106). According to Gramsci (*id.* at 436), 'the philosophy of praxis is precisely the concrete historicisation of philosophy and its identification with history'. This marked both a critique of prevalent liberal and idealist currents of thought and 'a critical return to and re-beginning from' certain foundational Marxist texts. (*See* Adam Morton, *The Firmly Comic Riddle of Hegemony in IPE: Where Is Class Struggle,* 26 POL. 118, 146 (2006)). In particular, it engaged Karl Marx's criticism of certain philosophical trends of the day, including the philosophical materialism of the young Hegelian Ludwig Feuerbach, who, Marx argued, had neglected the historical significance of human agency. It is believed that Gramsci had not read Marx's *Theses on Feuerbach,* which famously conclude that 'Philosophers have only *interpreted* the world in various ways; the point is to *change* it.' (*See* Karl Marx, *Theses on Feuerbach, in* THE PORTABLE KARL MARX (Eugene Kamensky ed., Penguin Books, 1983), 155, 158). However, Gramsci was influenced by Marx's critique of political economy 'that set out to overcome the essential separation of philosophy, economics, and politics' (*see* Morton, *supra,* at 54). Gramsci's formulation of the philosophy of praxis transcended both philosophical idealism and vulgar materialism in its focus on the historical significance of human actions and practices (*see* Morton, *supra,* at 53–54, and Adam Morton, *Historicizing Gramsci: Situating Ideas in and beyond Their Context,* 10 REV. INT'L POL. ECON. 118, 131 (2003).

[15] Historical materialism is a philosophy of praxis as well as a method of critical analysis. It conceptualizes world order as a historical bloc comprised of material, ideological and institutional forces that embody both traces of the past and seeds of the future. As a form of critical theory, it seeks to reveal the power relations that secure oppression and inequality in the world by de-reifying the apparent natural and neutral appearances of contemporary capitalism and thereby identifying openings for transformation to a better world. *See* A. Claire Cutler, *New Constitutionalism and the Commodity Form of Global Capitalism, in* NEW CONSTITUTIONALISM AND WORLD ORDER 45–63 (Stephen Gill & A. Claire Cutler eds., 2014) [hereinafter Cutler, *New Constitutionalism and the Commodity Form of Global Capitalism*]; A. Claire Cutler, *Toward a Radical Political Economy Critique of Transnational Economic Law, in* INTERNATIONAL LAW ON THE LEFT: REVISING MARXIST LEGACIES 199–219 (Susan Marks eds., 2008) [hereinafter Cutler, *Toward a Radical Political Economy Critique of Transnational Economic Law*]; and A. Claire Cutler, *Gramsci, Law, and the Culture of Global Capitalism,* 8 CRITICAL REV. INT'L SOC. & POL. PHIL. 527–42 (2005) [hereinafter Cutler, *Gramsci, Law, and the Culture of Global Capitalism*]. For adaptations of Gramsci's conceptions of historical bloc, social forces and hegemony to the analysis of the conditions of world order, see NEW CONSTITUTIONALISM AND WORLD ORDER, *supra;* ROBERT COX & TIMOTHY SINCLAIR, APPROACHES TO WORLD ORDER (1996); and STEPHEN GILL, POWER AND RESISTANCE IN THE NEW WORLD ORDER (2008).

non-state and corporate or *private* actors in the constitution of transnational authority and consequent concerns about their legitimacy as governors.[16]

This chapter examines private transnational authority beginning with ontological considerations and Jessup's famous definition of transnational law provided in the Storrs Lectures. Attention then turns to the disciplines of international law and international relations for insights into the nature and operation of transnational authority. The chapter argues that the dominant actor-centric conception of transnational authority obscures its significance as a domain of power, competition and contestation between states and a variety of private and public actors and institutions in the global political economy. These conflicts are shifting the balances between private and public power in the world and determining winners and losers with profound distributional consequences. The chapter argues that while Jessup was prescient in broadening his conceptualization of transnational law to embrace a plurality of actors and institutions, he missed the potentially threatening rise and significance of *private transnational authority* in structuring world affairs. The need for developing a critical political economy approach that grasps the darker side of private power and authority is advanced. The chapter accordingly analyses transnational authority as a mechanism of a 'new constitutionalism' that subordinates local societies and political economies to the discipline of private transnational capital accumulation.[17] The new constitutionalism is enhancing the power and authority of private actors, laws and institutions and forming new sites of authority that are constitutive of a *private transnational legal order*. However, the dominance of private transnational authority is argued to be incomplete. This is because two vectors of power, which are identified as constituting the dialectical foundations for

[16] *See* A. Claire Cutler, *Private Transnational Governance and the Crisis of Global Leadership, in* GLOBAL CRISES AND THE CRISIS OF GLOBAL LEADERSHIP 56–70 (Stephen Gill ed., 2012) [hereinafter Cutler, *Private Transnational Governance and the Crisis of Global Leadership*]; PRIVATE AUTHORITY AND INTERNATIONAL AFFAIRS (A. Claire Cutler, Virginia Haufler & Tony Porter eds., 1999); THE EMERGENCE OF PRIVATE AUTHORITY IN GLOBAL GOVERNANCE (Rodney Hall & Thomas Biersteker eds., 2002); KARSTEN RONIT & VOLKER SCHNEIDER, PRIVATE ORGANIZATIONS IN GLOBAL POLITICS (2000); NON-STATE ACTORS AND AUTHORITY IN THE GLOBAL SYSTEM (Richard Higgott, Geoffrey Underhill & Andreas Bieler eds., 2000); TRANSNATIONAL PRIVATE GOVERNANCE AND ITS LIMITS (J.C. Graz & A. Nölke eds., 2008); THE TRANSNATIONAL POLITICS OF CORPORATE GOVERNANCE REGULATION (Hank Overbeek, Bastiaan Van Apeldoorn & Andreas Nölke eds., 2007); and Bastiaan Van Apeldoorn & Laura Horn, *The Transformation of Corporate Governance Regulation in the EU: From Harmonization to Marketization, in* THE TRANSNATIONAL POLITICS OF CORPORATE GOVERNANCE REGULATION 77–97 (Hank Overbeek, Bastiaan Van Apeldoorn & Andreas Nölke eds., 2007).
[17] NEW CONSTITUTIONALISM AND WORLD ORDER, *supra* note 15.

private transnational authority, provide critical openings for its development as a progressive social and political force.

B THE ONTOLOGY OF 'PRIVATE TRANSNATIONAL GOVERNANCE'

Ontology is the study of reality and being and in this context means analysing and theorizing the existence of private transnational governance. This involves defining 'the transnational' and locating it as a domain of social and purposive activity, as well as identifying the *private* nature of the processes and participants that are authoritative in *governance*.[18] A significant criticism of extant scholarship on private transnational governance is that it is characterized by conceptual uncertainty and clear limitations on all three elements of the concept: 'transnational', 'private' and 'governance'.[19] While serious normative limitations and challenges also exist, these concerns will be addressed more fully later.

We will now turn to defining and locating the transnational as the prelude to addressing private transnational governance. Defining and locating 'the transnational' is more problematic than it might at first appear to be. This matter will be approached first from the perspective of international law and thereafter from that of international relations.

I *International Law and 'the Transnational'*

In the field of international law, we begin with Philip Jessup's now classic definition of *transnational law* as 'all law which regulates actions or events that transcend national frontiers. Both public and private international law are included, as are other rules which do not wholly fit into such standard categories.'[20] He further notes that '[t]ransnational situations, then, may involve individuals, corporations, states, organizations of states, or other groups'[21] and he points to private citizens, oil companies, international governmental organizations, such as the United Nations, and international non-governmental organizations, such as the International Chamber of

---

[18] *See* Horatia Muir Watt, *The Relevance of Private International Law to Global Governance, in* PRIVATE INTERNATIONAL LAW AND GLOBAL GOVERNANCE (Horatia Muir Watt & Diego F. Fernández eds., 2014), for the need for an epistemological and ontological interrogation of global governance dimensions of the discipline of private international law.

[19] *See, e.g.,* the contributions to TRANSNATIONAL PRIVATE GOVERNANCE AND ITS LIMITS, *supra* note 16.

[20] PHILLIP C. JESSUP, TRANSNATIONAL LAW 2 (1956).

[21] *Id.* at 3.

Commerce, as entities capable of engaging in transnational activities. Jessup
thus contemplated considerable pluralism as to the actors or agents engaged in
transnational legal regulation. Importantly, Jessup appears to hold that the
traditional orientation of legal scholarship as law between states is little more
than an unfounded fiction, and his examples help to demonstrate this point by
showing how transnational law actually operates across the traditional focus on
states. On this particular point, Jessup writes:

> The more wedded we become to a particular classification or definition, the
> more our thinking tends to become frozen and thus to have a rigidity which
> hampers progress toward the ever needed new solutions of problems whether
> old or new. Conflicts and laws are made by man. So are the theories which
> pronounce, for example, that international law cannot confer rights or
> impose duties directly on an individual because, says Theory, the individual
> is not a subject but an object of international law.[22]

Now, contrast this view with that of *Akehurst's Modern Introduction to
International Law*:

> International law ... primarily governs the relationships between states,
> whereas in the nineteenth century private international law was thought of
> as regulating transborder relationships between individuals, in the sense of
> the old 'law merchant' (or *lex mercatoria*), the usages among traders. ...
> Although some authors have advocated the idea of 'transnational law' com-
> prising both systems [public and private international law], in reality, there is
> no such thing. No legal order exists above the various national legal systems
> to deal with transborder interactions between individuals (as distinct from
> states). The problem is, therefore which of the various domestic laws should
> apply.[23]

This latter view, articulating the postulate that international law can only
derive from and operate among states, is possibly the most enduring 'truth'
of modern international law. It is bound up with a mythical story of origins
that dates the beginning of modernity back to the year 1648. The Peace of
Westphalia is generally regarded as establishing the system of sovereign states
as the fundamental constitutional principle of world order and forming the

---

[22] *Id.* at 7.
[23] AKEHURST'S MODERN INTRODUCTION TO INTERNATIONAL LAW 72 (Peter Malanczuk ed., 7th
   ed. 1997). This volume was substantially edited and revised by Peter Malanczuk, and it is
   difficult to determine whether this view is that of Akehurst or of the editor. The fifth edition
   (1984), written by Akehurst, does not contain reference to the term 'transnational law'. There
   was one further edition (1987) written by Akehurst that this author is attempting to locate. What
   is interesting is the seventh edition's categorical rejection of 'the transnational'.

analytical foundations of international law.[24] It also embodies an understanding of law as something that is inherently national in that it is conceptualized as located *within* and emanating *from* the state.[25] Thus, international law locates the state as the locus of political activity through the legal positivist doctrine governing international legal personality (only states are 'subjects' of international law) and the identification of the sources of international law with state consent (explicit consent in international treaties or implied consent in customary international law).[26] The authority and legitimacy of public international law (like national law) flow from the exercise of external (or internal) sovereignty, while private international law is reduced to municipal law regulating transactions that possess a trans-border element.[27] As a consequence, transnational law disappears as an analytical or theoretical possibility because it qualifies as neither international nor national law. The parochialism of this view is eclipsed only by its historical inaccuracy and by forgetting the legal agency or subjectivity exercised by the great trading corporations in the conduct of commerce and war, the treaties entered into by European imperial powers with indigenous peoples in the Americas and the operation for over a millennium of capital's own private, non-state system of law, *lex mercatoria*: the law merchant.[28]

---

[24] While it is common for scholars to recognize the diversity of participants in the international legal sphere, the analytical and theoretical foundations of international law remain stubbornly state-centric. *See* A. Claire Cutler, *Critical Reflections on Westphalian Assumptions of International Law and Organization: A Crisis of Legitimacy*, 27 REV. INT'L STUD. 133–50 (2001); and WILLIAM TWINNING, GLOBALIZATION AND LEGAL THEORY (2000). For debate over the historical significance of the Peace of Westphalia, see Cutler, *supra*.

[25] GIANFRANCO POGGI, THE DEVELOPMENT OF THE MODERN STATE: A SOCIOLOGICAL INTRODUCTION (1978).

[26] *See* Rosalyn Higgins, *Conceptual Thinking about the Individual in International Law*, in INTERNATIONAL LAW: A CONTEMPORARY PERSPECTIVE 476–93 (Richard Falk, Franz Kratochwil & Saul Mendolvitz eds., 1985); M.W. Janis, *Individuals as Subjects of International Law*, 17 CORNELL INT'L L.J. 61–78 (1984); and David Kennedy, *The Sources of International Law*, 2 AM. U. J. INT'L L. & POL'Y 1–96 (1987).

[27] Private international law is also known as conflict of laws and provides rules that determine what national law applies to transactions involving persons or corporations from different states when there is uncertainty as to the national law that should govern due to conflicting jurisdictional options arising from the international or transnational character of the transaction. *See* A. CLAIRE CUTLER, PRIVATE POWER AND GLOBAL AUTHORITY: TRANSNATIONAL MERCHANT LAW IN THE GLOBAL POLITICAL ECONOMY 39 (2003).

[28] *See id.*; Janet McLean, *The Transnational Corporation in History: Some Lessons for Today*, 79 IND. L.J. 363–77 (2003); Antony Anghie, *Finding the Peripheries: Sovereignty and Colonialism in Nineteenth Century International Law*, 40 HARV. INT'L L.J. 1–80 (1999); S. JAMES ANAYA, INDIGENOUS PEOPLES IN INTERNATIONAL LAW (1996).

However, more important than historical inaccuracy are the obstacles that
this apparently necessary association of law and state pose to understanding the
nature, significance and historical effectivity of transnational law today.
Indeed, Jessup articulated a conception of transnational law that anticipated
legal developments now associated with globalization, which 'break the
frames' of the historical unity of law and state.[29] Jessup identified changes in
practice that we today associate with a paradigmatic shift in the legal relations
between states and supra-state, sub-state and non-state actors involved in
transboundary social relations and economic transactions. In areas as diverse
as the peaceful settlement of disputes, the use of force, international criminal
law, the law of treaties, the recognition of states and governments, the protection of foreign investment, international legal subjectivity and the legal
regulation of the global commons, Jessup identified developments that pushed
beyond traditional conceptions of *international* law, giving rise to a conception he identified as *transnational law*. In *Modern Law of Nations*, Jessup
anticipated these developments in discussing the hypothesis that a modern-
ized international law should apply directly to individuals:

> In using the term 'individual' in connection with the hypothesis here under
> discussion, it should be understood that various types of groups or associations of
> individuals are included. International law, particularly in claims cases, is accus-
> tomed to dealing with corporations as 'citizens' or 'nationals' of states in the same
> way in which it deals with natural persons. . . . Accordingly, under the hypothesis,
> corporations or partnerships may also be subjects of international law.[30]

Indeed, individual actors have found a place in transnational law. But what
Jessup missed is the power differential between entities like transnational
corporations, weaker states and individual citizens and the distributional consequences of such asymmetries in power. While the transnational as a contested
domain seems to escape his analysis as regards a deeper scrutiny of the power
dynamics that characterize the emerging constellations, his recognition of non-
state actors can nevertheless be seen as an analytical contribution to the
recording of empirical developments in legal practice. Today, practicing transnational corporate lawyers would probably not stop for a moment to query

---

[29] *See* Gunther Teubner, *Breaking Frames: Economic Globalization and the Emergence of Lex
Mercatoria*, 5 EUR. J. SOC. THEORY 199–217 (2002); and A. Claire Cutler, *Legal Pluralism as the
'Common Sense' of Transnational Capitalism*, 3 OÑATI SOCIO-LEGAL SERIES 719–40 (2013)
[hereinafter Cutler, *Legal Pluralism*].

[30] PHILIP C. JESSUP, A MODERN LAW OF NATIONS 19–20 (1948) [hereinafter JESSUP, A MODERN
LAW OF NATIONS]. *See also* Philip C. Jessup, *The Subjects of a Modern Law of Nations*, 45
MICH. L. REV. 383–408 (1947).

whether or not transnational contract law is *really* law.[31] Indeed, the growing empirical 'reality' of transnational law is evident in efforts to analyse and theorize empirical developments in the law that are associated with the globalization of law, the transnationalization of the legal field,[32] entrepreneurial lawyering,[33] lawmaking by transnational law firms,[34] private business associations and business corporations,[35] disaggregated sovereignty[36] and the contractual regulation of global production through transnational value chains.[37] In fact, private lawmaking processes have transformed the fields of both public and private international law, blurring the distinction between the two[38] and creating tensions between national and transnational orders.

---

[31] For a discussion of the law of contractual agreements, see JESSUP, A MODERN LAW OF NATIONS, *supra* note 30, ch. 2.

[32] *See* D. Trubek, Yves Dezalay, Ruth Buchanan & John R. Davis, *Global Restructuring and the Law: Studies in the Internationalisation of the Legal Fields and Transnational Arenas*, 44 CASE W. L. REV. 407–97 (1994) [hereinafter Trubek, Dezalay, Buchanan & Davis, *Global Restructuring*]; THE TRANSNATIONAL LAW OF INTERNATIONAL COMMERCIAL TRANSACTIONS (Norbert Horn & Clive Schmitthoff eds., 1982); TRANSNATIONAL LEGAL ORDERS, *supra* note 8; and Peer Zumbansen, *Preface* (in this volume).

[33] *See* YVES DEZALAY & BRYANT GARTH, DEALING IN VIRTUE: INTERNATIONAL COMMERCIAL ARBITRATION AND THE CONSTRUCTION OF A TRANSNATIONAL LEGAL ORDER (1996) [hereinafter Dezalay and Garth, *Dealing in Virtue*]; and THE POLITICS OF PRIVATE TRANSNATIONAL GOVERNANCE BY CONTRACT, *supra* note 9.

[34] *See* A. Claire Cutler, *Transnational Law and Privatized Governance, in* GLOBAL ORDERING: INSTITUTIONS AND AUTONOMY IN A CHANGING WORLD 144–65 (Louis Pauly & William Coleman eds., 2008).

[35] *See* TRANSNATIONAL COMMUNITIES. SHAPING GLOBAL ECONOMIC GOVERNANCE (Marie-Laure Djelic & Sigrid Quack eds., 2010); Sigrid Quack, *Legal Professions and Transnational Lawmaking: A Case of Distributed Agency*, 14 ORG. 643–66 (2004) [hereinafter Quack, *Legal Professions*]; Glenn Morgan, *Transnational Actors, Transnational Institutions, Transnational Spaces: The Role of the Law Firms in the Internationalization of Competition Regulation, in* TRANSNATIONAL GOVERNANCE: INSTITUTIONAL DYNAMICS OF REGULATION 139–60 (Kerstin Sahlin & Marie-Laure Djelic eds., 2006); A. Claire Cutler, *Transnational Law and Privatized Governance, in* INSTITUTIONS, GOVERNANCE, AND GLOBAL ORDERING 144–65 (Louis Pauly & William Coleman eds., 2008) [hereinafter Cutler, *Transnational Law and Privatized Governance*]; Julian Arato, *Corporations as Lawmakers*, 56 HARV. INT'L L.J. 229–95 (2015) [hereinafter Arato, *Corporations as Lawmakers*]; and Peter Muchlinski, *Corporations and the Uses of Law: International Investment Arbitration as a 'Multilateral Legal Order'*, 1 OÑATI SOCIO-LEGAL SERIES (2011).

[36] Anne-Marie Slaughter, *Disaggregated Sovereignty: Towards the Public Accountability of Global Governance Networks*, 39 GOVERNMENT AND OPPOSITION 159–90 (2004).

[37] *See* Larry Catá Backer, *Regulating Multinational Corporations: Trends, Challenges and Opportunities*, 22 BROWN J. WORLD AFF. 153–73 (2015); and A. Claire Cutler, *Private Transnational Governance in Global Value Chains: Contract as a Neglected Dimension, in* THE POLITICS OF PRIVATE TRANSNATIONAL GOVERNANCE BY CONTRACT (A. Claire Cutler & Thomas Dietz eds., 2017).

[38] *See* Ralph G. Steinhardt, *The Privatization of Public International Law*, 25 GEO. WASH. J. INT'L L. & ECON. 523–53 (1991); John A. Spanogle, *The Arrival of Private Law*, 25 GEO. WASH. J. INT'L L. & ECON. 477–522 (1991); and CUTLER, *supra* note 27.

Conceptions of 'transnational liftoff and juridical touchdown'[39] have been proposed to capture the way in which transnationalized law is creating supra-territorial relations among people by delocalizing and denationalizing the law,[40] removing its creation, interpretation and application from the con-straints of territorial locations, while simultaneously re-localizing and renationalizing social relations when enforcing the laws.[41] David Schneider-man[42] and Gus Van Harten[43] analyse the investor-state regime that implicates states in transnational governance by subordinating them to the demands of securing and expanding global investment.[44] Similarly, the emerging global intellectual property regime, which is centred on the 1994 Agreement on Trade-Related Aspects on Intellectual Property Rights (TRIPS), was initiated by powerful private pharmaceutical, entertainment and software companies and is administered by the World Trade Organization. The TRIPS Agreement 'reaches deep into the domestic regulatory environment of states',[45] subjecting local economic activities to transnational legal disciplines.[46]

---

[39] Robert Wai, *Transnational Liftoff and Juridical Touchdown: The Regulatory Function of Private International Law in an Era of Globalization*, 12 COLUM. J. TRANSNAT'L L. 209, 209 (2001).

[40] BOAVENTURA DE SOUSA SANTOS, TOWARD A NEW LEGAL COMMON SENSE: LAW, GLOBALIZATION, AND EMANCIPATION (2d ed. 2002).

[41] *See* Harold Koh, *Transnational Public Law Litigation*, 100 YALE L.J. 8347–401 (1991); Harold Koh, *Why Transnational Law Matters*, 24 PENN ST. INT'L L. REV. 745–53 (2006); and A. Claire Cutler, *Transnational Business Civilization, Corporations, and the Privatization of Global Governance*, in GLOBAL CORPORATE POWER 199–226 (Christopher May ed., 2006) [hereinafter Cutler, *Transnational Business Civilization*].

[42] David Schneiderman, *How to Govern Differently: Neo-liberalism, New Constitutionalism and International Investment Law*, in NEW CONSTITUTIONALISM AND WORLD ORDER *supra* note 15, at 159–78.

[43] Gus Van Harten, *Private Authority and Transnational Governance: The Contours of the International System of Investment Protection*, 12 REV. INT'L POL. ECON 600–23 (2005).

[44] For an analysis of the investor-state regime as a modality of transnational capitalism, see A. Claire Cutler, *Transformations in Statehood, the Investor-State Regime and the New Constitutionalism*, 23 IND. J. GLOBAL LEGAL STUD. 96–126 (2016) [hereinafter Cutler, *Transformations in Statehood, the Investor-State Regime and the New Constitutionalism*]; and A. Claire Cutler, *The Judicialization of Private Transnational Power and Authority*, 25 IND. J. GLOBAL LEGAL STUD. 61–95 (2018) [hereinafter Cutler, *The Judicialization of Private Transnational Power and Authority*].

[45] SUSAN SELL, PRIVATE POWER, PUBLIC LAW: THE GLOBALIZATION OF INTELLECTUAL PROPERTY LAW 1 (2003).

[46] Across the world, large corporations, such as Monsanto, have been heavily marketing genetically modified plant varieties that are specially engineered to be resistant to the corporation's own herbicides. Farmers are thus compelled into a reliance on the company's pesticides as well. TRIPs grants Monsanto exclusive rights over any of its engineered varieties – making the altered variety a product of the corporation. Farmers are thus not only forced to buy the herbicides but must pay Monsanto royalties each time seeds are planted, even if they have not been purchased. Monsanto has gained a reputation by suing farmers whose farms contain

These developments challenge traditional analytical distinctions and definitions and remind us of Jessup's commitment to practical reason and his
invocation of Benjamin Cardozo's injunction that the '[l]aw and obedience
to law are facts confirmed every day to us all in our experiences of life. If the
result of a definition is to make them to be illusions, so much the worse for the
definition: we must enlarge it till it is broad enough to answer to realities.'[47]
Law must thus follow and adapt to changes in how we regulate life, suggesting
its evolution as a potential progressive, functional force.

Common to all of these approaches is the insight that transnational law
does not eclipse states and national laws but rather reconfigures the laws
governing the way states and peoples do business, immediately affecting
people's daily lives and practices. The transnational is thus not 'located'
outside but is implicated within the national, linking local and global political
economies and societies in complex ways.[48] In this vein, Dezalay and Garth
located an 'increasingly global private justice system' at the 'transnational
level', which they argued 'is best understood as a virtual space that provides
strategic opportunities for competitive struggles engaged in by *national*
actors'.[49] Trubek et al.[50] similarly emphasized that it is national legal fields
that are being reconfigured through the development of a transnational legal
field, which they conceptualize as 'the embedded practices of lawyers, judges,
and academics' who constitute the legal field and 'whose logics are being
transformed directly, and indirectly, by transnational interactions'.[51] As Quack
has noted more recently, transnational lawmaking refers to 'legal regulatory
activities that span across national borders without essentially having a global
dimension' and includes 'a variety of different types of actors and different
forms of law-making that transcend the scope of nation states without being
reducible to interstate law. The term thus encompasses not only private
international law-making, but also international and supranational law forms

---

genetically modified plants growing as weeds. In a much celebrated legal case, Monsanto
successfully sued a Canadian farmer in Canadian courts for infringement of its patent (deriving
from Canadian patent legislation bringing the TRIPS Agreement into effect) on genetically
modified canola seed, which was found to have contaminated his fields (Monsanto Can. Inc.
v. Schmeiser, [2004] 1 S.C.R. 902 (Can.)).
[47] PHILIP C. JESSUP, TRANSNATIONAL LAW 7 (1956), *quoting* BENJAMIN CARDOZO, THE NATURE
OF JUDICIAL PROCESS 127 (1920).
[48] CUTLER, PRIVATE POWER, *supra* note 27.
[49] DEZALAY & GARTH, DEALING IN VIRTUE, *supra* note 33, at 3.
[50] Trubek, Dezalay, Buchanan & Davis, *Global Restructuring, supra* note 32, at 411.
[51] *See* Anne-Marie Slaughter & William Burke-White, *The Future of International Law Is
Domestic (or, The European Way of Life,* 47 HARV. INT'L L.J. 327–52 (2006)).

that develop a life as legal institutions beyond interstate treaties from which they arose.'[52]

Those working within a legal pluralist framework have usefully challenged the state-centricity and methodological nationalism evident in traditional approaches to public and private international law. In this vein, Peer Zumbansen views transnational law 'primarily as a methodological approach' that seeks to capture the 'transformation of legal institutions in the context of an evolving complex society':[53]

> Focusing on the coexistence and competition between hard and soft, official and unofficial, public and private norms... transnational legal pluralism suggests studying law from a methodological angle in the context of evolving theories of social ordering, rather than as a contained discipline. Central to this undertaking is a shift in perspective, which leads to a focus on *actors*, *norms*, and *processes* as building blocks of the methodology of transnational law.[54]

Halliday and Shaffer similarly adopt an actor- and process-based approach and define 'transnational legal ordering' as 'a collection of formalized legal norms and associated organizations and actors that authoritatively order the understanding and practice of law across national jurisdictions' in which nation-states remain central'.[55] Their approach is informed by insights from 'new legal realism' that engages transnational law through a pragmatic, functional, problem-solving approach, reminiscent of Jessup's approach.[56]

Transnational law thus takes many forms: public international law, as in treaties and customary international law; lawmaking by a mixture of governmental and non-governmental actors, as in many environmental conventions; and private transnational lawmaking, as in international and transnational business law and the law governing international commercial arbitration.[57] It arises from a number of sources and a multiplicity of governance

---

[52] Quack, *Legal Professions*, *supra* note 35, at 644.

[53] Peer Zumbansen, *Defining the Space of Transnational Law: Legal Theory, Global Governance and Legal Pluralism*, 21 TRANSNAT'L L. & SOC. PROBS. 305, 308 (2012).

[54] *Id. See also* PEER ZUMBANSEN, *Manifestations and Arguments: The Everyday Operation of Transnational Legal Pluralism*, in OXFORD HANDBOOK OF GLOBAL LEGAL PLURALISM (Paul Schiff Berman ed., forthcoming 2019).

[55] TRANSNATIONAL LEGAL ORDERS, *supra* note 8, at 5.

[56] Gregory Shaffer, *The New Legal Realist Approach to International Law*, 28 LEIDEN J. INT'L L. 189–210 (2015).

[57] *See* Edward S. Cohen, *Private Arbitration as a Mechanism for the Construction of Contractual Norms in Private-Public Relationships: The Case of Investor-State Arbitration*, in THE POLITICS OF PRIVATE TRANSNATIONAL GOVERNANCE BY CONTRACT (A. Claire Cutler & Thomas eds., 2017) [hereinafter Cohen, *Private Arbitration*]; and Cutler, *Transformations in Statehood, the*

arrangements, including governance both with and without government.[58] However, what is missed in this optic is the deeper structuring influence of the political economy driving private actors and corporate power. The transnational is a domain of power and contestation that determines 'who gets what' in the global political economy.[59] It is therefore necessary to develop a better understanding of the social forces that are driving and benefiting from *private* transnational lawmaking. While the literature recognizes the practical activity of lawyers and legal institutions, such as transnational law firms, arbitration institutions and other private legal associations, who work the law creating and transmitting new legal forms and practices through their transnational networks[60] what is required is a critical understanding of the winners and losers in private transnational governance.

Although Jessup's recognition of transnational law contained a normative dimension in that it was inspired by a belief in the capacity for international law and institutions to contribute to a better world by developing and expanding international cooperation in the achievement of community norms, he did not consider law in distributional terms. While serving as a judge on the International Court of Justice, which he did from 1961 until 1970, Jessup ruled in a famous case that all states possess legal obligations to the international community as a whole.[61] This principle may appear unproblematic in its simplicity; however, it is easy to miss its potential subversiveness for positivist legal theory. In effect, it goes beyond stating that states under

Investor-State Regime and the New Constitutionalism, supra note 44. See also the chapters by Shahla Ali and Florian Grisel in this volume.

[58] See Cutler, *Transnational Law and Privatized Governance, supra* note 35.

[59] See Edward S. Cohen & A. Claire Cutler, *Law, Contestation and Power in the Global Political Economy: An Introduction,* 3 Oñati Socio-legal Series 611–21 (2013).

[60] See Jonathan V. Beaverstock, *Transnational Elite Communities in Global Cities: Connectivities, Flows and Networks,* 63:Z GaWC Res. Bull. (2001); Michael J. Powell, *Professional Innovation: Corporate Lawyers and Private Lawmaking,* 18 Law & Soc. Inquiry 423–52 (1993); Rules and Networks: The Legal Culture of Global Business Transactions (Richard P. Appelbaum, William L. Felstiner, & Gessner Volkmar eds., 2001); Diane Stone, *The Policy Roles of Private Research Institutions in Global Politics, in* Private Organizations in Global Politics (Karsten Ronit & Volker Schneider eds., 2000), 187–207; Alex Stone Sweet, *The New Lex Mercatoria and Transnational Governance,* 13 J. Eur. Pub. Pol'y 627–46 (2006); and Edward S. Cohen, *The Harmonization of Private Commercial Law: The Case of Secured Finance, in* Law and Legalization in Transnational Relations 58–80 (Christian Brütsch & Dirk Lehmkuhl eds., 2007).

[61] Barcelona Traction, Light & Power Co. Ltd., (Belg. v. Spain), Judgment, 1970 I.C.J. Rep. 3, ¶¶ 33–45 (Feb. 5), articulating the principle that states have obligations to the international community as a whole (*erga omnes*) that today is relied upon to root international humanitarian, human rights, environmental, and labour laws, as well as the emerging 'responsibility to protect'.

international law owe duties to each other, to provide that they also owe duties
to the international community. *The Modern Law of Nations* began to sketch
out the contours of the sorts of obligations that states might owe to the
international community.[62] He hypothesized that a contemporary law of
nations would go beyond recognizing and enforcing obligations between
states and individuals to include more general obligations to the international
community. His hypothesis that there is a 'community interest' reflects a
marriage of analytical and normative concerns that challenges the foundations
of analytical jurisprudence and the concern of separating the 'is' and the
'ought'. This is because Jessup was contemplating the infusion of international
anarchy and the decentralized, self-help system of sovereign states with an
aspiration to community, unity and solidarity. This move challenged the
formalistic and legal positivist association of international law with the state,
for it imputed greater purposes for international law than the summation of
the interests and purposes of states. Indeed, it contemplated public purposes
that extend, transnationally, beyond the boundaries of state sovereignty, anticipating current conceptions of a *transnational public space* mentioned at the
outset.[63] However, Jessup did not appear to question the vexing problem of
establishing the legitimacy of transnational public purposes in a world that
lacks a universal referent. Nor did he anticipate the even more acute problem
of the legitimacy of private lawmaking and governance, as hard binding law
gives way increasingly to soft, voluntary corporate social responsibilities. His
hypothetical challenges of state-centricity did not extend to critical political
economy, nor arguably could they emerge from his functional and pragmatic
analysis of transnational law and practice.

II *International Relations and 'the Transnational'*

Changing the register now away from international law to international
relations, how have international relations scholars fared in defining and
locating *the transnational*?[64] A brief review of significant analytical efforts in

---

[62] See PHILIP JESSUP, *The Subjects of a Modern Law of Nations, in* A MODERN LAW OF NATIONS,
supra note 30, at 15–42.

[63] For an interesting examination of the universalist teleology of international law, see Martti
Koskenniemi, *Law, Teleology and International Relations: An Essay in Counterdisciplinarity*,
26 INT'L REL. 3–34 (2011).

[64] See Bastiaan Van Apeldoorn, *Theorizing the Transnational: A Historical Materialist Approach*,
4 J. INT'L REL. & DEV. 142–76 (2004) [hereinafter *Theorizing the Transnational*] for an
excellent and comprehensive review of the development of transnational studies in
international relations.

international relations reveals a deep division between agentic and structural approaches to the subject, which reflect significant theoretical differences. The former reflects the dominant neorealist and liberal approaches to international relations and international political economy, while the latter reflects critical or radical understandings.[65] This division results in uncertainty over how the transnational is to be located vis-à-vis the state and, as will become evident, also implicates conceptualizations of *private transnational governance*.

In political science, concern with transnationalism may be traced back to pioneering studies of European integration and the formation of supranational security communities that were considered to significantly challenge the autonomy of states[66] but is typically marked in the field of international relations with the appearance of Keohane and Nye's *Transnational Relations and World Politics*.[67] In this work, the transnational is conceptualized as a plurality of actors and organizations on the world stage, next and often opposed to states. As Van Apeldoorn notes, the 'notion of transnational actors as rival to states and their interests, engaged in a "confrontation" that states may or may not win . . . [misses] how transnational actors by definition operate simultaneously *inside* different "national states" rather than "confronting" those states from the outside'.[68] By contrast, Keohane and Nye framed the transnational as an 'outside' or external challenge to the authority and political agency of the state. This reflects a focus on the agency of states shorn of historically constituting social structures; the state is both naturalized and reified as the locus of political significance facing external challenges to its authority.[69]

---

[65] *Id.*

[66] *See* ERNEST HAAS, THE UNITING OF EUROPE: POLITICAL, SOCIAL, AND ECONOMIC FORCES (1958); and KARL DEUTSCH et al., POLITICAL COMMUNITY AND THE NORTH ATLANTIC AREA: INTERNATIONAL ORGANIZATION IN LIGHT OF HISTORICAL EXPERIENCE 1957).

[67] TRANSNATIONAL RELATIONS AND WORLD POLITICS (Robert Keohane & Joseph Nye eds., 1971). *See also* TRANSNATIONAL ACTORS IN GLOBAL GOVERNANCE: PATTERNS, EXPLANATIONS AND IMPLICATIONS, *supra* note 9.

[68] Van Apeldoorn, *Theorizing the Transnational, supra* note 64, at 146.

[69] There is a voluminous literature that is critical of this agentic, state-centric focus of neorealism, the dominant theoretical approach in the field of international relations and in the subfield of international political economy. However, the most stinging indictment continues to be that of Richard K. Ashley, *The Poverty of Nationalism, in* NEOREALISM AND ITS CRITICS 225–300 (Robert H. Keohane ed., 1986). The focus on non-state actors developed along with liberal theories of international institutions and international regimes, at first mounting a clear challenge for neorealism. However, this challenge was short-lived, as liberal theories grew closer to neorealism by adopting a similar state-centric ontology. Both tend to focus on states as the main actors of international relations and international political economy and assess their

To the extent that the focus on transnational actors challenged the state-
centricity of dominant neorealist[70] approaches to the study of international
relations, this approach marked a potential innovation in international relations theory, for it opened the door to analysing the political significance of a
variety of non-state actors. This, though, was not to be, for the revival of Cold
War tensions resulted in the absorption of the transnational challenge by
dominant neorealist theorizations in the 1980s and 1990s and its reformulation
as a state-centric variant of neo-liberalism.[71] The return to state-centric conceptualizations reinforced the accuracy of one reviewer that 'many ghosts will
have to be laid before Professor Jessup's ideas on [transnational law] ... are
likely to secure general acceptance'.[72] Indeed, the focus on the state as the
locus of political agency worked to marginalize the activities of non-state
actors and the sphere of private corporate activity, which were theorized to
be apolitical domains of economic activity and thus not worthy of political
analysis.[73]

However, a focus on transnational corporations, which began in the 1970s,
persisted.[74] The growing subfield of international political economy, inspired

significance and influence according to their material capabilities. More recently,
constructivist theories have sought to account for the significance of non-material and
ideational influences on state behaviour and to explore the social constitution of the state, but
they remain within the dominant ontology. (See Ondej Císa, *The Transnationalisation of
Political Conflict: Beyond Rationalism and Constructivism*, 6 J. INT'L REL. & DEV. 6–22
(2003).) In contrast, critical theories, such as historical materialism, focus on the social origins
of state power and the embeddedness of states in structures that are in turn conditioned by
capitalist social relations. See Mark Rupert, *Alienation, Capitalism and the Inter-state System*,
in GRAMSCI, HISTORICAL MATERIALISM AND INTERNATIONAL RELATIONS (Stephen Gill ed.,
1993), 67–93.

[70] Kenneth Waltz is the seminal work on neorealism, which takes insights about the centrality of
state power to the conduct of world politics and international relations developed by classical
scholars of international relations, such as Hans Morgenthau and E. H. Carr, and attempts to
create a scientific theory of world politics that derives from the operation of the structure of the
international states system. As the theory implies, the focus is upon states as the primary
analytical agents of the international system. Non-state, private actors are regarded as super-
structural and epiphenomenal and, thus, not analytically or theoretically of political
significance as agents. (See KENNETH WALTZ, THEORY OF INTERNATIONAL POLITICS (1979)).

[71] Miles Kahler, *Inventing International Relations: International Relations Theory after 1945*, in
NEW THINKING IN INTERNATIONAL RELATIONS THEORY 20–53 (M.W. Doyle & G.J. Ikenberry
eds., 1997).

[72] Frederick Honig, Book Review, 34 INT'L AFF. 78, 79 (1958) (reviewing PHILIP C. JESSUP,
TRANSNATIONAL LAW (1956)).

[73] CUTLER, PRIVATE POWER, *supra* note 27, at 54–59.

[74] TRANSNATIONAL CORPORATIONS AND WORLD ORDER: READINGS IN INTERNATIONAL POLITICAL
ECONOMY (G. Modelski ed., 1979).

by the pioneering work of the late Susan Strange[75] regarding the political significance of transnational business corporations and markets, developed a deeper understanding of the political salience of transnational corporate actors, institutions and processes. But, as Van Apeldoorn noted[76], it was only really in the mid-1990s that theorizations of transnational relations reappeared in mainstream (neorealist and neo-liberal) international relations, with the publication of Risse-Kappen's *Bringing Transnational Relations Back In*.[77] There, 'transnational relations' are defined as '*regular interactions across national boundaries when at least one actor is a non-state agent or does not operate on behalf of a national government or an intergovernmental organization*' (original italics). A central thesis of that volume is that the domestic structures of states determine the impact of transnational actors and institutions upon the state. Notwithstanding the apparent concern with transnational *relations*, the focus remained more on transnational *actors*. Subjects of study include the European economic and monetary union, US and Japanese corporate practices, multinational corporations in East Asia, security policy in the USSR and Russia, social movements in Eastern Europe as well as transnational environmental coalitions. Again, the transnational is conceptualized through an actor-centred approach,[78] located 'outside' and acting *upon* and in competition *with* the state. This approach has been brought forward in other studies of multilevel governance,[79] transnational corporations,[80] transnational advocacy networks[81] and transnational social movements.[82]

Despite the focus of some studies on the governance roles of corporations and private business associations, the focus of the burgeoning literature on transnational relations has until recently been overwhelmingly on the non-profit sector.[83] The publication of Cutler, Haufler and Porter's *Private*

---

[75] See STRANGE, *supra* note 12; Susan Strange, *The Study of Transnational Relations*, 52 INT'L AFF. 333–45 (1976); Susan Strange, *Big Business and the State*, 20 MILLENNIUM: J. INT'L STUD. 245–50 (1991); and JOHN STOPFORD & SUSAN STRANGE, RIVAL STATES, RIVAL FIRMS: COMPETITION FOR WORLD MARKET SHARES (1991).

[76] Van Apeldoorn, *Theorizing the Transnational*, *supra* note 64, at 148.

[77] BRINGING TRANSNATIONAL RELATIONS BACK IN: NON-STATE ACTORS, DOMESTIC STRUCTURES AND INTERNATIONAL INSTITUTIONS 3 (Thomas Risse-Kappen ed., 1995).

[78] Van Apeldoorn, *supra* note 64, at 148.

[79] GOVERNANCE WITHOUT GOVERNMENT (James N. Rosenau & Ernst-Otto Czempiel eds., 1992).

[80] See ROBERT REICH, THE WORK OF NATIONS (1991); and Ruggie, *supra* note 1.

[81] MARGARET KECK & KATHRYN SIKKINK, ACTIVISTS BEYOND BORDERS: TRANSNATIONAL ADVOCACY NETWORKS IN INTERNATIONAL POLITICS (1998).

[82] See SIDNEY TARROW, THE NEW TRANSNATIONAL ACTIVISM (2005); and CONTESTING GLOBAL GOVERNANCE: MULTILATERAL ECONOMIC INSTITUTIONS AND GLOBAL SOCIAL MOVEMENTS (Robert O'Brien, A.M. Goetz, J. Aart & M. Williams eds., 2000).

[83] Thomas Risse, *Transnational Actors and World Politics*, *in* HANDBOOK OF INTERNATIONAL RELATIONS 426–53 (Walter Carlsnaes, Thomas Risse & Beth Simmons eds., 2002).

Authority and International Affairs marked an attempt to develop an analysis of the significance of business corporations and their private associations in the governance of the global political economy, in part to address the neglect in international relations of studying corporations as transnational participants in global governance.[84] The study began by asking, Do corporations 'rule the world?' and concluded that they 'increasingly do establish institutions that "govern" in the absence of or in coordination with governance arrangements involving states at the international level'.[85] The volume developed a typology of private authority, which includes informal industry norms and practices, coordination service firms, production alliances and subcontractor relationships, cartels, business associations and private international regimes, a typology that has been further developed in subsequent studies and more recent volumes.[86] The research findings in these volumes reveal the interconnectedness of state practice and inter-firm institutions and indicate that private authority does not mean the disappearance of the state.[87]

Recent scholarship on governance picks up and develops many of these themes and is particularly insightful in raising analytical concerns that require further examination. Conceptual imprecision in framing the analytical foundations of private international authority have been identified, and many analysts have reframed the problematic as one of *transnational* rather than of *international* concern. Indeed, for many, the inadequacy of notions of private *international* authority prompted the adoption of the increasingly common term 'private *transnational* authority'.[88] Nölke and Perry have observed that a 'popular analytical concept always runs the risk of becoming more and more diluted by frequent and imprecise use, until it finally may lose most of its content'.[89] They emphasized the analytical need to recognize that 'transnational private authority does not exist independently of the state, or

[84] PRIVATE AUTHORITY AND INTERNATIONAL AFFAIRS, *supra* note 16, at 5–7.
[85] *Id.* at 3, 370.
[86] *See* A. Claire Cutler, *Private International Regimes and Interfirm Cooperation, in* THE EMERGENCE OF PRIVATE AUTHORITY IN GLOBAL GOVERNANCE, *supra* note 16, at 23–40.
[87] Hall and Biersteker's volume, *Emergence of Private Authority in Global Governance*, extends the focus on private authority in global governance beyond the world of firms and political economy to encompass transnational social movements and other non-state actors, including *inter alia*, religious movements, transnationally organized crime, and the privatization of security. (*See* THE EMERGENCE OF PRIVATE AUTHORITY IN GLOBAL GOVERNANCE 23–40, *supra* note 16.)
[88] *See* Cutler, *Toward a Radical Political Economy Critique of Transnational Economic Law, supra* note 15, at 199–219.
[89] Andreas Nölke & James Perry, *Coordination Service Firms and the Erosion of Rhenish Capitalism, in* THE TRANSNATIONAL POLITICS OF CORPORATE GOVERNANCE REGULATION 111, 123 (Henk Overbeek, Bastiaan van Apeldoorn & Andreas Nölke eds., 2007).

even against it. Instead, private authority should be understood as having a mutually constitutive relation to state authority.'[90] As Saskia Sassen observed, globalization is not producing a territorially defined physical space somewhere outside, above or beyond the state, but is constituted very much within the 'national' and with the participation of local social forces possessed by global and transnational orientations.[91] As I have argued elsewhere, private transnational authority operates in many domains to reorient national societies and political economies to the demands of foreign investors, international trade, securities, banking and investment interests and the legal culture of transnational economic institutions, lawyers and arbitrators.[92] Indeed, critical political economy scholars have been criticizing dominant functional and actor-centric analysis for obscuring 'the transnational' as a domain of power and contestation where social forces compete over the nature and operation of private transnational governance as a modality of transnational capitalism.

C CRITICAL THEORY AND A PRAXIS CONCEPTION OF PRIVATE TRANSNATIONAL AUTHORITY

This chapter has argued that dominant analyses of private transnational governance have tended to neglect its role in structuring the global political economy, as well as the ways in which private transnational governance is itself shaped by global social, economic and political forces. The neglect of underlying socio-economic structures is ironic in light of the present 'era in which the transnationalization of capital has both accelerated and deepened and transnational private accumulation has taken on new extreme forms'.[93] Van Apeldoorn thus identifies the need to 'historicize transnational relations, asking how they came about, and examining how transnational actors and their identities are constituted by larger-than-national structures' in the form of 'historical materialist foundations'.[94] This sentiment reflects the concerns of a growing, non-mainstream and critical literature in the subfield of

---

[90] *Id.*

[91] SASKIA SASSEN, TERRITORY, AUTHORITY, RIGHTS: FROM MEDIEVAL TO GLOBAL ASSEMBLAGES (2006).

[92] CUTLER, PRIVATE POWER, *supra* note 27; Cutler, *Transformations in Statehood, the Investor-State Regime and the New Constitutionalism, supra* note 44; Cutler, *The Judicialization of Private Transnational Power and Authority, supra* note 44; and A. Claire Cutler, *New Constitutionalism and the Commodity Form of Global Capitalism, in* NEW CONSTITUTIONALISM AND WORLD ORDER, *supra* note 15, at 45–62.

[93] Van Apeldoorn, *Theorizing the Transnational, supra* note 64, at 149.

[94] *Id.* at 150.

international political economy that draws upon dependency theory as well as neo-Gramscian theorizations of the significance of deep historical structures to the analysis of transnationalism.[95] Critical political economy is informed by Robert Cox's oft-repeated distinction between 'problem-solving theory' and 'critical theory'.[96] The former takes the world as it is and focuses on solutions to global problems; the latter instead is transformative and seeks to bring about a more just world order.

Notable contributions are Gill and Law's pioneering work on global hegemony and the structural power of transnational capital and Gill's analysis of the constitutionalization of transnational capitalism through the development of transnational legal structures that lock states into neo-liberal disciplines.[97] This analysis is further developed in Gill and Cutler as a form of 'new constitutionalism' that subordinates national societies and political economies to legal disciplines that protect and advance transnational capital accumulation.[98] Thus, Van der Pijl focuses on a transnational managerial elite or cadre and capital as a sociopolitical force, asking 'how is disciplinary power organized at the transnational level,' which he defines in turn as 'the terrain where national social formations are at least partly integrated internationally'.[99] Van der Pijl identifies a cadre of 'private international authority' whose task it is to 'streamline all social forces along neo-liberal lines',[100] while I[101] identify the

---

[95] See GRAMSCI, HISTORICAL MATERIALISM AND INTERNATIONAL RELATIONS, *supra* note 9; MARK RUPERT, PRODUCING HEGEMONY: THE POLITICS OF MASS PRODUCTION AND AMERICAN GLOBAL POWER (1995); ANDREAS BIELER, GLOBALISATION AND ENLARGEMENT OF THE EU: AUSTRIAN AND SWEDISH SOCIAL FORCES IN THE STRUGGLE OVER MEMBERSHIP (2000); SOCIAL FORCES IN THE MAKING OF THE NEW EUROPE: THE RESTRUCTURING OF EUROPEAN SOCIAL RELATIONS IN THE GLOBAL POLITICAL ECONOMY (Andreas Bieler & David Morton eds., 2001); Andreas Bieler & David Morton, *The Gordian Knot of Agency-Structure in International Relations: A Neo-Gramscian Perspective*, 7 EUR. J. INT'L REL. 5–35 (2001); WILLIAM ROBINSON, A THEORY OF GLOBAL CAPITALISM: PRODUCTION, CLASS, AND STATE IN A TRANSNATIONAL WORLD (2004); A. Claire Cutler, *Gramsci, Law, and the Culture of Global Capitalism*, 8 CRITICAL REV. INT'L SOC. POL. PHIL. 527–42 (2003); Cutler, *Gramsci, Law, and the Culture of Global Capitalism*, *supra* note 15; Cutler, *Toward a Radical Political Economy Critique of Transnational Economic Law*, *supra* note 15.

[96] Robert Cox, *Social Forces, States and World Orders: Beyond International Relations Theory* 10 MILLENNIUM 126, 126–27 (1981).

[97] See STEPHEN GILL & DAVID LAW, THE GLOBAL POLITICAL ECONOMY: PERSPECTIVES, PROBLEMS AND POLICIES (1988); Stephen Gill & David Law, *Global Hegemony and the Structural Power of Capital*, 33 INT'L STUD. Q. 475–99 (1989); and STEPHEN GILL, POWER AND RESISTANCE IN THE NEW WORLD ORDER (2008).

[98] NEW CONSTITUTIONALISM AND WORLD ORDER, *supra* note 15.

[99] Kees Van der Pijl, *Two Faces of the Transnational Cadre under Neo-liberalism*, 7 J. INT'L REL. & DEV. 177, 178 (2004).

[100] *Id.* at 190.

[101] CUTLER, PRIVATE POWER, *supra* note 27.

transnational merchant class, or 'mercatocracy',[102] as constitutive of private transnational authority.[103]

Such analyses suggest that we need to rethink the nature of the relationship between governance and capitalism, as well as the significance of private transnational governance as constitutive of private transnational regimes of accumulation and legitimation. This rethinking involves analysing how expert, technical and legal knowledge and the culture of efficiency that characterize the dominant regulatory ethos work to legitimate strategies of private appropriation. For example, the corporate social responsibility movement, which advances soft, voluntary corporate responsibilities, might be fruitfully analysed as a legitimating mechanism – as a 'transnational private legitimacy regime'.[104] This involves opening up the 'black box of private authority' in order to theorize and better understand 'why and how private rules are accepted as authoritative' as well as '[w]hat kind of order is transnational private authority, what interests does it serve, for what purposes does it exist'.[105]

The role of experts is crucial in creating and legitimating private regimes that are resistant to oversight or accountability.[106] Expert opinion drives and legitimates a diversity of private transnational orders, ranging from the regulation of security by private security companies[107] to the regulation of trans-

---

[102] The term 'mercatocracy' or merchant class is adapted from the medieval law merchant or *lex mercatoria*, a private justice system that regulated overseas trade for over a millennium see CUTLER, PRIVATE POWER, *supra* note 27, at 4–5.

[103] *See* LESLIE SKLAIR, THE TRANSNATIONAL CAPITALIST CLASS (2001); ROBINSON, *supra* note 95; and KEES VAN DER PIJL, TRANSNATIONAL CLASSES AND INTERNATIONAL RELATIONS (1998).

[104] Paul Haslam, *Is Corporate Social Responsibility a Constructivist Regime? Evidence from Latin America*, 21 GLOBAL SOC'Y 269, 270 (2007). *See also* A. Claire Cutler, *Problematizing Corporate Social Responsibility under Conditions of Late Capitalism and Postmodernity*, in AUTHORITY IN GLOBAL POLITICAL ECONOMY 189–216 (Volker Rittberger & Martin Nettesheim eds., 2008); and Cutler, *Transnational Business Civilization*, *supra* note 41.

[105] Haslam, *supra* note 104, at 274–75.

[106] *See* Martti Koskenniemi, *The Fate of Public International Law: Between Technique and Politics*, 70 MOD. L. REV. 1–30 (2007).

[107] *See* Elke Krahmann, *Security: Collective Good or Commodity?* 1 EUR. J. INT'L REL. 379–404 (2008); Anna Leander, *The Power to Construct International Security: On the Significance of Private Military Companies*, 33 MILLENNIUM: J. INT'L STUD. 803–26 (2005); A. Claire Cutler, *The Legitimacy of Private Transnational Governance: Experts and the Transnational Market for Force*, 8 SOCIO-ECONOMIC REV. 113–30 (2010); and A. Claire Cutler & Stephanie Law, *Regulating Private Military and Security Companies by Contract: Between Anarchy and Hierarchy?*, in THE POLITICS OF PRIVATE TRANSNATIONAL GOVERNANCE BY CONTRACT 225–76 (A. Claire Cutler & Thomas Dietz eds., 2017).

national securities,[108] finance[109] and international investment.[110] Experts, in international security for example, gain legitimacy as risk entrepreneurs who are celebrated as business innovators and receive praise from the neo-liberal camp for the private provision of security as more efficient and cost-effective in comparison to state-based security. In this regard, they are responding to deep structural and, perhaps, discursive developments that are associated with the commodification of security and the individualization and privatization of responsibility to protect and secure against risk.[111] In Gramscian terms, they function as organic intellectuals by presenting privatized management of security risks as a collective and public good and by participating in the process of *trasformismo*,[112] which conceals and diffuses potential criticism or opposition to their activities.[113] We need to better understand how the construction of risk and its management delivers 'authority to experts' and constructs the neo-liberal subject as the prudent manager of risks.[114] This also involves exploring the fundamental contradiction between risk management as a commodity to be bought and sold and risk management as a form of governance or governmentality that is internalized by self-regulating subjects. This contradiction points to a tension between the elitism of expert risk management and neo-liberalism's commitment to the democratic self-realization and autonomy of its subjects and underlines the power and authority that has been granted to business corporations. As Julian Arato has argued in the context of the international investment regime, 'international legal doctrine has gone too far in empowering

[108] RODERICK MACDONALD, *When Lenders Have Too Much Cash and Borrowers Have Too Little Law: The Emergence of Secured Transactions*, in TRANSNATIONAL LEGAL ORDERS 114–53 (Terence C. Halliday & Gregory Shaffer eds., 2015).

[109] *See* Cutler, *Private Transnational Governance and the Crisis of Global Leadership*, *supra* note 16, at 56–70 (Stephen Gill ed., 2012); and A. Claire Cutler, *Strange Bedfellows? Bankers, Business(men) and Bureaucrats in Global Financial Governance*, in SUSAN STRANGE AND THE FUTURE OF GLOBAL POLITICAL ECONOMY: POWER, CONTROL AND TRANSFORMATION 126–51 (Randall Germain ed., 2016) [hereinafter Cutler, *Strange Bedfellows?*].

[110] Cohen, *Private Arbitration*, *supra* note 57; Cutler, *Transformations in Statehood, the Investor-State Regime and the New Constitutionalism*, *supra* note 44; and Cutler, *The Judicialization of Private Transnational Power and Authority*, *supra* note 44.

[111] Craig Calhoun, *The Privatization of Risk*, 18 PUB. CULTURE 257–64 (2006).

[112] *Trasformismo* is the process Gramsci describes whereby opposition and resistance to the hegemony of the dominant class is absorbed, diffused and neutralized. *See* GRAMSCI, *supra* note 13, at 57–59.

[113] *See* Adam Morton, *The Grimly Comic Riddle of Hegemony in IPE: Where Is Class Struggle?*, 26 POL. 62–72 (2006).

[114] Pat O'Malley, *Uncertain Subjects: Risks, Liberalism, and Contract*, 29 ECON. & SOC. 460, 462 (2000).

multinationals against the state, while remaining too hesitant to demand any form of corporate accountability'.[115]

Indeed, a praxis conception of private transnational governance assists in understanding the complex relationships between states and transnational legal ordering. I have argued elsewhere that private transnational governance is a central modality of capitalism in its contemporary form.[116] More recently, and drawing upon critical political economy, I have suggested that transnational law operates dialectically as the 'common sense' of transnational capitalism.[117] This common sense is embedded in a new constitutionalism that legitimizes and, indeed, fetishizes private corporate power and the subordination of local and national societies and political economies to the disciplines of private, foreign capital.[118] The dominant form of law is the commodity form of law that expands and deepens commodification locally and globally.[119]

This deepening is achieved through dialectical movements along two central vectors of power. The first vector is tension and contestation over international and transnational legality, while the second concerns the dialectical operations of hard and soft law. These two vectors work to empower transnational corporations by subjecting the societies in which they operate to the discipline of hard, enforceable corporate trade and investment rights, whilst limiting corporate social responsibility to soft, voluntary and unenforceable standards. However, this discipline is not total or hegemonic as there are fractures in this 'common sense'. This is illustrated in the evolution of the investor-state regime, from one heavily one-sided in favour of transnational corporate authority along the first vector and soft corporate responsibilities on the second vector of power. However, over time resistance to the regime developed, first by states like the United States and Canada, who, having been subject to punishing damage awards in investor-state arbitrations, rethought loss of public policy and legislative autonomy to the power of foreign investors

---

[115] Arato, *Corporations as Lawmakers*, *supra* note 35, at 229.
[116] See CUTLER, *supra* note 27; Cutler, *supra* note 29; Cutler, *Toward a Radical Political Economy Critique of Transnational Economic Law*, *supra* note 15; Cutler, *Strange Bedfellows?*, *supra* note 109; and Cutler, *The Judicialization of Private Transnational Power and Authority*, *supra* note 44.
[117] Cutler, *Legal Pluralism*, *supra* note 29.
[118] See NEW CONSTITUTIONALISM AND WORLD ORDER; Cutler, *Strange Bedfellows?*, *supra* note 109; and Cutler, *The Judicialization of Private Transnational Power and Authority*, *supra* note 44.
[119] Cutler, *New Constitutionalism and the Commodity Form of Global Capitalism*, *supra* note 15.

and the discretion of arbitrators. Other states have exited the regime for similar reasons,[120] while increasingly NGOs like the Centre for International Environmental Law and the International Institute for Sustainable Development have mobilized for changes in access to and procedures within investor-state arbitrations. Gradually the key investor-state arbitration institutions, ICSID and UNCITRAL, have also modified their rules permitting greater transparency and participation.[121] While they are not exactly revolutionary changes in the investor-state regime, these developments point to openings for contesting social forces to reconfigure the balance between transnational private and public authority.[122]

D CONCLUSION

This chapter has illustrated the growing analytical recognition of 'the transnational' as a domain of social, economic and political engagement in the fields of law and politics. It presents this domain as one of governance and legitimation, although arguably the former operation has received more attention than the latter. While Jessup was most prescient in identifying the trend to transnational governance and the increasing significance of non-state actors, institutions and laws, his focus was analytical and empirical and arguably normative only in its aspiration to the recognition of an international community interest. He did not adequately address the deeper forces contesting the nature and function of this hypothetical universal, transitional public space nor its role in legitimating transnational capitalism. Critical political economy assists in developing this part of the story, but studies are only just beginning to frame private transnational governance as a legitimating mechanism that is connected at a deeper level to the reproduction and expansion of transnational capitalism. In conclusion, we will highlight some of the outstanding analytical, theoretical and normative concerns that emerge from the analysis and require further study.

[120] Bolivia, Ecuador and Venezuela have withdrawn membership from ICSID, while South Africa and Indonesia have terminated their BITs.
[121] For a detailed review of these developments, see Cutler, *Strange Bedfellows?*, *supra* note 109; and Cohen, *Private Arbitration*, *supra* note 57.
[122] *See* JONATHAN GRAUBART, LEGALIZING TRANSNATIONAL ACTIVISM: THE STRUGGLE TO GAIN SOCIAL CHANGE FROM NAFTA's CITIZEN PETITIONS (2008); and Cutler, *Strange Bedfellows?*, *supra* note 109.

Analytically, there is considerable ambiguity over the definition and scope of private transnational governance. Must the scope and application of private transnational regulation extend beyond the reach of the *private* participants to regulate collective activities or to supply public goods in order to constitute governance? Some suggest that this is the case,[123] while others do not.[124] The latter identify private transnational authority and the authority of experts as distinct analytical categories.[125]

There is also uncertainty in characterizing the contemporary enhanced significance of private authority in the global political economy as one of *international* or *transnational* scope and operation. The weight of opinion appears to be in favour of the latter characterization. However, in the field of international relations, there is further disagreement as to whether an actor-specific focus on the *agents* involved or a focus on deeper *structural* forces is the appropriate conceptual approach to the study of private transnational governance. The latter involves situating private transnational governance in broader historical, material and ideological contexts.

Relatedly, there is some uncertainty over how to situate 'the transnational' vis-à-vis *the national* and *the global*. The nature of the relationship between private transnational governance and the state has, arguably, received greater attention than its relation to global structures and processes. Most analysts today argue that rather than displacing or replacing state authority, private transnational authority operates in relation with the state, involving re-regulation and recasting of the nature and role of contemporary states. However, the exact nature of this relationship is uncertain. Is it necessary that private authority operate with an explicit or implicit grant of state authority or in the 'shadow of the state' in order to constitute authority? Or is it sufficient that private governance be authorized by experts as a form of technical authority?[126] The formulation originally introduced by Cutler, Haufler and Porter can be seen as building in both state authorization and expert opinion as analytical requirements.[127] Here the conceptual status of private

---

[123] *See* David Bernstein & Benjamin Cashore, *Non-state Global Governance: Is Forest Certification a Legitimate Alternative to a Global Forest Convention?*, in HARD CHOICES, SOFT LAW: VOLUNTARY STANDARDS IN GLOBAL TRADE, ENVIRONMENT AND SOCIAL GOVERNANCE 33–63 (John Kirton & Michael Trebilcock eds., 2004) [hereinafter Bernstein & Cashore, *Non-state Global Governance*]; and Ruggie, *Reconstituting the Global Public Domain, supra* note 1.
[124] PRIVATE AUTHORITY AND INTERNATIONAL AFFAIRS, *supra* note 16.
[125] Tony Porter, *Private Authority, Technical Authority, and the Globalization of Accounting Standards*, 7 BUS. & POL. 1–30 (2005) [hereinafter Porter, *Private Authority*].
[126] *Id.*
[127] PRIVATE AUTHORITY AND INTERNATIONAL AFFAIRS, *supra* note 16.

transnational governance raises important legitimacy issues. Is state authority required to legitimate private governance, or can private governance structures operate legitimately without state recognition through the authority of experts[128] or markets?[129] Furthermore, how is the legitimacy of private trans-national governance to be assessed? If we employ democratic criteria of input, throughput and output legitimacy, are we conflating different analytical instances of authority (*in* and *an* authority) and also disabling an understand-ing of illicit authority?

These analytical ambiguities, in turn, have theoretical and normative implications. Theoretically, how do we account for the legitimacy of private transnational authority? Actor-specific studies tend to focus on output legitim-acy that stresses the functionality and efficiency of outcomes. They theorize private transnational governance in the context of liberal political theory and political economy and rationalist models of public goods provision and col-lective action. These theoretical approaches build a public dimension right into their analytical framework. As a result, the extent to which private transnational governance operates as an integral part of macro-regulation as a legitimating strategy for private processes of transnational capital accumula-tion escapes analysis. Questions concerning 'who benefits' from private trans-national regulation and critical examination of the 'publicness' of the goods provided do not form part of the inquiry.

Related functional theorizations similarly risk depoliticizing and naturaliz-ing private transnational governance, which emerges as a consequence of the pursuit of economic efficiencies through functional differentiation of the global system. The pressing normative issues concerning 'who gets what' and 'why' are possibly the least studied and most problematic dimensions of private transnational governance that require further interrogation. However, this is difficult given the apparent division between actor-centred and macro-structural analytical foci that reflect profound theoretical divisions concerning the political economy and purposes of private transnational governance. The legitimacy of private transnational governance turns on the *purposes* it serves, which should therefore constitute the core analytical and theoretical concerns of future research. It thus appears that a radical political economy critique has much to offer for our understanding of the legitimacy of private transnational governance. It reminds us that transnational law is neither neutral nor object-ive in nature, operation and effect but is rooted in contesting social forces with

---

[128] Porter, *Private Authority*, supra note 125.
[129] Bernstein & Cashore, *Non-state Global Governance, supra* note 123.

very different views of the purposes it does and should serve. Students of transnational law are thus wise to reflect upon Jessup's emphasis on the necessary accountability of states and non-state actors alike to community norms. The reference to a broader transnational community opens up space for a praxis conception of transnational law and for progressive social change.

14

Transnational Law as Drama

JOTHIE RAJAH

A INTRODUCTION: INTERDISCIPLINARITY AND TRANSNATIONAL LAW

For Philip Jessup, 'the authority to make the rules men live by'[1] extends from the familial injunction 'Wash your hands before supper'[2] to rules of procedure at the UN General Assembly.[3] He writes, 'Nowadays it is neither novel nor heretical to call all of these rules "law."'[4,5]

Jessup delivered this assertion sixty years ago. Ironically, his challenge to the domains, categories and disciplinary autonomy of law still seems, if not novel and heretical, at the very least boundary pushing, even in *our* day. Despite decades of contestation on the meaning and sites of law – much of which has unfolded in the social sciences and sociolegal scholarship[6] – contemporary legal education and mainstream understandings of law remain dominated by narrowly positivist conceptions.[7] In short, despite Jessup's sixty-year-old,

---

[1] Philip C. Jessup, Transnational Law 8 (1956).
[2] *Id.*
[3] *Id* at 9.
[4] *Id.*
[5] In addition to challenging legal doctrinal thinking, Jessup's range of examples also raises the intractable issue as to which normative orders can or should be called law. This issue is one that perhaps legal anthropologists have most potently tussled with, advancing analysis on law by recognizing, first, that 'the state was not the only source of obligatory norms' (*see* Sally Falk Moore, *Certainties Undone: Fifty Turbulent Years of Legal Anthropology, 1949–1999,* 7 J. Royal Anthropological Inst. 95 (2001) and, second, that definitional moves do much of the work in distinguishing law from other normative orders (*see* Sally Engle Merry, *Anthropology, Law, and Transnational Process,* 21 Ann. Rev. Anthropology 357–79 (1992)).
[6] *See* Eve Darian-Smith, Laws and Societies in Global Contexts: Contemporary Approaches 1–38 (2013).
[7] *See, e.g.,* Peer Zumbansen, *Where the Wild Things Are: Journeys to Transnational Legal Orders and Back,* 1 UC Irvine J. Int'l, Transnat'l & Compar. L. 161–94 (2016); Darian-Smith,

catholic conception of law and its transnational expressions, the need to challenge received thinking remains ongoing.

It is in the spirit of constructively contesting (legal doctrinal) understandings of law that I argue in this paper, through an analysis of an image that came to be known as the 'Situation Room photograph',[8] for approaching transnational law as drama. As elaborated below, the metaphor of law as drama inheres in Jessup's own turn to drama.[9] Yoking Jessup's turn to drama with anthropologist Victor Turner's notion of 'social drama as a device for describing and analysing episodes that manifest social conflict',[10] my paper asks, 'What does the Situation Room photograph tell us about contemporary law as a cultural and social activity?'

As a preliminary point, I should like to highlight Jessup's question 'What is the role of the scholar in treating international or transnational law?'[11] In answering this question, Jessup insists that 'it is essential that no complete detachment ever take place'.[12] The detachment that must not take place, he implies, is the detachment from bodies and facts.[13] In other words, transnational law must engage with the actual – with material realities. As an image that has been widely disseminated and viewed,[14] the Situation Room

---

supra note 6; Carrie Menkel-Meadow, *Why and How to Study 'Transnational' Law*, 1:1 UC IRVINE L. REV. 97128 (2011).

[8] This photograph is especially expressive of state power because it was taken by the White House's official photographer, Pete Souza. Minimally mediated by non-state sources, disseminated both through the White House Flickr website and major newspapers worldwide, this state-generated photograph, depicting state elites in a highly secretive state space, was assessed, at one point, to be the most viewed image on the internet. *See* Liam Kennedy, *Seeing and Believing on Photography and the War on Terror*, 24:2 PUB. CULTURE 265 (2012). *See* Obama White House, *P050111PS-0210*, FLICKR (May 1, 2011), https://www.flickr.com/photos/whitehouse/5680724572/in/album-72157626507626189/.

[9] *See* JESSUP, *supra* note 1, at 16–28.

[10] VICTOR TURNER, DRAMAS, FIELDS, AND METAPHORS: SYMBOLIC ACTION IN HUMAN SOCIETY 78 (1974).

[11] JESSUP, *supra* note 1, at 9

[12] *Id.* at 10.

[13] *Id.* Jessup writes, 'If what the scholar says is not subject to criticism, it might as well be left unsaid. Without disparaging the contribution of pure reason he need not take the position of Grotius, who wrote … "If anyone thinks that I have had in view any controversies of our own times, either those that have arisen or those which can be foreseen as likely to arise, he will do me an injustice. With all truthfulness I aver that, just as mathematicians treat their figures as abstracted from bodies, so in treat law I have withdrawn my mind from every particular fact." I have not tried to emulate Grotius in this respect; to the contrary, I agree with Max Radin: "it is essential that no complete detachment ever takes place."' *See Id.*

[14] *See* Kennedy, *supra* note 8, at 255–66.

photograph is undoubtedly an important facet of communicative materiality.[15] After Foucault, we understand discourse broadly, as words, representations, ideas, beliefs, values and more.[16] Even if contingent and relational, these and other attributes of the social shape our material environments, our institutions, our sense of self and the ways we relate.

Before delving into the specifics of the Situation Room photograph, I should like to account, in some detail, for the analytic and interpretive move of approaching transnational law as drama. First, I take seriously Jessup's turn to drama. Departing from the style and language of conventional legal scholarly argument for a brief seven pages to demonstrate, as his title to Chapter 1 indicates, the 'universality of human problems', Jessup crafts 'three dramas, each one in two scenes'.[17] These pairs mirror each other in terms of power dynamics and conflicts, but are enacted in very different spheres. For example, Drama No. 1 pairs the intensely personal spheres of marriage, divorce and traditional gender roles in the lives of Mary and Frank, with the imperial relations of domination and subordination unfolding between Morocco and France.

Jessup characterizes his 'experiment with three dramas'[18] as motivated thus: 'In spite of vast organizational and procedural differences between the national and the international stage, if we find there are common elements in the domestic and the international dramas, may not the greater experience with the solution of the former aid in the solution of the later?'[19] Mining analogy as an analytic resource, Jessup expands the scale and relational dimensions of transnational law by embracing the 'individual, corporate, interregional, and international' as transnational actors and situations.[20] Additionally, his turn to drama suggests an effort to overcome a constraint inherent to the language and logics of conventional (legal) scholarly argument – a constraint vaulted over through the playful, imaginative strategy of pairings of dramatic scenes.

---

[15] For a more detailed analysis of the Situation Room photograph in relation to law as record, see Jothie Rajah, *Law as Record: The Death of Osama bin Laden*, 13 No FOUNDATIONS 46–69 (2016).

[16] *See, e.g.*, MICHAEL FOUCAULT, POWER/KNOWLEDGE: SELECTED INTERVIEWS & OTHER WRITING 1972–1977 (Colin Gordon ed. 1980).

[17] JESSUP, *supra* note 13, at 16.

[18] *Id.*

[19] *Id.*

[20] *Id.*

Taking Jessup's turn to drama seriously is not as whimsical as it may seem. Introducing his 1985 collection of essays, *Heracles' Bow: Essays on the Rhetoric and Poetics of the Law,* James Boyd White writes:

> Law is ... a language, but it is also like drama and poetry and rhetoric and narrative. ... Part of my object is to establish a way of thinking by drawing analogies, by making metaphors – by talking about one thing in terms of another – ... not as proposing comparisons between law and other things, ... but as manifesting a bent of mind, a disposition and a method, that works by looking at law as one cultural and social activity among others.[21]

In other words, by illuminating law's enmeshments and coexistence with other spheres and dynamics of life, metaphor dismantles law's imagined disciplinary autonomy. From Sally Falk Moore's influential analogy, law as process,[22] to the more specific explorations of law as drama,[23] we find ourselves today with vistas opened by the recent and ongoing 'Law As ...' project led by Christopher Tomlins.[24] 'Law As ...' sets out to dismantle the conventional sociolegal framework of 'law and' that has dominated sociolegal studies. The sociolegal 'law and' framework 'perpetuates the idea that, even though law is situated in society, law is distinct from society'.[25] Departing from the modernist segregations of 'law and', 'Law As ...', with the radical openness of the ellipses, perceives law's sites and expressions capaciously and metaphorically, probing the insights facilitated by

> deploy[ing] history as an interpretive practice – that is, as a theory, a methodology, and even a philosophy – by which to engage in research on law. Simultaneously it proposes history as a substantive arena in which other interpretive research practices – those of anthropology, literature, political economy, political science, political theory, rhetoric, and sociology – can engage with law. The result is a capacious interdisciplinary jurisprudence inflected by history rather than by the positivism of the social sciences, which holds out the possibility, a century after their divorce, of reuniting metaphysics with materiality.[26]

---

[21] JAMES BOYD WHITE, HERACLES' BOW: ESSAYS ON THE RHETORIC AND POETICS OF THE LAW viii (1985).

[22] SALLY FALK MOORE, LAW AS PROCESS: ANTHROPOLOGICAL APPROACH (1978).

[23] *See, e.g.,* WHITE, *supra* note 21; J.M. Balkin & Sanford Levinson, *Law as Performance, in* LAW AND LITERATURE 729–51 (Michael Freeman & Andrew D.E. Lewis eds., 1999).

[24] For a review of the 'Law as ...' project, *see* Christopher Tomlins, *Foreword: 'Law As ...' III – Glossolalia: Toward a Minor (Historical) Jurisprudence,* 5 UC IRVINE L. REV. 239–61 (2015).

[25] Catherine L. Fisk & Robert W. Gordon. *Foreword: 'Law As ...': Theory and Method in Legal History,* 1:3 UC IRVINE L. REV. 519–41 (2011).

[26] *See* TOMLINS, *supra* note 24, at 239.

This long-overdue reuniting of metaphysics with materiality relates, in part, to a recovery of justice and ethical relations as inextricable aspects of law.[27] As a lens for interdisciplinary scholarship on law, 'Law As ...' dwells 'on the conditions of possibility for a critical knowledge of the here and now'.[28] In search of a critical knowledge of law in the here and now, I excavate legitimizing scripts from the Situation Room photograph, engaging in an interpretive practice in order to illuminate insidious rule- and norm making represented in texts we tend not to think of as legal.

In keeping with Jessup's effort to dismantle legal doctrinal constraint, and the expansive interdisciplinary resources of 'Law As ...', I read into Jessup's turn to drama a recognition of the communicative resources associated with drama or theatre, such as affect, images, soundscapes, narrative and shared understandings of genre, myth, character, archetypes and symbols. I also draw on Turner's analytic model of social drama (described in section B below). Turner's conception of social drama is invaluable for its grasp of dramatic events as historically and culturally embedded expressions of social conflict.

A final note on methodology relates to the close reading of text and the approach of entering broad social questions through single textual examples. This paper draws on the sociolinguistic subfield of critical discourse analysis (CDA).[29] CDA is informed by critical theory on language and power, in particular the work of Foucault, Bourdieu and Habermas. CDA seeks to render explicit underlying meanings and social relations so as to uncover that which may be hidden or normalized. In CDA, close reading of text is highly valued because each and every instance of text is understood to yoke the macrocosm of society to the microcosm of a particular text.[30] Because every instance of text expresses the conditions of possibility that are the larger structures of the social, the task for the scholar is to uncover the histories, politics, ideologies and social relations embedded in, and occluded from, a text. Thus, through the lens of CDA, a single instance of text can validly lead

---

[27] Shaun McVeigh, *Afterword: Office and the Conduct of the Minor Jurisprudent*, 5 UC IRVINE L. REV. 499–512 (2015); Christopher Tomlins & John Comaroff, *'Law As ...': Theory and Practice in Legal History*, 1 UC IRVINE L. REV. 1039–79 (2011).

[28] *See* TOMLINS & COMAROFF, *supra* note 27, at 1044.

[29] NORMAN FAIRCLOUGH, LANGUAGE AND POWER (1989). Critical discourse analysis informs an extensive body of scholarship attending to the relationship between language and power. In addition to Fairclough's own considerable body of work, see (for example) the scholarship of Allan Luke on pedagogy, literacy and race; Carmen Luke on critical media and cultural studies, feminism, and globalization; Teun A. Van Dijk on mass communications, race and ideology; and Ruth Wodak on critical sociolinguistics. Blommaert & Bulcaen (2000) offer a useful review of CDA.

[30] Christopher N. Candlin, *General Editor's Preface* to FAIRCLOUGH, *supra* note 29, at viii.

to an excavation of broader social and political dynamics. Through close analysis of text, the goal is to analyse the ways in which one text relates to other texts (intertextuality) as well as to historical and synchronic contexts.[31]

In short, obedient to Jessup's prescription that lawyers should disavow detachment from bodies and facts, be alert to the communicative and social dynamics of drama and be ready participants in Jessup's project of challenging disciplinary parameters, I draw on interdisciplinary scholarship on law informed by critical theory and cultural studies to read the Situation Room photograph as an instance of transnational law as drama.

B SOCIAL DRAMA

In *Dramas, Fields, and Metaphors*, Turner uses 'the notion of social drama as a device for describing and analysing episodes that manifest social conflict'.[32] Turner identifies social drama as consisting of a four-stage model. The first stage is breach, 'of some relationship regarded as crucial in the relevant social group'.[33] The second is crisis, 'when sides are being taken, coalitions formed and fissures spread and deepen'.[34] Stage three is the 'legal or ritual means of redress or reconciliation between the conflicting parties',[35] and finally, with stage four, 'either the public and symbolic expression of reconciliation or else of irremediable schism'.[36]

As a dramatic episode in transnational law, the killing of bin Laden is a key component of the US state's official narrative relating to post-9/11 national identity and legitimacy.[37] In the US narrative, the events of 9/11 constitute that

---

[31] Ruth Wodak, *Critical Linguistics and Critical Discourse Analysis, in* HANDBOOK OF PRAGMATICS 204–10 (Jef Verschueren et al. eds., 1996).

[32] *See* TURNER, *supra* note 10, at 78. Set out in this manner, social drama may look straightforwardly sequential, but Turner highlights, 'there are a number of variations possible with regard to the sequence of the phases and to the weight accorded to them. Again, when there is a rapid sequence of social dramas, it is hard to tell whether what one is observing at a given moment in the series is breach, crisis, . . . or the application of redressive machinery.' *See id.* at 79.

[33] *Id.* at 78.

[34] *Id.* at 79.

[35] *Id.* at 78.

[36] *Id.* at 79.

[37] *See* Jothie Rajah, *Sinister Translations: Law's Authority in a Post-9/11 World*, 21:1 IND. J. GLOBAL LEGAL STUD., 107–43 (2014).

initiatory phase one – breach of a crucial relationship – and the killing of bin Laden constitutes phase three: a moment of legal redress.[38]

However, narratives, and accounts of blame and innocence, cause and effect, are, as we know, highly ideological. In her essay 'Human Rights and National Insecurity', Alison Brysk argues that *human* security – as distinct from national security – would be enhanced by perceiving 'terrorism as an expression of social conflict reflecting comprehensible grievances (albeit not necessarily justifiable)'.[39] But, she highlights, the potential to address social conflict as expressions of comprehensible grievances is lost when 'challengers are defined as "evildoers" beyond the scope of human community [and] [w]hen terrorists are inscribed as part of a state of nature – a transhistorical plague, or "enemies of humanity"'.[40]

Bearing in mind Brysk's caution that acknowledging comprehensible grievances is not equivalent to justifying violence, it is important to note, as Bruce Lawrence and Aisha Karim put it, that bin Laden 'could be dismissed as a jingoistic psychopath except that he projects a representation of himself as virtuous and his enemy as vile that resonates with many Muslims throughout Asia, Africa, and the Arab world'.[41] In other words, if 9/11 and the killing of bin Laden are episodes in the same drama of social conflict, from the perspective of the non-US party to this conflict (and I apologize for deploying a reductive 'West and the rest' binary), 9/11 is unlikely to be the initiatory phase one moment of breach.[42] The geopolitical and historical dis-embedding inherent to characterizing terrorists as trans-historically evil atomizes actors and events, extracting moments like 9/11 from a larger picture that Turner frames as the conflictual processes constituting social drama.

---

[38] In his announcement on the killing of bin Laden, President Obama avoided the term 'law', using instead the category 'justice'. In Obama's account, bin Laden bore culpability for perpetrating an extreme violence that has caused the American people extreme grief and trauma. Obama presented counterterrorism, intelligence and military personnel as a new cast of determined and heroic justice actors, able to shift the nation away from grief and trauma and towards the victory of killing bin Laden. In so doing, these new justice actors enact the greatness of the United States as nation and repaired the trauma of 9/11. The killing becomes emblematic of justice as a redemptive and retributive *felt* substitute for law. For an elaboration, see *id.*

[39] Alison Brysk, *Human Rights and National Insecurity, in* National Insecurity and Human Rights 4 (Alison Brysk & Gershon Shafir eds., 2007).

[40] *Id.*

[41] On Violence: A Reader 540 (Bruce B. Lawrence & Aisha Karim eds., 2007).

[42] Lawrence and Karim make this point and offer a simple example when they include, in their reader, an excerpt of bin Laden's 1996 rationale, 'projected as a fatwa or juridical decree'. *See id.* at 539.

In her influential analysis of post-9/11 hate violence in the United States, Leti Volpp highlights the role played by 'the redeployment of old Orientalist tropes' in which '[h]istorically, Asia and the Middle East have functioned as phantasmic sites on which the U.S. nation projects a series of anxieties regarding internal and external threats to the coherence of the national body. The national identity of the United States has been constructed in opposition to those categorized as "foreigners", "aliens," and "others".'[43] Orientalist tropes, famously traced by Edward Said in his seminal *Orientalism* (1978), have been among the ideological and cultural pillars accompanying the founding violence of European colonialism. As such, Orientalist thinking has enjoyed Euro-Atlantic (and, by extension, global) dominance for (at least) some four hundred years or more. George W. Bush's infamous invocation of a post-9/11 crusade is but one illustration of the ease with which medieval hatreds can be revitalized for contemporary purposes.[44] In short, marking the 9/11 attacks as the moment at which this particular social conflict was initiated is patently inadequate, yet when the Situation Room photograph dominates mediatized global culture's representations of the bin Laden killing, alongside the US state's meaning-making narratives, it is, one-dimensionally, the US perspective that is disseminated. Absent from the picture are other perspectives on this death, other voices to this social conflict. The drama becomes politically and ideologically a self-absorbed monologue, closed to addressing other points of view, other experiences. Strikingly, because of the dramatic nature of the event, we – the globalized, mediatized, subject 'we' – tend not to notice that only one perspective in this conflict is given airtime.

The value of Turner's model of social drama to transnational law is twofold. First, for Turner it is important to highlight the processual structure of social action. 'The social world', he emphasizes, 'is a world in becoming not a world in being.'[45] In the dynamic moments between phases, liminal moments hold the potential of radical openness: 'all previous standards and models are subjected to criticism, and fresh new ways of describing and interpreting sociocultural experience are formulated'.[46] Nothing, he stresses, is fixed by grand design when it comes to 'living action for the human species'.[47]

---

[43] Leti Volpp, *The Citizen and the Terrorist*, 49 UCLA L. Rev. 1575, 1586 (2002).
[44] There is extensive scholarship on the deployment of Orientalist tropes in post-9/11 discourse. For one example of comprehensive and detailed analysis, see Richard Jackson, Writing the War on Terrorism: Language, Politics, and Counter-Terrorism (2005).
[45] *See* Turner *supra* note 10, at 24.
[46] *Id.* at 15.
[47] *Id.* at 13.

For us, in this era of perpetual war, with vast public resources devoted to battling *imagined* precarity such that populations are left unprotected from *actual* precarity,[48] Turner's model of social drama offers an alternative way forward. Through social drama, Turner shows us one way to turn the conceptual gaze of transnational law away from the episodic and the dis-embedded. Turner emphasizes that the episodes in social drama can unfold rapidly or over centuries. If transnational law situates events as phases in social drama, there is a better chance of thoughtful action towards legal redress or reconciliation, a better chance of avoiding polemical, ahistorical interpretations that escalate conflict. Or if social conflict arrives at 'irremediable schism' rather than reconciliation, we can bring more awareness to the manner in which law's violence navigates that schism.

C TRANSNATIONAL LAW'S DRAMA IN THE SITUATION ROOM PHOTOGRAPH

I *The Transnational Citizenry of Photography*

The Situation Room photograph has been disseminated and viewed worldwide,[49] speaking both to bin Laden's death as a global media event, and to the vitality of contemporary visual culture. In keeping with the project of exploring transnational law as drama, I ask, How does this photograph represent contemporary law? What values, venues and actors are represented as those of transnational law in the Situation Room photograph, and how might we understand its erasures and displacements?

My analysis of the Situation Room photograph relies, in part, on Ariella Azoulay's lens on photographs as simultaneous expressions of, and platforms for, political relations that exceed nation state ideology.[50] For Azoulay, photographs establish a civil and political sphere embracing all actors involved in photography's social and technological encounter, including photographer, photographed subject, camera, viewer/spectator, processes of dissemination and remembering and those present at a photographic event who are not captured in the image.[51]

---

[48] JOSEPH MASCO, THE THEATER OF OPERATIONS: NATIONAL SECURITY AFFECT FROM THE COLD WAR TO THE WAR ON TERROR (2014).

[49] *See* Kennedy, *supra* note 8, at 265–66.

[50] ARIELLA AZOULAY, THE CIVIL CONTRACT OF PHOTOGRAPHY 12 (2008).

[51] *See id.; see* Ariella Azoulay, *What Is a Photograph? What Is Photography?*, 1:1 PHIL. PHOTOGRAPHY 9–13 (2010).

Azoulay's complex and sometimes elusive argument is effectively encapsulated by Justin Carville in his discussion of her 2008 monograph:

> The invention of photography is [. . .] identified as not only the beginning of a new technological means of producing images but as the emergence of a radical reorganization of social and political relations within and through the visual. The very breadth of this 'community of photography' – everyone who has had some relation to photography – what Azoulay terms the 'citizenry of photography' is what establishes it as 'borderless and open,'[52] positioning photography as having agency in 'de-territorializing citizenship.'[53] Photography's invention is thus identified as marking a moment when a political space emerged within the arena of the visible in which all those governed are able to participate as citizens.[54]

Given the global engagement with the Situation Room photograph, and the layers of meaning held within it, Azoulay's bold reimagining of photographs as sites for transnational civil and political relations is of particular value for an effort to recognize the dramatic as a feature and a platform of transnational law.

II *Obscuring Law's Violence*

The Situation Room photograph depicts Obama's national security team watching a screen we cannot see.[55] With the exception of the uniformed Brigadier General Webb, who is working on his laptop, this room full of powerful state actors watches the screen beyond the photograph with intense concentration and fixed expressions. In this image, the United States is pictured as omnipresent watcher, managing territory beyond its borders. The image subsumes the world to a US sphere of action and control with no suggestion that this expansive jurisdiction needs to be explained or justified. Extraterritorial power is seamlessly presented as taken for granted – the proper order of things.

---

[52] *See* Azoulay, *supra* note 50, at 97.
[53] *Id.* at 25.
[54] Justin Carville, *Intolerable Gaze: The Social Contract of Photography*, 3:3 PHOTOGRAPHY & CULTURE 355 (2010).
[55] While a discussion of gender is beyond the scope of this paper, it is noteworthy that the Situation Room photograph depicts an especially masculine space: only two women are visible in a room otherwise populated by men. One of these women is Secretary of State Hillary Clinton, and her gesture, of a hand held over her mouth, is the most dramatic betrayal of an affective response from anyone in the image. The other woman, Audrey Tomason, director for counterterrorism, stands at the back of the room.

Perhaps the most striking feature of the Situation Room photograph is its displacement of the primary scene of violence. In representing 'spectatorship and virtualization'[56] instead of the operation[57] against bin Laden, this photograph captures a double paradox: first, it simultaneously reveals and conceals a killing; and second, in spite of hyper-mediatization, we see *less* of law's violence.[58] Cumulatively, the effect of this double paradox is the near erasure of the other party to this social drama. The killing of bin Laden is represented even as bin Laden is displaced.

In what it does show, the Situation Room photograph captures a major strand of law in our present: it expresses that law in which the authority of state resides in a national security team rather than in a (peacetime) cabinet or an apex court. With the national security team centre stage, alternative configurations of state are displaced even as the photograph reinscribes a post-9/11 context of 'terror as normality'[59] and a militarized civil sphere.[60] The uniformed brigadier general embodies this militarized civil sphere,[61] while personnel from counterterrorism and intelligence agencies embody surveillance and hidden limbs of state power. The national security state, we are shown, is composed of key civil members of cabinet, the brute violence of military, the covert violence of intelligence agencies and the compound body of the president/commander-in-chief.

III *The Drama of Liberal Democratic Virtue*

In her discussion of political idealization, Wendy Brown explores 'the relationship between citizenship, loyalty, and critique [...] as they are configured by a time of crisis and by a liberal democratic state response to that crisis'.[62] In exploring the psychoanalytic dimensions of the state–citizen relation, Brown focuses on 'the place of *idealization* and *identification* in generating political

---

[56] *See* Kennedy, *supra* note 8, at 265.

[57] 'Operation' is the term Obama uses in his announcement of the killing, an announcement characterized by the significant avoidance of the term law. In the affiliations of 'operation' with the spheres of medicine and the military, 'operation' is surely designed to evoke the technical expertise of surgical precision and military calculations *See* Rajah, *supra* note 37, at 121.

[58] I am grateful to Alejandra Azuero for this point.

[59] *See* Joseph Masco, *Terror as Normality*, 69 BULL. ATOMIC SCIENTISTS 26–32 (2013).

[60] *See* Catherine Lutz, *Anthropology in an Era of Permanent War*, 51:2 CANADIAN ANTHROPOLOGY SOC'Y 367–79, (2009).

[61] Music critic Chris Richards notes that the brigadier general takes the seat usually occupied by the president; *see* Chris Richards, *Breaking Down the Situation Room*, WASH. POST (May 5, 2011), http://www.washingtonpost.com/wp-srv/lifestyle/style/situation-room.html.

[62] WENDY BROWN, EDGEWORK: CRITICAL ESSAYS ON KNOWLEDGE AND POLITICS 18 (2005).

fealty and conditioning the specific problem of dissent amid this fealty'.[63]
Brown draws on Freud to explain the dynamics of collective political idealization typical of conventional patriotism:

> [I]ndividuals replace their natural rivalry toward one another with identifica-
> tion, an identification achieved by loving the same object [...] e.g., the
> image of the nation, or the power of the nation [...] However, the attach-
> ment, [...] produces two very significant, indeed troubling effects for demo-
> cratic citizenship even as it binds citizens into a nation; first, the attachment
> achieved through idealization is likely to glory in the *power* of the nation, a
> power expressed in state action; second and relatedly, because individual ego
> ideals have been displaced onto the nation, citizenship and patriotism are
> rendered as both passive and uncritical adoration of this power. Power thus
> replaces democracy as the love object, and passivity, obeisance, and uncrit-
> ical fealty replace active citizenship as the expression of love.[64]

Delving into the complexity of identification informing civic love, Brown
explains the work of imaginary and symbolic identification in maintaining
political idealization, as well as in 'maintaining the kind of identification upon
which a liberal democratic patriotic ideal depends'.[65] Drawing on the work of
Slavoj Žižek, and on Rey Chow's discussion of Žižek, she writes:

> [I]n an image of America as good, free, and true, but injured by evildoers who
> 'hate our way of life', imaginary identification involves identifying with
> wounded goodness, while symbolic identification identifies with the power
> that generates this image. [...] If imaginary identification tends toward
> identification with powerlessness in such scenes, symbolic identification
> identifies with power, but dissimulates this identification in the image of
> purity or woundedness through which it is achieved.[66]

In the Situation Room photograph, the tense demeanours of the national
security team, augmented by Clinton's gesture of concern – her hand held
over her mouth – facilitate our spectator–subject identification with the
wounded goodness of liberal democracy.[67] In the concern and tension, we
see affect appropriate to the liberal democratic state displayed: when lives are
at stake, decisions and actions are informed not by untrammelled bloodlust
but by intense concentration and a sombre gravitas.

---

[63] *Id.* at 27; emphasis in original.
[64] *Id.* at 30; emphasis in original.
[65] *Id.* at 32.
[66] *Id.* at 32–33.
[67] I am grateful to Bonnie Honig for this point.

The displacement of the primary scene of violence facilitates the other limb of political idealization: symbolic identification. Symbolic identification 'generate[s] a patriotic ideal that disavows its imbrications with state violence, imperial arrogance, aggression toward outsiders'.[68] Instead of seeing the Abbottabad raid – the chaos of sudden military attack in an extraterritorial residential arena and the affect generated by people confronting, risking or experiencing imminent and violent death – what we *do* see is a clean, orderly room populated by clean, orderly people. State elites clad in corporate attire[69] suggest the (peacetime) quotidian regularity of bureaucracy and state institutions.

A further representation of conduct appropriate to a liberal democratic state might be read into the photograph's apparent delivery of transparency. Even as it displaces the primary scene of violence, the Situation Room photograph appears to supply transparency by taking us into the immediacy and intimacy of the inner workings of state power. Liam Kennedy has characterized this move as the construction of visibility as a species of transparency and legitimacy.[70]

All in all, in appearing to deliver transparency by showing us an otherwise secret state space populated by clean, orderly, concerned people, mostly dressed for work in corporate settings, and taking their work very seriously indeed, the fraught legitimacy, contested legality and brute violence of the killing of bin Laden is simply not represented. The image thus facilitates identification with the wounded goodness of the United States' liberal democratic virtue even as it 'disavows its imbrications with state violence'.[71]

In a contemporary context of globalized media culture, and processes by which 'nation-states themselves are receding, however slowly and unevenly, as the basis of collective identification and collective action',[72] the impact of the Situation Room photograph far exceeds that of state citizen within the container of US domestic relations. In addition to Azoulay's point that 'photography [. . .] de-territorializes citizenship',[73] it is important to highlight that the United States is, uniquely, 'the one and only *global* state, with

---

[68] See Brown, *supra* note 62, at 33.
[69] The potentially discordant note introduced by the one sartorial exception – the uniformed brigadier general – is muted by his exceptional status, the formal military dress rather than battle fatigues and the mundane activity of his working on a laptop.
[70] See Kennedy, *supra* note 8, at 267.
[71] See Brown, *supra* note 62, at 33.
[72] *Id.* at 19.
[73] See Azoulay, *supra* note 50, at 25.

strategic interests and military deployments spread across the entirely of the globe'.[74] When US-based and owned media corporations disseminate to audiences worldwide, it is not unlikely that 'global media corporations [...] actually export the perspective of the U.S.'.[75] As participants in these global processes, the 'we' who are not US citizens are also likely to read into this image the liberal democratic virtue structuring a political idealization of the one and only global state. Given that '[t]he idealization that symbolic identification generates and lives off of are extremely powerful as legitimation strategies',[76] it is important to highlight that the audience for the Situation Room photograph's scripts of legitimation is a transnational spectator subject.

IV *Transnational Law as Revenge Drama*

Significantly, what we are not shown – the chaos and violence of the action unfolding in the Abbottabad compound – is more akin to law as vengeance than what we *are* shown. The arresting power of this photograph rests, in part, in the action and state actors we *imagine*, even as we gaze upon the suspense and stillness of the photograph. The dynamic watching Azoulay calls for – injecting movement and time into the stillness of the photograph – becomes part of what we *see* even though we are not shown it.[77]

These different strands of law – liberal democratic virtue, law in the national security state and law as vengeance – converged when the conservative group, Judicial Watch, filed Freedom of Information Act lawsuits against the US Department of Defense and the Central Intelligence Agency. Judicial Watch sought 'all photographs and/or video recordings of Osama (Usama) bin Laden taken during and/or after the U.S. military operation in Pakistan on or about May 1, 2011'.[78] At both first instance[79] and on appeal,[80] the courts

---

[74] *See* Richard Falk, *Encroaching on the Rule of Law: Post 9/11 Policies within the United States in*, National Insecurity and Human Rights 18 (Alison Brysk & Gershon Shafir eds., 2007); emphasis in original.

[75] *See* Judith Butler, Frames of War: When Is Life Grievable? xv (2010).

[76] *See* Brown, *supra* note 62, at 33.

[77] *See* Azoulay, *supra* note 50, at 25.

[78] *See* Letter from Judicial Watch to Office of Freedom of Information, OSD/JS FOIA Requester Service Center (May 2, 2011), http://www.judicialwatch.org/document-archive/foia-request-for-osama-bin-laden-photos/.

[79] *See* Judicial Watch, Inc. v. U.S. Dep't of Def. & Cent. Intelligence Agency, 1:11-cv-890 (D.C. Cir. 2012); *see* Bill Mears, *Federal Judge Blocks Release of bin Laden Death Photos*, CNN (Apr. 27, 2012), http://www.cnn.com/2012/04/26/justice/bin-laden-photos/.

[80] *See* Judicial Watch, Inc. v. U.S. Dep't of Def. & Cent. Intelligence Agency., 1:11-cv-890 (D.C. Cir. 2013), https://www.cadc.uscourts.gov/internet/opinions.nsf/ C82B0A642E2CDCB485257B72004F25D6/$file/12-5137-1437137.pdf; Mears, *supra* note 78.

upheld the US government's position that legitimate national security interests barred public release of these images.[81] The courts agreed with the state's assessment that America and Americans were safer if the killing and burial were not evidenced by images. At first instance, Judge James Boasberg said, 'A picture may be worth a thousand words. And perhaps moving pictures bear an even higher value. Yet in this case, verbal descriptions of the death and burial of Osama bin Laden will have to suffice, for this court will not order the release of anything more.'[82]

The word/image distinction that marks the official record of bin Laden's death – telling us with words what it will not show us with images[83] – illustrates Foucault's insight that the archive is 'a system of enunciability [...] first the law of what can be said, the system that governs the appearance of statements as unique events'.[84] Visual culture augments the law of what can be said, with the factor of what can be *shown*, when state and judicial actors acknowledge the impossibility of controlling responses to images that will be seen worldwide. In Azoulay's words, 'within this space of photography [...] no sovereign power exists'.[85] As cultural text, the plurality of meaning ascribable to photographs, and the expansive, transnational civil political sphere of the visual,[86] shapes the law of what can be *shown* differently from the law of what can be said. Through the lens of transnational law as drama, scholars and practitioners are able to become more attentive to images, and dramatic events, as sites and texts of transnational law.

In the challenge to the state launched by Judicial Watch, there is a striking commonality between plaintiff and defendant: the legality of the killing, in and of itself, is unquestioned. This extraterritorial, extralegal killing is understood by both plaintiff and defendant as belonging to a register of post-9/11 violence that 'creates its own interpretive conditions and so suspends ethical and legal conventions of response to its enactments'.[87] Before the courts, Judicial Watch invokes the Freedom of Information Act, and principles of democratic transparency, with no apparent awareness of its complicity in

[81] Judicial Watch, Inc. v. U.S. Dep't of Def. & Cent. Intelligence Agency (U.S. District Court for the District of Columbia, Civil Action No. 11-890 (JEB)); Mears, *supra* note 79.
[82] See Mears, *supra* note 79.
[83] See Rajah, *supra* note 15.
[84] See MICHEL FOUCAULT, THE ARCHEOLOGY OF KNOWLEDGE AND THE DISCOURSE OF LANGUAGE 129 (1972).
[85] See Azoulay, *supra* note 50, at 25. The US state's wary attention to the potency of images cannot but recall the continuing horror – a horror unregulated by nation-state affiliation – precipitated by images of prisoner abuse at Abu Ghraib and Guantánamo Bay.
[86] *Id.*
[87] See Kennedy, *supra* note 8, at 265.

a re-scripting of humanist principles of law and justice.[88] In the web of
meanings tied to the Situation Room photograph – law as vengeance, liberal
democratic virtue and law as the national security state – law as vengeance,
and as the national security state, are the accounts of law privileged by the
state, the courts and the public, who seem to recognize that state and society
cannot be antagonistic when friend or enemy is at work.

D CONCLUSION: THROUGH DRAMA TO JUSTICE

Just as Jessup's concept of transnational law addresses the disjuncture between
the actualities of transnational situations and the conceptual limitations of
national and international law, Turner's social drama addresses the disjuncture between law's very constrained and limited sense of time and event and
the very different operations of time, social memory and meaning making
informing the conduct of social actors in conflict.

As a text of transnational law, the Situation Room photograph illuminates
the normalizing and legitimizing of the national security state even as gestures
and representations of law associated with liberal democracy thread through
the image – compounding law in the national security state with liberal
legality. Scrutinizing transnational law as drama enables us, as non-state
subjects, to discard the uncritical passivity engendered by scripts of political
idealization generated when a liberal democratic state is in crisis.[89] Transnational law as drama illuminates the gap between what is officially disclosed
to us and what we are not shown: the missing voices, actors, narratives,
histories and perspectives of other parties to this social conflict. If we perceive
conflict as part of a larger social drama, we are compelled, as subjects, to
address the astonishing ideological coherence evident in the mediatized and
transnational public sphere, and the ways in which we are constituted by
global media culture. In prompting these processes and understandings,
transnational law as drama may repudiate and challenge the numbing and
apparently unending force of law's subordination to the expansive discourse of
national security. If law is to pursue the promise of justice, conceiving of law
as transnational and as drama may be one path through which promise and
potential become material and real.

---

[88] *See, e.g.,* Austin Sarat, *Situating Law between the Realities of Violence and the Claims of
Justice: An Introduction in* LAW, VIOLENCE, AND THE POSSIBILITY OF JUSTICE 3–16 (Austin
Sarat ed., 2001).

[89] *See* BROWN, *supra* note 62.

15

Transnational Law as Unseen Law

NATASHA AFFOLDER[*]

A INTRODUCTION: THIRTEEN WORDS THAT CHANGED THE WORLD

With thirteen words in the Storrs Lecture in 1956, Philip Jessup created an incurable itch for legal scholars.[1] This itch emerges from a conception of transnational law that was at once clarifying and obscuring in its specification that 'public and private international law are included *as are other rules which do not wholly fit into such standard categories*'.[2] With these words, Jessup expressed discontent with the inadequacy of existing terminology and approaches to conceptualizing border-crossing law. He flagged the profound misalignment between a solely state-mediated view of law underlying much international legal theory and his own experience of law in the world. In so doing, he created space to acknowledge law's *other* sources, legal rules and sources of knowledge about law that matter in practice but ill fit standard categories. Usefully, Jessup did not offer a restrictive list of what these misfits might be. The concept of transnational law he advanced was therefore not so much a singular and fully embellished fait accompli as it was the refreshing creation of a new intellectual holding pen for ideas about law and its border-crossing movements.

Part of the allure of Jessup's description of transnational law lies in its promise of capturing something beyond the *visible* bodies of public and private international law – in its invocation to uncover unseen law, other

---

[*] I am grateful to the organizers and participants of Jessup's Bold Proposal: Engagements with *Transnational Law* after Sixty Years for stimulating these ideas and ongoing conservations. I also thank Nicholas Healey for his excellent research assistance.

[1] PHILIP C. JESSUP, TRANSNATIONAL LAW (1956).

[2] *Id.* at 2.

law, law that is important in practice but neglected in scholarship. There have been many recent attempts to frame and name this unseen law: through raising awareness of informal international lawmaking,[3] in identifying the turn to stealthier means of transnational legal ordering,[4] by revealing the 'hidden world' of World Trade Organization governance,[5] by disclosing the 'hidden tools' that populate international investment law[6] and in unveiling the obscured interactions of private international law on public international law.[7] Such contributions emerge in studies variously described as international, transnational, comparative and global. Yet they invoke a Jessup-inspired approach to transnational law in the sense that they draw on 'a larger storehouse of rules to apply' and fail to 'worry whether public or private law applies in certain cases'.[8]

Vocabularies of visibility and invisibility continue to permeate transnational law discourse. Jessup's project of '*illuminating* a transnational space'[9] addresses 'the *empty space* left by the existing doctrinal perspectives'.[10] Transnational law is '*a lens*' through which particular relationships between national laws become *visible*.[11] Bringing transnational law '*into view*' demands seeing transnational law as a whole; if not, 'then many of its features will be *lost to sight*, the programmatic development of the system will be *obscured*, and the systematic absence of concern for legality and human rights will be *hidden*'.[12] In such a way, transnational law, whether viewed predominantly as a

---

[3] J. Pauwelyn, R. A. Wessel & J. Wouters, Informal International Lawmaking (2012).

[4] G. Shaffer & C. Coye, *From International Law to Jessup's Transnational Law, From Transnational Law to Transnational Legal Orders*, UC Irvine School of Law Research Paper No. 2017-02.

[5] A. Lang & J. Scott, *The Hidden World of WTO Governance*, 20:3 Eur. J. Int'l L. 575–614 (2009).

[6] P. Fox & C. Rosenberg, *The Hidden Tool in a Foreign Investor's Toolbox: The Trade Preference Program as a 'Carrot and Stick' to Secure Compliance with International Law Obligations*, 34 Nw. J. Int'l L. & Bus. 53–80 (2013).

[7] A. Mills, *Rediscovering the Public Dimension of Private International Law*, 24 Hague Y.B. Int'l L. 11–23 (2011); A. Mills, *Variable Geometry, Peer Governance, and the Public International Perspective on Private International Law*, in Private International Law and Global Governance 245–61 (H. Muir Watt & D. Fernández Arroyo eds., 2014).

[8] Jessup, *supra* note 1, at 15.

[9] B. Bowling & J. Sheptycki, *Global Policing and Transnational Rule with Law*, 6:1 Transnat'l Legal Theory 141, 146 (2015).

[10] G.-P. Calliess & P. Zumbansen, Rough Consensus and Running Code 11 (2010).

[11] P. Zumbansen, *Defining the Space of Transnational Law: Legal Theory, Global Governance and Legal Pluralism* 21 Transnat'l L. & Contemp. Probs. 305, 307 (2012).

[12] Neil Boister, *Further Reflections on the Concept of Transnational Criminal Law*, 6:1 Transnat'l Legal Theory 9, 30 (2015).

body of substantive law or as a methodology, implicates an enlarging of law's vision field.

Despite the appetite for viewing border-crossing law in expansive ways, the task of making visible the actualities of law *and practice* comprising transnational law involves slippery methodological questions that legal scholars seem particularly skilled at sidestepping. Jessup himself invoked the need to more fully capture an expansive view of the sources of international law and suggested some unconventional methods for elucidating these sources.[13] Neither Jessup nor the scholars who have individually taken up the task of revealing hidden aspects of transnational law, though, have squarely tackled the question of how best to address not only the *unseen* aspects of transnational law but also the disparity between the *known* and the *unknowable*.

This short chapter takes some first steps towards filling this gap. First, the chapter examines the intellectual holding pen created by Jessup for *other* rules and sources of law, his 'larger storehouse of rules'. While this initiative was firmly aimed at expanding the view of law to see beyond *the state* and to centre *practice* in its vision field, the tools and methods for studying and elucidating such a vision of law remain unclear. Second, the chapter interrogates the meaning of the practice-enriched perspective that transnational law claims to deliver, arguing that those who invoke *practice* in fact mean many different things. Finally, the chapter grounds its somewhat abstract reflections on visibility and invisibility in an examination of the difference such issues make to transnational environmental law research. By identifying four 'black boxes' that limit access to knowledge, the challenge of discovering unseen law becomes more apparent. Jessup himself acknowledged the partiality of the peekaboo views of transnational processes that populate scholarship.[14] Emerging from an awareness that the transnational law 'lens' delivers but a selective view, and that forms and manifestations of legal knowledge continue to elude us, are tantalizing possibilities for future research.

---

[13] Jessup offered methodological suggestions as to how transnational law could be mapped by scholars, drawing on 'useful precedents' from maritime law including usages, codes, conferences, practices 'codified by the voluntary action of shipping interests', inclusion of rules in bills of lading and the adoption of identical domestic legislation in maritime states: JESSUP, *supra* note 1, at 109–10.

[14] Jessup, for example, noted the challenges in accessing 'secret archives' and the barriers on new knowledge imposed by 'unfamiliar scientific terminology' and 'official security classifications': P.C. Jessup & H.J. Taubenfeld, *Outer Space, Antarctica, and the United Nations*, 13 INT'L ORG. 363, 363 (1959).

B TRANSNATIONAL LAW AS AN INTELLECTUAL HOLDING PEN: JESSUP'S 'LARGER STOREHOUSE OF RULES'

In the sixty years that have passed since the Storrs Lectures, scholars have flocked to Jessup's definition of transnational law as a safe haven – a place for exploring the multiple sites and manifestations of transnational legality that comprise 'all law which regulates actions or events that transcend national frontiers'.[15] Transnational law has become a form of intellectual shorthand, a terminology that unites scholars who share a dissatisfaction with versions of public international law that are too limited in their vision, too erasing of people, places, sites of lawmaking and sources of knowledge about law. Transnational law equally provides respite from a view of private international law that is too blind to its public-facing and political dimensions. Not surprisingly, much of the intellectual energy that has emerged in transnational law scholarship is based on critique (both explicit and implicit) of what non-transnational law misses.

The resulting shared project of mapping and understanding the interactions between private and public, and the intermeshing of state and non-state actors in lawmaking, has worked to advance Jessup's aspiration of engaging with actualities and to fill the 'gaps' in knowledge that Jessup's concept of transnational law hinted at but failed to definitively diagnose. These compulsions are expressed not only in scholarship that self-identifies with a transnational law label but can be seen in recent public international law and private international law literatures that aim to better elucidate how international law 'works in practice'.[16]

Jessup's unwillingness to define and restrict the 'larger storehouse of rules' he evoked in defining transnational law was a genius move. It effectively secured transnational law's enduring appeal by hinting at this term's ongoing capacity to capture a wider vision field. Transnational law has secured its place in legal thought by serving, given this flexibility, as a much-needed place-holder for contemporary anxieties. It has created space for scholars yearning to better reflect the important, diverse and intermeshed roles of the state and non-state in lawmaking to reject compartmentalized views of public and

---

[15] JESSUP, *supra* note 1, at 2.
[16] *See, e.g.*, Gráinne de Búrca, *Human Rights Experimentalism*, 111 AMER. J. INT'L L. 277–316 (2017). This compulsion can also be traced through scholarship on global legal pluralism, global administrative law, transnational legal process, transnational legal orders, trans-governmental regulatory networks, international organizations as lawmakers, and new legal realism and international law.

private international law, to take practice seriously as a source of both norms and legal knowledge, and to embrace a plurality of legal sources in capturing the 'larger storehouse of legal rules'.[17]

But framing an inquiry as 'transnational' does not only reveal previous blind spots. It also provides an opportunity to reintroduce or perpetuate partial visions of law. A transnational law framing will emphasize certain ideas, inquiries and actors at the expense of others. While it is easy to applaud the task of more expansively covering law 'as it is experienced in the world', it is harder to soberly measure how well scholars are achieving this goal. It is, however, evident that there is a scholarly appetite for seeking to make *visible* obscured dimensions of law's function and features as it crosses borders. An example of this is a recent study of commercial lawmaking within the United Nations that describes itself in this way: 'We focus on the *least visible* of lawmaking institutions: international organizations that function more like legislatures... As an empirical investigation, this book penetrates the *zones of invisibility* that cloud the production of legal norms that govern international commerce and trade.'[18] Feminist scholarship provides a useful reminder to those contemplating transnational law's selective gaze of the potentially problematic nature of *both* visibility and invisibility. Marginalized groups are often shown to occupy positions of hyper-visibility[19] while the experiences of dominant communities enjoy a claim to universality as the hegemonic norm that conceals their domination.[20] In other situations, feminists describe invisibility as a situation of marginalization[21] from which women, and particularly certain groups of women, are deprived of political agency. A central occupation for many feminist scholars is *identifying* the unknown and, in response, making known what is hidden by legal processes.[22] Feminist theory thus offers an

---

[17] JESSUP, *supra* note 1 at 15.

[18] S. BLOCK-LIEB & T.C. HALLIDAY, GLOBAL LAWMAKERS: INTERNATIONAL ORGANIZATIONS IN THE CRAFTING OF WORLD MARKETS 23 (2017) (emphasis mine).

[19] S. Arat-Koç, *Invisibilized, Individualized, and Culturalized: Paradoxical Invisibility and Hypervisibility of Gender in Policy Making and Policy Discourse in Neoliberal Canada*, 29 CANADIAN WOMAN STUD. 6–18 (2012).

[20] R. Simpson & P. Lewis, *An Investigation of Silence and a Scrutiny of Transparency: Re-examining Gender in Organization Literature through the Concepts of Voice and Visibility*, 58 HUM. REL. 1253, 1263–64 (2005).

[21] M. YAMADA, *Invisibility is an Unnatural Disaster: Reflections of an Asian American Woman*, in THIS BRIDGE CALLED MY BACK: WRITINGS BY RADICAL WOMEN OF COLOR 35 (C. Moraga & G. Anzaldúa eds., 1981).

[22] *See* R. Ahlers & M. Zwarteveen, *The Water Question in Feminism: Water Control and Gender Inequities in a Neo-liberal Era*, 16:4 GENDER PLACE & CULTURE 409, 414–16 (2009) (exposing the practices of water resource management through which neo-liberal discourse renders unseen the political nature of decision-making); F. Johns, *The Invisibility of the Transnational*

ever-present reminder that facts, events, vocabularies, outcomes, processes and people can all be erased by methodological choices and starting points.

Mariana Valverde's *Chronotopes of Law* identifies how a scale shift in feminist legal thought to embrace the transnational has, perhaps unintentionally, relegated certain feminist critiques to the background. These include feminist critiques of marriage and unpaid housework.[23] A shift in scale to the transnational tends to focus attention on 'flows, networks and governance assemblages'[24] and divert attention away from the individual people who comprise these processes.[25] This work is a powerful reminder that a scale shift, such as that to the transnational in studying law, does not only lead to productive new fields of vision; it also implies abandoning other sights and sites of legal activity. Feminist critiques of 'the male gaze' highlight the stakes that are implicated in the very act of *seeing*.[26]

C WHAT IS A PRACTICE-ENRICHED PERSPECTIVE?

'Practice' is a single word that denotes many things. It is invoked so often and in so many different ways that it is worth spending some time thinking about why and how scholars use 'practice' and 'practices' to illuminate law and legal processes. Jessup's own appeal to the *practical* was not singular. He invokes practice in multiple ways, including (1) through focusing on *problems* applicable to the 'complex interrelated world community'[27] (the lived reality of law), (2) by appealing to practitioner knowledge (what lawyers know), (3) by drawing on his own diplomatic and government experience (personal experience of international diplomacy), (4) by clarifying that law's problems transcend legal sub-disciplines (highlighting the practical need for intra-disciplinary problem-solving), (5) with alertness to the extralegal (arguing that law includes processes that go beyond adjudication such as business negotiations and renegotiations),[28] (6) employing an explicit attempt to align legal concepts

Corporation: An Analysis of International Law and Legal Theory, 19 MELBOURNE U. L. REV. 893, 917–19 (1994) (employing feminist critiques of the public–private divide and jurisdictional doctrines to reveal how transnational corporations hide their damaging exploitation of women's labour).

[23] M. VALVERDE, CHRONOTOPES OF LAW: JURISDICTION, SCALE AND GOVERNANCE 106 (2015).

[24] *Id.*

[25] N. Affolder, *Transnational Environmental Law's 'Missing People'*, 8 TRANSNAT'L ENVTL. L. (2019) (forthcoming).

[26] Valverde, *supra* note 23, at 58.

[27] JESSUP, *supra* note 1, at 1.

[28] *Id.* at 6 ('One notes that the problem of extracting and refining oil in Iran may involve – as it has - Iranian law, English law, and public international law. Procedurally it may involve – as it

and their definition with 'realities' (law in action)[29] and (7) by applauding those scholars and judges whose work has a practical real-world impact on international politics.[30]

These multiple uses of *practice* can all be seen in the Storrs Lectures. In those lectures, Jessup explicitly distinguishes his own approach to law from that of Grotius, who detached himself from 'every particular fact', agreeing with a characterization of Grotius as 'a scholar, and his only authority was that of a scholar'.[31] While Jessup, like many others, implies that 'practice' gives one 'authority' beyond that of a scholar, the nature of that authority and the qualification threshold for claiming it remain underspecified.

Beyond invoking the value of legal practice and citing diplomatic experience as informing real-world knowledge, Jessup suggests that rules emanate from 'practices' as diverse as those of General Motors, secret societies, towns, cities, states.[32] Jessup did not himself include the word 'practices' in his own definition of transnational law in the Storrs Lectures. Yet subsequent scholars have made such an insertion, claiming that '"Law" for Jessup is composed of all rules *and practices* which regulate actions and events.'[33]

In the sixty years since Jessup's Storrs Lectures, appeals to practice in legal scholarship appear to have multiplied. The common vocabulary of 'practice', and 'practices' circulating through this scholarship may hide the fact that quite different things are being invoked: 'law in action' as opposed to 'law on the books', an understanding of law common to law's practitioners as opposed to 'detached' scholars, the real world of international politics and diplomacy, social practices of institutions and groups of non-state actors. Indeed, as legal scholarship exhibits a growing comfort with sociolegal and ethnographic methodologies that seek to understand law through social practices, it remains difficult to elucidate whether the 'practices' being referred to are indeed seen as social practices, legal practices or something else entirely. Unfortunately,

---

has – diplomatic negotiations, proceedings in the International Court of Justice and in the Security Council, business negotiations with and among oil companies, and action in the Iranian Majlis'.).

[29] *Id.* at 7. He thus approvingly quotes Justice Cardozo's own Storrs Lecture: 'Law and obedience to law are facts confirmed every day to us all in our experience of life. If the result of a definition is to make them seem to be illusions, so much the worse for the definition; we must enlarge it till it is broad enough to answer to realities.'

[30] *Id.* at 10–11, acknowledging that Grotius 'and succeeding scholars have not been without their influence on developments in international politics'.

[31] *Id.* at 10 (quoting Max Rodin).

[32] *Id.* at 9.

[33] N. de B. Katzenbach, (Book Review) 24 U. CHI. L. REV. 413, 413 (1957) (reviewing JESSUP, *supra* note 1) (emphasis mine).

the language of practice seems to be invoked somewhat more often than effort is put into articulating what is indicated by it. And at times, invoking 'practical relevance' is simply an undisguised critique of the lack of utility of theory. Such uses accompany calls to redirect legal scholars to the mission of serving 'the profession', invoking past glory days when law professors were 'strictly at the service of the practical profession – the judges and practicing lawyers. Law professors aspired to Utility rather than Truth. Their demeanor and attire were professional, worldly (as were their incomes), in comparison to the mild bohemianism by which the true don proclaimed (and proclaims) his independence from the quotidian.'[34]

Simply put, legal scholarship seems to have sidestepped the detailed methodological debates that have marked the 'practice turns' in other disciplines such as international relations or history.[35] The consequence is that *legal* practice tends to be invoked as some non-contentious and non-political body of common knowledge without being subjected to the usual questions of legitimacy given to sources of law and sources of knowledge about law. Practice, in such a way, acquires an assumed, rather than an up-for-debate, rationality. The reason that the methods for studying, or revealing, practice matter, in particular, to a collection of essays exploring Jessup's legacy, is that a practice-informed perspective was so central to Jessup's vision of transnational law. The value of studying practices to reveal *unconscious* knowledges that might be taken for granted or obscured, and *unseen* dynamics of socialization,[36] remain no less relevant to current transnational law scholarship.

The fact that the meaning, and particular authority, resident in law's practice claims remains little explored suggests that there is room for more explicit scholarly discussion about how lawyers and legal scholars, *and which ones*, get to access and represent legal practice in producing those more complete/accurate/true-to-life visions and versions of law that 'practice-informed perspectives' claim, at least implicitly, to provide. Who gets to draw on the experience of their own lives with a sense that their experience of practice is of more than anecdotal value? As legal scholars, do we unwittingly reproduce very selective 'practice-informed perspectives' by our unspoken assumptions as to whose practice and whose perspective on that practice is worth capturing in text? Do we need to adopt more deliberate, and different,

---

[34] R.A. Posner, *Legal Scholarship Today* 45 STAN. L. REV. 1647, 1648 (1993).

[35] J. Kustermans, *Parsing the Practice Turn: Practice, Practical Knowledge, Practices*, 44:2 MILLENNIUM J. INT'L STUD. 175–96 (2016).

[36] T. SCHATZKI, *Introduction: Practice Theory, in* THE PRACTICE TURN IN CONTEMPORARY THEORY 10, 13 (T. Schatzki, K. Cetina & E. von Savigny eds., 2001); M. Polyakov, *Practice Theories: The Latest Turn in Historiography?* (2012) 6 J. PHIL. HIST. 218, 218–19.

methodologies to ensure that varied, diverse and thus widely representative 'practice-informed perspectives' are shared? And what is it exactly that a practice-informed perspective is seeking to offer – a fuller, wider or just different vision of law or a more 'true-to-life' vision, and if so, true to whose life?

Many of these anxieties trace to the fact that legal scholarship can be marked by methodological timidity, and sometimes even an aversion to saying much at all about methodological choices. In her book *Non-legality in International Law*, Fleur Johns adopts the term 'quasi-ethnography' to reference the ways in which her scholarship draws upon her experiences in legal practice.[37] By being explicit about the practice base upon which she personally draws, Johns's references to practice take on greater meaning and clarity. Other scholars find ways to clarify their conceptions of practice and practices by defining practices by what they are not. For example, human rights scholars differentiate *practices* of human rights from human rights *discourses*, taking care to note that the two are mutually constitutive.[38]

Ethnographic work has illuminated the difference a practice-informed perspective makes in the sense of revealing law through its 'lived practices and techniques'.[39] Such work, for example, allows scholars to adjust where they direct their gaze in understand global supply chains, revealing the importance of detailed scrutiny of practices that occur not only in but around the chain.[40] Studying legal knowledge in this way can involve looking at quite diverse sites of practice, including viewing law as the product of specialized elites[41] or analysing law as the product of automation and routinized practices.[42] As transnational sites of knowledge production increasingly attract the interest of legal scholars, law's visual field is adjusted by a willingness to examine how legal knowledge is formed through material practices.

---

[37] F. JOHNS, NON-LEGALITY IN INTERNATIONAL LAW 22 (2013); *see* B. OWEN, IN THE MIX: STRUGGLE AND SURVIVAL IN A WOMEN'S PRISON (1998).

[38] M. Goodale, *Locating Rights, Envisioning Law between the Global and the Local, in* THE PRACTICE OF HUMAN RIGHTS: TRACKING LAW BETWEEN THE GLOBAL AND THE LOCAL 1, 18 (M. Goodale & S.E. Merry eds., 2007). This chapter title again draws on the language of visibility in its exercise of *envisioning* law.

[39] *See* S.E. Merry, *New Legal Realism and the Ethnography of Transnational Law* 31:4 LAW & SOC. INQUIRY 975–95 (2006).

[40] *See* B. Reinke & P. Zumbansen, *Transnational Liability Regimes in Contract, Tort, and Comparative Law: Comparative Observations on 'Global Supply Chain Liability', in* LE DEVOIR DE LA VIGILANCE (S. Schiller ed., 2019).

[41] Y. DEZALAY & B.G. GARTH, THE INTERNATIONALIZATION OF PALACE WARS (2002).

[42] *See, e.g.,* A. RILES, COLLATERAL KNOWLEDGE: LEGAL REASONING IN THE GLOBAL FINANCIAL MARKET 230 (2011); Johns, *supra* note 37, at 64.

Many of the scholars writing practice-inspired accounts of international law and transnational regulation do so after a career-long engagement with practice and draw on their own lives in creating practice-informed perspectives. Martti Koskenniemi, for example, has explicitly drawn attention to the importance of his long career practicing international law with the Finnish Ministry of Foreign Affairs in shaping the starting points for *From Apology to Utopia*.[43] David Kennedy, a scholar whose own writing is animated by deep suspicions about expert rule and its tendency to marginalize opportunities for contestation, writes in an anecdote-rich way that reveals the depth of his expertise, his networks and his experience in professional practice.[44]

While personal experience-rich accounts such as Kennedy's and monumental interview-based and practice-reflecting texts like John Braithwaite and Peter Drahos's *Global Business Regulation* provide models of practice-informed scholarly writing, they are exceptional examples of such work. Kennedy provides a rich view of the 'field' from social and professional interactions without the interruptions of footnotes denoting interview numbers and ethics approvals, but, in reality, produced based on unparalleled access to both grass-roots and elite military, economic and humanitarian actors. Braithwaite and Drahos document a decade-long process of interviewing 500 'international leaders in business and government'.[45] They explain the purpose of undertaking such a monumental number of interviews as revealing 'what the formal language of international intellectual property agreements does not: *the informal dynamic of power* that determines the choice of words, their meaning, and subsequent utilization'.[46]

Jessup's conception of transnational law presents us with the challenge of creating 'practice-informed; perspectives of law. Such a task demands being explicit about how we are creating these accounts. What methodological safeguards might ensure that the visions of practice that do inform accounts of transnational law do not unwittingly reproduce the very patterns of privilege and marginalization of sources of knowledge that they seek to address?

---

[43] M. KOSKENNIEMI, FROM APOLOGY TO UTOPIA: THE STRUCTURE OF INTERNATIONAL LEGAL ARGUMENT 562 (2005).

[44] D. Kennedy, *The Politics of the Invisible College: International Governance and the Politics of Expertise*, 5 EUR. HUM. RTS. L. REV. 463–97 (2001); D. KENNEDY, A WORLD OF STRUGGLE: HOW POWER, LAW, AND EXPERTISE SHAPE GLOBAL POLITICAL ECONOMY 2 (2016); D. KENNEDY, THE DARK SIDES OF VIRTUE: REASSESSING INTERNATIONAL HUMANITARIANISM xvi (2004).

[45] J. BRAITHWAITE & P. DRAHOS, GLOBAL BUSINESS REGULATION (2000).

[46] P. DRAHOS & J. BRAITHWAITE, INFORMATION FEUDALISM: WHO OWNS THE INFORMATION ECONOMY? (2002), preface.

Acknowledging that there are 'black boxes' of knowledge about law, the task of
the next section, might be one first step.

D ACCESSING TRANSNATIONAL ENVIRONMENTAL LAW'S
'SECRET ARCHIVES'

The next section of the chapter looks to some concrete challenges in realizing
the Jessup-inspired ideal, a version of practice-informed, problem-addressing
transnational law. Jessup did not hesitate to acknowledge the gaps in public
and private international law nor the impediments to accessing information
contained in 'secret archives'.[47] He was not explicit about what those 'secret
archives' were but cited scientific knowledge and official security classifications as examples.[48] Applying the idea of 'secret archives' to the research
context of the contemporary transnational environmental law scholar,
I explore below four examples of 'black boxes' that limit access to knowledge.
They are far from an exhaustive list of problem areas for accessing rich and full
views of transnational legal problems. A more complete list might more
comprehensively target the geographic imbalances of the available data of
'global' environmental law, the consequences of language barriers (and
English-language defaults), search engine biases (and online-research
defaults), the obscuring of environmental issues most pressing to women,
the ways in which environmental terminology is complicated by disparate
meanings and the relative silence surrounding the place of indigenous law in
accounts of global environmental law processes.

Indeed, transnational environmental law presents a particularly rich venue
for observing such tensions up close. For scholars interested in environmental
problems, accessing the specialized knowledge of different regimes (trade,
investment, intellectual property, international criminal law) requires confronting immediate challenges. Fragmentation and the resulting limits of
'insider knowledge' make it harder to know what scholars fail to see and what
sources are 'hidden from view'.[49] The challenges of classifying various aspects
of 'global background law',[50] or 'fuzzy law',[51] that populate environmental law

---

[47] Jessup & Taubenfeld, *supra* note 14, at 363.
[48] *Id.*
[49] *See* N. Affolder, *Looking for Law in Unusual Places: Cross-Border Diffusion of Environmental
Norms*, 7:3 TRANSNAT'L ENVTL. L. 425–49 (2018).
[50] R. Michaels, *The UNIDROIT Principles as Global Background Law*, 19:4 UNIFORM L. REV.
643–68 (2014).
[51] O. PEREZ, *Fuzzy Law: A Theory of Quasi-legality, in* LAW AND THE NEW LOGICS 236 (P. Glenn
& L. Smith eds., 2017).

practice explain the allure of Jessup's transnational law terminology as a 'catch-all'.

I *The Partial Knowledge Base of Arbitration*

In transnational law scholarship, international arbitration (both investment arbitration and international commercial arbitration) has occupied a privileged place as providing precisely that 'larger storehouse of rules' that Jessup invoked. International arbitration is a familiar area of study for those explicitly adopting a transnational law lens in their work and well fits the practice-informed, problem-addressing, public–private divide jumping context set out by Jessup as transnational law's domain. Transnational environmental law scholars eager to capture the influence of these legal rules on environmental problems, though, remain stymied by the limits on access to information from and about arbitral processes.

Many scholarly works on arbitration treat transparency as a normative issue,[52] rather than focusing descriptively on what information is available and what remains off limits to the public and interested researchers. Scholars thus argue that while 'arbitral decision-making of yesteryear occurred in a virtual black box', '[t]oday the situation is quite different'.[53] This comment seems to include both international commercial arbitration and investor–state arbitration in its scope while the transparency issues at stake in each form of arbitration differ.[54] The cited improvements in the transparency of arbitral processes most often relate to reforms making 'the rules that regulate decision-making' more readily available to interested parties and to the growing number of voluntary and involuntary disclosures.[55] While these reforms may go some way to disclosing information on challenges to arbitrators and creating clearer guidance on arbitrator standards of conduct, they do little to increase the disclosure to interested scholars of what disputes are reaching arbitration.

---

[52] This scholarship traces back to the detailed case for the publication of arbitration awards made in J.D.M. LEW, *The Case for the Publication of Arbitration Awards, in* THE ART OF ARBITRATION 22–42 (J.C. Schultz & J. van den Berg eds., 1982); and T.E. Carbonneau, *Rendering Arbitral Awards with Reasons: The Elaboration of a Common Law of International Transactions*, 23:3 COLUM. J. TRANSNAT'L L. 579–614 (1985).

[53] C.A. Rogers, *Transparency in International Commercial Arbitration* 54 U. KAN. L. REV. 1301, 1312–13 (2006).

[54] Rogers usefully canvasses the multiple possible means of transparency. *Id.*

[55] *Id.* at 1313.

At the same time as scholars are reporting that more arbitral awards are being voluntarily published,[56] it is impossible to know what 'tip of the iceberg' these awards represent. Ginsburg notes that the subset of awards that are published represents 'an explicitly biased sample' as the International Chamber of Commerce, for example, seeks to publish 'particularly interesting or unusual awards'.[57] But for non-experts, it may be the 'uninteresting' and 'usual' awards that equally illuminate. It is easy to calculate that there is a large disparity between the sparse number of published awards and the documented caseload of arbitral institutions, which shows thousands of arbitrations taking place each year.[58]

For environmental law research, this offers many dead ends. While the attractiveness of arbitration as a venue for resolving environmental disputes is widely advertised,[59] it is challenging to discover how often arbitration clauses are used, how many environmental disputes (or commercial disputes that include environmental issues) ever reach an arbitral panel and if so with what results. This limits an awareness of how partial, or how representative, discussions of arbitral practices are when they draw on a small sample of reported cases. Further, as still little is known about the composition of the 'invisible college' of arbitrators,[60] the extent to which arbitrators possess, or are open to, specialized environmental and scientific knowledge remains unknown.

An added challenge emerges from the patterns of redaction common to arbitral reporting, which complicate searching environmental content, reducing carbon trading to 'services' and environmental goods to 'products'. In practice, the much-applauded reforms to disclosure that are in the interests of parties and voluntarily introduced might not be the same sort of reforms needed to produce more informed and robust knowledge. Interview-based studies help elucidate hidden aspects of arbitral practice, yet they run into some of the same problems of 'trust me' default visions of expertise described

---

[56] *See* D.M. Gruner, *Accounting for the Public Interest in International Arbitration: The Need for Procedural and Structural Reform*, 41:3 COLUM. J. TRANSNAT'L L. 923, 959 (2003) ('Today, several arbitral institutions, as well as independent publishers, have started to regularly publish arbitral awards.').

[57] T. Ginsburg, *The Culture of Arbitration*, 36 VAND. J. TRANSNAT'L L. 1335, 1340 (2003).

[58] Such data is reproduced in J. JEMIELNIAK, LEGAL INTERPRETATION IN INTERNATIONAL COMMERCIAL ARBITRATION 91 (2014).

[59] *Carbon Mission*, THE LAWYER (Oct. 28, 2009), https://www.thelawyer.com/issues/online/carbon-mission/.

[60] S.D. Franck et al., *The Diversity Challenge: Exploring the 'Invisible College' of Arbitration*, 53 COLUM. J. TRANSNAT'L L. 429–506 (2015) (offering a 'glimpse' of this college through disaggregating data on conference attendance).

above. The challenge then is not simply that knowledge about arbitration remains out of reach, but that it is difficult to know how little one knows.

II *Tracing Transplants*

Scholars alert to transnational environmental law's movements are increasingly attentive to the movement of environmental law ideas, models and forms across borders.[61] Discourses of diffusion, emphasizing and assuming environmental law's transferability, have become central to the way in which new environmental law ideas and approaches are developed and communicated.[62] Yet the tasks of tracing the movement of law and its underlying ideas are impeded by the many forces that obscure the processes by which transnational influences shape both the substance of legislative 'transplants' and legislative drafting processes.

For example, a 2017 Climate Legislation Study calculated that more than 1200 laws to curb climate change have now been passed, an increase from about sixty laws in place two decades ago.[63] Econometric research drawing on this data set of legislation points to the practice of international policy diffusion whereby the climate action a country undertakes is likely to depend on prior climate legislation by other countries.[64] While these assertions are made and justified by regressing climate legislation against the number of laws passed in all other countries in the sample, little analysis is made of the pressures shaping legislative form and content.[65] Such studies make valuable contributions to an understanding of the proliferation of climate laws, but they also point to the underlying methodological challenges implicit in trying to provide a comprehensive 'global' image of legislative activity, as well as a dynamic image of how law moves from place to place and why. Moreover, they reveal how hard it is to come up with a satisfactory definition of what counts as climate legislation.

---

[61] N. Affolder, *Contagious Environmental Lawmaking*, 31 J. ENVTL. L. 187–212, (2019); J.B. Wiener, *Something Borrowed for Something Blue: Legal Transplants and the Evolution of Global Environmental Law*, 27 ECOLOGY L.Q. 1295–372 (2001).

[62] For example, Peel and Osofsky contemplate existing rights-based judgments as offering a 'model or inspiration' for climate litigation decisions in other jurisdictions. J. Peel & H. Osofsky, *A Rights Turn in Climate Litigation*, 7 TRANSNAT'L ENVTL. L. 37, 37 (2018).

[63] M. NACHMANY, S. FANKHAUSER, J. SETZER & A. AVERCHENKOVA, GLOBAL TRENDS IN CLIMATE CHANGE LEGISLATION AND LITIGATION 4 (2017).

[64] S. Fankhauser, C. Gennaioli, & M. Collins, *Do International Factors Influence the Passage of Climate Change Legislation?* 16 CLIMATE POL'Y 318–31 (2016).

[65] A. Boute, *The Impossible Transplant of the EU Emissions Trading Scheme: The Challenge of Energy Market Regulation*, 6 TRANSNAT'L ENVTL. L. 59–85 (2017).

Attempts to trace diffusion of environmental law models contribute to understandings of global power dynamics and national influence. The EU's claimed position of climate leadership can thus be partially traced to its creation of models capable of transplantation elsewhere.[66] The EU's Emission Trading Scheme has served as a model for many countries looking to introduce the legal infrastructure necessary for domestic carbon markets. But it is a model that is proving challenging to export.[67] In other areas of transnational environmental law, accounts of 'borrowing' European law models for environmental legislation are equally easy to find[68] but largely unsystematic, and often reveal examples rather than 'thick description' of how these models were tailored for local needs. Rarely on offer is a view of how such one might adjust or fine-tune these universal or borrowed prescriptions to particular local contexts.[69] This gap reveals the larger challenge for environmental law research emerging from limited qualitative and quantitative data on the environmental law practices of non-OECD countries.[70]

These issues go further to the point that legislative drafting processes generally operate in a context of limited transparency and under a veil of secrecy. In many countries, the confidentiality of legislative drafting materials is protected through statutes.[71] This prevents a full understanding of the significance of transnational influences on the domestic enactment of

[66] K. Kulovesi, *Climate Change in the EU External Relations: Please Follow My Example (or I Might Force You to), in* THE EXTERNAL ENVIRONMENTAL POLICY OF THE EUROPEAN UNION: EU AND INTERNATIONAL LAW DIMENSIONS 115–48 (E. Morgera ed., 2012).

[67] Boute, *supra* note 65.

[68] Jörgens, for example, traces the influence of European concepts of sustainable development through 'diffusion' of global policies, documenting the key role of the World Bank. H. Jörgens, *Governance by Diffusion: Implementing Global Norms through Cross-National Imitation and Learning, in* GOVERNANCE FOR SUSTAINABLE DEVELOPMENT: THE CHALLENGE OF ADAPTING FORM TO FUNCTION 246, 269–71 (W. Lafferty ed., 2004). Scott's work on REACH discusses the influence of this EU on the development of US law, and specifically on the amendments to California's health and safety code. J. Scott, *From Brussels with Love: The Transatlantic Travels of European Law and the Chemistry of Regulatory Attraction*, 57 AM. J. COMP. L. 4897, 910–12.

[69] This despite a long history of recognition that the failure of decades of 'law and development' initiatives can be traced to a blindness to addressing localized contexts and challenges.

[70] For example, a recent book review of an edited environmental governance collection explains the dominant focus on the experience of OECD countries in this 'comparative work' as not due to the OECD countries' historic responsibility for climate change but rather due to the 'availability of data on these countries': J. Barandiaran, *Review of Duit, Andreas, Ed. 2014. State and Environment: The Comparative Study of Environmental Governance*, 16 GLOBAL ENVTL. POL. 108, 109 (2016).

[71] For example, provisions limit access to these materials for 90 years in New Zealand, 100 years in the Canadian province of Ontario and (with possible redactions) after 30 years in the United Kingdom. S. Tomlinson, *Public Access to Legislative Drafting Files*, 21 RECORDS MGMT. J. 28, 28, 33 (2011).

environmental legislation. The reality of such transnational influence must instead be gleaned from reports of the practice of drafting including either voluntary or mandatory consideration of international 'best practices',[72] reliance on foreign legislative drafting consultants,[73] the sponsorship of drafting initiatives by international financial institutions and international organizations,[74] 'study tours' of other countries to inform climate legislation,[75] job advertisements for international consultancy work on legislative drafting[76] and the curricula of international legislative drafting conferences[77] and graduate training programs[78]. Yet these sources still afford only a partial glimpse of such practices.

Authors who 'divulge' transnational influences and processes shaping their own legislative drafting experiences do so in the spirit of describing their work

---

[72] The Kenya Law Reform Commission's Guide to the Legislative Process in Kenya prescribes '[undertaking] comparative research to ensure that the draft legislative instrument benefits from international best practices' as a step in drafting bills. KENYA LAW REFORM COMMISSION, A GUIDE TO THE LEGISLATIVE PROCESS IN KENYA 51 (2015), http://www.klrc.go.ke/index.php/reports-and-publications/562-a-guide-to-the-legislative-process-in-kenya. Moldova's Law on Legislative Acts includes a similar provision requiring comparative analysis of the proposed bill with 'useful information contained in the legislation of other countries, and principles of main systems of the world applied': T. St. John & N. Bates, *Legislating for Drafting: The Moldavian Experience*, 30 STATUTE L. REV. 123, 125–26 (2009).

[73] Nain discusses Fiji's reliance on foreign legal drafters since the former colony gained independence. N. Nain, *Teaching Legislative Drafting: The Pacific Experience*, 1 INT'L J. LEGIS. DRAFTING & L. REFORM 28, 29 (2012).

[74] UNEP's Partnership for the Development of Environmental Law and Institutions in Africa has been influential in developing national environmental laws in Africa. E. Kasimbazi, *Application of International Standards in Drafting Environmental Legislation and Law Reform Projects: The African Experience*, 1 INT'L J. LEGIS. DRAFTING & L. REFORM 10–27 (2012). The Asian Development Bank has taken on similar roles in Asia including the reform of Chinese water pollution legislation, China's framework Environmental Protection Law, and Land Administration and Natural Resource legislation. ASIAN DEV. BANK, REFORM OF ENVIRONMENTAL AND LAND LEGISLATION IN THE PEOPLE'S REPUBLIC OF CHINA (2000).

[75] Stritih and Simonič comment on the 'study tour' of the UK undertaken by members of government and expert advisors tasked with producing Slovenia's climate change legislation. J. Stritih & B. Simonič, *Drafting a Climate Change Act: Lessons Learned*, 42 ENVTL. POL'Y & L. 46, 46 (2012).

[76] UN CAREERS, LEGISLATIVE DRAFTING OF THE CLIMATE CHANGE BILL, MBABANE, https://uncareer.net/ vacancy/legislative-drafting-climate-change-bill-consultancy-mbabane.

[77] *See, e.g.*, Fourth International Conference on Legislation and Law Reform, held at the World Bank in D.C. (Nov. 17–18, 2016), which included sessions on Legislative Drafting for Sustainable Development and the Importance of Drafting in Implementing Sustainable Development Goals. Available at https://ilegis.org/files/iLegis-2016-Agenda.pdf.

[78] Nagoya University School of Law advertises a programme in *Cross-Border Legal Institution Design*, the objective of which is to 'produce Asia-literate professionals who can design legal institutions for cross-border transplantation': Nagoya University, available at http://www.law.nagoya-u.ac.jp/~leading/en/index-e.html.

rather than through formalized research studies. The very few empirical studies of legislative drafting processes, such as Gluck and Bressman's interview-based analysis of US congressional practices, only confirms the methodological difficulties with gaining access to the relevant people to pierce a deep culture of confidentiality surrounding legislative drafting.[79]

III *Judges and 'the Project' of Environmental Law*

Interest in how legal norms travel has attempted to incorporate the insight that judges also travel, and their travel involves 'messy and diverse' processes of judicial interaction.[80] Judges clearly occupy a privileged place in legal analysis, yet thinking about judges as research subjects exposes still more black boxes. A wide view of transnational lawmaking invites questions about judicial practices well beyond written court decisions. These questions transcend current interest in 'what judges do', which tends to centre around issues of judicial 'independence', framing 'extrajudicial' activities as transgressions.[81] They move analysis beyond the more easily traceable practices of explicit trans-judicial borrowing reflected in the use of foreign law materials in domestic courts.

Appreciating the multifaceted dimensions of the professional lives of judges brings into view different dimensions of judicial work, including speaking, writing and advocacy, some of which will be directly related to the judicial function (for example, advocating for specialized tribunals and the form they should take), some not. Scholars are adopting diverse strategies for attempting to access the 'black box' of judicial lives outside of their courtrooms. Kendall and Sorkin traced financial disclosures to track the sponsors and funders of private judicial conferences that 'represent a veiled attempt to lobby the judiciary under the guise of judicial education'.[82] A report on the feasibility and structure of a specialized environmental court for England and Wales revealed the involvement of a range of judges from other

---

[79] A.R. Gluck & L.S. Bressman, *Statutory Interpretation from the Inside – An Empirical Study of Congressional Drafting, Delegation, and the Canons: Part I*, 65:5 STAN. L. REV. 901, 922 (2013) ('congressional staffers are a notoriously difficult population to study, both because of the difficulty of identifying the relevant staffers and also because of the strong culture of confidentiality and the fear of "leaks" that permeates Congress'.)

[80] A.M. Slaughter, *Judicial Globalization*, 40:4 VA. J. INT'L L. 1103, 1104 (2000).

[81] J.C. Blue, *A Well-Tuned Cymbal? Extrajudicial Political Activity*, 18 GEO. J. LEGAL ETHICS 1–63 (2004).

[82] D.T. Kendall & E. Sorkin, *Nothing for Free: How Private Judicial Seminars are Undermining Environmental Protections and Breaking the Public's Trust*, 25 HARV. ENVTL. L. REV. 405, 405 (2001).

jurisdictions.[83] Environmental law perhaps offers a particularly vivid exposure to the 'project' of environmental protection motivating a select group of judges who have taken on openly public advocacy roles speaking in conferences, publishing scholarship and writing judicial opinions to advance particular environmental law reforms and projects.[84]

Little is, however, systematically known about environmental law judges' efforts to influence law and policy as opinion leaders, network builders, publicists and law reform advocates – efforts referred to as off-bench judicial mobilization[85] – or about judicial practices of off-bench resistance.[86] A strong sense of the common 'project' of environmental protection being advanced through the judiciary can be gleaned from articles like Lord Carnwath's 'world tour'[87] of exceptional environmental law judges and his celebration of the crucial role that 'judges for the environment' have to play, both individually and collectively.[88] It is equally evident from the work and choice of issue focus of judicial networks, such as the ASEAN Chief Justices' Roundtable on the Environment.[89]

Biographies and autobiographies offer additional and valuable glimpses of the people who animate the projects of transnational environmental law. Judge Jessup's refusal to clinically separate public and private international law is rendered more palpable from an understanding of his prior legal practice that included work as a legal adviser to the governments of foreign states at the same time as representing a private non-governmental organization.[90] While still rare, examples of 'life writing' by and about judges, as well as

[83] M. GRANT, ENVIRONMENTAL COURT PROJECT: FINAL REPORT xviii–xix (2000).

[84] *See, e.g.,* Brian Preston, *Benefits of Judicial Specialization in Environmental Law: The Land and Environment Court of New South Wales as a Case Study,* 29 PACE ENVTL. L. REV. 396–440 (2012); Antonio Herman Benjamin, We, *the Judges, and the Environment,* 29 PACE ENVTL. L. REV. 582–91 (2012).

[85] O. Bakiner, *Judges Discover Politics: Sources of Judges' Off-Bench Mobilization in Turkey,* 4:1 J. L. & CTS. 131–57 (2016).

[86] A. Trochev & R. Ellett, *Judges and Their Allies: Rethinking Judicial Autonomy through the Prism of Off-Bench Resistance,* 2 J. L. & CTS. 67–91 (2014).

[87] R. Carnwath, *Judges and the Common Laws of the Environment – At Home and Abroad,* 26 J. ENVTL L. 177, 182 (2014).

[88] R. Carnwath, *Judges for the Environment: We Have a Crucial Role to Play,* GUARDIAN (June 22, 2012), https://www.theguardian.com/law/2012/jun/22/judges-environment-lord-carnwath-rio.

[89] See R. Pepper, *The Role of Judicial Networking in Information Sharing in Promoting and Implementing Environmental Law,* NSW LAND AND ENVIRONMENT COURT (Nov. 12, 2016), http://www.lec.justice.nsw.gov.au/Documents/Speeches%20and%20Papers/PepperJ/PepperJ%20Judicial%20Networking%20in%20Promoting%20Mutual%20Assistance.pdf.

[90] PHILIP C. JESSUP'S TRANSNATIONAL LAW REVISITED: ON THE OCCASION OF THE 50TH ANNIVERSARY OF ITS PUBLICATION 12 (C. Tietje, A. Brouder & K. Nowrot eds., 2006).

about international law scholars and practitioners, provide one route into this particular black box of transnational law practice.[91]

IV *The Private Lives of Contractual Texts*

A final disparity I draw attention to here is that which exists between growing scholarly interest in exploring the significance of global value chains as aspects of environmental governance and the still limited knowledge base of contracting upon which this research is based. Environmental law is heavily implicated in global value chains and multiple and intersecting sources of law surround and engage with supply chain contracts.[92] Yet a full scholarly view of how these legal obligations move across time and space through contractual practices is hampered by the challenge of accessing private contractual texts.[93] This is not a problem of shallow or unambitious scholarly efforts. It is a problem of the limited access to 'private' sources of transnational law.

In a variety of fields, scholars see great potential in contracts as accountability mechanisms for private actors operating in international legal spaces.[94] Yet scholarship and commentary on global value chains may emerge from a limited view of the actual content of these contracts. Scholars attempt to find a variety of ways around the problem of the 'black box' of contractual texts. They may base their analysis on existing knowledge of global value chains, rather than the contracts that comprise those chains.[95] They may

---

[91] *See, e.g.*, Judge Weeramantry's writings. C.G. WEERAMANTRY, TREAD LIGHTLY ON THE EARTH: RELIGION, THE ENVIRONMENT AND THE HUMAN FUTURE (2009). Attempts to present fuller practice-reflecting views of international law emerge from recent collections, including THE LAW OF INTERNATIONAL LAWYERS: READING MARTTI KOSKENNIEMI (W. Werner, M. de Hoon & A. Galan eds., 2017); INTERNATIONAL LAW AS A PROFESSION (J. d'Aspremont, T. Gazzini, A. Nolkaemper & W. Werner eds., 2017).

[92] L.C. Backer, *Are Supply Chains Transnational Legal Orders? What We Can Learn from the Rana Plaza Factory Collapse*, 1 UC IRVINE J. INT'L, TRANSNAT'L & COMP. L. 11–66 (2015).

[93] For a more extensive discussion of the challenge of accessing reliable information about contracting practices, see Affolder, *supra* note 49.

[94] Dickinson, whose scholarship looks at private military contracts, is enthusiastic about the potential of contracts governments enter into with non-state actors to include provisions that would help to create both standards of behaviour, performance benchmarks and a means of providing some measure for public accountability. She acknowledges that 'in many cases it is impossible for the public or a watchdog group even to obtain the text of the contracts, either because government officials have kept them secret for security reasons or because the contractors have exercised what is essentially a veto, under the Freedom of Information Act (FOIA), for certain types of commercial information'. L. Dickinson, *Public Law Values in a Privatized World*, 31 YALE J. INT'L L. 383, 386, 402 (2006).

[95] K.B. Sobel-Read, *Global Value Chains: A Framework for Analysis*, 5 TRANSNAT'L LEGAL THEORY 364–407 (2014).

analyse contracting practices from standard form contracts that are publicly available on corporate websites.[96] Or they may ground their analysis in interviews of supply chain participants rather than textual review of the contracts themselves.[97] Scholars also may secure access to a select handful of contractual examples[98] or offer a deep analysis based on a single example[99] or rely on codes of conduct as a proxy for examining contracts.[100] This work is enriched by explicit acknowledgment of 'the dense veil of confidentiality that often accompanies outsourcing' and the significant selection biases that prevent scholarship from being generalizable to the broader population of outsourcing deals.[101]

Further heroic attempts to provide a fuller view of contracting practices, and texts, emerge from the efforts of scholars to use their access as in-house counsel to comment on contractual forms[102] and from NGOs campaigning for greater transparency and contractual disclosure in natural resource project settings.[103] In some situations, the selective visibility of contracts might be mitigated by access to other sources, such as the data emerging from interviews of managerial motivations to adopt CSR measures[104] and from

[96] K.P. Mitkidis, *Using Private Contracts for Climate Change Mitigation*, 2 GRONINGEN J. INT'L L. 54, 71 (2014).

[97] R.A. Mulhall & J.R. Bryson, *The Energy Hot Potato and Governance of Value Chains: Power, Risk, and Organizational Adjustment in Intermediate Manufacturing Firms*, 89 ECON. GEOGRAPHY 395, 397–98 (2013).

[98] F. Cafaggi & P. Iamiceli, *Inter-firm Networks in the European Wine Industry*, 19 EUI WORKING PAPERS 13 (2010); R.J. Gilson, C.F. Sabel & R.E. Scott, *Contracting for Innovation: Vertical Disintegration and Interfirm Collaboration*, 109 COLUM. L. REV. 431, 458–71 (2009).

[99] D. Danielsen, *How Corporations Govern: Taking Corporate Power Seriously in Transnational Regulation and Governance*, 46 HARV. INT'L L.J. 411–25 (2005).

[100] Lin analyses codes of conduct as a proxy for actual contracts, noting that 'contracts between private entities are usually confidential'. L.W. Lin, *Legal Transplants through Private Contracting: Codes of Vendor Conduct in Global Supply Chains as an Example*, 57 AM. J. COMP. L. 711, 722 (2009).

[101] G.S. Geis, *An Empirical Examination of Business Outsourcing Transactions*, 96 VA. L. REV., 241, 254, 260 (2010).

[102] *See, e.g.*, Danielsen, *supra* note 99, at 416.

[103] *See, e.g.*, the confidentiality clause examples in P. ROSENBLUM & S. MAPLES, CONTRACTS CONFIDENTIAL: ENDING SECRET DEALS IN THE EXTRACTIVE INDUSTRIES 65–85 (2009); Amnesty International's work accessing contractual documents for the Baku–Tbilisi–Ceyhan and Chad–Cameroon pipelines: AMNESTY INTERNATIONAL, HUMAN RIGHTS ON THE LINE: THE BAKU-TBILISI-CEYHAN PIPELINE PROJECT (2003); AMNESTY INTERNATIONAL, CONTRACTING OUT OF HUMAN RIGHTS: THE CHAD-CAMEROON PIPELINE PROJECT (2005). Global Witness's work on the Mittal Steel investment contract in Liberia: GLOBAL WITNESS, HEAVY MITTAL? A STATE WITHIN A STATE: THE INEQUITABLE MINERAL DEVELOPMENT AGREEMENT BETWEEN THE GOVERNMENT OF LIBERIA AND MITTAL STEEL HOLDINGS (2006).

[104] B. Sheehy, *Understanding CSR: An Empirical Study of Private Self-Regulation*, 32:2 MONASH L. REV. 103–27 (2012).

ethnographic accounts of corporate cultures.[105] But the generalizability of these 'partial views' is questionable. The extent of the practical problem of access to private contracts is highlighted in contexts such as that of cobalt mining in the Democratic Republic of the Congo, where corporations allege that contractual measures guarantee their compliance with human rights standards yet watchdogs are unable to access these contracts or measure their implementation.[106]

Knowledge of individual, localized contracts can also obscure another reality that only meta-analysis might unveil, the extent to which seemingly customized deals incorporate pressure for standardization, resulting in the use of standard templates rather than highly unique contractual terms.[107] Thus, the documentary lens of the deal can 'prevent people from realizing that deals are not as unique and creative as advertised'.[108] Deal documents that might appear as 'the embodiment of choices' in another light might be seen as composed almost entirely of recycled and recyclable parts.[109]

The 'black boxes' I discuss here were not ones that likely troubled Jessup. He had his own. By acknowledging that 'secret archives' do exist and that there is a 'larger storehouse of rules' worth accessing, Jessup issued an open invitation to continue to think about what legal knowledge is not satisfactorily captured in existing understandings of private and public international law. Accessing knowledge about law and about legal knowledge that operates in any kind of global space is far from straightforward. It points to the complexity of the task facing not only lawyers and legal scholars but many others who are 'beginning to ask how precisely can any idea be understood "in context" if context is now defined to encompass intercontinental communications, multilingual communities, or the expansion of world systems'.[110]

---

[105] M. WELKER, ENACTING THE CORPORATION: AN AMERICA MINING FIRM IN POST-AUTHORITARIAN INDONESIA (2014).

[106] AMNESTY INTERNATIONAL, 'THIS IS WHAT WE DIE FOR': HUMAN RIGHTS ABUSES IN THE DEMOCRATIC REPUBLIC OF THE CONGO POWER THE GLOBAL TRADE IN COBALT 64 (2016).

[107] On the pressures to standardize procurement and finance processes in P3 deals and how this leads to the return of standard templates, *see* M. Valverde, F. Johns & J. Raso, *Governing Infrastructure in the Age of the 'Art of the Deal': Logics of Governance and Scales of Visibility*, 41:S1 POLAR: POL. & LEGAL ANTHROPOLOGY REV. 118–32 (2018).

[108] *Id.* at 120.

[109] *Id.* at 124.

[110] D. Armitage, *The International Turn in Intellectual History, in* RETHINKING MODERN EUROPEAN INTELLECTUAL HISTORY 232, 244 (D.M. McMahon & S. Moyn eds., 2013).

E CONCLUSION: FROM SEEN/UNSEEN TO KNOWN/UNKNOWABLE

As this collection of essays celebrating the sixtieth anniversary of Jessup's Storrs Lecture reveals, transnational law scholarship is full of exciting and far-reaching initiatives to *make visible* aspects of lawmaking that narrowly targeted engagements with state-based law might miss. This chapter's perhaps overly sober comments on methodology are not designed to take away from the larger celebration of the depth and breadth of new knowledge of transnational processes, and of law, that has emerged, inspired by Jessup's own writing.

Two particular dimensions of transnational law serve as the focal points for this chapter. The first is transnational law's preoccupation with *visibility*, a concern that permeates attempts to transcend narrow conceptions of law, law's sources and its relevant actors. The second is the privileged place that transnational law reserves for *practice*. On both fronts, there is an opportunity for scholars to be much more forthcoming in articulating how a transnational law approach might illuminate new visions of law and, in so doing, how it might employ practice. I would suggest that there is much low-hanging fruit here. The methodological bases for many practice-based insights are easily known. They are just rarely written down. The solution may be sometimes as simple as overcoming a reluctance to situate ourselves and our professional lives in our texts.

It is less obvious how to overcome the challenges of selective vision and partial knowledge. Indeed, this chapter's foray into some of the 'black boxes' that complicate efforts to understand transnational environmental lawmaking reveals that, despite best efforts, some knowledge of law and legal processes remains off-limits. But scholars are finding new and creative ways to access sources and gain forbidden knowledge, as this chapter suggests. They are successfully breaking into transnational law's 'black boxes'. To conclude, as did Jessup sixty years ago, there is still work for the 'headlong scholar' to go where the 'foreign offices, the legislatures, and the courts' fear to tread.[111]

---

[111] JESSUP, *supra* note 1, at 113.

16

The *Cri de Jessup* Sixty Years Later

Transnational Law's Intangible Objects and Abstracted Frameworks

LARRY CATÁ BACKER[*]

We have learned that history is something that takes no notice whatever of our expectations.[1]

Revolutionaries learn from one another, even if they aim for different goals.[2]

A JESSUP'S *CRI DE VALMY*

In 2016 the Dickson Poon School of Law of King's College London, its Transnational Law Institute and its inaugural director, my friend and colleague Peer Zumbansen, brought together a group of scholars on the occasion of the institute's first two years of successful operation.[3] The event concluded with an international conference, organized by the Transnational Law Institute, to commemorate the sixtieth anniversary of the publication of Philip Jessup's landmark study *Transnational Law*.[4] This chapter grew out of the challenge at the core of that conference – to again take up Jessup's *cri de guerre* or, better put, its *cri de Valmy* from which one could date a new era in the history of the world.[5] This chapter takes up that challenge at yet another

---

[*]   My thanks to Miaoqiang Dai (SIA MIA expected May 2019) and Bethany Salgado (SIA MIA expected May 2020) for their excellent research assistance on this project.

[1]   OSWALD SPENGLER, MAN AND TECHNICS: A CONTRIBUTION TO A PHILOSOPHY OF LIFE (Alfred A. Knopf 1963) (1932).

[2]   Ralf Michaels, *The New European Choice of Law Revolution*, 82 TUL. L. REV. 1607, 1644 (2008).

[3]   Symposium, *Transnational Law: What's in a Name?*, held Apr. 27, 2016, to celebrate the inauguration of the Transnational Law Institute, https://www.kcl.ac.uk/law/newsevents/newsrecords/tli/transnational-law-whats-in-a-name?TaxonomyKey=0/1/2/17.

[4]   PHILIP C. JESSUP, TRANSNATIONAL LAW (1956).

[5]   Georges Gusdorf, *Le Cri de Valmy*, 45 COMMUNICATIONS 117–55 (1987) ("Image d'Epinal. En haut de la colline, devant le moulin qui la couronne, le général Kellermann, chapeau brandi à la pointe du sabre, se dresse sur ses étriers, et de toute la force de sa voix crie: 'Vive la nation!'

386

transitional moment in history but one that is no longer comfortably well nestled within an orthodox consensus of a trajectory of development of regulatory orders[6] that have threatened old international law and international relations orthodoxies.[7] Long past, it seems, are the days where the community of scholars wholeheartedly believed in the promise of concepts such as "global governance" or even of the state and its international system as the apex of organized legitimate political power.[8] Jessup reminds us still, however, of the power of that old consensus even in its supposed decline.[9]

Sixty years ago, the original *cri de Jessup* gave the transnational *within* law the means to distinguish itself from other legal orders.[10] It gave form to what might have morphed into a liberation movement of sorts from orthodoxy in law,[11] inspiring a generation of those who followed Jessup to advance this globalizing extrasovereign movement against the colonialism and imperialism of statist legal orthodoxy.[12] Yet even sixty years after the *cri de Jessup*, the transnational remains tied from its moorings in ancient conceptions of nation, of enterprise, and of law. Sixty years after Jessup's first effort at liberation, is it still possible to be driven by Jessup's transnational ululations?

This contribution is divided into three sections. The starting point also a point of departure. Section B's "Transnational Law as Manifesto" explores the contemporary approach to transnational law and its more radical possibilities.

Cri aussitôt repris par la masse des troupes rangées en bataille derrière le commandant en chef. En ce 20 septembre 1792, le cri de Valmy possède une valeur emblématique si puissante que Goethe, correspondant de guerre dans l'armée d'en face et témoin de l'incident, croit pouvoir dater de ce moment une nouvelle ère dans l'histoire du monde." *Id.* 155).

[6] Larry Catá Backer, *Economic Globalization Ascendant: Four Perspectives on the Emerging Ideology of the State in the New Global Order*, 17 BERKELEY LA RAZA L.J. 141 (2006).

[7] Adam Irish, Charlotte Ku & Paul F. Diehl, *Bridging the International Law-International Relations Divide: Taking Stock of Progress*, 41 GA. J. INT'L & COMP. L. 357–88 (2013).

[8] Consider, for example, the arc of orthodoxy from WESTEL W. WILLOUGHBY, THE FUNDAMENTAL CONCEPTS OF PUBLIC LAW (1924) to JOSÉ E. ALVAREZ, INTERNATIONAL ORGANIZATIONS AS LAW-MAKERS (2006).

[9] Reza Dibadj, *Panglossian Transnationalism*, 44 STAN. J. INT'L L. 253 (2008).

[10] GRALF-PETER CALLIESS & PEER ZUMBANSEN, ROUGH CONSENSUS AND RUNNING CODE: A THEORY OF TRANSNATIONAL PRIVATE LAW (2010); TRANSNATIONAL LEGAL ORDERING AND STATE CHANGE (Gregory Shaffer ed., 2013).

[11] Larry Catá Backer, *The Emerging Normative Structures of Transnational Law: Non-state Enterprises in Polycentric Asymmetric Global Orders*, 31 BYU J. PUB. L. 1 (2016).

[12] Lawrence M. Friedman, *Borders: On the Emerging Sociology of Transnational Law*, 32 STAN. J. INT'L L. 65 (1996). Yet it is important to understand subtext; law, like other social systems, is subject to the dynamics of dependencies on a metropolitan center. *See* FRANTZ FANON, BLACK SKIN, WHITE MASKS (Charles Lam Markmann trans., Grove Press, 1967) (1952). *Cf.* Martin T. Berger, *Decolonisation, Modernisation and Nation-Building: Political Development Theory and the Appeal of Communism in Southeast Asia, 1945–1975*, 34 J. SE. ASIAN STUD. 421–48 (2003).

These possibilities are radical not in the sense of requiring a substantial break with the past but in the sense of suggesting the ways in which Jessup's vision ultimately requires a shifting of perspectives about the relationship of law to the state, the state to the societal sphere, and both to transnational law and the multinational enterprise. That potential for shifting vision is then examined in the two sections that follow.

Section C, "Jessup's Big Bang and Beyond," starts with Jessup's core premise – that the transnational is situational, ad hoc nature, and residual, in the sense that the transnational is what is left when no traditional legal order is available – and then moves beyond it.[13] Moving beyond becomes a greater challenge when Jessup's situationalism has itself spawned an important and influential set of templates. These approaches have substantially advanced Jessup's transnational project with great fidelity to Jessup's situational and ad hoc approach. But it is also confined by Jessup's residualism, one that assumes that the transnational remains firmly anchored to the state and its legal regimes.[14] The power of this template and its multiple current manifestations is particularly acute when speaking to the transnational enterprise.

The last section, "From Transnational Law to the Law of Transnational Spaces," considers the parallel development of the problem of transnational law and of the transnational enterprise. To that end, it applies an actor-network (norm) process framework[15] inward within and to the enterprise. Like

---

[13] The residuary ad hoc situationalism inherent in classical transnationalism echoes the traditional cultures of equity within which Jessup learned his trade. *Cf.* Stephen N. Subrin, *How Equity Conquered Common Law: The Federal Rules of Civil Procedure in Historical Perspective*, 135 U. PA. L. REV. 909 (1986).

[14] One understands this in the way that Maitland, for example, understood the way that equity remained tied to the structures and sensibilities of common law and ecclesiastical practice as it developed as a residuary well of justice. FREDERIC W. MAITLAND, EQUITY, ALSO THE FORMS OF ACTION AT COMMON LAW (1909).

[15] This framework has strong connection not merely to legal process, Adriana Espinosa Bonilla, *Frames y prácticas discursivas entre Estado y poblaciones negras en Colombia: Racismo estructural y derechos humanos*, 78 REVISTA HUMANÍSTICA 308–30 (2014). It also has resonance to origins within the sociology of technology. *See, e.g.*, John Steen, *Actor-Network Theory and the Dilemma of the Resource Concept in Strategic Management*, 26 SCANDINAVIAN J. MGMT. 324–31 (2010). And, to my mind, it connects to an action-norm process approach at the heart of contemporary transnational law discourse. Calliess and Zumbansen approach this convergence quite neatly in the construction of the "rough consensus running code" model "as a methodological approach top productively unfold the dramatic paradox which haunts all of transnational law." CALLIESS & ZUMBANSEN, supra note 10, at 134. These notions are more specifically developed in Peer Zumbansen, *Defining the Space of Transnational Law: Legal Theory, Global Governance, and Legal Pluralism*, 21 TRANSNAT'L L. & CONTEMP. PROBS. 305, 308 (2012) are the subject of the discussion *infra* section D. *Cf.* Elinor Ostrom, *Collective Action and the Evolution of Social Norms*, 14 J. ECON. PERSP. 137–58 (2000).

transnational law itself, the transnational (business) enterprise under this framework might be simultaneously assumed to be an object external to law, an autonomous system internalizing framework for law and as a reconstitution of production chains and the object of those chains themselves. That, in turn, suggests a progression from the most orthodox theoretical foundation (and the one most compatible with the current consensus on framing transnational law) to the least conventional perspective. It ends by suggesting that while the development of transnational law and the transnational enterprise have come very far, neither has moved very much from the conceptual orbit of an ideology that conflates law and the state. Both transnational law, as a governance order, and the transnational enterprise, as a management order, remain at the margins of an ideology the core object of which is to protect the integrity of a system that preserves an identity between state and law and that sees in both transnational law and the transnational enterprise a means of filling gaps. Both transnational law and enterprise serve as a complement to domestic legal orders and its territorial boundaries. They are the embodiment for the law and space of the "in-between" and absent the reorientation of perspective suggested in the opening section will remain at the margins of law and institutional governance.

B TRANSNATIONAL LAW AS MANIFESTO

There is a certain ritual in discussions of transnational law.[16] This ritual is built on anxiety to remain faithful to the group feelings (*assabiyah*)[17] that define fields of human activity, in this case the contemporary expression of the ancient ideological structures of "law-through-the-state."[18] That is, the ritual requires situating the transnational within law and law within the state.[19] It is the essence of the ritual to produce a revelation, to conduct a divination (through the traditional rituals of academic knowledge production) about transnational *law* by contriving a connection to or a derivation from out of

---

[16] *Cf.* OSCAR G. CHASE, LAW, CULTURE, AND RITUAL: DISPUTING SYSTEMS IN CROSS-CULTURAL CONTEXT (2005), 30–45; ERIC A. FELDMAN, THE RITUAL OF RIGHTS IN JAPAN 141–63 (2000); Richard G. Dillon, *Ritual Resolution in Meta-legal Process*, 15 ETHNOLOGY 287–99 (1976).

[17] ABD AL-RAHMAN IBN KHALDUN, THE MUQADDIMAH: AN INTRODUCTION TO HISTORY (Franz Rosenthal trans., Princeton Classics abridged ed. 2015).

[18] Harold Hongyu Koh, *Why Transnational Law Matters*, 24 PENN ST. INT'L L. REV. 745 (2005–2006); *cf.* Sally Engle Merry, *New Legal Realism and the Ethnography of Transnational Law*, 31:4 LAW & SOC. INQUIRY 975–95 (2006).

[19] Larry Catá Backer, *Are Supply Chains Transnational Legal Orders? What We Can Learn from the Rana Plaza Factory Building Collapse*, 1 UC IRVINE J. INT'L, TRANSNAT'L & COMP. L. 11–65 (2016).

what now passes for the entirety of the reality that is orthodox "law."[20]
Likewise, rituals produce an ordering of legal realms that mimic those of the
law-through-state systems through which connection is established and
legitimacy asserted. It is not for nothing that one sees in the constitutionalization of the enterprise the ritualization of the legal-political ordering of the
state.[21] Through these rituals almost anything is possible,[22] as long as one does
not stray too far.[23] I am a great advocate of ritual;[24] it is a useful performance
and affirmance of a necessary orthodoxy that separates society from its natural
state.[25] But I mean to invoke a quite different orthodoxy: to that end I want to
invert the conventional ritual to situate law and the state *within* the transnational.[26] The orthodox legalities of states (including the laws of their
political apparatus) are necessarily delegated from and must be understood

[20] Craig M. Scott, *"Transnational Law" as Proto Concept: Three Concepts*, 10 GERMAN L.J. 859–76 (2009).

[21] Peer Zumbansen, *The Incurable Constitutional Itch: Transnational Private Regulatory Governance and the Woes of Legitimacy, in* NEGOTIATING STATE AND NON-STATE LAW: THE CHALLENGE OF GLOBAL AND LOCAL LEGAL PLURALISM 83–110 (Michael Helfand ed., 2015); Larry Catá Backer, *Transnational Corporations' Outward Expression of Inward Self-Constitution: The Enforcement of Human Rights by Apple, Inc.*, 20 IND. J. GLOBAL LEGAL STUD. 805–79 (2013).

[22] Gunther Teubner, *"Global Bukowina": Legal Pluralism in the World Society, in* GLOBAL LAW WITHOUT A STATE (Gunther Teubner ed., 1997); Peer Zumbansen, *Transnational Law, Evolving, in* ELGAR ENCYCLOPEDIA OF COMPARATIVE LAW 899 (Jan Smits ed., 2d ed, 2012).

[23] PAUL SCHIFF BERMAN,GLOBAL LEGAL PLURALISM: A JURISPRUDENCE OF LAW BEYOND BORDERS (2012), 141–94; A. Claire Cutler, *Legal Pluralism as the "Common Sense" of Transnational Capitalism*, 3 OÑATI SOCIO-LEGAL SERIES 719–40 (2013). It is in that that plural law may not stray far from the shadow of the state nor from the forms of the law, that one might read in a more constrained way efforts to conceive of a grand theory of pluralist jurisprudence "involves the recognition of non-state law in a way that is independent of both the agency and the authority of states." NICOLE ROUGHAN & ANDREW HALPIN, *Introduction, in* IN PURSUIT OF PLURALIST JURISPRUDENCE 3 (Nicole Roughan & Andrew Halpin ed., 2017). The rituals of transnational law require even that independence to be measured against and to proceed from the performance of law within the state and its internal and external instrumentalities.

[24] Larry Catá Backer, *Emasculated Men, Effeminate Law in the United States, Zimbabwe and Malaysia*, 17 YALE J.L. & FEMINISM 1 (2005); Larry Catá Backer, *Retaining Judicial Authority: A Preliminary Inquiry on the Dominion of Judges*, 12 WM. & MARY BILL OF RIGHTS J. 117 (2003); Larry Catá Backer, *Chroniclers in the Field of Cultural Production: Interpretive Conversations Between Courts and Culture*, 20 B.C. THIRD WORLD L.J. 291 (2000); Larry Catá Backer, *Inventing a "Homosexual" for Constitutional Theory: Sodomy Narrative and Antipathy in U.S. and British Courts*, 71 TUL. L. REV. 529 (1996).

[25] A. John Simmons, *Locke's State of Nature*, 17 POL. THEORY 449–70 (1989). *See also* Edward Craig, *Knowledge and the State of Nature*, 183 REVUE PHILOSOPHIQUE DE LA FRANCE ET DE L'ETRANGER 620–21 (1990); BEATE JAHN, THE CULTURAL CONSTRUCTION OF INTERNATIONAL RELATIONS: THE INVENTION OF THE STATE OF NATURE (2000).

[26] DETLEF VON DANIELS, THE CONCEPT OF LAW FROM A TRANSNATIONAL PERSPECTIVE 169–81 (2010) (with a focus on linkages).

against the great principles of transnational law – that is the revolutionary
revaluation of values[27] emerging sixty years on from the *cri de Jessup*.

To situate law and the state within the transnational, it is necessary to start
with law within the state in order to embed it within a more authoritative and
broader context.[28] That exercise might most fruitfully be undertaken in the
classroom rather than in the more abstract spaces traditionally devoted to the
production of knowledge.[29] When I taught a course called Introduction to US
Law and Legal Systems,[30] I usually started with the fundamental question of
the character of law. The object was not to produce an answer to an intractable problem of legal philosophy (the familiar spectrum from "nothing is law
if everything is" to the irrelevance of precisely drawn legal categories)[31] but
rather to begin a process of detaching the concept of law from the concept of
the state. That process of detachment leads the class to a consideration of law's
fundamental normative principles rather than its attachment to an apparatus

---

[27] This is a task that requires both values and their revaluation. "Whatever has value in the present
world has it not in itself, according to its nature – nature is always value-less – but has rather
been given, granted value." FRIEDRICH NIETZSCHE, THE GAY SCIENCE 301 (Bernard Williams
ed., Josefine Nauckhoff & Adrian del Caro trans., Cambridge Univ. Press 2001). For the
hierarchy- and values-obsessed elites in the West, who have embedded legal hierarchies as the
essential foundational premise of law (*cf.* Dinah Shelton, *Normative Hierarchy in International
Law*, 100 AM. J. INT'L L. 291–323 (2006)), a revaluation of values takes as the starting point of
their valuation – the state and its attached legal hierarchies at the apex of which are
constitutional orders (and for the more "progressive among them perhaps also *jus cogens* and
assorted other hierarchically arranged international norms"). These are reordered to suit the
times. Here one is confronted with a variation of Deleuze's notion of revaluation's core as
"change and reversal in the element from the which the value of values derives." GILLES
DELEUZE, NIETZSCHE & PHILOSOPHY 163 (Hugh Tomlinson trans., Columbia Univ. Press
2006). That revaluation has as its starting point the relational axis of law, state, and what we
have come to call the transnational (now understood as the principles for ordering polycentric
systems as well as the core normative principles of that system itself). "For it may be doubted,
firstly, whether antitheses exist at all; and secondly, whether the popular valuations and
antitheses of value upon which metaphysicians have set their seal, are not perhaps merely
superficial estimates, merely provisional perspectives, besides being probably made from some
corner, perhaps from below – 'frog perspectives,' as it were, to borrow an expression current
among painters." FRIEDRICH NIETZSCHE, BEYOND GOOD AND EVIL: A PRELUDE TO A
PHILOSOPHY OF THE FUTURE ch. 1, ¶ 2 (Helen Zimmern trans., 2003) (1886) (Project
Gutenberg ebook) [hereinafter NIETZSCHE, BEYOND GOOD AND EVIL].

[28] LARRY CATÁ BACKER, *Governance without Government: An Overview, in* BEYOND
TERRITORIALITY: TRANSNATIONAL LEGAL AUTHORITY IN AN AGE OF GLOBALIZATION 87–123
(Günther Handl, Joachim Zekoll & Peer Zumbansen eds., 2012).

[29] *Cf.* PAULO FREIRE, PEDAGOGY OF THE OPPRESSED (Continuum, 1993) (1968).

[30] From a book of materials to be published as LARRY CATÁ BACKER, ELEMENTS OF LAW AND THE
UNITED STATES LEGAL SYSTEM (forthcoming 2019).

[31] RALF MICHAELS, *Law beyond the State, in* INTRODUCTION TO LAW AND SOCIAL THEORY (Reza
Banakar & Max Travers eds., 2d ed. 2013).

of production.[32] Let's call these principles a cluster of normative values around a concept of justice, along with its core process values centering on principles of certainty and predictability.[33]

But quickly we come to understand justice and process as relational and contextual. Justice is understood in relation to the values of the community, which would bind itself by a set of values, while process would be understood as just or fair in the context of the particular transaction or occurrence to which it relates. These relational and contextual elements are well in evidence in the formative sources of the great legal systems of global civilization. Justinian's Institutes, for example, speak to justice as the systematization of the core principle of giving everyone their due.[34] Marxist–Leninist systems speak to justice as bound up in the societal movement toward the establishment of a communist society.[35] Religions speak to justice as a relational connection to a divine or natural source whose command or essence incarnates the principle.[36] Even the most rigid system takes as its starting point a relation between ideal and the realities of the communities to which it is directed or from which it arises.[37]

All of these points can and have been contested by orthodox establishments, and they form part of a lively debate that appears to be going both nowhere, for those in the fruitless search for truth (at the moment a particularly strong affliction among influential elements of American and European intellectuals and their institutional sponsors but also one to which Chinese intellectuals are becoming attached), and everywhere, for those who might understand in

---

[32] Larry Catá Backer, *Reifying Law – Government, Law and the Rule of Law in Governance Systems*, 26 PENN ST. INT'L L. REV. 521–63 (2008).

[33] *Cf.* Paul Heinrich Neuhaus, *Legal Certainty versus Equity in the Conflicts of Laws*, 28 LAW & CONTEMP. PROBS. 795–807 (1963); James Maxeiner, *Legal Certainty and Legal Methods: A European Alternative to American Legal Indeterminacy?*, 15 TUL. J. INT'L & COMP. L. 541 (2007); John Braithwaite, *Rules and Principles: A Theory of Legal Certainty*, 27 AUSTRALIAN J. LEGAL PHIL. 47–82 (2002); Jeremy Waldron, *Stare Decisis and the Rule of Law: A Layered Approach*, 111 MICH. L. REV. 1–31 (2012).

[34] CAESAR FLAVIUS JUSTINIAN, THE INSTITUTES OF JUSTINIAN (J.B. Moyle trans., 5th ed. 1913), https://www.gutenberg.org/files/5983/5983-h/5983-h.htm.

[35] Larry Catá Backer, *Party, People, Government, and State: On Constitutional Values and the Legitimacy of the Chinese State-Party Rule of Law System*, 30 B.U. INT'L L.J. 331–408 (2012).

[36] In the West, JOHN FINNIS, NATURAL LAW AND NATURAL RIGHTS (2d ed. 2011).

[37] ARISTOTLE, POLITICS: A TREATISE ON GOVERNMENT (William Ellis trans., J.M. Dent & Sons Ltd. 1912) ("For a law derives all its strength from custom, and this requires long time to establish; so that, to make it an easy matter to pass from the established laws to other new ones, is to weaken the power of laws. Besides, here is another question; if the laws are to be altered, are they all to be altered, and in every government or not, and whether at the pleasure of one person or many? all which particulars will make a great difference; for which reason we will at present drop the inquiry, to pursue it at some other time.").

these conversations the value of the power of narrative to control the boundaries of an orthodox political reality that can be policed and to whose benefit
they might be turned.[38] Still, even accounting for these caveats, the insights
can then usefully take us back to the key frameworks around which the
relational and contextual can be fixed.[39] It takes the class back to the starting
point – first to custom and tradition,[40] and through those, to fundamental
notions of consent[41] and their respective ironies.[42] The former expresses the
lived realities of the community, however (re)constructed, and thus points to

---

[38] FRIEDRICH NIETZSCHE, THE ANTICHRIST (H.L. Menken trans. Alfred A. Knopf 1923 ("People
erect a concept of morality, of virtue, of holiness upon this false view of all things; they ground
good conscience upon faulty vision; they argue that no other sort of vision has value any more,
once they have made theirs sacrosanct with the names of 'God,' 'salvation' and 'eternity.' . . .
Whatever a theologian regards as true must be false: there you have almost a criterion of truth.
His profound instinct of self-preservation stands against truth ever coming into honour in any
way, or even getting stated."). Of course, that provocation itself is the subject of substantial
contestation. The point though is the possibility rather than any always false effort at truth freed
of context.

[39] One can understand the term fixed in a number of ways, for example as set, or as repaired in
accordance with the desires of those in the business of fixing. Thus, for example, the basic line
of the Chinese Communist Party fixes the political and economic model of that society, as do
the social and political constitutions of Western liberal democracies. On the concept of fixity,
see the interesting ideas in D.H. Mellor, *McTaggert, Fixity, and Coming True, in* TIME AND
CAUSATION 325–44 (Michael Tooley ed., 1999).

[40] *Cf.* the usual starting point: FERDINAND TÖNNIES, COMMUNITY AND SOCIETY (Charles
P. Loomis trans., Martino Fine Books 2017) (1887). The notions remain vital outside of the
global "metropolis" and do not always point in the expected political direction (at least from
the Western progressive perspective). *See, e.g.,* Peter Burns, *Custom, That Is before All Law, in*
THE REVIVAL OF TRADITION IN INDONESIAN POLITICS: THE DEPLOYMENT OF ADAT FROM
COLONIALISM TO INDIGENISM 68–86 (Jamie S. Davidson & David Henley eds., 2007); Terence
Ranger, *The Invention of Tradition in Colonial Africa, in* PERSPECTIVES ON AFRICA: A READER
IN CULTURE, HISTORY AND REPRESENTATION 450–61 (Roy Richard Grinker, Stephen C.
Lubkemann & Christopher Steiner eds., 2d ed. 2010).

[41] *E.g.,* "Consent cannot simply be understood as a subjective fact, a fact about the psychology of
the individual. It has to be understood primarily as a legal fact about the divine order of nature."
John Dunn, *Consent in the Political Theory of John Locke,* 10 HIST. J. 153, 156 (1967). Also, in
the international arena, Jan Klabbers, *Law-Making and Constitutionalism, in* THE
CONSTITUTIONALIZATION OF INTERNATIONAL LAW 81 (Jan Klabbers, Anne Peters & Geir
Ulfstein eds., 2009); Nico Krisch, *The Decay of Consent: International Law in an Age of Global
Public Goods,* 108 AM. J. INT'L L. 1–40 (2014); Andrew Guzman, *Against Consent,* 52 VA.
J. INT'L L. 747 (2011–2012); Bruce L. Benson, *Customary Law as a Social Contract:
International Commercial Law,* 3 CONST. POL. ECON. 1–27 (1992).

[42] Oliver Wendell Holmes, *Natural Law,* 32 HARV. L. REV. 40 (1918–1919) ("Deep-seated
preferences cannot be argued about – you cannot argue a man into liking a glass of beer – and
therefore, when differences are sufficiently far reaching, we try to kill the other man rather than
let him have his way. But that is perfectly consistent with admitting that, so far as appears, his
grounds are just as good as ours.")

the way it practices its rules and values in itself and against others.[43] The latter touches on assent and its philosophy; it points to the practices that are performed.[44] This assent comes in a variety of forms, from an internalized and socialized embrace of practices and values to mere forms of consent that must be policed by an outside force, to an assent to received custom and practice, and everything in between.

From custom, tradition, and consent, it is possible then – and only then – to consider law's systemic character. These include its disciplines, usually classified by a variety of types. In Anglo-America these include the usual fields of tort, contract, criminal, family law, etc. These suggest taxonomies of obligations. However, that layering also includes the architecture of its expression – again in Anglo-America, these include common law, equity, statute, administrative regulation and decisions, and privatized authority. These suggest taxonomies of structure and the allocation of authority to discipline. Together, taxonomies of obligation and of structure then become the self-reflexive organism that can be described as systems of law.[45]

Only then – only after one has exposed the normative architecture of law in and of itself, only after one has developed its self-referencing expressive forms – only then do we introduce the state and its institutional apparatus into the discussion. This introduction has important consequences. *It diminishes law from an architecture of behaviors to an object and expression of politics.*[46] Here one encounters the first of our revaluation of values – *from* law *to* the state and *from* the individual *to* the representative. With the state, law mutates and shrinks. The effect can be understood in two principal respects. First law shrinks as a set of self-referencing practices and values autonomous of the state because it is now bound by and reduced to the outer boundaries of the *ideological expression* of the state – that is law is reduced to consequential

---

43 J. Richard Broughton, *The Jurisprudence of Tradition and Justice Scalia's Unwritten Constitution*, 103 W. VA. L. REV. 19 (2000–2001); Bruce Rigsby, *Custom and Tradition: Innovation and Invention*, 6 MACQUARIE L.J. 113 (2006); Robert E. Park, *Human Nature and Collective Behavior*, 32 AM. J. SOC. 733–41 (1927).

44 Roscoe Pound, *What of Stare Decisis?*, 10 FORDHAM L. REV. 1 (1941).

45 GUNTHER TEUBNER, LAW AS AN AUTOPOIETIC SYSTEM (1993) (law's autonomy in the self-reproduction of a communication network and understands its relation to society as interference with other autonomous communication networks); Niklas Luhmann, *The Self Reproduction of Law and Its Limits*, in DILEMMAS OF LAW IN THE WELFARE STATE 111–27 (Gunther Teubner ed., 1988); and see, in contrast, Jürgen Habermas, *Law as Medium and Law as Institution*, in DILEMMAS OF LAW IN THE WELFARE STATE, *supra*, at 203–20.

46 "The nation exists prior to everything. Its will is always legal. It is the law itself." EMMANUELE JOSEPH SIEYÈS, *What Is the Third Estate?*, in EMMANUELE JOSEPH SIEYÈS, POLITICAL WRITINGS 92, at 136 (Michael Sonencher ed. & trans., Hackett Pub. 2003) (1789).

expression of politics. Its expression is practiced through state-managed reme-
diation mechanics, and it is generally subject to state oversight.[47] But more
deeply, law is reduced to only that conception possible and compatible with
the conception of the state itself. Second, law shrinks as an instrumental
institutional expression of the state itself. It is in this sense that the ideology
of the state merges law into itself. As law and the state merge, law becomes *the*
tool through which politics can be performed. Its transnational elements are
quite evident at national frontiers – especially the frontiers of the state as an
economic institution.[48] Law ceases to be a thing in itself (but was it ever?);[49] it
becomes rather the means by which the state can express *itself* through its
apparatus. The political representative may be the means by which the state
expresses itself; but the exercise of that expression is undertaken by the
administrator.[50] Thus, the second great revaluation of values – from the
political to the bureaucratic.[51] The context and relational aspects of justice
become the context and relational aspects of justice within the state and its
institutional apparatus.

But the introduction of the state also complicates law in another way. It
requires the production of another law – a law of laws that binds law to the
state and the state to law.[52] This is the rule of law in its institutional context. It
is with the introduction of the state that a metalegality becomes necessary.[53]
This metalegality is all the more needed the more completely law is subsumed
within the institutional apparatus of the state. We tended to shepherd that

---

[47] For example, Complaint for Declaratory & Injunctive Relief, California v. Trump, No. 3:19-cv-
00872 (N.D. Cal. Feb. 18, 2019; available https://int.nyt.com/data/documenthelper/620-
california-lawsuit-against-tru/8e2f7958e51b7fbf4c78/optimized/full.pdf#page=1.

[48] Dustin Tingley, Christopher Xu, Adam Chilton & Helen V. Milner, *The Political Economy of*
Inward FDI: Opposition to Chinese Mergers and Acquisitions, 8 Chinese J. Int'l Pol. 27–57
(2015); Joel Slawotsky, *The National Security Exception in US-China FDI and Trade: Lessons*
from Delaware Corporate Law, 6 Chinese J. Comp. L. 228–64 (2018).

[49] John Burnet, *Law and Nature in Greek Ethics,* 3 Int'l J. Ethics 328–33 (1897).

[50] *Cf.* Max Weber, *Science as a Vocation, in* From Max Weber Essays in Sociology 129–56
(H.H. Gerth and C. Wright Mills trans., 1958) ("Today the routines of everyday life challenge
religion. Many old gods ascend from their graves; they are disenchanted and hence take the
form of impersonal forces. They strive to gain power over our lives and again they resume their
eternal struggle with one." *Id.* at 148).

[51] Benedict Kingsbury & Lorenzo Casini, *Global Administrative Law Dimensions of International*
Organizations Law, 6 Int'l Organizations L. Rev. 31958 (2009); Alfred C. Aman,
Globalization, Democracy, and the Need for a New Administrative Law, 10 Ind. J. Global
Legal Stud. 125–55 (2003).

[52] Larry Catá Backer, *From Constitution to Constitutionalism: A Global Framework for Legitimate*
Public Power Systems, 113 Penn St. L. Rev. 671–732 (2009).

[53] Anthony I. Ogus, *Law and Spontaneous Order: Hayek's Contribution to Legal Theory,* 16 J.
L. & Soc'y 393 (1989).

metalegality into the corral of constitutional law. It comes as no surprise that this constitutional metalaw arises with the constitution of the state itself from out of the rubble of the more disordered sovereignties of the age that preceded the French and American revolutions.

Further, metalegalities also produce another consequence – the need for communications among these reified law systems now incarnated as states.[54] If law is the state and the state is law, then a language of interpersonal relations must be developed. There is a horizontal language – the language of comparative law – that makes communication among those subject to states possible. And there is the language of international law – that law that makes relations among states and between them, that permits concerted action when it suits, all the more possible. It is at this point that Jessup enters – enters a world so well ordered and so well protected by its own systems that the possibility of conceiving it other than as it is becomes inconceivable. What is left, then, to him and those who follow are the bits and pieces that poke out from under the tent that the law-in-state enterprise ideology has created. Jessup focused on the messy situations that are produced as a consequence of the inability of states to keep their people and property at home. Others, among the best, focus on a harmonizing ideology.[55]

So ... when we speak to law, generally, we have come to assume that it is embedded within and expressed through the state. This becomes the unremarkable reality of a remarkable appropriation. That appropriation is made possible by the insinuation of an ideology of politics – of the character, nature, power, and status of the state – into an ideology of law. That ideology transforms the former into the incarnation of popular will and vests that popular will with an extraordinary instrumental power over its customs and traditions. And it transforms the latter from an autonomous expression of the accumulated expressions of norms to the instrument of the expression of will as managed by and through the apparatus of state – managed not only by a representative body but by that singularly powerful apparatus of regulatory and administrative mechanisms to which law has been delegated and, thus delegated, absorbed into its own body. The ideology of the state is, as well, the transformation of law from normative expressions of justice to the managed

---

[54] Poul F. Kjaer, *Law of the Worlds – Towards an Inter-systemic Theory, in* Recht Zwischen Dogmatik Und Theorie: Marc Amstutz Zum 50 Geburtstag 159–75 (Stefan Keller & Stefan Wiprächtiger eds., 2012).

[55] *Cf.* Christiana Ochoa, *Towards a Cosmopolitan Vision of International Law: Identifying and Defining CIL Post Sosa v. Alvarez-Machain*, 74 U. Cin. L. Rev. 105–45 (2006).

"cage"[56] within which administrative discretion may be exercised.[57] If law is the state and the state is law, one must also admit that both are now exercised as discretionary applications by the apparatus of the state itself.

Our conceits about, and the construction of, a political ideology of the state have appeared to fuse law and the state in a permanent union and in the process diminished law. We have come to believe that law wears the collar of the state. In the manner of the ancient way on which law referenced a married couple by identifying the husband by name and the wife merely by status – John Doe *et uxor*[58] – contemporary ideology speaks to the name of the state by name ... and its law generically.

But Philip Jessup, innocently enough, as he sought to embed those human activities that could not be confined to the state, or even among them, within the state, began a process that has proven that the union of law and the state is not merely loveless but has made it possible to consider the possibility that this union is also a perversion that explains only a small part, though a part potent enough, of the capacities of law in the construction and operation of human organization.

And thus, my provocation: half a century from now, in gatherings like this one, our grandchildren (for I write this provocation *for them* and *not to those here and now*) may look back and marvel at the lunatic arrogance of a project that sought to confine law in and to the state in the manner that our twentieth-century thinkers thoughtlessly found unproblematic.

Our grandchildren may conclude that the madness of the Enlightenment, of metastasized scientism, of Napoleon and Marx, and of Anglo-American pragmatists, and those who followed them, who sought to classify and confine law to the state – for that is what their ideological lenses constrained them to see – that this ideological madness did the enterprise of law a great injury.[59] Its

---

[56] Xi Jinping, *Keep Power Reined within the Cage of Regulations* 48 CHINESE L. & GOV'T 458 (2016).

[57] *Cf.* Peer Zumbansen, *Administrative Law's Global Dream: Navigating Regulatory Spaces between "National" and "International,"* 11 INT'L J. CONST. L. 506–22 (2013).

[58] Glanville L. Williams, *The Legal Unity of Husband and Wife*, 10 MOD. L. REV. 16–31 (1947).

[59] As I write this, I am reminded of the way that Eric Stein started one of his articles on the European Union, during a more hopeful time, with a reference to a letter from Thomas Jefferson to Samuel Kercheval; Eric Stein, *The European Community in 1983: A Less Perfect Union?*, 20 COMMON MKT. L. REV. 641–56 ("But I also know that laws and institutions must go hand in hand with the progress of the human mind. As that becomes more developed, more enlightened, as new discoveries are made, new truths disclosed, and manners and opinions change with the change of circumstances, institutions must advance also and keep pace with the time." *Id.* at 641). The reminder is ironic. MAX HORKHEIMER & THEODOR W. ADORNO, DIALECTIC OF ENLIGHTENMENT (Edmund Jephcott trans., Stanford Univ. Press 2002) (1947); considered critically in Jürgen Habermas & Thomas Y. Levin, *The Entwinement of Myth and*

domestication within the apparatus of state produced first formal barriers and then conceptual blockages the reaction against which have produced the exotic forms of nonlaw law that have arisen around it.[60] And yet it is precisely the arc of the role of the social engineer that has yet to reach its apogee – technology has now made possible the substitution of law by data-driven governance in furtherance of the project of scientism in the management of individuals and the societies in which they are embedded.[61]

Our grandchildren may also conclude that the law that binds people, communities, enterprises, states – indeed that the law that binds itself – is not merely transnational but that it is transinstitutional as well.[62] One already sees glimmerings in that project of (elite) transnational anxiety – the European Union.[63] In the process the distinction between public and private, between political and economic, and between social and religious may also fall away even as the systems built on these distinctions seek to maintain these boundaries and their regulatory potentials.

They may further conclude that one ought to study the "law of and in the state" in the way we presume today to approach the study of transnational law.[64] That would presume that this law of the state ought to be understood as a derivative legal category subsumed within transnational law rather than the other way around. That is, what passes for traditional law ought to be treated as a subset of a much broader and more complex terrain of governance with an infinite variety, scope, jurisdiction, and practice that are closed or complete.[65]

Enlightenment: Re-reading Dialectic of Enlightenment, 6 CRITICAL THEORY & MODERNITY 13–30 (1982).

[60] *Cf.* Roger Cotterrell, *Transnational Communities and the Concept of Law*, 21 RATIO JURIS 118 (2008).

[61] Larry Catá Backer, *Next Generation Law: Data-Driven Governance and Accountability-Based Regulatory Systems in the West, and Social Credit Regimes in China*, 28 S. CAL. INTERDISC. L.J. (2019); Shoshana Zuboff, *Big Other: Surveillance Capitalism and the Prospects of an Information Civilization*, 30 J. INFO. TECH. 75–89 (2015).

[62] Gunther Teubner & Peter Korth, *Two Kinds of Legal Pluralism: Collision of Transnational Regimes in the Double Fragmentation of World Society*, in REGIME INTERACTION IN INTERNATIONAL LAW: FACING FRAGMENTATION 23–54 (Margaret Young ed., 2010).

[63] William Phelan, *What Is Sui Generis about the European Union? Costly International Cooperation in a Self-Contained Regime*, 14 INT'L STUD. REV. 367–85 (2012); Larry Catá Backer, *The Extra-National State: American Confederate Federalism and the European Union*, 7 COLUM. J. EUR. L. 173 (2001).

[64] *Cf.* Chris Thornhill, *Niklas Luhmann: A Sociological Transformation of Political Legitimacy?*, 7 DISTINKTION 33–53 (2011).

[65] This turns on its head the traditional understanding of national law as closed by positing that it is transnational law that is closed or complete and that national law is necessarily open and incomplete because it is incapable of determining applicable rules for all legal issues that may arise in and through its territory. "According to a widely held view, all legal orders are logically

That would further presume that this law of and in the state would be subsumed within a common set of metaprinciples that distinguish law from other forms of compulsion and from the exercise of personal discretion applicable to a range of law attached and detached from the state. But it would also require acknowledging that such a radical inversion of the study of law of the state within the transnational rather than the study of transnational law attached to or derivative of the law of the state would require a change in the approach to the way in which we understand politics, representation, consent, and justice. And with that we return to where we started – the consideration of the connection between law and justice, not between law and the state.

They would also conclude that principles of polycentric governance[66] – of the simultaneous and coordinated application of systems of law to objects, persons, conditions, and transactions – will reorient and help broaden the increasingly inadequate mechanics of conflicts of law,[67] itself still largely confined to the state and among them.[68] In the process, transnational choice-of-law rules will necessarily emerge, ones that overturn the differential privileging of states over nonstate actors as "lawmakers" in contexts of multi-level governance – for example in the context of so-called corporate social responsibility[69] or in the production chain itself.[70]

closed or complete in the sense that for every legal question that can be asked with reference to a legal system there is a determinate answer according to a norm of this legal order. If there is no specific rule to provide the answer, the universal legal principle 'Whatever is not legally prohibited is legally permitted,' is said to provide the answer." Ilmar Tammelo, *On the Logical Openness of Legal Orders – A Model Analysis of Law with Special Reference to the Logical Status of Non Liquet in International Law*, 8 AM. J. COMP. L. 187, 188 (1959).

[66] *E.g.*, Elinor Ostrom, *Beyond Markets and States: Polycentric Governance of Complex Economic Systems*, 100 AM. ECON. REV. 641–72 (2010); Chris Skelcher, *Jurisdictional Integrity, Polycentrism, and the Design of Democratic Governance*, 18 GOVERNANCE 89–110 (2005).

[67] *Cf.* Christopher A. Whytock, *Conflict of Laws, Global Governance, and Transnational Legal Order*, 1 UC IRVINE J. INT'L, TRANSNATIONAL, & COMP. L. 117–40 (2016); Larry Catá Backer, *The Private Law of Public Law: Public Authorities as Shareholders, Golden Shares, Sovereign Wealth Funds, and the Public Law Element In Private Choice of Law*, 82 TUL. L. REV. 1801 (2008).

[68] Ralf Michaels, *The New European Choice of Law Revolution*, 82 TUL. L. REV. 1607–44 (2008).

[69] Marc Amstutz, *The Evolution of Corporate Social Responsibility: Reflections on the Constitution of a Global Law for Multinational Enterprises*, 3 SZW/RSDA 189, 198 (2015): "CSR can only be understood in legal terms by abandoning the notion that the function of law is tied to the political construct of the nation-state, where its role is to stabilize expectations. In world society, the law takes on a new function, which consists in the providing of direction for cognitive processes."

[70] Gary Gereffi, John Humphrey & Timothy Sturgeon, *The Governance of Global Value Chains*, 12 REV. INT'L POL. ECON. 78–104 (2015).

And lastly, our grandchildren might conclude that arguments over the character of transnational law – as method, field, substance, etc. – fail to recognize its metacharacteristics. That is that the domestic legal orders of states, their constitutional traditions, the universe of governance norms increasingly legalizing the societal sphere in both traditionally public and private areas of human activity, are themselves merely specific manifestations of the principles of transnational law. Just as one can today at least understand the entire enterprise of international law as normatively founded on the human rights embedded in all individuals (and other juridical personalities), tomorrow one might at last be able to discern public and private law as founded on the great principles of law, the essence of which is transnational. And thus, the inversion of our ritual is complete.

In his *Twilight of the Idols*,[71] Nietzsche once famously worried about the four great errors – of inverting cause and effect, of false causes, of imaginary causes, and of the illusion of free will.[72] The relationship today of the law of state to transnational law reminds one of at least the first three of these errors. The contemporary rituals that serve as the acceptable discursive patterns around the "transnational" invert the cause and effects of law as it constructs an ideology built on the assumption that law derives from the state rather than the state deriving from law. The rituals perpetuate false causation built on a notion of transnational law that is conceived as possible only through and from out of the state and then only as a means of ordering communication between and among the legal orders of states. It imagines a causality grounded in a first principle of state. That imaginary redefines law as something that cannot exist, as such, beyond the state. And it supposes that states acquire a free will to order their domestic law when such a possibility is both illusory and especially for states downstream of global production chains largely fantasy. We are reminded that purpose in this context is imposed from outside – it is a political act enforced through the social forces it is meant to order and legitimate.[73]

---

[71] FRIEDRICH NIETZSCHE, TWILIGHT OF THE IDOLS; OR, HOW TO PHILOSOPHIZE WITH A HAMMER (Duncan Large trans., Oxford University Press reissue ed. 2009).

[72] *Id.* at ch. 6, ¶¶ 1–8.

[73] "We invented the concept 'purpose'; in reality purpose is altogether lacking. One is necessary, one is a piece of fate, one belongs to the whole, one is in the whole, – there is nothing that could judge, measure, compare, and condemn our existence, for that would mean judging, measuring, comparing and condemning the whole. But there is nothing outside the whole!" *Id.* at ch. 6, ¶ 8.

In the face of the realities of globalization, which itself might be understood as an effort to return to a more "natural" state of law,[74] we academics do ourselves a great harm by continuing to serve as the shills of an ideology that itself may be remote from reality.[75] To fail to acknowledge the emerging realities makes us complicit in the maintenance of ideologically necessary constructs of inverted, false, or imaginary causes in the service of a peculiar and quite specific view of the state – but not necessarily of law.

One comes at last to the product of sixty years of development, even a grudging one, and of the thrust of the revaluation of values that the *cri de Jessup* perhaps even inadvertently put in (slow) motion.

That is transnational law made visible;[76] that is this manifesto of transnational law.

C JESSUP'S BIG BANG AND BEYOND

Manifestos can be grand gestures. Manifestos can be made even grander as they are autopsied by the thought leaders of conventional elites (even lovingly), who on that basis pronounce the manifesto messianic in language tending toward pathos and bathos.[77] Is it possible to make relevant the alarming manifesto of the first section of this contribution?[78] Or is the transnational doomed to be an elitist project?[79]

---

[74] *Cf.* Marc Amstutz, *Eroding Boundaries: On Financial Crisis and an Evolutionary Concept of Regulatory Reform, in* THE FINANCIAL CRISIS IN CONSTITUTIONAL PERSPECTIVE 258 *et seq.* (Poul F. Kjaer et al. eds., 2011).

[75] "Not only do we try to find a certain kind of explanation as the cause, but those kinds of explanations are selected and preferred which dissipate most rapidly the sensation of strangeness, novelty and unfamiliarity, – in fact the most ordinary explanations. And the result is that a certain manner of postulating causes tends to predominate ever more and more, becomes concentrated into a system, and finally reigns supreme, to the complete exclusion of all other causes and explanations." NIETZSCHE, *supra* note 71, at ch. 6, ¶ 5.

[76] Martin Puchner, *Manifesto = Theater*, 54 THEATER J. 449, 449 (2002): "Both terms, manifesto and theatre, refer to the act of making visible"; Galia Yanoshevsky, *Three Decades of Writing on Manifesto: The Making of a Genre*, 30 POETICS TODAY 257–86 (2009).

[77] J.H.H. Weiler, *The Political and Legal Culture of European Integration: An Exploratory Essay*, 9 INT'L J. CONST. L. 678, 683 (2011): "It is interesting to reread the [Schuman] declaration through the conceptual prism of political messianism. . . . The messianic feature is notable in both its rhetoric and substance. Note, first, the language used-ceremonial and 'sermonial,' with plenty of pathos (and bathos)."

[78] This is undertaken with a bit of irony, the irony of moralizing utility. NIETZSCHE, BEYOND GOOD AND EVIL, *supra* note 27 ("Ye Utilitarians – ye, too, love the UTILE only as a VEHICLE for your inclinations, – ye, too, really find the noise of its wheels insupportable!" *Id.* at ¶174).

[79] Ralf Michaels, *Does Brexit Spell the Death of Transnational Law?*, 17 GERMAN L.J. 51 (2016).

To that end it may be useful once again to return to the *cri de Jessup*'s conventional foundations in order to extract its contemporary possibilities. This section, then, starts with Jessup's core premise – that the transnational is situational, ad hoc nature, and residual, in the sense that the transnational is what is left when no traditional legal order is available.[80] It first considers the templates that have grown up around that situational and ad hoc approach to the transnational, one firmly anchored in the shadow of the state and its legal regimes. It then briefly considers the power of this template and its multiple current manifestations when speaking to the enterprise.[81]

Jessup's deceptively simple and deceptively naive "'Big Bang" has framed the problem of transnational law from its inception: "What, then, is the general problem: This planet is peopled with human beings whose lives are affected by rules."[82] This suggests, first, the external interplay of legal orders by, for, and on its individual subjects and objects. But it also evidences a reticence about a positive definition. Jessup's focus was on the transnational ad hoc situation.[83] That focus produced a three-part analytical framework. It requires *first the identification of the individuals* on whom actions precipitate response (the ad hoc).[84] Second, it requires an *articulation of the actions* or transactions that produce an effect in search of redress (the situation). And third, that amalgamation of individuals and transaction *cannot be addressed through the application of national domestic legal orders* nor adequately assigned by the application of the conflict-of-laws rules that traditionally serve as routers for resolution of legal disputes in the context of which it is possible to solve the problem through the creation of ordered networks for action that can be legal, extralegal, and metajuridical (the ad hoc transnational situation).

Jessup's framework and the structure of analysis continues to shape thinking about the transnational. That shaping now sixty years on has produced a so-called common understanding about the fragmentation of transnational law – that is on the insight that there is no "there" there.[85] But this consensus also

---

[80] JESSUP, *supra* note 2, and discussion below.

[81] Larry Catá Backer, *The Problem of the Enterprise and the Enterprise of Law: Regulating the Multinational Enterprise as Entity, as a Network of Links, and as a Process of Production*, in OXFORD HANDBOOK OF TRANSNATIONAL LAW (Peer Zumbansen ed., forthcoming 2019).

[82] JESSUP, *supra* note 2.

[83] *Id.*

[84] The ad hoc understood in the way that adjudication is the ad hoc element of common law and now of administrative law in the United States. Warren E, Baker, *Policy by Rule or Ad Hoc Approach: Which Should It Be?*, 22 LAW & CONTEMP. PROBS. 658–71 (1957)

[85] Martti Koskenniemi & Pävi Leino, *Fragmentation of International Law? Postmodern Anxieties*, 15 LEIDEN J. INT'L L. 553, 56of. (2002); Gerhard Hafner, *Pros and Cons Ensuing from Fragmentation of International Law*, 25 MICH. J. INT'L L. 849 (2003–2004).

rests on a failure to understand the consequences of a theoretical approach grounded at its core on *ad hoc* situations beyond the reach of states and their law, as well as a misreading of the implications of the rise of so-called global and the resulting fragmentation of the unity of the law-state nexus.[86] It has also tended to produce a significant set of stabilizing projects. Among the most influential of these are (1) transnational legal process,[87] (2) networked communities,[88] (3) legal pluralism,[89] (4) societal constitutionalism,[90] (5) running codes,[91] and (6) transnational legal orders.[92] These stabilizing projects flesh out and frame the situational and ad hoc character of Jessup's analytical Big Bang framework. But by embracing its core premise – that transnational law arises from and is sourced in those "in-between" spaces, in other words, *that transnational law is the law of governance gaps* – the transnational is treated the way the Cuban state treats private markets in a planned economy[93] as subordinate and complementary to the central reality of the state into whose embrace and under whose guidance all is possible (even the nonstate governance sector).[94] What that suggests, then, is a hierarchy of law norms, one in which transnational law is reduced to a sometimes complex suture – but a

---

[86] Koskenniemi & Leino, *supra* note 85; Andreas Fischer-Lescano & Gunther Teubner, *Regime-Collisions: The Vain Search for Legal Unity in the Fragmentation of Global Law*, 25 MICH. J. INT'L L. 999 (2004).

[87] Harold Hongju Koh, *Transnational Legal Process*, 75 NEB. L. REV. 181 (1996); Gregory Shaffer, *Transnational Legal Process and State Change*, 37 LAW & SOC. INQUIRY 229–64 (2012).

[88] Oren Perez & Ofir Stegmann, *Transnational Networked Constitutionalism*, 45 J. LAW & SOC'Y S135–62 (2018); Neil Walker, *The Shaping of Global Law*, 8 TRANSNAT'L LEGAL THEORY 360 (2017); Andrea Hamann Hélène Ruiz Fabri, *Transnational Networks and Constitutionalism*, 6 INT'L J. CONST. L. 481–508 (2008); Fabrizio Cafaggi, *New Foundations of Transnational Private Regulation*, 38 J. LAW & SOC'Y 20–49 (2011); Karl-Heinz Ladeur, *Towards a Legal Theory of Supranationality – The Viability of the Network Concept*, 3 EUR. L.J. 33 (1997).

[89] Sally Engle Merry, *Legal Pluralism*, 22 LAW & SOC'Y REV. 869 (1988); Gunther Teubner, *The Two Faces of Janus: Rethinking Legal Pluralism*, 13 CARDOZO L. REV. 1443 (1991–1992); Brain Z. Tamanaha, *Understanding Legal Pluralism: Past to Present, Local to Global*, 30 SYDNEY L. REV. 375 (2008); PAUL SCHIFF BERMAN, GLOBAL LEGAL PLURALISM: A JURISPRUDENCE OF LAW BEYOND BORDERS (2012); BOAVENTURA DE SOUSA SANTOS, TOWARD A NEW LEGAL COMMON SENSE: LAW, GLOBALIZATION AND EMANCIPATION 89ff. (2d ed. 2002).

[90] GUNTHER TEUBNER, CONSTITUTIONAL FRAGMENTS: SOCIETAL CONSTITUTIONALISM AND GLOBALIZATION (2012); DAVID SCIULLI, THEORY OF SOCIETAL CONSTITUTIONALISM: FOUNDATIONS OF A NON-MARXIST CRITICAL THEORY (1992).

[91] CALLIESS & PEER ZUMBANSEN, *supra* note 10.

[92] TRANSNATIONAL LEGAL ORDERS (Terence C. Halliday & Gregory Shaffer eds., 2015).

[93] LARRY CATÁ BACKER, CUBA'S CARIBBEAN MARXISM: ESSAYS ON IDEOLOGY, GOVERNMENT, SOCIETY, AND ECONOMY IN THE POST FIDEL CASTRO ERA (2018).

[94] JESSUP, note 2, at 108–09.

suture all the same – connecting proper law-norm orders to enhance the traditional centers of their production and utilization.[95]

It may follow that, for all this work, it is possible to conclude that building *beyond Jessup* is not really on the agenda – either for transnational law or for the so-called law of the transnational (or multinational) enterprise – other than as a piece of intellectual propaganda in the service of a long-term political objective, the specific contours of which remain hazy. In both cases, the state gets in the way – conceptually at least.[96] The notion of the transnational as the law of the "in-between" peaks out from the consideration of regulatory (transnational?) responses to, for example, sustainability[97] and human rights[98] consequences (the "situation") of economic activity by enterprises (the "ad hoc").[99] But that peeking is possible only when one moves beyond the piecemeal and serendipity of traditional approaches to the transnational – something now possible in part because of the space created where the ideologies of the state and the market meet.[100]

The "situation" still dominates a discourse grounded in the interplay of actors, networks, process. These three factors form the baseline for the analytical approaches of post-Jessup transnationalism for the stabilizing projects of the distinct schools of post-Jessup transnational theory. Actors serve as the building blocks of these projects. Networks build with these actor "blocks." And process provides the building block assembly instructions. Actors, networks, and structures are well suited to a field built on the core premise that all transnational situations are ad hoc and require a form methodology for

[95] Ulrich Mückenberger, *Civilising Globalism: Transnational Norm-Building Networks as a Lever of the Emerging Global Legal Order?*, 1 TRANSNAT'L LEGAL THEORY 523–73 (2015).

[96] *E.g.*, Ralf Michaels, *The True Lex Mercatoria: Law beyond the State*, 4 IND. J. GLOBAL LEGAL STUD. 447 (2007); Simon Roberts, *After Government? On Representing Law without the State*, 68 MOD. L. REV. 1–24 (2005). *Cf.* LARRY CATÁ BACKER, *Governance without Government: An Overview*, *in* BEYOND TERRITORIALITY: TRANSNATIONAL LEGAL AUTHORITY IN AN AGE OF GLOBALIZATION 87–123 (Günther Handl, Joachim Zekoll & Peer Zumbansen eds., 2012).

[97] John G. Ruggie, *Trade, Sustainability and Global Governance*, 27 COLUM. J. ENVTL. L. 297 (2002).

[98] Andrew Crane, Genevieve LeBaron, Jean Allain & Laya Behbahani, *Governance Gaps in Eradicating Forced Labor: From Global to Domestic Supply Chains*, 13 REG. & GOVERNANCE 86–106 (2017).

[99] Sara L. Seck, *Home State Regulation of Environmental Human Rights Harms as Transnational Private Regulatory Governance*, 13 GERMAN L.J. 1363 (2012).

[100] Larry Catá Backer, *Theorizing Regulatory Governance within Its Ecology: The Structure of Management in an Age of Globalization*, 24 CONTEMP. POL. 607–30 (2018).

concocting a contextual ordering of the rules that are applicable one ad hoc situation at a time.[101]

Jessupian and *post-Jessupian* transnational law theory, then, each is simultaneously *situational* and *ad hoc*. That approach has a consequence much in evidence in theoretical approaches of the last thirty years or so. These are constructed on the premise that transnational law is not a field but a method[102], an identification formula, and a process for application. That identification and process approach centers on *people* – natural and bodies corporate who live in a world in which a singular rule order has now passed into history. It consumes *law*, which has been transformed from monocultures of consumable crops (the law state) to wild fields of hyperhybridized consumable vegetation. It is focused on the *identification of context* – principles for organizing context in a local and authoritative form, the *context cookbook* from which people cook up this gathered law and concoct a meal to suit the situation. And lastly, these families of transnational law theory converge around *process* – an orderly logical arrangement usually in steps of people and law in context; such "meals" are contingent, dynamic, and malleable, but the people, food stocks, kitchen, *and the need to eat* remain constant.

At first blush, transnational law's engagement with the enterprise reflects the situational and ad hoc approach of the transnational law project. That project appears to focus on the enterprise as an actor apart, like the state, within transnational law's *ad hoc* situational processes. Like states, enterprises are governance singularities into which law can be poured, extracting coherent action. As a consequence, transnational law might move the enterprise from the construction of a category to a consequential instrumentalism, a tool through which the ad hoc situationism of transnational law might be applied. Yet there is a curious parallel interplay between the core *problematique* of transnational law and of the transnational enterprise. The problem is framed by a set of parallel challenges centering on their respective: (1) existence;[103]

---

[101] Peer Zumbansen, *Where the Wild Things Are: Journeys to Transnational Legal Orders, and Back*, 1 UC IRVINE J. INT'L, TRANSNAT'L & COMP. L. 161 (2016).

[102] For the argument that transnational law is a framework of legal methodology, see Zumbansen, *supra* note 22, and the introduction to this volume.

[103] PHILLIP I. BLUMBERG, THE MULTINATIONAL CHALLENGE TO CORPORATION LAW: THE SEARCH FOR A NEW CORPORATE PERSONALITY (1993); Fleur Johns, *The Invisibility of the Transnational Corporation: An Analysis of International Law and Legal Theory*, 19 MELBOURNE U. L. REV. 893 (1993–1994). *Cf.* KARL POLANYI, THE GREAT TRANSFORMATION: THE POLITICAL AND ECONOMIC ORIGINS OF OUR TIME (1944).

and (2) construction[104] in (a) law,[105] (b) sociology (broadly understood),[106] and (c) political economy.[107] Yet these challenges raise questions worth considering: Does this relationship between the enterprise and transnational law construct the enterprise too restrictively? Does it fail to describe the reality of the enterprise (the problem of definition)? Ought one to consider enterprises as a transnational legal order in its own right (the systems issue)? Ought one instead to consider enterprises as the constitution of production chains (the conflation/inversion issue)?

If we acknowledge the relationship between enterprise and transnationalism as challenge, then the manifesto with which this contribution began suggests an approach out from the constraints of the ad hoc situationalism and its stabilizing theoretical elaborations. The objective might then be to focus on the enterprise *within transnational law* (as object) and *as transnational law* (as subject). In that sense it might be worth positing that transnational law both constructs and deploys the enterprise to suit its situational and ad hoc focus. But the enterprise also constructs and deploys transnational law as a consumable object critical to production and constructs and deploys the state as a service provider to enhance the value of its global

---

[104] *E.g.*, D.M. Jaehne, M. Li, R. Riedel & E. Mueller, *Configuring and Operating Global Production Networks*, 47 INT'L J. PRODUCTION RES. 2013–30 (2009); Jöran Wrana & Javier Revilla Diez, *Can Multinational Enterprises Introduce New Institutions to Host Countries? An Explorative Study About MNEs' Training Programs with Educational Institutes and Their Potential Influence on Vietnam's Vocational Education Sector*, 104 GEOGRAPHISCHE ZEITSCHRIFT 158–82 (2016).

[105] JEAN PHILIPPE ROBÉ, *Multinational Enterprises: The Constitution of a Pluralistic Legal Order, in* GLOBAL LAW WITHOUT A STATE 45–78 (Gunther Teubner ed., 1997); CLAIRE CUTLER, *Globalization, Law and Transnational Corporations: A Deepening of Market Discipline, in* POWER IN THE GLOBAL ERA GROUNDING GLOBALIZATION 53–66 (Theodore H. Cohn, Stephen McBride & John Wiseman eds., 2000); Antoine Duval, *Lex Sportiva: A Playground for Transnational Law*, 19 EUR. L.J. 822–42 (2013); Larry Catá Backer, *Multinational Corporations, Transnational Law: The United Nations' Norms on the Responsibilities of Transnational Corporations as a Harbinger of Corporate Social Responsivity in International Law*, 37 COLUM. HUM. RTS. L. REV. 287 (2005–2006); Sally Engle Merry, *New Legal Realism and the Ethnography of Transnational Law*, 31 LAW & SOC. INQUIRY 975–95 (2006).

[106] Philip Liste, *Geographical Knowledge at Work: Human Rights Litigation and Transnational Territoriality*, 22 EUR. J. INT'L REL. 217–39 (2015); Roger Cotterrell, *Spectres of Transnationalism: Changing Terrains of Sociology of Law*, 36 J. L. & SOC'Y 481–500 (2009); David Harvey, *The Sociological and Geographical Imaginations*, 18 INT'L J. POL., CULTURE & SOC'Y 211–55 (2005); essays in THE SOCIOLOGY OF FINANCIAL MARKETS (Karin Knorr-Cetina & Alex Preda eds., 2005); and SASKIA SASSEN, *Spatialities and Temporalities of the Global, in* GLOBALIZATION 260–78 (Arjun Appadurai ed., 2001).

[107] WILLIAM K. CARROLL, THE MAKING OF A TRANSNATIONAL CAPITALIST CLASS: CORPORATE POWER IN THE 21ST CENTURY (2010); Ilkka Kauppinen, *Towards Transnational Academic Capitalism*, 64 HIGHER EDUC. 543–56 (2012).

production footprint.[108] The enterprise is neither contained by legal structures nor by the state, even as it embeds itself deeply within the structures of both. And transnational law is in turn constructed from this deployment of the enterprise in that space around, through, and above the state. These hypotheses require one to reframe the static questions of ad hoc situationalism as a more dynamic self-referencing dialectic: What can transnational law tell us about TNCs? What can TNCs tell us about transnational law?

D FROM TRANSNATIONAL LAW TO THE LAW OF TRANSNATIONAL SPACES

To that end it might be useful to apply the actors-norms-processes framework[109] inward within and to the enterprise. To that end the enterprise might be simultaneously assumed to be (1) an object external to law, (2) an autonomous system internalizing framework for law, and (3) as a reconstitution of production chains and the object of those chains themselves.[110] That, in turn, suggests a progression from the most orthodox theoretical foundation (and the one most compatible with the current consensus on framing transnational law) to the least conventional perspective.

The enterprise as an object external to law. This describes the traditional construction of the enterprise in transnational law. Here, transnational law assumes a quite conventional discursive trope – the enterprise and its partners parallel the old feudal view of the relation between the king and his vassals. This is an easy approach because it draws on a large tool kit of old forms and

---

[108] James K. Feibleman, *Institutions, Law and Morals*, 31 TUL. L. REV. 503–16 (1956–1957) ("When the state features its law, or when the law takes precedence over the state as an institution, so that outsiders attracted by its principles come under its protection voluntarily . . . then we have a law dominated state . . . . The consumption of law may be said to be the order secured by the adherence to it." *Id.* at 511). *See also* Marina Kurkchiyan, *The Professionalization of Law in the Context of the Russian Federation, in* A SOCIOLOGY OF JUSTICE IN RUSSIA 12–39 Marina Kurkchiyan & Agnieszka Kubal eds., 2018) ("During the first two decades of social engineering, the consumption of law shifted back and forth between legal nihilism and extreme legal instrumentalism." *Id.*). *Cf.* DAVID SCIULLI, CORPORATE POWER IN CIVIL SOCIETY: AN APPLICATION OF SOCIETAL CONSTITUTIONALISM (2001).

[109] Peer Zumbansen posits this approach as the core of a transnational legal pluralism project, one which "suggests studying law from a methodological angle in the context of evolving theories of societal ordering, rather than as a contained discipline. Central to this undertaking is a shift in perspective, which leads to a focus on actors, *norms, and processes* as building blocks of a methodology of transnational law." Peer Zumbansen, *Defining the Space of Transnational Law: Legal Theory, Global Governance, and Legal Pluralism*, 21 TRANSNAT'L L. & CONTEMP. PROBS. 305, 308 (2012), and the introduction to this volume.

[110] Backer, *supra* note 81.

relationships now applied to situations that on the surface appear to be similar. First, of course, is the complex and deeply comfortable legal universe of the corporation. The corporation creates an abstraction onto which law (in its most traditional forms) can be applied. And it can also serve as a site for the delegation of regulatory authority framed through law. The enterprise as functional equivalent of the corporation provides a site through which trans-national law can be sourced and applied. It is in this context that the large cornucopia of efforts at global regulation of economic activity have found a foundation: disclosure regimes, corporate social responsibility regimes, the normative structuring of the human rights obligations of economic actors exemplified by the UN *Guiding Principles of Business and Human Rights*[111] and the OECD's *Guidelines for Multinational Enterprises*[112] (and its National Contact Points process),[113] evidence the increasingly layered (and thus con-ventionally transnational) framework built on the assumption of enterprise corpus.[114]

But that construct also represents a bit of wishful thinking. It ignores or reconstructs legal basis for enterprise organization, layered over or through national legislation.[115] It also propels traditional law in new directions whose

---

[111] Human Rights Council, *Report of the Special Representative to the Secretary-General on the Issue of Human Rights and Transnational Corporations and Other Business Enterprises, John Ruggie: Guiding Principles on Business and Human Rights: Implementing the United Nations "Protect, Respect and Remedy" Framework*, U.N. Doc. A/URC/17/31 (Mar. 21, 2011), http://www .business-humanrights.org/media/documents/ruggie/ruggie-guiding-principles-21-mar-2011.pdf [hereinafter UNGP].

[112] ORGANISATION FOR ECONOMIC CO-OPERATION AND DEVELOPMENT [OECD], OECD GUIDELINES FOR MULTINATIONAL ENTERPRISES (2011), https://www.oecd.org/daf/inv/mne/ 48004323.pdf [hereinafter OECD GUIDELINES].

[113] Juan Carlos Ochoa Sanchez, *The Roles and Powers of the OECD National Contact Points Regarding Complaints on an Alleged Breach of the OECD Guidelines for Multinational Enterprises by a Transnational Corporation*, 84 NORDIC J. INT'L L. 89–126 (2015).

[114] Karin Buhmann, *The Danish CSR Reporting Requirement as Reflexive Law: Employing CSR as a Modality to Promote Policy Objectives Through Law*, 24 EUR. BUS. L. REV. 187–216 (2013); Sandra Cossart, Jérôme Chaplier & Tiphaine Beau de Lomenie, *The French Law on Duty of Care: A Historic Step towards Making Globalization Work for All*, 2 BUS. HUM. RTS. L.J. 317–23 (2017).

[115] Consider how the UNGPs and the OECD guidelines confront the issue of the organization of the MNE. The OECD guidelines suggest a definition beyond the boundaries of law: "A precise definition of multinational enterprises is not required for the purposes of the Guidelines. These enterprises operate in all sectors of the economy. They usually comprise companies or other entities established in more than one country and so linked that they may co-ordinate their operations in various ways. While one or more of these entities may be able to exercise a significant influence over the activities of others, their degree of autonomy within the enterprise may vary widely from one multinational enterprise to another. Ownership may be private, State or mixed." (OECD GUIDELINES, *supra* note 112, at 17–18, ¶ 4). On the other

consequences remain shrouded in ambiguity.[116] Here, one enters the brave
new world of the instrumental use of veil piercing,[117] the bloodied battlefields
of the rise (and fall) and rise again of enterprise liability,[118] the hopes for a new
law of agency,[119] and the tireless, if somewhat circular, engagements with the
concept of fiduciary duty (as regards monitoring and mediation) in corporate
and contract relations.[120]

The enterprise as an autonomous system creating transnational law. Here,
one encounters (and grudgingly among those who still center analysis on the
state) the enterprise as a regulating object.[121] That enterprise of regulatory is
emerging in two principle variations. The first unpacks the enterprise in a
variety of ways. It might reduce the enterprise to its structural dimension
(subsidiaries, contract relations). Or it might focus on the enterprise's
governance dimension (enterprise a self-reflexive legal universe). It is an
approach that seeks to preserve the unity of the enterprise unity as against
outside law and reveals its intersystemic quality for internal governance. The

---

hand, the UNGP offers a more ambiguous approach, though one centered on the construction
of an entity: "The responsibility of business enterprises to respect human rights applies to all
enterprises regardless of their size, sector, operational context, ownership and structure."
UNGP, *supra* note 111, ¶ 14. The commentary expands on the black letter, focusing on
something like an "effects" test. "The means through which a business enterprise meets its
responsibility to respect human rights may also vary depending on whether, and the extent to
which, it conducts business through a corporate group or individually. However, the
responsibility to respect human rights applies fully and equally to all business enterprises." *Id.*
In one instance, the MNE is constructed as a group bund together through ties of influence. In
the other the MNE is constructed as a function of "means." In both cases, the analysis proceeds
backwards from behaviors to connection.

[116] Philip I. Blumberg, *Asserting Human Rights against Multinational Corporations under United States Law: Conceptual and Procedural Problems*, 50 AM. J. COMP. L. SUPP. 493 (2002); Steven R. Ratner, *Corporations and Human Rights: A Theory of Legal Responsibility, in* HUMAN RIGHTS AND CORPORATIONS (David Kinley ed., 2009).

[117] Rolf H. Weber & Rainer Baisch, *Liability of Parent Companies for Human Rights Violations of Subsidiaries*, 27 EUR. BUS. L. REV. 669–95 (2016); Peter Rott & Vibe Ulfbeck, *Supply Chain Liability of Multinational Corporations?*, 23 EUR. REV. PRIV. L. 415–36 (2015).

[118] Gwynne Skinner, *Rethinking Limited Liability of Parent Corporations for Foreign Subsidiaries' Violations of International Human Rights Law*, 72 WASH. & LEE L. REV. 1769 (2015); René Reich-Graefe, *Changing Paradigms: The Liability of Corporate Groups in Germany*, 37 CONN. L. REV. 785 (2004–2005).

[119] *E.g.*, Chandler v. Cape Plc [2012] 1 WLR 3111 (Eng.); Lubbe v. Cape Plc [2000] UKHL 41 (appeal taken from Eng.).

[120] Cynthia A. Williams and John M. Conley, *Is There an Emerging Fiduciary Duty to Consider Human Rights?*, 74 U. CIN. L. REV. 75 (2005–2006). This approach has recently been thought applicable to the state as well. Evan Fox-Decent & Evan J. Criddle, *The Fiduciary Constitution of Human Rights*, 15 LEGAL THEORY 301–36 (2009).

[121] Gunther Teubner, *Self-Constitutionalizing TNCs? On the Linkage of "Private" and "Public" Corporate Codes of Conduct*, 18 IND. J. GLOB. LEG. STUD. 617–38 (2011).

second reconstructs the enterprise as corporation. Here one encounters the growing literature of the so-called apex corporation, an active regulatory object objectifying its downstream components.

In either variation, the enterprise here serves as a site of legal tension. Three well-known examples provide context. The first centers on the highly inflammatory issue of extraterritoriality (national law embedded in the global operations of the enterprise).[122] The second touches on the literature of "good governance," itself grounded in systemic effects of the enterprise.[123] The third seeks to attach the enterprise to the state as an informal or privatized administrative organ.[124] The enterprise here is transformed into a law/standard maker and in this way is effectively incorporated into the administrative state – through regulatory delegation principally. In this context the state owned enterprise poses its own challenges.[125]

This last reflex transforms the enterprise system into an adjunct to the governmental system attached either to states or to international organizations with oversight authority. The enterprise (and transnational law) then is here

---

[122] UNGP, *supra* note 111, ¶ 2, appears to approve the extension of MNE regulation extraterritorially. "States should set out clearly the expectation that all business enterprises domiciled in their territory and/or jurisdiction respect human rights throughout their operations." The commentary makes clear that extraterritoriality is an accepted form of extranational regulation through national law. "At present States are not generally required under international human rights law to regulate the extraterritorial activities of businesses domiciled in their territory and/or jurisdiction. Nor are they generally prohibited from doing so, provided there is a recognized jurisdictional basis." *Id.* The OECD guidelines are an excellent example of extraterritoriality applied through soft law frameworks. JENNIFER A. ZERK, EXTRATERRITORIAL JURISDICTION: LESSONS FOR THE BUSINESS AND HUMAN RIGHTS SPHERE FROM SIX REGULATORY AREAS: A REPORT FOR THE HARVARD CORPORATE SOCIAL RESPONSIBILITY INITIATIVE TO HELP INFORM THE MANDATE OF THE UNSG'S SPECIAL REPRESENTATIVE ON BUSINESS AND HUMAN RIGHTS (2010).

[123] For an interesting approach, see CORNELIUS B. PRATT, *Reformulating the Emerging Theory of Corporate Social Responsibility as Good Governance, in* PUBLIC RELATIONS THEORY II (Carl H. Botan & Vincent Hazelton eds., 2009); Ned P. Vanda, *The "Good Governance" Concept Revisited,* 603 THE ANNALS OF THE ACADEMY OF POLITICAL AND SOCIAL SCIENCES 269–83 (2006); MERILEE GRINDLE, *Good Governance: The Inflation of an Idea, in* PLANNING IDEAS THAT MATTER: LIVABILITY, TERRITORIALITY, GOVERNANCE, AND REFLEXIVE PRACTICE 259–82 (Bishwapriya Sanyal, Lawrence J. Vale & Christina D. Rosan eds., 2012).

[124] PUBLIC-PRIVATE POLICY PARTNERSHIPS (Pauline Vaillancourt Rosenau ed., 2000); Paul R. Verkuil, *Public Limitations on Privatization of Government Functions,* 84 N.C. L. REV. 397 (2005). In its human rights dimensions, Alfred C. Aman, Jr., *Privatization, Prisons, Democracy, and Human Rights: The Need to Extend the Province of Administrative Law,* 12 IND. J. GLOBAL LEGAL STUD. 511 (2005); Antenor Hallo De Wolf, *Modern Condotierri in Iraq: Privatizing War from the Perspective of International and Human Rights Law,* 13 IND. J. GLOBAL LEGAL STUD. 315–56 (2006).

[125] Mikko Rajavuori, *How Should States Own? Heinisch v. Germany and the Emergence of Human Rights–Sensitive State Ownership Function,* 26 EUR. J. INT'L L. 727–46 (2015).

recast not as process or method but as an enterprise for the orderly administration of the privatization of law and the governmentalization of the private sector.[126] The enterprise is simultaneously a means of hardening soft law.[127] It serves as the space through which the governance conditionality of international financial institutional lending may be furthered. It serves as the framework through which it may be possible to develop robust systems for human rights due diligence. And it serves as an alternative space for the creation of nonstate, nonjudicial grievance mechanisms.[128]

The enterprise as the reconstitution of the production chain. Here the enterprise shifts form object to a metaphor; it is a metaphor for the organization of production in which the enterprise serves as an organizing object (the corporation or business), as the relationships that are themselves the producers of rules and as the system that consumes rules. At its limit, the enterprise here falls away as an object or self-constituted system. It becomes instead both the objectification of production chains and a factor in the constitution and operation of production chains. It is transformed into part of, or transposed into, production systems themselves. Yet this does not result in the disappearance of the enterprise within production chains. Rather it shifts the prime object of regulation – the constitution of regulatory space – *from an object* (the enterprise, a body corporate mimicking the state) *to a process*. It is within that

---

[126] Larry Catá Backer, *Text of My Remarks, "Transnational Legal Orders and Global Regulatory Networks": to be delivered as part of the 2017 Global Law Week and the International Francqui Symposium on Global and Transnational Law Today*, LAW AT THE END OF THE DAY (May 12, 2017, 4:11 PM), http://lcbackerblog.blogspot.com/2017/05/text-of-my-remarks-transnational-legal.html.

[127] Friends of the Earth v. Rabobank, OECDWATCH (June 26, 2014), https://complaints .oecdwatch.org/cases/Case_330; Benjamin Thompson, *Dutch Banking Sector Agreement on Human Rights: An Exercise in Regulation, Experimentation or Advocacy?*, 14 UTRECHT L. REV. 84 (2018).

[128] In 2014 the Office of the High Commissioner for Human Rights initiated a multiyear project to advance objectives of better operationalizing the remedial pillar of the UNGP. Human Rights Council Res. 32/10, U.N. Doc. A/HRC/RES/32/10 (July 15, 2016). This Accountability and Remedy Project "aims to deliver credible and workable recommendations to enable more consistent implementation of the UN Guiding Principles on Business and Human Rights in the area of access to remedy." OHCHR *Accountability and Remedy Project: Improving Accountability and Access to Remedy in Cases of Business Involvement in Human Rights Abuses*, UN OFFICE OF THE HIGH COMMISSIONER ON HUMAN RIGHTS, https://www.ohchr.org/EN/ Issues/Business/Pages/OHCHRaccountabilityandremedyproject.aspx (last visited Apr. 5, 2019). The project was divided into three phases, each generating its own sets of reports and together mapping a transnational space for remedial mechanisms: ARP I, enhancing effectiveness of judicial mechanisms in cases of business-related human rights abuse; ARP II, enhancing effectiveness of state-based nonjudicial mechanisms in cases of business-related human rights abuse; ARP III, enhancing effectiveness of non-state-based grievance mechanisms in cases of business-related human rights abuse. *Id.*

process that objects (the state and the enterprise included) operate. And here one returns to the revolutionary revaluation of values suggested extractable from the *cri de Jessup* in part 2's manifesto, the territorialization of institutions, of control, and of production; more generally the premise that economic rather than political communities can serve as the basis for the construction of institutions that functions like states through law. Here one again quits the transnational for the extranational. And the transnational law project again merges itself into its most profound implications.

Yet more radically, the enterprise serves as a site for the privatization of politics. It becomes a mediating form through which multilateralism can be effectively privatized. One can see this transformation in a number of well-known contemporary examples: the accord and alliance in the context of the Rana Plaza building collapse,[129] the Rabobank agreement to adopt Round Table for Responsible Palm Oil,[130] and the Norwegian Sovereign Wealth Fund governance architecture.[131] Even this, though, is understood as complementary to the project of law under the leadership of states. One engages in these tasks and delegates this authority when one has no choice. It is in this light that one can understand better the discursive tropes about the transnationalism of the enterprise in the context of, and as a necessary element for, the management of failed states,[132] of conflict zones,[133] of market failures,[134] and of capacity building.[135] Yet this remains exceptional and always subject to

---

[129] Discussed in Backer, *Are Supply Chains Transnational Legal Orders?*, *supra* note 19.

[130] Friends of the Earth v. Rabobank, *supra* note 127.

[131] BENT SOFUS TRANØY, *Norway – The Accidental Role Model, in* THE POLITICAL ECONOMY OF SOVEREIGN WEALTH FUNDS 177–201 (X. Yi-chong & G. Bahgat eds., 2010); Larry Catá Backer, *Sovereign Investing and Markets-Based Transnational Rule of Law Building: The Norwegian Sovereign Wealth Fund in Global Markets*, 29 AM. U. INT'L L. REV. 1–122 (2013).

[132] Dirk Hanekom & John Manuel Luiz, *The Impact of Multinational Enterprises on Public Governance Institutions in Areas of Limited Statehood*, 55 MGMT. DECISION 1736–48 (2017).

[133] NICOLE DEITELHOFF KLAUS DIETER WOLF, *Corporate Security Responsibility: Corporate Governance Contributions to Peace and Security in Zones of Conflict, in* CORPORATE SECURITY RESPONSIBILITY? 1–25 (N. Deitelhoff & K.D. Wolf eds., 2010); Larry Catá Backer, *Corporate Social Responsibility in Weak Governance Zones*, 14 SANTA CLARA J. INT'L L. 297 (2016).

[134] Mingfang Li, Kannan Ramaswamy & Barbara S. Pécherot Petitt, *Business Groups and Market Failures: A Focus on Vertical and Horizontal Strategies*, 23 ASIA PACIFIC J. MANAGEMENT 439–52 (2006).

[135] Ryan Goodman & Derek Jinks, *How to Influence States: Socialization and International Human Rights*, 54 DUKE L.J. 621 (2004). This last one is particularly interesting, both as to its premise that a certain socialization is required in order to better manage across political and economic boundaries but also as to its politics – that is in the choice of the normative architecture that is to be normalized. This latter point, once indisputably Western, has now been challenged by rising powers, especially China. *See* Colom Lynch, *China Enlists U.N. to Promote Its Belt and Road Initiative*, FOREIGN POLICY (May 10, 2018), https://foreignpolicy

the general assumption of the primacy of the state and its domestic legal order, which is like a black hole into which objects are consumed.

This brief sketching of an analytical framework leads to a potentially destabilizing insight for the stabilization projects that seek to protect and project the conventional view of Jessup's legacy. *It suggests that transnational law both constitutes and is constituted by an abstraction it seeks to objectify.* A considered reply would require substantially more space than allocated here. But one can outline an approach. One starts with traditional Jessup and the task of seeking to fit these abstractions into ancient systems of classifications. Jessup also reminds us that these ancient systems of classification are no longer relevant in many of those areas where they reveal gaps. The task, then, is to fill the gaps. On the other hand, the most radical lesson that Jessup tried to teach those who followed him moved toward the decoupling of law regulation from the institutions through which it might be expressed, especially in the societal sphere. This more radical revaluation of values inherent in the *cri de Jessup* has been hard to internalize.[136]

Moreover, the *constitutes-constituted*, the self-reflexive relationship between transnational law and the MNE, might be unremarkable, at least by analogy. It appears to be the essence of the modern relationship between the state and law. Yet that itself is the remarkable part. The power of that analogy is built on the premise of the complementary role of transnational law. If it is possible to adhere to the notion of a core basis of transnational law in the relationship between law and the state, surely, then, it should be equally possible to structure the self-reflexive character of law and its transnational complement in the societal sphere. That is certainly plausible – though built on premises that themselves remain contestable. Perhaps it becomes more plausible still where the objectified abstraction is meant to serve as a state substitute in the societal sector. And that is the key to this connection. The enterprise becomes the *perfect vehicle for the territorialization of economic activity organized into global production chains.* If one can import the ideologies and sensibilities embedded in the construction and management of states into the enterprise, one can produce a parallel nonstate system that differs only by the identity of the body corporate at the apex of lawmaking. It was this notion that animated

.com/2018/05/10/china-enlists-u-n-to-promote-its-belt-and-road-project/. In any case, what transnationalization implies, however, is that this approach is as easily applied to economic institutions as to the institutions of state. For a careful treatment of the complexities of socialization, see Jean Frédéric Morin & E. Richard Gold, *International Socialization and the State and Individual Levels: Mixed Evidence from Intellectual Property*, 29 CAMBRIDGE REV. INT'L AFF. 1375–95 (2016).

[136] See, Section B.

the drive to develop the *Norms on the Responsibilities of Transnational Corporations*[137] which ended in a great disappointment in the first decade of this century.[138] The remarkable element, though, was that the *Norms*, by seeking to privatize human rights, would have resulted in a delegation to an institution that, through the agency of that delegation, would have acquired the characteristics (and the responsibilities) of states, thus effectively using transnational concepts to re-create a state system within the societal sphere.[139] More than that, it would have created in the enterprise a site for both the consumption and production of norms (and its expression as regulation) in ways that would position the enterprise both within and beyond the state (as regulator).[140] Similar dynamics mark the approach to the development of a comprehensive international instrument for business and human rights since 2014,[141] a project that remains ongoing[142] and controversial.[143] Like the abandoned *Norms* project, the elaboration of a legally binding instrument – a

---

[137] David Weissbrodt & Muria Kruger, *Norms on the Responsibilities of Transnational Corporations and Other Business Enterprises with Regard to Human Rights*, 97 AM. J. INT'L L. 901 (2003). *Cf.* Larry Catá Backer, *Multinational Corporations, Transnational Law: The United Nation's Norms on the Responsibilities of Transnational Corporations as a Harbinger of Corporate Social Responsibility as International Law*, 37 COLUM. HUM. RTS. L. REV. 287–389 (2006).

[138] U.N. Econ. & Soc. Council Dec. 2004/279, U.N. Doc. E/DEC/2004/279 (July 22, 2004). Discussed in U.N. Econ. & Soc. Council, Comm'n on Human Rights, Interim Rep. of the Special Representative of the Secretary-General on the Issue of Human Rights and Transnational Corporations and Other Business Enterprises, U.N. Doc. E/CN.4/2006/97 (Feb. 22, 2006) ("Instead, the Norms exercise became engulfed by its own doctrinal excesses. Even leaving aside the highly contentious though largely symbolic proposal to monitor firms and provide for reparation payments to victims, its exaggerated legal claims and conceptual ambiguities created confusion and doubt even among many mainstream international lawyers and other impartial observers. Two aspects are particularly problematic in the context of this mandate. One concerns the legal authority advanced for the Norms, and the other the principle by which they propose to allocate human rights responsibilities between states and firms." *Id.* ¶ 59).

[139] David Kinley & Rachel Chambers, *The UN Human Rights Norms for Corporations: The Private Implications of Public International Law*, 2 HUM. RTS. L. REV. 447, 481–83 (2006).

[140] David Weissbrodt, *Business and Human Rights*, 74 U. CIN. L. REV. 55 (2005); David Weisbrodt, *Human Rights Standards Concerning Transnational Corporations and Other Business Entities*, 23 MINN. J. INT'L L. 135 (2014). Critical discussion in John G. Ruggie, *Business and Human Rights: The Evolving Agenda*, 101 AM. J. INT'L L. 819 (2007); Backer, *Multinational Corporations, Transnational Law, supra* note 137.

[141] Human Rights Council Res. 26/9, U.N. Doc. A/HRC/RES/26/9 (July 14, 2014).

[142] *E.g.*, BUILDING A TREATY ON BUSINESS AND HUMAN RIGHTS: CONTEXT AND CONTOURS (Surya Deva & David Bilchitz eds., 2017).

[143] Larry Catá Backer, *Moving Forward the UN Guiding Principles for Business and Human Rights: Between Enterprise Social Norm, State Domestic Legal Orders, and the Treaty Law That Might Bind Them All*, 38 FORDHAM INT'L L.J. 457, 517–39 (2015).

comprehensive treaty for business and human rights – also attempts the remarkable. It constructs an institution ("the enterprise") as a subset of the universe of the forms through which economic activity is conducted[144] in law and through law. The "in and through law" construct is possible where the transnational is both situational and residual: transnational law provides the normative foundation; that is, it serves as the initiating agent (the treaty) and then disappears within domestic legal orders of states, only to reappear within the regulatory orders of transnational enterprises charged in the first instance with the articulation and implementation of the normative objectives overseen by states.[145]

Understood as a project of the construction of the multinational enterprise as a *societal* state within those spaces where the *political* state (by its very nature) is not permitted access,[146] the MNE serves to enhance the traditional power arrangements and dependencies between law and an institutional architecture. And it reaffirms the marginal – complementary – role of the transnational in that complex. But that reconstruction of the MNE as a state-like organ also permits its placement within the hierarchies of political

---

[144] H.R.C. Res. 26/9, *supra* note 141, n.1 ("'Other business enterprises' denotes all business enterprises that have a transnational character in their operational activities, and does not apply to local businesses registered in terms of relevant domestic law.").

[145] Carlos López, *Human Rights Legal Liability for Business Enterprises: The Role of an International Treaty, in* BUILDING A TREATY ON BUSINESS AND HUMAN RIGHTS, *supra* note 142; Larry Catá Backer, *Shaping a Global Law for Business Enterprises: Framing Principles and the Promise of a Comprehensive Treaty on Business and Human Rights*, 42 N.C. J. INT'L L. 417–504 (2016).

[146] States, of course, may project their power wherever their power permits them. THUCYDIDES, THE PELOPONNESIAN WAR 331 (Richard Crawly trans., Modern Library 1951) (c. 400 B.C.E.) ("right, as the world goes, is only in question between equals in power, while the strong do what they can and the weak suffer what they must"). The nature references, then, is the nature of the normative frameworks of classical international law (rather than of international relations or economics, both of which tend to rationalize their own structures in their own ways). It is marked by the framework of the UN Charter's principles of sovereign equality (U.N. Charter art. 2, ¶ 1) and non-interference in internal affairs (U.N. Charter art. 2, ¶ 7). Interference is understood as a function of collective rather than of individual action, and thus, there are spaces where the state is not permitted access except as part of a collective and subject to at least theoretically robust constraints. PETER MUCHLINSKI, MULTINATIONAL ENTERPRISES AND THE LAW (2d ed. 2007). One sees this quite clearly in the recent jurisprudence of the US Supreme Court. *See, e.g.*, WesternGeco LLC v. ION Geophysical Corp., No. 16-1011, slip op. (June 22, 2018) (patents); F. Hoffmann-La Roche Ltd. v. Empagran S.A., 542 U.S. 155 (2004) (antitrust); Jesner v. Arab Bank, 138 S. Ct. 1386 (2018) (corporations and Alien Tort Claims Act). These constraints arise out of a conception of the nature of the state that, to say the least, is likely to undergo transformation in the face of the challenges of globalization, and ironically enough, of the transnational. One notes this, for example, in the efforts to reconsider the constraints of extraterritoriality

authority. It permits the development of a political hierarchy now open to nonstate actors but in which these nonstate actors remain subordinate to the state in relation to law yet responsible for governance within the scope of its delegated authority. One moves here to the reconfiguration of subsidiary political territories from territorially fixed provinces to functionally differentiated managers of global production. The Chinese Belt and Road Initiative provides a great blueprint for this model.[147]

At first blush, then, for both enterprises and transnational law this means that a functional response may be more satisfactory in the long run. One can move toward a mediating role for both TNCs and transnational law. However, this approach requires a rejection of the situationalist and the residualist approach at the heart of Jessup's transnational project. We move here from the *cri de Jessup* to the consequences of the manifesto with which this contribution started. To that end one must start where Jessup ended – at the point in which we can be free to reconceptualize the vessels into which we pour law, the way law manifests, and the interplay between institutions that now simultaneously consume and produce law around their interactions.

This may entail the simultaneous recasting of both the enterprise and its transnational law as (1) a bridging device (legal coordination), (2) as a coordinating device (conflicts of law), (3) as a signaling device (choice of law), and (4) as instruments (delegation). But these functional responses also point to more transforming responses. This would require a return to Jessup's "Big Bang," and back to his definition but to acknowledge the vastness of the yet uncharted terrain. Jessup's core question might today better be reframed in some distance from his initial situational and ad hoc grounding in "transnational problems"; that is, from a transactional foundation to a *constituting one*. But constituting moves us beyond Jessup in the sense that that object of the constitution is no longer responsive to an ad hoc situation (with its sui generis premise) nor undertaken only as a last resort (when a legitimately regulating state is nowhere to be found). What one is constituting, in this case, is the enterprise and law in the sort of self-reflexive binary that characterizes the relationship between states and law. In both contexts, the transnational will remain outside, as the gap filler and the law in search of those in-between territories that cannot be constituted.

[147] Hong Yu, *Motivation behind China's "One Belt, One Road" Initiatives and Establishment of the Asian Infrastructure Investment Bank*, 26 J. CONTEMP. CHINA 353–68 (2017); Yiping Huang, *Understanding China's Belt & Road Initiative: Motivation, Framework and Assessment*, 40 CHINA ECON. REV. 314–21 (2016).

That, in turn, opens the real question for transnational law in this century (as opposed to the question that was critical to the century in which Jessup operated): namely, the question of *what* is being constituted. For the enterprise it is the production chain that is being constituted as a regulatory space and as a regulatory object.[148] For transnational law it is its own dispositive and constitutive character that is being given form.[149] Just as the enterprise can now be understood as a component of a more comprehensive system of production, so transnational law can be recognized as the expression of a regulatory reflex that both creates and regulates the systems and objects that are the sources of its own constitution. Process is essential as the mediating modality of constitution;[150] but it is the constitutive element itself that moves away from the ad hoc to a normative terrain.

E CONCLUDING THOUGHTS

Both (transnational business) *enterprises* and transnational *law* have been constructed and used as a complementary means by which states might extend legal regimes to cover governance gaps. That construction and use, however, have been based on *ad hoc* and situational methodologies. Enterprises are objects of transnational law production. But enterprises are also sources of transnational law production. Furthermore, enterprises are mutually dependent sites for the resolution of transnational situations. And enterprises are transnational law systems. In all these instances, these objects acquire their shape and character not in and of themselves but in relation to the state. Sixty years after the *cri de Jessup*, transnational law remains essentially the law of the in-between, and the enterprise remains the object reified as spatial gap filler in the management of economic relations. Yet together they may well rise above their conceptual limitations as a complement to "real" law arising when necessary to fill gaps or as a space into which to project law when the traditional bases in territory are insufficient.

Is transnational law simultaneously the law of corporate bodies and the expression of itself through bodies corporate? That question requires a more

---

[148] Peter Dicken & Nigel Thrift, *The Organization of Production and the Production of Organization: Why Business Enterprises Matter in the Study of Geographical Industrialization,* 17 Transactions of the Institute of British Geographers 279–91 (1992); Backer, *supra* note 81.

[149] Larry Catá Backer, *Next Generation Law: Data Driven Governance and Accountability Based Regulatory Systems in the West, and Social Credit Regimes in China,* 28 USC Interdisc. L.J. (forthcoming 2019).

[150] Zumbansen, *supra* note 22.

intense interrogation of that meeting point between the expression of these bodies corporate and the means through which they express themselves – the enterprise, the state, the institutions of religion, of indigenous peoples, of peoples without a state, and of other human communities. Conventional transnational legal theory offers self-reflexive approaches to these questions that seek to preserve the old order from out of which the challenges of transnational law arose sixty years ago. But that is no longer enough. Transnational law ought not to be bound by a political subtext grounded in fidelity to the state, its *Recht-* and *Sozialstaat* structures, as privileged sites whose principles are incapable of effective transposition. That fidelity has resulted in developmental delays for transnational law. The here-offered contribution started with the suggestion that the fundamental question of transnational law ought to be inverted, from out of the state to into the state. And it suggests the very small movement that the profound transformations that are economic globalization and its governance orders has generated from Jessup's initial vision. Thus, this contribution ends with a question that still is in search of an answer: Have we come far but not moved very much? The answer may lie not in process and method but in the institutionalization of a normative ordering of rule-producing entities.

17

The Private Life of Transnational Law

Reading Jessup from the Post-Colony

PRABHAKAR SINGH[*]

A THE BIRTH OF JESSUP'S *TRANSNATIONAL LAW*

There are many reasons why the development of legal theory in Europe took a new, . . . mistaken direction after Kant. The chief reason seems to be that the major political preoccupation of Europe in the nineteenth century after Kant's death was with imperialism and expansionism.[1]

Phillip C. Jessup authored *Transnational Law* in 1956.[2] Jessup's account concerned the birth of the non-European states from decolonization and with 'imperialism'.

The seeds of Jessup's *Transnational Law*, however, lie in his Julius Rosenthal Foundation lecture at the Northwestern University School of Law given in April 1947.[3] The *Illinois Law Review* published it soon after. In a very lucidly penned piece, 'The International Court of Justice and Legal Matters', Jessup banked on the existing American cases and settlements of awards by tribunals to articulately present a case for the sources of international law.[4] Agreeing to the power of publications as sources of law, Jessup noted that 'the opinions of our courts more and more cite law review articles'.[5] 'The writers',

---

[*] I presented this paper at the American University in Cairo in March 2015, at Kings College London in June 2016 and at the Erasmus University Law School, Rotterdam, on 16 November 2018. I thank the National University of Singapore, TLSI King's College and Erasmus Law School for funding my trips to Cairo, London and Rotterdam.
[1] CHHATRAPATI SINGH, LAW FROM ANARCHY TO UTOPIA 5–6 (1985).
[2] PHILIP C. JESSUP, TRANSNATIONAL LAW (1956).
[3] PHILLIP C. JESSUP, *The International Court of Justice and Legal Matters*, 42 ILL. L. REV. 273–291 (1947).
[4] *Id.* at 276–80.
[5] *Id.* at 278.

according to him, 'have played a notable role in the development of international law and their contribution cannot be discredited just by calling them
"Professors"'.[6]

Clearly, Jessup presented the role of publicists as a source of law within
Art. 38(1)(d) of the International Court of Justice (ICJ) Statute in explicit
words. 'It is the publicists', Jessup wrote, 'who now have important claim to
consideration in connection with the progressive development of international law and its codification which is being undertaken by the General
Assembly of the United Nations in accordance with the obligation imposed
upon it by Article 13, par. 1(a) of the [United Nations] Charter'.[7] Jessup's
imaginative piece drove the role of publicists of the various 'civilized nations'
as sources of international law to the forefront. Jessup, a diplomat in the
American administration, a professor at the Columbia Law School and an
ICJ judge, was doubtless one of the most respected publicists of the post–
World War II world. His writings certainly qualify as subsidiary sources of law
pursuant to Art. 38(1)(d) of the ICJ Statute.

What is 'civilization' in international law, however? During the nineteenth
century, a state was called civilized if its laws offered economic and physical
protection to the Western aliens. This meant that most of the Western
European states, North America, Japan and Russia before the October Revolution of 1917 would qualify as civilized. These are also the states that the
twentieth century's first textbook, Oppenheim's *International Law*, marked as
states proper without doubts or any ambiguity about their sovereign character.
Japan defeated Tsarist Russia in 1905, allowing Japan to become civilized in
Oppenheim's textbook, which came out the very same year. Contrarily,
Oppenheim found the 'position' of 'Persia, Siam, China, Korea, Abyssinia'
somewhat 'doubtful' as 'their civilisation ha[d] not yet reached that condition
which is necessary to enable their Governments and their population in every
respect to understand and to carry out the command of the rules of International Law'.[8]

Little surprise that the civilized states alone produced civilized publicists.
The protection and promotion of capital, as evinced in the economic protection of alien, controlled the entry of states into the club of the civilized. Before
the formation of the UN, the world was part of the empire, British or
otherwise; the League of Nations had only forty-four participants. There was
no possibility of finding 'teachings' of the non-civilized publicists as sources.

---

[6] *Id.* at 279.
[7] JESSUP, *supra* note 2, at 297.
[8] LASSA OPPENHEIM, INTERNATIONAL LAW 33 (1905).

More particularly, the dominance of the capital exporting "civilized" states controlled the production of customary international law, a primary source of international law. Sornarajah has offered a statistical critique of the capital-led formation of the customary international law:

> Takings in pursuance of economic programmes came to be debated after the Russian revolution. The Eastern bloc states maintained that such taking was non-compensable … there were two regions, Eastern Europe and Latin America, where European attitudes to state taking were questioned. With the independence of Africa and Asia, two more regions were added, and there were four regions that stood outside the European sphere … [thus] it is futile to suggest that any customary international law would have developed on this point, despite the suggestions of some writers to the contrary.[9]

So much for the democratic legitimacy of international legal doctrines! Further, the *Shufeldt* tribunal found the Guatemalan legislation regarding cancellation of a concession contract subject to review by an international court, even though in the tribunal's view the issues involved were only contractual.[10] Very surprisingly, the *Shufeldt* arbitration awarded to the investor compensation based, among other things, as Sornarajah points out, on the 'anxiety of mind'.[11] After World War II, the preliminary draft prepared in 1957 by Garcia Amador explicitly provided that international obligations whose breach entails state responsibility are those 'resulting from any of the sources of international law'.[12] Although coming from civilized states, whether the investor's 'anxiety of mind' covers subsidiary sources remains an interesting question.

---

[9] M. SORNARAJAH, THE INTERNATIONAL LAW ON FOREIGN INVESTMENT (3d ed. 2010) 366. B.S. CHIMNI, *Customary International Law: A Third World Perspective*, 112 AM. J. INT'L L. 1–46 (2018), takes a clear Marxist position on CIL. *See* P.S. Rao, *The Identification of Customary International Law: A Process That Defies Prescription*, 57 INDIAN J. INT'L L. 221–58 (2018).

[10] Decision of the Arbitrator in claim by the United States *ex rel.* P.W. Shufeldt v. Guatemala, Decision of the Arbitrator (July 24, 1930), *reprinted in* 24 AM. J. INT'L L. 799 (1930).

[11] SORNARAJAH, *supra* note 9, at 158.

[12] A typical way for the ILC to start a proposition is to think of what writers have said. 'The works of writers who have discussed the international responsibility of States give but scanty treatment in their works to the question of the possible significance of the source of the international obligation breached. Many writers are content merely to state that an internationally wrongful act and, hence, international responsibility, exist if there has been a breach of an international obligation.' *See* [1976] 2 Y.B. Int'l L. Comm'n pt. 1, at 11, U.N. Doc. A/CN.4/SER.A/1976/Add.l (pt. 1), 11. *Cf.* E. Jiminez de Arechaga, *Application of the Rules of State Responsibility to the Nationalization of Foreign-Owned Property, in* LEGAL ASPECTS OF THE NEW INTERNATIONAL ECONOMIC ORDER 229–30 (Kamal Hossain ed. 1980).

On the general relationship between colonialism and international law, as Chimni says, Mohammed Bedjaoui took a position more radical than Anand.[13] Anghie, while in agreement with the general arguments of both Anand and Bedjaoui, made an original conclusion that colonialism is central, not peripheral, to the making of international law.[14] Sornarajah's contribution has been the exposition that Western publicists have rigged the primary sources of international law in favour of the investors.

My reading of *Transnational Law* has a postcolonial context. The *Suez* crisis, although diplomatic in nature, bordering territorial aggression by the Western powers, was one of the proxies for the unfolding Cold War.[15] The *Suez* crisis naturally inspired Abi-Saab's views on international law just as the *Right of Passage* case ushered legal postcolonialism in India.[16] It is hardly surprising that India's Nehru and Egypt's Nasser were allies of the Non-Aligned Movement, although ironically aligned to the Soviet Russia. Much of the legal arguments that sprang up from Asia, with Africa still under colonialism, came from the Soviet view on colonialism and imperialism after the October Revolution of 1917. This supplanted the Latin American views expressed in the last quarter of the nineteenth century. This had the effect of pitting all of Latin America, Asia and Africa against *Transnational Law*'s alleged innovation.

This chapter argues that (1) Jessup was the second-best student of Lord McNair's school of public international lawmaking by private law principles after Lauterpacht and (2) Jessup's *Transnational Law* had the effect of ossifying the decolonization goals of the United Nations. My findings and arguments in this chapter are in many ways the restatement of the works of Abi-Saab,[17] Sornarajah and Anghie.[18] More particularly, I read the application of the transnational law doctrine in the *Suez* episode in Egypt.

---

[13] B.S. Chimni, *Towards a Radical Third World Approach to Contemporary International Law*, 5 ICCLP Rev. (2002) 18–21.

[14] Antony Anghie, Imperialism, Sovereignty and the Making of International Law 3–4 (2006).

[15] *See* James Gathii, *War's Legacy in International Investment Law*, 11 Int'l Community L. Rev. 252–86 (2009).

[16] Prabhakar Singh, *India before and after the Right of Passage Case*, 5 Asian J. Int'l L. 176–208 (2015).

[17] G. Abi-Saab, *The Newly Independent States and the Rules of International Law: An Outline*, 8 Howard L.J. 97–121 (1962).

[18] Anghie, *supra* note 14, at 223–35.

B ARBITRATIONS AND THE MAKING OF COMMERCIAL
TRANSNATIONAL LAW

Even though the idea of sovereignty came to the fore in Europe, in investor–state arbitrations before and after the First World War, the Latin American states were its most frequent users. Such arguments of sovereignty arose when the North American investors took Latin American states to arbitrations about American investment in former Spanish colonies. In almost all cases, investments in Latin America would succeed 'concession contracts'. Typically, the main legal questions to arise from disputes involving the breach of such concession contracts were whether such contracts are treaties and the issue of the 'choice of law'.

In 1927, Lauterpacht lamented the attempt by publicists to distinguish between contract and treaties, foretelling that such attempts are 'doomed to failure'.[19] Lauterpacht, known for his doctrine of the legalization of political disputes, was a true disciple of Lord McNair, who prefaced Lauterpacht's treatise saying, 'it is essential that the resources of private law should be exploited ungrudgingly and to the full'.[20]

Jessup turned out to be McNair's most obedient student after Lauterpacht; Jessup often drew inspiration from Lauterpacht.[21] Jessup heeded to McNair's appeal for 'resort[ing] to rules and conceptions of private law for the purpose of the development of international law'.[22] Moreover, the opening pages of *Transnational Law* quotes Georges Scelle saying that international law should not be 'taken exclusively in its Latin etymology'.[23] What Jessup meant was that in commercial matters, one must not take sovereignty very seriously.

Independent kingdoms (Siam/Thailand),[24] failing Asian empires (the Ottoman) or fledgling Latin American states were preferred choices for Western

---

[19]   *See* H. LAUTERPACHT, PRIVATE LAW SOURCES AND ANALOGIES OF INTERNATIONAL LAW 156 (1927).

[20]   MacNair, *Foreword* to LAUTERPACHT, *supra* note 19, at v. *Cf.* V.S. Mani, *Audi Alteram Partem: Journey of a Principle from the Realms of Private Procedural Law to the Realms of International Procedural Law*, 9 INDIAN J. INT'L L. 381 (1969).

[21]   'In regard to the nature and value of dissenting opinions, I am in complete agreement with the views of a great judge, a former member of this Court – the late Sir Hersch Lauterpach – who so often and so brilliantly contributed to the cause of international law and justice his own concurring or dissenting opinions.' South West Africa (Eth. v. S. Afr.; Liber. v. S. Afr.), Second Phase, Judgment, 1966 I.C.J. Rep. 6, 325 (July) (dissenting opinion of Jessup, J.).

[22]   MacNair, *supra* note 20, at v.

[23]   JESSUP, *supra* note 2, at 1.

[24]   Contextual reading of Cheek v. Siam (1898) 'proves that both private law and public international law are structurally rigged against ex-semi-colonial nations'. P. Singh,

investments.[25] Concessions contracts were the usual way to legalize the relationship. When dispute arose, civilized arbitrators wrote for civilized investors.

Examples abound. The *Cedroni* v. *Guatemala* arbitration found the one-sided termination of the contract by Guatemalan government illegal.[26] Similarly, in *Company General of the Orinoco* case before the 1902 French-Venezuelan Mixed Claims Commission, the termination of the contract by Venezuela was held to give rise to an international liability.[27] In *May* v. *Guatemala*, the investor was awarded damages against the government of Guatemala.[28]

The line of such cases is rather large.[29] The outcomes of these cases produce intrigue. While investors claimed to have come to such poor countries rich in resources on the logic of development of such countries. Yet in *Czechoslovakia* v. *Radio Corporation of America*, the arbitrator said that the state has not realized its expectations of profit could not be considered a reason sufficient enough from releasing it from its obligation pursuant to the 'concession contracts'.[30] The *Radio Corp* v. *China* arbitration had suggested that '[t]he Chinese Government can certainly sign away a part of its liberty of action'.[31]

One feels as though the civilized arbitrators, while decidedly putting much in store by the term 'contract', forgot to stress upon 'concession'. After all, the

---

Of International Law, Semi-colonial Thailand, and Imperial Ghosts, 9 ASIAN J. INT'L L. 46–74 (2019).

[25] Cheek v. Siam, Award of Mar. 21, 1898, 5 MOORE, INT'L ARB. 5069, 5071 (1899); JACKSON HARVEY RALSTON, INTERNATIONAL ARBITRATION FROM ATHENS TO LOCARNO 218, 219 (1929). Czechoslovakia v. Radio Corporation of America, Award of Apr. 1, 1932, 30 AM. J. INTL L. 523 (1936).

[26] Cedroni (Italy) v. Guatemala, Award of Oct. 12, 1898, H. LA FOUNTAINE, PASICRISIE INTERNATIONALE 606 (1902).

[27] Company General of the Orinoco (France) v. Venezuela, Opinion of Umpire Plumley, July 31, 1905, RALSTON REP. 244, 322 (1906).

[28] R.H. May v. Guatemala, Award of Nov. 16, 1900, *reprinted in* PAPERS RELATING TO THE FOREIGN RELATIONS OF THE UNITED STATES 659, 672 (1900).

[29] El Triunfo (U.S. v. El Sal.), U.S. FOREIGN REL. 838–62 (1900); Milligan v. Peru, U.S.-Peruvian Claims Commission under Convention of Dec. 4, 1868, 2 MOORE, INT'L ARB. 1643–44 (1898) (*ex gratia*); North and South American Construction Co. USA v. Chile, 3 MOORE, INT'L ARB. 2318; Hammeken v. Mexico, Mexican Claims Commission under Convention of July 4, 1868, 4 MOORE, INT'L ARB., 3470–72; Central and South American Telegraph Co v. Chile, U.S.-Chilean Claims Commission under Convention of August 7, 1892, 2 MOORE'S DIGEST 1477 (1898); Punchard, McTaggart, Lowther & Co. v. Colombia, Award of Oct. 17, 1899, H. LA FOUNTAINE, PASICRISIE INTERNATIONALE 544; Aboilard (France) v. Haiti, Award of July 26, 1905, 12 REVUE GÉNÉRALE DE DROIT INTERNATIONAL PUBLIC, Docs. 12–17 (1905); Landreau v. Peru, Award of Oct. 26, 1922, 17 AM. J. INT'L L. 157 (1923).

[30] *Czechoslovakia, supra* note 25, at 534.

[31] Radio Corporation of America v. Republic of China, AM. J. INT'L L. 535, 540 (1930).

tribunals were interpreting 'concessions' contract and not private law con-tract.[32] Secondly, by exploiting private law principles, in McNair's words 'ungrudgingly and to the full', the civilized arbitrators while uprooting con-tracts from the soil of 'concessions' deposited them in the province of inter-national law. This obliteration of the history of the development of law had the impact of transferring the cost of legal production to poor states even as the profits, often acquired in colonies and reinvested in Latin America, made capitalists richer. International investment law was born after ghostwriters of favourable legal norms went to bed with capitalism.

If the Permanent Court of International Justice (the PCIJ) cases are any-thing to go by, the public international law, as it were, of 'concession con-tracts' uses arbitration between private investors and non-Western sovereign states as sources.[33] In the *Serbian Loan* case, the PCIJ tried to settle this question. Two years after Lauterpacht's *Private Law Analogies of International Law* came out, the PCIJ noted:

> Another difficulty arises from the fact that this is not a dispute between States but a controversy between a State and private individuals. This is the question what rules are to be applied. The Parties have only invoked contracts and laws. But a loan contract or a bearer bond is subject to municipal law, so that only municipal legislation must be applied to them. And yet the Court, whose mission it is to enforce international law and which has been created to apply such law, must apply this law (Article 38 of the Statute). Hitherto it has done so, and though sometimes it may have applied municipal law, this has only been in a subsidiary manner. In the present case it is however obliged to apply municipal law and nothing but municipal law.[34]

The PCIJ, moving away from Lauterpacht, said, 'In regard to national systems of law, the Court has already had occasion to state in previous cases that it could not undertake to pass upon questions of municipal law but must simply take such law and the relevant doctrine as it found it.' The public inter-national law of concession contracts thus emerged from, as Carlston puts it, 'living law' of investor–state contracts.[35]

---

[32] Prabhakar Singh, *The Rough and Tumble of International Courts and Tribunals*, 55 INDIAN J. INT'L L. 329–66 (2015).

[33] Mavrommatis Jerusalem Concessions (Greece v. U.K.), 1925 P.C.I.J. (ser. A) No. 5 (Mar. 26) (governmental action interfering with exclusivity of a concession, admission by respondent government of the lack of power under treaty to effect expropriation).

[34] Payment of Various Serbian Loans Issued in France (Fr. v Yugoslavia.), 1929 P.C.I.J. (ser. A) No. 20 (July 12).

[35] K.S. Carlston, *Concession Agreements and Nationalization*, 52 AM. J. INT'L L. 260 (1958).

In 1957–8, McNair made a bid to internationalize contracts based on the 'general principles of law' in ICJ Statute Art. 38(1)(c) that directed towards law 'recognized by civilised nations' for the choice of applicable law.[36]

Roughly a decade ago, the ICJ had, with McNair as its president in the *Anglo-Iranian Oil* case, refused to see a concessionary contract as a treaty between the United Kingdom and Iran:

> [T]he subject-matter of the dispute between the United Kingdom and Iran in 1932 and 1933 arose out of a private concession. The conclusion of the new concessionary contract removed the cause of a complaint by the United Kingdom against Iran. It did not regulate any public matters directly concerning the two Governments. It could not possibly be considered to lay down the law between the two States.[37]

Already between the PCIJ and ICJ, we see some correction on the position on private law and international law. Nevertheless, at the time of the *Anglo-Iranian* litigation, Asia had decolonized but not much of Africa. Six years later, in the *Right of Passage* case, the treaty-versus-contract debate continued in the presence of Lauterpacht who replaced McNair at the ICJ for the British seat. Portugal contended that the 'Treaty' of 1779 'ceded' the 'sovereignty over the enclaves' to them by the 'Mahratha ruler', while India alleged that 'Portugal acquired only certain revocable fiscal rights with regard to the enclaves, and that the sovereignty over them was retained by the Mahratha State'.[38]

Meanwhile, the civilized arbitrators next targeted the international law of 'permanent sovereignty' over natural resources.[39] Even so, Art. 2 of the *Charter of Economic Rights and Duties of States* provided that '[e]very State has and shall freely exercise full and permanent sovereignty, including full possession,

---

[36] A. McNair, *The Applicability of 'General Principles of Law' to Contracts between a State and a Foreign National*, ABA Sec. Min. & Nat. Resources L. Proc. 168, 170 (1957). Arnold McNair, *The General Principles of Law Recognized by Civilized Nations*, 33 Brit. Y.B. Int'l L. 1 (1958). Wolfgang Friedmann, *The Uses of 'General Principles' in the Development of International Law*, 57 Am. J. Int'l L. 279–99 (1963). M.C. Bassiouni, *A Functional Approach to 'General Principles of International Law'*, 11 Mich. J. Int'l L. 768 (1990).

[37] Anglo-Iranian Oil Co. Case (U.K. v. Iran), Judgment, 1952 I.C.J. Rep. 93, at 113 (July 22).

[38] Right of Passage over Indian Territory, Preliminary Objection, 1957 I.C.J. Rep. 125, at 164 (Nov. 26) (dissenting opinion of Klaestad, J.).

[39] Permanent Sovereignty over Natural Resources, G.A. Res. 1803, U.N. Doc. A/5217 (1962); Saudi Arabia v. Arabian American Oil Co., 27 I.L.R. 117 (1963).

use and disposal, over all its wealth, natural resources and economic activities.'[40] The rejection by arbitrators in *Aminoil* saying the 'contention' of permanent sovereignty 'lacks all foundation' is now a familiar story.[41]

I *International Law after* Transnational Law: *Ideologies as Legal Doctrines*

During the interwar period, and in the decades after the World War II, the most highly qualified publicists of the various Western nations—Borchard, Cheng, Delson, Verdross and Wortle, among others—all wrote on expropriation, concession contracts and international law.[42] Some of the students of these publicists are Amerasinghe, Domke, Dolzer and Schwebel.[43] Pro-capital views of international law did not go unchallenged as Soviet writers opposed

---

[40] The Charter of Economic Rights and Duties of States, G.A. Res. 3281, U.N. Doc. A/9631 (1973), at 49.

[41] Government of Kuwait v. American Independent Oil Co., 21 I.L.M. 976, 1021 (1982). Naturally, in *AGIP v. Congo*, the arbitration panel tethered Congo to the provisions of a concession contract against the sovereign will. AGIP v. Popular Republic of Congo, 21 I.L.M. 726 (1982).

[42] They are as follows: CLYDE EAGLETON, THE RESPONSIBILITY OF STATES IN INTERNATIONAL LAW 165 (1928); C.C. Hyde, *Confiscatory Expropriation*, 32 AM. J. INT'L L. 758, 760–61 (1938); B.A. Wortley, *Expropriation in International Law*, 33 GROTIUS SOC'Y TRANSACTIONS 25, 30, 31 (1947); J.N. Hyde, *Permanent Sovereignty over Natural Wealth and Resources*, 50 AM. J. INT'L L. 854, 862 (1956); D.P. O'CONNELL, THE LAW OF STATE SUCCESSION 107 (1956); A. Nussbaum, *The Arbitration Between the Lena Goldfields, Ltd. and the Soviet Government*, 36 CORNELL L.Q. 30, 38–39 (1950); E.M. BORCHARD, THE DIPLOMATIC PROTECTION OF CITIZENS ABROAD OR LAW OF INTERNATIONAL CLAIMS (1925); H. Herz, *Expropriation of Foreign Property*, 35 AM. J. INT'L L. 243 (1941); J.L. Kunz, *The Mexican Expropriations*, 17 N.Y.U. L.Q. REV. 327 (1940); F.A. Mann, *The Law Governing State Contracts*, 21 BRIT. Y.B. INT'L L. 11 22 (1944); N.R. Doman, *Postwar Nationalization of Foreign Property in Europe*, 48 COLUM. L. REV. 1125 (1948); S.J. Rubin, *Nationalization and Compensation: A Comparative Approach*, 17 U. CHI. L. REV. 458 (1950); B. Cheng, *Expropriation in International Law*, 21 SOLIC. 98, 100 (1954); D.P. O'Connell, *A Critique of Iranian Oil Litigation*, 4 INT'L COMP. L Q. 267 (1955); F. Morgenstern, *Recognition and Enforcement of Foreign Legislative, Administrative and Judicial Acts Which Are Contrary to International Law*, 4 INT'L L.Q. 326, 329 (1951); see, however, R. Delson, *Nationalization of the Suez Canal Company: Issues of Public and Private International Law*, 57 COLUM. L. REV. 755, 776–78 (1957); G.A. van Hecke, *Confiscation, Expropriation and the Conflict of Laws*, 4 INT'L L.Q. 345 (1951); Seidl-Hohenveldern, *Extraterritorial Effects of Confiscations and Expropriations*, 49 MICH. L. REV. 851 (1951); Seidl-Hohenveldern, *Chilean Copper Nationalization before the German Courts*, 69 AM. J. INT'L L. 110, 111–12 (1975); E.D. Re, *Nationalization of Foreign Owned Property*, 36 MINN. L. REV. 323 (1952); A. Drucker, *Compensation for Nationalized Property: The British Practice*, 49 AM. J. INT'L L. 477 (1955); C.J. Olmstead, *Nationalization of Foreign Property Interests, Particularly Those Subject to Agreements with the State*, 32 N.Y.U. L.Q. REV. 1122 (1956).

[43] S.M. Schwebel, *International Protection of Contract Arrangements*, 53 ASIL PROC. 266, 266 (1959).

restrictions on sovereign powers.[44] International law thus became a normative battlefield between apologists of capitalism and protagonists of a socialist view of international law.

The doctrine of *rebus sic stantibus* stands for the fundamental change in circumstances that can lead to limiting a state's obligations arising from treaties.[45] While diluting the importance of *rebus sic stantibus*, Brierly compares treaties with contracts.[46] Subsequently, Art. 62 of the Vienna Convention on the Law of Treaties (VCLT) restricted the application of *rebus sic stantibus* on boundary establishing treaties to save *uti possidetis* principle. McNair and Lauterpacht rejected *rebus sic stantibus* fiercely.[47]

For the development of international law, Lauterpacht sought to 'reduce the emanations of the so-called *rebus sic stantibus* doctrine to the manageable confines of a general principle of law applied by an international tribunal at the instance of the state which claims to be released from the treaty on account of a change in vital circumstances' bolstering *pacta sunt servanda* at the same time.[48] In 1927, Lauterpacht saw *rebus sic stantibus* as a cause of 'embarrassment to international publicists'.[49]

More recently, the issue of *pacta sunt servanda* versus *rebus sic stantibus* resurfaced at the ICJ in the *Gabčíkovo-Nagymaros Project* case.[50] Hungary in this case presented arguments in support of the lawfulness of the termination of a treaty using the doctrine of *rebus sic stantibus*. Hungary argued that it was entitled to invoke a number of events that, cumulatively, would have constituted a 'fundamental change of circumstances' understood within the

---

[44] G.E. Vilkov, *Nationalisation and International Law*, SOVIET Y.B. INT'L L. 58, 77 (1960); V.I. Sapozhnikov, Neocolonialistic Doctrines of International Protection of Foreign Concessions, SOVIET Y.B. INT'L L. 90, 98 (1968). See, for a perspective, A.F.M. Maniruzzaman, *State Contracts in Contemporary International Law: Monist Versus Dualist Controversies*, 12 EUR. J. INT'L L. 309 (2001).

[45] O.J. Lissitzyn, *Treaties and Changed Circumstances (Rebus Sic Stantibus)*, 61 AM. J. INT'L L. 895–922 (1967). Wright had noted the East–West difference on *rebus sic stantibus. See* Q. Wright, *The Strengthening of International Law*, 98 RECUEIL DES COURS 78 (1959).

[46] J.L. BRIERLY, THE LAW OF NATIONS 337 (Sir Humphrey Waldock ed., 6th ed. 1963).

[47] ARNOLD McNAIR, *So-Called State Servitudes*, 6 BRIT. Y.B. INT'L L. 122 (1925), *cited in* MATHEW CRAVEN, THE DECOLONIZATION OF INTERNATIONAL LAW 367 (2007).

[48] H. Lauterpacht, *Codification and Development of International Law*, 49 AM. J. INT'L L. 16, 17 (1955). J. Kunz, *The Meaning and the Range of the Norm Pacta Sunt Servanda*, 39 AM. J. INT'L L. 180, 190 (1945).

[49] LAUTERPACHT , *supra* note 19, at 167. *Cf.* Statement of Indian Delegate in the Security Council During the Kashmir Debate, U.N. SCOR, 12th Sess., 764th mtg. at 26, U.N. Doc. S/PV.764 (1957). Denunciation of the Treaty of Nov. 2nd, 1856, Between China and Belgium, 1927 P.C.I.J. (ser. A) No. 8, at 4–5, discussed in CRAVEN, *supra* note 47, at 367–68. D. Kennedy, *The Sources of International Law*, 2 AM. U. J. INT'L L & POL'Y 57–60 (1987).

[50] Gabčíkovo-Nagymaros Project (Hung./Slovk.), 1997 I.C.J. Rep. 7, at 59.

meaning of VCLT Art. 62.[51] However, the ICJ noted that 'the negative and conditional wording of Article 62 of the VCLT is a clear indication' and 'the stability of treaty relations requires that the plea of fundamental change of circumstances be applied only in exceptional cases'.[52] Judge Rezek explained the theory of *pacta* in the following words:

> [T]he rule *pacta sunt servanda* means that the treaty creates reciprocal rights between the parties on the basis of a convergence of interests, a pooling of sovereign wills which in all probability will continue to coincide over time. When on both sides of the treaty process, there is a lack of rigour in doing what has been agreed, the commitment weakens and becomes vulnerable to formal repudiation by one of the parties, irrespective of the question of which party was the first to neglect its duties, and it hardly matters that the parties lacked rigour in different ways. Treaties derive their force from the will of the States which conclude them. They do not have an objective value which makes them sacred regardless of those common intentions.[53]

Notably, elevating one legal principle over another is not governed by any doctrine or rule of law. The preference for one over other are ideological positions clothed as a legal argument. For example, Dolzer found the 'flow of capital' was 'crucial' for the 'stabilizing' of 'the economy of the developing countries in particular'.[54] In 1961 Guha Roy thought that 'what at first sight appear to be generous sacrifices of acquired rights and interests of considerable value but are really in most cases no more than either belated justice or overdue rectifications of past wrongs'.[55]

Clearly, Dolzer puts much store by the investor's 'legitimate reliance' and 'good faith' even as he rejects the application of 'unjust enrichment' on private investors.[56] Thus, if one proves with statistics that the flow of capital does not 'stabilize' economies, even ignoring the corrupt practices that investors use to seal deals, Dolzer's theory would fall down.

Moreover, the right of every state to freely choose its economic system as an aspect of the (economic) sovereign equality of states was introduced in the Declaration on Principles of International Law Concerning Friendly

---

[51] *Id.* at 64.

[52] *Id.* at 65.

[53] *Id.* at 86 (declaration by Rezek, J.). Cf. A d'Amato, *Treaties as a Source of General Rules of International Law*, 3 Harv. Int'l L. Club Bull. 1, 13 (1961–1962).

[54] R. Dolzer, *New Foundations of the Law of Expropriation of Alien Property*, 75 Am. J. Int'l L. 553, 580 (1981).

[55] S.N. Guha Roy, *Is the Law of Responsibility of States for Injuries to Aliens a Part of Universal International Law?* 55 Am. J. Int'l L. 891 (1961).

[56] T. Hassan, *Good Faith in Treaty Formation*, 21 Va. J. Int'l L. 443 (1981).

Relations and Co-operation Among States.[57] A writer's doctrinal and supporting political and geopolitical environment morphs into applicable legal principles when an 'invisible college of lawyers' sitting on the same side of the
ideological fence invoke it.[58] Irony is heightened when such a college papers
over the UN declarations.[59]

The international law of concession contracts is thus a worthy candidate
primed for a historical analysis. It is therefore understandable that developing
countries sought to outlaw economic coercion using Art. 52 of the VCLT,
holding that 'a treaty is void if its conclusion has been procured by the threat
or use of force in violation of the principles of international law embodied in
the Charter of the United Nations'.[60]

II *The Publicists' Reception of* Transnational Law

During the 1950s, international arbitrations and decisions involving expropriations or nationalizations of concessions, owned wholly or predominantly by
foreign nationals, placed the newly conceptualized transnational law into the
context of private property. Legally speaking, these concession agreements
were half contract and half legislation, and half treaty and half ordinary
municipal contract.[61]

This 'schizophrenic nature' – the result of an agreement between a state
and a foreign corporation or individual – led to controversy about these
agreements' international status.[62] The Western judicial scheme, in this case
the American system, as Dickstein explains, 'is predicated upon the notion
that particular cases will be tried upon the merits of their particular facts'.[63]
Thus, previous misapplications of the law would have no effect upon its

---

[57] See further U.N. Secretary-General, *Progressive Development of the Principles and Norms of
International Law Relating to a New International Economic Order*, ¶ 3, U.N. Doc A/39/504/
Add.1 (Oct. 23, 1984).

[58] *See generally* Patrick M Norton, A *Law of the Future or a Law of the Past? Modern Tribunals
and the International Law of Expropriation*, 85 AM. J. INT'L L. 474 (1991).

[59] G. Abi-Saab, *Permanent Sovereignty over Natural Resources, in* INTERNATIONAL LAW:
ACHIEVEMENTS AND PROSPECTS 600 (M. Bedjaoui ed., 1991).

[60] Vienna Convention on the Law of Treaties, art. 52, 1155 U.N.T.S. 331, 8 I.L.M. 679 (1969); S.
Malawer, A *New Concept of Consent and World Public Order*, 4 VAND. J. TRANSNAT'L L. 1, 28
(1970).

[61] M.E. Dickstein, *Revitalizing the International Law Governing Concession Agreements*, 6 INT'L
TAX & BUS. L54 (1988).

[62] *Id.*

[63] *Id.* at 60.

proper application to a present set of facts.[64] A presumption of the innocence of history is therefore used as a tool for interpreting international law.

Furthermore, Friedmann saw Jessup addressing the 'increasing fluidity of the traditional distinction between public and private international law' through transnational law, which would, instead of sovereignty or power, work on 'the premise that jurisdiction is essentially a matter of procedure which could be amicably arranged among the nations of the world'.[65] Dillard, the president of the American Society of International Law at the time, noted that the society was 'acting as a catalyst for the exchange of ideas and documents among practicing lawyers, government officials, teachers of law, political scientists, and corporate officials' helping to foster new concepts in transnational law.[66]

Ramazani of the University of Virginia likewise noted that '[w]ith the proliferation of international oil contracts, the problem of the choice of law ... deserves investigations by the students of "transnational law".'[67] For Amerasinghe, the fact that a tribunal is disconnected from any municipal legal system makes the tribunal 'a transnational one'.[68] Discussing state contracts in international law, Jennings, invoking Jessup, noted 'that there is a great wealth of legal material from which answers to these problems may be fashioned whether by judicial elaboration or otherwise'.[69]

Authors are not alone in accepting transnational law. Among practitioners, Domke was perhaps the most ardent student of transnational law.[70] He noted that Jessup's transnationalism, 'far from being an outgrowth of only Western concepts, is indeed an expression of fundamental principles embodied in long established legal systems throughout the world'.[71] All of this has been said, of course, without first clearing the dichotomy that colonialism wedged into the

---

[64] *Id.*

[65] W.G. Friedmann, *Corporate Power, Government by Private Groups, and the Law*, 57 COLUM. L. REV. 155, 176 n.60 (1957).

[66] H.C. Dillard, *A Tribute to Philip C. Jessup and Some Comments on International Adjudication*, 62 COLUM. L. REV. 1138, 1140 n.5 (1962).

[67] R.K. Ramazani, *Choice-of-Law Problems and International Oil Contracts: A Case Study*, 11 INT'L COMP. L.Q. 503, 518 (1962).

[68] C.F. Amerasinghe, *Some Legal Problems of State Trading in Southeast Asia*, 20 VAND. L. REV. 257, 269 (1967). For an uncritical reception of transnational law, see C. Ku & P.F. Diehl, *International Law as Operating and Normative Systems: An Overview, in* INTERNATIONAL LAW: CLASSIC AND CONTEMPORARY READINGS 1, 10 (Charlotte Ku & Paul F Diehl eds., 3d ed. 2009).

[69] R.Y. Jennings, *State Contracts in International Law*, 55 BRIT. Y.B. INT'L L. 156, 178 (1961).

[70] M. Domke, *The Settlement of International Investment Disputes*, 12 BUS. LAW. 264, 271 (1957).

[71] M. Domke, *Foreign Nationalizations: Some Aspects of Contemporary International Law*, 55 AM. J INT'L L. 585 (1961).

sources of international law.[72] 'A truly realistic analysis of the law', Alfred von
Verdross wrote much earlier, shows 'that every positive juridical order has its
roots in the ethics of a certain community, that it cannot be understood apart
from its moral basis'.[73] One wonders if Verdross' idea of 'forbidden treaties'
could be extended to void colonial treaties as sources of law based on moral
arguments given the context of colonial servitude, slavery, violence and
colonial capture in which they were contextualized – a position that is
antithetical to *jus cogens*.[74]

That said, it took two World Wars for the world to condemn colonialism as
an issue of jus cogens. The 1984 *Second Report on the Draft Code of Offences
against the Peace and Security of Mankind* noted this with disappointment
mixed with astonishment:

> The condemnation of colonialism falls within the sphere of jus cogens, and it
> is surprising that no reference should have been made to this phenomenon in
> a draft code drawn up in 1954. It was necessary to wait until 1960 for the
> adoption of the well-known Declaration on the Granting of Independence to
> Colonial Countries and Peoples, outlawing colonialism. However, the Char-
> ter of the United Nations itself already contained the principle of the
> condemnation of colonialism.[75]

Perhaps to express a condemnation of colonialism would have struck at the
universality of the protection of Western aliens in international law. Besides,
white settler states, like South Africa and Australia, appeared even more
determined to continue with neocolonialism, to which the convenient forgetting of the colonial pilfering of native resources was an important dimension.

C THE SUEZ CRISIS: THE EAST VERSUS THE WEST ON
TRANSNATIONAL LAW

The presence of the Suez Canal in Egyptian territory drove substantial
Western investment interest in Egypt. In 1856, the Khedive of Egypt made a
concession to Ferdinand de Lesseps to dig a canal across the Isthmus of Suez.

---

[72] SORNARAJAH, *supra* note 9, at 19.
[73] Alfred von Verdross, *Forbidden Treaties in International Law*, 31 AM. J. INT'L L. 571, 576 (1937).
[74] For a discussion on jus cogens and the reaction of various governments, see Sir Humphrey
Waldock (Special Rapporteur), *Fifth Rep. on the Law of Treaties*, ¶¶ 20–30, U.N. Doc. A/
CN.4/183 & Add.1-4 (1966), *reprinted in* [1967] 2 Y.B. Int'l L. Comm'n, U.N. Doc. A/CN.4/
SER.A/1966/Add.1.
[75] Doudou Thiam, Special Rapporteur, *Second Rep. on the Draft Code of Offences against the
Peace and Security of Mankind*, ¶ 48, Int'l Law Comm'n, 36th Sess., U.N. Doc. A/CN.4/377 &
Corr.1 (Feb. 1, 1984).

The concession contract was confirmed by a *firman* (executive order) of the sultan of Turkey in 1866 and established the Universal Suez Maritime Canal Company. Egypt, along with a consortium of largely British shareholdings, financed the canal, which was opened to traffic in 1868.[76] The duration of the concession was ninety-nine years, and its terms provided free and equal navigation of the canal and a system for the distribution of tolls.

The fact that 'official Egyptian attitudes' toward 'international legal order in general' has been a subject of scholarly study demonstrates the importance of the Suez Canal for international trade and commerce.[77] Indeed, just as the *Lotus* case was Turkey's first legal dispute with France, the canal occasioned Egypt's first diplomatic showdown with the West after the Second World War. The 1965 nationalization of the canal by the then president Abdel Nasser augmented a crisis.

The principal legal issue involved in Egyptian nationalization was 'whether or not the Company was Egyptian'.[78] Egypt argued in the affirmative, while the Western powers, whose nationals had invested in the Suez Company, maintained that the 1888 Constantinople Convention and the international nature of the investment furnished the canal with international legal status.[79] Huang, for instance, after careful examination of relevant documents and most importantly, the 'international law of concessions', argued that the Declaration of the Ottoman Porte of 1 December 1873 gave the company an international legal status.[80] Based on its unique status, the French government contended that the Suez Canal Company was amenable not solely to Egyptian law but also to French and international law.[81]

Naturally, in *Saudi Arabia v. the Arabian American Oil Company*, decided two years after Suez nationalization, arbitrators wrote 'that public international law should be applied to the effects of the Concession, when objective reasons lead it to conclude that certain matters cannot be governed by any rule of municipal law of any state'.[82]

---

[76] Q. Wright, *Interventions, 1956*, 51 AM. J. INT'L L. 257, 261 (1957).
[77] Kathryn B Doherty, *Rhetoric and Reality: A Study of Contemporary Official Egyptian Attitudes toward the International Legal Order*, 62 AM. J. INT'L L. 335, 336 (1968).
[78] *Id.* at 347.
[79] *Transcript of Secretary Dulles' News Conference*, 35 DEPT. OF STATE BULL. 406, 407 (1956) [hereinafter *Dulles' Transcript*].
[80] T. Huang, *Some International and Legal Aspects of the Suez Canal Question*, 51 AM. J. INT'L L. 307 (1957).
[81] U.N. SCOR, 12th Sess., 764th mtg., supra note 49, at 286.
[82] Saudi Arabia v. Arabian American Oil Co., 27 I.L.R. 117; F.A. Mann, *The Proper Law of Contracts Concluded by International Persons*, 35 BRIT. Y.B. INT'L L. 34, 47–49 (1959).

Nasser's action led the British cabinet to proposition that 'the use of armed force against Egypt' was in this commercial context 'a legitimate measure'.[83] This was in complete contravention to the UN Charter principle that made the old law of aggression illegal. The British cabinet sought to build its case for the use of force in commercial matters, a position that needed 'wider international grounds' for justification.[84]

Little wonder that publicists again came in aid of the British executive position. Professor Arthur Goodhart published a letter in *The Times* on 11 August 1956, opining that the view that under 'international law force must never be used except to repel direct territorial attack ... cannot be accepted, as the use of force is not so limited'.[85] This legal opinion was then used by the then British cabinet member Viscount Kilmuir to support Britain's decision to attack Egypt.[86]

Among the many geopolitical reasons, Nasser is said to have nationalized the canal after the United States reneged on a promise to provide funds for construction of the Aswan Dam on the Nile River.[87] Though such economic considerations were certainly important, as Doherty says, for Egypt 'the deeper motivation appears to be political: the attainment of full sovereignty and national dignity'.[88] Indeed, secretary to then US President, Eisenhower, Mr Dulles, while answering whether he felt that the Suez crisis would have developed if the United States had not withdrawn its aid offer for the Aswan Dam, replied in the affirmative:

> I feel quite confident that it would have happened in any event. Indeed President Nasser did not, and does not, attempt to justify his action on the ground of the withdrawal of aid to the Aswan Dam. That would indeed be a very feeble ground upon which to justify it. He justifies it as a step in his program of developing the influence of Egypt, what he calls the 'grandeur' of Egypt, and as a part of his program of moving from "triumph to triumph." He puts it on these broad grounds and says he himself has been studying it for over 2 years.[89]

[83] G. Marston, *Armed Intervention in the 1956 Suez Canal Crisis: The Legal Advice Tendered to the British Government*, 37 INT'L COMP. L.Q. 776 (1988).
[84] *Quoted in id.*
[85] *Quoted in id.* at 778. *Cf.* M.K. Nawaz, *Limits of Self-Defence: Legitimacy of Use of Force Against Economic Strangulation*, 16 INDIAN J. INT'L L. 252 (1976).
[86] *Quoted in* Marston *supra* note 83, at 778.
[87] JAN JANSEN & JÜRGEN OSTERHAMMEL, DECOLONIZATION 94 (2017).
[88] Doherty, *supra* note 77, 238 n.89.
[89] *Dulles' Transcript, supra* note 79, at 407–08.

Notably, the same Mr Dulles, when at the 1919 Paris Peace Conference, had suggested that Egyptian demands for self-determination from British colonialism 'should not even be acknowledged'.[90] Huang's study of the international law of concession contracts, which came a year after Jessup's *Transnational Law*, read the latter favourably.[91] For no obvious reasons, newly independent states were subjected to harsher standards, these arguments rooted in the questionable judicial formulations of the civilized publicist.[92]

Nasser's move of 1956 was judged in the light of his allegiance to the Non-aligned Movement and good relations with the Soviet Union.[93] The Egyptian press quoted President Nasser's astonishment on American observation that the 1888 Constantinople Convention had given an international character to the Suez Canal.[94] Egypt now prepared for litigation as it accepted the ICJ's 'compulsory the jurisdiction'.[95] Meanwhile, the American media asked Secretary Dulles to explain 'the meaning of "international" in that connection'.[96] Secretary Dulles replied:

> [T]he Suez Canal was, of course, built before Egypt was an independent state, when it was still a part of the Ottoman Empire, and at that period it was internationalized by the treaty of 1888, which provides that it shall be a waterway freely open in time of peace and war to the traffic of all of the nations. That treaty was signed by the nations at that time principally interested in the canal and constituting the then "great powers" of the world. It was open for adherence by all countries of the world.[97]

---

[90] Cited in PANKAJ MISHRA, FROM THE RUINS OF EMPIRE: THE REVOLT AGAINST THE WEST AND THE REMAKING OF ASIA 200 (2013). Quite notably, the accounts of Dulles's diplomacy has been the subject of both emotional heat and scholarly detachment. *See* Coral Bell, *The Diplomacy of Mr. Dulles*, 20 INT'L J. 90 (1965).

[91] Huang, *supra* note 80, at 289–97.

[92] A.A. Fatouros, *International Law and the Third World*, 50 VA. L. REV. 811 (1964); Doherty, *supra* note 77, at 362.

[93] Secretary Dulles of the United States spoke that almost throughout the entire London conference, the Soviet Union 'was carrying on an extreme form of propaganda through its Arab-language radio in Egypt, designed to make it extremely difficult for President Nasser to accept even a fair solution'. *See Dulles' Transcript, supra* note 79, at 407.

[94] *Id.* at 408.

[95] Declaration Recognizing as Compulsory Jurisdiction of the International Court of Justice in Conformity with Article 36, Paragraph 2, of the Statute of the International Court of Justice and in Pursuance and for the Purposes of Paragraph 9 (b) of the Declaration of the Government of Egypt of 24 April 1957 on the Suez Canal and the Arrangements for its Operation (July 18, 1957), 272 U.N.T.S. 225, *reprinted in* 1958–1959 Int'l Ct. Just. Y.B. 127, 142.

[96] *Dulles' Transcript, supra* note 79, at 407.

[97] *Id.*

For Dulles it was not necessary to think of the problem in terms of 'these great slogans, such as the slogans of "nationalism versus internationalism," or "nationalism versus colonialism", or "Asia versus Europe", or any such things"'.[98] The British were upset at the canal's nationalization and sought the support of France, which believed that Nasser was supporting rebels in the French colonial rule of Algeria. Secretary Dulles, who represented the United States at the London Conference on Suez Crisis, summed up the Soviet propaganda in the following words: 'That propaganda was, in effect, saying to the Egyptian people: Any solution that comes out of the London conference is colonialism, is imperialism, and if you accept it you will have subordinated Egypt again to the colonial rule which you have thrown off.'[99]

I *The Transnational Law of the Suez Crisis*

The representative of Egypt maintained that the mere fact that the 1888 Convention mentioned the concession agreement did not confer upon it the status of a treaty.[100] If McNair and Lauterpacht had already internationalized contractual principles, 'agreement' was a piece of cake during the Cold war years. Hyde already now read the concession contracts as 'international economic development contracts'.[101] In opposition, Carlston wrote 'legal rules could not be fully understood or evaluated without a fairly clear understanding of the social facts which they were designed to regulate."[102]

Many of these 'international economic development contracts' concealed behind the verbiage of legal drafting, the past of callous (even corrupt) rulers in the developing world, privateers and the subsequent direct colonial capture or imperial control. In the post UN Charter world, self-determination and sovereign equality were the touchstone standards by which every international legal rule was judged. The principle of good faith was a central means through which those principles were to be implemented. Yet writers found investors in need of 'good faith' effectively imposing taxes on the fledgling states' independence. Regardless, Huang bluntly postulated that "political pressure and indirect means ... exerted to secure the grant does not

[98] *Id.* 407.
[99] *Id.*
[100] U.N. SCOR, 12th Sess., 764th mtg., *supra* note 49, at 1, 7.
[101] J.N. Hyde, *Permanent Sovereignty over Natural Wealth and Resources*, 50 AM. J. INT'L L. 854, 862 (1956).
[102] Carlston, *supra* note 35, at 260.

necessarily invalidate the concession if the laws of the conceding state have been complied with."[103]

Effectively, (1) the principle of good faith was used to protect colonial concession contracts and related rights and interests and (2) this was achieved by characterizing the concession as an international treaty, obligations under which should be satisfied using good-faith and arm's-length obligations and without reference to any colonial context.

II *The Suez Crisis, Publicists and Applied* Transnational Law

In response to the nationalization of the Suez Canal, on 12 February 1957, the French government introduced a bill declaring the *Compagnie Universelle de Suez* to be a wholly owned French company not subject to the laws of a foreign state. The Americans also contemplated 'creative thought [to] devis[e] new forms of protection for American investments'.[104] Martin Domke, the then vice president of the American Arbitration Association, noted that the 'Suez Canal crisis demonstrates that international law failed to offer new solutions adequate to meet new problems'.[105] He wrote that the legal protection of the investor, in both the 'judicial determination of his rights in the foreign country as well as on the international level, requires a new approach to a time-old remedial aspect'.[106] Domke turned to Jessup's *Transnational Law*[107] and the work of Friedmann to form a new approach to the Suez crisis:[108]

> This development shows a new international "law" governing the taking of property of foreigners when in the national interest of a country in which such assets are located. Economic development, not only in underdeveloped countries, may require appropriation of public resources for public use. It has been labelled the sovereign right of countries to dispose of natural resources

[103] Huang, *supra* note 80, at 292.
[104] M. Domke, *American Protection against Foreign Expropriation in the Light of the Suez Canal Crisis*, 105 U. PA. L. REV. 1033, 1034 (1957).
[105] *Id.* at 1042. Fitzmaurice, who became a judge of the ICJ, prepared a paper, 'Why the Egyptian Action in Nationalising the Suez Canal is Illegal', for the London Conference. FO 800/747; the copy in the Law Officers' Department file bears at its head the handwritten comment: 'This is not a considered legal opinion but was intended to give us talking points at the Conference' (LO 2/825).
[106] Domke, *supra* note 104, at 1042.
[107] *Id.* at 1043.
[108] *Id.*, quoting Friedmann, *Corporate Power, Government by Private Groups, and the Law*, 57 COLUM. L. REV. 155, 169 (1957). It is little wonder that the law bulletin established by Friedmann was later named *Columbia Journal of Transnational Law*.

and wealth, without mentioning an express or implied obligation to compensate foreign investors. The resolution of the General Assembly of December 21, 1952 recognized such a right and in spite of the criticism encountered [...][109]

'We have to face the fact that competitive coexistence', Domke noted in 1957, 'in one form or the other, is here to stay, bringing about new challenges which the Western world has to meet by new approaches to international legal relations'.[110] Most importantly, 'creative thought', he pondered, 'will become necessary to cope with new challenges'.[111] Domke wrote in the vocabulary of what might be referred to as reverse colonialism: 'We are, of course, aware of the fact that the Suez Canal crisis is not solely – or even principally – concerned with the nationalization of the Suez Canal Company.'[112]

More is involved, namely the unilateral abrogation by a foreign government of contracts voluntarily entered into that it decides no longer to respect.[113] Domke uncritically assumes that such contracts were 'voluntarily entered'. These attitudes were part of litigation strategies, with several Western publicists replying to the 'nationalization' of colonial properties by Iran, Egypt, Indonesia and Cuba in the 1950s through an astute transnationalization of international law. Indeed, many legal innovations sprang from the writing of publicists citing other publicists.[114]

International law was thus read as accepting colonialism as a matter of property law transnationalized. Naturally, Judge Guha Roy wrote, 'international law which the worldwide community of states today inherits is the law which owes its genesis and growth, first, to the attempts of these states to regulate their mutual intercourse in their own interests and, secondly, to the use made of it during the period of colonialism'.[115] Dezalay and Garth echo these views:

> The law and legal practices directed to the north-south disputes ... developed to reflect the interest of Western businesses in avoiding national courts and laws. And merchants found the services useful and valuable also because the perceived autonomy and universality of the *lex mercatoria* enabled the Western merchants to ensure – at least statistically – their

[109] Domke, *supra* note 103, at Domke, *supra* note 104, 1034.
[110] *Id.*
[111] *Id.*
[112] *Id.*
[113] *Id.*
[114] M. Domke, Foreign Nationalizations: *Some Aspects of Contemporary International Law*, 55 AM. J. INT'L L. 585, 596 (1961).
[115] Guha Roy, *supra* note 55, at 866.

domination and their profits in their business relations with ex-colonial governments.[116]

Commercial arbitrations that Dezalay and Garth talk about prepared the bed for international investment law to grow and flower. As such, transnationalism arose as a counterargument to decolonization. The subsequent international investment law allowed Western publicists to internationalize contracts to defend colonial property rights without first resolving the doctrinal and moral puzzles that colonialism presented.

Although international law gave legal protection to property built on conquered land, it did not critically question the temporal attachment of property to colonial land. Ironically, the role of equity and fairness in expropriation became part of the doctrine only after decolonization for the benefit of the investors. The arguments of equity should have been first used to highlight the colonial nature of property acquisition.

D CONCLUSION

I conclude with the caveat that although *Transnational Law* by making individuals the subjects of international law has been liberating in human rights, it all began with first making investment law the human rights of the investor and multinational corporations. Phillip C. Jessup's *Transnational Law* challenges the state as the sole maker of international law. The doctrine of transnational law advocated the disrobing of new-found sovereignty acquired after decades of nationalist struggles in Asia and then in Africa. American corporate lawyers curried favour from the transnational law doctrine to expand their practice in international commercial arbitration. Next, in disputes arising from the expropriations by new states of property acquired from concession contracts investors found transnational law profitable.

Effectively, *Transnational Law*, restoring a colonial status quo through its doctrine, facilitated the post-war internationalization of contracts to develop the law of economic protection of aliens. The transnational law doctrine wantonly focused far too much on 'contracts' forgetting conveniently the concessional nature and history of the 'concession contracts'. The doctrine of transnational law grew from the McNair–Lauterpacht school of thought, which 'exploited ungrudgingly and to the full' the 'rules' of 'private law for the

---

[116] Y. DEZALAY & B. GARTH, DEALING IN VIRTUE: INTERNATIONAL COMMERCIAL ARBITRATION AND THE CONSTRUCTION OF A TRANSNATIONAL LEGAL ORDER 98 (1996). A. Martineau, *A Forgotten Chapter in the History of International Commercial Arbitration: The Slave Trade's Dispute Settlement System*, 31 LEIDEN J. INT'L L. 219–41 (2018).

purpose of the development of international law'. The Suez crisis was the first instance of the application of the transnational law doctrine.

To better understand the history of international law, it is, as I have shown, necessary to rethink the context and conditions under which transnationalism flourished. In this context, it is important to highlight the role and power of scholarly writings in using transnationalism as an argument to continue colonial power dynamics. Scholarly writings played a crucial functional role in the making of international law. Transnationalism as a legal argument sought to puncture the sovereignty of newly decolonized states and to protect the properties accrued though colonialism.

Transnational law demonstrates the creativity of arguments within international law and at the same time, upon critical reflection, disrobes the idealism and universalism that international law purportedly covers itself with. Transnationalism was pushed into the sphere of international legal argumentation for purely commercial needs of the erstwhile colonizers. The *Suez* crisis explains and contextualizes the reasons for the growth of the doctrine of the internationalized contracts in international law. The concept of the internationalized contract presented in the *Suez* case was derived from the comparison of concession agreements to treaties. By turning contracts into treaty, a legal fiction was created permitting international law to govern these arrangements. This international law got renamed *Transnational Law*.

18

After the Backlash

A New PRIDE for Transnational Law

RALF MICHAELS[*]

A INTRODUCTION

What a difference a few years make. It seems like yesterday that transnational law – that idea introduced by Philip Jessup more than sixty years ago and since refined by scholars, practitioners and activists all over the world – presented itself as the most attractive candidate for both the theory and the practice of law in a globalized world.[1] Transnational law promised not only to overcome the distinctions between public and private, domestic and international law, but also the distinction between law and society. Transnational law, far from being an apologist for neoliberalism and economic globalization, promised to provide tools not only to understand global injustices but also to overcome them. Transnational law was worthy of our pride.

Alas, no progress without backlash; no move to the future without nostalgia for the past, and no winning without losers. The dual shock of 2016 – the Brexit referendum in the United Kingdom and the election of Donald Trump as president in the United States – threw a wrench into the progress story of transnational law. Sure, nationalism and populism, racism, and xenophobia, those enemies of the transnational project, had raised their ugly heads before. But they had been considered to be on the way out, not supposed to garner majorities of votes – especially not in those cradles of democracy, as which we still view the UK and the United States. Now that they have, what shall we

[*] An earlier version of sections A and B was published as Ralf Michaels, *Does Brexit Spell the Death of Transnational Law?*, 17 GERMAN L.J. 51–61 (2016). Besides the additions, both text and references have been slightly amended. Earlier versions were presented at the Jessup conference in London 2016, at a Duke Law School faculty retreat in 2017, and at the AALS conference in San Diego in 2018.
[1] PHILIP JESSUP, TRANSNATIONAL LAW (1956).

make of the transnational project? Is the time of transnational law over? Or
can transnational law be renewed and revived?

It is worth remembering that Brexit and Trump are not isolated events of
antitransnationalism. The most successful transnational movement today is,
ironically, nationalism. Nationalists and populists in other EU member states
hoped to ride the Brexit wave and inaugurate their own exits in the name of
national sovereignty (although the chaotic discussions in the UK concerning
the Brexit negotiations have made leaving the EU less attractive to nationalist
movements elsewhere). And such nationalism, often with clear racist tendencies, goes beyond Europe and North America. In India, Modi has instituted a
new Hindu nationalism. In Russia, Putin is deploying a cynical form of
nationalism. In Brazil, Bolsonaro managed to double down on Donald
Trump's racist and discriminatory electoral campaign to win office. This
transnational nationalism is thus about more than just membership in the
EU. It is a movement for (perceived) national strength, for closed borders, for
controlled or restricted trade, for homogeneity. It wants to reestablish a
traditional idea of a sovereign nation state.

Brexiteers, like Trump voters, have been called stupid, selfish, and xenophobic, among other things. Even if this were true (it clearly is for some and
clearly not for all), this would not prove much. In a democracy, everyone has
the right to be stupid and also, up to a point, selfish and xenophobic. This is
not petty: we leave to democratic votes precisely those questions of politics that
we feel we cannot decide objectively on a scientific basis, and we trust people
to determine for themselves what is best for them and the country. Whether
membership in the EU should be open to a referendum is quite contestable.
But once a referendum is called, it is not easy to reject the result and
simultaneously celebrate democracy. The arguments must be taken seriously,
even if we refuse to accept them. And they must inform our thinking about
transnational law, even if we refuse to adopt them.

B BACKLASH AND NOSTALGIA

I *Brexit as Rejection of Transnational Law*

Brexit must be understood as a rejection of transnational law because, in many
ways, the European Union is the epitome of transnationalism.[2] Jessup himself,

---

[2]   *See, e.g.,* Karl-Heinz Ladeur, *European Law as Transnational Law – Europe Has to Be
      Conceived as an Heterarchical Network and Not as a Superstate!,* 10 GERMAN L.J. 1357 (2009);
      Christian Calliess, *Europe as Transnational Law – The Transnationalization of Values by*

although primarily interested in Asia, acknowledged as much. When his *Transnational Law* was first published, Jessup could only mention the European Coal and Steel Community, but he already rejoiced that it had "blazed a trail for supranational authorities."[3] In *Transnational Law*, Jessup famously defined transnational law "to include all law which regulates actions or events that transcend national frontiers. Both public and private international law are included, as are other rules which do not wholly fit into such standard categories."[4] This fit the new European Union quite well, as Jessup himself explained elsewhere:

> The basic treaties are pure international law, as is the rule which makes these treaties binding – pacta sunt servanda. But the jurisprudence of the Court of Justice of the European Communities shows that to a great extent the law of the Communities is something different – something which I would call "transnational," which may be in part international law in the sense in which that term is used in Article 38 of the Statute of the International Court of Justice, and partly law which has certain other characteristics.[5]

The core for our understanding of both transnational law and European law (and, incidentally, also of Brexit) is to understand their relation to the state and to national sovereignty. For Jessup, states were only one of many sets of actors, besides individuals, organizations and corporations, and also supranational organizations. Sovereignty, for him, did not disappear or become irrelevant, but it had become relative. Already in 1942, Jessup said as much: "If we can remove the snobbery and the selfishness from our international thinking, really admitting that the principle of sovereignty is not a sacred and unlimited

---

European Law, 10 GERMAN L.J. 1367 (2009); Christoph J.M. Safferling, *Europe as Transnational Law – A Criminal Law for Europe: Between National Heritage and Transnational Necessities*, 10 GERMAN L.J. 1386 (2009); *see also Symposium: Law, Lawyers, and Transnational Politics in the Production of Europe*, 32 LAW & SOC. INQUIRY 75 (2007).

[3] JESSUP, *supra* note 1, at 113. Later, Jessup reflected: "In Europe, sixteen years ago, I was noting the trail-blazing steps of the Coal and Steel Community, not anticipating in detail the further developments of the European Community which are now so familiar." Philip C. Jessup, *The Present State of Transnational Law, in* THE PRESENT STATE OF INTERNATIONAL LAW AND OTHER ESSAYS WRITTEN IN HONOUR OF THE CENTENARY CELEBRATION OF THE INTERNATIONAL LAW ASSOCIATION 1873–1973 339, 340 (Maarten Bos ed., 1973).

[4] JESSUP, *supra* note 1, at 2. Later in the book, in a less-often-quoted passage, he clarifies: "Transnational law then includes both civil and criminal aspects, it includes what we know as public and private international law, and it includes national law, both public and private." *Id.* at 106. On this, see also Peer Zumbansen's introduction to this volume, at n.39.

[5] Philip Jessup, *Diversity and Uniformity in the Law of Nations*, 58 AM. J. INT'L L. 341, 347–48 (1964).

thing, we shall be well on our way toward true international democracy."[6] In *Transnational Law*, he argued that "in fact the sovereign's power is neither exclusive nor absolute within its own territory, and that this is true whether one is talking in terms of legal or extralegal power."[7] He could have been speaking of the EU. Member states still play a role, but they are one set of actors between individuals and regions, on the one hand, and the supranational organization of the EU, on the other hand. Sovereignty does not disappear, but it is shared, as in Neil MacCormick's insightful analysis of constitutional pluralism that generated a whole field.[8]

The Brexit movement, in rejecting the EU, rejected quite precisely the transnational law character of the EU, even if this was not overt in every aspect. At its heart, Brexit represented a fundamentally legal concern: rules for the UK should be made by the UK and its institutions. This links lawmaking and sovereignty with the idealized sovereign state of nineteenth-century international law:[9] a largely homogeneous population without foreigners and immigrants, a firmly controlled territory isolated by closed borders, and a sovereign UK government that need not share authority with Brussels. And, remarkably, they also emphasize the fourth element named as a requirement for a state in international law: its ability to enter into relations with other states on its own terms. In other words, what the "leave" voters wanted was traditional sovereignty, both in its internal and its external aspects: a Westphalian model of the world, in which states are internally sovereign, and in which international relations are exclusively dealt with as matters between states.

II *The Nostalgia of the Nation State*

Much of this desire is driven by nostalgia for a past that never was. On the one hand, there is the right-wing nostalgia for a United Kingdom that was not only powerful and prosperous but also, by and large, white. Some of this is nostalgia for the British Empire, as evidenced by the hope to reestablish enhanced trade with former colonies (including the United States) and the rather nonchalant

---

[6] *Jessup Calls International Democracy Post-War Ideal*, COLUM. DAILY SPECTATOR June 2, 1942, at 1.

[7] JESSUP, *supra* note 1, at 41.

[8] Neil MacCormick, *Beyond the Sovereign State*, 56 MOD. L. REV. 1 (1993); Neil Walker, *Constitutional Pluralism Revisited*, 22 EUR. L.J. 333 (2016).

[9] *See* art. 1 of the Montevideo Convention on Rights and Duties of States, *opened for signature* Dec. 26, 1933, 165 L.N.T.S. 19 (entered into force Dec. 26, 1934).

treatment of the former British colony of Ireland.[10] Some of it is the nostalgia for an ethnically based nation state. On the other hand, there is the left-wing nostalgia for a functioning welfare state, for a strong left that can actually improve workers conditions, that can fight understandable fights with understandable enemies (workers against capitalists), against a neoliberal techno-cratic government in Brussels.[11]

This hope for a return to the nation state is misguided. There is no way back. The nation state, like the empire, in its nineteenth-century idealized form is a mirage, and self-regulation in isolation can no longer work.[12] Start with the idea of sovereignty. We know it to be a construct and a highly problematic one. Krasner has (supportively) called it, with some justification, organized hypocrisy.[13] Jessup made the point earlier, from a realist perspective:

> The very existence of a government of a state is a fiction, for a state is an intangible, and our international law picture of a sovereign state never had life. Sovereignty is essentially a concept of completeness. It is also a legal creation, and as such, is a paradox, if not an absolute impossibility, for if a state is a sovereign in the complete sense, it knows no law and therefore abolishes, at the moment of its creation, the jural creator which gave it being. All juristic persons, indeed, as Charles De Visscher has pointed out, are fictions created by a superannuated doctrine which should be discarded.[14]

But the idea of the state as the fundamental entity is problematic in other ways too. Insofar as the dream of the "leavers" is to go back to the nation state with a shared identity, the futility of the dream is showing, not least from the voting results. A country cannot easily be said to have a clear national identity if, in a referendum, it splits almost evenly on what that identity is. Notably, the split is not random but tracks various societal differentiations: young versus old, urban versus rural, educated versus uneducated. The idea of one country with one identity and one national interest is refuted by the results of the very referendum that sought to reclaim the notion.

Indeed, the UK is one of the stranger models for a nation state, not least because it consists of several nations: besides England, there are Wales,

---

[10] Ireland was colonized before it became a kingdom, though whether it was a colony in a technical sense remains disputed. *See* Stephen Howe, *Questioning the (Bad) Question: "Was Ireland a Colony?"*, 36 Irish Hist. Stud,, 138 (2008).

[11] *E.g.*, Costas Lapavitsas, The Left Case against the EU (2018).

[12] *See* Jo Guldi, *The Case for Utopia: History and the Possible Meanings of Brexit a Hundred Years On*, 14 Globalizations 150 (2017).

[13] Stephen D. Krasner, Sovereignty: Organized Hypocrisy (1999).

[14] Philip C. Jessup, *International Law in the Post-war World*, 36 Am. Soc'y Int'l L. Proc. 46, 49 (1942).

Scotland, and Northern Ireland. Scotland and Northern Ireland voted with
significant majorities to remain in the EU. Scotland considered an exit from
the UK before and is suggesting it might still initiate this. Northern Ireland
creates the problem that may still bring Brexit down altogether. The "leavers"
run into a conundrum familiar from international law discussions on seces-
sion and self-determination: If the UK can split from the EU, why should not
Scotland split from the UK? Why is it wrong for Brussels to make rules for
London but right for London to make rules for Glasgow? Who is the *self* in
self-governance?

There is one answer to the lack of unity, and it should not be dismissed out
of hand.[15] One might say that sovereignty does not require homogeneity of a
shared identity. Quite the contrary: the state is that very institution that
provides robust procedures to create decisions that can be accepted among
diverse views. Nation states (especially the UK with its parliamentary supremacy) provide the relevant institutions for democratic decision-making. They
have functioning parliaments, a functioning court system, a functioning
government. And they have elected officials who can be held accountable.
This seems plausible in theory, but it has two shortcomings. First, it is not
clear that voters actually accept decisions made under the procedures provided by the state; the referendum itself remains a test case. Second, and more
importantly, it is not clear that the state's institutions are particularly well-
versed for transnational problems. These institutions remain national in their
setup and in their functioning. As they stand, these institutions are adequate
for national, less so transnational, issues.

This is where the second mirage becomes evident, the mirage of self-
governance. When Jessup suggested that "the sovereign's power is neither
exclusive nor absolute within its own territory," he expressed an important
fact. There are many issues that are effectively decided outside of the sovereign. There are issues on which states are almost bound to follow the demands
from other states – not by law but by necessity. Neighbors of the EU know of
the need to enact EU legislation in order to be compatible. Even seemingly
robust states strive to comply with EU data privacy standards in order to serve
as "safe havens." Poorer countries have even less choice. They have to enact
certain product and labor standards in order to be allowed to export. They may
have to grant foreign investors specific privileges. Their sovereignty is formal,
but in effect they are regulated from elsewhere through economic pressures,

---

[15] *See, e.g.,* Richard Tuck, *The Left Case for Brexit,* DISSENT (June 6, 2016), https://www
.dissentmagazine.org/online_articles/left-case-brexit.

even without the formalities of a system like the EU. Jessup knew about this interdependence. British proponents of Brexit, if they did not, are learning it.

Jessup's focus, in positing transnational law, was especially on problems that transcend borders – which defines, at least traditionally, the limited competences of the EU. But Jessup already demonstrated that there is no clear boundary between domestic and transnational problems and that traditional distinctions tend to be arbitrary.[16] Realistically, an increasing number of problems must be characterized as transnational, and it is therefore not surprising therefore that the EU has claimed ever broader competences. Now, these transnational problems cannot be resolved through isolated self-regulation on the level of the nation state. By necessity, citizens in or from several countries are involved – the very justification for regulation at the EU level.[17] Immigration concerns, one of the biggest drivers of the referendum's outcome, are a good example. Immigration control can be defined as a national problem, but that is artificial.[18] Immigration is by definition a trans-national problem: it concerns the immigration country, the emigration country, the refugees in transit between the two, and also other countries that will need to bear the costs of one country's permissive or restrictive immigration policies. Much was made of the claim that Angela Merkel, in recognizing the European duty under international law to accept masses of refugees, was indirectly imposing on other countries as well. But the Brexit demand for self-regulation – in itself the demand that the UK should be allowed to regulate refugees – is effectively also an imposition on other countries, without giving them a say. That may be justifiable, but not as pure self-regulation.

Again, there is a more sophisticated version of this argument. It says that even when problems are transnational, they need not be regulated on a supranational level. It would be better to resolve them through coordination among individual states, and such regulation requires sovereign states. The "leavers" made much of the UK's enhanced ability to enter into agreements, both with third countries and with the EU. And indeed, in many ways, such decentralized regulation is often superior to supranational regulation. But it seems questionable, to say the least, that such coordination is easier from outside than from inside the EU. One can well speculate that a vote for Brexit is really largely a vote against coordination, not for better coordination.

---

[16] Jessup, *supra* note 1, at 11.
[17] See (critically) Alexander Somek, *The Darling Dogma of Bourgeois Europeanists*, 20 Eur. L.J. 688 (2014).
[18] *See, e.g.,* Tendayi Achiume, *Migration as Decolonization*, 71 Stan. L. Rev. (2019).

This is not to say that the EU is the optimal mechanism for coordination. It is not a mere coordination institution, and one may well argue that its impulse for harmonization has gone too far, that its technocratic nature is antidemocratic, and that the lack of a Europe-wide social welfare system restricts its space of meaningful and legitimate action. But the "leavers" grossly overestimate the space for political freedom that Brexit creates. In view of existing networks, it will be very difficult for the UK to independently negotiate better conditions and, thus, essentially secure more regulatory space for itself than would have been possible from within the EU. Switzerland and Norway are sometimes named as models. But one would think the UK's ambition goes beyond the autonomy and authority of these countries. Leaving the EU means escaping from some outside influence, but it results in the UK losing even more influence.

III *The Nostalgia of Transnational Law*

If the desire to return to the nation state is a sign of nostalgia, then why is it that so many people prefer it over transnational law? One answer, I suggest, is perhaps surprising: transnational law itself is marred by its own nostalgia. Nostalgia for Jessup can be viewed, perhaps, in the frequency with which his book *Transnational Law* is invoked as a book for our, not its, time. Nostalgia for the European Union can be viewed, for example, in the curious statement from June 25, 2016, in which the foreign ministers of the six original founding member states invoke the community's founding in 1957 and assure themselves of that project's continued importance,[19] or a novelist's (made-up) claim that Walter Hallstein called for a united Europe in Auschwitz.[20] Both invoke a time that is no longer ours. Just as we cannot go back to the nineteenth-century sovereign state, so we cannot go back to the midcentury world.

In many ways, reading Jessup's *Transnational Law*, like reading other statements from the time of the founding of the European Communities, is

---

[19] *See* Press Release, Common Statement by the Foreign Ministers of Belgium, France, Germany, Italy, Luxemburg and the Netherlands (June 25, 2016), http://www.auswaertiges-amt .de/EN/Infoservice/Presse/Meldungen/2016/160625_Gemeinsam_Erklaerung_ Gruenderstaatentreffen_ENG_VERSION.html.

[20] Robert Menasse, The Capital (2019); *see also* Robert Menasse, Enraged Citizens, European Peace and Democratic Deficits; or, Why the Democracy Given to Us Must Become One We Fight For (2016). Menasse invented not only Hallstein's Auschwitz speech but also Hallstein quotes to the effect that the goal of the EU was to overcome the nation state and is being criticized for it.

a journey into another time, the era of the Pax Americana. That era was influenced by the recent experience of the catastrophe of two World Wars, and it was characterized by an emerging Cold War. The first of these experiences suggested the risk of nationalism; the second suggested the risk of collectivism. Transnationalism and individualism in the form of free markets, were the apt responses. But this describes only what was to be rejected – in that time and in that place. Beyond that, both *Transnational Law* and the European Community were hopeful projects. Jessup's *Transnational Law* exudes the optimism of its time: problems exist, but they can be solved. There is some utopian quality to it, but it is a very finely chiseled and detailed utopia. It is a manifesto of a generation that sees big tasks ahead but feels up to resolving them, with the right instruments and the right attitude.

Instead of such nostalgia, it is necessary to consider carefully what the instruments and attitude of the time were. Jessup's approach to transnational law was influenced by legal realism. He suggested that one should start with concrete problems rather than abstract categories. What was needed was expertise – not expertise in legal doctrine but expertise in real-world problems and their solutions. Jessup trusted institutions and officials to display this kind of expertise. He praised mixed arbitral tribunals for their creativity in developing new and attractive rules in the lack of established ones and suggested that national judges should be able to do something similar. At least in principle this is still the approach that the EU takes in its lawmaking. Most secondary law is formulated as a response to a concrete problem that has surfaced, based on preparatory work by experts and a complex political process.

What could be wrong about all this? For one, Brexit demonstrates that governance by experts is unpopular. This should not be dismissed as merely irrational. David Kennedy demonstrates some of the problems of expert-based governance and how it can lead to injustice.[21] Among the many reasons for this, the simplest may be that it risks being undemocratic. Expert-based governance depoliticizes decisions and turns them into observable truths. Such depoliticization may have seemed appropriate in view of the experience with the unhampered politics of Nazi Germany and the Soviet Union. Today it has become problematic. In the light of such expert opinions, it appears that Brexit supporters relied on the power they had: they may be wrong, their vote may not even be to their benefit, but at least they are able to stick it to the "expert-ocracy."

---

[21] David Kennedy, A World of Struggle: How Power, Law & Expertise Shape Global Political Economy (2016).

This leads to a broader problem for transnational law, the problem of democratic responsibility. In *Transnational Law*, Jessup discussed the wealth of rules, he discussed jurisdiction, and he discussed choice of law, but he did not discuss accountability. Admittedly, Jessup spoke forcefully for international democracy elsewhere.[22] But even there, this democracy often seemed more instrumental than intrinsically good. Democracy was important to fend off the Soviet Union (which did not support it, at least in the Western way). But it is not clear that it played a role for the development of transnational law. And as for the EU, its democratic deficit has never been fully resolved, and it is not clear that there is enough political will to fix it. In many ways, the EU was set up precisely in order to overcome the narrow national interests that make their way into national legislation.

Indeed, arguably, this antidemocratic position was once a virtue. In the aftermath of the experience with Nazi Germany, the idea of populist control was deeply suspicious, at least for Europe. In the European postwar mind, the depoliticization of important questions seemed a good thing: it made it possible to ensure that rational decisions would be taken. In this story, what made the postwar world prosper and what made transnational law successful was precisely that it held populist control in check. The international human rights movement spoke truth to power, even where that power rested in overwhelming popular majorities and even where the "truth" was normative and contestable. The emerging transnational commercial law was successful because it was able to free itself from state control, democratic or not. And the EU was able to hold national governments accountable not just vis-à-vis foreigners but also vis-à-vis their own citizens, an aspect that Christian Joerges has emphasized. The disdain for the "leave" voters as populists is a successor to the disdain for Nazis as populists. Discord may exist within, not about, the system. This somewhat restrained view of democracy is now seeing its limits: people revolt against a decision-making process in which they do not feel represented.

This leads to a further aspect. For Jessup and for the European Union, the focus on the individual was closely linked to a preference for competition and capitalist markets. This project has been successful: party autonomy has been greatly expanded, and private ordering has been celebrated. Not all individualism in transnational law has this focus on markets; the human rights movement is, in parts, anticapitalist. Nonetheless, it appears that individualism itself is being rejected. In Brexit we see this with particular strength. The hope of

---

[22] *See, e.g.*, Jessup, *supra* note 5; Philip C. Jessup, *Democracy Must Keep Constant Guard for Freedom*, 25 Dep't St. Bull. 220 (1951).

many of the "leavers" was to avoid the harsh individual competition of the common market in favor of a national community, whether in the leftist view of solidarity and the welfare state or the rightist view of a racially homogeneous nation.

A final aspect follows from this, and it may be the most important one: transnational law is potentially elitist. Transnational law, like increased Europe-wide competition benefits some and injures others: it benefits the British elites and the famous Polish plumber; it hurts the British worker. If, as we know, more educated voters were against Brexit and more uneducated ones were for it, that need not suggest that votes for Brexit were simply dumb; it may also suggest that the EU benefits the educated more than it benefits the uneducated. Similarly, it is undoubtedly xenophobic and selfish to oppose human rights, including rights for refugees. But it is at least not irrational in view of the fact that, of course, human rights for some individuals have spillover effects on others. This is a reason why we usually do not leave decisions on human rights to a majority vote; the fact that the Brexit referendum has such effects is one of the most unfortunate aspects.[23]

The elitist potential of transnational law is no accident. It is a reflection of the new stratification of world society, creating a transnational upper class that travels and communicates freely across borders and a national underclass that remains local and cannot participate in the benefits of the upper class. In this sense, the solidarity among nationalists worldwide is not paradoxical (though it is often hypocritical, given that many of its proponents are themselves members of transnational elites). Transnational law, insofar as it concerns transnational problems, threatens to be the law of that transnational elite. It may care for the transnational underclass (especially migrants), but it has difficulties with the local underclass, especially where that underclass is racist. As such, it is no surprise that the underclass opposes it.

C   A NEW PRIDE

All of this does not suggest that transnational law is dead. The simple return to the nation state is not the answer, despite the nostalgia that surrounds it. Transnational problems are not solved by national laws in isolation. There is no alternative to transnational law. But we must realize that transnational law has a dark underbelly. That underbelly was not so visible in the 1950s, and maybe it was not so important. Today it is important and should not be

---

[23] *See* Lauren Fiedler, *Is Nationalism the Most Serious Challenge to Human Rights: Warnings from Brexit and Lessons from History*, 53 TEX. INT'L L.J. 211 (2018).

underestimated. Transnational law, like any other area, benefits some and hurts others. It must be developed without nostalgia. That means that some aspects that are often underappreciated must be addressed and that transnational law must adapt to the challenges of the present.

What does it take for transnational law to respond to the wave of nationalism and populism? Obviously, a fully fledged program would be impossible to draft here; it would also, arguably, be in contrast to the evolutionary and learning character of transnational law itself. Nonetheless, a program which I want to call "PRIDE" would include five programmatic points: politicization, redistribution, inclusion, democratization, energization. I do not claim novelty for these points, but I think it may be helpful to spell them out together. Let me discuss each of these in brief.

I *Politicization*

A first need for transnational law is politicization. In the 1950s, the politicization of law may have seemed a threat in view of the experience with Nazi Germany. Jessup's alternative was a kind of natural law;[24] the European Communities endorsed a rather technocratic approach to the creation and regulation of common markets. Both placed hope in law as a rational alternative to the unpredictability of politics.[25] The hope was that proper solutions could be found through prudence and did not require political struggle.

We still see remnants of both. There is still a variant of human rights law that is intrinsically apolitical (or even antipolitical); it ignores not only local context and but also local decision-making – in fact, it is formulated with the explicit goal to isolate certain core values from political decision-making processes. This variant claims an inherent superiority to human rights over their alternative and therefore sees no need to engage with opponents. Moreover, some (by far not all) human rights law is focused on individual rights protection without concern for the eminently political problem of distributive justice.[26] The deliberately apolitical character of this variant of human rights law is also its weakness; the backlash against human rights from rightist

---

[24] Early reviewers of JESSUP, *supra* note 1, already pointed this out: Nicholas de B. Katzenbach, Book Review, 24 U. CHI. L. REV. 413, 414 (1957); Hessel E. Yntema, Book Review, 6 AM. J. COMP. L. 364, 365 (1957); *see also* Matthias Mahlmann, *Theorizing Transnational Law – Varieties of Transnational Law and the Universalistic Stance*, 10 GERMAN L.J. 1325 (2009).

[25] *See, e.g.*, PHILIP C. JESSUP, THE USE OF INTERNATIONAL LAW (1959).

[26] Thus the criticism from SAMUEL MOYN, NOT ENOUGH – HUMAN RIGHTS IN AN UNEQUAL WORLD (2018); but see the sharp defense of existing human rights practice by Gráinne de Búrca, Book Review, 16 INT'L J. CONST. L. 1347 (2018) (reviewing MOYN, *supra*).

populists and leftist critics emerges in large part from the denial of politics. And although the technocratic character of EU law is otherwise entirely different from the natural law variant of human rights law, both share an apolitical character. Like human rights law, EU law interferes with domestic legal processes. Like human rights law, its claim is that correct decisions can be found elsewhere; in this case, in expertise. And like human rights law, EU law is criticized for its denial of politics.

What would politicization look like? We actually already see a lot of it in current transnational law debates. The new human rights movement not only views itself as a political project; it also assigns a space to politics within the regimes it proposes and defends. The European Union has been faced with demands for a more political concept, be it in the calls for a European contract law based on social justice a decade ago[27] or in proposals for a new European Union in response to the Greek crisis.[28] In similar ways, transnational law as a discipline needs to be understood as political in a dual way: it must integrate politics in addition to legal doctrine and culture, and it must itself be understood as a political, engaged project.[29] It must, in other words, leave behind the dual antipolitical postwar nostalgia of natural law and technocracy and explicitly endorse an understanding of law as political.

II Redistribution

Closely related to politics is the question of inequality and the likely response of redistribution. Jessup was already aware of the power the have-nots could yield if their concerns remained unaddressed:

> When such issues as we have been describing attain certain proportions or degrees of intensity, something is done about it. If it is not done by the haves, the have-nots may resort to domestic violence, or to international war, or to the General Assembly of the United Nations.[30]

[27] E.g., *Study Group on Social Justice in European Private Law, Social Justice in European Contract Law: A Manifesto*, 10 Eur. L.J. 653 (2004); Ugo Mattei & Fernanda Nicola, *A "Social Dimension" in European Private Law? The Call for Setting a Progressive Agenda*, 41 New Eng. L. Rev. 1 (2006); Martin Hesselink, *Five Political Ideas of European Contract Law*, 7 Eur. Rev. Contract L. 295 (2011).

[28] Óscar García Agustín, *European Counterpublics? DiEM25, Plan B and the Agonistic European Public Sphere*, 13 J. Civ. Soc. 323 (2017).

[29] Peer Zumbansen, *Theorizing as Activity: Transnational Legal Theory in Context, in* Law's Ethical, Global and Theoretical Contexts: Essays in Honour of William Twining 280 (Christopher McCrudden et al. eds., 2015).

[30] Jessup, *supra* note 1, at 32.

The prediction has (unsurprisingly) come true in all three regards; we see
violence, war, and involvement of the UN: the abolition of poverty is the first
of the UN Development Goals. Renewed populism is not only about economic uncertainty, but this is certainly one of its drivers. Inequality in the law
used to be, for many, a domestic problem, to be resolved through domestic
institutions like a welfare system and progressive taxation. Global inequality
seemed less pressing. But globalization has had a triple impact on inequality.
First, although it has enhanced the opportunities for transnational elites, who
can move between different countries and arbitrage, and for the global poor,
who have had chances of rising either in their own countries or for moving, it
has decreased these opportunities for lower classes in developed countries,
who now fear reductions to the welfare system and increased competition
from immigrants. Second, globalization has restricted the regulatory discretion for states, partly through regulatory competition, partly through obligations under trade treaties and investment treaties. Third, globalization has
increased visibility of global inequalities. In this sense (and not in every sense),
the nationalism behind Brexit and Trump is also a reflection of distributive
issues. And transnational law must take this into account.

Of course, transnational law has always considered inequality. But the
avoidance of politics has meant that it had difficulties dealing with it. Inequality within the state was left to states themselves (which have social welfare
systems); international inequality seemed impossible to tackle in the absence
of strong supranational institution. Short of institutions, the hope for transnationalists long lay in growth, but growth is no longer a solution, not least
because of its impact on climate change. Moreover, although transnational
law often likes to take on the fate of the poor elsewhere – exploited workers in
Bangladesh, environmental victims in Ecuador – it has not always sufficiently
endorsed the issues of the have-nots at home, especially where these have-nots
display unattractive characteristics such as racism and xenophobia. Only
recently have discussions about inequality come to the center of debates,
encouraged especially by economists.[31] Equality has become a core concern
that transnational law, no matter in what ideological variant, has to deal with.
It is heartening therefore that it is becoming a core concern in transnational
law conferences.[32]

[31] *E.g.*, THOMAS PIKETTY, CAPITAL IN THE TWENTY-FIRST CENTURY (2014); BRANKO MILANOVIC,
   GLOBAL INEQUALITY – A NEW APPROACH FOR THE AGE OF GLOBALIZATION (2016).
[32] See references to two conferences in Berlin and Sydney respectively: Thomas Dollmaier,
   *Messing with the Mess We Are In – Notes from the Transregional Academy on 'Redistribution
   and the Law in an Antagonistic World' from 21–30 August 2017 in Berlin*, VÖLKERRECHTSBLOG
   (Sept. 8, 2017), https://voelkerrechtsblog.org/messing-with-the-mess-we-are-in/; *Programme*,

III *Inclusion*

If politicization and redistribution are responses to substantive concerns among Brexiteers and Trumpists, inclusion goes to a formal concern: the sense of exclusion. This seems ironic from the perspective of traditional transnational law. After all, it was the exclusionary (and in the case of Nazi Germany, murderous) nationalism that had led to destruction. The hope in transnational law was one of inclusion of everyone and everything. Everyone: a law that crosses borders and covers everyone who is affected. Everything: a law that "includes both civil and criminal aspects, it includes what we know as public and private international law, and it includes national law, both public and private."[33] An all-inclusive law, in other ways.

Such an all-inclusive law is a mirage, as Hans Lindahl shows, focusing especially on laws with a universal appeal like trade law and human rights law.[34] Legal orders are always about something, which also means that they must exclude what stands in the way of that something. We can see this easily in transnational law, when it excludes nationalism and racism from its program. It is no wonder, therefore, that nationalists and racists feel excluded from an ostentatiously all-including law.[35] This does not mean that nationalism and racism must be included as normative positions. But it does mean that transnational law must explicitly account for what it excludes and justify this exclusion instead of invoking a false universal character.

If transnational law views populists only as outsiders to what is otherwise perceived as a common project, the danger becomes that of elitism. Transnational law, by and large, is a project made by a transnational elite, a transnational network of scholars and decision makers. It is also, widely, supported by a network made for a transnational elite, namely those who benefit from transnationalism, whether in its market liberal form or its human rights form. Market-liberal transnationalists let the weak collapse; leftist transnationalists let the xenophobes collapse. As a consequence, weak xenophobes most vociferously reject transnationalism. The Brexit voters are those who felt

Transnational Law Summer Institute 2017, "Inequality: Reproduction, Alienation, Intervention," KING'S COLLEGE LONDON, https://www.kcl.ac.uk/law/tli/tlsi/programme.aspx; *TLSI 2017: Inequality – Reproduction, Alienation, & Intervention, Program,* KING'S COLLEGE LONDON, https://www.kcl.ac.uk/law/tli/tlsi/TLSI-2017-Programme-Overview-June-2017.pdf.

[33] *See* JESSUP, *supra* note 1, 106, See also ibid., 2.
[34] HANS LINDAHL, AUTHORITY AND THE GLOBALISATION OF INCLUSION AND EXCLUSION (2018).
[35] *See also* Thomas J. Scotto, David Sanders & Jason Reifler, *The Consequential Nationalist–Globalist Policy Divide in Contemporary Britain: Some Initial Analyses,* 28 J. ELECTIONS, PUB. OPINION & PARTIES 38–58 (2018).

excluded, and the disdain that we pour on them suggests that they are not wrong in feeling that way. Transnational law will need to include them too in some way, without necessarily yielding to their demands.

IV *Democratization*

A concrete way in which exclusion manifests itself is decline in democracy. Populists feel excluded in part because they feel that their voice is not heard, that they have no say in decisions over their (and everybody else's) future. Indeed, the four most populous democracies are currently ruled by populists.[36] If both Brexit and the Trump election were at least in part fueled by a desire to "take back control," this could be read as a desire for more democracy.

It is easy to point out that this was not successful. Domestically, power remains in the hands of elites. The UK government's desire to restrict the power of Parliament in matters of Brexit is no more ironic than the way in which Trump fulfilled his promise to "drain the swamp" by putting in his cronies and enriching himself. Internationally, Brexit undoubtedly leads to a loss of influence for the UK (and thus for its voters); Trump's strategy of "America first" has a similar effect. Populism of this kind, it can be said, is not good for democracy. But such analyses hide a bigger problem: if indeed it is not practically possible to "take back control" through nationalizing in a globalized world, then how and where is democracy possible at all? After World War II, hope lay in a world government or at least in a strongly centralized UN. Jessup himself, though skeptical about world government itself, endorsed at least certain paths toward centralization.[37] During the Cold War, a core concern was establishing democracy (Western-style) outside of the West, meaning in socialist countries and in former colonies. Inherent in all of these programs was the idea, opposed by populism, that important decisions should be taken out of the democratic decision-making process and shifted to experts.

Today our faith in both projects has been shattered, but the democratization of transnational decision-making remains a challenge for a transnational law that goes beyond issues of both legal technique and substantive justice.[38] Existing projects like global constitutionalism and global administrative law

---

[36] Yasha Mounk & Jordan Kyle, *What Populists Do to Democracies*, Atlantic, Dec. 26, 2018.

[37] Philip C. Jessup, The International Problem of Governing Mankind (1947).

[38] *See, e.g.*, Oren Perez, *Normative Creativity and Global Legal Pluralism: Reflections on the Democratic Critique of Transnational Law*, 10 Ind. J. Glob. Leg. Stud. 25 (2003).

are, at least in part and insofar as they transfer experiences from the nation state to the global sphere, still somewhat mired in the thinking of democracy as a relation between citizens and a centralized government. They also face the remaining problem of decision-making by experts – only that the experts are now lawyers and legal scholars. The lack of global institutions likely requires a decentered democracy for which we have no true model. Thus, democratization beyond the nation state remains a challenge.

V *Energization*

A final plea for transnational law is what I want to call energization. Populists are energized, and this has been one root of their success. Transnationalists have long been worried by energization, viewing it as closely related to demagogy and ideology. Jessup's own response, predating international legal realism, was a cool-headed one: Instead of ideology, we should focus on problem solving: looking at problems and finding concrete solutions.[39] The European Union was established on a similar idea: by providing essentially technical solutions to problems, it should be possible to take out emotions and to overcome ideology. Inherent in this was a great faith in the power not just of law but also of technocracy and the superiority of experts in solving problems.

But today we realize that the problem-solving approach underestimates the importance of emotions in politics and law, as well as the symbolic value of law.[40] The Brexit nostalgia for the British state is also a nostalgia for the symbolism of nationally made law, which has more attraction than Brussels. Trump's success has emerged from his appeal to raw emotions, even if many of these appear ugly. And populists have been carried by an energy that finds no match on the other side. True, meetings among transnational legal scholars can be both exciting and energizing. But what it will take is to carry this energy on into society at large, to present a powerful counterweight to the allures of an exclusionary nationalism.

How can such energy be established? Do we need a new populism that is not racist and nationalist, as Chantal Mouffe, among others, has proposed?[41] Or is the idea of populism, even in an antiessentialist form, too close to that of a people, with its implications of ethnic homogeneity and nationalism? And if

---

[39] *See* Gregory Shaffer, *Legal Realism and International Law*, in INTERNATIONAL LEGAL THEORY: FOUNDATIONS AND FRONTIERS (Jeffrey L. Dunoff & Mark A. Pollack eds., 2019).

[40] THE AFFECT EFFECT – DYNAMICS OF EMOTION IN POLITICAL THINKING AND BEHAVIOR (Russell Neuman et al. eds., 2007).

[41] CHANTAL MOUFFE, FOR A LEFT POPULISM (2018).

so, can transnational law generate enough excitement to carry the day? This remains to be seen. What we know is that transnational law must move beyond both a merely defensive role (of avoiding war or racism) and an arrogation of superiority (vis-à-vis the narrow-minded nationalists). It must, again, become a matter of pride – or, better perhaps, as I suggest here, of PRIDE.

PART IV

Conclusion

Epilogue

Difficulties for Every Solution
Defining Transnational Law at the Edge of Transdisciplinarity

VIK KANWAR

A INTRODUCTION

[S]ome lawyers find solutions for every difficulty while other lawyers find difficulties for every solution.

Philip C. Jessup (after Lord Denning)[1]

The solution suggested here is that, for the time being at least, we avoid further classification of transnational problems and further definitions of transnational law.

Philip C. Jessup[2]

In 1956, Philip C. Jessup, in *Transnational Law*, defined transnational law (TL) as "all law which regulates actions or events that transcend national frontiers. Both public and private international law are included, as are other rules which do not wholly fit into such standard categories." The book, defining the *object* of study, crystalized over the next generation as a *field* of study, if not quite yet a methodology and not yet a discipline. Philip Jessup's definition of TL was formulated within the horizon of a particular phase of disciplinary engagement, which has been broadly characterized as postwar "pragmatism," though this category hides as much as it reveals.[3] The current

---

[1] PHILIP C. JESSUP, TRANSNATIONAL LAW 6 (1956).
[2] *Id.*
[3] On the postwar style of international legal thought, characterized across opposing camps as pragmatic, functionalist, and liberal, see, e.g., David Kennedy, *The International Style in Postwar Law and Policy*, 1994 UTAH L. REV. 7, 11 (1994) [hereinafter Kennedy, *International Style*]; David Kennedy, *Thinking Against the Box: When Renewal Repeats*, 32 N.Y.U. J. INT'L L. & POL. 335 (1999) [hereinafter Kennedy, *Thinking Against the Box*]; Justin Desautels-Stein, *At War with the Eclectics: Mapping Pragmatism in Contemporary Legal Analysis*, 2007 MICH. ST. L. REV. 565 (2007); Hengameh Saberi, *Love it or Hate it, but for the Right Reasons: Pragmatism and the New Haven School's International Law of Human Dignity*, 35 B.C. INT'L & COMP. L. REV. 59 (2012).

book arrives at a different moment, and if future intellectual historians take us at our word, they will characterize us with a similarly imprecise term: *interdisciplinary*. This epilogue will diverge in its task from what the essays above have done so ably: investigating TL as an account of regulatory actors, norms, and processes discoverable in the world. It will open a window instead upon TL as a project for producing knowledge.[4] This means viewing the book through the lens of its purposes, motives, and habits in producing TL as a kind of knowledge. It also means recognizing that the particular image of TL captured in the present book is highly specific, implicitly opposed to other conceptions, and that is true even if representatives of every faction are present and accounted for.

The essays presented in this book arise out of a series of presentations and performances at the Transnational Law Institute, King's College London, in 2016, commemorating the sixtieth year of Philip Jessup's Storrs Lectures (1956), published as *Transnational Law*, inaugurating a concept and definition that have been a source of inspiration and bewilderment in the decades since. Today, it has become so routine to cite to Jessup's definition as a point of departure, whether or not one agrees with his original articulation, that the effort may appear mechanical and superficial. Yet the production of knowledge takes place through moments alternately experienced as ritual and routine, as play and conflict, and even the quotidian habits of citation and definition may contain layers of significance we have not yet considered. This essay proceeds through four attempts to define TL in light of this book and its approach. The first two sections, "Defining a Concept" and "Defining a Project," contrast the purposes behind two definitions of TL: Jessup's and the one presented in the introduction to this book. The third section, "Defining as Disciplinarity," revisits what we know about the various intellectual projects that have taken on the name "transnational law" since 1956, locating the current project in a flight from systematization to eclecticism and from interdisciplinarity to transdisciplinarity.[5] The fourth and final, called "Definition between Deference and Distinctiveness," returns us to the opening

---

[4] As with many modern disciplinary formations, TL maintains the reciprocal senses of "domain of knowledge" as well as "object of study," but along with most fields of law, it is additionally a "field of regulation." Thus, TL scholars pursue an actors-norms-processes triad, but it should be apparent that there is a continuum of possible connections between expert communities involved in the production of knowledge and governance. *See, e.g.*, TRANSNATIONAL COMMUNITIES: SHAPING GLOBAL ECONOMIC GOVERNANCE (M.L. Djelic & S. Quack eds., 2010).

[5] MARTTI KOSKENNIEMI, THE GENTLE CIVILIZER OF NATIONS: THE RISE AND FALL OF INTERNATIONAL LAW 1870–1960 (2002).

gestures of definition and conceptualization, revisiting what binds us to Jessup's text, this time *refracted* through disciplines rarely engaged in the already thoroughly interdisciplinary TL literature, intentionally multiplying the *manner* as well as the motive of definition. Taken together, these few final meditations and thought experiments point to the specificity of the knowledge assembled here and celebrate the willful eclecticism that holds it together despite any definitional, conceptual uncertainties that haunt TL as a disciplinary project and discourse.[6]

B DEFINING A CONCEPT

For its quotability, concision, and enduring influence, Philip Jessup's 1956 definition of TL remains unsurpassed.[7] It provides a shared point of reference for the major subsequent applications of the concept, including in each of the essays presented in this book.[8] The central features of this definition should be familiar to us by now. First, TL scrambles the traditional two-by-two matrix of law as public or private and domestic or international; these are no longer viewed as fixed or mutually exclusive domains of legal activity ("either/or") but as contingent and potentially interoperable ("both/and" or "if/then").[9]

---

[6] For a view that a canon of concepts is useful even a conceptually unstable discipline, see CONCEPTS FOR INTERNATIONAL LAW: CONTRIBUTIONS TO DISCIPLINARY THOUGHT (Jean d'Aspremont & Sahib Singh eds., 2019).

[7] *See* JESSUP, *supra* note 1, at 2 ("[A]ll law which regulates actions or events that transcend national frontiers. Both public and private international law are included, as are other rules which do not wholly fit into such standard categories."); *id.* at 106 expands the grid slightly ("Transnational law then includes both civil and criminal aspects, it includes what we know as public and private international law, and it includes national law, both public and private."). For an argument that TL neither properly a definition nor a concept, see, e.g., Craig Scott, *Transnational Law as Proto Concept: Three Conceptions*, 10 GERMAN L.J. 859 (2009).

[8] Of course, the consistent foregrounding of Jessup's definition here owes partly to the commemorative nature of this volume, and as we would expect, the passage is similarly ubiquitous in a volume commemorating the lecture a decade ago. *See* PHILIP JESSUP'S TRANSNATIONAL LAW REVISITED: ON THE 50TH ANNIVERSARY OF ITS PUBLICATION 17–43 (Christian Tietje, Alan Brouder & Karsten Nowrot eds., 2006). More importantly, there is scarcely an article on TL that does not quote the passage prominently. A telling example is that at least five essays in a book dedicated to the work of another transnational law scholar, Detlev Vagts, cite Jessup's definition in approximately the same way. MAKING TRANSNATIONAL LAW WORK IN THE GLOBAL ECONOMY: ESSAYS IN HONOUR OF DETLEV VAGTS (Pieter H.F. Bekker, Rudolf Dolzer & Michael Waibel, eds., 2010).

[9] *See, e.g.*, Pierre Schlag, *The Aesthetics of American Law*, 115 HARV. L. REV. 1047 (2002). ("Recall the grid thinkers. They slice and dice. They maintain the boundaries. For them, the key issues in law are questions of limits and classification. . . . The energy thinkers evaluate, quantify, and commensurate. Law, for them, is not so much about drawing lines and setting limits, but rather about balancing considerations and furthering policies"): Neil Walker,

Second, TL is sometimes manifest in "other rules which do not wholly fit into such standard categories" ("neither/nor"). This unspecified category suggests not only a toolbox of gap-filling norms but gestures beyond the positivist doctrines of legal sources in both domestic and international law.[10] Yet for all its inclusivity, Jessup's definition – formed as it was within a particular intellectual and historical context – provides neither a map nor a detailed itinerary for what we encounter in this book: the subsequent development of the concept of TL into a diversified project of intellectual inquiry. Thus, in the introduction to this volume, editor Peer Zumbansen offers a *second definition*, effectively bridging this gap and bringing us to date on the state of TL as an intellectual and *critical* project:

> Transnational law aims at confronting the doctrinal and conceptual dimensions of law through an interdisciplinary analysis of how legal rules emerge, how they are disseminated and which actors are involved and where. It is, thus, both a theory of law in the tradition of sociolegal analysis of law's norms, actors and processes *and* a project of legal critique in the tradition of critical social theory. . . . Transnational law breaks the mirror of a legal conception that associated law too easily with "the state" without scrutinizing – empirically, conceptually and epistemologically – the meaning and materiality of norm-creation processes today. . . . Transnational law, then, emerges as a call to arms to empirically and conceptually scrutinize the actors, norms and processes as well as the pitfalls of lawmaking, on the one hand, and the conditions of accessing, challenging and using law in, through but also in contestation of the legal system, on the other.[11]

Even in this slightly truncated form, this redefinition sacrifices concision in favor of precision, avoiding reduction to easily recited elements. It extends Jessup's lawyerly focus on "rules" to a more broadly empirical focus on "actors, norms, and processes."[12] Within this understanding of TL as both an *object* of

---

Beyond Boundary Disputes and Basic Grids: Mapping the Global Disorder of Normative Orders, 6 INT'L J. CONST. L. 373 (2008).

[10] Mapping the more traditional versions of "sources" doctrine in public international law; see David Kennedy, *The Sources of International Law*, 2 AM. U. INT'L L. REV. 196 (1987). Mapping emerging postpositivist concepts, including "legal hybridity, transnational law, legal pluralism, inter-legality, and legal perspectivism"; see, e.g., Kaarlo Tuori, *Transnational Law: On Legal Hybrids and Legal Perspectivism, in* TRANSNATIONAL LAW: RETHINKING EUROPEAN LAW AND LEGAL THINKING 11–58 (Miguel Maduro, Kaarlo Tuori & Suvi Sankari eds., 2014).

[11] See the introduction to this volume: Peer C. Zumbansen, *Transnational Law, with and beyond Jessup, in* THE MANY LIVES OF TRANSNATIONAL LAW 63–64 (Peer Zumbansen ed., 2019).

[12] As with anything called law, TL has quite easily (and in a way Jessup anticipated) picked up the reciprocal senses of "domain of knowledge" as well as "object of study." *See, e.g.,* Carrie Menkel-Meadow, *Why and How to Study Transnational Law*, 1 UC IRVINE L. REV. 97 (2011)

study and a domain of knowledge, it downplays certain canonical features (the obligatory reference to "the state" and to the grid of public/private–domestic/international)[13] in favor of seemingly less obvious ones, particularly three characteristics not immediately apparent in Jessup's work: (1) interdisciplinarity,[14] (2) legal pluralism,[15] and (3) criticality.[16] As theoretical-methodological-attitudinal interventions, these refractive lenses bend the possibilities of TL in different directions, but one wonders whether they are essential to the definition itself or offer a new grid to graft upon the concept of law. Instead, each in its way challenges a relatively stable conception of law itself: *interdisciplinarity* is a rejection of law's autonomy; *legal pluralism* is a rejection of law's pedigree in a sovereign source; and *criticality* casts doubt on (among other things) the identification of legality with legitimacy, law's claim to coherence, or its adherence to underlying norms. The accretion of these elements into the intellectual practice of TL tracks closely the sustained effort to develop and document the theory and practice of TL over the past two decades at least, often formulating and reformulating TL in relation to overlapping fields. All

---

("the study of legal phenomena, including law-making processes, rules, and legal institutions, that affect or have the power to affect behaviors beyond a single state border").

[13] Just beyond the definition, Zumbansen makes reference to the elements of the grid: "It is through the invocation of something like 'transnational law' that one can point at the transformation of law's architectures through an increasing interpenetration of local, national and international, formal and informal, state and non-state based norm making processes." Perhaps the point of removing these elements from the definition is that these coordinates, whether treated as a presence or an absence, should not somehow (once again) *become* the definition.

[14] For explorations of interdisciplinarity, see, e.g., Peer C. Zumbansen, *Sociological Jurisprudence 2.0: Updating Law's Interdisciplinarity in a Global Context*, 21 IND. J. GLOBAL LEGAL STUD. (2014); Peer C. Zumbansen, *Transnational Law, Evolving, in* ENCYCLOPEDIA OF COMPARATIVE LAW 899 (Jan Smits ed., 2012). Peer C. Zumbansen, *The Politics of Relevance: Law, Translation and Alternative Knowledges* (Comparative Research in Law & Political Economy, Research Paper No. 45/2013, Oct. 15, 2013), https://ssrn.com/abstract=234069 [hereinafter Zumbansen, *The Politics of Relevance*].

[15] For connections to legal pluralism, see, e.g., Peer C. Zumbansen, *Defining the Space of Transnational Law: Legal Theory, Global Governance and Global Pluralism*, 21 TRANSNAT'L. L. & CONTEMP. PROB. 305 (2012); Peer C. Zumbansen, *Law and Legal Pluralism: Hybridity in Transnational Governance, in* REGULATORY HYBRIDIZATION IN THE TRANSNATIONAL SPHERE 49–70 (Poul Kjaer, Paulius Jurcys & Ren Yatsunami, eds., 2013); Peer C. Zumbansen, *Neither Public nor Private, National nor International: Transnational Corporate Governance from a Legal Pluralist Perspective*, 38 J.L. & SOC'Y 50–75 (2011).

[16] For encounters with critical theory, see, e.g., Peer C. Zumbansen, *Theorizing as Activity: Transnational Legal Theory in Context, in* LAW'S ETHICAL, GLOBAL AND THEORETICAL CONTEXTS: ESSAYS IN HONOUR OF WILLIAM TWINING 280–302 (Christopher McCrudden, Upendra Baxi & Abdul Paliwala eds., 2015); Peer Zumbansen, *Can Transnational Law Be Critical? Reflections on a Contested Idea, Field & Method, in* RESEARCH HANDBOOK ON CRITICAL INTERNATIONAL THEORY (Emilios Christodoulidis ed., forthcoming 2019).

of this is happening within an endeavor that at minimum seeks to locate and describe the law.

Placed side by side, there remains between the two definitions an unsettling lack of symmetry. This is not an asymmetry merely of scale or style but of essential purpose. Here is a reconfigured version of what Zumbansen's definition might have looked like if he had attempted a "thicker" accounting of TL *as a concept*:

1. **Transnational law.** Norms and processes, beginning with those commonly called law, which can be private and/or public (but potentially also those that fit neither category) and which can be international and/or national (but also potentially those that fit neither category). The open category of rules "that fit neither category" may exist on a continuum between formal and informal, subnationally, supranationally, and extranationally, so that they detach from proximate state promulgation or interpretation. These norms and processes as well as the actors that carry them out, as well as the actors impacted by them, are the primary object of study for a domain of knowledge also called TL (see definition two).

2. **Transnational law (i.e., transnational legal studies, transnational legal theory, or transnational legal method).** A disciplinary subfield of interdisciplinary legal studies, focused on empirical and/or conceptual aspects of lawmaking (which can be constructive and/or critical) and/or law using (which can be constructive [called "accessing"] and/or critical [called "challenging"]), particularly in the context of increasing interpenetration of local, national and international, formal and informal, state- and non-state-based norm-making processes.

3. **Transnational law.** Consists of specialized theoretical extensions and variations of definitions one and two, or possibly both, to connote a concept, a definition, a proposal, an evolving object of study, or an evolving domain of knowledge.

4. **Transnational law.** In a rarely used sense, a direct synonym for *law*, understood in contentious multiple senses, narrow or broad, and usually incorporating examples drawn from definitions one and two above. (See also *legal pluralism*.)

This redefinition, if anything, is even more cumbrous than Zumbansen's definition, but its structure is obvious: it stays close to Jessup's grid, with all the new definition's functionality and modern fittings (even, in their way, the three refractive lenses) piped together with Jessup's either/or, neither/nor, both/and, this/that/the other, or if/then. Indeed, one might notice it is not a single concept but four related concepts or senses of a concept that lean on each other more than supplant or contradict one another. Yet if it were worth pursuing definitional criteria at all, why not prefer a definition of this kind? Perhaps this is to misunderstand the "problem of definition" being posed in the first place.

If one understands the problem of "definition" to be a conceptual one, then there are plenty of solutions of this kind to be proposed. Upon closer examination, the latter is not actually a definition of a concept. As we will see, it works instead as the definition of a "project." The divergence between the two definitions (each answering the question "What is transnational law?") should be understood as the difference between two different definitional tasks. To understand the difference quickly, one may see this as the difference between Wittgenstein's dilemma on the problem of "games," on one side,[17] and the fabrication of unity in a self-consciously historicized intellectual project (e.g., the TWAIL/Third World Approaches to International Law movement) on the other. Each "definitional" task involves the difficulties of unifying in light of complicated differences, but only the first hinges on conceptual clarity. One could find conventional ways of dealing with the problem that are neither "once and for all" or "I know it when I see it" (implicitly a "free-for-all").[18] TL is undoubtedly not only a concept confounding (as concepts do) multiple examples but most likely also multiple concepts, and each of its meanings may have to run through some of the same procedures in order to be defined.

However, the problem is of a different kind altogether. For Zumbansen, whether or not any of these procedures for eliminating conceptual doubt seem promising, they are no longer relevant. Nor is this to make an unnecessary virtue of conceptual skepticism, like Musil's *Man without Qualities*, "viewing a thing from many sides without comprehending it wholly – for a thing wholly

---

[17] Wittgenstein famously asked and then answered a question about the definition of *games*, asserting that "games" (chess, tennis, poker, baseball, jacks, and a child's game of pretend) had no central unifying criterion bringing all examples together. Wittgenstein's solution of "family resemblances" or overlapping similarities despite innumerable dissimilarities. Transnational law might pose a similar challenge. What is it that unifies the examples of the asserted privatized norms of the *lex mercatoria* to the procedural dilemmas of Alien Tort litigation in the United States? LUDWIG WITTGENSTEIN, PHILOSOPHICAL INVESTIGATIONS (Blackwell 2001) (1953). *See also* HANS SLUGA, WITTGENSTEIN ch. 5 (2011).

[18] Were this the relevant "problem," one could turn alternatively to actual lexicographers, where, for example, the *OED* divides *games* into two major senses (those that are played competitively and those that are not). It proceeds to coordinate other usages (a "game" of chess as the particular match, the particular game board and its pieces, or to the historical "game of chess") according to these two. The *OED* approach is more or less what has been attempted in the "thickening" of Jessup's concept above. Compare *Games*, THE COMPACT EDITION OF THE OXFORD ENGLISH DICTIONARY (1971).

comprehended instantly loses its bulk and melts down into a concept."[19] Instead, what one finds in a conceptual journey is "a somewhere" in the attempt, a drift toward complication or toward greater clarity about one's motivation in defining. Once one becomes attentive to the active and historical sense of "definition" (now a verb, not a noun), two more insights seem to grant a permission to abandon the conceptual exercise of producing a "once-and-for-all" definition, without instituting in its place a "free-for-all" or "anything goes."[20] The first is the question of power. Just as a few years earlier, Zumbansen had asked, in light of a postrealist sensibility, "... why then further invest our energy into definition games[?] We know well enough that these only raise further questions as to who does the defining, to which purpose and to which effect[.]"[21] The other insight, also having matured a few years earlier, involves disciplinary and theoretical lenses: the horizon of our questions is constituted by disciplinary, theoretical, and political constraints and corresponding commitments. Even conceptual disagreement, which treats the question of definition passively, "can be attributed mostly to the different doctrinal and theoretical backgrounds of those employing it."[22] The "definition" of a project (certainly like TWAIL and one might guess at least one version of TL) is explicitly a reference to aspirations and therefore is not reducible to present examples, least of all a promulgation of positive law. This is most likely where the motivation comes in to abandon the attempt to define in this sense and to embrace a definition suitable to a thought community united in an agenda. It is in moving away from a "concept" (especially one assumed to mirror a set of legal rules) that we are prompted to reflect on moving toward *defining a "project."* This explains part of the appeal to Zumbansen's approach: less like Wittgenstein's dilemma, more like TWAIL. Once one appreciates its purpose, one can better appreciate the need for the definition framing this book (slightly unwieldy, disclaiming conceptual finality), even if we never quite reach that elusive "simplicity on the other side of complexity."[23]

[19] 1 ROBERT MUSIL, THE MAN WITHOUT QUALITIES 297 (Eithne Wilkins & Ernst Kaiser trans., Picador 1982) (describing protagonist Ulrich's demeanor as the manner of an essay: "the haphazard, paralysing, disarming manner against logical systematisation").

[20] RALF MICHAELS, *Law beyond the State, in* INTRODUCTION TO LAW AND SOCIAL THEORY (Reza Banakar & Max Travers eds., 2d ed. 2013).

[21] Zumbansen, *The Politics of Relevance,* supra note 14, at 16.

[22] Peer Zumbansen, *Transnational Law, Evolving, in* ENCYCLOPEDIA OF COMPARATIVE LAW 899 (Jan Smits ed. 2006), *reprinted in* King's College London Dickson Poon School of Law Legal Studies Research Paper Series, Paper No. 2014-29 (2012), at 6.

[23] Here I paraphrase a dictum more familiar (and often more elegant) in its misquoted forms but traceable to this original: "The only simplicity for which I would give a straw is that which is on

C DEFINING A PROJECT

When we move from "defining a concept" to "defining a project," even our usage of the word *defining* changes. Of course, the concept of a "project," for all its ambition and ambiguity, requires our attention, and here the answer comes in layers. The critical international legal scholar David Kennedy has written a series of articles and books redescribing his own field of public international law as a subject of study inseparable from the production of that knowledge.[24] As such, he has departed from traditional approaches treating international law as either "sovereigns with sources" or "agents in structures" to "people with projects." Projects, understood as encompassing political, personal, and intellectual levels,[25] are intentional thought communities implicated in "projects of affiliation and disaffiliation, commitment and aversion, and with wills to power and to submission."[26] Elsewhere, taking the (increasingly paradigmatic) example of TWAIL, Kennedy remarks:

> I tend to think about projects ... in several registers – as intellectual efforts to intervene in disciplinary knowledge we have about how our society is organized, as personal projects of identity, assertion and community, as political efforts to write a new world into being, and institutional efforts to routinize, establish, reproduce and extend those political, personal and intellectual projects.[27]

Having finally formulated a definition of TL adequate to its diverse manifestations, Zumbansen remains skeptical of the finality of a "once-and-for-all-satisfying definition." Unlike Jessup, however, whose provisional suggestion was that we "avoid further classification of transnational problems and further definitions of transnational law," Zumbansen and, indeed, most of the authors in this book keep the engine of descriptivism running, deferring, it seems, to

the other side of the complex – not that which never has divined it." HOLMES-POLLOCK LETTERS: THE CORRESPONDENCE OF MR. JUSTICE HOLMES AND SIR FREDERICK POLLOCK, 1874–1932 109 (Mark DeWolfe Howe, ed., 2d. ed. 1961).

[24] David Kennedy, *The Disciplines of International Law*, 12 LEIDEN J. INT'L L. 9, 88–101 (1999)

[25] David Kennedy, Keynote Address, TWAIL Conference, Albany, N.Y. (Apr. 20, 2007), http://www.law.harvard.edu/faculty/dkennedy/speeches/TwailKeynote.htm ("I tend to think about projects... in several registers – as intellectual efforts to intervene in disciplinary knowledge we have about how our society is organized, as personal projects of identity, assertion and community, as political efforts to write a new world into being, and institutional efforts to routinize, establish, reproduce and extend those political, personal and intellectual projects.").

[26] *See* David Kennedy, Kormendy Lecture, Ohio Northern University, Pettit College of Law: The Mystery of Global Governance (Jan. 25, 2008), http://www.law.harvard.edu/faculty/ dkennedy/ speeches/ GlobalGovernance(2).htm.

[27] *See* Kennedy, *supra* note 26.

"people with projects." "More than what TL means, the authors here illustrate what the concept means to them."[28] The point here is not to say everyone can provide an equally valid definition to a concept but that we expect they will engage with TL *as a project*. Insofar as we see differing usages coexist, this "can be attributed mostly to the different doctrinal and theoretical backgrounds of those employing it."[29] Projects such as TL link personal but also collective efforts, though they are never entirely idiosyncratic or monolithic.[30] Thus, what feels then initially like an incongruity emerges instead a historically specific technique of knowledge production. Instead of thinking of the content of each definition as the crucial issue, one can see the form of each as representing a certain mode of the production of knowledge. We see this in the chapters in this volume. This understanding of "the project," as a critical but also a self-critical one, has been influential among some overlapping groups of scholars but has not been applied with such explicitness to TL as of yet. If this book is a milestone in the development of TL discourse, it is perhaps precisely this, where a shifting aspiration tracks a moving target (TL as concept, TL as method, TL as project) and finally catches up.

A subset of "defining a project," one that is recurrent in the life of a project, is what can be called "defining a problem." Though Zumbansen and Jessup may differ in treating TL itself as a concept or a project, they both cut off any further conceptualization to work on other "problems." A similar approach is reflected in the preceding chapters. Thus both Jessup and Zumbansen, after some initial attempts at defining the concept of TL, eventually move on. The former is seemingly satisfied that this working concept succeeds as a commonsense definition, and the latter is seemingly unconcerned that there might never emerge a common concept. The contributors to the present

[28] Zumbansen, *supra* note 11.

[29] Zumbansen, *supra* note 22, at 6.

[30] On a notion of the "project" emphasizing the layers of individual and collective agency, see, e.g., JEAN-PAUL SARTRE, BEING AND NOTHINGNESS 481 (Hazel Barnes trans., Philosophical Library 1956): ("Our particular projects, aimed at the realization in the world of a particular end, are united in the global project which we are. But precisely because we are wholly choice and act, these partial projects are not determined by the global project. They must themselves be choices; and a certain margin of contingency, of unpredictability, and of the absurd is allowed to each of them."). For related conceptions of the "project," see Vik Kanwar, *"Not a Place but a Project": Bandung, TWAIL, and the Aesthetics of Third-ness, in* Luis Eslava, Michael Fakhri & Vasuki Nesiah eds., BANDUNG, GLOBAL HISTORY AND INTERNATIONAL LAW: CRITICAL PASTS AND PENDING FUTURES (Luis Eslava, Michael Fakhri & Vasuki Nesiah eds. 2017); Vik Kanwar & Jaya Neupaney, *Transnational Art Law, in* OXFORD HANDBOOK OF TRANSNATIONAL LAW (Peer Zumbansen ed. forthcoming 2019); LUC BOLTANSKI & EVE CHIAPELLO, THE NEW SPIRIT OF CAPITALISM (2006); PETER OSBORNE, ANYWHERE OR NOT AT ALL: PHILOSOPHY OF CONTEMPORARY ART (2013).

quasi-commemorative project delve deep into engagements with TL as project – in a wide variety of *transnational problems*. As one sees in both Jessup's
lectures and subsequent textbooks and collections (including this one), the TL
canon runs deep with references to such "problems." A problem, like a
project, is among other things "something to work on." *Defining a problem*
and deciding to treat something as such are each regular if not routinized
dilemmas in the everyday life of a project of interdisciplinary knowledge. In an
interdisciplinary project, we may each perceive and each choose to pursue
different problems. What we can learn looking across interdisciplinary
endeavors is that consensus or dissent on how we divide "problem" from a
"nonproblem" is rarely announced, even though it should be obvious that we
all have variable thresholds for tolerating or resolving ongoing doubts. We
think of lawyers as problem solvers. It is part of their job. Nevertheless, their
training will attune them to a certain perceptible frequency of a problem,
which will not be the conceptual puzzles of language, at least not very often or
to the degree considered by Wittgenstein. Law-trained scholars (who have the
reputation of being lowercase-*p* "pragmatic," in a nonphilosophical sense)
tend to move quickly to postconceptual issues in order to find a conventional
solution (like agreeing to agree or agreeing to disagree) for issues that might
not be determinative to other goals. However, one need not be a Wittgen-
steinian to want to slow down and work though a "problem" that a lawyer
perceives to be a "nonproblem." Pragmatic divisions of intellectual labor and
temporalities are not always an option. If someone stays behind to resolve the
conceptual uncertainty and everyone else has moved on, it becomes an issue
of epistemology large enough to accommodate the interproject or if the
project is large enough to contain multiple epistemologies. With the best
methods for finding out what things mean, we still need to invest in methods
for reflection on how and when to just agree to disagree or actually even agree
to suspend a project when we fall short of the justificatory thresholds coun-
seled by each discipline.

D DEFINING AS DISCIPLINARITY

Philip Jessup's definition of TL was formulated within the horizon of a
particular phase of disciplinary, intradisciplinary, and interdisciplinary engagement and was originally understood within a limited argumentative space of
postwar pragmatism. Six decades after *Transnational Law* – as in TL the book,
the lecture, the concept" – TL the discipline has not yet emerged. Yet every
subsequent avatar of TL carries with it problems of "disciplinarity." We can
plausibly refer to TL as an interdisciplinary *discourse*, one that can exist wholly

within or wholly outside parent disciplines such as public international law or sociolegal studies.[31] The positioning of TL in dialogue, exchange, or contrast with different disciplines runs like a red thread through this book from the first to the last chapter.

Whose lives are the *Many Lives of Transnational Law* recognized in the title to this book? Is it the concept alone? Is it a reference to the works and lives of prominent scholars, to the collective lives of generations, to the everyday lives of people with projects, or to the longer life spans of disciplines? An answer might lie in drawing some rough grids, beginning with bootstrapping Jessup's TL proposal to structural and historical accounts of midcentury public international law and the projects of the next generation to other disciplines or interdisciplinary perspectives. We can find *within* virtually any discipline or project, sociology of knowledge, art history, analytic philosophy, and literary criticism, among others, a small subgenre of works aspiring to providing (viewed from the air) "metatheories" or (viewed from the ground) "auto-ethnographies" of their respective fields.[32] Some lean toward abstraction and others toward intimacy; some toward structures and others toward motives. Mapping the production of disciplinary knowledge can be attempted from a certain height of abstraction[33] or with the intimacy of participation,[34] and some memorable works of legal scholarship engage both levels consciously.[35] Though this is too large of a task to begin here, we can hope to see attempts from within and without, mapping the history and consciousness of the TL discourses.[36]

---

[31] *See, e.g.,* Jean Piaget, *The Epistemology of Interdisciplinary Relationships, in* INTERDISCIPLINARITY: PROBLEMS OF TEACHING AND RESEARCH IN UNIVERSITIES 127–39 (L. Apostel, G. Berger, A. Briggs & G. Michaud eds., 1972).

[32] For eclectic models from a variety of disciplines, see, e.g., RANDALL COLLINS, THE SOCIOLOGY OF PHILOSOPHIES: A GLOBAL THEORY OF INTELLECTUAL CHANGE (1998); STANLEY BARRETT, THE REBIRTH OF ANTHROPOLOGICAL THEORY (1992); GRISELDA POLLOCK. AVANT-GARDE GAMBITS 1888–1893: GENDER AND THE COLOR OF ART HISTORY; (1992); HAROLD BLOOM, THE ANXIETY OF INFLUENCE (1973); RICHARD RORTY, CONTINGENCY, IRONY, SOLIDARITY (1989); THOMAS S. KUHN, THE STRUCTURE OF SCIENTIFIC REVOLUTIONS (1962); LUDWICK FLECK, GENESIS AND DEVELOPMENT OF A SCIENTIFIC FACT (Thaddeus J. Trenn & Robert K. Merton eds., Frederick Bradley & Thaddeus J. Trenn trans., 1979) (1935).

[33] *See, e.g.,* MARTTI KOSKENNIEMI, FROM APOLOGY TO UTOPIA: THE STRUCTURE OF INTERNATIONAL LEGAL ARGUMENT (1989, 2004).

[34] *See, e.g.,* DAVID KENNEDY, THE DARK SIDES OF VIRTUE: REASSESSING INTERNATIONAL HUMANITARIANISM (2004).

[35] *See, e.g.,* DUNCAN KENNEDY, A CRITIQUE OF ADJUDICATION: FIN DE SIÈCLE (1997).

[36] *See, eventually,* Vik Kanwar, *International Legal Discourses: Images, Objects, and People with Projects* (forthcoming); *see, e.g.,* David Kennedy, *The Disciplines of International Law,* 12 LEIDEN J. INT'L L. 9 (1999). One will see throughout this paper numerous references to the works produced by David Kennedy. This is largely because except for one or two sentences,

Today, over 120 years after Jessup's birth,[37] over 60 years after his TL lectures, and over 30 years after his death, we still only count two generations of TL scholarship. For now, the simplest division of intellectual generations would be to treat as a first generation (TL_1) the period between Jessup's lectures and the end of his life (1956–86), reserving the designation "TL_2" for the subsequent period, including our own (1986–present). This periodization begins in convenience but even upon closer examination retains merit. Within each of the two generations of TL, we can identify three rival schools of thought, claiming different qualities and strengths, as in a game of rock-paper-scissors. The TL_1 period primarily sees the reception of Jessup's concept into the three existing schools of thought in public international law, located at Columbia, Yale, and Harvard, but also a stabilizing presence in practice-oriented discourses, which allowed it to survive into a second generation. In the TL_2 period, we see TL emerge as an independent discourse, foregrounded in the name "transnational legal process" (TLP), staking a claim to each of the three previous schools, attempting a grand synthesis of the midcentury streams of thought.[38] Alongside TLP, we see the emergence of two rival perspectives based on differing styles of interdisciplinary investigation, an eclectic critical project known as transnational legal theory (TLT) and a more systematized social-science-style project called transnational legal ordering (TLO).[39]

I *The Midcentury Grid: TL_1 as Jessup's Eclecticism among Pragmatists*

In the first period (TL_1), TL was incorporated separately into each of the postwar American schools of public international law, located at Columbia

---

and as compatible as his framework is with what is being discussed, Kennedy seems to have left a gap for "transnational law" in his discussion of histories of "international legal disciplines," one that deserves to be addressed.

[37] Jessup's generation was the first to view itself meaningfully as belonging to a "generation" as a marker of shared identity and experience. *See* CHRISTOPHER LASCH, THE TRUE AND ONLY HEAVEN: PROGRESS AND ITS CRITICS (1991) 107. "For the generation born around 1900, the century's youth, prematurely cut off by war, coincided with their own, and it was easy to see the history of the twentieth century as the life history of their own generation."

[38] *Cf.* Koh, *infra* notes 48 and 54.

[39] COLLINS, *supra* note 32, at 191, has proposed a stable structure of rivalry three and only as many as six rival positions vying within the same intellectual attention space. Within previous attempts to map TL, most categorizations hover around three. *See also* Ralf Michaels, *State Law as a Transnational Legal Order*, 1 UC IRVINE J. INT'L TRANSNAT'L & COMP. L. 141 (2016). At the upper end, Larry Catá Backer's essay in this book identifies six "stabilizing projects" that might be candidates for TL_2: (1) transnational legal process; (2) networked communities; (3) legal pluralism; (4) societal constitutionalism; (5) running codes; and (6) transnational legal orders.

(Manhattan School Liberal Internationalism), Yale (New Haven School of Policy Science), and Harvard (International Legal Process). They each embodied distinctive commitments and concepts, intertwined with Jessup's biography as well. By breaking down the rigidity of the grid between national and international, public and private, without reformulating PIL as a project of renewal, he gave support to the pragmatic moves toward principle, policy, and process.[40] Jessup was a sympathetic "eclectic" among the contending pragmatists, and it should be emphasized that *eclecticism* is not the same as *interdisciplinarity.* Jessup kept the concerns slightly separate; though he had a pragmatic perspective on international law, it was not his intention to subsume the traditional doctrines under a new supradiscipline. We see here the pull of "relevance" of a certain kind. The question of where a project falls on a *spectrum of disciplinarity* should be treated separately from whether a project aims at *systematicity versus eclecticism.* In the first generation of TL, Jessup was an *eclectic,* informed by a more traditional education in international law but active engagement with new institutions. In Jessup's case his eclecticism probably helped prevent him from being drawn into the New Haven "system" or any other fashionable "call to order" posing as science or social science.

The question of Jessup's interdisciplinarity ought to be opened up to a serious intellectual biography, but the nearest answer as of now seems to be that if he was interdisciplinary, the word is not meant in the way we would now ordinarily use it. Moves to interdisciplinarity or even transdisciplinarity in TL projects have to be viewed in context of their respective historical periods and contexts. Jessup was *not,* however, *interdisciplinary* in the sense of what was possible either then or now. If anything, the project was *intra*disciplinary, pulling together legal fields and jurisdictions that had been separated on a grid (which, again, is also evidence of his eclecticism, more the softening of a system than the creation of one.)[41] Had he been inclined to articulate a parallel system (as was being done at New Haven), he would have. To have

---

[40] Kennedy, *Thinking against the Box, supra* note 3. But by the postwar period, these lines were blurring, and schools of thought distributed themselves across two spectrums: one between international community and sovereign autonomy and the other between formalism and anti-formalism They struggled not only with each other, where they differed more on scholarly style than fundamental beliefs, but also within a particular problem space, guarding the relevance of the discipline against neighboring disciplines, like international relations and domestic public law theory (the true political realists, the true legal realists, and the true formalists).

[41] To look at this in the opposite way, and not confine TL_1 to Jessup's lectures, it is true that if we consider part of the TL_1 project to have been allied to at least one major interdisciplinary PIL project of the time, the New Haven School, it was possible to engage with TL in an interdisciplinary way. This does not become a way of understanding TL until the next generation. By then, New Haven style syntheses seem thoroughly monodisciplinary.

participated in anything analogous to the kind of interdisciplinarity in play in this volume would have had to have, at the very least, crossed the commons at Columbia to meet with his distinguished colleagues teaching in the social sciences and humanities. Overlapping his student and teaching years, Columbia University was home to towering figures of midcentury thought throughout the social sciences and humanities, including Margaret Mead, Franz Boas, C. Wright Mills, Robert K. Merton, Herbert Gans, Lionel Trilling, Erich Fromm, Arthur Danto, John Dewey, and Kenneth Waltz, among many others. There is no evidence that he sought any guidance from or synthesis with their disciplines, just as he never joined any collaborative efforts of the kind Yale's NHS was attempting. As a participant in the building the postwar world order, at the UN as well as Bretton Woods, Jessup would have certainly encountered the ideas of political realists and economists. However, the kind of interdisciplinary that is evident *in the current book* would be difficult to find or to import Jessup's formulation of TL.[42] While one could extrapolate from his proposals the need to pay attention to legal pluralism or emerging transnational networks, there is no evidence that he would have recognized the pluralist literatures of his time or ours into his program.[43] The survival of TL into the next generation was not due to Jessup's devising a plan that would accommodate interdisciplinary, critical, and pluralist literature. Nevertheless, some of these developments were underway.

Otherwise, the kind of "relevance" that helped TL survive into the next decades had little to do with interdisciplinary or renewal projects but its insertion into pedagogy and the reframing of practice. First, we must (as some of the contributors have) look beyond North American legal academy and trace the influence or noninfluence of Jessup on some practice relevance to European circles writing about arbitration. These tie to debates on arbitrability and a revival of the lex mercatoria concept. The appearance of "practice-readiness" in the law school context and "practice relevance" in bridging international concepts to the real world seems to have some force on both

---

[42] None of this means Jessup was underinformed or intellectually incurious. Instead, only by today's standards would he appear to be more a "hedgehog" than "fox," his contemporaries noted that in terms of practical, doctrinal, and contextual knowledge of his field, he was "no less than a Modern Blackstone." See Grisel, this volume, first page, citing Cecil J. Olmstead, *Jessup: Transnational Law*, 32 N.Y.U. L. Rev. 1024, 1026–27 (1957).

[43] Natasha Affolder, in this volume, seems to believe Jessup did in fact contemplate something like legal pluralism, referring to "rules not fitting standard categories." Affolder asserts that these "other rules" of Jessup's original articulation were left undefined with the consequence that the concept of transnational law has developed into a powerful placeholder for "otherness" and "misfits" in legal thought and methodology. Affolder also highlights Jessup's reference to a "larger storehouse of rules." Affolder, in this volume.

sides of the Atlantic.[44] Second, there was an infrastructural component as well, best seen in the confluence of three pedagogically based projects. By 1968, having already left Columbia for the International Court of Justice, Jessup's concerns were commemorated on the *Columbia Journal of Transnational Law*, which had been founded some years before, by Friedmann: "This Journal is dedicated to the concept of 'transnational law' – as articulated by Professor Philip C. Jessup, now a Judge of the International Court of Justice." The editors go on to quote the classic definition from *Transnational Law* as above. Mirroring this, a few years later, in the first issue of the journal that would become the *Yale Journal of International Law*, the editor-in-chief wrote, "The New Haven School does not [view legal processes] through a dichotomy of national and international law ... it describes them in terms of the interpenetration of multiple processes of authoritative decision of varying territorial compass."[45] Though it stopped short of citing Jessup and adopting the term TL, this confirmed the compatibility of TL and NHS overall to a degree that today a compatibility between the two approaches is taken for granted. And yet, it was at neither Columbia nor Yale but at Harvard where the context for a meaningful continuation of Jessup's project into the next decades was provided. In a development roughly contemporaneous with the creation of the first TL journals, Jessup's TL approach was incorporated into a textbook and course at Harvard by Steiner and Vagts, entitled *Transnational Legal Problems*, with editions in 1968 and 1976. In the third edition (1986), they offer the following definition:

> The problems that have some foreign dimension and may require a special response within a national legal system take many forms. ... How a nation reacts to these and related problems ... necessarily affects other countries and their nationals. Thus, such expressions of national legal systems can be viewed as having a transnational character. Together with public international law and with regulation by international organizations, such phases of national law form a complex of rules, policies, principles, attitudes and processes bearing upon relationships among nations or among their

---

[44] The contemporary debates on *lex mercatoria* are by now too vast and contentious to summarize in a single note or a single source. A comprehensive bibliography, consisting of over one thousand entries, is available at https://www.trans-lex.org/biblio/of-transnational-law-(lex-mercatoria); *see also* Zumbansen, *Introduction*.

[45] Eisuke Suzuki, *The New Haven School of International Law: An Invitation to a Policy-Oriented Jurisprudence*, 1 YALE J. WORLD PUB. ORD. 1, 6 (1974).

nationals. It is that complex to which with book refers as "transnational legal problems" or "transnational law."[46]

This definition, which survived at least until the third edition (1986), elaborates the concept and the field in both general and the specific directions. The general, systematizing leap is to a complex of rules, policies, principles, attitudes, and processes. Importantly, this "stand-in" definition was removed in 1994, and Jessup's definition returned.[47] Unlike Jessup's Storrs Lectures, crystallized permanently in 113 pages, Steiner and Vagts had the necessity and opportunity to update their book throughout the latter decades of the twentieth century and adapt to palpable changes in the subdisciplines, their context, and the salient problems identified. The early focus of the legal process movement was on the study of legal institutions, "reasoned elaboration," neutral principles, and the optimism that rational but orderly policy change could be achieved through pluralistic political process. Insofar as this approach anticipated a nonexhaustive list of "problems" a legal practitioner might actually face in a law office, and not only the exotic few employed by the State Department or an international organization, the "transnational problems" TLP approach was probably more adequate to the task of educating (primarily American) lawyers in something their employers would call "international law."[48] It is not that the public international law was discarded, but it was supplemented: not "either/or" but "both/and." Whereas there is a lack of symmetry between the terms "private" and "public" international law, international business transactions and public international law, TLP filled the gap. The necessary companion to public international law doctrine was not simply the "private international law" (choice of laws or conflict of laws) but all aspects of national law, substantive and procedural, civil and criminal, putting nations and nationals in potential disputes. Jessup did not spend much time on the anxieties we attribute to public international law as a field in the United States: anxieties over disciplinary status based not only on explanatory power coherence but also over perceptions of policy relevance, market

---

[46] HENRY J. STEINER & DETLEV VAGTS, TRANSNATIONAL LEGAL PROBLEMS: MATERIALS AND TEXT (1968).

[47] HENRY J. STEINER, DETLEV F. VAGTS & HAROLD H. KOH TRANSNATIONAL LEGAL PROBLEMS: MATERIALS AND TEXT (4th ed. 1994). This was perhaps as a tribute to Jessup, or as a sign of the influence of the newest coeditor, Harold Koh, to whom we will return in the next section.

[48] Harold Hongju Koh, *Transnational Legal Process*, 75 NEB. L. REV. 181, 206 (1996). Koh reveals here that the original textbook also owed much to unpublished course materials by Abram Chayes and Andreas Lowenfeld at Harvard in international legal process, and updating MILTON KATZ & KINGMAN BREWSTER, LAW OF INTERNATIONAL TRANSACTIONS AND RELATIONS (1960).

relevance, and practice relevance). This approach solved a series of curricular dilemmas of teaching international legal issues in American law schools in particular, which recognized that "private international law" did not mean what one might have supposed and "international business transactions" was taken to comprise less than what one might need to know. Both such courses continue to exist at the fringe of today's JD curriculum if they are not, in one way or the other, being made part of courses with variations on the title "International Law." Meanwhile, their conception of TL remained relatively static and, conceptually at least, legible to Jessup himself at the time of his death. If Yale claimed but failed to establish coherent claims to "policy relevance," Harvard's approach was toward "practice relevance."[49] If this work had not bridged the gap, one would have to look away from the United States for any discussion on TL (at least by that name) from the period between the 1960s and the 1990s.[50]

II *The Millennial Grid: TL₂ in the Context of Interdisciplinary Thought*

Building on varieties of "pragmatism", the later period could be called varieties of "interdisciplinarity." In the TL_2 period, we see TL emerge as an independent discourse, foregrounded in the name TLP, whereby a claim is being staked to each of the three previous schools and a grand synthesis of the midcentury streams of thought is attempted. Alongside TLP, we see the emergence of two rival perspectives based on differing styles of interdisciplinary investigation, an eclectic critical project (evident in the present book) known as TLT and a more systematized social science style project called TLO. Here are a few observations on each.

1 Transnational Legal Process (TLP)

The first of the three contending schools of TL_2 is TLP, which in name and method is the most direct continuation of the TL_1 tradition, particularly the TLP textbook that had begun in 1968. As mentioned above, by 1994, Steiner and Vagts had added a third author, Harold Koh, a codescendant of the Harvard legal process and Yale policy science schools who had graduated

---

[49] Over time, the extant doctrines of TL came to be summarized in RESTATEMENT (THIRD) OF THE FOREIGN RELATIONS LAW OF THE UNITED STATES (AM. LAW INST. 1987).

[50] Mathias Reimann, *From the Law of Nations to Transnational Law: Why We Need a New Basic Course for the International Curriculum*, 22 PENN. ST. INT'L L. REV. 397–415 (2004). STEINER, VAGTS & KOH, *supra* note 47.

from the former and was teaching at the latter.[51] TLP places transnationalism, at last, at the center of formidable perspective within contemporary international legal thought, fulfilling Jessup's call for a scholarly vanguard where the "foreign offices, the legislatures, and the courts" lagged behind.[52] Koh's ambitious intellectual project would be to synthesize all three of the postwar schools into a comprehensive perspective called TLP. Koh, who is also versed in the relevant intellectual history (at least the US-based part of it), takes up concepts from all three schools, placing up front Jessup's contribution, TLP, but also Steiner and Vagts, and the New Haven School. Though Koh's definition of the scope of TLP seems inconsistent, the best way to understand it is that it has both nonnormative, neutral "process" factors,[53] and considered separately, a substance based on policy science normativism.[54] From the Manhattan School, it inherited not only Jessup's terms, the Liberal "fighting faith" and the functional view that that international law must be capable of providing normative compulsion.[55]

In short, TLP is from one perspective midcentury TL, fully "actualized." From another, however, it is an ambivalent thickening of a couple of aspects not developed by Jessup: interdisciplinarity and legal pluralism. While TLP would have absorbed a certain amount of the midcentury interdisciplinary outlook from Yale and given lip service to interdisciplinary insights, at least initially Koh also placed his revival of "mainstream" legal thinking against the trend toward criticality and interdisciplinarity in international legal scholarship.[56] On this last point, he is in TLP; Koh finds a new constitutive boundary for TL, and since national, international, and other categories are not available, and he has already assimilated all the previous schools of thought, looking to the left there is a growing "critical" literature, and to the right there is prevalence of law and economics models. However, later, speaking as dean of Yale Law School on the subject of a revival of the New Haven School (which is explicitly framed as the same project as TLP), he places interdisciplinarity as a core aspect of the project. Still bearing the traits of synthesis of the by then "classic" theoretical schools of earlier decades and of a counterrevolution against his critical and interdisciplinary contemporaries it nevertheless found itself drawing on, not even the neologisms of NHS but

---

[51] STEINER, VAGTS & KOH, *supra* note 47.

[52] JESSUP, *supra* note 1, last page.

[53] Koh, *supra* note 48, at 181, 183–84.

[54] Harold H. Koh, *Is There a "New" New Haven School of International Law?*, 32 YALE J. INT'L L. (2007).

[55] *Id.* at 184.

[56] Koh, *supra* note 48, at 206.

public choice theories, positive political theory, and new economic institutionalism. This ambivalent embrace of interdisciplinarity is accompanied by a selective incorporation of legal pluralism. Thinking usually of a framework that overlaps US federalism, the salient international institutions of the postwar order, and a few venerable doctrines of PIL, TLP has not ruled out a nonanthropological, nonsociological literature on legal pluralism, most notably the global legal pluralism of Paul Schiff Berman.[57] This newer legal pluralism, truncated from its theoretical grounding, is largely in the service of partial though experiments in "reimagining" with Anne-Marie Slaughter[58] the international world as one in which all sorts of actors – states, individuals, NGOs, IGOs, multinational corporations – apply international rules of differing degrees of binding power.[59] Finally, TLP takes over the practicebased tradition of Steiner and Vagts and retextures it with "public law litigation" and "impact litigation," including human rights litigation in US courts.[60] It remains in many ways a primarily American discipline in both its process and policy aspects and at its best represents both a practitioner perspective and a policy perspective.

2 Transnational Legal Theory (TLT)

The second modern school, TLT, which is represented by the editorial strategy of the current book, emerges as a clear "scholarly" and "interdisciplinary" alternative to TLP. TLT was the first North American wing of TL discourse to refer meaningfully to theoretical developments from outside the United States and to foreground theory at all. Thus rather than moving smoothly from Jessup to Steiner and Vagts and adding Koh, thus redeeming all of the lost opportunities of past coalitions through the new synthesis, one has to pay attention to what has happened elsewhere, beginning as far back as the 1950s. TL survived in a modest form through a practitioneroriented textbook at Harvard as well as some works of social theory and *lex mercatoria* practice in Europe. Without even getting into a game of retroactive cross-disciplinary lineage claiming, there is a clear line between the TLT work

---

[57] *See, e.g.,* PAUL SCHIFF BERMAN, GLOBAL LEGAL PLURALISM: A JURISPRUDENCE OF LAW BEYOND BORDERS (2012). Paul Schiff Berman, *The Globalization of Jurisdiction*, 151 U. PA. L. REV. 311 (2002).
[58] Anne-Marie Slaughter, *International Law in a World of Liberal States*, 6 EUR. J. INT'L L. 503, 505 (1995).
[59] Koh, *supra* note 56, at 184.
[60] *See also* Harold Hongju Koh,, The *"Haiti Paradigm" in United States Human Rights Policy*, 103 YALE L.J. 2391, 2395 n.20, 2406 (1994).

being done today and work on arbitration in the 1960s; from there this expands
to ambitious social theory, on one hand, and empirical studies, on the other.
What has been emerging here over the last two decades, and canonized in
cross-citations and in theoretical as well as practice and advocacy-oriented
collaborations, is lively interdisciplinary coalition:

> Manifesting the value of creating critical analogies and comparisons between
> the domestic trajectories of legal theory, critical legal studies, "law & society"
> and "law in context", on the one hand, and the emerging critical projects
> under the rubric of transnational law, including transnational/global legal
> pluralism, transnational legal anthropology, transnational legal geography,
> transitional justice as well as – fundamentally – postcolonial and alternative
> epistemological studies, on the other, this book is meant as an invitation to
> think seriously and critically and to work empirically and conceptually in
> confronting the question of law's role today.[61]

We can notice a few things right away. The first is this that this list reclaims
Koh's outcasts, the critical and interdisciplinary scholars against whom he
defined TLP in the first place. It also makes official the alternative genealogies
as in "systems theory" and "legal pluralism," which began in parallel or even
before TLP, outside the US legal academy. The sociolegal and law and society
groupings around the world have already canonized some of this work. TLT[62]
may be viewed as an eclectic school as well as an interdisciplinary one. It
imports and develops from influences from systems theory, institutional economics, critical legal theory, and legal pluralism, among other interdisciplinary projects. Under the rubric of TL, including transnational/global legal
pluralism, transnational legal anthropology, transnational legal geography,
transitional justice as well as – fundamentally – postcolonial and alternative
epistemological studies,

In contrast to the more clearly accentuated US origin of TLP and its
elaboration in the context of American pragmatism and domestic/inter-
national legal policy making, TLT's origins are harder to place. Though the
designation "TLT" approximates a relation to the Canadian-based journal
cofounded by Zumbansen, it is only slightly misleading, not all theory, and
one might do well to look again at infrastructural and pedagogical materiality.
With important works on *lex mercatoria* published in France, Germany, and
the UK as well as in the United States and Canada, the same transnationality

---

[61] Zumbansen, *Introduction*.
[62] TLT is identified as such for the work of the Canadian-based law journal of the same name,
where Peer Zumbansen served as founding coeditor.

can be recognized, for example, in the intricate combination of comparative law and sociolegal studies present in trailblazer projects such as the *German Law Journal*[63], the first peer-reviewed law online review. *Transnational* legal publication and collaboration projects in TL of this sort comprise today online resources such as the *Electronic Journal of Comparative Law*, the *Utrecht Law Review*, but also *SUR*, which publishes in Spanish and English. Meanwhile "in Europe," TL work continues to have many roots in both the practice and the scholarly elaboration of arbitration. Engaging legal practice, on the one hand, but also questions regarding TL as a "body of law" versus a "method of decision-making," this work continues in considerable distance from Jessup's US-based academic heirs. While the earliest cited[64] texts date back to the 1960s, Duval – in this volume – identifies the crucial contribution of François Rigaux, a Belgian scholar of both public and private international law, who first theorized the "transnational space"[65] by retexturing Jessup's concept. His book *Droit public et droit privé dans les relations internationals*, published in 1977, may have been the first attempt to embed the framework in some of the classic social theoretical debates elaborated by sociologists from Durkheim and Weber onward.[66] Whether under the heading of *lex mercatoria* or trans-national commercial arbitration, US-based arbitration as well as law and society scholars and their European counterparts documented and engaged transnational forms of arbitration. Very visibly in Europe, less so in the United States, this work was picked up by scholars such as Gunther Teubner, who, drawing on Niklas Luhmann, recontextualized it in a sophisticated socio-logical theory of a "world society," the law and politics of which he identified as no longer comprehensible by references to the dualism of "state and

[63] *See* www.germanlawjournal.com. Another journal with Zumbansen's hand in founding, *GLJ* was originally established in Germany as a twice-monthly, English-language newsletter edited in at the time seven different countries and, since its move into the internet in 2001, remains a freely available source for legal analysis from countries around the world, freely available and with a subscriber basis of tens of thousands of readers.

[64] *See, e.g.,* Emmanuel Gaillard, *Transnational Law: A Legal System or a Method of Decision Making?* 17 ARB. INT'L 59, 6263 (2001).

[65] *See* Duval, this volume. (Attributing to Rigaux proposals for "the constitution of a new type of law specifically tailored to the needs of 'transnational' relations, a law stemming from the specific community of international business and on which multinational enterprises exercise a decisive influence.")

[66] The contemporary debates on *lex mercatoria* are by now too vast and contentious to summarize in a single note or a single source. A comprehensive bibliography is available at https://www.trans-lex.org/biblio/of-transnational-law-(lex-mercatoria).

society," but only through an engagement with the particular rationalities of a highly differentiated universe of "social systems."[67]

In a discourse where the grid lines of public/private and formal/informal are erased, unleashing fascinating variety in informal and private mechanisms of self-ordering, one might at least defer for later consideration some questions about legitimacy and legitimation. In this unfamiliar topography, without a normative or even positivist map, there is always a risk that one becomes enamored with notions like "autonomy," "private ordering," or "self-restraint" and grapple too late with these as emergent forms of coercion. Against this, fortunately, new configurations of "the political" are being organized from within the TLT tradition. In other words, some scholars in this tradition have moved beyond confirming with precision the operations of unrestrained global (private) power and used their critical tools to describe these on behalf of those excluded. TLT, in this vein, has begun to turn its attention to transnational legal problems around equality, exclusion, and access. Sites of conflict are egregious labor practices and human rights violations in land rights disputes in the extractive industry or in the context of global supply chains. The "norms" under scrutiny comprise codes of conduct, human rights guidelines for multinationals as well as labor standards, for example.

3 Transnational Legal Ordering (TLO)

Back in the United States, but looking beyond it, there has now emerged a third modern TL school, known as TLO. TLO has a decidedly interdisciplinary and systematizing orientation. If the tendency of TLP was to cultivate ideas of policy and practice and TLT could be described as focusing, arguably, on the area of *understanding* that overlaps the theoretical and methodological goals of the qualitative social sciences and humanities, TLO has its origins in both political science (and its sustained interest – and belief – in the state) and sociology (and its analysis of societal stakeholders and the dynamics of their interactions). Halliday and Shaffer place the issue of "defining a problem" at the center of the TLO methodology:

> The construction of a "problem" related to the purposes or goals of salient actors in creating a TLO. In an actor's generic purposes are to produce order, the particular purposes derive from imagined alternatives to existing

---

[67] For the entire progression, see GUNTHER TEUBNER, CRITICAL THEORY AND LEGAL AUTOPOIESIS: THE CASE FOR SOCIETAL CONSTITUTIONALISM (2019). For a distillation, see Gunther Teubner, *Breaking Frames Economic Globalization and the Emergence of Lex Mercatoria* 5 EUR. J. SOC. THEORY 199, 206 (2002).

problems. Put another way, a struggle over definition or specification of a problem lays the foundation for a struggle over a set of prescriptions to produce a particular outcome.[68]

In terms outside but analogous to TLO, a project space is renewed by organizing a "problem-space," and participants negotiate openly or not "particular questions that seem worth asking and the kind of answers that seem worth having."[69] It takes not only important steps toward methodological precision but also aims at "systematization." However, unlike TLT, which tends to posit TL *as* methodology, TLO defines very clearly its purposes and methods by never straying too far from an engagement with processes of "recursive" norm generation, dissemination, and settlement within the layers of state (domestic), IO (international), and NGO (crossing these divides and existing in each of these universes). TLO is perhaps the least hospitable of the three to bringing within its ambit of study classic legal pluralism. TLO accepts "law *beyond* the state" (an uncontroversial description of international law, comparative law, international relations) but never "law *without* the state" (a charge that could be leveled at legal pluralism and some branches of anthropology as well as private ordering in economics). Framing its interdisciplinarity not with reference to any of the schools of the TLP synthesis (not even New Haven, though this fealty could carry over with many of the scholars conscripted into the project) but to legal realism is as its core legal theory, TLP is in some ways a descendant of an even older generation of pragmatism. Within the bounds of successor disciplines (law, IR, sociology), TLO is trans*national* insofar as the state is still present; trans*law* insofar as state policy does not disappear.

In short, if Jessup's project was eclectic and just on the verge of interdisciplinarity, subsequent TL projects have sought refinements. TLP limits the interdisciplinarity (in the form of criticality) to be eclectically practice and policy relevant; TLO contains the eclecticism to be interdisciplinary and systematic. TLT limits neither in the name of gathering more contexts and more experimentation, putting its "methodologies" at the service of

---

[68] Terence C. Halliday & Gregory Shaffer, *Transnational Legal Orders, in* TRANSNATIONAL LEGAL ORDERS 8 (Terence C. Halliday & Gregory Shaffer eds. 2015).

[69] DAVID SCOTT, CONSCRIPTS OF MODERNITY: THE TRAGEDY OF COLONIAL ENLIGHTENMENT 4 (2004). Scott defines "problem-space" as "an ensemble of questions and answers around which a horizon of identifiable stakes (conceptual as well as ideological-political stakes) hangs . . . [W]hat defines this discursive context are not only the particular problems as such . . . but the particular questions that seem worth asking and the kind of answers that seem worth having . . . a problem-space is very much a context of dispute, a context of rival views, a context . . . of knowledge and power."

interdisciplinary inquiry, and places the discourse on the verge of transdisci-plinarity. Yet, in the present book, further afield into the wilderness of inter-disciplinarity, legal pluralism, and criticality, there is a strong case to be made that it remains close to the orbit of Jessup's project. In light of these, trends, let us return once again to the significance of Jessup and his definition in all of this.

E DEFINITION BETWEEN DEFERENCE AND DISTINCTIVENESS

We will end approximately where we began, but the imperfection of proximity is important. In the decades since Jessup's lectures, it has become routine to cite Jessup's lectures as a point of departure. Let us first discuss two possible (and roughly opposite) implications of the persistence of Jessup's definition, in this book and elsewhere. The first would be to assume that Jessup's definition has been a working draft of a framework that, if treated as a scientific hypothesis, has been applied and refined but not falsified. As Jessup himself would have expected, a book like this would have been served as a contextual-ization or example-gathering exercise as a series of illustrations of Jessup's proposed concept, starting with the definition. Each case study have concret-ized the concept, instantiating its coherence and utility, inviting further case studies to test and help substantiate its validity. Now let us consider a very different implication. The persistent reference to Jessup's formulation of TL shows nothing of the sort. Instead, both Jessup and his term have been emptied of any meaning so that the concept of TL is simply a *floating signifier*, which, rather than carrying any specific meaning, receives whatever meaning is grafted upon it.[70] These apparent solutions hardly remove further difficul-ties. The apparently mechanical superficiality of citing Jessup is all too apparent, and if even imagination is lacking, then almost certainly the act of citing Jessup's definition would be emptied of all meaning. However, everyday machines and avant-garde artists know better and suggest there is more to the ritual density and complexity of the act of defining within a disciplinary project. In light of a postconceptual, divergent, project-based, and potentially transdisciplinary phase of TL scholarship sketched above, how do we define precisely what we are doing in this book?

---

[70] ERNESTO LACLAU, *Why Do Empty Signifiers Matter to Politics?*, in EMANCIPATION(S) 36–46 (Verso 1996); ERNESTO LACLAU & CHANTAL MOUFFE, HEGEMONY AND SOCIALIST STRATEGY: TOWARDS A RADICAL DEMOCRATIC POLITICS 112 (2d ed. 2001) ("Even in order to differ, to subvert meaning, there has to be a meaning").

The relationship to Jessup in this book is slightly less rote, slightly less reverential, but ultimately more joyful in its way. In 2010, Gralf-Peter Calliess and Peer Zumbansen wrote, probably correctly, "the consequences of Jessup's concept of TL are both rich and incoherent. Its legacy is that it – perhaps – has none, if we were to measure its success by its ability to enter doctrinal, black-letter terminology. Instead, the concept has been spurring legal imagination."[71] Of course, just as nothing we do is pure science, nothing is pure jouissance. It should take nothing away from a commitment to either to say law-related discourses are hybridized and complicated. Imagination must be extended to a self-conscious fabrication of one's collective intellectual project.

There are a number of ways in which the seemingly mechanical repetition of this citation to Jessup could be determined to be internalized to create meaning in a project (as well as distinctiveness) to bind us not as much to a founder as to each other. We risk opening too many nested dolls, and we must stop somewhere. Yet is is worth opening a final set, to propose a small, non-exhaustive set of thought experiment. Each closes the "project" of defining as four kinds of *deference through reference: as signal, as data set, as ritual,* and *as specificity.*

I As Signal

This is not about Jessup or a concept but about membership in a discursive community. To the extent that we adopt Jessup as a precursor, it shows our knowledge of the traditions of experience, placing us in a lineage, regardless of our views on his actual claims. Deference is not the same thing as reverence, but neither is it as weighty as an anxiety of influence.[72] It is not a dead metaphor or an empty signifier, but it is the kind of flag you use to flag down a fellow traveler lost in a crowd (as opposed to the kind you run up a flagpole to salute). First, there is a specificity to working with Jessup's TL concept as well. It is a mark of the project's distinctiveness; it is a sixty-plus-year tradition of thought, continuous, discontinuous, recursive, and revisable. Like the definition, which does not quite fit our self-image of how we usually use definitions, separately on relevance, "Jessup" has become a marker of prestige and a glimpse of a claim to practicality and relevance usually missing in public international law. This seems less like a citation to an overturned authority, or

---

[71] GRALF-PETER CALLIESS & PEER ZUMBANSEN, ROUGH CONSENSUS AND RUNNING CODE: A THEORY OF TRANSNATIONAL PRIVATE LAW 12 (2010). Here we will expand a sense of what that imagination entails.

[72] BLOOM, *supra* note 32.

deference to an influence (and there is certainly no anxiety of influence), but another kind of signaling, a performative threshold. We invoke him, but if not for citational authority, then for charismatic authority. To invoke Jessup conjures up some other purpose. It establishes our membership in an argumentative community, competent to establish things about international law, yes, but beyond that as well.[73] Commemorating works and rituals of such regularity that it might surprise nonscholars, there is a more mundane ritual that we participate in as academics, the invocation and citation of Jessup reinforces his preeminence in the field; it potentially establishes our authority to surpass him; but more surely, he remains where he is. To invoke Jessup is performatively sufficient not for everything we are setting out to do but for at least two things. First, it recognizes every origin of the TL project in a conceptual exercise (probably abandoned) but one that marks us as belonging to the inside of an interpretative community.

II *As Data Set*

The proliferation of publicly available data sets and interpretation tools has had a marked effect upon the humanities. It has also offered alternative ways of thinking about our subjects even when our personal-professional corners of our respective projects are not quantitative in nature.[74] The field of computational linguistics has offered the concept of the n-gram, the measurable frequency of unique characters and words following one another. The Google N-Gram Viewer compares frequency of "mentions" in a corpus of published books and other archived material daring back to 1500. One notices, for example, brief moments that Marx and Freud eclipsed references to Plato before settling into modest numbers. One notices large differences between different academic fields and doctrinal areas of law, that philosophy dwarfs the social sciences and the well-known philosophers of a period, and that in recent years, media-salient terms like "globalization" and "United Nations" have had palpable points where they crossed from specialized to generalized use. What if we were to think of the conjunction and prevalence of "Jessup" and "TL"

---

[73] STANLEY FISH, DOING WHAT COMES NATURALLY: CHANGE, RHETORIC, AND THE PRACTICE OF THEORY IN LITERARY AND LEGAL STUDIES 294, 303 (1989). ("[A]s a fully situated member of an interpretive community, be it literary or legal, you 'naturally' look at the object of the community's concerns with eyes already informed by community imperatives, urgencies, and goals.")

[74] Jean-Baptiste Michel et al., *Quantitative Analysis of Culture Using Millions of Digitized Books*, 331:6014 SCI. 176–82 (2011).

not as a matter of subjective or intersubjective meaning or a ritually dense signal but as the probability of one unique letter following another within a comprehensive data set? The bare salience of terms within the universe of published books does not take away from a search for meaning; it provides a different layer.

Using this tool, one finds around 1956 Jessup's salience in these books peaks; for the first and last time, his name exceeded mentions of his field mentions, "public international law" – that in 1956, the frequency of the mention of Jessup's name was as high as it had ever been. This personal triumph was short lived, but a second thing occurred that year. Professor Jessup dropped into our collective lexicon the term TL. It would take another fifteen or twenty years for mentions of TL to surpass Jessup for the first time, and this term continues to trend upward while Jessup trends downward. By 2008, the frequency of Professor Jessup's name declined, and the frequency of the use of the term he popularized grew; the two had switched places in terms of the 1956 numbers. In numerical terms, it took less than fifty years for the words *Philip C. Jessup* to be replaced in our collective lexicon by the words *transnational law*. You would find he began to vanish into the concept of TL, and like the portrait of Dorian Gray, its fortune seemed to improve as he disappeared. Like Dorian Gray and his picture, one weakened the other. This is a bit puzzling in some ways, particularly because nearly every academic treatment of the term is accompanied by an obligatory citation to the same quotation as above. Even if there is more literature than ever on TL and Jessup is appropriately cited, entire books are written on TL with only one citation to Jessup, the same pages, and same passages. One can compare the decline of his notoriety and the growth of his concept relative to others who have coined or popularized a term (for example, the French sociologist Alfred Sauvy, who first used the term *tiers monde*, or "Third World"). In most cases one will see this kind of relationship. If the book is an edited anthology, the mentions of that passage can be multiplied by the number of individual essays. Jessup's influence is wide but not deep. If we apply that inquiry to this book, something similar might emerge, with the Jessup and his definition appearing somewhere in the first five sentences of each piece and then quickly dropping off after that. In a newly open attention space, the significance of our citation and reference practice changes. The data set reveals something we did not know, but it is possible to think in ways the machine has not yet learned. What accompanies the apparent superficiality of such a reference may not be apparent to machine learning: the ritual density and complexity of the relationship within a disciplinary project. In this way, the deeper the epistemic gap between Jessup and his successors, the more meaningful the invocation of Jessup becomes.

III *As Ritual*

The conference at the Transnational Law Institute at King's College London came together to celebrate the sixtieth year of Philip Jessup's Storrs Lectures. It embraced TL, all at once, as the book, the definition, and concept. Because of its relation to a commemorative ceremony, a celebration, the reciting of a definition earlier recited in a lecture becomes at minimum a performance. As a citation in an article, it becomes a reference. There is plenty of information in the sections and indeed the chapters above that adds layers of complications and might call into question a meaningful continuity between Jessup's conception of TL and the various versions that we see in circulation today. In light of the many difficulties pertaining to definition, concept, field, or methodology raised in this text and invariably acknowledged by the authors, what becomes the function of a book such as this? Taken together, the here-collected engagements with TL become rituals of deference, of reciting Jessup's famous definition, before also encoding it into the third or fourth sentence of an opening paragraph, before launching into deeply differing projects of expertise, critique, and emancipation. Now what if we were to view citation as a routine and invest something like the invocation of a founding disciplinary text with ritual significance? Not only initiation, but commemorate origins in the same. Here, the terms ritual and routine are not opposites but belong on a spectrum. Ritual and routine are concepts that both describe repeated actions and differ only in one's embeddedness in a system of meaning or one's subjective perception of significance. Either way, the more "meaningful" one perceives an activity to be, the more applicable the term *ritual*. In the scholarly production of knowledge, where passionate commitment and mundane requirements exist in constant proximity, there is a zone of uncertainty. Second, there is a routine/non-routine ritual significance to citing Jessup's page 2 definition. To the extent that we adopt Jessup as a precursor, it shows our knowledge of the traditions of experience, placing us in a lineage, regardless of our views on his actual claim; it is to his articulation we refer, seemingly defer, but more likely we differ as we continually redefine TL.[75]

---

[75] This sequence of these terms is borrowed from art historian Griselda Pollock, who defines these as a strategic "gambit." First comes "reference," positioning oneself within the concerns current (salient) within a subcultural milieu. Deference is our imitation of the recognized master within the subculture. Finally, there is "difference," the subtle repositioning and overtaking of the master, through the introduction of something distinctive and "new." GRISELDA POLLOCK, AVANT-GARDE GAMBITS 1888–1893: GENDER AND THE COLOR OF ART HISTORY (1992).

IV *As Specificity*

Finally, we can refer to these processes by reference to specificity. It is difficult to gesture at the merits or even the meaning of specificity without taking an excursion in the opposite direction.

To hint finally at the complexity beyond that simplicity (even putting aside all things "transnational"), let us unpack for even a moment what we already inherit in this thing called "law" in its vernacular, disciplinary, and discursive variety. We find in law the reciprocal senses of "domain of knowledge" as well as "object of study." We see an area constituted by experts and one that coproduces the conditions of their expertise. We see a system of regulation that resembles codified morality, natural coordination, explicit coercion, interpretative meaning, and a near synonym of justice. We see the aspiration toward a self-contained science in a preempirical sense, a domain of exact knowledge. We see a branch of the social science providing crucial context, a professional vocation tied to codes of ethics, and a branch of the humanities whose study may be undertaken without topical or vocational utility. We see the possibility of aesthetic and interpretive understandings that shock us out of a naturalized common sense, deepen our commitments to culture and belief, and heighten our awareness of our location in world. We see in our vocation both rituals and routines; the daily call of problem solving; our symbolic, intellectual, and actual capital and labor; our abjection but also our participation in exploitation of others.[76]

Along with the erasure of disciplines, there is a rising indistinction between academic work and play, though we are not always better for it.[77] Disciplines do not only call us to order, and interdisciplinarity does not only teach us new ways to work. Together they teach us new ways to *play*, to *critique our work*, and to *critique our play*. We see all of these across multiple realms we call theory and practice. With all of this, and everything contained with it, grafted onto a map called the transnational, edging toward the horizon called the transdisciplinary, is there anything left outside this description, any "other" left to encounter?

Thus, we return to the need to look at projects in their specificity and their struggle for distinctiveness. Jessup is a call to specificity. The specificity of belonging to and working within an epistemic and interpretive community,

---

[76] *See, e.g.,* Saskia Sassen, Expulsions: Brutality and Complexity in the Global Economy (2014).
[77] *See e.g.,* Stefano Harney & Fred Moten, The Undercommons: Fugitive Planning & Black Study (2013).

whose shared lingua franca in TL will allow them to gain some fluency across borders and recognize links among heterogeneous problems within an intentional project space. Brought into a room by a reference to Jessup, a European systems theorist will see the anthropology of legal pluralism as necessary interlocutor, a public lawyer will seek to understand soft law mechanisms, and a sociologist of immigration practice near the Rio Grande River will tune in at the mention of *lex mercatoria*. In this way, TL is more properly our relation to Jessup and his formulation than it is the everything-ification of everything. It is to not hide behind a word like *transnational* and believe it means everything under the sun.

F CONCLUSION

Perhaps sixty years from now, a future generation of scholars (or autopoetic androids, by then self-replicating and seeking autonomously the knowledge we once sought) will be asking the question "What was transnational law?" They would eventually have to make their way back through the debates presented in this book and others like it, dwell on our disagreements briefly before discovering a convergence of citations leading to a series of lectures delivered in New Haven in the middle of last century. The personal biography of the lecturer would take them back further through the Cold War and the conflagrations of the two World Wars, the birth of international organizations, a map of colleagues and rivals, a receding horizon of intellectual influences directly from the nineteenth century. This much we know. Whatever knowledge we produce about TL between now and then, Jessup (TL the book, the lecture, the concept, the definition) seems to be connected firmly to its beginnings. What we cannot know is whether they would think to ask the question, what they mean when they seek a definition, and whether they are interested in definite answers or the nature of our disagreements. Projecting ourselves forward and asking the question in the past tense ("What was transnational Law?") contemplate at least two other possibilities. Either the concept will fail to gain salience among competing discourses (ambitious neighbors with names like "global governance" and "global normative orders" or more distinctive names as yet unformulated), or it will succeed to a degree that it will lose all distinctiveness, evaporating into a transdisciplinary cloud inseparable from "common sense." Perhaps in a context where the term *globalized world* is finally eliminated from grammatical use for redundancy, the notion of TL will seem similarly redundant; leaving only for intellectual historians (perhaps a critical school of robots) the underlying crises, the footnoting of what we do not think to think about and scholarly rivalries that fueled its use and disuse, rise and/or fall. Jessup smuggled more than one crossing under the term *transnational*, gliding past the literal understanding of cross-border law, to "crossing" law and nation in multiple ways, and reshuffling public and private for good measure. Already, one gets the sense that for Jessup transnational was neither simply "across," spanning, even shuttling, or "beyond" but also as "overcoming," so that transborder law did not capture the concept – rather something like law unbound by borders. It was also transsectoral (public/private), transintensity (hard/soft), transformal, transcontextual (merchant law but also public law). In short, Jessup's project was translegal on the verge of interdisciplinarity. The second generation is eclectic, encyclopedic, on the verge of transdisciplinarity. In this way, the very minimalism of Jessup's definition left open the multiple sites of transcendence or overcoming, and this will be a disciplinary resource whether or not we cross a transdisciplinary frontier.[78]

---

[78] Darian-Smith & Philip C. McCarty The Global Turn: Theories, Research Designs and Methods for Global Studies (2017); Eve Darian-Smith & Philip McCarty, *Beyond Interdisciplinarity: Developing a Global Transdisciplinary Framework*, 7 Transcience 1–26 (2016).

Index of Names

Abel, Richard, 35
Abi-Saab, Georges, 422
Affolder, Natasha, 37, 51, 475
Ali, Shahla, 49
Alstott, Alison, 316
Aman, Alfred C., Jr., 35
Anghie, Antony, 422
Appleby, Joyce, 109
Arnaud, René, 194
Arthurs, Harry W., 36
Ashley, Richard, 335
Azoulay, Ariella, 356–57, 360–62

Backer, Larry Catá, 27, 411, 473
Baxi, Upendra, 43
Bell, John, 201
Berger, Klaus Peter, 228–32
Berger, Martin T., 5
Berman, Paul Schiff, 36, 480
Biersteker, Thomas, 338
bin Laden, Osama, 353–56, 358, 360–62
Bingham, Lord, 201–2
Blackett, Adelle, 36
Borchard, Edwin M., 427
Bourdieu, Pierre, 352
Braithwaite, John, 373
Brennan, Chief Justice Sir Gerard, 218, 222
Brown, Wendy, 358–60
Brysk, Alison, 354
Buchanan, Ruth, 35
Bush, George W., 355

Calliess, Gralf-Peter, 35, 113, 119, 274, 388, 486
Canfield, Matthew, 37
Cardozo, Benjamin, 224, 331, 370
Carlston, K. S., 425, 436

Carville, Justin, 357
Catá-Backer, Larry, 36
Chapsos, Ioannis, 113
Charnovitz, Steve, 11
Chen Zhu (陈竺), 78, 82, 184
Cheng, Bin, 427
Chimni, B. S., 421
Choudhury, Cyra, 311
Chow, Rey, 359
Císa, Ondej, 336
Cohen, Edward, 344
Cooper, Melinda, 315
Cotterrell, Roger, 20–21, 36, 108
Cox, Robert, 340
Cutler, A. Claire, 35, 43, 50–51, 337, 340–41, 344–45

D'Amato, Al, 429
Darian-Smith, Eve, 37
Deng, Xiaoping, 183
Dezalay, Yves, 35, 228, 234, 331, 438–39
Dickstein, M. E., 430
Dietz, Thomas, 35
Dillard, H. C., 431
Dilling, Olaf, 113
Dolzer, Rudolf, 427, 429
Domke, Martin, 427, 431, 437–38
Drahos, Peter, 373
Duval, Antoine, 49, 277, 285, 482

Eslava, Luis, 23

Falk, Richard, 7
Farer, Tom, 20
Feichtner, Isabel, 10
Foucault, Michel, 350, 352, 362

Fouchard, Philippe, 228
French, Chief Justice Robert, 202, 216, 221
Friedmann, Wolfgang G., 11, 21, 431, 437, 476

Gaillard, Emmanuel, 230–32
Garth, Bryant, 35, 228, 234, 331, 438–39
Gathii, James, 20
Gill, Stephen, 340
Gleeson, Chief Justice Murray, 209, 219, 221
Goldman, Berthold, 228, 271
Goode, Roy, 235
Goodwin, Morag, 22
Gramsci, Antonio, 322–23, 340, 342
Grisel, Florian, 48–49, 333, 475
Gupta, Priya S., 37

Habermas, Jürgen, 352, 394, 398
Hacker, Daphna, 310
Halliday, Terence C., 30–32, 36, 47–48, 73, 77, 110, 179, 283, 311–13, 332, 483
Han Changfu (韩长赋), 184
Hart, H. L. A., 117, 277
Haufler, Virginia, 337, 345
Heraclitus of Ephesus, 105
Higgins, Rosalyn, 98, 203
Horrigan, Bryan, 48–49, 217
Hu, Zhouke, 47
Huang, Thomas, 433, 435–36
Hyde, J. N., 7, 59, 436

Ihering, Rudolf, 30, 33
Isaacs, Nathan, 16, 219

Jennings, Robert Yewdall, 431
Jessup, Philip
  A *Modern Law of Nations* (author of), 64, 328
  Cecil Olmstead and, 195
  colonialism and, 387, 419, 431
  diplomacy of, 61
  drama and, 349–52
  eclecticism and, 474
  Elihu Root and, 2–3
  family and, 298
  global dispute resolution and, 49, 225–26
  global governance and, 3
  globalized markets and, 192
  Hersch Lauterpacht and, 423
  inequality and, 453
  interdisciplinarity and, 474–75, 477, 492

international agreement and, 64
international agreements and, 68
International Court of Justice and, 2, 191, 193, 195, 333, 420, 476
international democracy and, 450
international law and, 6, 73, 479
the international lawyer, 5
jurisdiction and, 93, 266
legal pluralism and, 475
legal realism and, 449, 457
McCarthy committee/inquiry and, 2, 126
norms and, 22–23, 26
Oscar Schachter and, 11
Peer Zumbansen and, 281–82, 470, 486
practice and, 369–70
public and private international law, 24, 45, 374, 381, 384, 431
rules and, 80, 82, 89, 115–16, 187, 348, 366–67, 370, 464
sovereignty and, 63, 423, 443, 445–46
state and, 397
state power and, 62–63
Storrs Lectures at Yale (1956), xviii, 2, 5–6, 11, 29, 44, 58, 65, 114–15, 126–27, 142, 144–45, 151, 179, 186, 189–90, 224, 269–70, 298, 364, 385, 462, 473–74, 477, 485, 489
transnational adjudication and, 197–200
Transnational Law (author of), 1, 3–4, 10–11, 13–19, 58–59, 62, 66, 70, 73–74, 76, 93–94, 99, 124, 188–89, 193–94, 224, 239–40, 386, 419, 422, 435, 437, 439, 443, 448, 450, 461
transnational law and, 3–4, 7, 12–13, 23, 25, 28, 48, 51, 68–69, 73–76, 78, 80–81, 84, 87, 110, 114–15, 126, 130, 140, 147, 152, 186–88, 195, 267, 271–72, 274, 278–81, 283, 292, 324–26, 328, 333, 344, 347, 349, 363–67, 371, 373, 375, 388, 396, 402, 413, 416, 443, 447, 452, 461–64, 466, 470–72, 475–78, 485–89, 491–92
transnational problems and, 64, 75–78, 82, 469
transnational situations and, 28, 64, 128
trasnational law and, 6, 217
US ambassador, 59, 66, 70, 126, 195
UN and, 62–63, 65–66, 70, 456

Kahn, Philippe, 228
Karim, Aisha, 354
Kennedy, David, 373, 449, 469, 472
Kennedy, Liam, 360

Kiefel, Chief Justice Susan, 219
Kirby, Justice Michael, 221–22
Knöpfel, Laura, xvii
Koh, Harold Hongju, 36, 92, 95, 110, 188, 477–81
Koskenniemi, Martii, 373
Kotiswaran, Prabha, 311

Lauterpacht, Hersch, 422, 425–26, 428, 436, 439
Lawrence, Bruce, 354
Lhuilier, Gilles, 37
Li Bin (李斌), 184
Likosky, Michael, 35
Luo, Haocai, 170

Malanczuk, Peter, 326
Malynes, Gerard, 228
Maniruzzaman, A. F. M., 428
Mares, Radu, 112
Markesinis, Sir Basil, 207
Markus, Till, 113
Marx, Karl, 322, 397, 487
Mason, Chief Justice Sir Anthony, 202, 214, 218–19, 221–22
McCarthy, Joseph, 1–2, 126
Merry, Sally Engle, 35
Michaels, Ralf, 27, 36, 53, 299, 305
Minas, Stephen, 24, 37, 45
Moore, Sally Falk, 154, 348, 351
Morton, Adam, 323
Muchlinski, Peter, 415
Mückenberger, Ulrich, 112
Muir Watt, Horatia, 36, 97, 295, 305

Ni, Lili, 47, 164, 169, 177
Norton, Patrick, 430
Nowrot, Karsten, 46–47, 107, 114

Obama, Barack, 51, 354, 357
Olmstead, Cecil, 186, 195
Oppenheim, Lassa, 420
Osofsky, Hari, 377

Paternotte, David, 313–14
Peel, Jacqueline, 377
Porter, Tony, 337, 345

Quack, Sigrid, 331

Rajah, Jothie, 51
Ramazani, R. K., 431

Ridi, Niccolò, 45–46
Risse-Kappen, Thomas, 337
Rittich, Kerry, 317
Ruggie, John, 414

Said, Edward, 355
Sanders, Pieter, 194
Sassen, Saskia, 283, 339
Schaack, Beth van, 25
Schachter, Oscar, 2–4, 11, 20, 59
Schmitt, Carl, 16
Schmitthoff, Clive, 228
Schultz, Thomas, 45–46, 272, 277
Schwebel, Stephen M., 427
Schwöbel-Patel, Christine, 10
Scott, Craig M., 36, 96, 281
Shachar, Aylet, 302
Shaffer, Gregory, 16, 30–32, 36, 47–48, 110, 114, 126, 129, 179, 283–84, 311–13, 332, 483
Shaw, Martin, 22
Singh, Prabhakar, 52–53
Slaughter, Anne-Marie, 24, 100, 209, 480
Slobodian, Quinn, 6
Snyder, Francis, 35, 47, 169, 177, 180, 182
Song, Gongde, 170
Sornarajah, Muthucumaraswamy, 53, 421–22
Strange, Susan, 337
Sullivan, Gavin, 37

Teubner, Gunther, 35, 228, 276, 284, 394, 482
Tietje, Christian, 111
Tomlins, Christopher, 351
Trubek, David, 35, 331
Trump, Donald, 149, 441–42, 454–57
Tsoukala, Philomila, 316–17
Turner, Victor, 349, 352–56, 363
Twining, William, 36

Vagts, Detlev F., 35, 281, 463, 476–78, 480
Valcke, Catherine, 36
Valverde, Mariana, 369
Van Apeldoorn, Bastiaan, 335, 337
Van der Pijl, Kees, 340
Van Harten, Gus, 330
Verdross, Alfred, 427, 432
Viellechner, Lars, 37, 284
Volpp, Leti, 355

Waldron, Jeremy, 203, 207, 216
Waltz, Kenneth, 336, 475

White, James Boyd, 351
Whytock, Christopher, 37, 45, 73,
    85, 128
Wouters, Jan, 140

Xavier, Sujith, 37
Xi Jinping (习近平), 184, 397

Zitelmann, Ernst, 228
Žižek, Slavoj, 359
Zuboff, Shoshana, 26
Zumbansen, Peer, 106, 111–12, 115, 181, 199,
    228–29, 232, 281–82, 294, 296, 312,
    314, 332, 386, 388, 407, 464–70,
    481–82, 486

Subject Index

2015 Food Safety Law (FSL) (China), 170, 176, 184–85
Abbottabad, 360–61
acceptable daily intakes (ADI), 165
accountability, 33, 140, 214, 217, 346
  corporate, 343
  government, 213, 215
  Jessup on, 450
  judicial, 213, 215, 217
  legal, 113
  mechanisms of, 128, 130, 133, 151, 215
  minimal, 65
  private, 341, 382
  public, 382
  Schaack on, 25
adjudication, 81, 96
  as governance function, 78–79, 83
  Australia, 218–19, 221
  common law, 208
  democratization of, 53
  extralegal, 369
  international, 98
  psychological dimension of, 17
  relationship between domestic and international law in, 200, 203–4, 208, 212, 216–18
  role of judge in, 17
  sovereign nature of, 93
  transnational, 48, 74, 86, 200, 206–10, 215, 217–18, 222–23
  tribunals, 236
administrative law, 26
  domestic, 402
  global, 284, 367, 456

Administrative Measures for Examination and Approval of the Export of Hazardous Waste, 156
affect, 359–60
aggression, 360, 422, 434
Agreement on Comprehensive Economic Partnership (ASEAN-China), 166
Agreement on Trade-Related Aspects of Intellectual Property, 130–31, 147, 330–31
Agreement on Trade-Related Aspects of Intellectual Property Rights, 130
agrochemical industry, 181
agrochemicals, 171
Ahmadou Sadio Diallo (Republic of Guinea v. Democratic Republic of the Congo) (ICJ case), 192
Ainu, 133, 138–39
Alien Tort Claims Act (ATCA), 415
Alien Tort Statute (ATS), 24–25, 97
alignment, 99, 166, 172–73, 422
All-China Federation of Trade Unions (ACFTU), 158
analogy, 10, 15, 277, 350–51, 413
Anglo-Commonwealth law, 203
anthropology, 26–27, 35, 39, 53, 265, 351, 481, 484, 491
Anticybersquatting Consumer Protection Act (ACPA), 247–54
anti-formalism, 474
arbitral awards, 142, 148, 187, 194, 232, 236–37, 376
arbitral jurisprudence, 49, 239, 290

arbitration, 96, 189, 194, 226–27, 233, 235, 375, 475, 481–82
  commercial, 12–13, 48, 87, 142, 192–94, 225, 227, 234, 238, 332, 375, 439, 482
  delocalized, 234
  environmental, 376
  international, 187, 194–95, 236, 239, 277, 375, 430
  investment, 190, 344, 375, 424–25, 427, 431
  law, 80, 235, 238
  religious, 302
  transnational, 49, 148, 192, 210, 225–27, 232, 234, 239
  tribunals, 99, 226
archetypes, 352
arrogance, 360, 397
Asia-Pacific Economic Cooperation (APEC), 166
Asia-Pacific Economic Cooperation (APEC) Secretariat, 166
Association of South East Asian Nations (ASEAN), 166, 381
Atkins v *Virginia*, 206
attention space, 473, 488
austerity measures, 312, 317
Australia, 202, 211, 219, 222
  chief justice of, 209, 214, 221
  Constitution of, 202, 221
  constitutional system, 218
  High Court of, 219–22
  international law, 219–21
  jurisprudence, 218
Australian
  Bar Association, 209
authority, 16, 20, 22, 78, 116, 123, 143, 200, 204, 242–43, 280, 346, 371, 448, 487
  adjudicative, 216
  administrative, 168
  allocation, 84–85, 94, 128, 147, 150, 264, 394, 412
  corporate, 192, 342–43
  domestic, 201
  expert, 342, 345
  foreign, 201
  in global legal system, 75, 84–86
  jurisdictional, 243, 264, 267
  law enforcement, 258
  legislative, 168
  norm-making, 169–70, 414
  political, 322, 416
  private, 44, 50, 86, 112, 193, 322, 324–25, 338–39, 341, 344–45, 394

  public, 194, 241, 327, 344
  regulatory, 408
  sovereign, 99, 212
  state, 226, 335, 339, 345, 358, 390
  transnational, 65, 324, 338, 410
automation, 264, 372

Bangladesh Accord, 26
Barcelona Traction, Light and Power Co., Ltd. (Belgium v. *Spain)* (ICJ case), 191, 333
Barcelona.com, Inc. v. *Excelentisimo Ayuntamiento de Barcelona*, 251–55
Basel Convention on the Control of Transboundary Movements of Hazardous Wastes and Their Disposal, 155
Bills/charters of rights, 202–4, 211, 218
Bitcoin, 262–63
blame, 354
blockchain, 262–63
breach, 287, 306, 353–54, 421, 423
Brexit, 53, 218, 441–44, 446–51, 454–57

Canada, 53, 122, 191–92, 209, 220, 260, 262, 302, 343, 481
capitalism, 26, 323
  constitutionalization of, 340
  domestic labour, 308–9
  global, 322, 339
  governance and, 341, 343
  transnational, 330, 344
  transnational law and, 343, 425, 428
Carta Mercatoria, 228
Catalogue of Hazardous Chemicals (2015) (China), 156, 160, 176
Center for Transnational Law (CENTRAL), 229
Certification and Accreditation Administration (CNCA) (China), 159
character
  of ILO measures, 159
  of law, 58, 112, 123, 391, 400, 413, 452
Chemical Registration Centre (CRC) (China), 172
chemical risks, 159, 162
China
  Communist Party, 62, 168
  Environmental Protection Law, 162
  intellectual property, 131–33
  International Labor Organization, 156, 158
  pesticide regulation in, 48, 153–85
  subnational rule-making, 174

United Nations, 62
White Paper, 60
World Trade Organization, 183
China REACH, 171–72
ChinaGAP, 159
Chinese State Council Regulations on
Pesticide Administration, 170, 175, 177
choice of law, 75, 127, 241
citizens, 91, 168, 178, 265
immigration, 450
international law, 325, 328, 447
photography, 357
relations to state, 358, 360–61, 457
transnational data, 241, 243–44, 248, 251, 256,
259
citizenship
de-territorializing. *See* de-territorializing
citizenship
political idealization, 358
women's, 307
civilization
global, 392
in international law, 420
climate change
governance, 9
growth and, 454
impacts of, 39
law, 39, 41–42, 377, 379
responsibility for, 378
climate legislation, 377, 379
CLOUD Act, 256
Code of Practice, 158–60, 167
Codes of Conduct, 119, 161, 312, 383, 483
Codex Alimentarius Commission, 164–65
standards, 164–67, 172–74
Codex Committee on Pesticide Residues
(CCPR), 164–66, 173, 183
colonialism, 355, 387, 422, 435–36, 438–39
condemnation of, 432
international law, 422, 431, 438, 440
post-, 9, 422
reverse, 438
settler, 300
comity, 46, 91, 94–95, 99
critiques, 89
definition, 89, 91
doctrine, 91–92, 94, 101
domestic law, 94–95, 246, 250
international legal regime, 95, 98–100, 202
judicial, 101
legal, 101

operation of, 46, 88, 90, 92, 95–97, 99, 101
prospective, 96
sovereignty and, 95–99
as a technique, 98
commercial arbitration, 12, 48, 142, 225, *See*
abitration:commercial
transnational, 87, 194, 227, 237–38, 332, 375,
439, 482
Communications Decency Act, 261
communicative resources, 352
Communist Party of China (CPC or CCP),
168, 183–84
comparative law, 4, 35, 38, 76, 231, 396, 482,
484
concepts, 108, 119, 181, 213, 216, 279, 467, 474,
479, 489
global governance, 387
international, 475
international law, 463
Jessup and, 1, 11
legal, 199, 369
of the state, 21
of transnational legal ordering and
transnational legal orders, 126–27, 130, 147
old, 7, 107
post-positivist, 464
private law, 305
sustainable development, 378
transnational, 414
transnational law and, 431
Western, 431
conditions of possibility, 352
Conflict of Laws, 74, 80, 82, 84, 85, 87, 242,
399, 416
Constitution of the Communist Party of China
(CPC), 168
constitutional law, 261
family law and, 316
human rights and, 221
municipal, 219
public law regimes, 212
continental shelf, 14
contract
as accountability, 382
choice-of-law clauses in, 85, 189
code of conduct as, 383
colonialism and, 305, 438–39
concession, 421, 423–27, 430, 433, 435–36,
439
disputes, 232
domain name, 252

contract (cont.)
   family law and, 300
   fiduciary duty in, 409
   global value chains and, 382
   international economic development,
     436
   international law and, 230, 329
   international trade and, 230, 234
   internationalized, 440
   investor–state, 425
   Jessup on, 14–15
   labour, 287
   lex mercatoria and, 278
   military, 382
   private, 32, 285
   scholars on, 382–84
   supply chain, 382
   surrogacy and, 310–11
   termination of, 424
   transnational private governance and, 306
   as treaty, 423, 426, 428, 430, 440
contracting
   choice-of-law clauses in, 186, 189
contracts
   international law and, 191
   Jennings on, 431
   rules and, 81
Convention on the Recognition and
   Enforcement of Foreign Arbitral Awards
   (1958), 142, 187, 194
corporate social responsibility, 210, 343, 399,
   408
cosmopolitan pluralism, 240, 266–67
cosmopolitanism, 266
Council of Europe, 124
counterterrorism, 209, 295, 354, 358
Court of Arbitration for Sport, 276, 289–92
Court of Justice of the European Union, 303
courts
   American, 96, 150, 246, 361
   Australian, 219
   Austrian, 237
   Canadian, 260, 331
   choice of law and, 16, 85, 95, 127, 254
   comity and, 92, 94, 100–1
   commercial awards and, 278
   conflicts of law and, 241
   family law and, 303–4, 316
   foreign law and, 202, 205, 212, 217–19
   French, 237, 302
   German, 288

   global community and, 100
   global law and, 74
   global legal system and, 75, 79
   human rights and, 139, 143, 203, 301, 310, 480
   in common law countries, 208–9, 218
   indigenous rights in, 134–36
   intellectual property and, 131
   international, 28, 46, 72–73, 86–87, 90,
     97–98, 100, 144, 313
   international arbitration and, 194
   international commercial, 210
   international law and, 128, 209
   international legal system and, 72, 74
   international treaties and, 150
   judicial transnationalism and, 205, 216
   national, 72, 74, 79, 100, 200, 209, *See*
     national courts
   norms and, 251
   patent law and, 131
   public international law and, 148
   sports and, 290
   supranational, 296
   transnational law and, 200, 209, 217
   Western, 302
crisis
   Berlin, 61–62
   climate, 53
   debt, 316
   Greek, 453
   of democratic governance, 45, 53
   SARS, 183
   social drama and, 353, 363
   Suez, 422, 433–34, 437–38, 440
   Wendy Brown on, 358
critical discourse analysis, 352
critical legal studies, 53, 481
critical political economy, 324, 334, 339–40, 344
critical theory, 53, 318, 323, 340, 352–53, 465
criticality, 465, 479, 484
CropLife International, 165
crusade, 355
CSR, 341, 383, 399
cultural text, 362
customary law, 15, 136, 227–28

Das v. George Weston Ltd., 25
decolonization, 5, 422, 439
deference, 91, 94, 250–51, 462, 486, 489
definition
   community, 264, 266
   of games, 467

of gender and sexuality, 314
of global legal system, 74
of international criminal law, 118
of law, 267
of multinational enterprises, 408
of private transnational goverance, 345
of site of governance, 180
of soft law, 170
of sustainable development, 67
of transnational law, 28, 34–43, 76, 81, 110,
    115, 130, 179, 225, 279, 324–25, 367, 370,
    461, 463–69, 471, 476–77, 485–86, 488–89,
    492
of transnational legal pluralism, 479
of transnational problems, 75–77, 86
of transnational situations, 28
delegation, 59, 126, 164, 168, 408, 410, 414, 416
democracy, 213, 218, 442, 450
    adaptation of, 211, 213, 215–16
    Cold War and, 456
    constitutional, 214
    corporate, 66
    decentred, 457
    decline in, 456
    definition of, 213, 457
    desire for more, 456
    international, 444, 450
    judges and, 211, 216
    liberal, 359, 363
    parliamentary, 66
    participatory, 215, 217
    referendums and, 442
    Ronald Dworkin on, 211
    shareholder, 23
    sovereignty and, 214
    undermined by international law, 212
    Wendy Brown on, 359
democratic citizenship, 359
detachment, 190, 266, 349, 353, 391, 435
de-territorialization, 241, 247, 255, 264, 267
de-territorializing citizenship, 357, 360, *See*
    citizenship:de-territorializing
diffusion, 313, 370, 377
diplomacy
    Cold War, 59
    Dulles and, 435
    international, 195, 369
    Jessup and, 2, 4–5, 57–61, 71
    judges and, 209
    parliamentary, 60
    United Nations, 6, 60, 62–63, 65

disciplinarity, 462, 466–71, 474
discourse, 122, 140, 350, 372
    interdisciplinary, 9, 282, 471
    law-related, 486
    neo-liberal, 368
    Orientalist, 355
    practice-oriented, 473
    surrogacy and, 311
    transnational, 304, 308
    transnational law, 29, 365, 388, 463, 470,
        472–73, 478, 480
dispute resolution
    clauses, 85
    framework, 137
    international arbitration as, 187
    private, 73, 79, 111, 227, 274
    sports, 277, 289
    transnational, 49, 73, 210, 224–25, 227,
        239
dissent
    judicial, 423
    political, 359
District of Columbia v. *Heller*, 206
diversity, 174, 302
domain names, 248–50, 254
domination, 368
    imperial, 350, 439
    in family law, 309
    male, 307
drones, 240, 264
dualism, 204, 219, 482
dynamic watching, 361

EC – *Hormones* case, 165
eclecticism, 462–63, 473–78, 484
elitism, 342, 455
embeddedness, 46, 291, 297, 336, 489
endosulfan, 164
epistemologies, 322, 471
ethics
    codes of, 490
    community, 432
Europe, 148, 151, 442
    Eastern, 337, 421
    football in, 286
    imperialism, 419
    legal theory in, 419
    transnational legal ordering, 149
European Convention on Human Rights,
    303
European Court of Justice, 144, 257, 288

European Union, 80, 109, 146, 149, 210, 316,
    397–98, 442–43, 448, 450, 453, 457
Euro-Retailer Produce Working Group, 159
extraterritoriality, 87, 244, 255, 410, 415

fake pesticides, 182
family law, 49–50, 294
    choice of law norms and, 148
    gender equality and, 304
    global politics of 'private', 308–11
    globalization and, 294
    international, 310
    neoliberalism and, 314–17
    private/public distinction in, 306–8
    sharia and, 303
    transformations of the welfare state and,
        311–12
    transnational, 49, 318
    transnational legal pluralism and, 298–304
FAO–WHO Joint Meeting on Pesticide
    Residues (JMPR), 165
Fédération Internationale de Football
    Association (FIFA), 278, 286–89
feminist theory, 309, 368
Filártiga v. *Peña-Irala*, 24
financial regulation, 9, 146
First Amendment, US Constitution, 244–46,
    261
Food and Agriculture Organization (FAO),
    148, 160–61, 164–65
force, use of, 119–21, 125, 328, 430, 434
foreign law
    definition of, 200
    EU courts and, 304
    Horrigan on, 48
    human rights and, 206
    national judicial reference to, 197, 201–5,
        208, 212–13, 217–22, 303, 380
    relationship to domestic law, 94, 200, 206,
        217
    Sitaraman, Ganesh, on, 205–6
    transnational law and, 197
formalism, 218, 314, 474
fragmented authoritarianism, 174
France
    courts in, 237
    family law in, 303, 350
    ICC and, 194
    lex mercatoria and, 481
    Lotus case and, 433
    Suez crisis and, 436

transnational surrogacy in, 301
    United Nations and, 61
    Yahoo! and, 242, 244, 260, 262
Freedom of Information Act, 361–62, 382
French Cour de Cassation, 237, 301, 303
Full Faith and Credit Clause, US
    Constitution, 245

gap filling, 416–17
GB 2763-2016 National Food Safety Standard –
    Maximum Residue Limits for Pesticides
    in Food, 172
gender equality, 303–4
    family law and, 302–4
    multiculturalism and, 303
    surrogacy and, 310
gender inequalities, 296
genre, 352, 472
geography, 9, 22, 27, 35, 116
    legal, 53, 481
    physical, 247–48, 265
    transnational, 44
geopolitical, 24, 354, 430, 434
global administrative law, 3, 284, 367, 456
global dispute resolution, 49, 225–26
global governance, 73, 325, 338, 491
    asymmetries of, 296
    belief in the promise of, 387
    corporations and, 338
    Jessup on, 3
    Shaffer and Coye on, 47
    theoretical approaches to, 33
global law, 32, 74, 80, 219
    formal properties of, 42
    judges and, 211, 219
    without a state, 233
    without the state, 274
    theories of, 22, 39
global legal pluralism, 38, 53, 78, 153, 181, 481
    family law and, 295
    local contexts and, 179
    Paul Schiff Berman's, 480
    scholarship on, 154, 367
global legal system, 74, 76, 82, 85–87
    components of, 74
    concept of, 45, 73–74, 77, 81–82, 86
    definition of, 75
    dimensions of choice and, 84
    four pillars of, 74
    functional approach to, 76
    governance functions of, 74

institutions of, 80, 86
teaching and, 86
global market, 22, 46, 48, 90, 93–96
transnational surrogacy and, 311, 316
Global Programme of Action on Sustainable
Development, 162
GLOBALG.A.P., 159, 181
globalization, 20–21, 30, 312
challenge, 22, 415
changes associated with, 322
corporate, 26
economic, 418, 441
family law and, 294–95
inequality and, 454
law and, 27–34, 50, 188, 294, 297–98, 328–29,
401
nation and, 339
regulatory problems and, 47, 454
use of the term, 487
Globally Harmonized System of Classification
and Labelling of Chemicals (GHS), 160,
176
GlobalSantaFe Corp. v. *Globalsantafe.com*,
247–51
Good Agricultural Practice (GAP), 159, 161
Google Spain SL v. *Agencia Española de
Protección de Datos*, 257–58
Google v. *Equustek Solutions*, 261
governance
arrangements, 332, 338
big data and algorithmic, 34
capitalism and, 341
climate change. *See* climate change:
governance
conflict of laws and, 85
data-driven, 398
definition of, 78
democratic, 9, 45, 53, 213
economic, 317
environmental, 378, 382
expert, 449, 462
global, 9, 45, 73, 195, 296, 321, 325, 338, 387,
491, *See* global governance
global legal system and, 77–78
institutional, 52, 389
international, 107
inter-systemic, 209
law and, 14, 398, 403
market, 295
multilevel, 337, 399
multi-modal, 211–18

municipal, 182
non-legal, 106
non-state, 403, 416
norms, 400
of intellectual property, 133
polycentric, 399
power, 85
private, 26, 81, 87, 111, 128, 306, 334, 337, 345,
405, 409–12, 417
private transnational, 325, 333, 335, 339, 341,
343–46
public, 312
regulatory, 50
risk management as, 342
scholarship on, 338
self, 314, 446
sites of, 153–54, 180–82, 185
soft law and, 146
technologies of, 128
tools, 68
transnational, 14, 22, 39, 50–51, 323, 330, 344
transnational law as, 389
WTO, 365
Graham v. *Florida*, 206
Greece, 316–17
Green v. *Mizuho Bank, Ltd*, 263
guidance documents, 172
Guidance for the Implementation of the
Catalogue of Hazardous Chemicals
(China), 160

hard law, 113, 119–20, 122, 146, 169–72, 182
erosion of, 46
instruments, 110
international, 115, 119, 123
and non-binding regulatory instruments,
107, 116
and non-binding steering instruments, 108,
120–21
High Court of Australia, 219–22
historical materialism, 323, 336
human rights, 452
abuses, 25, 78, 134, 306, 483
activists, 6, 139, 296, 310, 450, 453
agreements, 220
business and, 122, 305, 384, 408–11, 414,
483
constitutionally protected, 206, 221–22
courts and, 25, 203, 301, 313, 480
democracy and, 213
discourses, 372

human rights (cont.)
  domestic, 110, 112, 135, 139, 203, 214
  elites and, 455
  enterprise system and, 411
  family law and, 295–97, 301, 306, 310
  global, 112
  governance of, 143
  groups, 82, 138
  high commissioner for, 411
  international, 410
  international criminal law and, 120
  judges and, 97, 210, 212, 218
  labour and, 24
  law, 110, 112, 121–22, 134, 139, 203, 219, 301,
    365, 400, 452
  law school and, 20
  lawyers, 143
  litigation, 24, 96, 110
  of capital, 6
  opposition to, 6, 451–52
  populism and, 9, 452
  practices, 372
  private, 414
  protection of, 214
  same-sex marriage and, 313
  scholarship on, 312, 372
  state and, 206
  trade law and, 455
  treaties, 142
  United Nations and, 65, 135, 138, 149
  universal, 28, 204, 211, 214, 223
  Universal Declaration of, 124, 137, 143
human security, 354

idealization
  political, 358–61, 363
identification
  imaginary, 359
  political, 358–60, 402, 405
  spectator–subject, 359
  symbolic, 359–61
ILO Code of Practice on Safety and Health in
    Agriculture, 158
ILO Convention concerning Safety in the Use
    of Chemicals at Work (Chemicals
    Convention), 156
ILO Convention on Safety and Health in
    Agriculture, 157
ILO Tripartite Declaration of Principles
    concerning Multinational Enterprises
    and Social Policy, 158

image, 51, 349, 352, 356–57, 359–63, 377
imperialism, 436
  anti-trust, 97
  arrogance and, 360
  Egypt under, 436
  European, 327, 419
  France and Morocco, 350
  Jessup on, 419
  of statist legal orthodoxy, 387
  Societ view on, 422
In re Search Warrant No. 16-960-M-01 to
    Google, *In re* Search Warrant No. 16-1061-
    M to Google, 256
India
  English common law and, 209
  family law in, 300
  Hindu nationalism in, 442
  legal postcolonialism in, 422
  Non-aligned Movement and, 422
  patents in, 131
  Portuguese colonialism in, 426
  transnational surrogacy and, 310
indigenous rights
  as emerging transnational legal order, 140
  international, 138
  law, 148
  movement, 138
  norms, 129
inequalities, 8, 453–55
  capitalism and, 323
  domestic, 454
  family law and, 309
  gender, 296
  global, 297, 454
  globalization and, 454
  Jessup on, 453
  transnational surrogacy and, 316
informal rule-making, 106–7
innocence, 354, 431
Integrated Pesticide Management (IPM), 161
intellectual history, 479
intellectual projects, 462, 469
intelligence, 354
  agencies, 358, 361
  as function of international legal system, 78
  function, 82
interdisciplinary, 21, 27, 38, 40, 86–87, 294, 298,
    317, 352–53, 461–62, 474–75, 479–81,
    483–84
  analysis of how legal rules emerge, 464
  discourse, 282

framework, 309
international law, 86
Jessup as, 474
jurisprudence, 351
knowledge, 471
legal studies, 466
perspective of transnational law, 282
perspectives, 472
resources, 352
transnational law literature, 463
international and transnational legality, 343
international arbitration, 277
  in 1950s, 48, 430
  as dispute resolution mechanism, 186
  evolution of, 195
  Jessup and, 187–88, 194–95, 375
  private and public collaboration in, 187
  rules of, 236
  transnational actors in, 192
  transnational law in, 234
  transnational processes in, 194
  transnational rules in, 190
  UNCITRAL Model Law and, 239
International Centre for the Settlement of
    Investment Disputes (ICSID), 187–88,
    190–91
  Convention, 189, 192
  membership of, 344
  transparency and participation in, 344
International Chamber of Commerce (ICC),
    187, 193–94, 232, 237, 326, 376
International Code of Conduct for Security,
    113
International Code of Conduct on Pesticide
    Management, 161
International Code of Conduct on the
    Distribution and Use of Pesticides,
    160
international community, 3, 6, 13–14, 67, 84,
    96, 280, 333–34, 474
  interest, 3
  interests, 3–4, 15, 344
  of merchants, 237
  organization of, 60
  regulation of international trade and, 183
International Court of Justice (ICJ), 144
  Anglo-Iranian Oil case and, 426
  Barcelona Traction case and, 191
  binding judgment and, 144
  Breard case and, 100
  Congo v. *Uganda* and, 119

domestic courts as sources of international
    law and, 203
Egypt and, 435, 437
Gabčíkovo-Nagymaros Project case, 428
Iranian oil and, 370
Jessup and, xvii, 1–2, 71, 191, 195, 333, 420,
    443, 476
Lauterpacht and, 426
Nicaragua v. *United States* and, 119
on formation of customary international law,
    119
South West Africa cases and, 119
Statute Article 38(1)(c), 426
international courts, proliferation of, 46, 90, 97
International Labour Organization (ILO), 71,
    156, 158–60, 167
international law
  commercial, 210, 229–30
  consequential and formalistic, 120–21, 123–24
  criminal, 118, 120–21, 124, 328, 374
  environmental, 144, 344
  flexible and encompassing, 120, 122
  humanitarian, 113, 121, 124
  informal rule-making. *See* informal rule-
    making
  softification, 105–25
  sources of, 72, 203, 327, 366, 419, 421, 432
  stagnation, 105, 140
international legal personality, 327
international legal system, 45, 58, 72–73, 78, 101
international legal theories, xvii
international normative repertoire, 154, 181
International Olympic Committee, 275, 289
international organizations, 15, 39, 70, 106,
    367–68, 379, 410
  agreements and, 64
  Barcelona Traction case and, 191
  Belize and, 133
  birth of, 491
  family law and, 310
  international legal system and, 72, 128
  lawmaking and, 109, 146
  legitimizing function of, 140
  as norm-generating actor, 310
  participatory rights and, 23
  practice of transnational law and, 17
  regulation by, 476
  resistance and, 149
  rules made by, 12, 116
  SDGs and, 65
  as supplier of transnational law, 78

international organizations (cont.)
  transnational legal processes and, 188
  Yearbook of, 145
international regimes, 181, 335, 338
international relations, 4
  centrality of states to, 24, 70, 335, 444, 484
  international law and, 24, 64, 67, 86–87, 122,
    324–25, 387
  scholarship, 47, 76, 129, 187, 345
  transnational law and, 69, 334–39
international relations theory, 336
international standards, 164–66, 172–74, 179,
  183
internet, 241
  advertisements, 260
  *Barcelona.com, Inc. v. Excelentisimo
    Ayuntamiento de Barcelona*, 251–55
  conflicts-of-law cases, 255
  GlobalSantaFe Corp. v. Globalsantafe.com,
    247–51
  *Google Spain SL v. Agencia Española de
    Protección de Datos*, 257–58
  Google v. Equustek, 260–62
  LICRA v. Yahoo!, 242
  Procureur-General v. Yahoo! Inc., 258–60
  United States v. Microsoft, 255–57
interpretive practice, 351–52
investment arbitration, 190, 375
investor–state regime, 330, 343
Ireland, 209, 255, 445–46
ius ad bellum, 119

Japan, 6, 133, 138–40, 173, 263, 337, 420
judge-made law, 207
judgment recognition, 242, 245–46, 255, 262
judicial decision-making, 197
judicial transnationalisation, 197, 201, 203–11,
  214, 216–18, 222–23
  theory of, 216
judicial tribunal, 17, 226, 280
Judicial Watch, 361–62
jurisdiction
  blockchains and, 263
  comity and, 92–95, 97–99, 101
  compulsory the, 436
  conflict of laws and, 242, 264, 327
  customary international law of, 78
  deterritorialization of data and, 264–65
  domestic law and, 201
  extraterritorial, 25
  family law and, 296, 298, 306, 312–13

harmonization and, 203, 209
human rights and, 214, 410
in *GlobalSantaFe Corp. v. Globalsantafe.
  com*, 249–51
in humanities and social sciences, 265–67
international, 97–98
International Court of Justice and,
  191, 431
international courts and, 98
international law and, 93
international normative repertoire and, 181
internet and, 258–60, 263
judicial transnationalisation of law and,
  218–22
in *LICRA v. Yahoo!*, 242
multinational corporate activity and, 240
non-state, 295
norms and, 283, 302, 304
power and, 62, 127
public international law and, 80, 84
in rem, 248
sports and, 289
theories of, 225
transnational adjudication and, 207
transnational arbitration and, 226
in *Transnational Law*, 14, 59, 93, 224, 280
transnational law and, 13, 29, 200, 212, 217,
  299, 431
transnational legal orders and, 127, 154, 181
treaties and, 202
UNCITRAL Model Law and, 238
jurisprudence
  analytical, 12, 334
  arbitral, 49, 239, 290
  Australia's, 218
  constitutional, 206
  Court of Arbitration for Sport, 276, 278
  Court of Justice of the European
    Communities, 443
  death penalty, 206
  human rights, 203, 219, 222
  intellectual property law and, 132
  interdisciplinary, 351
  international law, 137
  Jessup and, 114, 224
  legal formalism and, 218
  Mason era, 221
  nationalist, 95
  pluralist, 390
  transnationalist, 92
  US Supreme Court, 207, 415

justice, 392
  belated, 429
  concept of, 392
  context and relational aspects of, 395
  discretionary, 14
  distributive, 452
  global private justice system, 331
  humanist principles of, 363
  in commercial field, 227
  judicial transnationalization and, 214
  law and, 352, 363
  Marxist–Leninist systems and, 392
  normative expressions of, 396
  Obama's use of the category, 354
  private justice system, 341
  social, 453
  substantive, 456
  system, 168
  transitional, 53, 481

Kiobel v. *Royal Dutch Petroleum*, 96
Kuwait v. *Aminoil* case, 189

law
  as cultural and social activity, 349, 351
  as drama, 51, 349–51, 353, 356, 362–63
  as narrative, 351–52
  as poetry, 351
  as rhetoric, 351
law merchant, 228, 230, 292, 326–27, 341
Law on the Quality and Safety of Agricultural
    Products (LAPQS) (China), 170
Lawrence v. *Texas*, 206
legal doctrine, 8, 14, 39, 342, 421, 427–30, 449,
    453
legal doctrines, 149
legal education, 18, 348
  transnational, 20
legal harmonization, 46
legal practice, 41–42, 51, 151, 271, 371
  Fleur Johns and, 372
  Jessup and, 328, 370, 381
  methods of choice in, 85
  norms and, 140
  north–south disputes and, 438
  scholarship on, 482
  social contexts and, 293
  transnational dynamics in, 227, 235
legal practices
  scholarship on, 370
legal realism, 17, 332, 367, 449, 457, 484

legal regulation, 204, 282, 309, 326,
    328
legal scholarship, 202, 472, 479
  continental, 274
  foreign, 202
  Jessup and, 57–58, 65–70, 326, 370
  methodologies and, 370–72
  socio-, 348
  transnational, 47, 270, 292
legal strategies, 42, 149, 180–81
legal theory
  development in Europe, 419
  domestic, 53
  international. *See* international legal
      theories
  Jessup and, 57
  legal realism and, 484
  positivist, 333
  postcolonial, 38, 299
  transnational, 297, 317, 418, 461–80
  transnational commercial law and, 226
  transnational law and, 199
legality, 360
Legislation Law (2015 Amendment) (China),
    167, 174
legislative drafting
  consultants, 379
  international conferences, 379
  materials, 378
  processes, 377–78, 380
legitimacy, 47, 52, 205, 353, 360, 465, 483
  democratic, 211, 421
  family law and, 296, 308
  global governance and, 45
  jurisdiction and, 264
  legal practice and, 371
  of national judicial reference to
      international and foreign law, 48, 197
  of newly formed legal structures, 298
  of non-state actors, 324
  of power, 214
  of private lawmaking, 334
  of private transnational authority, 346
  of public international law, 327
  ritual and, 390
  of sporting legal order, 275
  transnational governance and, 46, 346
  transnational law and, 33, 272
  transnational private, 341
  of transnational public purposes, 334
  trasnational governance and, 346

legitimising scripts, 352
lex mercatoria, 109, 230–35, 271–72, 274–75,
    341, 467, 491
    as autonomous legal system, 230
    de facto autonomy of, 231
    de facto harmonization of, 230
    debates over, 29
    discourse on, 277
    doctrinal debates around, 274
    English view on, 233
    existence of, 278
    history of, 227–29, 438
    lex sportiva versus, 277–78
    nature and sources of, 231
    new, 229, 292
    rediscovery of, 271
    revival of, 273, 475
    scholarship on, 476, 480–82
    transnational, 233
    as transnational legal order, 274
    UNIDROIT Principles and, 232
lex sportiva, 49, 270–93
liberal democratic state, 358–60, 363
liberal legality, 363
LICRA v. Yahoo!, 242

materiality
    communicative, 350
    of contemporary legal conflicts, 22
    metaphysics and, 351
    normative, 38
    of norm creation processes, 40, 464
    pedagogical, 481
    of transnational legal formations and
        practices, 37
maximum pesticide residue limits (MRLs), 161,
    166–67, 172–74
Maya, 126–38
McDonald v. Chicago, 206
meaning and sites of law, 348
Measures on Environmental Administration of
    New Chemical Substances (MEANCS)
    (China), 171–72
media
    American, 435
    corporations, 361
    culture, 363
    globalized, 360
    Modern Law of Nations and, 4
    social, 255, 258
    theory, 51

melamine scandal, 183
mercatocracy, 341
metaphor, 351, 411
    dead, 486
    of law as drama, 349
metaphysics, 351
methodologies, 220, 372, 484
    ethnographic, 370
    situational, 417
    transnational law, 296
Microsoft v. United States, 255
migration, 447
    laws, 287
    norm-, 300, 316
Millennium Development Goals,
    66–67
Ministry of Agriculture (MOA) (China), 153,
    160, 171–73, 177, 184–85
Ministry of Environmental Protection (MEP)
    (China), 171
monism, 204, 219
myth, 352

narrative
    convergionist, 312
    convergionist legal, 313
    ideology and, 354
    law as, 351–52
    power of, 393
    progress, 105
    same-sex marriage, 313
    subordination/objectification, 311
    transnational law as drama and,
        363
    US, 353, 355
nation, 84–85, 91, 99, 114, 265, 269,
    394
    EU and, 448
    governance of, 213, 215
    international and, 75, 225
    international law and, 73
    judges and, 217
    law and, 491
    power of the, 359
    transnational law and, 64, 476
national courts, 203
    avoidance of, 438
    commercial awards and, 278
    displacement of, 148
    foreign law in, 220
    global affairs and, 72

global legal system and, 74, 79
international law in, 72, 128, 218, 220
international legal order and, 209
international relations and, 87
international sports and, 289, 291
Jessup and, 127, 200
multi-modal governance, regulation and
    democracy, 211–18
transnational view of, 211
national food safety standards, 165, 172
National Health and Family Planning
    Commission (China), 166, 172–73, 184
national identity, 353, 355, 445
National Implementation Plan (NIP) (China),
    157
national law
    arbitration and, 234, 236, 271
    Chinese, 167–68
    choice-of-law clauses and, 85
    courts and, 150
    extraterritoriality and, 410
    global law and, 233
    international and foreign law and, 204, 207,
        217
    international law and, 72, 81, 128, 152, 211,
        327, 476–77
    international organizations and, 146
    lex mercatoria and, 231, 233, 236–37
    maritime law and, 18
    nations and, 80
    rules of, 82
    scholarship on, 87
    sharia's influence on, 303
    sovereignty and, 327
    sustainable development and, 162
    third-party ownership and, 287
    transnational law and, 11, 17, 32, 73, 80, 84,
        89, 110, 115, 198, 279, 282, 292, 327, 331,
        365, 398, 443, 455, 463
    transnational problems and, 451
    tribunals and, 236
National People's Congress (China), 163,
    167–68, 184
national security, 362
    discourse of, 363
    human security versus, 354
    state, 358, 361, 363
    team, 51, 357–59
National Strategy (China), 160
nationalism, 441, 449
    as transnational movement, 442

Brexit and, 454
exclusionary, 457
Hindu, 442
methodological, 18, 332
Nazi, 455
Putin's, 442
racism and, 442, 455
transnational, 442
nation states, 5, 21–22, 26, 255, 264, 332, 445–47
    coalitions of, 204
    definition of, 266
    democratization beyond, 457
    economic globalization and, 180
    global law and, 30
    globalization of law and, 215
    globalized media and, 360
    interdependence among, 28
    international law and, 28, 30
    model law and, 238
    multinational corporate activity and, 240
    nostalgia of, 444–48, 451
    relations among, 153
    return to, 53
    sovereign, 10, 442
    transnational law and, 6, 198, 200, 331
neo-liberalism, 305, 311, 342
    birth of, 297
    family law and, 314–17
    transnational law and, 441
new constitutionalism, 324, 340, 343
New Zealand, 209, 220, 378
NGOs, 11, 39, 140, 344, 383
    CCPR and, 165
    international, 145–46, 325
    international law and, 11, 204
    same-sex maarriage and, 313
    transnational labor law and, 41
non-legally-binding measures, 159
non-state actors, 39, 57, 62, 64–66, 68–69, 72,
    77, 111, 122, 328, 336, 338, 370, 382, 416
    international law and, 72, 204
    international organizations and, 70
    norms and, 123, 300, 346
    scholarship on, 335
    transnational governance and, 344
non-state norm-generating communities, 267
norms, 16, 30, 81, 133, 185, 396, *See* governance:
    norms
    advanced by maginalized groups, 129
    Chinese, 168, 170, 183–85
    choice of law, 148, 251

norms (cont.)
  community, 333, 346
  creation of, 29, 368, 414
  cross-border development of, 28
  domestic, 152, 168, 314
  enforceable, 200
  family, 296, 300, 303, 306, 308, 315,
    317
  First Amendment, 244
  free speech, 245
  global law and, 30
  hard and soft law, 146
  hierarchy of, 154
  human rights, 25, 301, 306
  indigenous rights and, 133, 139
  industry, 338
  institutionalization of, 147
  intellectual property law, 129, 131
  international, 24, 152, 219, 313, 391
  international investment law and,
    425
  international law and, 128
  judges and, 17, 211, 242
  jus cogens, 80
  legal and non-legal, 22
  legally binding, 172, 179
  non-binding, 117
  non-legal, 122
  non-state, 23, 267, 304
  operation of, 32
  private, 73, 152, 291, 332, 467
  public and private, 4, 11, 15
  soft law, 128, 170, 179
  specification of, 168
  sports, 49
  state, 300
  transnational, 115, 312
  transnational law and, 10, 13–15, 20, 31,
    38, 40, 43, 108, 111, 198, 200, 295–96,
    466
  transnational legal order and, 31–32, 127, 140,
    147, 154, 180–81, 283
  types of, 13
  US constitutional, 245
  value-neutral, 30
nostalgia, 53, 441, 444–53, 457

Obergefell v. *Hodges*, 207
OECD Guidelines for Multinational
  Enterprises, 122, 204, 408, 410
Orientalism, 355

Orientalist tropes, 355
outsiders, 53, 360, 407, 455

pacta sunt servanda, 428, 443
PAN International List of Highly Hazardous
  Pesticides, 163
Paris Convention for the Protection of
  Industrial Property, 130, 254
patriotism, 359
perpetual war, 356
personal spheres, 350
Pesticide Eco-Alternatives Centre (PEAC)
  (PAN China), 163
pesticides, 47–48, 153–85
Pesticides Action Network (PAN), 163
Philip C. Jessup Collection (Library of
  Congress), 187
philosophy of praxis, 322
photography, 356–57, 360, 362
political fealty, 359
politicized situations, 46
populism, 9, 441, 452, 454, 456–57
positivism, 3, 92, 101, 351
  legal, 17, 218
post-9/11, 353, 355, 358, 362
postcolonial, 199
  -ism, 9
  legal, 422
  legal theory, 38, 299
  societies, 297
  studies, 4, 52–53, 296–97, 481
post-war, 4, 67, 450, 461, 473, 475, 479
  pragmatism, 461, 471
power
  allocation of, 150–51
  asymmetries, 8, 305, 328
  binding, 480
  colonial, 440
  corporate, 214, 322, 333, 343
  disciplinary, 340
  economic, 272
  extraterritorial, 357
  global, 378
  governance. *See* governance:power
  imperial, 327
  informal dynamic of, 373
  Jessup on, 62–63
  judicial, 277
  jurisdictional, 94, 251
  language and, 352
  law and, 62, 70, 152, 457

legal arcanum of, 16
legitimacy of. *See* legitimacy:of power
national courts and, 127
norm-making, 168
of narrative, 393
of the nation, 359
political, 166, 229, 387
politics, 7
private, 50, 324, 483
public, 215
regulatory, 305
sovereign, 267, 362, 428, 444, 446
state, 62, 304, 336, 349, 358, 360, 415
symbolic, 51
transnational, 333, 339
treaty, 150, 425
practice, 369–74, 475
in international relations, 122
international law, 107, 119, 367, 382
of law, 181, 375, 378, 441
legal. *See* legal practice
lex mercatoria and, 231, 278, 480
of transnational law, 10–19, 198, 366, 465
state, 63, 143
transnational law, 43, 292, 328, 334, 382, 385,
439, 475, 482
transnational law as, 19–28
transnational legal orders and, 127–28, 312,
332
transnational legal processes and, 188
practice-informed perspective, 12, 371–73
pragmatism, 2–3, 280, 461, 478, 484
American, 481
real-world, 88
precarity
actual, 356
imagined, 356
principles of equity, 15, 226
principles of law, 15, 189, 195, 226, 229, 235, 274,
276, 363, 400, 426
private authority. *See* authority:private
private international law, 92
American, 91
comity and, 91–92, 94, 101
conflict of laws and, 5, 25, 74, 80, 82, 84, 85,
87, 327, 477
European, 295
global legal system and, 45
Hague Conference on, 310
interaction with public international law,
147–49, 152, 305, 327, 329, 365

Jessup and, 12, 127, 374, 381, 431, 461
legal pluralism and, 301, 332
lex mercatoria and, 234
nineteenth century, 326
Rigaux on, 273
transnational human rights litigation and,
24
transnational law and, 12, 17, 20, 47, 81,
115, 188, 197–99, 225, 325, 364, 367,
443, 463
treaties of, 19
private regulation, 182, 271, 287, 289, 314
private transnational authority, 11, 324, 338–45
problem-solving theory, 340
Procureur General v. *Skype*, 258
Procureur-General v. *Yahoo! Inc*, 258–60
production of knowledge, 391, 462, 470, 489
progress, 7, 58, 63, 105, 279, 326, 397, 441
public health, 161, 175, 183
public law, 149, 206, 304–5
contract, 14
international, 3, 12, 17, 20, 23–24, 28, 35, 45,
81, 92, 115, 145, 188, 198–99, 225, 272,
325–26, 329, 332, 364, 367, 374, 381, 431,
443, 455, 461, 463, 482
litigation, 110, 480
regimes, 212
theory, 474
transnational law and, 129
transnational legal order and, 152
public standards, 159

rebus sic stantibus, 428–29
reconciliation, 353, 356
recursivity, 42, 312
redress, 353–54, 356, 402
reform and opening (China), 183
refugees, 447, 451
regimes, 46, 183, 374
arbitration, 14
corporate social responsibility, 408
disclosure, 408
domestic legal, 311
domestic trademark, 255
functional, 20
human rights, 295, 297
international, 181, 335
international human rights, 110
legal, 121, 267, 388, 402, 417
legal-regulatory, 27, 46
ordinary domestic law, 212

regimes (cont.)
  private, 341
  private international, 338
  private transnational, 341
  public law, 212
  regulatory, 185, 282
  steering, 111, 121, 123
  transboundary steering, 47, 108, 116, 123
  transnational adjudication, 48
  transnational governance, 22
  transnational law, 111
  transnational legal, 301
  transnational policy, 321
  transnational regulatory, 46, 306
  treaty, 192
regional measures, 154, 166, 169
regulation
  self-, 229, 445, 447
  transnational, 316, 345–46, 373
Regulation on Control of Agrochemicals (State Council Decree 677) (China), 171
Regulations on Pesticide Administration (China), 162, 170, 175, 177–78
Regulations on Procedures for the Formulation of Rules (China), 167
Regulations on the Safe Management of Hazardous Chemicals in China (Decree No. 591), 160
regulatory governance
  private, 26
  transnational, 44, 50–51
  transnational law as, 46–50
  transnational private, 26
relative authority, 242
resistance, 343
  against dominant class, 342
  against human rights movement, 6
  against neo-liberalism, 316–17
  off-bench, 381
  popular, 149
  to transnational legal ordering, 149
  underground movements, 60
  against WTO, 130
right to be forgotten, 257, 260
Rio Declaration on Environment and Development, 162
risk regulation, 153
robotics, 264
Roper v. *Simmons*, 206

Rotterdam Convention on the Prior Informed Consent Procedure for Certain Hazardous Chemicals and Pesticides in International Trade, 156
rule of law, 32, 44, 119, 213, 216, 395, 429
  global, 321
  values of, 213
rules, 81, 115, 182, 201
  administrative, 169, 175
  of allocation, 84
  allocation and, 85
  anti-doping, 285
  arbitration, 234–36, 238, 375, 449
  of authority, allocation, and party autonomy, 85
  of behaviour, 119, 123
  China and, 169
  choice-of-law, 265, 399
  codification of, 232
  community, 394
  competition, 94
  conflicts-of-laws, 15, 74, 80, 82, 233, 242, 402
  of constitutional, statutory, and common law interpretation, 203
  customary, 239
  domestic, 85, 150, 301
  ecclesiastical, 12, 116
  enforcement of, 78
  family, 116, 300
  family law, 50, 295, 304, 315
  FIFA, 287
  for internet expression, 244
  for taking evidence, 148
  global, 286
  global law and, 74, 79–80, 82
  governance and, 78
  in international arbitration, 188–90
  international, 145, 480
  international arbitration and, 277
  international law and, 62, 72, 80, 98, 420
  international law scholarship and, 24
  international legal, 24
  international normative, 121
  international organizations and, 15
  international trade and, 271
  international trade law, 130
  interstate law and, 120
  of investor–state arbitration institutions, 344
  Jessup on, 22, 89

Jessup's larger storehouse of, 367–69, 375, 384, 475
jurisdictional, 92, 94, 98, 240, 265
jurisdiction-regulating, 98
labour, 287
of law, 235, 290
law and, 12, 81, 88, 116, 370
legal, 81–82, 229, 231, 264, 364, 375, 436, 464, 468
legal field and, 8
legal pluralism and, 475
legally binding, 82, 116
of the *lex mercatoria*, 231, 233, 278
of the *lex sportiva*, 290
local administrative, 168, 170
mandatory, 112
marriage, 300
multinational enterprises and, 3
national, 174, 177
national law and, 398
non-binding, 81, 107, 117, 121
non-legal, 81
non-legally-binding, 82, 111
non-state, 290
pesticide, 177, 179
of precedent, 218
private, 81, 195, 285, 291, 341
private international law and, 94, 234, 327
private law, 423, 439
privately generated, 46
production chain, 411
public, 291
public international law and, 28
secret societies and, 12, 116
self-made, 273
self-regulatory, 112
of the SGBs, 291
shishi xize, 168, 170
soft law and, 170
sports, 288, 292
third-party ownership, 287
transboundary, 120
transnational, 231, 236, 405
transnational law and, 3, 19–20, 28, 40, 42, 59, 70, 74, 77–78, 80–81, 109, 111–12, 115, 119, 126, 147, 187–88, 198–99, 225, 236, 325, 364–66, 402, 443, 450, 461, 463–64, 466, 476–77
transnational problems and, 82
UK and, 444
UN, 348

same-sex marriage, 307
constitutionality of, 207
reforms, 296, 298, 301
transnational legal ordering and, 306–12
Sarajevo Code of Conduct for Private Security Companies, 113
SARS, 183
scale, 350, 369, 466
screen, 149, 247, 357
security
collective, 6
commodification of, 338, 342
companies, 113, 341
food, 47
human. *See* human security
international, 322, 342
national. *See* national security
policy in the USSR and Russia, 337
post-9/11, 140
relations, 6
supranational security communities, 335
self-governance. *See* governance:self-
service providers, 113, 244, 258, 261, 274
Shaanxi Province, 175, 177–78
Shandong Province, 175–78
sharia family laws, 302–3
site of governance. *See* governance:sites of
Situation Room photograph, 51, 349–50, 352–53, 355–61, 363
social action, 355
social conflict, 349, 352–56, 363
social drama, 349, 352–56, 358, 363
soft law, 81, 107, 117–18, 141, 145–46, 151, 159, 166, 170
Chinese, 160
definition of, 170
enterprise and, 411
frameworks, 410
hard law and, 111–12, 123, 169–72, 182, 343
ILO and, 159, 167
instruments, 110, 119–20
measures, 170
mechanisms, 491
norms, 41, *See* norms:soft law
transnational law as, 46
soundscapes, 352
sovereignty, 88, 90–93, 200, 213–14, 292, 327, 444–46
age of, 21
Brexit and, 442–43
comity and, 46, 90, 95–98

sovereignty (cont.)
  decolonization and, 52, 434, 439–40
  democratic, 21
  disaggregated, 329
  erosion of, 45
  fiction of, 63
  foreign, 95
  formal, 446
  history of, 426–27, 444
  idea of, 423
  investors and, 423
  Jessup and, 423
  joint, 60
  jurisdiction and, 264
  of the people, 213–14
  orientation, 167
  principle of, 63, 443
  reconceptualization of, 216
  state, 13, 60, 230, 334
  traditional, 444
  unlimited, 63
spatialization, 27, 42
specification, 33, 155, 168, 178, 364, 484
spectatorship, 358
standards, 24, 111, 177–78, 183, 435
  alignment and, 172–74
  of behaviour, 382
  Codex, 167
  of conduct, 375
  data privacy, 446
  emission, 41
  Forest Stewardship Council's, 148
  human rights, 28, 384
  international. *See* international standards
  international legal, 220
  of the International Organization for Standardization, 148
  labour, 156, 446, 483
  legally binding, 167
  of the *lex mercatoria*, 229
  private, 153, 159
  public. *See* public standards
  technical, 183
  voluntary, 159, 161
state
  administrative, 410
  anti-doping and, 286
  authoritative legal system and, 20
  based law, 4, 52
  birth of, 336, 419
  -centric legal studies, 293

-centric understanding of law, 11, 180
choice-of-law and, 85, 251
civilized, 420–21
colonialism and, 438, 440
comity and, 92, 94, 99, 246
concession contracts and, 424
concessions and, 437
de-colonized, 52
domestic labour and, 308
enterprise and, 410–11, 414–15, 417
family law and, 300, 302–3
FIFA and, 288
global, 360–61
global legal system and, 78, 87
globalization and, 339, 415, 454
human rights and, 112, 306, 314, 414
indigenous rights and, 133
inequality and, 8, 454
inter-, 21
international agreements and, 64
international community and, 333–34
international dispute settlement mechanisms and, 97
international investment regimes and, 343
international law and, 52, 64, 107, 119, 126, 128, 130, 140, 151–52, 204, 225, 326–27, 333–34, 396, 433, 439, 444–45
international legal subsystems and, 79
international normative order and, 111
international order and, 292
international relations and, 68–69, 86–87
–investor disputes, 188–91
Judicial Watch and, 362
jurisdiction, 13, 29, 70, 84, 295
law, 30, 297–99
law and, 10, 327, 388–90, 394–400, 403, 407, 412–13, 416, 484
law through the, 389–90
legal pluralism and, 298, 300, 332
lex sportiva and, 278
liberal democratic. *See* liberal democratic state
market and, 21, 34
nation. *See* nation states
national legal systems and, 79
neo-liberalism and, 44, 336, 340
neorealism and, 335–36
norms and, 32, 41, 300, 304, 310, 348, 465–66, 484
oversight bodies and, 140

patriotism and, 359
power, 304, 358
practice of transnational law and, 17
private actors and, 13
private authority and, 338
private legal relations and, 305
regulation, 41
rules and, 85, 116
security, 342, 358
society and, 21, 182, 482
as source of legitimation, 181
sovereignty, 45, 60, 63, 92–93, 230, 280, 426, 429, 443–48, *See* sovereignty:state
sovereignty and, 444
supra-, 111
theory, 21
totalitarian, 17
transformation, 22
transnational, 323
transnational arbitration and, 234
transnational authority and, 324
transnational commercial law and, 450
transnational governance and, 330, 343, 345
transnational law and, 11, 28, 40, 78, 140, 188, 197, 226, 233, 272, 292–93, 298–99, 326, 328, 331, 334, 346, 366, 385, 388, 390, 400, 404, 407, 418, 464–65
transnational legal normativity and, 317
transnational legal orders and, 32, 133, 140, 149, 274, 283, 483–84
transnational problems and, 77
transnational relations and, 337
transnational situations and, 29, 64, 68, 114, 325
transnationalism and, 335, 337
treaties and, 16, 19, 141–42, 150, 428–29
unity of law and, 328
violence, 360, *See* violence:state
violence and, 307
visual culture and, 362
welfare, 311, *See* welfare state
State Administration of Work Safety (SAWS) Measures for the Administration of Physical Hazard Identification and Classification of Chemicals (China), 160
state contracts, 431
state centrism, 21
state citizen, 358, 360
states
  norms and, 415
statutory law, 143, 208

Stockholm Convention on Persistent Organic Pollutants (POPs), 157, 164, 166
Stored Communications Act, 255–56
Storrs Lectures, xvii, 1, 57–58, 65, 114–15, 126, 179, 186–87, 189–90, 198, 200, 224, 269, 280, 324, 462, 477, 489
subordination, 304, 311, 343, 350, 363
  women's, 307
Suez crisis. *See* crisis: Suez
supply chain contracts. *See* contract:supply chain
supply chains, global, 372, 483
Supreme People's Court (SPC) (China), 132, 167, 169
Supreme People's Court Provisions on Several Issues concerning the Adjudication of Administrative Cases Relating to International Trade (China), 167
Supreme People's Procuratorate (SPP) (China), 169
surveillance, 358
  capitalism, 26
  of workers, 159
sustainability, 67, 404
Sustainable Development Goals, 45, 57, 65–70
symbolic identification. *See* identification: symbolic
symbols, 352

talaq, 302–4
territoriality, 254
  doctrine of, 254
  principle of, 253–54, 280
  resurfacing of, 97
  rule, 91
territory, 88, 91, 180, 241, 248, 250, 263, 265–66, 357, 398, 410, 417, 444, 446
  -based protection of human rights, 112
  Egyptian, 432
terrorism, 354
  counter-. *See* counterterrorism
Texaco Calasiatic v. Libya, 195
text, 352–53, 363
Third World, 467, 488
trademark law, 247–48, 250, 252–54
transnational arbitration. *See* arbitration: transnational
transnational capitalism, 330, 339–40, 343–44
transnational corporations, 26, 122, 328, 336–37, 343, 369, 414
transnational enterprises, 415

transnational feminism, 296
transnational human rights litigation, 24
transnational law
  adjudication and, 207, 209
  capitalism and, 343
  conflicts of law/private international law and, 81, 147, 180, 198–99, 225, 242, 304–6, 328, 331, 333, 367
  definition. *See* definition:of transnational law
  as drama, 349–50, 353, 355–56, 361–63
  as elitist, 451, 455
  family law and, 294–98, 312
  as field, 33, 37, 41, 52, 77, 400
  global dispute resolution and, 227–30
  global law and, 39, 75, 82
  global legal pluralism and, 78, 154
  as governance order, 389
  inequality and, 454
  international arbitration and, 187, 190, 194–95, 234–37, 375
  international law/public international law and, 8–9, 58, 73, 81, 127–29, 151, 180, 198–99, 225, 269, 304–6, 328, 367, 443, 463
  judicial reference to, 207
  as law of governance, 403
  law of transnational spaces and, 417
  legal pluralism and, 298–306
  legal realism and, 449
  as method, 39–40, 42–43, 182, 296, 332, 365, 400, 405, 407
  postcolonial legal theory and, 422, 430, 439
  as practice, 10–28, 328, 334, 366, 382, 385, 441, 465
  private transnational authority and, 324
  as regulatory governance, 46–50
  revival of, 109, 270
  rules and. *See* rules:transnational law and
  sovereignty and, 216
  Storrs Lectures on. *See* Storrs Lectures
  transnational legal orders/ordering and, 126–27, 129–33, 273
  as transnational politics, 43–44
transnational legal ordering, 48, 50, 283, 321, 483–85
  concept of, 30, 73, 127, 130, 311
  definition of, 127, 332
  family law and, 317
  international law and, 140
  national contexts and, 283

nation states and, 32
norms and, 133, 140, 152
public international law and, 47, 128, 151
public international law with private international law, 147–48
public law and, 152
rise and fall of, 149–51
same-sex marriage and, 312–14
scholarship on, 31, 283, 473
soft law and, 145
states and, 343
transnational law and, 47
WTO and, 365
transnational legal orders, 31–32, 149, 179, 275, 312, 403
  autonomy from nation state legal institutions, 32
  concept of, 30, 110, 126–27, 180, 273
  connection to nation states, 32
  definition of, 127, 181
  denationalized, 281
  emergence of, 274
  family regulation and, 304
  norms and, 181
  proliferation of, 146
  public international law and, 151–52
  regulation of pesticides in China as, 48, 154, 163, 183
  scholarship on, 47, 283, 313, 367
  sports and, 276
  surfacing of, 99
  theory of, 32
  transnational law and, 42, 47, 127, 129–40, 147, 180, 182, 274, 281
transnational legal pluralism, 281–83, 298–304
  anti-doping and, 286
  Peer Zumbansen on, 181, 332, 407
transnational merchant class, 341
transnational problems, 74, 77–78, 81–82, 86, 129, 140, 147, 151, 416, 446, 471, 477
  domestic and, 447
  Jessup on, 12, 15, 18, 63, 82, 115, 224–25, 279, 469
  national laws and, 451
  norms and, 47
  public international law and, 152
  transnational law and, 127, 451
transnational surrogacy, 297, 301, 309–11
transnational transactions, 226
transparency, 344, 360, 362, 375, 378, 383
transplants, 132, 377–80

treaties, 128, 141, 150, 202
  of 1779, 426
  of 1888, 435
  between European imperial powers and
    indigenous peoples in the Americas, 327
  bilateral, 141
  bilateral investment, 142
  colonial, 432
  commercial, 142
  concession agreements and, 430, 436, 440
  concessionary contract versus, 426
  constitutional review of, 150
  contracts as. *See* contracts:as treaty
  creation of, 65, 83
  domestication of, 143
  expropriation and, 425
  for business and human rights, 415
  forbidden, 432
  foreign investments and, 191
  government-to-government, 256
  human rights. *See* human rights:treaties
  ICC and, 194
  international, 135, 145, 148, 150, 167, 170–71,
    327, 437
  international courts and, 144
  international law and, 72, 443
  interstate, 332
  investment, 192, 454
  law, 80
  law of, 328
  monitoring bodies of, 138
  multilateral, 141
  negotiations, 146, 150, 187
  new, 144
  norms and, 312
  North Atlantic and Warsaw, 6
  of friendship, navigation and commerce, 142
  of private international law, 19
  pacta sunt servanda and, 429
  peace, 226
  power of, 150
  power to make, 19
  public international law and, 332
  rebus sic stantibus and, 428
  regimes, 192
  release from, 428
  sports and, 288
  termination of, 428, 430
  trade, 454
  transnational law and, 194
  UN, 16, 141
  US domestic application of, 150
  uti possidetis principle and, 428
  types of norms (China), 13, 168, 170

UN Conference on Environment and
  Development (UNCED), 144, 160, 162
UN Guiding Principles on Business and
  Human Rights, 204, 411
UNCITRAL, 146, 228, 238–39, 344
UNCITRAL Model Law, 227, 238–39
UNIDROIT Principles, 85, 229, 232–33, 235,
  237
United Kingdom, 53, 91, 143, 151, 378, 426, 441,
  444
United Nations, 24, 65, 69, 454, 487
  Charter, 6, 125, 415, 420, 430, 432, 434, 436
  China and, 62
  commercial lawmaking within, 368
  Commission on International Trade Law.
    See UNCITRAL
  Committee on the Elimination of All Forms
    of Racial Discrimination, 135
  Committee on the Elimination of Racial
    Discrimination, 134
  Conference on Environment and
    Development, 144, 159, *See* UN
    Conference on Environment and
    Development (UNCED)
  Convention of the Recognition and
    Enforcement of Foreign Arbitral Awards.
    See Convention of the Recognition and
    Enforcement of Foreign Arbitral Awards
    (1958)
  Declaration on the Rights of Indigenous
    People, 133, 135–37, 139
  decolonization and, 422
  democratization of, 66
  diplomacy, 6
  Economic and Social Council of the, 193
  environmental agreements, 144
  Food and Agricultural Organization. *See*
    Food and Agricultural Organization
    (FAO)
  formation of, 420
  General Assembly, 2, 16, 65, 119, 125, 133, 135,
    193, 348, 420, 453
  Guiding Principles on Business and Human
    Rights. *See* UN Guiding Principles on
    Business and Human Rights
  human rights and, 135, 138, 149
  Human Rights Committee, 134, 139

United Nations (cont.)
  Human Rights Council, 82, 122, 139, 408
  Jessup and, 1, 6, 10, 45, 57–65, 70–71, 126, 456, 475
  Millennium Declaration, 66
  Monitoring, Verification and Inspection Commission, 195
  New York Convention and, 194
  participatory rights in, 23
  pesticides and, 159
  Secretary General, 65, 141
  Security Council, 83
  United Nations International Children's Emergency Fund, 188
United States, 262
  antitrust law, 94
  Bretton Woods conference and, 126
  Congress, 16
  constitutional norms. *See* norms:US constitutional
  domain names and, 250, 254
  family law, 316
  human rights and, 25
  intellectual property law and, 130–31
  Jessup and, 2, 62
  Jessup on, 63
  national identity, 355
  private international law, 91
  prohibition laws, 13
  Suez crisis and, 434, 436
  Supreme Court. *See* US Supreme Court
  Third Reich industry litigation and, 96
  trademark law, 253
  transnational enforcement doctrines and, 91
  transnational law and, 19
  transnational legal ordering and, 149
  Trump and, 149, 441
  United Nations and, 59, 61
  United States v. *Microsoft*, 255–57
United States v. *Windsor*, 207
Universal Declaration of Human Rights, 124, 137, 143
US Department of Defense, 361
US Supreme Court, 95, 150, 206–7, 219, 415
uti possidetis, 428

value chains, global, 382
values
  common global, 74
  community, 202, 392, 394

conflicts-of-law, 242
core process, 392
discourse and, 350
family, 315
family law, 309
liberal democratic, 211
normative, 76, 304, 392
plurality of, 295
preconstitutional, 212
religious and cultural, 294
revaluation of, 391, 394–95, 401, 412–13
rule-of-law, 44, 213
shared, 15
value of, 391
vengeance, 361, 363
vertical (*tiao*) and horizontal (*kuai*) relations, 174
violence
  against women, 307, 453
  hate, 354
  international law and, 23
  justification of, 354
  law's, 356–58
  of 9/11, 354
  of European colonialism, 355, 432
  of the killing of bin Laden, 360–61
  post-9/11, 362
  primary scene of, 358, 360
  state, 360
  UN and, 454
virtualization, 358
visibility
  of contracts, 383
  of global inequalities, 454
  of harmonization, 239
  hyper-, 368
  and invisibility, 365–66, 368
  transnational law and, 385
  as transparency and legitimacy, 360
visual culture, 356, 362

welfare state, 11, 451
  continuing transformation of, 297, 312, 314
  dismantling of, 315
  functioning of, 315, 445
  industrial era, 315
  law and, 314
  Western, 312
World Health Organisation (WHO), 164–65
World Intellectual Property Organization (WIPO), 252

World Trade Organisation (WTO) Appellate
Body, 165
World Trade Organization (WTO), 130, 141,
148, 165, 167, 172–73, 182–83, 330, 365

Xi'an, 175, 178–79

Yahoo!, Inc. v. *La Ligue Contre le
Racisme et l'Antisémitisme,*
245
Yale Law School, xvii, 1, 198, 224,
479
Yunnan Province, 163